Tanzania

Lake Victoria
p246

Northern
Tanzania
p153

Central Tanzania
p237

Northeastern
Tanzania
p126

Zanzibar
Archipelago
p75

Western
Tanzania
p263

⊙ Dar es Salaam
p52

Southern
Highlands
p281

Southeastern
Tanzania
p315

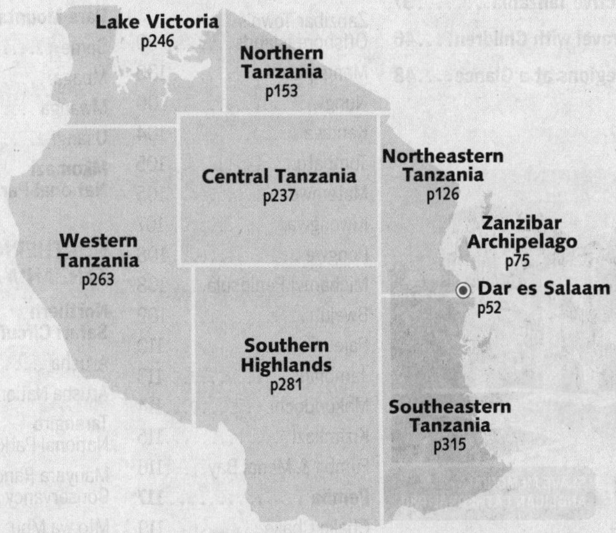

Mary Fitzpatrick,
Ray Bartlett, David Else, Anthony Ham, Helena Smith

PLAN YOUR TRIP

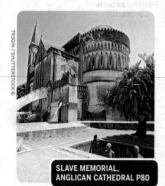

SLAVE MEMORIAL,
ANGLICAN CATHEDRAL P80

MAASAI WARRIORS P187

ON THE ROAD

Contents

Welcome to Tanzania

Wildlife, beaches, friendly people, fascinating cultures – Tanzania has all these and more wrapped up in one adventurous, welcoming package.

Captivating Cultures

Wherever you go in Tanzania, opportunities abound for getting to know the country's people and cultures. Meet red-cloaked Maasai warriors. Spend time with semi-nomadic Barabaig. Experience the hospitality of a local meal and the rhythms of traditional dance. Chat and barter at local markets. More than anything else, it is the Tanzanian people – with their characteristic warmth and politeness, and the dignity and beauty of their cultures – that make visiting Tanzania so memorable. Chances are you'll want to come back for more, to which most Tanzanians will say *'karibu tena'* (welcome again).

Idyllic Beaches

Tanzania's Indian Ocean coastline is magical, with tranquil islands and sleepy coastal villages steeped in centuries of Swahili culture. Travel back in time to the days when the East African coast was the seat of sultans and a linchpin in a far-flung trading network extending to Persia, India and beyond. Relax on powdery beaches backed by palm trees and massive baobabs; take in magnificent, pastel-hued sunrises; immerse yourself in languid coastal rhythms; and sit beneath the billowing sails of a wooden dhow, listening to the creaking of its rigging and the gentle slap of the sea against its prow.

Mt Kilimanjaro

Sending its shadow across Tanzania's northern plains, Mt Kilimanjaro beckons visitors with its graceful, forested flanks and stately snow-capped summit. It is Africa's highest peak and the world's highest free-standing volcano. It is also home to the Chagga people, and to a wealth of birds and wildlife. Climbers by the thousands venture here to challenge themselves on its muddy slopes, rocky trails and slippery scree. The rewards: the thrill of standing at the top of Africa; magnificent views of Kilimanjaro's ice fields; and witnessing the sunrise.

Wonderful Wildlife

More than almost any other destination, Tanzania is *the* land of safaris. Wildebeest stampede across the plains. Hippos jostle for space in muddy waterways. Elephants wander along seasonal migration routes and chimpanzees swing through the treetops. There are unparalleled opportunities to experience this natural wealth: take a boat safari down the Rufiji River past snoozing crocodiles in Selous Game Reserve; watch giraffes silhouetted against ancient baobab trees in Ruaha National Park; sit motionless as waterbirds peck in the shallows around Rubondo Island; and hold your breath while lions pad around your vehicle in Ngorongoro Crater.

Why I Love Tanzania

By Mary Fitzpatrick, Writer

I love Tanzania because of the light, colours and life in almost every scene, especially at dawn, when the rising sun floods the cool grasslands with gold, schoolchildren walk along the roadsides and vendors set out their wares. Nature surrounds you in all its exuberance: the largest animals mingle with the most minute; bird calls fill the air; trees blossom with flowers; hills roll into the horizon; and fishing dhows set sail in coastal waters. Amid all this, the real highlight is getting to know Tanzanians, with their equanimity, charm, dignity and warm welcome.

For more about our writers, see p416

Above: Giraffes under a baobab tree (p300)

Tanzania

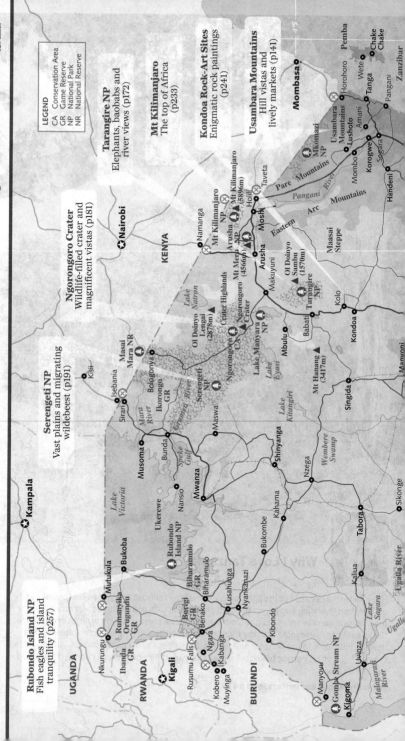

Rubondo Island NP
Fish eagles and island tranquility (p257)

Serengeti NP
Vast plains and migrating wildebeest (p191)

Ngorongoro Crater
Wildlife-filled crater and magnificent vistas (p181)

Tarangire NP
Elephants, baobabs and river views (p172)

Mt Kilimanjaro
The top of Africa (p233)

Kondoa Rock-Art Sites
Enigmatic rock paintings (p241)

Usambara Mountains
Hill vistas and lively markets (p141)

LEGEND
CA Conservation Area
GR Game Reserve
NP National Park
NR National Reserve

200 km
120 miles

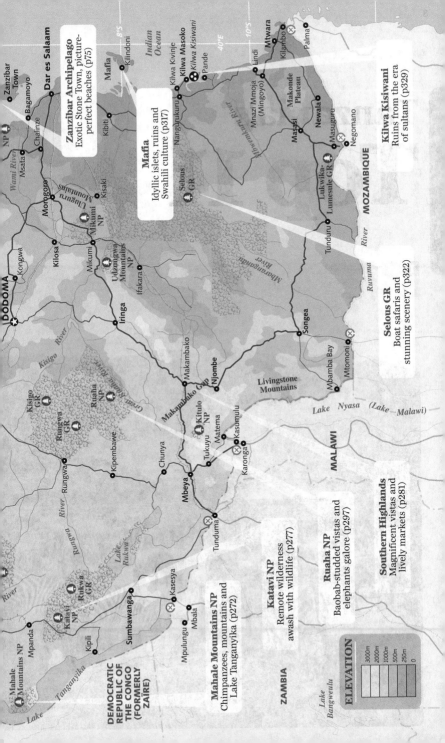

Dar es Salaam

Zanzibar Town

Bagamoyo

Zanzibar Archipelago
Exotic Stone Town, picture-perfect beaches (p75)

Mafia

Mafia
Idyllic islets, ruins and Swahili culture (p317)

Kilindoni

Indian Ocean

Kilwa Kivinje
Kilwa Masoko
Kilwa Kisiwani

Pande

Mtwara

Kilambo
Palma

Lindi

Mnazi Mmoja (Mingoyo)

Kilwa Kisiwani
Ruins from the era of sultans (p329)

Makonde Plateau

Masasi

Newala

Masuguru

Negomano

MOZAMBIQUE

Nangurukuru

Selous GR

Lukwika Lumesule GR

Tunduru

Ruvuma River

Selous GR
Boat safaris and stunning scenery (p322)

Mbwemkuru River

Mbarangandu River

Songea

Mbamba Bay

Mtomoni

Livingstone Mountains

Lake Nyasa (Lake Malawi)

Southern Highlands
Magnificent vistas and lively markets (p281)

DODOMA

Kongwa

Morogoro

Uluguru Mountains

Kilosa

Mikumi NP

Kisaki

Kibiti

Chalinze

Msata

Matata

Wami River

NP

Udzungwa Mountains NP

Ifakara

Iringa

Kilombero River

Makambako

Njombe

Makambako Gap

Kisigo

Kisigo GR

Rungwa GR

Ruaha NP

Kipembawe

Great Ruaha River

Rungwa River

Rungwa

Chunya

Tukuyu

Kitulo NP

Matema

Kasumulu

Karonga

MALAWI

Kibembawe

Mbeya

Tunduma

Lake Rukwa

Rukwa GR

Katavi NP

Katavi NP
Remote wilderness awash with wildlife (p277)

Ruaha NP
Baobab-studded vistas and elephants galore (p297)

Sumbawanga

Kasesya

Mpulungu
Mbala

Kipili

Lake Tanganyika

Mahale Mountains NP

Mahale Mountains NP
Chimpanzees, mountains and Lake Tanganyika (p272)

Mpanda

DEMOCRATIC REPUBLIC OF THE CONGO (FORMERLY ZAÏRE)

River

ZAMBIA

Lake Bangweulu

ELEVATION

3000m
2000m
1000m
500m
250m
0

Tanzania's
Top 11

Ngorongoro Conservation Area

1 The magic of Ngorongoro (p181) starts while you're up on the rim, with its tangled forest wreathed in mist and sublime views over the enormous crater. From here, descend onto a wide plain cloaked in hues of blue and green and teeming with wildlife. It's easy to imagine primeval Africa, with an almost constant parade of animals streaming past against a quintessential East African backdrop. Surrounding the crater are the magnificent Crater Highlands, home to calderas, forests, open plains and roaming wildlife.

Serengeti National Park

2 The sound of pounding hooves on the Serengeti Plains draws closer. Suddenly, thousands of animals stampede by as the great wildebeest migration (pictured below) – one of earth's most impressive natural spectacles – plays out. Despite the drama, time seems to stand still in this superlative park. Lions sit majestically on lofty outcrops, giraffes stride gracefully into the sunset, crocodiles bask on riverbanks. Wildlife watching is outstanding year-round. Whether you stay for two days or a week, it never seems to be long enough to take in all the Serengeti (p191) has to offer.

JAMIE FRIEDLAND / GETTY IMAGES ©

JULIAN W / SHUTTERSTOCK ©

Zanzibar's Stone Town

3 Whether it's your first visit or your 50th, Stone Town (p77) – the historic quarter of Zanzibar Town – never loses its touch of the exotic. First, take in the skyline, with its many minarets, the spires of St Joseph's Cathedral and the massive Old Fort. Later, wander through narrow alleyways, where surprises are revealed at every turn. Linger in dusty shops scented with cloves, watch as men wearing white, robe-like *kanzu* play a game of *bao,* and let island rhythms take over as mainland life slips away.

Beaches & Diving

4 With exotic archipelagos and over 1000km of Indian Ocean coastline, you'll be spoiled for choice with Tanzania's beaches. Zanzibar Island's coastline is developed but lovely, with white sand, palm trees and rewarding diving. To get away from the crowds, head to Mafia (p317) with its strong Swahili culture and diving. Pemba offers lush greenery, placid coves and challenging dives, while the mainland near Pangani has beaches and ruins. In the far south, between Kilwa Masoko and the Mozambique border, be sure not to miss tiny Mikindani and lively Lindi. Nungwi (p100)

Local Life

5 Abundant wildlife, forest-clad mountains, lovely beaches and Swahili ruins are but a backdrop to Tanzania's most fascinating resource – its people. Tanzanian culture is accessible and diverse: hunt up cultural tourism programs to get acquainted with the Maasai, learn about the burial traditions of the Pare and experience a local market day with the Arusha people (pictured above). The Usambara area (p144), with its lively markets and hill vistas, is one of many good places to start your explorations. Wherever you go, Tanzania's rich cultures are fascinating to discover.

Mt Kilimanjaro

6 It's difficult to resist the allure of climbing Africa's highest peak, with its snow-capped summit and views over the surrounding plains. Thousands of trekkers complete the climb each year, with a main requirement for success being adequate time for acclimatisation. But there are also other rewarding ways to experience Kilimanjaro (p233). Take a day hike or bicycle on the mountain's lush lower slopes, learn about local Chagga culture or sip a sundowner from one of many nearby vantage points with the mountain as a backdrop.

Chimpanzee Tracking

7 Climb steep muddy paths, stumble over twisted roots and make your way through dense vegetation – chimpanzee tracking is hard work. But the struggle and sweat is all forgotten once you spot the chimps. Tanzania's remote western parks – Mahale Mountains (p272) and Gombe – are among the best places anywhere to get close to our primate cousins. Combine chimpanzee tracking with a safari in Katavi National Park or an exploration of the Lake Tanganyika shoreline for an unforgettable adventure well off the beaten track.

Selous Game Reserve

8 Vast Selous (p322), with its tropical climate, profusion of greenery and the massive Rufiji River, is a complete change of pace from Tanzania's northern parks. Take a boat safari, and as you glide past borassus palms, slumbering hippos, cavorting elephants and the stealthy shapes of motion-less crocodiles, watch as well for the many smaller attractions along the riverbanks. These include majestic African fish eagles, stately Goliath herons and tiny white-fronted bee-eaters – all part of the daily natural symphony in Africa's largest wildlife reserve.

GUNTER ZIESLER / GETTY IMAGES ©

NIGEL PAVITT / GETTY IMAGES ©

Ruaha National Park

9 Rugged, baobab-studded Ruaha National Park (p297), together with surrounding conservation areas, is home to one of Tanzania's largest elephant populations. An ideal spot to watch for the giant pachyderms is along the Great Ruaha River at sunrise or sundown, when they make their way down to the banks to snack or to swim in the company of hippos, antelopes and over 400 different types of birds. A visit here, together with a journey through the surrounding Southern Highlands, is far removed from the more popular northern circuit and unfailingly rewarding.

Lake Victoria

10 Lake Victoria – Africa's largest lake and the world's second-largest freshwater lake – is well off most Tanzania itineraries, but a delight to explore. Rubondo Island National Park (p257), with its African fish eagles, abundant water birds and tranquility, is a particular highlight. Prosperous Bukoba, near the heartland of the ancient Haya kingdom, is also well worth exploring. Other attractions include: lively Musoma, with its mix of tribes and pretty vistas; bustling Mwanza, the main city on the Tanzanian lakeshore; and the fascinating Bujora museum of Sukuma culture. African darter, Rubondo Island National Park (p257)

Ruins & Rock Art

11 Tanzania offers a wealth of attractions for history buffs. The most impressive of the many coastal ruins are those at Kilwa Kisiwani (p329; pictured above) – a Unesco World Heritage Site harking back to the days of sultans and far-flung trade routes that linked inland gold fields with Persia, India and China. Standing in the restored Great Mosque, you can almost hear the whispers of bygone centuries. Inland, armed with a sense of adventure and a taste for rugged travel, head for the enigmatic Kondoa Rock-Art Sites, spread throughout central Tanzania's Irangi hills.

Need to Know

For more information, see Survival Guide (p369)

Currency
Tanzanian shilling (Tsh)

Languages
Swahili, English

Visas
Required by most travellers and best acquired in advance. Proof of yellow fever vaccination may also be requested at entry.

Money
ATMs accepting Visa and MasterCard only are in most major towns. Credit cards are not widey accepted for payment. National park fees must be paid with Visa card.

Mobile Phones
Local SIM cards work in European and Australian phones. Other phones must be set to roaming.

Time
East Africa Time (GMT/UTC plus three hours)

When to Go

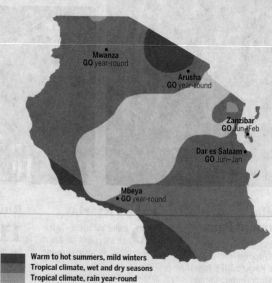

Warm to hot summers, mild winters
Tropical climate, wet and dry seasons
Tropical climate, rain year-round
Desert, dry climate

Mwanza
GO year-round

Arusha
GO year-round

Zanzibar
GO Jun–Feb

Dar es Salaam
GO Jun–Jan

Mbeya
GO year-round

High Season
(Jun–Sep)

➡ Weather is cooler and dry.

➡ Hotels in popular areas are full, with high-season prices.

➡ Animal-spotting is easiest, as foliage is sparse and animals congregate around dwindling water sources.

Shoulder
(Oct–Feb)

➡ Weather is hot, especially December through to February.

➡ From late October, the *mvuli* (short rains) fall and the *kusi* (seasonal trade wind) blows.

➡ High-season prices from mid-December to mid-January.

Low Season
(Mar–May)

➡ Heavy rains make secondary roads muddy and some areas inaccessible.

➡ It seldom rains all day, every day. Landscapes are lush and green.

➡ Some hotels close; others offer discounts.

Useful Websites

Lonely Planet (www.lonely planet.com/tanzania) Destination information, hotel bookings, traveller forum and more.

Tanzania Parks (www.tanzania parks.go.tz) Background info on all of Tanzania's national parks.

Tanzania Tourist Board (www. tanzaniatourism.com) Official site.

Zanzibar.net (www.zanzibar. net) Helpful background and travel information.

SafariBookings (www.safari bookings.com) Background information and booking links for Tanzania's parks and wildlife.

HerdTracker (www.discover africa.com/herdtracker) Track the Serengeti wildebeest migration.

Important Numbers

Landline telephone numbers are seven digits plus area code; mobile numbers are six digits plus a four-digit provider code. Area codes must be used for landline numbers. There are no central police or emergency numbers.

| Country code | ☑255 |
| International access code | ☑000 |

Exchange Rates

Australia	A$1	Tsh1776
Canada	C$1	Tsh1804
Europe	€1	Tsh2791
Japan	¥100	Tsh2036
Kenya	KSh100	Tsh2207
New Zealand	NZ$1	Tsh1636
South Africa	R10	Tsh1863
UK	UK£1	Tsh3165
US	US$1	Tsh2245

For current exchange rates, see www.xe.com.

Daily Costs

Budget: Less than US$50

➜ Camping per person: US$5–15

➜ Bed in a hostel or budget guesthouse: US$15–25

➜ Meal in a local restaurant: US$2–5

➜ Long-distance bus fares: US$5–25

Midrange: US$50–200

➜ Double room in a midrange hotel: US$50–150

➜ Restaurant meal: US$5–10

➜ Vehicle hire per day: from US$100

Top End: More than US$200

➜ Double room in an upmarket hotel: from US$150

➜ Upmarket safari packages per person per day: from US$250

➜ Domestic one-way flights: US$75–300

Opening Hours

Opening hours are generally as follows:

Banks and government offices 8am to 3.30pm Monday to Friday

Restaurants 7am to 9.30am, noon to 3pm and 6.30pm to 9.30pm; reduced hours low season

Shops 8.30am to 5pm or 6pm Monday to Friday, 9am to 1pm Saturday; often closed Friday afternoon for mosque services

Supermarkets 8.30am to 6pm Monday to Friday, 9am to 4pm Saturday, 10am to 2pm Sunday

Arriving in Tanzania

Julius Nyerere International Airport (Dar es Salaam) A taxi to the city centre (from Tsh35,000 to Tsh45,000) will take 30 minutes to 1½ hours, depending on traffic.

Kilimanjaro International Airport Taxis charge Tsh50,000 to Moshi or Arusha. Airline minivan shuttles charge Tsh10,000. For both: 45 minutes to Moshi, one hour to Arusha.

Zanzibar International Airport Take a taxi (Tsh20,000 to Tsh45,000, 15 minutes) into Zanzibar Town.

Kigoma Ferry service from Zambia on the MV *Liemba* arrives here. Walk (five to 10 minutes) from the port to the town centre and hotels. Visas can be obtained on the boat.

Overland Cross-border bus service to/from Kenya, Uganda and Rwanda; for other countries, get Tanzania transport once across the border. Don't change money at borders and arrange visas in advance if possible.

Getting Around

Tanzania is large, and time spent getting around is a major part of many visitors' itineraries.

Air The most efficient option for bridging long distances.

Bus Inexpensive and often gruelling, but the main way of getting around and a good way to get to know the 'real' Tanzania.

Car A treat if you can afford it. Try self-drive if you already have Africa driving experience. Driving is on the left.

Train Inexpensive, slow, scenic and a great cultural experience.

For much more on **getting around**, see p386

If You Like...

Wildlife

Serengeti National Park Outstanding year-round wildlife watching, and the famed great wildebeest migration. (p191)

Ngorongoro Crater The steep walls of this ancient caldera offer a backdrop for abundant, easily spotted wildlife. (p181)

Tarangire National Park Over 3000 elephants and other migrants gather to drink from the Tarangire River during the dry season. (p172)

Selous Game Reserve Sublime riverine scenery, plenty of wildlife and the chance for boat safaris. (p322)

Katavi National Park Hippos, buffaloes and more congregate by the hundreds at dry season water sources in this remote park. (p277)

Mahale Mountains National Park Verdant mountains soar up from Lake Tanganyika's crystal-clear waters while chimpanzee hoots echo through the forest. (p272)

Ruaha National Park Rugged, riverine panoramas and a unique mix of animals including elephants and wild dogs. (p297)

Mikumi National Park Easy-to-reach Mikumi offers reliable year-round wildlife watching. (p286)

Arusha National Park This lush, scenic park makes an easy, rewarding day trip from Arusha for low-key wildlife experiences. (p167)

Beaches & Islands

Zanzibar Island Turquoise-hued waters, powdery white sands, island rhythms and intriguing Stone Town work their magic. (p77)

Pangani The coastline running north and south of Pangani is beautiful and uncrowded. (p132)

Mafia A stronghold of Swahili culture, with a collection of pampered upmarket getaways plus snorkelling and dhow cruises. (p317)

Lake Tanganyika Remote and stunning, with sandy coves backed by lush, green mountains. (p276)

Masoko Pwani This long, palm-fringed stretch of fine, white sand is one of the southeast's hidden gems. (p327)

Southeastern coast Sleepy and slow-paced, Tanzania's southern beaches offer a glimpse into traditional coastal life. (p315)

Sange Beach Tucked away between Pangani and Saadani National Park is this magnificent, seldom-visited stretch of sand. (p130)

Lake Nyasa The quiet, mountain-fringed beaches here are ideal for families and those travelling off the beaten track. (p309)

Pemba Hilly, green Pemba holds many surprises, with hidden coves, challenging diving and an intriguing culture. (p117)

Fanjove Private Island Try this Robinson Crusoe–style getaway for coastal culture, relaxation and snorkelling. (p331)

Trekking & Hiking

Mt Kilimanjaro Take the ultimate challenge and trek to Africa's roof or explore the mountain's lower slopes. (p233)

Usambara Mountains Hike from village to village through pine forests, maize fields and lovely landscapes. (p40)

Mt Meru Tanzania's second-highest peak is a fine destination in itself, or as a warm-up for Kilimanjaro. (p40)

Crater Highlands Experience the rugged beauty and Rift Valley vistas with a Maasai guide. (p40)

Udzungwa Mountains National Park Forested slopes, rushing streams, tumbling waterfalls and 10 species of primates. (p289)

Mt Hanang Tanzania's fourth-highest peak offers a straightforward climb and an introduction to local Barabaig culture. (p244)

Kitulo National Park The park's rugged, magnificent setting, filled with orchids and wildflowers, is ideal for well-equipped hikers. (p302)

Top: Wild dolphin off the coast of Zanzibar (p75)

Bottom: Beach near Saadani National Park (p130)

Southern Highlands The areas around Tukuyu, Njombe and Iringa offer many lovely walks. (p41)

Mahale Mountains As remote as Tanzania gets, with pristine mountain peaks surrounded by wildlife and jungle. (p272)

Birdwatching

Rubondo Island National Park This tranquil group of islands is an outstanding birding destination, with a wealth of waterbirds. (p257)

Amani Nature Reserve Lush montane forest rich with unique bird species. (p142)

Selous Game Reserve The Rufiji River's banks are covered with nests; the river and its tributaries offer outstanding birding. (p322)

Northern Safari Circuit The northern parks host a wealth of avian species, with Lake Manyara a particular birding highlight. (p168)

Udzungwa Mountains Fine destination home to endemics including the Udzungwa forest partridge, plus many wetland species. (p289)

Lake Natron With its millions of flamingos, this otherworldly lake is not to be missed. (p188)

Mkomazi National Park Birding is a highlight in this offbeat park, especially around Dindera Dam. (p152)

Creature Comforts

Selous Game Reserve The Selous has wonderful lodges, each rivalling the next in setting and ambience. (p322)

Northern Safari Circuit Tanzania's northern parks are awash with excellent choices, both within and outside the park boundaries. (p153)

PLAN YOUR TRIP IF YOU LIKE...

Ngorongoro Crater Try an exclusive lodge overlooking the crater or in the nearby highlands around Karatu. (p181)

Ruaha National Park This park has a great collection of comfortable camps and lodges; try a few nights at each. (p297)

Mafia Unique lodges where you can pamper yourself, enjoy fine dining and take in the beautiful ocean views. (p317)

Zanzibar Archipelago The islands abound in comfortable choices, on the beaches as well as in Stone Town. (p75)

Lake Tanganyika Relax in an 'African Zen' bungalow overlooking the lake. (p276)

Diving & Snorkelling

Zanzibar Island The north has excellent fish diversity and many pelagics, while Stone Town offers wrecks and reefs. (p77)

Mnemba There is outstanding snorkelling around this tiny private island, just opposite Zanzibar Island's Matemwe village. (p106)

Pemba Challenging, spectacular dives off the Kigomasha Peninsula, and snorkelling around tiny Misali Island. (p117)

Mafia Island Marine Park Excellent corals, lots of fish and no crowds are the highlights of this marine park. (p319)

Lake Tanganyika The lake's clear, deep waters are home to many species of colourful cichlids. (p276)

Maziwe Marine Reserve A tiny patch of sand offshore from Pangani that makes a good offbeat snorkelling destination. (p135)

Fanjove Private Island Dive and snorkel in uncharted waters from this low-key island northeast of Kilwa. (p331)

Mnazi Bay-Ruvuma Estuary Marine Park Rewarding diving well away from the crowds. (p339)

Offbeat Travel

Lake Tanganyika Take the MV *Liemba* to Mahale Mountains park or reach Gombe park via lake taxi. (p270)

Western Tanzania Visit Tabora and safari in Katavi National Park for an introduction to Tanzania's wild west. (p265)

Lake Nyasa Laze on the lakeshore, paddle in a dugout canoe or visit a local pottery market. (p309)

Southern Highlands Explore the hills around Mbeya and Njombe, hike in Kitulo National Park and relax around Iringa. (p303)

Southeastern Tanzania Immerse yourself in coastal history, with stops in Mafia, Kilwa, Mikindani, Lindi and Mtwara. (p315)

Pangani Relax on lovely beaches, visit ruins and finish with a boat trip to Zanzibar Island. (p132)

Saadani National Park Saadani safaris offer the chance to experience bush and beach at the same time. (p130)

Lake Victoria Island-hop at Rubondo Island National Park or explore the lively lakeside towns of Bukoba and Musoma. (p257)

Lake Eyasi Take in Lake Eyasi's stark landscapes and meet the local Hadzabe. (p180)

Ruins & Rock Art

Kilwa Kisiwani & **Songo Mnara** Haunting echoes from Kilwa's days as linchpin of far-flung trading networks to Persia and the Orient. (p329)

Bagamoyo Ruins at nearby Kaole and a wealth of historical buildings document sleepy Bagamoyo's long history. (p128)

Pangani & **Tongoni** Crumbling Pangani and nearby overgrown Tongoni were once major centres along the Swahili coast. (p132)

Mafia The atmospheric ruins on Chole and Juani islands hark back to the Mafia Archipelago's Shirazi-era heyday. (p318)

Kondoa Rock-Art Sites These sites in central Tanzania's Irangi hills are Tanzania's most recently designated Unesco World Heritage Site. (p242)

Travelling on a Budget

Usambara Mountains Hike through the hills, following the cycle of local market days. (p141)

Local-Style Dining Dine like a local in a *hoteli* (local eatery). (p365)

Bus Travel Taking the bus costs a fraction of car rental and is an eye-opener into local life. (p388)

Church Singing Tanzania's churches are packed to overflowing; Sunday services are long, but the singing is outstanding. (p54)

MV Liemba A sail down Lake Tanganyika on this ageing ferry is one of Africa's classic journeys. (p270)

Cultural Tourism Programs Seek out these community-run ventures for reasonably priced introductions to local life and culture. (p156)

Pare Mountains Spend time here hiking and learning about burial and other traditions. (p149)

Ruaha Cultural Tourism Program Cattle-herd with the Maasai and take lessons in traditional cooking. (p298)

Southern Tanzania The Southern Highlands and southeastern coast are ideal regions for exploring on a budget. (p281)

Month by Month

January

The weather almost everywhere is hot, especially along the coast. It's also dry, including on Kilimanjaro, and this dry, warm season from December into February can be an ideal time to scale the mountain.

✨ Zanzibar Swahili Festival

This art and cultural festival is held every four months on Zanzibar Island, each time with a different focus.

February

The weather continues to be hot, but in parts of the country the rains start falling, giving relief from the drought and bringing green landscapes, flowers and birds.

◉ Orchids in Kitulo National Park

The blooms of orchids (over 40 species have been identified) as well as irises, geraniums and many other wildflowers carpet Kitulo Plateau in Tanzania's Southern Highlands. It's the rainy, muddy season here, but hardy, well-equipped hikers will be rewarded. (p302)

✨ Sauti za Busara

This three-day music and dance festival (www.busaramusic.org) in Zanzibar Town's Stone Town is centred on all things Swahili, both traditional and modern.

◉ Wildebeest Calving Season

In one of nature's greatest spectacles, over 8000 wildebeest calves are born each day in the southern Serengeti, although about 40% of these will die before they are four months old.

March

The long rains move into full swing by late March, although it seldom rains all day or every day. Some hotels close. Those that remain open often offer low-season discounts, and you'll have many areas to yourself.

✨ Jalada Mobile Literary & Arts Festival

Dates and locations vary for this mobile festival, which travels throughout East Africa celebrating cultural diversity and promoting cross-cultural literary and artistic exchanges with workshops, performances, film screenings and more.

🏃 Kilimanjaro Marathon

This marathon (www.kilimanjaromarathon.com) is something to do around Kilimanjaro's foothills, in case climbing to the summit isn't enough; it's held in late February or early March in Moshi, with a half-marathon, a 10km wheelchair marathon and a 5km fun run also available.

✗ Nyama Choma Festival

Self-described as 'the largest barbecue showcase festival in East Africa', this is the place to try one of Tanzania's favourite meals, prepared in seemingly infinite variety by master chefs. Held several times annually in Dar es Salaam and other locations (www.facebook.com/nyamachomafest).

April

The rains begin to taper off in some areas, although much of the country remains wet. Green landscapes, wildflowers and birds, plus continued low-season prices, make this a delightful time to travel, if you can avoid the mud.

☉ Wildebeest Migration Begins

The wildebeest – until now widely scattered over the southern Serengeti and the western reaches of Ngorongoro Conservation Area – begin to form thousands-strong herds that start migrating north and west in search of food.

June

With the ending of the rains, the air is clear and landscapes are slowly beginning to dry out. Temperatures are also considerably cooler.

✦ Bulabo Dance Festival

This festival features rival dance teams; each competes to win the most audience members using animals such as snakes, hyenas and porcupines. It's held in late May or June and timed to coincide with the Christian Corpus Christi feast day (www.sukumamuseum.org).

☉ Serengeti Wildebeest Migration

As the southern Serengeti dries out, vast wildebeest

Top: Mara River crossing (p193)

Bottom: Swahili Fashion Week (p58), Dar es Salaam

herds continue migrating northwestward in search of food, crossing the Grumeti River en route. The timing of the crossing (which lasts about a week) varies from year to year, anywhere from May to July.

July

Cool, dry July marks the start of peak travel season, with higher prices (and crowds) for safaris and lodges. It's an optimal wildlife-watching month, with sparse vegetation and animals congregating at dwindling water sources.

◉ Dry Season Wildlife Watching

As rivers and streams dry out, animals congregate around remaining water sources, and it's common to see large herds of elephants and more. Katavi and Tarangire parks are particularly notable for their dry season wildlife watching in late July and August.

🎎 Festival of the Dhow Countries

This two-week extravaganza of dance, music, film and literature from Tanzania and other Indian Ocean countries has the Zanzibar International Film Festival (www.ziff.or.tz) as its centrepiece. It's held in early to mid-July at various locations in the Zanzibar Archipelago.

🎎 Mwaka Kogwa

This sometimes raucous four-day festival in late July marks Nairuzim (the Shirazi New Year). Festivities are best in Makunduchi on Zanzibar Island.

🏃 Ruaha Marathon

This marathon (www.ruahamarathon.org) in and around Iringa is a good way to test your fitness and to see the Southern Highlands. There are also races for runners with disabilities.

August

Dry weather continues, as does the Serengeti wildebeest migration. Wildlife watching almost everywhere is at its prime.

◉ Mara River Crossing

By August – often earlier – the wildebeest make their spectacular crossing of the Mara River into Kenya's Masai Mara, before roaming south again in anticipation of the rains.

September

September is a delightful month throughout the country, with pleasant temperatures, dry weather, good animal-spotting and many things to do.

🎎 Bagamoyo International Festival of Arts & Culture

This is a somewhat unorganised but fascinating week of traditional music, dance, drama, acrobatics, poetry reading and more, sponsored by the Bagamoyo College of Arts (www.tasuba.ac.tz) and featuring local and regional ensembles. Dates vary.

◉ Dar es Salaam Charity Goat Races

Tanzania's answer to the Royal Ascot, with proceeds going to charity. Sponsor a goat or three, and come join in the festivities (www.goatraces.co.tz). Dates vary.

October

The weather is mostly dry throughout the country, with a profusion of lavender jacaranda blossoms in higher-lying towns and some rain. It's still a fine time for wildlife watching, without the crowds of July and August.

November

Increasing temperatures are mitigated by the arrival of mango season and by the short rains that are now falling in many areas. It's still a pleasant travel time, before the holiday travel high season.

🎎 Karibu Music Festival

This lively festival (http://karibumusic.org) has grown fast, and is now one of Tanzania's largest music festivals. It's held in Bagamoyo; dates vary.

December

December's holidays and hot, dry weather bring many visitors. It's an ideal time to climb Mt Kilimanjaro and to see the wildebeest in the southern Serengeti.

◉ Swahili Fashion Week

The largest showcase for East African design (www.swahilifashionweek.com), this event is held annually in December.

Itineraries

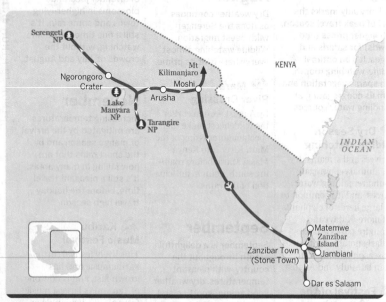

Serengeti NP

Ngorongoro Crater

Lake Manyara NP

Tarangire NP

Mt Kilimanjaro

Moshi

Arusha

KENYA

INDIAN OCEAN

Matemwe

Zanzibar Island

Zanzibar Town (Stone Town)

Jambiani

Dar es Salaam

2 WEEKS Tanzania's Greatest Hits

This route combines wildlife watching or trekking with gorgeous beaches and the alluring 'Spice Islands'. It's a popular itinerary, with plenty of accommodation and dining choices at all stops.

Fly into Kilimanjaro International Airport. Starting at **Arusha**, spend your first week exploring a few of the northern parks. Good wildlife-watching combinations include **Ngorongoro Crater** and **Serengeti National Park** or Ngorongoro plus **Lake Manyara National Park** and **Tarangire National Park**. Alternatively, head from the airport to **Moshi** and embark on a **Mt Kilimanjaro** trek. For either of these options (epic wildlife watching or serious mountain trekking), there are also numerous opportunities for hiking and cultural interaction around Arusha and Moshi.

Give the second half of your adventure over to less energetic pursuits. First, either fly to **Zanzibar Island** or travel overland from Moshi or Arusha and then catch a boat. Once here, divide your week between exploration of **Stone Town** (Zanzibar Town's historic quarter) and relaxation on the island's beaches – **Matemwe** and **Jambiani** are just two of the possibilities for getting your fill of white sand. Fly out again from Zanzibar Island, or from nearby Dar es Salaam.

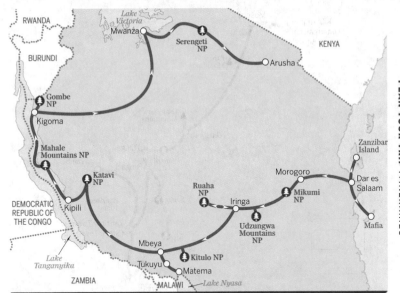

6 WEEKS Southern Highlands & Western Tanzania

The Southern Highlands is one of Tanzania's most scenic regions, appealing especially to adventure-loving travellers with at least several weeks at their disposal. For those with more time and a taste for the offbeat, the region links nicely with western Tanzania.

From **Dar es Salaam**, head west to **Morogoro** for cultural tours and hiking, or to **Mikumi National Park**, with its easily spotted wildlife. Next stop: **Udzungwa Mountains National Park**, for hiking up the steep, lushly vegetated slopes or exploring the surrounding Kilombero area. Alternatively, continue from Mikumi to **Iringa**, which makes a relaxing base. From Iringa, a two- or three-night detour to **Ruaha National Park** is well worth the effort, before heading down the Tanzam Hwy to **Mbeya**. En route are several lovely spots to relax and explore.

Once in Mbeya, there is plenty to do in the surrounding area. Options include hiking in the scenic hills around **Tukuyu**; canoeing, exploring and hiking around Lake Nyasa, using **Matema**, with its picturesque beach and lush mountains, as a base; and hiking in lovely **Kitulo National Park**, with its wildflowers and wide vistas.

Taking your time, it would be easy enough to spend the first three weeks of your itinerary up to this point. With the remaining time, you could return the way you came, with several days left over at the end for a short stay on **Zanzibar Island** or **Mafia**. On Mafia, don't miss a day of diving or snorkelling from a wooden dhow.

For those wanting more adventure, we recommend continuing northwest from Mbeya via Sumbawanga to **Katavi National Park**. This park deserves at least two days, especially in the dry season when wildlife watching is at its best. From Katavi, double back and head down the escarpment to Lake Tanganyika for several days relaxing at **Lake Shore Lodge** near Kipili before taking the MV *Liemba* to **Mahale Mountains National Park**, or on to **Kigoma** and perhaps an overnight at nearby **Gombe National Park**. From Kigoma, take a train, bus or plane back to Dar es Salaam. Alternatively – but this will require two to three additional weeks – you can continue overland from Kigoma to **Mwanza** and Lake Victoria, from where you could proceed into the **Serengeti** and on to **Arusha**.

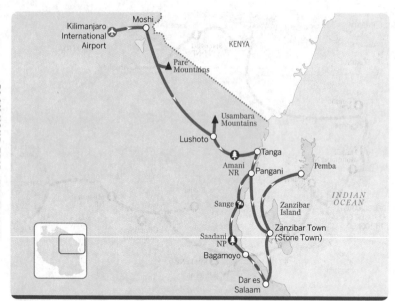

4 WEEKS Northeastern Tanzania

Northeastern Tanzania has accommodation options and transport connections for all budgets, and a delightful mix of beach, cultural and historical attractions and bush. For combination itineraries, it's also conveniently sandwiched between Tanzania's northern circuit wildlife parks and Mt Kilimanjaro to the northwest, and the Zanzibar Archipelago to the east.

From Kilimanjaro airport, spend time in **Moshi** before heading southeast to the **Usambara Mountains** around **Lushoto**. It's easy to spend up to a week here hiking, exploring and enjoying the hill panoramas. Botanists and birders can venture further to **Amani Nature Reserve** in the eastern Usambaras, with its cool forest walks and nighttime symphony of insects. With extra time and a tolerance for off-the-beaten-track travel, another possible detour before reaching Lushoto is to the **Pare Mountains** for hiking and getting to know local Pare culture.

Once you've finished exploring the mountains, travel eastwards to **Tanga**. This coastal town, with its relaxed ambience, wide streets filled with cyclists, nearby beaches and many nearby excursions, is one of Tanzania's most pleasant urban areas. It's also the starting point for exploring the **Pangani** area, with its quiet coastline and long history. Many travellers wind up staying here longer than planned.

Zanzibar Island is just across the channel from Pangani, and there are regular boat and plane connections linking the island with Pangani and with nearby Tanga. Once on Zanzibar Island, get to know Zanzibar Town's **Stone Town**, relax on a beach or two or three and perhaps also venture to **Pemba** for a complete change of pace. After you have finished your exploration of the archipelago, frequent boat and plane connections make it easy to get to **Dar es Salaam**. Allow a day or several in this crowded, bustling city to see the sights, do some final shopping, enjoy the array of good eateries and perhaps even visit nearby historical **Bagamoyo** or (with a bit more time) tiny **Saadani National Park**. An enjoyable way to incorporate these latter destinations into your travels is by making your way down the coast from Pangani to Bagamoyo via lovely **Sange beach**.

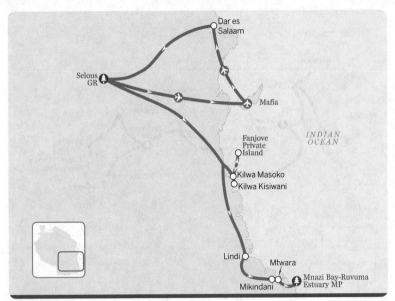

10 DAYS Selous, Mafia & Beyond

This itinerary is ideal for those wanting to get a glimpse of Tanzania's wildlife and beaches away from the more standard northern circuit–Zanzibar Archipelago combination. Allow about 10 days for a straight Selous–Mafia combination, and up to four weeks for extended versions taking in Kilwa and Mikindani, further south.

Starting in **Dar es Salaam**, spend several days enjoying the city's restaurants and craft shopping, visiting a museum or taking a cultural tourism tour.

From Dar es Salaam, there are daily buses in the dry season to **Selous Game Reserve**, but it's a long, rough ride. There's also a slow train, and daily flights. The Selous is a magnificent reserve, and well worth at least three to four days enjoying its fine lodges, boat safaris, wildlife and amazing night sounds, especially hippos grunting in the Rufiji River.

From Selous, there are daily flights to **Mafia**, just offshore. Spend the remaining few days of your stay here in one of the lovely island lodges, diving and snorkelling, trying to spot whale sharks or sailing to some of the smaller islands to get a glimpse into the archipelago's fascinating Swahili culture and long history. From Mafia, take one of the several daily flights back to Dar es Salaam.

For adventurous travellers with more time and a taste for the offbeat, continue from Selous Game Reserve (or from the mainland coast opposite Mafia island, for those who depart Mafia by boat) to Tanzania's far south. Sleepy **Kilwa Masoko** makes a pleasant destination for a day or two. The town is also the springboard to the famed ruins at **Kilwa Kisiwani**, just offshore. Another possible excursion from Kilwa Masoko is to nearby **Fanjove Private Island**, which has a lovely, upmarket lodge, and which is easily combined with both Mafia and Kilwa. Once you've finished exploring in the Kilwa area, continue by bus south via **Lindi** to the **Mtwara** area, where **Mikindani** – with its coconut plantations and long history – and the beach at Msimbati, in the **Mnazi Bay-Ruvuma Estuary Marine Park**, are the highlights.

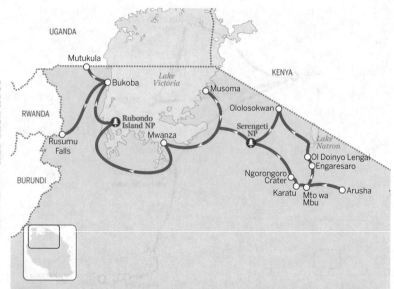

Lake Victoria & Serengeti National Park

3 WEEKS

Lake Victoria is a fascinating region with much to offer those who enjoy exploring off the beaten track. It's also easily combined with wildlife watching in Serengeti National Park.

From **Arusha**, head west to Serengeti, stopping en route in **Karatu** to enjoy the cool and stunning highlands, and in **Ngorongoro Crater** for wildlife and magnificent views from the crater rim. Following exploration of central **Serengeti**, continue into the park's Western Corridor, which is especially rewarding around May and early June. Exit the park at Ndabaka gate, from where it's an easy bus ride on good tarmac north to lively **Musoma**.

With extra time and a taste for adventure, consider varying the above approach to the Serengeti to arrive in the park via Lake Natron: after leaving Arusha, continue west on good tarmac toward Karatu. Before reaching Karatu, turn north at the lively market village of **Mto wa Mbu** toward **Engaresero** and **Lake Natron**. Spend at least one night at Lake Natron, ideally two or three. Nearby, and dominating vistas, is the starkly majestic **Ol Doinyo Lengai** – a rewarding trek for adventurous travellers. Once finished exploring the Lake Natron area, continue northwest via Loliondo village and the honey-producing village of **Ololosokwan** to enter the Serengeti via the park's northerly Klein's gate. Spend several days exploring the northern Serengeti before heading south toward central Serengeti, then joining the main route through the Western Corridor toward Musoma.

In Musoma, it's easy to spend several days becoming acquainted with the region's many cultures and enjoying sunrise and sunset views over Lake Victoria. Once ready to move on, take the bus south to **Mwanza**, with its low-key vibe and good facilities.

Continue west around the lake toward pretty, prosperous **Bukoba** and the heart of the ancient Haya kingdom. There are many cultural tours to see waterfalls, cave paintings and rural homesteads that offer an excellent introduction to Haya life and culture. En route to Bukoba, don't miss **Rubondo Island National Park**, with its magnificent birding. Once finished, connections are easy into Rwanda (at **Rusumu Falls**) or Uganda (**Mutukula**). This itinerary can be rearranged with Mwanza as the starting point, with the advantage that Serengeti safaris are generally cheaper to arrange from Mwanza than from Arusha.

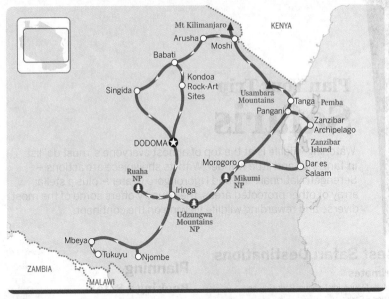

6 WEEKS Tanzania Circuit

Road conditions in central Tanzania have improved greatly, opening up the chance for circuit itineraries combining northern and central Tanzania with the Southern Highlands, the coast and northeastern Tanzania. Four weeks is the minimum, but there's enough to do to keep you busy for twice that long.

Arusha makes a convenient starting point. Allow up to a week here, perhaps taking in a northern circuit safari or some cultural tourism activities. From Arusha, head southwest toward **Babati**, where you can detour for a hike up Mt Hanang. Afterwards, continue on to Dodoma via **Singida**, which is completely off the beaten track. Take a stroll near Lake Singidani and visit Singida's small museum. Alternatively, head south from Babati directly to Dodoma, stopping en route at the **Kondoa Rock-Art Sites**.

Dodoma itself – Tanzania's official capital – is worth a day or two, walking the wide streets, admiring the religious architecture and possibly visiting the Bunge (parliament). From Dodoma, continue south on a recently upgraded road to **Iringa**, as well as the gateway to the lovely Southern Highlands to the southwest. From here, you could travel southwest toward **Njombe**, **Mbeya** or **Tukuyu**. Otherwise, head northeast toward Morogoro, stopping en route at **Udzungwa Mountains National Park** for several days of hiking, and at **Mikumi National Park** for wildlife watching. Wildlife watching is also easily incorporated into this itinerary in **Ruaha National Park**, which is readily accessed from Iringa.

In **Morogoro**, allow a day or two to explore the Ulugurus on a cultural tourism program tour before continuing east to **Dar es Salaam** or northeast toward **Pangani** and **Tanga**. Once on the coast, it's easy to arrange a detour to the **Zanzibar Archipelago**, with flights from Dar es Salaam, Pangani and Tanga and sea connections from Pangani and Dar es Salaam. After relaxing along the coast, head to the **Usambara Mountains** for hiking in the hills before continuing on to **Moshi**, home of the Chagga people and of **Mt Kilimanjaro**. It's easy to spend several days here exploring the mountain's lower slopes and enjoying Moshi's laid-back vibe. From Moshi, take the bus back to Arusha or to Kilimanjaro airport and your flight home.

Plan Your Trip
Safaris

Watching wildlife is at the top of almost everyone's 'must do' list in Tanzania, and little wonder. With its showpiece attractions – Serengeti National Park and Ngorongoro Crater – plus a stellar array of other protected areas, the country offers some of the most diverse and rewarding wildlife viewing on the continent.

Best Safari Destinations

Primates
Mahale Mountains National Park, Gombe National Park

Elephants
Tarangire National Park, Selous Game Reserve

Predators
Serengeti National Park, Ruaha National Park

Offbeat Safaris
Katavi National Park, Rubondo Island National Park

Birdwatching
Lake Manyara National Park, Serengeti National Park, Rubondo Island National Park, Selous Game Reserve

Active Safaris
Lake Manyara National Park, Kilimanjaro National Park, Udzungwa Mountains National Park

Dry Season
Katavi National Park, Tarangire National Park, Ruaha National Park, Selous Game Reserve

Wet Season
Serengeti National Park, Kitulo National Park

Planning

Booking a Safari

Arusha is the best base for organising visits to the northern parks. Mwanza-based operators also organise safaris into western Serengeti. For the southern parks, there's no comparable hub, although most southern-focused operators have offices in Dar es Salaam. For Gombe and Mahale Mountains, Kigoma is the base for independent and budget travellers, while most upper-end safaris to these parks, and to Katavi, are organised out of Arusha as fly-in packages or – for Mahale and Katavi – as fly-in add-ons to a Ruaha safari. For land-based safaris to Katavi, good bases are Lake Shore Lodge (p276) in Kipili and Mpanda town. Mwanza and Bukoba are the starting points for Rubondo Island National Park.

Booking and paying for a safari before arriving in Tanzania is recommended if you'll be travelling in popular areas during the high season. If you wait to book your safari once in Tanzania, allow time to shop around and don't rush into any deals.

Normally, major problems such as vehicle breakdown are compensated for by adding additional time to your safari. If this isn't possible (eg if you have an onward flight), reliable operators may compensate you for a portion of the time lost. However, don't expect a refund for 'minor' problems such as punctured tyres and so on. Park fees are also non-refundable. If you do get taken for a ride, the main avenue of recourse is to file a complaint with both the **Tanzania Tourist Board** (TTB; www.tanzaniatourism.com) and the **Tanzanian Association of Tour Operators** (TATO; ✆0754 535637, 027-250 6430, 027-254 5208; www.tatotz.org; Philips St, just off Simeon Rd, Arusha). The police will be of little help, and it's unlikely that you will see your money again.

Costs

Most safari quotes include park entrance fees, accommodation and transport costs to/from the park and within the park, but confirm before paying. Drinks (alcoholic or not) are generally excluded, although many operators provide one bottle of water daily. Budget camping safari prices usually exclude sleeping bag rental (US$5 per day to US$30 per trip).

If accommodation-only prices apply, you'll need to pay extra to actually go out looking for wildlife, either on wildlife drives, boat safaris or walks. There is usually the chance for two of these 'activities' per day (each about two to three hours). Costs range from around US$30 per person per activity up to US$300 per vehicle per day for wildlife drives.

Budget Safaris

Most budget safaris are camping safaris. To minimise costs, you'll likely camp outside national park areas (thereby missing early-morning prime viewing time, but saving on park admission and camping fees) or stay in budget guesthouses. Budget operators also save costs by working with larger groups to minimise per-person transport costs, and by keeping to a no-frills setup with basic meals and a minimum number of staff. Most budget and many midrange safaris place daily kilometre limits on the vehicles.

Expect to pay from US$150 to US$200 per person per day for a budget safari with a registered operator. To save money, bring drinks with you, especially bottled water, as it's expensive in and near the parks. Snacks, extra food and toilet paper are other worthwhile backpack additions. During the low season it's often possible to find a lodge safari for close to the price of a camping safari.

Midrange Safaris

Midrange safaris usually use lodges, where you'll have a room and eat in a restaurant. Overall, safaris in this category are comfortable, reliable and reasonably good value. A disadvantage is that they may have somewhat of a packaged-tour or production-line feel, although this can be minimised by selecting a safari company and accommodation carefully, by giving attention to who and how many other people you travel with, and by avoiding the large, popular lodges during the high season. Midrange lodge safaris cost from US$200 to US$300 per person per day.

Top-End Safaris

Private lodges, luxury tented camps, and sometimes private fly camps, are used in top-end safaris, all with the aim of providing guests with as authentic and personal a bush experience as possible, while not forgoing the comforts. For the price you pay (from US$300 up to US$600 or more per person per day), expect a full range of amenities, and high-quality guiding. Even in remote settings without running water you will be able to enjoy hot, bush-style showers, comfortable beds and fine dining. Expect a good level of personalised attention and an often intimate atmosphere (many places at this level have fewer than 20 beds).

TIPPING

Tipping is an important part of the safari experience (especially to the driver/guides, cooks and others whose livelihoods depend on gratuities), and this will always be in addition to the price quoted by the operator. Many operators have tipping guidelines; expect to tip from about US$10 or US$15 per group per day to the driver and/or guide, and from about US$10 per group per day to the cook – more for top-end safaris or if an especially good job has been done. It's never a mistake to err on the side of generosity while tipping those who have worked to make your safari experience memorable. Whenever possible, give your tips directly to the staff whom you want to thank.

When to Go

Getting around is easier throughout the country in the dry season (late June to October), and in many parks this is when animals are easier to find around waterholes and rivers. Foliage is also less dense, making it easier to spot wildlife. However, as the dry season corresponds in part with the travel high season, lodges and camps become crowded and accommodation prices are at a premium. Some lodges and camps, mainly in Selous Game Reserve and in the western parks, close for a month or so around April and May.

Apart from these considerations, when to go depends in part on what your interests are. For birding, the rainy season months from November/December through to April are particularly rewarding. For walking in wildlife areas, the dry season is best. For general wildlife viewing, tailor your choice of park according to the season.

Large sections of Katavi, for example, are only accessible during the dry season, and almost all of the camps close during the rains. Tarangire National Park, although accessible year-round, is another park best visited during the dry season, when wildlife concentrations are significantly higher than at other times of the year. In the Serengeti wildlife concentrations are comparatively low (although still spectacular) during the dry season; it's during the wet season that you'll see the enormous herds of wildebeest massed in the park's southeastern section before they begin their migration north and west in search of food. The dry season, however, is best for lions and other predators. If you are planning your safari around specific events such as the Serengeti wildebeest migration, remember that the timing varies from year to year and is difficult to accurately predict in advance.

WHAT TO BRING

- [ ] binoculars
- [ ] good-quality sleeping bag (for camping safaris)
- [ ] mosquito repellent
- [ ] rain gear and waterproofs for wet-season travel
- [ ] sunglasses and sunscreen
- [ ] camera
- [ ] extra contact lens solution and your prescription glasses (the dust can be irritating)
- [ ] mosquito net (many places have nets, but it doesn't hurt to bring one along)
- [ ] lightweight, long-sleeved/legged clothing in subdued colours, a head covering and sturdy, comfortable shoes (for walking safaris)
- [ ] field guides (look for: *The Kingdon Field Guide to African Mammals* by Jonathan Kingdon; *The Safari Companion – A Guide to Watching African Mammals* by Richard Estes; *Birds of Kenya and Northern Tanzania* by Dale Zimmerman, Donald Turner and David Pearson; and *Field Guide to the Birds of East Africa* by Terry Stevenson and John Fanshawe, also available as an app)

Types of Safaris

Vehicle Safaris

In many parks, due to park regulations, vehicle safaris are the only option. In the northern parks, vehicle safaris must be done in a 'closed' vehicle, which means a vehicle with closed sides, although there is often an opening in the roof that allows you to stand up, get a better view and take photographs. These openings are sometimes just a simple hatch that flips open or comes off, or (better, as it affords some shade) a pop-up style roof. In Selous Game Reserve, some of the southern parks and Katavi National Park, safaris in open vehicles are permitted. These are usually high vehicles with two or three seats at staggered levels and a covering over the roof, but open on the sides and back. If you have the choice, open vehicles are best as they are roomier, give you a full viewing range and minimise barriers. The least-preferable option is minibuses, which are sometimes used, especially in the north. They accommodate too many people for a good experience, the rooftop opening is usually only large enough for a few passengers to use at a time and at least some passengers will get stuck in middle seats with poor views.

Whatever type of vehicle you are in, avoid overcrowding. Sitting uncomfortably scrunched together for several hours over

Top: Lake Magadi,
Ngorongoro Crater
(p181)

Bottom: Vehicle safari,
Ngorongoro Crater
(p181)

BLUEORANGE STUDIO / SHUTTERSTOCK ©

SAFARI STYLE

While price can be a major determining factor in safari planning, there are other considerations, too:

Ambience Will you be staying in or near the park? (If you stay well outside the park, you'll miss the good early-morning and evening wildlife-viewing hours.) Are the surroundings atmospheric? Will you be in a large lodge or an intimate private camp?

Equipment Mediocre vehicles and equipment can significantly detract from the overall experience. In remote areas, lack of quality equipment or vehicles and appropriate back-up arrangements can be a safety risk.

Access and activities If you don't relish the idea of hours in a 4WD on bumpy roads, consider parks and lodges where you can fly in. Areas offering walking and boat safaris are best for getting out of the vehicle and into the bush.

Guides A good driver/guide can make or break your safari. With low-budget operators trying to cut corners, chances are that staff are unfairly paid, and are not likely to be knowledgeable or motivated.

Community commitment Look for operators that do more than just give lip service to 'ecotourism' principles, and that have a genuine, long-standing commitment to the communities where they work. In addition to being more culturally responsible, they'll also be able to give you a more authentic experience.

Setting the agenda Some drivers feel that they have to whisk you from one good 'sighting' to the next. If you prefer to stay in one place for a while to experience the environment and see what comes by, discuss this with your driver. Going off in wild pursuit of the 'Big Five' means you'll miss the more subtle aspects of your surroundings.

Extracurriculars On the northern circuit, it's common for drivers to stop at souvenir shops en route. While this gives the driver an often much-needed break from the wheel, most shops pay drivers commissions to bring clients, which means you may find yourself spending more time souvenir shopping than you'd bargained for. Discuss this with your driver at the outset, ideally while still at the operator's offices.

Less is more If you'll be teaming up with others to make a group, find out how many people will be in your vehicle, and try to meet your travelling companions before setting off.

Special interests If birding or other special interests are important, arrange a private safari with a specialised operator.

bumpy roads puts a definite damper on the safari experience. Most safari quotes are based on groups of three to four passengers, which is about the maximum for comfort in most vehicles. Some companies put five or six passengers in a standard 4WD, but the minimal savings don't compensate for the extra discomfort.

Night drives are permitted in Lake Manyara and Tarangire National Parks, and in wildlife areas adjoining Tarangire.

Walking Safaris

Places where you can walk in 'big game' areas include Selous Game Reserve, and Ruaha, Mikumi, Katavi, Tarangire, Lake Manyara, Serengeti and Arusha National Parks. There are also several parks – notably Mt Kilimanjaro, Udzungwa Mountains, Mahale Mountains and Gombe National Parks – that can only be explored on foot. Short walks are easily arranged in Rubondo Island National Park.

Most walking safaris offered are for one to two hours, usually done in the early morning or late afternoon and then returning to the main camp or lodge or, alternatively, to a fly camp. Not much distance is covered; the pace is measured, with the main goal discovering your surroundings in depth rather than spotting lots of large animals. En route there will be stops for observation, or for your guide to pick up an animal's track. Some walking safaris are done within park boundaries, while others are in adjacent areas that are part of the park ecosystem. Multiday walks are possible in Ngorongoro Conservation Area, Serengeti National Park and Selous Game Reserve.

Walks are always accompanied by a guide, who is usually armed, and with whom you will need to walk in close proximity.

Boat & Canoe Safaris

The best place for boat safaris is along the Rufiji River in Selous Game Reserve. They're also possible on the Wami River bordering Saadani National Park, although the wildlife cannot compare. Canoe safaris are possible on the Momella Lakes in Arusha National Park, and sometimes on Lake Manyara (water level permitting).

Itineraries

Don't be tempted to try to fit too much in to your itinerary. Distances in Tanzania are long, and at the end, hopping from park to park is likely to leave you tired, unsatisfied and feeling that you haven't even scratched the surface. More rewarding: longer periods at just one or two parks, exploring in depth what each has to offer, and taking advantage of cultural and walking opportunities in park border areas.

Northern Circuit

Arusha National Park (p167) is easily visited as a day trip. Tarangire (p172) and Lake Manyara (p176) parks are frequently accessed as overnight trips from Arusha, although both deserve more time to do them justice. For a half-week itinerary, try any of the northern parks alone (for the Serengeti, it's worth considering flying at least one way, since it's a full day's drive from Arusha), or Ngorongoro Crater together with either Lake Manyara or Tarangire. With a week, you will have just enough time for the classic combination of Lake Manyara, Tarangire, Ngorongoro and the Serengeti, but it's better to focus on just two or three of these. The Serengeti alone, or in combination with Ngorongoro Crater, could easily keep you happy for a week. Many operators offer a standard three-day tour of Lake Manyara, Tarangire and Ngorongoro (or a four- to five-day version including the Serengeti). However, distances to Ngorongoro and the Serengeti are long, and the trip is likely to leave you feeling that you've spent too much time rushing from park to park and not enough time settling in and experiencing the actual environments.

In addition to these more conventional itineraries, there are countless other possibilities combining wildlife viewing with visits to other areas. For example, you might begin with a vehicle safari in Ngorongoro Crater followed by a climb of Ol Doinyo Lengai (p190), trekking elsewhere in the Ngorongoro Conservation Area (p181), relaxing at one of the lodges around Karatu (p178), or visiting Lake Eyasi (p180). Alternatively, combine travel around Lake Victoria (p246) and a visit to

---

TIPS FOR WILDLIFE WATCHING
David Lukas

➡ Your best bet for seeing black rhinos is Ngorongoro Crater. Here they are used to vehicles, while elsewhere in Tanzania they are secretive and occur in remote locations.

➡ Let the vervet monkeys tell you if there's a predator in the neighbourhood. Listen for their screeching alarm calls and look in the direction they're facing.

➡ During the July to October dry season, Tarangire National Park provides outstanding wildlife viewing. Over 3000 elephants and many other migratory animals come here to drink from the Tarangire River.

➡ Hundreds of thousands of flamingos may be seen at Lake Manyara National Park, though they move from lake to lake as water levels and composition change, and their presence is never predictable.

➡ Don't forget a high-quality pair of binoculars. Practise using them at home before departing because some animals, especially birds, don't wait around for you to learn how to aim and focus in the field.

Rubondo Island National Park (p257) with the western Serengeti.

Southern Circuit

Mikumi (p286) and Saadani (p130) National Parks are good destinations from Dar es Salaam if you only have a couple of nights. Three to four days would be ideal for Selous Game Reserve (p322), or for Ruaha National Park (p297), if you fly. Together, Mikumi and Udzungwa Mountains National Park (p289) offer an enjoyable safari-hiking combination. Recommended week-long combination itineraries include Selous and Ruaha, or Ruaha and Katavi, in the west, both of which allow you to sample markedly different terrain and wildlife populations. The Ruaha-Katavi combination is increasingly popular given the availability of flights between the two parks. The expanded flight network linking the southern and western parks with the coast has opened up the possibility for longer itineraries combining time on the coast or islands with safaris in Ruaha, Mahale and/ or Katavi. Selous and Mafia or Zanzibar Island is also a recommended safari-beach combination.

Western Parks

For Katavi National Park (p277) alone, plan at least two to three days. For a six- to seven-day itinerary, Katavi and Mahale (p272) make a fine combination, and many fly-in safari schedules are built around this. Budget extra days to relax in between on Lake Tanganyika (p276). Katavi is easily and rewardingly combined with Ruaha, and a Ruaha-Katavi-Mahale grouping is also quite feasible; plan on at least nine or 10 days. For Gombe (p271), budget two days. Adventurous overland travellers can bring Rubondo Island park into a western Tanzania itinerary. At least two days on the island is recommended.

Other Areas

Mkomazi National Park (p152) is an intriguing stop for birders on any itinerary linking Dar es Salaam or the northeastern coast with Arusha and the northern circuit. Kitulo National Park (p302) can be worked into itineraries in the Mbeya-Tukuyu area, or from Iringa. Diving in Mafia Island Marine Park (p319) is easily incorporated into a stay on Mafia island.

Do-It-Yourself Safaris

It's quite feasible to visit the parks with your own vehicle, without going through a safari operator. However, unless you're based in Tanzania or are particularly experienced at bush driving and self-sufficient for spares and repairs, the cost savings will be offset by the ease of having someone else handle the logistics.

For most parks and reserves, you'll need a 4WD. There's a US$47.20 per day vehicle fee for foreign-registered vehicles (Tsh23,600 for locally registered vehicles). Guides are not required, except as noted in the individual park entries. However, taking one can help you find your way, and to locate the best wildlife areas. Hiring a guide also helps the local economy, and helps people see wildlife as a resource that is worth protecting. If you try to go solo, you lose their knowledge of the area and may just wander around flailing, whereas a guide can take you right to where you want to go.

Carry extra petrol, as it's not available in any of the parks, except (expensively) at Seronera in the Serengeti.

You can rent safari vehicles in Dar es Salaam, Arusha, Mwanza, Karatu and Mto wa Mbu and sometimes near Katavi National Park. Otherwise, there's no vehicle rental at any of the parks or reserves.

Operators
Northern Circuit

The following are recommended companies focusing on the northern circuit, including Mt Kilimanjaro.

Access2Tanzania (www.access2tanzania.com) Customised, community-focused itineraries throughout Tanzania and into neighbouring Rwanda.

Africa Travel Resource (ATR; www.africatravel resource.com) Web-based safari broker that matches your safari ideas with an operator and offers excellent background information on its website.

African Scenic Safaris (☑0783 080239; www. africanscenicsafaris.com) Well-organised cultural tours, northern circuit safaris and Kilimanjaro treks.

Anasa Safaris (www.anasasafari.com) Customised mobile safaris in the northern circuit. Also runs lodges in Mkomazi National Park, Lake Eyasi and Lake Victoria.

Base Camp Tanzania (Map p158; ☎027-250 0393; www.basecamptanzania.com; Golden Rose Arcade, Colonel Middleton Rd, Arusha) Northern circuit safaris and treks.

Dorobo Safaris (☎0744 366335; www.dorobo safaris.com) ✈ Culturally-oriented wildlife safaris and treks.

Duma Explorer (☎0787 079127; www.duma explorer.com) Northern Tanzania safaris, Kilimanjaro and Meru treks and cultural tours.

Hoopoe Safaris (Map p158; ☎027-250 7011; www.hoopoe.com; India St, Arusha; ⊙8.30am-5.30pm Mon-Fri, to 2pm Sat) ✈ Highly regarded company offering community-integrated luxury camping and lodge safaris in the northern circuit; also has its own tented camps at Lake Manyara and mobile camps in the Serengeti.

IntoAfrica (☎0797 4975723; www.intoafrica.co.uk) ✈ Reliable, long-standing company offering fair-traded cultural safaris and treks in northern Tanzania, including a highly praised seven-day wildlife-cultural safari in Maasai areas.

Just Kilimanjaro (☎0789 743272; www.just-kilimanjaro.com) ✈ Small, highly regarded operator offering expertly guided Kilimanjaro treks.

Maasai Wanderings (☎0755 984925; www.maasaiwanderings.com) Tanzania safaris and treks focusing primarily on the northern circuit parks, but also with some itineraries on the coast and in southern Tanzania.

Makasa Safaris (☎0767 699006, 0767 453454; www.makasatanzania.com; 🖥) Northern circuit

---

CHOOSING AN OPERATOR

When booking safaris and treks, especially budget level, the need for careful research can't be overemphasised.

➡ Get personal recommendations, and talk with as many people as you can who have recently returned from a safari or trek with the company you're considering.

➡ Be sceptical of quotes that sound too good to be true and don't rush into any deals. If others have supposedly registered, ask to speak with them.

➡ Don't give money to anyone who doesn't work out of an office, and don't arrange any safari deals on the spot, at the bus stand or with touts who follow you to your hotel room.

➡ Check the blacklist of the Tanzania Tourist Board (TTB) Tourist Information Centre (p165) in Arusha – although keep in mind that this isn't necessarily the final word. Also check the Tanzanian Association of Tour Operators (p29) list of licensed operators. TATO isn't the most powerful of entities, but going on safari with one of its members will give you some recourse to appeal in case of problems.

➡ Ask to see a valid, original TALA (Tourist Agents Licensing Authority) licence – a government-issued document without which a company can't bring tourists into national parks. For wildlife parks, a tour or safari operator designation on the licence suffices; for Kilimanjaro treks, a TALA mountaineering licence is required. Be sceptical of claims that the original is with the 'head office' elsewhere in the country.

➡ Go with a company that has its own vehicles and equipment. If you have any doubts, don't pay a deposit until you've seen the vehicle (and tyres) that you'll be using and remember that it's not unknown for an operator to show you one vehicle, but then arrive in an inferior one on the day.

➡ Go through the itinerary in detail and confirm what is planned for each stage of the trip. Check that the number of wildlife drives per day and all other specifics appear in the contract. While two competing safari company itineraries may look the same, service can be very different. Beware of client swapping between companies; you can end up in the hands of a company you were trying to avoid.

➡ Watch for sham operators trading under the same names as companies listed in guidebooks. Don't let business cards or websites fool you; they're no proof of legitimacy.

safaris plus some southern Tanzania itineraries, family safaris and cultural excursions around the lower slopes of Mt Kilimanjaro.

Milestone Safaris (Map p227; ☑0767 551190; www.milestonesafaris.com; 400m southwest of Marangu Rd, at Honey Badger Lodge, Moshi) ✔ Kilimanjaro climbs, northern circuit safaris, safaricoast combination itineraries and cultural tours around Moshi.

Nature Discovery (☑027-254 4063; www. naturediscovery.com) A reliable and long-standing operator offering northern circuit safaris, and trekking on Kilimanjaro, Meru, the Crater Highlands and elsewhere in northern Tanzania.

Peace Matunda Tours (☑0787 482966, 0757 198076; www.peacematunda.org) ✔ Cultural walks and tours around Arusha, plus northern circuit wildlife safaris. Profits go to support the organisation's school and other community projects.

Roy Safaris (Map p158; ☑027-250 2115; www. roysafaris.com; Serengeti Rd, Arusha; ☺8am-5.30pm) A long-standing, reliable operator offering budget and semiluxury camping safaris in the northern circuit, as well as luxury lodge safaris, and Kilimanjaro and Meru treks.

Safari Makers (www.safarimakers.com; Suye-Kimandolo Rd, Arusha) No-frills northern circuit camping and lodge safaris and treks.

Shaw Safaris (Map p170; ☑0768 945735; www. shawsafaris.com) Northern circuit self-drive safaris.

Summit Expeditions & Nomadic Experience (☑0787 740282; www.nomadicexperience.com) Expertly guided Kilimanjaro treks, cycling, walks and cultural excursions on the mountain's lower slopes, and customised northern circuit wildlife safaris.

Tanzania Journeys (☑0787 834152, 027-275 4295; www.tanzaniajourneys.com) ✔ Northern circuit, community-focused vehicle, active and cultural safaris, including Kilimanjaro treks, day hikes and cultural tours in the Moshi area.

TinTin Tours (Map p228; ☑0657 123766; www. tintintours.org; Kibo Rd, Moshi) ✔ Low-key outfit offering Kilimanjaro treks and northern circuit safaris.

Wayo Africa (Green Footprint Adventures; ☑0784 203000, 0783 141119; www.wayoafrica.com) Northern circuit active safaris, including Serengeti walking safaris, cycling around Lake Manyara, canoeing in Arusha National Park and much more.

Wilkinson Tours (☑0784 805259; www.wilkinson -tours.com) Northern circuit safaris, plus Meru and Kilimanjaro climbs and add-on excursions to Zanzibar and other coastal destinations.

Southern Circuit

The following outifts do southern-circuit safari bookings, and combination itineraries involving Mikumi, Ruaha and Katavi National Parks, Selous Game Reserve, Zanzibar Island and Mafia.

Afriroots (☑0787 459887, 0713 652642, 0732 926350; www.afriroots.co.tz) Hiking and cycling safaris in the Udzungwa and Usambara mountains.

Authentic Tanzania (Map p62; ☑0786 019965; www.authentictanzania.com; Senga Rd, Mikocheni) Wilderness walking safaris, treks with chimpanzees, fly-camps, mountain biking, horse riding and more, in parks throughout western and southern Tanzania.

Bateleur Safaris & Tours (☑0765 735261, 0762 921825; www.bateleursafaris.co.tz; ☺8am-7pm) Excursions to Ruaha (including night safaris) and Mikumi National Parks, plus cultural tours around Iringa.

Essential Destinations (Map p62; ☑022-260 1747; www.ed.co.tz; Slipway, Slipway Rd, Msasani, Dar es Salaam) Long-established outfit with its own fleet of planes, and safari camps and lodges in Ruaha, Selous, Mafia and elsewhere.

Foxes African Safaris (www.foxessafaricamps.com) This long-standing family-run operation has lodges and camps in Mikumi, Ruaha and Katavi National Parks, on the coast near Bagamoyo, in the Southern Highlands and in Selous Game Reserve; it organises combination itineraries using plane and road.

Hippotours & Safaris (Map p62; ☑0754 267706, 0733 128662; www.hippotours.com; Kinondoni Rd, Ground Fl, Hugo House, Dar es Salaam) This long-standing operator runs customised safari itineraries focusing on southern and western Tanzania.

Tent with a View (☑0737 226398, 0713 323318; www.tentwithaview.com) This long-standing outfit specialises in southern circuit tours, especially in Selous, Saadani and on Zanzibar, where it has its own camps and hotels.

Wild Things Safaris (www.wildthingssafaris.com) Pioneering sustainable tourism safaris in conjunction with local communities, Wild Things will take you well off the beaten track with mobile camps, trekking and cultural tours in Ruaha, Mikumi, the Udzungwa Mountains and the remote Kilombero Valley.

Elsewhere in Tanzania

Lake Tanganyika Adventure Safaris (www. lakeshoretz.com) Organises highly recommended adventure safaris focusing on Katavi and Mahale Mountains National Parks and Lake Tanganyika.

Mt Kilimanjaro National Park (p233)

Plan Your Trip
Active Tanzania

Tanzania offers its famous wildlife safaris, plus much more, with diving, snorkelling, birdwatching, kitesurfing, chimpanzee tracking, cycling, hiking and trekking just some of the highlights. Plan your holiday around one of these options, or sample several.

Tanzania's Best

Trekking & Hiking

Mt Kilimanjaro, Mt Meru, Usambara Mountains, Crater Highlands

Diving & Snorkelling

Zanzibar, Pemba Island, Mafia Island Marine Park

Walking Safaris

Selous Game Reserve, Ruaha National Park, Mikumi National Park

Birdwatching

Lake Manyara National Park, Selous Game Reserve, Rubondo Island National Park

Times to Go

Trekking and hiking June through February

Diving and snorkelling September through February

Walking safaris June through October

Birding Any time, but best from December through June

Trekking & Hiking

Tanzania has rugged, varied terrain and a fine collection of peaks, rolling hills and mountain ranges. Landscapes range from the forested slopes of the eastern Udzungwa Mountains to the sheer volcanic cliffs of the inner wall of Mt Meru's crater, the rolling hill landscapes of the Usambaras and the final scree-slope ascent of Mt Kilimanjaro. Treks and hikes range from village-to-village walks to bush hikes.

Throughout the country, almost all trekking can be done without technical equipment, by anyone who is reasonably fit. However, most excursions – and all trekking or hiking in national parks and wildlife areas – require being accompanied by a guide or ranger. This usually also entails adhering to set (sometimes short) daily stages.

Booking

General booking considerations are similar to those for safaris (p28). The best places

for booking Kilimanjaro treks are Moshi and Marangu, followed by Arusha. Meru treks can be organised independently with park staff at the gate, or booked in Arusha if you'll be going through a trekking operator. Treks in the Crater Highlands and climbs up Ol Doinyo Lengai are best organised in Arusha.

Costs

Treks on Kilimanjaro and in the Crater Highlands are expensive. Most other treks in Tanzania can be done on a reasonable budget with a bit of effort, and a few are cheap. The following are among the least-expensive trekking areas, all of which are accessible via public transport:

Usambara, Pare and Uluguru Mountains All can be done as part of local cultural tourism programs or independently (a guide is recommended); no national park fees.

Mt Hanang and Mt Longido Both can be climbed as part of local cultural tourism programs; no national park fees.

Udzungwa Mountains National Park Main costs will be for park entry and guide fees.

When to Go

The best times for trekking are during the dry, warmer season from mid-December to February, and the dry, cooler season from June to October. The least favourable time is from mid-March to mid-May, when the heaviest rains fall. That said, trekking is possible in most areas year-round, with the exception of the Udzungwa, Usambara, Pare and Uluguru Mountains, where conditions become extremely muddy during the March to May rains.

Types of Treks

Stage-by-stage fully equipped trekking accompanied by guides and porters is the norm for treks on Mt Kilimanjaro and Mt Meru (although climbing Meru doesn't require porters). Ol Doinyo Lengai is also a relatively structured and generally fully equipped venture, given the rugged conditions and difficulties of access, as is most trekking in the Crater Highlands. The Usambaras, and to a lesser extent the Pares, involve comparatively easy village-to-village walks where you can stock up on basic food items as you go along. Most other areas are somewhere in between, requiring that you stock up in advance on basics and have a guide (or a GPS and some basic Swahili), but with flexibility as to routes and guiding.

What to Bring

For Mt Kilimanjaro and Mt Meru, you'll need a full range of waterproof cold-weather clothing and gear. Particularly on Kilimanjaro, waterproof everything, especially your sleeping bag, as things rarely dry on the mountain. In all of Tanzania's mountain areas, expect rain at any time of the year and considerably cooler weather than along the coast. Nights can be very chilly, and a water- and wind-proof jacket and warm pullover are essential almost everywhere.

Guides & Porters

Guides are required for treks on Mt Kilimanjaro, Mt Meru, in the Crater Highlands and in Udzungwa Mountains National Park. Elsewhere, although not essential, a local guide is recommended to show you the way, to provide introductions in remote places, and to guard against occasional instances of hassling and robberies in some

areas. If you decide to hike without a guide, you'll need to know some basic Swahili. Wherever you trek, always be sure your guide is accredited, or affiliated with an established company. On Kilimanjaro, this should be taken care of by your trekking company, and on Mt Meru and in Udzungwa Mountains National Park, guides are park rangers. The Ngorongoro Conservation Area also has its own guides. In other areas, check with the local tourist office or guide association before finalising your arrangements. Avoid going with freelancers.

Porters are commonly used on Mt Kilimanjaro, and sometimes on Mt Meru, though not elsewhere. In the Crater Highlands, donkeys may be used to carry gear.

Tipping

Tipping for guides and porters is an important budgetary consideration when planning treks on Mt Kilimanjaro and Mt Meru, and the main source of income for those who helped you on your trek. In other mountain areas, assuming service has been satisfactory, guides will expect a modest but fair tip. A good guideline is about 10% to 15% of your per-day hiking fees.

RESPONSIBLE TREKKING

➡ Carry out all your rubbish, including sanitary napkins, tampons, condoms and toilet paper (which burns and/or decomposes poorly).

➡ Take minimal packaging and reusable containers or stuff sacks.

➡ Use toilets where available. Otherwise, bury waste in a small hole 15cm (6in) deep and at least 100m (320ft) from any watercourse. Cover the waste with soil and rocks.

➡ Don't use detergents or toothpaste, even biodegradable ones, in or near watercourses.

➡ For washing, use biodegradable soap and a water container at least 50m (160ft) away from the watercourse. Disperse the waste water widely so the soil filters it fully.

➡ Wash cooking utensils 50m (160ft) from watercourses with a scourer, not detergent.

➡ Stick to existing trails and avoid short cuts; avoid removing the plant life that keeps topsoils in place.

➡ Don't depend on open fires for cooking. Cutting firewood in popular trekking areas can cause rapid deforestation. Cook on a lightweight kerosene, alcohol or Shellite (white gas) stove and avoid those powered by disposable butane gas canisters.

➡ If trekking with a guide and porters, supply stoves for the whole team. In cold areas, see that all members have sufficient clothing so that fires aren't necessary for warmth.

➡ Don't buy items made from endangered species.

Trekking Areas

Tanzania's most famous trek is Mt Kilimanjaro, but there are many other options.

Mt Kilimanjaro

Africa's highest mountain (5896m), and Tanzania's most famous trek, Kilimanjaro (p233) offers a choice of routes, all making their way from the forested lower slopes through moorland and alpine zones to the snow- and glacier-covered summit. There are also many walks on Kilimanjaro's lower slopes, with lush vegetation, waterfalls and cultural opportunities centred on local Chagga villages. Marangu and Machame make good bases, and Moshi- and Marangu-based tour operators are the best contacts.

Mt Meru

Although languishing in the shadow of nearby Kilimanjaro, Mt Meru (4566m) is a fine destination in its own right, and considerably less costly than its famous neighbour. It's also worth considering as a preparatory trek for the higher peak and, as part of Arusha National Park (p167), is well suited for safari-trek combination itineraries. The climbing is nontechnical and straightforward, although there's an extremely challenging open ridge walk as you approach the summit that many trekkers feel makes the overall Meru experience even more difficult than scaling Kilimanjaro.

Mt Hanang

Tanzania's fourth-highest peak (3417m), Mt Hanang offers a comparatively easy trek along well-worn but often overgrown footpaths to the summit. It's also relatively inexpensive to organise, and makes an intriguing destination if you're interested in combining trekking with an introduction to local cultures.

Crater Highlands & Ngorongoro Conservation Area

Together with adjoining parts of the Ngorongoro Conservation Area, the Crater Highlands offer rugged, rewarding and generally expensive trekking. The spectacular terrain includes steep escarpments, crater lakes, dense forests, grassy ridges, streams and waterfalls, plus the still-active volcano of Ol Doinyo Lengai (p190). This is just north of the Ngorongoro Conservation Area (p181) boundaries and can also be accessed from Lake Natron. Apart from the Maasai people who live here, you'll likely have most areas to yourself.

Usambara Mountains

The western Usambaras offer village-to-village walks along well-worn footpaths, ranging from a few hours to a week or more. There are enough local guesthouses that carrying a tent is unnecessary. Lushoto is the main base, although there are many other options, including Soni and Mambo. The main centre for hikes in the eastern Usambaras is Amani Nature Reserve (p142), where there is a network of short forest footpaths. Hikes combining the two regions (allow five to six days) are also possible.

Pare Mountains

The Pares (p149) offer relatively short hikes along mostly well-trodden mountain footpaths. There is only minimal tourism development, so hikers should come well prepared, and walk with a guide. Accommodation is generally camping or in very basic local guesthouses.

KILI'S TOPOGRAPHY

The Kilimanjaro massif has an oval base about 40km to 60km across, and rises almost 5000m above the surrounding plains. The two main peak areas are Kibo, the dome at the centre of the massif, which dips inwards to form a crater that can't be seen from below, and Mawenzi, a group of jagged pinnacles on the eastern side. A third peak, Shira, on the western end of the massif, is lower and less distinct than Kibo and Mawenzi. The highest point on Kibo is Uhuru Peak (5896m), the goal for most trekkers. The highest point on Mawenzi, Hans Meyer Point (5149m), cannot be reached by trekkers and is only rarely visited by mountaineers.

Kilimanjaro is considered an extinct volcano, although it still releases steam and sulphur from vents in the crater centre.

Walking safari

Udzungwa Mountains

The lush Udzungwas (p289) are fascinating from a botanical perspective, with more unique plant species than almost anywhere else in the region. They are also a prime destination for birders. There is only a handful of fully established trails, ranging from short walks to multiday mountain hikes, for which you will need a tent and have to be self-sufficient with food.

Uluguru Mountains

If you happen to be in the gateway town of Morogoro, it's worth setting aside time for hiking in the densely populated Ulugurus (p286) – of interest culturally and botanically. Hikes (most for half a day or a day) range from easy to moderately stiff excursions. Guides are readily organised in Morogoro, and costs are reasonable.

Southern Highlands & Kitulo National Park

Until recently, the rolling hill country in southwestern Tanzania, stretching southward roughly between Makambako and Mbeya, had little tourist infrastructure.

With the recent gazetting of Kitulo National Park (p302) and a slowly expanding network of accommodation, this is gradually beginning to change, although you will still be very much on your own in many areas. Shorter hikes and excursions as well as longer hikes are best organised from Mbeya or Tukuyu.

Mahale Mountains

Mt Nkungwe in Mahale Mountains National Park (p272) makes a rugged but scenic three-day trek. Getting to this remote wilderness takes determination but the rewards are great: intimate glimpses of chimpanzee populations, stunning vistas from the peak and the entire range of African wildlife – from big cats to hippos and crocodiles. Hikers will need to hire an armed ranger for all journeys as protection against animal attacks.

Trekking Operators

Arusha

If you're organising a Kilimanjaro trek in Arusha, look for operators that organise treks themselves rather than subcontracting to a Moshi- or Marangu-based operator.

MINIMISING COSTS

Organised-trek costs vary considerably and depend on the length of the trek, the size of the group, the standard of accommodation before and after the trek, the quality of bunk-houses or tents, plus the knowledge and experience of guides and trek leaders. To minimise costs:

➡ trek or hike outside national parks (to avoid park entry fees)

➡ carry your own camping equipment (to cut down on rental costs)

➡ avoid treks that necessitate vehicle rentals for access

➡ consider trekking out of season, when you may be able to negotiate discounted rates

It's not worth cutting corners where reliability is essential, however, such as on Kilimanjaro. Always check that there are enough porters, a cook and an assistant guide or two (in case the group splits or somebody has to return due to illness). Beware of unscrupulous budget companies charging you for, say, a five-day trek but only paying mountain and hut fees for four days. And be wary of staff stories about 'running out of money' while on the mountain, as promises of refunds are usually forgotten or denied when you get back to base.

Dorobo Safaris (p35) Community-oriented treks in and around the Ngorongoro Conservation Area and wilderness treks in Tarangire National Park border areas and in the Serengeti.

Kiliwarrior Expeditions (www.kiliwarrior expeditions.com) Upmarket Kilimanjaro climbs and treks in the Ngorongoro Conservation Area.

Summits Africa (☎0784 522090; www.summits -africa.com) High-quality treks and walks in the northern circuit and beyond.

Marangu

Most Marangu hotels organise Kilimanjaro treks. Also worth noting is the 'hard way' option of Marangu Hotel (p232), in which the climber pays park fees, crew fees and transport to the trailhead, plus providing all food and equipment. The hotel will take care of hut reservations and provide the necessary guides and porters.

Moshi

Moshi-based companies focus on Kilimanjaro treks; most can also organise day hikes on the mountain's lower slopes.

African Scenic Safaris (p34) Customised Kili treks and wildlife safaris.

Just Kilimanjaro (p35) A small, highly regarded operator offering expertly guided Kilimanjaro treks.

Kessy Brothers Tours & Travel (☎027-275 1185, 0754 803953; www.kessybrotherstours.com) Kilimanjaro treks.

Milestone Safaris (p36) Kilimanjaro climbs, northern circuit safaris and cultural tours around Moshi.

Moshi Expeditions & Mountaineering (MEM Tours; Map p228; ☎027-275 4234; www.mem tours.com) Kilimanjaro treks.

Shah Tours (Map p228; ☎0787 141052, 027-275 2998; www.shah-tours.com) Kilimanjaro and Meru treks, plus treks in the Ngorongoro highlands and on Ol Doinyo Lengai.

Summit Expeditions & Nomadic Experience (p386) Expertly guided Kilimanjaro treks, cultural excursions on the mountain's lower slopes and Usambara Mountains cycling tours.

Tanzania Journeys (p36) Kilimanjaro treks plus day hikes and cultural tours in the Moshi area.

TinTin Tours (p36) Kilimanjaro treks and northern circuit safaris.

Diving & Snorkelling

Tanzania's underwater marvels are just as amazing as its terrestrial attractions, with a magnificent array of hard and soft corals and a diverse collection of sea creatures, including manta rays, hawksbill and green turtles, barracuda and sharks. Other draws of the local diving scene include wall dives, especially off Pemba; the fascinating cultural backdrop; and the opportunity to combine wildlife safaris with underwater exploration. On the downside, visibility isn't reliable, and prices are considerably higher than in places such as the Red Sea or Thailand. Another thing to consider – if you're a serious diver and coming to the archipelago exclusively for diving – is that unless you do a live-aboard arrangement, you'll need to travel, often for up to an hour, to many of the dive sites. Inland, there's rewarding diving in Lake Tanganyika.

Seasons & Conditions

Diving is possible year-round, although conditions vary dramatically. Late March until mid-June is generally the least favourable time because of erratic weather patterns and frequent storms. July or August to February or March tends to be the best time overall, although again, conditions vary and wind is an important factor. On Pemba, for example, the southeastern seas can be rough around June and July when the wind is blowing from the south, but calm and clear as glass from around November to late February when the monsoon winds blow from the north. The calmest time is generally from around September to November during the lull between the annual monsoons.

Water temperatures range from lows of about 22°C in July and August to highs of about 29°C in February and March, with the average about 26°C.

Costs & Courses

Costs are fairly uniform, with Pemba and Mafia islands slightly pricier than elsewhere along the coast. Expect to pay up to US$500 for a four-day PADI open-water course and from about US$50 to US$80 for a single dive (with better prices available for multi-dive packages). Most places discount about 10% if you have your own equipment, and for groups. In addition to open-water certification, many operators also offer other courses, including Advanced Open Water, Medic First Aid, Rescue Diver and speciality courses, such as underwater photography.

Most dive operators also offer snorkelling. Equipment rental costs US$5 to US$15; when you're selecting it, pay particular attention to getting a good mask. Most of the best snorkelling sites along the coast are only accessible by boat. Trips

Diving off the coast of Zanzibar Island (p77)

average US$20 to US$50 per person per half-day, often including a snack or lunch.

Where to Dive

Generally speaking, Zanzibar Island (p77) is known for the corals and shipwrecks offshore from Zanzibar Town's Stone Town, and for fairly reliable visibility, high fish diversity and the chance to see pelagics around the island's north and northeast. While some sites are challenging, there are many easily accessed sites for beginning and midrange divers.

Unlike Zanzibar, which is a continental island, Pemba (p117) is an oceanic island located in a deep channel with a steeply dropping shelf. Because of this, diving tends to be more challenging, with an emphasis on wall and drift dives, though there are some sheltered areas for beginners, especially around Misali island. Most dives are to the west around Misali, and to the north off the Kigomasha Peninsula.

Mafia (p319) offers divers excellent corals, good fish variety including pelagics, and uncrowded diving, often from motorised dhows.

The far south, in Mnazi Bay-Rovuma Estuary Marine Park (p339), is offbeat, with still-unexplored areas. Also offbeat is Lake Tanganyika, which offers crystal-clear waters and snorkelling.

Wherever you dive, allow a sufficient surface interval between the conclusion of your final dive and any onward/homeward flights. According to PADI recommendations, this should be at least 12 hours, or more than 12 hours if you have been doing daily multiple dives for several days. Another consideration is insurance, which you should arrange before coming to Tanzania. Many policies exclude diving, so you may need to pay a bit extra – well worth it in comparison to the bills you will need to foot should something go wrong.

Choosing an Operator

When choosing a dive operator, quality rather than cost should be the priority. Consider the operator's experience and qualifications; knowledgeability and competence of staff; and the condition of equipment and frequency of maintenance. Assess whether the overall attitude of the organisation is serious and professional, and ask about safety precautions – radios, oxygen, emergency evacuation procedures, boat reliability and back-up engines, first-aid kits, safety flares and life jackets. On longer dives, do you get a meal, or just tea and biscuits? An advantage of operators offering PADI courses is that you'll have the flexibility to go elsewhere in the world and have what you've already done recognised at other PADI dive centres.

RESPONSIBLE DIVING & SNORKELLING

➡ Never use anchors on the reef, and take care not to ground boats on coral.

➡ Avoid touching or standing on living marine organisms or dragging equipment across the reef. If you must hold on to the reef, only touch exposed rock or dead coral.

➡ Be conscious of your fins. Even without contact, the surge from fin strokes near the reef can damage delicate organisms. Take care not to kick up clouds of sand, which can smother organisms.

➡ Practise and maintain proper buoyancy control. Major damage can be done by divers descending too fast and colliding with the reef.

➡ Take care in underwater caves. Spend as little time within them as possible as your air bubbles may be caught within the roof and thereby leave organisms high and dry. Take turns to inspect the interior of a small cave.

➡ Resist the temptation to collect or buy corals or shells.

➡ Take home all your rubbish. Plastics in particular are a serious threat to marine life.

➡ Don't feed fish.

➡ Never ride on the backs of turtles.

There's a decompression chamber in Matemwe (otherwise the closest one is in Johannesburg, South Africa), and you can check the **Divers Alert Network Southern Africa** (DAN; www.dansa.org) website, which lists some Tanzania-based operators that are part of the DAN network. If you choose to dive with an operator that isn't affiliated with DAN, it's highly recommended to take out insurance coverage with DAN.

Other Activities

Birdwatching

Tanzania is an outstanding birding destination, with well over 1000 species, including numerous endemics. In addition to the national parks and reserves, top birding spots include the eastern Usambara Mountains and Lake Victoria. Useful websites include the Tanzania Bird Atlas (www.tanzaniabirdatlas.net), the Tanzania Hotspots page on www.camacdonald.com/birding/africatanzania.htm and Tanzanian Birds & Butterflies (www.tanzaniabirds.net).

Dhow sailing boat, Zanzibar Island (p77)

Boating, Sailing & Kayaking

Local dhow trips are easily arranged along the coast. They are generally best booked for short sails rather than longer journeys. Ask your hotel for recommendations or contact one of the coastal or island hotels, many of which have private dhows that can be chartered for cruises. Catamarans and sailboats can be chartered on Zanzibar Island, on Pemba and in Kilwa, and Dar es Salaam and Tanga have private yacht clubs.

Chimpanzee Tracking

Gombe National Park (p271) and Mahale Mountains National Park (p272) have both hosted international research teams for decades, and are outstanding destinations if you are interested in observing chimpanzees at close quarters.

Fishing

Mafia, the Pemba channel and the waters around the Zanzibar Archipelago and the Songo Songo Archipelago have long been insider tips in deep-sea fishing circles, and upmarket hotels in these areas are the best places to arrange charters. Other contacts include Mwangaza Hideaway (p328) in Kilwa Masoko and upper-end hotels in most coastal destinations. In Dar es Salaam, anglers can enquire at Sea Breeze Marine (p58) and at the **Dar es Salaam Yacht Club** (Map p62; www.daryachtclub.co.tz; Yacht Club Rd, Msasani; 🚗).

Inland, Lake Victoria is renowned for its fishing, particularly for Nile perch. Contacts here include Lukuba Island Lodge Resort (p248) and Wag Hill Lodge (p253).

Horse Riding

Riding safaris are possible in the West Kilimanjaro and Lake Natron areas. Contacts include **Makoa Farm** (Map p227; ☑0625 312896, 0754 312896; www.makoa-farm.com) and **Kaskazi Horse Safaris** (☑0766 432792; www.kaskazihorsesafaris.com). At the time of research, horse-riding safaris were also scheduled to begin in 2018 in Kitulo National Park, down to Matema on Lake Nyasa. Contact Maua Café & Tours (p305) in Mbeya.

Plan Your Trip
Travel with Children

Tanzania may initially seem daunting for travel with children: prices for accommodation and park entry fees can be high, road distances are long and vehicle rental is costly. But for those with a sense of adventure, it's a destination with wonderful attractions, including wildlife, beaches, friendly people and good weather.

Best Regions for Kids

Northern Tanzania

Tanzania's north is safari country and Maasai country. It's not cheap, but kids will love seeing the animals, as well as the many colourful cultures. There are many child-friendly hotels and restaurants.

Zanzibar Island

Zanzibar Island's gentle beaches alone are enough to make the island the perfect family destination. Many hotels also have swimming pools (ideal for passing time while the tide is out) and spacious grounds, and there's a wide choice of child-friendly cuisine.

Southern Highlands

The highlands offer plenty of space for kids to run around, wildlife parks, Lake Malawi and family-friendly accommodation.

Northeastern Tanzania

Low-key beaches, family-friendly lodging, historical Bagamoyo and the chance to spot wildlife in Saadani National Park make this region a child-friendly choice.

Tanzania for Kids

Wildlife Watching

Tanzania's wildlife areas, especially Serengeti, Tarangire and Ngorongoro Crater, offer almost guaranteed animal-spotting, often at very close range. If staying inside the park, choose a lodge or safari camp with a pool where the kids can expend their energy between wildlife drives. Alternatively, base yourself outside the park at a hotel with a pool and/or large grounds for running around. Venture into the park on one well-timed animal-spotting foray (with snacks or a picnic), while also taking advantage of cultural tours, night drives and other activities outside the park.

Beaches

Tanzania's beaches are wonderful, although there can be seaweed and cloudy waters at certain times of year. Ask hotel staff about good areas and times to swim safely.

Transport

Renting a vehicle with driver is a good investment for family travel in Tanzania, giving you some control over driving speeds and the chance to stop for bathroom breaks when you'd like. Many families also happily explore the country on public transport, particularly the train.

Staying Safe

Tanzania's parks are completely unfenced, as are the park lodges and camps. The necessity of carefully supervising your children while in camp cannot be overemphasised. Wild animals frequently enter public areas, and a child should not be allowed to walk alone around camp, even for short distances. Exercise particular vigilance in the evenings.

Children's Highlights

Beaches

➡ **Zanzibar Island** Lovely east-coast beaches with soft sand and gentle waters, plus resort swimming pools for when the tides are out. In Stone Town, Tembo House Hotel (p90) is a good family-friendly choice.

➡ **Pangani** Quiet beaches and sheltered coves, plus family-friendly resorts, including Peponi (p133) and Fish Eagle Point (p139).

➡ **Lake Nyasa** Matema beach (p310) is wonderful for families, except during the heavy rains (March through May) when waves can be big.

➡ **Mafia** (p317) Small, quiet beaches, dhow rides and snorkelling.

Wildlife

➡ **Saadani National Park** (p130) Beach plus wildlife.

➡ **Arusha National Park** (p167) Small and manageable; easy day trip from Arusha.

➡ **Ngorongoro Crater** (p181) Guaranteed wildlife; nearby family-friendly accommodation.

➡ **Southern safari circuit** (p34) Ideal for older children; also offers safaris in open vehicles.

Exploring

➡ **Iringa area** Rolling hill panoramas, plenty of space, hiking, Ruaha National Park (p297) and family-friendly accommodation – especially Kisolanza – The Old Farm House (p296).

➡ **Usambara Mountains** (p141) Lovely mountain scenery, cool temperatures, hiking and family-friendly accommodation.

PLANNING TIPS

➡ The June through September cooler, dry season is best, and mosquitoes tend to be fewer (although anti-malaria precautions should still be taken).

➡ Check with your doctor about recommended vaccinations and use of malarial prophylactics. It's essential to bring along mosquito nets and ensure that your children sleep under them. Bring long-sleeved shirts, trousers and socks for dawn and dusk and always use mosquito repellent (from home).

➡ At beaches, keep in mind the risks of hookworm infestation in populated areas, and watch out for sea urchins while wading in the shallows and snorkelling. Take care about bilharzia infection in lakes, and thorns and the like in the bush. A fully stocked child-oriented first-aid kit is essential.

➡ Street food isn't generally suitable for children, and 'healthy snacks' are difficult to find on the road. Stock up on fresh and dried fruit and kids' juices in major cities. Bring a pocket knife from home for peeling fruit. Plain yoghurt (*mtindi*) is available in major towns.

➡ Baby changing areas are rare. Bring a small blanket or changing mat.

➡ Processed baby foods, powdered infant milk, disposable nappies, baby wipes and similar items are available in major towns. Child seats for hire cars and safari vehicles should be arranged in advance.

➡ Many wildlife lodges and safari camps have restrictions on accommodating children under 12.

➡ Most hotels and all national parks offer discounted entry and accommodation rates for children, but you'll need to specifically request these, especially when booking through tour operators.

➡ Lonely Planet's *Travel with Children* has more tips for keeping children and parents happy while on the road.

Regions at a Glance

Distances between places are long in Tanzania, and it is well worth keeping this in mind when planning your itinerary. One popular two-week combination is northern Tanzania's wildlife parks, followed by a Kilimanjaro trek or relaxation on Zanzibar Island.

With more time at your disposal, and an adventurous bent, the rest of the country opens up. Head west for chimpanzee tracking and exploring Lake Tanganyika and Lake Victoria. Travel through the Southern Highlands for hiking, lovely hill panoramas and vibrant markets. Southeastern Tanzania is ideal for wildlife (in Selous Game Reserve) and for getting to know traditional Swahili culture (along the coast), while northeastern Tanzania offers hiking, beaches and history. Bustling Dar es Salaam has an international airport and good shopping and dining.

Dar es Salaam

Shopping
Architecture
History

Markets & Boutiques

Whether it's Mwenge carvers' market, the weekend craft fair at Msasani Slipway or chic boutiques in upmarket hotels, Dar es Salaam has a wealth of options.

Eclectic Architecture

Discover a jumble of architectural styles, from the German-era colonial buildings lining Kivukoni Front to stately Karimjee Hall, Indian-influenced architecture around Jamhuri St and modern high-rises near the harbour.

Museums

History buffs will enjoy the National Museum, with its displays on Olduvai Gorge and the Shirazi civilisation of Kilwa. Head to the Village Museum for an intro to traditional life and cultures.

p52

Zanzibar Archipelago

Beaches
Zanzibar Town
Diving

Stone Town

With its maze of alleyways, shops scented with cloves, Arabic-style houses, bustling bazaars, long history and rich cultural melange, this World Heritage Site never loses its appeal.

White Sands

Zanzibar Island's combination of powdery white sands, swaying palms, turquoise waters, picturesque dhows and pastel-hued sunrises make its beaches – especially those on the island's east coast – hard to beat.

Abundant Sealife

Clear waters filled with colourful corals and fish entice divers of all abilities. There are also fine snorkelling opportunities, especially around Mnemba island.

p75

Northeastern Tanzania

Beaches
Hiking
History

Palms & Baobabs

The beaches north and south of Pangani are lovely, dotted with stands of palms and baobabs. They are also almost deserted, compared with those on Zanzibar Island, just across the channel.

Hill Panoramas

Lushoto and surrounding villages, with their walking trails and hill panoramas, and Amani Nature Reserve, with its many unique plants, are highlights of hiking in this mountainous region.

Relics & Ruins

Bagamoyo makes a fascinating stop, with its museum, German colonial-era buildings and nearby ruins. Pangani's sleepy streets are also full of history. Just south are the 14th-century Tongoni ruins.

p126

Northern Tanzania

Wildlife
Trekking
Culture

Safaris

Ngorongoro, Serengeti, Tarangire, Lake Manyara – Tanzania's northern safari circuit offers some of the best wildlife watching anywhere on the continent.

Challenging Summits

Both Mt Kilimanjaro and Mt Meru have challenging treks to the summit for anyone who is reasonably fit and well acclimatised. Other highlights: the Crater Highlands and Ol Doinyo Lengai.

Colourful Tribal Groups

The Maasai are just one of northern Tanzania's tribal groups, but there are many more to get to know. These include the Chagga on Mt Kilimanjaro, the Iraqw around Karatu and the Hadzabe around Lake Eyasi.

p153

Central Tanzania

Culture
History
Exploration

Traditional Cultures

Among the best-known tribes are the semi-nomadic Barabaig around Mt Hanang. Central Tanzania is also home to Maasai, Sandawe, Iraqw and others; visiting the Katesh market gives a fascinating introduction.

Rock Art

The Kondoa Rock-Art Sites are time-consuming to access, but intriguing to explore.

Off the Beaten Track

Few travellers make it to this part of the country, but for those who do, it is fun to discover. Try Dodoma, with its outsized street layout and grandiose buildings, climb Mt Hanang or take a cultural tour in the market town of Babati.

p237

Lake Victoria

Birdwatching
History
Islands

Birding

Lake Victoria offers fine birdwatching opportunities. The highlight is Rubondo Island National Park, with its wealth of waterbirds and migrants.

Museums

Two intriguing museums are tucked away near Lake Victoria: the Sukuma Museum outside Mwanza, and the Mwalimu Julius K Nyerere Museum in Butiama, near Musoma.

Relaxation & Tranquillity

Choose between tranquil Rubondo Island National Park, tiny Lukuba Island near Musoma, Musira Island near Bukoba or Ukerewe Island, offshore from Mwanza. All are scenic and relaxing, and give glimpses of traditional lakeshore life.

p246

Western Tanzania

Lake Tanganyika
Exploration
Wildlife

Chimpanzees

Mahale Mountains and Gombe National Parks offer excellent opportunities to observe chimpanzees up close. Both parks are also highly scenic, and adventurous to reach.

Lake & Shoreline

Clear fish-filled waters, secluded coves, isolated villages and the MV *Liemba* make Lake Tanganyika and its hinterlands a delight to explore. Don't miss Kigoma, Ujiji and inland Tabora.

Hippos & Buffaloes

Enjoy superb dry season wildlife watching at Katavi National Park, with its giant pods of hippos and massive buffalo herds, followed by relaxation on the lakeshore around Kipili.

p263

Southern Highlands

National Parks
Hiking
Landscapes

Safaris

Both Ruaha and Mikumi National Parks offer outstanding wildlife watching and evocative landscapes. Don't miss Ruaha's elephants and hippos, or Mikumi's zebras and giraffes.

Waterfalls & Winding Footpaths

Exploring the steep, waterfall-laced slopes of the Udzungwas is a highlight. Other hiking options: guided walks around Mbeya or rugged jaunts on the orchid-filled Kitulo Plateau.

Hills & Wildflowers

The wide swathe from Iringa down to Lake Malawi is beautiful, with rolling hills, wildflower-carpeted valleys, ancient stands of baobabs, vast tea plantations and jacaranda-shaded towns.

p281

Southeastern Tanzania

Coastal Life
History
Wildlife

Beaches

With its mangrove-shaded waterways and lively local traditions, Mafia is a delightful intro to Swahili culture. On the mainland, Lindi, Mtwara and Kilwa Masoko also offer glimpses into traditional coastal life.

Ruins

At the evocative Kilwa Kisiwani ruins, imagine the days of sultans and monsoon-driven trading networks stretching as far afield as India and China.

Boat Safaris & Underwater Wonders

Selous Game Reserve is a regional highlight, with sublime vistas, boat safaris and many large animals. For offshore 'wildlife', dive around Mafia island and Mnazi Bay-Ruvuma Estuary Marine Park.

p315

On the Road

Dar es Salaam

📞 022 / POP 4.36 MILLION

Best Places to Stay

➡ Alexander's Hotel (p61)

➡ Southern Sun (p60)

➡ Friendly Gecko Guesthouse (p71)

➡ Ras Kutani (p74)

➡ Dar es Salaam Serena Hotel (p60)

➡ Hyatt Regency Dar es Salaam (p60)

Best Places to Eat

➡ Oriental (p64)

➡ Mamboz Corner BBQ (p64)

➡ Chapan Bhog (p64)

➡ Zuane Trattoria & Pizzeria (p65)

➡ Addis in Dar (p65)

Why Go?

Over the last century, Dar es Salaam has grown from a sleepy Zaramo fishing village into a thriving tropical metropolis of over four million people. Straddling some of the most important sea routes in the world, it is East Africa's second-busiest port and Tanzania's commercial hub. Despite this, and its notorious traffic jams, the city has managed to maintain a low-key down-to-earth feel.

Rimming the central area is Kivukoni Front, with a bustling fish market where dhows dock at dawn to offload the night's catch. Excellent craft markets and restaurants abound, and nearby sandy beaches and islands beckon.

Dar es Salaam's architecture is a mixture of African, Arab, Indian and German, although much of this is now dwarfed by towering high-rises. Many travellers bypass 'Dar' completely; those that linger will encounter the city's eclectic cultural mix and languid vibe.

When to Go
Dar es Salaam

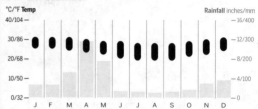

Mar–May Low season, cheaper rates, fewer tourists, but some coastal lodges are closed.

Jun–Sep Dry, cool weather and low humidity make this a comfortable season to explore the city.

Dec & Jan Christmas/New Year holidays on nearby beaches, the arrival of migratory birds.

History

In 1862 Sultan Seyyid Majid of Zanzibar alighted on the Zaramo fishing village of Mzizima as the location for his new summer palace. He named it Dar es Salaam (Haven of Peace), a name that reflected its isolated location on a broad natural bay, making it perfect for the new trading depot he envisaged. Yemeni Arabs from the Hadrumat were invited to plant coconuts inland while Indian merchants contributed to the fledgling economy.

Majid's sudden death in 1870 brought an abrupt end to the development, as his succeeding brother, Barghash, had little interest in the new port. So it wasn't until the late 1880s, when the German East Africa Company established a trading station, that the city really began to evolve. By 1887 Dar was the capital of the new German protectorate. The colonial administration was moved from Bagamoyo and the construction of a railway line accelerated the city's growth, facilitating trade with Central Africa via Lake Tanganyika.

As the city grew, social and political awareness grew too. Ironically, WWI was to prove the catalyst for revival of African institutions such as the Tanganyika African Association, which was sanctioned by the postwar British administration in 1922. This organisation ultimately merged with the Tanganyika African National Union (TANU) to form the basis for the nationalist movement, which achieved independence for the country in 1961. Since then Dar es Salaam has remained Tanzania's undisputed political and economic capital, even though the legislature and official seat of government were transferred to Dodoma in 1973.

In the newly independent Tanzania, Dar fared poorly. President Julius Nyerere favoured a socialist economic model, and one in which urban areas were de-emphasised in favour of rural investment. As Tanzania's primary city, Dar es Salaam languished while a newly nationalised labour market and centralised government spawned Byzantine levels of bureaucracy and corruption. Still, the close ties of friendship between Nyerere and China started to pay dividends when socialism was abandoned in favour of liberalisation in the 1990s. Since then Chinese investment has transformed the city from a quaint colonial backwater into a high-rise metropolis and Beijing is now Dar es Salaam's biggest trading partner. Investment is focused on large-scale projects such as roads, bridges, railways, apartments and pipelines. Most notably, though,

Dar es Salaam Highlights

❶ **Offshore Islands** (p73) Heading out to Mbudya and Bongoyo for snorkelling and picnics.

❷ **Coco Beach** (p58) Joining hardworking locals living it up at the city's main weekend beach hang-out.

❸ **Wonder Workshop** (p67) Shopping for wonderfully wacky, upcycled souvenirs.

❹ **Local Life** (p58) Getting to know the real Dar es Salaam on a bicycling, cultural or walking tour.

❺ **Dekeza Dhows** (p73) Enjoying being on the water and exploring by dhow or kayak.

❻ **Ras Kutani** (p74) Escaping to this luxuriously unspoilt headland where turtles come to nest.

❼ **Cuisine** (p64) Savouring Dar es Salaam's diverse cuisine, including *dhoklas*, barbecued meat, spiced tea and coconut-crusted fish.

❽ **Birding** (p58) Getting acquainted with Dar es Salaam's avian wealth on a bird walk.

there is significant investment in the new city of Kigamboni over the bay, where the future of Dar es Salaam lies in a 20-year, US$11.6 trillion project set for completion in 2032.

◉ Sights

Dar es Salaam's centre runs along Samora Ave. Northeast of here is Uzunguni, the old colonial centre where all the sights are located. Southwest are Kisutu and Mchafukoge, the Asian quarter, with its many Indian merchants and traders. It is here that the city is at its most exotic, with dozens of shops selling everything from lighting fixtures to textiles and spicy samosas. Further west and southwest a jumble of earthy neighbourhoods takes over, including Kariakoo, Temeke and Ilala. In these areas – seldom reached by travellers – sandy streets wind past densely packed houses and thriving street markets.

North of the centre, across Selander Bridge, are the upmarket residential areas of Oyster Bay and Msasani, with their Western-style dining and shopping, and the city's main stretch of sand, Coco Beach.

Nafasi Art Space   GALLERY
(Map p72; ☑ 0753 334310, 0673 334314; www.nafasiartspace.org; Eyasi Rd, Light Industrial Area, Mikocheni B; ☉ 10am-5.30pm Mon-Fri, 10am-2pm Sat) Aiming to be the leading contemporary art centre in Tanzania, Nafasi is a complex of studios housed in an old industrial warehouse in Mikocheni. Many local member artists work there alongside regional and international residencies, all of whom exhibit in the on-site gallery. The centre provides a platform for training and cross-cultural discourse, which it promotes through monthly events such as Chap Chap, which combines an exhibition and open workshops with evening music, theatre and dance.

National Museum & House of Culture   MUSEUM
(Map p56; ☑ 022-211 7508; Shaaban Robert St; adult/student Tsh6500/2600; ☉ 9.30am-6pm) The National Museum houses a copy of the famous fossil discoveries of *zinjanthropus* ('nutcracker man') from Olduvai Gorge, plus other archaeological finds. Wander through the History Room and ethnographic collection for insights into Tanzania's past and its mosaic of cultures, including the Shirazi civilisation of Kilwa, the Zanzibar slave trade, and the German and British colonial periods. Despite renovations, however, the museum still has much work to do on appropriate

displays and the curation of a coherent narrative. For vintage auto aficionados, there's a small special collection, including the Rolls-Royce used first by the British colonial government and later by Julius Nyerere.

Village Museum   MUSEUM
(Map p62; ☑ 022-270 0437, 0718 525682; New Bagamoyo Rd; adult/student Tsh6500/2600; dance & drum performance Tsh2000; ☉ 9am-6pm) This open-air museum features a collection of authentically constructed dwellings illustrating traditional life in various parts of Tanzania. Each house is furnished with typical items and surrounded by small plots of crops, while 'villagers' demonstrate traditional skills such as weaving, pottery and carving. Traditional tribal dance performances also take place daily, whenever there is sufficient demand.

The museum is 9km north of the city centre; Mwenge dalla-dallas run there from New Posta transport stand (Tsh400, 45 minutes). Get off at 'Makumbusho'; the museum is across the street.

St Joseph Cathedral   CHURCH
(Map p56; www.daressalaamarchdiocese.or.tz/st-joseph-cathedral; Sokoine Dr) This spired, Gothic-style, Roman Catholic cathedral was built at the turn of the 19th century by German missionaries. In addition to the striking stained-glass windows behind the main altar (best viewed late in the afternoon), it still contains many of the original German inscriptions and artwork, including the carved relief above the main altar.

Azania Front Lutheran Church   CHURCH
(Map p56; www.azaniafront.org; cnr Azikiwe St & Sokoine Dr) A striking edifice, with a red-roofed belfry overlooking the water, a rather stern Gothic interior and a marvellous, new handmade organ, this is one of the city's major landmarks. The church was built in 1898 by German missionaries and was the centre of the German mission in Tanzania; now it is the cathedral for the diocese and is still in active use for services and choir rehearsals (beautiful – you can sometimes hear the singing from the street).

Services in English are held Sunday mornings at 9am; all other services are in Swahili.

Fish Market   MARKET
(Map p56; Kivukoni Front; ☉ 6am-sunset) Head down to the Kivukoni fish market in the early morning to see fishers flog their catch to restauranteurs and homemakers with all the zeal of Wall St stockbrokers. The market is

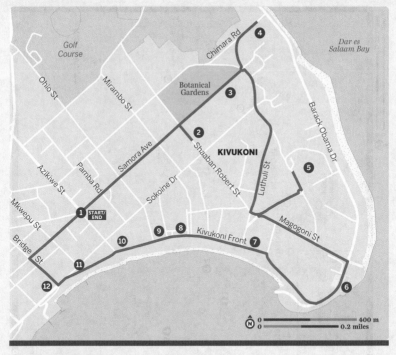

City Walk
Historic Dar es Salaam

START CNR SAMORA AVE & AZIKIWE ST
END CNR SAMORA AVE & AZIKIWE ST
LENGTH 4.5KM; TWO HOURS

Begin at ❶ **Askari monument** (Samora Ave & Azikiwe St), a bronze statue dedicated to Africans killed in WWI. Head northeast along Samora Ave to Shaaban Robert St and the ❷ **National Museum** (p54). Continue northeast along Samora Ave for half a block. On the right is ❸ **Karimjee Hall**, the former house of parliament where Julius Nyerere was sworn in as president. Continue along Samora Ave to Luthuli St. To the northeast is ❹ **Ocean Rd Hospital**, built in 1897. The small, white, domed building just before is where Robert Koch carried out his pioneering research on malaria and tuberculosis around the turn of the 20th century.

Head south along Luthuli St. On your left is the ❺ **State House** (p57), originally built by the Germans and then rebuilt after WWI by the British. Just southeast on the seafront is the ❻ **Fish Market** (p54).

From the fish market, head west along Kivukoni Front (Azania Front). To the right are ❼ **government buildings**, including the Ministry of Foreign Affairs, Ministry of Justice and Bureau of Statistics, all dating from the German era. Left is the seafront. Continue straight to the old ❽ **Kilimanjaro Hotel** (now Hyatt Regency Dar es Salaam).

Just beyond is ❾ **Azania Front Lutheran Church** (p54), with its landmark red-roofed belfry. The church was built at the turn of the 20th century by German missionaries. Continuing along the waterfront are, first, the ❿ **Old Post Office** and, then, the ⓫ **White Fathers' Mission House**, one of the city's oldest buildings. One block beyond this is ⓬ **St Joseph Cathedral** (p54), another landmark. The cathedral, also built by German missionaries, contains many original German inscriptions and some artwork, including the carved relief above the main altar. From St Joseph's, head one block north along Bridge St to Samora Ave. Follow this east, back to the Askari monument.

Central Dar es Salaam

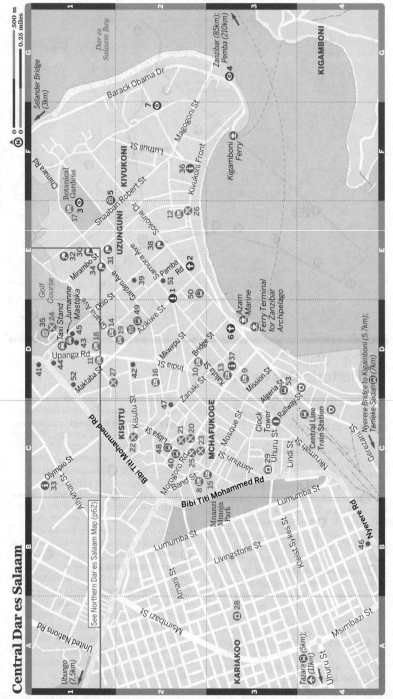

Central Dar es Salaam

◉ Sights
1 Askari Monument.....................................E2
2 Azania Front Lutheran Church.............E2
3 Botanical Gardens E1
4 Fish Market G3
5 National Museum & House of
  Culture F1
6 St Joseph Cathedral D3
7 State House F2

⊜ Sleeping
Dar es Salaam Serena Hotel........ (see 35)
8 Econolodge C2
9 Harbour View Suites..............................D3
10 Heritage Motel...D2
11 Holiday Inn D1
12 Hyatt Regency Dar es Salaam..............E2
13 Rainbow Hotel D3
14 Ramada Encore D1
15 Safari Inn C3
16 Sleep Inn D2
17 Southern Sun...E1
18 YMCA D1
19 YWCA D2

✪ Eating
20 Akberali Tea Room...................................C2
  Al Basha ....(see 10)
21 Ali's C2
22 Chapan Bhog C2
23 Chef's Pride C2
24 Kibo Bar D1
25 Mamboz Corner BBQ C2
26 Oriental E2
27 Patel Samaj...D1
  YMCA ....(see 18)

◉ Drinking & Nightlife
Level 8 Bar ....(see 12)
Rouge...(see 12)

◎ Shopping
28 Kariakoo Market.......................................A3
29 Mnazi Moja Textile Vendors C3

ℹ Information
30 British High Commission.......................E1
31 Canadian High Commission..................E1
  German Embassy ....(see 30)
32 Indian High Commission........................E1
33 Marine Parks & Reserves Unit C1
34 Mozambique High
  Commission E1
  Netherlands Embassy.................(see 30)
  Serena Forex Bureau ....(see 35)
35 Serena Hotel Business
  Centre..D1
36 Surveys & Mapping Division
  Map Sales Office................................F2
37 Tanzania Tourist Board
  Information Centre............................D3
  YMCA Internet Café ....(see 18)
38 Zambian High Commission....................E2

ℹ Transport
39 Air Tanzania...E2
40 Dar Express C2
41 Egyptair..D1
42 Emirates Airlines.....................................D2
43 Ethiopian Airlines....................................D1
44 Fast Track Tanzania D1
  Fastjet...(see 9)
45 First Car Rental...D1
46 Green Car Rentals B4
47 Kearsley Travel C2
  Kenya Airways............................. (see 41)
48 Kilimanjaro Express..................................C2
  KLM ....(see 41)
  Linhas Aéreas de
   Moçambique ....(see 44)
  Malawi Airlines.............................(see 44)
49 New Posta Transport Stand...................D2
50 Old Posta Transport Stand E2
51 Precision Air E2
  RwandAir ....(see 41)
52 South African Airways D1
53 Stesheni Transport Stand D3

divided into two main sections, comprising eight zones, one of which is the auction. In other sections fish are cleaned, cooked and resold at marked-up prices. It's colourful and chaotic, and you could walk away with a handsome snapper for as little as Tsh3000.

State House ARCHITECTURE
(Map p56; Luthuli St) An imposing complex set amid large grounds, the State House was originally built by the Germans and rebuilt after WWI by the British.

Botanical Gardens GARDENS
(Map p56; Samora Ave; ⊙6am-6pm) FREE Although in danger of disappearing beneath development, these botanical gardens provide an essential shady oasis in the city. They were established in 1893 by Professor Stuhlman, the first Director of Agriculture, and were initially used as a testing ground for cash crops. They're still home to the Horticultural Society, which tends the indigenous and exotic plants, including scarlet flame trees, several species of palm, cycads and jacaranda.

🏃 Activities

For swimming, try the **pool** (Map p62; ☏022-260 0288; www.goldentulipdaressalaam.com; Toure Dr; per person Tsh20,000) at the Golden Tulip

DAR ES SALAAM CULTURAL TOURS

Amid the clamour of Dar's development boom it can sometimes be hard to get a sense of the city's history and culture. If you have time, it's rewarding to take a walking or other cultural tour for a glimpse of life at street level.

Afriroots (☎ 0732 926350, 0713 652642, 0787 459887; www.afriroots.co.tz; tours per person US$40-50) Runs a history walk around the city centre, exploring Dar's evolution from the Omani sultanate to key ANC (African National Congress) and Frelimo hot spots in the struggle for independence, as well as a 'behind-the-scenes' cycle tour where you'll get to meet locals and hear their stories about living in the city, and a 'Dar by Night' tour to get acquainted with local nightlife.

Kigamboni Community Centre (Map p72; ☎ 0788 482684, 0753 226662; www.kccdar. com; Kigamboni) This impressive, locally run centre provides education, talent development and vocational training for Kigamboni-area youth. For visitors, it can organise traditional dance, drumming, acrobatic, cooking and Swahili lessons, plus walking and cycling tours. Monday through Saturday from 5pm to 6pm is the best time to visit. With luck, you'll catch one of the free talent shows; call ahead to confirm. To get here, take the ferry to Kigamboni and get a *bajaji* (tuk-tuk) to the centre; it's opposite the Kigamboni police station next to Kakala bar.

Hotel. Guided **bird walks** can be arranged in and around Dar es Salaam with **Andrew Majembe** (☎ 0658 490399, 0784 490399).

Tanzaquatic FISHING, CRUISE
(Map p62; ☎ 0786 058370, 0654 454535; www. facebook.com/tanzaquatic; Slipway, Slipway Rd, Msasani; glass-bottom boat per person US$10-20) Enjoy the natural beauty of Msasani Bay on sunset cruises, glass-bottom boat trips, fishing excursions (from US$450 per half-day for four people) and snorkelling and picnic trips to Bongoyo, Mbudya and Sinda. They can also be contacted through **Sea Breeze Marine** (Map p62; ☎ 0754 783241; www.seabreezemarine.org; Slipway, Slipway Rd, Msasani).

Bongoyo Boat Trips OUTDOORS
(Map p62; ☎ 0713 328126; Slipway, Slipway Rd, Msasani; return adult/child Tsh46,500/23,250; ⊙ four departures daily 9.30am-3.30pm, minimum four passengers; ⚑) If you don't have a car, the quickest and easiest way to enjoy some offshore island fun is to hop on the ferry from the Slipway to Bongoyo Island in the Dar es Salaam Marine Reserve System (p73). The last boat returns at 5pm and the marine reserve fee is included in the price. The crossing takes about 30 minutes.

Coco Beach BEACH
(Map p62; Toure Dr) North of the city centre, the Msasani Peninsula is fringed with a long stretch of sand and coral rag beach along its eastern side. Swimming is only possible at high tide, but it's a favourite weekend spot for locals, when the beach is dotted with food stalls, coconut stands and beer sellers.

Bounce AMUSEMENT PARK
(Map p72; ☎ 0776 865854, 0685 619599; Mkuki House Mall, Nyerere Rd; over/under 10s Tsh10,000/7000, plus socks Tsh5000; ⊙ 2-10pm Tue-Fri, 11am-10pm Sat & Sun; ⚑) Billed as East Africa's first trampoline park, Bounce is a good way for kids to work off some extra energy.

✯✯ Festivals & Events

Goat Races CULTURAL
(www.goatraces.co.tz; The Green, Kenyatta Dr; adult/child Tsh20,000/10,000; ⊙ Sep) Each September, have a flutter on Dar's finest racing goats. If your billy goat comes first you get the cash; if not, your money goes to support charities.

Nyama Choma FOOD & DRINK
(☎ 0719 217550; www.facebook.com/nyamachoma fest; Tunisia Rd, at Leader's Club, off Ali Hassan Mwinyi Rd; entry Tsh30,000; ⊙ Mar, Jun, Sep, Dec; ⚑) The largest barbecue block party in East Africa, this quarterly festival showcases the skills of Dar's finest pit-masters alongside live bands, soccer matches and a kids' corner.

Swahili Fashion Week CULTURAL
(www.swahilifashionweek.com; 104 Kenyatta Dr; ⊙ Dec) Get a heads-up on Tanzania's sartorial trends at this annual fashion show, which serves as the largest platform for East African designers.

🛌 Sleeping

Dar es Salaam has a wide variety of accommodation. Most budget hotels and some midrange places are in the city centre, with several midrange options also on the quieter Msasani Peninsula. For top-end hotels expect to pay from US$200 per room. The closest places for camping are along South Beach, on the southern side of Kurasini Creek.

🛏 City Centre & Upanga

Most of the reliable budget and midrange lodgings are located in the city centre neighbourhoods of Kisutu and Mchafukoge, which are packed with food stalls and restaurants, and are walkable from the ferry terminal. Comfortable high-end accommodation and flagship hotels like the Hyatt and Dar es Salaam Serena are located in the old colonial quarters of Uzunguni and Kivukoni, in the heart of the city centre. There are also several options in the Upanga residential district, on the edge of the city centre and just southwest of Selander Bridge.

YMCA   HOSTEL $
(Map p56; ☎ 0758 097733, 0754 645103, 022-213 5457; Upanga Rd; dm/s/d Tsh15,000/25,000/28,000; @) This YMCA offers no-frills rooms that are fairly quiet considering the city-centre location. It's in a small compound around the corner from the post office, and also has a canteen (p64) with inexpensive meals. Men and women are accepted. Downstairs is a small internet cafe (p68).

YWCA   HOSTEL $
(Map p56; ☎ 0713 622707; Maktaba St; dm/tr Tsh15,000/50,000, s/d with shared bathroom Tsh20,000/30,000) Located on a small side street between the main post office and St Alban's Anglican church, this YWCA has basic rooms with concrete floors, fans, sinks and clean, shared bathrooms. Rooms get a fair amount of street noise, although those around the inner courtyard are quieter. Men and women are accepted, and the restaurant serves inexpensive local-style meals.

Safari Inn   HOTEL $
(Map p56; ☎ 022-213 8101, 0754 485013; www.safari inn.co.tz; Band St; s/d with fan Tsh28,000/35,000, with air-con Tsh35,000/45,000; ❄@🛜) A popular and long-standing travellers haunt in Kisutu, with English-speaking staff, the Safari Inn has 42 rooms, 10 of which are air-conditioned. All rooms have mosquito nets.

Econolodge   HOTEL $
(Map p56; ☎ 022-211 6049, 022-211 6048; econolodge@raha.com; Band St; s/d/tr with fan Tsh28,000/38,000/48,000, with air-con Tsh38,000/48,000/55,000; ❄) Clean, bland, but good-value rooms hidden away in an aesthetically unappealing high-rise close to the Kisutu St bus booking offices. There are no mosquito nets, but rooms have fans and air-con for circulation. Cash only.

Harbour View Suites   BUSINESS HOTEL $$
(Map p56; ☎ 0784 564848, 022-212 4040; www.harbourview-suites.com; Samora Ave; r US$125-175; ❄🛜🏊) Well-equipped, centrally located business traveller apartments with views over the city or the harbour. Some rooms have mosquito nets, and all have modern furnishings and a kitchenette. There's a business centre, a fitness centre, a restaurant and a blues bar. Very popular and often full. Underneath is JM Mall shopping centre, with an ATM and supermarket.

Holiday Inn   HOTEL $$
(Map p56; ☎ 022-213 9250, 0684 885250; www.holidayinn.co.tz; cnr Maktaba St & Upanga Rd; r from US$136; P❄@🛜) This popular downtown hotel offers modern rooms, courteous service, a handsome buffet breakfast and a rooftop restaurant. Add to that a free daily shuttle service to/from Jangwani Sea Breeze Lodge for guests wanting a swim, plus travel advice on booking charter flights to Zanzibar Island and Pemba. Rates are higher when booked on-site (ie not online).

Heritage Motel   HOTEL $$
(Map p56; ☎ 0787 464683, 022-211 7471; www.heritagemotel.co.tz; cnr Kaluta & Bridge Sts; s/d/tw/tr US$60/80/85/90; ❄🛜) Good-value rooms in a central location just 15 minutes' walk from the ferry terminal. Rooms are spacious, clean and comfortable, with a mini-fridge, TV, and flyscreens on the windows. Al Basha restaurant (p65) next door serves the hotel breakfast plus good Lebanese food.

Ramada Encore   BUSINESS HOTEL $$
(Map p56; ☎ 022-234 3434; www.ramadaencore dar.com; 542 Ghana Ave; s/d from US$128/140; P❄🛜) A new addition to Dar es Salaam's business traveller hotels, the high-rise Ramada Encore has small but reasonably well-appointed rooms, an overwhelming red-grey-black colour scheme, and good views from some of the rooms over the green grounds of the Gymkhana Club and the sea in the distance.

Rainbow Hotel
HOTEL **$$**

(Map p56; ☑ 022-212 0024, 0754 261314; www.
rainbow-hoteltz.com; Morogoro Rd; s US$45-55, d
US$65-90; ❄️🛜) Centrally located right in
the thick of things on Morogoro Rd, just a
five-minute walk from the Zanzibar ferry ter-
minal, Rainbow distinguishes itself with its ef-
ficient staff, decent restaurant and serviceable,
tidy rooms, which all have firm beds, TVs and
air-conditioning. Taxis are located just outside
the front door. Two-bedroom apartments are
also available for families (US$130 to US$150).

Sleep Inn
HOTEL **$$**

(Map p56; ☑ 0754 362866, 022-212 7341, 022-212
7340; www.sleepinnhoteltz.com; Jamhuri St; s/d
US$60/75; ❄️🛜) This high-rise hotel has a
convenient location in the heart of the Asian
Quarter and basic but clean rooms with fan,
air-con, refrigerator and small double bed.
Check several rooms, as their size and condition vary. Breakfast is included; for other
meals there are many restaurants nearby.

★ Southern Sun
HOTEL **$$$**

(Map p56; ☑ 0757 700000, 022-213 7575; www.
tsogosunhotels.com; Garden Ave; s/d from
US$202/228; 🅿️❄️🛜🏊♿) With its Afro-
Islamic decor, popular restaurant and pro-
fessional service, the Southern Sun punches
way above its weight. Rooms are furnished
with plush, comfortable beds and all mod-
cons, while the generous buffet breakfast
can be enjoyed on a terrace overlooking the
Botanical Gardens. Modest rate reductions
are available on weekends.

Dar es Salaam Serena Hotel
HOTEL **$$$**

(Map p56; ☑ 022-221 2500, 022-211 2416; www.
serenahotels.com; Ohio St; s/d from US$242/268;
🅿️❄️@🛜🏊♿) Serena has an unbeatable
location in enormous gardens overlooking
the golf course of the Gymkhana Club, and
a lovely, large swimming pool. Rooms offer
all the bells and whistles you'd expect from
a five-star hotel.

Hyatt Regency Dar es Salaam
HOTEL **$$$**

(The Kilimanjaro; Map p56; ☑ 0764 704704, 0764
701234; www.daressalaamkilimanjaro.regency.hyatt.
com; 24 Kivukoni Front; r from US$300; 🅿️❄️🛜🏊)
'The Kilimanjaro' has been a Dar landmark
since its opening in the mid-1960s and has
hosted a stream of pop stars and dignitaries.
In 2006 a huge refurbishment transformed
its tired decor into a sleek, marble-clad hav-
en of luxury with ultramodern rooms, two
stylish restaurants, a harbour-view bar and
rooftop infinity pool.

Protea Courtyard
HOTEL **$$$**

(Map p62; ☑ 022-213 0130; https://protea.marriott.
com; Barack Obama Dr; s/d US$200/230; 🅿️❄️@
🛜♿) Opened in 1948 by her Royal Begum
Om Habibeh Aga Khan, this art deco hotel
preserves a slice of Dar's history. Among its
prominent guests are African independence
leaders Jomo Kenyatta and Kenneth Kaunda. There's a small pool in the flower-filled
courtyard, as well as a wood-panelled bar,
business facilities and a terrace restaurant
serving good Indian food.

🛏️ Msasani Peninsula

If you have some extra time and don't mind
paying for taxis or travelling the distance
from the airport (about 20km), the hotels on
the Msasani Peninsula offer a break from the
urban bustle. If you decide to stay here, bear
in mind the traffic bottleneck over Selander
Bridge, which should be avoided at all costs
during rush hour.

Slipway Studio Apartments
APARTMENT **$$**

(Map p62; ☑ 0713 888301, 0713 408696; Slip-
way, Msasani; r without breakfast US$75; 🅿️🛜)
Straightforward self-catering apartments
adjoining the Slipway shopping complex.

Hotel Slipway
HOTEL **$$**

(Map p62; ☑ 022-260 0893, 0713 888301; www.
hotelslipway.com; Slipway, Msasani; s US$120-260,
d US$135-275, tr US$170-290; 🅿️❄️🛜🏊♿) In-
tegrated into the seafront Slipway shopping
complex, this apart-hotel offers good-value
accommodation. Rooms and apartments are
bright and breezy, with handcrafted wooden
furniture, bright Indian bed throws, sea-
facing balconies and, in the apartments, well-
equipped kitchenettes. On your doorstep you
also have three standout restaurants, including the popular Waterfront (p65).

Baobab Village Apartments
APARTMENT **$$**

(Map p62; ☑ 0769 395501; Baobab Village Rd;
apt US$80; 🅿️❄️🛜🏊) Straightforward one-
bedroom furnished, serviced apartments
with kitchen, located about 1.5km north of
the Slipway and just east of Chole Rd. Mini-
mum stay is usually five nights.

Triniti Guesthouse
GUESTHOUSE **$$**

(Map p62; ☑ 0755 963686, 0769 628328; www.
triniti.co.tz; 26 Msasani Rd; s/d from US$70/80;
🅿️❄️🛜) Triniti offers informal lodge-like
accommodation in detached wooden bungalows set in a mature garden. While rooms
are small, they are painted spotlessly white
and are decorated with local artworks and

colourful furnishings. Breakfast is a communal affair with homebaked doughnuts, fruit and eggs to order. On Friday night the bar hosts a live band and DJ.

★ **Alexander's Hotel** BOUTIQUE HOTEL $$$
(Map p62; ☑0754 343834; www.alexanders-tz.com; Maryknoll Lane; s/d from US$150/185; ❈🕸☀🍴) With its Le Corbusier–style modernist lines, spacious rooftop terrace and shady courtyard, family-run Alexander's is a true boutique hotel. Its 17 stylish rooms have comfortable beds, plump pillows and bright *kikoi* throws, and all front a shaded pool. Breakfast is served in the art- and book-filled dining room, while sundowners and dinners are enjoyed on the upstairs terrace.

Sea Cliff Hotel HOTEL $$$
(Map p62; ☑022-552 9900, 0764 700600; www.hotelseacliff.com; Toure Dr; r from US$320; 🅿❈@🕸☀) Sea Cliff has an excellent setting overlooking the ocean at the northern tip of Msasani Peninsula. The extensive facilities include a fitness centre, a beauty salon, a casino and restaurants. The best feature, however, is the large cliff-top garden and pool. When booking, it's worth enquiring about special deals.

Coral Beach Hotel HOTEL $$$
(Map p62; ☑0784 260192; www.coralbeach-tz.com; Coral Lane, Masaki; s/d from US$110/135; 🅿❈@🕸☀) A quiet hotel (part of the Best Western chain) with front-row views of the sunset over Oyster Bay. Rooms, in new and old wings, are large and comfortable, with louvred shutters and coral print throws. Many in the old wing don't have views, so check when you're booking.

Protea Hotel Oyster Bay HOTEL $$$
(Map p62; ☑0784 666665, 022-266 6665; http://protea.marriott.com; cnr Haile Selassie & Ali Hassan Mwinyi Rds; s US$220, d US$250, 2-bedroom apt US$320; 🅿❈🕸☀) Part of the South African Protea chain, this hotel is styled something like a motel, with accommodation units (all with kitchenettes) arranged around an internal garden and pool. Rooms have rather bland, modern decor but are well furnished and service is friendly and professional. There's also a gym and conference facilities, making it popular with the business crowd.

🏠 Mikocheni & Kawe Beach

The residential area of Mikocheni can take ages to reach from the city centre during rush

---

DAR ES SALAAM FOR CHILDREN

Dar es Salaam is full of fun things to do with children:

➡ Boat trips (p58) to Bongoyo for grilled fish and snorkelling.

➡ Drumming or acrobatics classes at the Kigamboni Community Centre (p58).

➡ Kunduchi Wet 'n' Wild (p71) water-park fun.

➡ Trampolining at Bounce (p58).

➡ Sunset kayaking up Siwatibe Creek with Dekeza Dhows (p73).

➡ Swimming in the pool at the Golden Tulip (p57).

➡ Watching the kitesurfers at Coco Beach (p58).

---

hour. However, it's convenient for self-drivers heading north towards Jangwani and Kunduchi Beaches or on towards Bagamoyo. It also has easy access to good restaurants and shopping. Nearby Kawe Beach is tranquil and serene once you arrive, with some appealing restaurants and nightlife venues nearby.

Taste of Mexico B&B $
(CEFA; Map p72; ☑022-278 0425; www.tasteofmexico.co.tz; off Old Bagamoyo Rd, Mikocheni B; s/d/tr/q Tsh50,000/70,000/100,000/120,000; 🅿🕸🍴) This place offers simple, spacious rooms in an attractive, Mediterranean-style building. There's also a breezy rooftop bar and restaurant featuring Mexican dishes. The property is signposted and is one block in from Old Bagamoyo Rd (the turn-off is three blocks north of Bima Rd and about 2km north of Mikocheni B cemetery).

Mediterraneo Hotel HOTEL $$$
(Map p72; ☑0754 812567, 0777 812567; www.mediterraneotanzania.com; Tuari Rd, Kawe; s/d US$130/160; 🅿❈@🕸☀🍴) With its clubby weekend vibe and spacious garden rooms the Mediterraneo is a great family-friendly option. Rooms have wrought-iron beds and colour-washed walls, while the popular open-sided restaurant serves Italian food overlooking Kawe Beach. Its all-night beach party on the third Saturday of the month is either to be awaited or avoided, depending on your mindset. Significant discounts for online bookings.

Northern Dar es Salaam

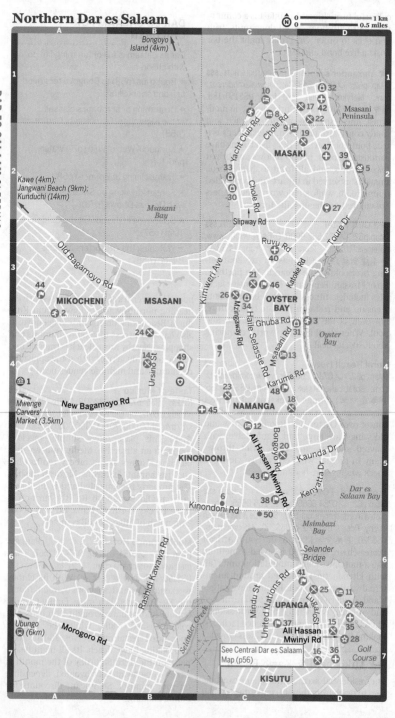

Northern Dar es Salaam

🛏 Ubungo

For travellers transiting through Ubungo bus terminal, there are several inexpensive hotels just west of the terminal and in Ubungo village to the south. Taxis, located just outside the terminal, should cost no more than Tsh5000.

Rombo Green View Hotel   HOTEL **$**
(Map p72; ☎ 0784 461042; www.rombogreen viewhotel.com; Shekilango Rd; s with shared bathroom US$25, s/d/tr from US$30/45/60; P ❄ @) This large, undistinguished hotel offers inexpensive although very mediocre rooms.

Room size and condition vary considerably, so ask to see several. There's also a bar and a restaurant. It's about 700m east of the Ubungo bus terminal, just off Morogoro Rd.

Moveck Hotel   HOTEL **$**
(Map p72; ☎ 0768 688343, 0713 984411; moveck hotel@gmail.com; Maziwa Rd; r with fan Tsh30,000, r with air-con Tsh40,000-50,000; ❄) Located in Ubungo village is this three-storey hotel with basic, serviceable double-bed rooms with mosquito nets, fans (some also have air-con) and en suite hot showers. There's a restaurant next door serving *nyama choma*

(barbecued meat). It's located 500m south of the main bus station in Ubungo.

Eating

Dar es Salaam has a fine selection of restaurants catering to the city's cosmopolitan population. Most of the cheaper Tanzanian and Indian restaurants are located in the city centre, with Euro-centric and upmarket seafood restaurants in Msasani. Many of the high-end hotels offer Sunday lunch buffets and/or brunch. Note that many city-centre restaurants are closed on Sunday.

City Centre & Upanga

★Chapan Bhog   INDIAN $
(56 Bhog; Map p56; ☎0685 401417; www.facebook.com/56Bhog; Kisutu St; meals Tsh6000-15,000; ۞7am-10pm; ✿) Chapan Bhog's Gujurati *dhoklas* (savoury steamed chickpea cakes), South Indian dosas (fermented crêpes) and thalis are a vegetarian nirvana in a sea of *nyama choma* (roasted meat). The all-vegetarian menu is extensive, and the restaurant has a prime position on temple-lined Kisutu St.

Mamboz Corner BBQ   BARBECUE $
(Map p56; ☎0784 243734; cnr Morogoro Rd & Libya St; mains Tsh5000-12,000; ۞6.30-11.30pm Wed-Mon) This streetside place is home to what many claim is Dar's best grilled chicken, including spicy gujarr chicken, lemon chicken and chicken *sekela* (with tamarind sauce), as well as dry fried fish and bowls of *urojo* (Zanzibar mix).

Akberali Tea Room   INDIAN $
(A Tea Room; Map p56; cnr Morogoro Rd & Jamhuri St; snacks Tsh500-3000; ۞7.30am-5pm) Enjoy tasty samosas, kebabs, chapati and other snacks plus a delicious cup of chai (tea) with the locals in this classic corner place.

Barbecue House   BARBECUE $
(Map p62; Nkomo St, just off Ali Hassan Mwinyi Rd; meals Tsh6000-12,000; ۞6-10pm) This informal eatery is a Dar institution. Choose from grilled chicken, fish or beef plus delicious sauces and sides, including green chilli, red chilli and tamarind sauces and coconut chutney. Plates of shredded raw cabbage and sides of fries or *ajam* (similar to naan bread) top things off.

Ali's   BARBECUE $
(Map p56; Mwisho St; meals Tsh6000-15,000; ۞from 6pm Wed-Mon) Huge beef, chicken and fish *mishikaki* (marinated, grilled kebabs), barbecue chicken and freshly baked garlic naan in a streetside setting.

Patel Samaj   INDIAN $
(Patel Brotherhood; Map p56; off Maktaba St; mains Tsh8000-20,000; ۞7-11pm; ✿✤) This large compound is a favourite evening spot for local Indian families, with reasonably priced Indian veg and non-veg meals (thali, chicken biryani and more). Service can be slow at peak times, but there's plenty of local atmosphere to soak up while you're waiting. It's a social club so an additional Tsh2000 entry fee per person is charged to non-members.

From Maktaba St opposite Holiday Inn, follow the small alleyway down to the well-signposted entry gate. There's also a children's play area.

Chef's Pride   TANZANIAN $
(Map p56; Chagga St; meals Tsh6000-12,000; ۞6am-11pm, closed during Ramadan; ✿) This long-standing and popular local eatery serves roasted chicken, biryani and coconut-crusted fish. In addition, the large menu features fast-food favourites such as pizza, Indian and vegetarian dishes. It's popular with families and hungry office workers.

YMCA   TANZANIAN $
(Map p56; ☎022-213 5457; Upanga Rd; meals Tsh5000-8000; ۞11am-8pm) The YMCA canteen serves inexpensive, tasty local food.

Under the Mango Tree   EUROPEAN $$
(Map p62; ☎0788 512322, 022-213 1406; www.facebook.com/umtdar; off Ali Hassan Mwinyi Rd, at Alliance Française; meals US$8-20; ۞9am-6pm Mon-Fri) This bright courtyard-style place serves well-prepared crêpes, burgers, pasta and other light meals. It's worth checking its Facebook page for announcements about frequent evening special events.

Delhi Darbar   INDIAN $$
(Map p62; ☎0784 202111, 0784 573445; Magore St, Upanga; meals Tsh15,000-25,000; ۞noon-3pm & 6-10pm Tue-Sun; ✿) This upmarket Indian restaurant serves tasty North Indian cuisine featuring rich, creamy curries seasoned with chillies, saffron, yoghurt and nuts alongside some tasty tandoori and kebabs. It also has a branch on Zanaki St in the town centre with a lunchtime buffet (Tsh12,000).

★Oriental   ASIAN $$$
(Map p56; ☎0764 701234; 24 Kivukoni Front, Hyatt Regency Dar es Salaam; meals from US$30; ۞6-10.30pm; ☏) From the high sheen of the

marble-tiled floors to the elegant Asian-inspired furnishings, gloved waiters and immaculate sushi bar, the Hyatt's gourmet Asian restaurant aims to seduce and impress. Fortunately, the expertly prepared sushi, bright papaya salads and intensely spiced curries and seafood live up to the opulent surroundings. Bookings recommended.

Kibo Bar
EUROPEAN $$$

(Map p56; ☑ 022-211 2416; Dar es Salaam Serena Hotel, Ohio St; meals Tsh20,000-35,000; ☺ noon-11.30pm; ☎) Pricey but tasty pub fare and other meals at this upmarket sports bar at the Dar es Salaam Serena Hotel.

Al Basha
LEBANESE $$$

(Map p56; ☑ 022-212 6888; Bridge St; mains Tsh20,000-35,000; ☺ 7-10am & noon-11pm) Dar's best Lebanese restaurant serves a good selection of hot and cold meze dishes, shish kebabs and salads. No alcohol is served but there are fresh juices. There's also a branch at Sea Cliff Village on the Msasani Peninsula.

🍴 Msasani Peninsula

Gembros Eatery
TANZANIAN $

(Map p62; Mwaya St; meals Tsh3000-7000; ☺ 6am-4pm Mon-Sat) This efficient local-style eatery has tasty grilled fish, rice, ugali and other standards. Service is fast, and there is pleasant outdoor seating under the trees.

Grace Shop
TANZANIAN $

(Map p62; Bongoyo Rd; meals Tsh5,000; ☺ 11.30am-2.30pm Mon-Fri) This informal eatery shares space with a bridal hire shop. There's no menu, but the lunchtime meal (ready around noon) includes tasty local staples such as ugali, spiced pilau, beans, *mchicha* (a dark green vegetable similar to spinach), cabbage, fried chicken, fish and goat.

Fairy Delights Ice Cream Shop
ICE CREAM $

(Map p62; Slipway, Slipway Rd, Msasani; per scoop from Tsh5000; ☺ 10am-9pm) Many flavours of homemade ice creams and sorbets.

Jackie's
TANZANIAN $

(Map p62; Haile Selassie Rd; meals from Tsh6000; ☺ 11am-11pm) *Mishikaki* (marinated, grilled kebabs), plus *chipsi mayai* (omelette mixed with French fries) and other local staples, and a mix of local and expat clientele in the evenings after work.

⭐ Addis in Dar
ETHIOPIAN $$

(Map p62; ☑ 0713 266299; www.addisindar.com; 35 Ursino St; meals Tsh10,000-25,000; ☺ 5.30-10.30pm Mon-Sat; ☎) Addis in Dar is decorated with embroidered umbrella lampshades, hand-carved seats and woven tables where food is served communally. Try a combination meal to sample a range of flavours. Everything is served on a large platter covered with *injera* (sourdough flatbread made of fermented teff flour); tear it off in pieces and use it to scoop up the spicy curries.

Ristorante Bella Napoli
ITALIAN $$

(Map p62; ☑ 022-260 0326, 0778 497776; www.bellanapolitz.com; 530 Haile Selassie Rd; mains Tsh12,000-25,000; ☺ 6-10pm Tue-Fri, noon-10pm Sat & Sun; ☎ 🍴) Delicious pizzas and Italian food served in a pleasant garden setting or in the air-con dining room, plus a children's playground.

Épi d'Or
BAKERY, CAFE $$

(Map p62; ☑ 0786 669889, 022-260 1663; www.epidor.co.tz; cnr Chole & Haile Selassie Rds; meals Tsh10,000-30,000; ☺ 8am-7pm Mon-Sat) This French-run bakery-cafe has a tempting selection of freshly baked breads, pastries, light lunches, paninis, banana crêpes and Middle Eastern dishes, plus good coffee.

Rohobot
ETHIOPIAN $$

(Map p62; ☑ 0784 235126; Karume Rd, Namanga; meals Tsh10,000-20,000; ☺ noon-2.30pm & 6-10.30pm Mon-Sat, 6-10.30pm Sun; ☎ 🍴) This small, informal place, next to the well-signposted Wonder Workshop (p67), has delicious Ethiopian cuisine.

Waterfront
EUROPEAN $$

(Map p62; ☑ 0762 883321; www.hotelslipway.com; Slipway, Slipway Rd, Msasani; meals Tsh15,000-35,000; ☺ noon-midnight; 🍴) Located in the Slipway shopping complex, this place is Dar's most popular sundowner spot, with westerly views over Msasani Bay. Palm-thatched umbrellas shade tables overlooking the water, and happy hour merges seamlessly into dinners of seafood, steaks and oven-fired pizza.

Zuane Trattoria & Pizzeria
ITALIAN $$$

(Map p62; ☑ 0766 679600; www.zuanetrattoria pizzeria.com; Mzingaway Rd; meals Tsh20,000-50,000; ☺ noon-2.30pm & 6-10.30pm Mon-Sat; 🍴) With its luxuriant garden setting this Italian trattoria housed in an old colonial villa is one of Dar's most atmospheric dining options. The menu features classics such as wood-fired pizzas, *melanzana parmigiana* (an aubergine- and Parmesan-layered bake), pastas, seafood and grilled fillet steak. There's also a children's playground in the garden. Book ahead; it's very popular.

Coral Ridge Spurs
STEAK $$$

(Map p62; ☑0764 700657; www.spurinternation al.com/tanzania; Sea Cliff Village, Toure Dr; meals Tsh20,000-50,000; ⏰10am-10pm Sun-Thu, 10am-11pm Fri & Sat; 🛜👶) Burgers, steaks, a salad bar, birthday celebrations, yummy desserts, fast service and a children's play area with video games make this place a favourite spot for families and children. Evenings, it's almost always crowded.

Terrace
INTERNATIONAL, SEAFOOD $$$

(Map p62; ☑0755 706838; www.hotelslipway.com; Slipway, Slipway Rd, Msasani; meals Tsh30,000-50,000; ⏰6am-11pm) Dine beneath a starry night sky on creative, contemporary dishes such as herb-crusted grouper, spicy jerk chicken and tuna carpaccio. The trendy, open-air terrace is dotted with candlelit tables arranged around a luminous swimming pool.

Self-Catering

Food Lover's Supermarket
SUPERMARKET $

(Map p62; ☑0762 500005; www.flm-tz.com; Msasani Rd; ⏰9am-8pm) A well-stocked and reasonably priced supermarket.

Village Supermarket
SUPERMARKET $$

(Map p62; ☑022-260 1110; www.village-super market.com; Sea Cliff Village, Toure Dr; ⏰8.30am-9pm) Pricey, but with a wide selection of Western foods and imported products.

Shopper's Supermarket
SUPERMARKET $$

(Map p62; Shopper's Plaza, Old Bagamoyo Rd, Mikocheni; ⏰8.30am-8.30pm) A large supermarket; for self-catering.

🍷 Drinking & Nightlife

Dar's biggest party nights are Friday and Saturday, with most bars staying open until the wee hours. Upmarket places usually charge a cover (Tsh5000 to Tsh15,000). On Saturday and Sunday, Coco Beach (p58) is a popular late-afternoon party venue with local vendors supplying inexpensive beers and snacks. If you decide to hang out here, stay with the crowd and avoid isolated areas of the beach.

Slipway Waterfront
BAR

(Map p62; ☑022-260 0893; Slipway, Slipway Rd, Msasani; ⏰11.30am-midnight) A popular place for sundowners, with prime sunset views. Meals are also available.

Triniti Bar & Restaurant
BAR

(Map p62; ☑0755 963686; www.triniti.co.tz; Msasani Rd; ⏰6pm-late) Happy hours, steak-and-wine Wednesdays, live music on Fridays

DAR BY NIGHT

Dar has a richly textured music scene that remains largely off-limits to travellers due to a dearth of information on popular bands and current hot venues. Bypass the problem on one of the Afriroots (p58) 'Dar by Night' tours (US$60 to US$100 per person) for insights into some of the city's best clubs, community centres and bars. The fee includes pick-up and drop-off at your hotel, entrance to clubs and an authentic BBQ dinner.

and big-screen weekend sports. There's a Tsh10,000 entry fee for some events.

George & Dragon
PUB

(Map p62; ☑0717 800002; Haile Selassie Rd, Msasani; ⏰5pm-midnight Tue-Fri, 2pm-midnight Sat, 1-11pm Sun) A bona fide English pub where they pull pints, broadcast Premier League games and serve pub grub like fish and chips (meals Tsh12,000 to Tsh 22,000). There's a DJ in the garden twice a week.

Level 8 Bar
BAR

(Map p56; ☑0764 701234; 8th fl, Hyatt Regency Dar es Salaam, Kivukoni Front; ⏰5pm-1am) The Hyatt's chic rooftop bar has wonderful views over the harbour, lounge seating and live music some evenings.

Rouge
CLUB

(Map p56; ☑0764 701234; Hyatt Regency Dar es Salaam, Kivukoni Front; ⏰10pm-4am Fri & Sat) This upmarket nightclub (entry Tsh15,000) with DJ is on the rooftop of the Hyatt Regency, and attracts a mixed crowd of locals and foreigners.

⭐ Entertainment

Alliance Française
DANCE, LIVE MUSIC

(Map p62; ☑022-213 1406; www.afdar.com; off Ali Hassan Mwinyi Rd; ⏰9am-6pm Mon-Fri, 9am-1pm Sat) Traditional and modern dance, live music and more at the monthly Barazani multicultural nights. It's held on the second or third Wednesday of the month; the schedule is on its website.

Village Museum
DANCE

(Map p62; ☑022-270 0437, 0718 525682; New Bagamoyo Rd; per adult/student Tsh6500/2600) *Ngoma* (drumming and dancing) performances daily (Tsh2000 per person), whenever there is sufficient demand, plus occasional special afternoon programs highlighting the dances of individual tribes.

Russian Cultural Centre ARTS CENTRE
(Map p62; ☑ 022-213 6578; http://tza.rs.gov.ru/en; Ocean Rd) Occasional art exhibitions and cultural performances.

🔒 Shopping

★ Wonder Workshop ARTS & CRAFTS
(Map p62; ☑ 0754 051417; info@wonder-workshop. org; 1372 Karume Rd, Msasani; ☺ 8.30am-6pm Mon-Fri, 10am-6pm Sat) 🏃 At this excellent workshop, artists with disabilities create world-class jewellery, sculptures, candles, stationery and other crafts from old glass, metal, car parts and other recycled materials. There's a small shop on the grounds. Crafts can also be commissioned (and sent abroad), and Monday through Friday you can watch the artists at work.

Tingatinga Centre ARTS & CRAFTS
(Map p62; www.tingatinga.org; Morogoro Stores, off Haile Selassie Rd; ☺ 9am-6pm) 🏃 This excellent centre is at the spot where Edward Saidi Tingatinga originally marketed his designs, and it's still one of the best places to buy Tingatinga paintings and to watch the artists at work.

Slipway SHOPPING CENTRE
(Map p62; www.slipway.net; Slipway Rd, Msasani; ☺ 9.30am-6pm) This waterfront shopping centre features upmarket boutiques plus a craft market, eateries, an ice-cream parlour and fine sunset views.

Mwenge Carvers' Market ARTS & CRAFTS
(Map p72; Sam Nujoma Rd; ☺ 8am-6pm) This market is packed with vendors, and you can watch woodcarvers at work. Take the Mwenge dalla-dalla from New Posta transport stand to the end of the route, from where it's five minutes on foot down Sam Nujoma Rd.

A Novel Idea BOOKS
(Map p62; ☑ 022-260 1088; www.anovelideatz. co.tz; Slipway, Slipway Rd, Msasani; ☺ 10am-7pm Mon-Sat) Dar es Salaam's best bookshop, with classics, modern fiction, travel guides, Africa titles, maps and more.

Kariakoo Market MARKET
(Map p56; off Msimbazi St; ☺ 6am-9pm) Dar es Salaam's biggest and busiest market occupies several city blocks and the former barracks of the British Carrier Corp. It heaves with people morning, noon and night and you can find virtually anything here. Take

the usual precautions against pickpockets and don't come with expensive cameras or wearing jewellery.

Oyster Bay Shopping Centre SHOPPING CENTRE
(Map p62; cnr Toure Dr & Ghuba Rd; ☺ 10am-6pm) Set around a garden courtyard, this small shopping centre is the beating heart of upmarket Oyster Bay. Here you'll find an organic grocer as well as some great craft shops, giftware from Moyo Designs and the Ngozee leather shop, as well as La Petite Galerie, with contemporary art and sculpture.

Green Room ARTS & CRAFTS
(Map p62; ☑ 0757 279405; www.thegreenroom tz.com; ☺ 10am-6pm Mon-Sat, noon-5pm Sun) A great place for unusual souvenirs, where high-quality giftware, home furnishings, jewellery and artworks are made from upcycled materials.

Sea Cliff Village MALL
(Map p62; Toure Dr; ☺ 9.30am-6pm) An upmarket shopping mall set around a garden courtyard. There are several restaurants, a supermarket, a children's play area and a selection of shops, including a number of jewellers selling tanzanite.

Mnazi Moja Textile Vendors CLOTHING
(Map p56; around Bibi Titi Mohammed Rd & Uhuru St; ☺ hours vary) For kangas (printed cotton wraparounds worn by many Tanzanian women) and other colourful textiles, try the vendors and wholesale shops in the Mnazi Moja area.

ⓘ Information

EMERGENCIES
Central Police Station (Map p56; Sokoine Dr) Near the Central Line Train Station.
Oyster Bay Police Station (Map p62; Old Bagamoyo Rd) Opposite the US Embassy.
Traffic Police Headquarters (Map p56; Sokoine Dr) Near the Central Line Train Station.

IMMIGRATION
Immigration Department (Uhamiaji; Map p72; ☑ 022-285 0575/6; www.immigration.go.tz; Uhamiaji House, Loliondo St, Kurasini; ☺ visa applications 8am-noon Mon-Fri, visa collections until 2pm) Just off Kilwa Rd, about 3.5km from the city centre.

INTERNET ACCESS
Most hotels, even budget ones, now have either a fixed internet point or wi-fi. Internet cafes abound in the city centre; the more professional

ones are tucked away in commercial centres such as Harbour View and Osman Towers. Most charge between Tsh1000 and Tsh2000 per hour.

Main Post Office (Map p56; Azikiwe St; ⊙8am-4.30pm Mon-Fri, 9am-noon Sat) Has terminals (Tsh1500 per hour).

Serena Hotel Business Centre (Map p56; Dar es Salaam Serena Hotel, Ohio St; per 10min Tsh1000; ⊙7.30am-7pm Mon-Fri, 8.30am-4pm Sat, 9am-1pm Sun)

YMCA Internet Café (Map p56; Upanga Rd; per hour Tsh1000; ⊙8am-7.30pm Mon-Fri, to 2pm Sat)

MEDICAL SERVICES

There are good pharmacies at all the main shopping centres, including the Slipway (p67) and Sea Cliff Village (p67).

Aga Khan Hospital (Map p62; ☑022-211 5151, 022-211 5153; www.agakhanhospitals.org; Barack Obama Dr) A multi-speciality hospital with internationally qualified doctors offering general medical services and specialist clinics.

Amref Flying Doctors (Map p62; ☑0719 881887, 0784 240500, in Kenya 020-699 2299; www.flydoc.org; Ali Hassan Mwinyi Rd) For emergency air evacuations.

IST Clinic (Map p62; ☑022-260 1307, 24hr emergency 0754 783393; www.istclinic.com; Ruvu Rd, Msasani; ⊙8am-6pm Mon-Thu, 8am-5pm Fri, 9am-noon Sat) Fully equipped Western-run clinic, with a doctor on call 24 hours.

JD Pharmacy (Map p62; ☑022-286 3663, 022-211 1049; www.jdpharmacy.co.tz; opposite Sea Cliff Village, cnr Toure Dr & Mhando St; ⊙9am-8pm Mon-Sat, 9am-2pm Sun) Well-stocked pharmacy, with several branches.

ⓘ DANGERS & ANNOYANCES

Take the usual precautions in Dar es Salaam:

➡ Watch out for pickpocketing in crowded areas, and for bag snatching through vehicle windows.

➡ Stay aware of your surroundings and leave your valuables in a reliable hotel safe.

➡ At night, always catch a taxi rather than taking a dalla-dalla or walking.

➡ Avoid walking alone along the path paralleling Barack Obama Dr, on Coco Beach, and at night along Chole Rd.

➡ Only use taxis from reliable hotels or established taxi stands. Avoid taxis cruising the streets, and never get in a taxi that has a 'friend' of the driver or anyone else already in it.

Premier Care Clinic (Map p62; ☑0752 254642, 0715 254642; www.premiercareclinic.com; 259 Ali Hassan Mwinyi Rd, Namanga; ⊙8am-5pm Mon-Fri, to noon Sat) Western standards and facilities; also has a branch in Masaki.

The Pharmacy (Map p62; ☑0782 994709; www.thepharmacy.co.tz; Haile Selassie Rd, Shoppers Plaza, Masaki; ⊙9am-9pm) Well-stocked pharmacy; also has a number of other branches around town.

MONEY

Forex bureaus give faster service and marginally better exchange rates than the banks. There are many scattered around the city centre, particularly on or near Samora Ave, where you can easily compare rates. All are open standard business hours.

All the big hotels also offer currency exchange, but their rates are less favourable. The worst rates of exchange are generally at the **Galaxy Forex Bureau** (Map p72; ⊙6am-11pm) in the arrivals hall at the airport, although it's useful for doing reverse exchanges at the end of your travels. In town, try **Serena Forex Bureau** (Map p56; Ohio St; ⊙8am-8pm Mon-Sat, 10am-1pm Sun & public holidays).

There are ATMs all over the city, and in all the major shopping centres.

POST

Main Post Office (Map p56; Azikiwe St; ⊙8am-4.30pm Mon-Fri, 9am-noon Sat)

TELEPHONE

Starter packs and top-up cards for mobile-phone operators are widely available at shops throughout the city.

TOURIST INFORMATION

Tanzania Tourist Board Information Centre (Map p56; ☑022-213 1555, 022-212 8472; www.tanzaniatourism.com; Samora Ave; ⊙8.30am-4pm Mon-Fri, to noon Sat) Free tourist maps and brochures, and limited city information.

TRAVEL AGENCIES

For flight and hotel bookings, try the following:

Coastal Travels (Map p62; ☑0713 325673, 022-284 2700; www.coastal.co.tz; Slipway, Slipway Rd, Msasani; ⊙8.30am-6pm Mon-Fri, to 2pm Sat) Especially good for travel to the Zanzibar Archipelago, and for flights linking northern and southern safari circuit destinations (for which it has its own airline). Also offers reasonably priced city tours, day trips to Zanzibar Island, and Mikumi National Park excursions.

Fast Track Tanzania (Map p56; ☑022-213 4600, 022-213 6663; www.fasttracktanzania.

com; ground fl, Peugeot House, Bibi Titi Mohammed Rd; ☺8.30am-5pm Mon-Fri, 8.30am-1pm Sat) The agent for Linhas Aéreas de Moçambique and Malawi Airlines.

Kearsley Travel (Map p56; ☑022-213 7713, 022-213 7711; www.kearsleys.com; 16 Zanaki St; ☺9am-6pm Mon-Fri, to 1pm Sat) One of the oldest travel agencies in Dar. As well as the usual flight, car and hotel bookings, it also offers southern circuit safaris. Also has an office at Sea Cliff Village (p67).

ⓘ Getting There & Away

AIR

Julius Nyerere International Airport (DAR; Map p72; ☑022-284 2402; www.taa.go.tz) is Tanzania's hub airport. It has two terminals, with domestic and international flights departing from Terminal Two, and charters and light aircraft departing from Terminal One ('old terminal'). Verify the departure terminal when purchasing your ticket.

A third terminal is being constructed to increase capacity to six million arrivals per year. Once completed, all international flights will move to Terminal Three, while Terminal Two will serve domestic routes.

Airlines connecting Dar es Salaam with elsewhere in Tanzania:

Air Tanzania (TC; Map p56; ☑022-211 3248; www.airtanzania.co.tz; Ohio St, 1st fl, ATC House; ☺8am-5pm Mon-Fri, 9am-2pm Sat)

Coastal Aviation (Map p62; ☑0713 325673, reservations 022-284 2700; www.coastal.co.tz; Slipway, Slipway Rd, Msasani; ☺9am-5pm Mon-Fri, 9am-3pm Sat)

Fastjet (Map p56; ☑0784 108900; www.fastjet.com; Samora Ave; ☺8am-4.30pm Mon-Fri, 8.30am-1pm Sat)

Precision Air (Map p56; ☑0787 888417, 022-213 0800; www.precisionairtz.com; cnr Samora Ave & Pamba Rd; ☺8am-5pm Mon-Fri, 9am-1pm Sat)

Tropical Air (Map p72; ☑024-223 2511, 0687 527511; www.tropicalair.co.tz; Terminal One, Airport)

ZanAir (Map p72; ☑0716 863857, 024-223 3670; www.zanair.com; Terminal One, Airport)

BOAT

The main passenger route is between Dar es Salaam and Zanzibar Island, with some boats continuing on to Pemba, and from there to Tanga. The **ferry terminal** (Map p56; Sokoine Dr) is in the city centre, opposite St Joseph Cathedral.

The only place at the port to buy legitimate ferry tickets is the tall, blue-glass building at the southern end of the ferry terminal on Kivukoni Front. The building is marked 'Azam Marine – Coastal Fast Ferries', and has ticket offices and a large waiting area inside. Avoid the smaller offices just to the north of this building. It's also possible to purchase tickets online through **Azam Marine** (Map p56; ☑022-212 3324; www.azammarine.com; Kivukoni Front).

Don't fall for touts at the harbour trying to collect extra fees for 'doctors' certificates', departure taxes and the like. The only fee is the ticket price (which includes the US$5 port tax). Also, avoid touts who want to take you into town to buy 'cheaper' ferry tickets, or who offer to purchase ferry tickets for you at resident rates.

Depending on the season, the ferry crossing can be choppy; most lines pass out seasickness bags at the start of each trip.

To/From Zanzibar

Four fast Azam Marine catamarans operate daily between Dar and Zanzibar Island (economy/VIP US$35/50, economy child US$25), leaving between about 7am and 4pm. All take around two hours, with a luggage allowance of 25kg per person. VIP tickets get you a seat in the air-con hold, but arrive early if you want to sit together.

To/From Pemba

The large Azam *Sealink I* ferry to Pemba (adult/child US$70/50, 18 hours including a stop at Zanzibar Island) departs Dar twice weekly. This ferry also takes vehicles. Tickets are purchased at the same blue Azam Marine building selling Zanzibar Island tickets. However, the departure point is about 200m further south along Kivukoni Front, just before the unmissable, boat-shaped Tanzania Ports Authority high-rise – look for the long, cement driveway leading down to the water. There is also a weekly connection on the *Sealink* between Tanga and Pemba (US$35, four hours).

BUS

Except as noted, at the time of research all buses were departing from and arriving at the main **Ubungo Bus Terminal** (Map p72; 8km west of the city centre on Morogoro Rd, from where you can connect on the new Dar Rapid Transit (DART) bus network to the city centre (Tsh650, about 20 minutes), or take a taxi (from Tsh30,000, about one hour, more with heavy traffic). Some lines terminate about 500m east along Morogoro Rd, at the junction of Sheikilango Rd ('Ubungo-Sheikilango'). However, a lot is due to change with full implementation of the new DART bus network, when all upcountry transport will be switched to Mbezi (past Ubungo on the Morogoro Rd). Ubungo itself will also benefit from a new terminal, which will replace the current sprawling lot and hopefully tame its notorious touts and hustlers.

As always keep an eye on your luggage and your wallet and try to avoid arriving at night. If you arrive at Ubungo via taxi, ask your taxi driver to take you directly to the ticket office window for the line you want to travel with. Avoid dealing with touts.

Bus tickets can be purchased at Ubungo, and – for Dar Express and Kilimanjaro Express – at their city offices on Libya St. Only buy tickets inside the bus offices.

Buses to Kilwa Masoko, Lindi and Mtwara depart from south of the city, at **Temeke–Sudan Market Area** (Temeke Sudani; Map p72; cnr Mbagala & Temeke Rds) and **Mbagala–Rangi Tatu** (Map p72).

Following are some sample prices from Dar es Salaam. All routes are serviced at least once daily.

Destination	Fare (Tsh)
Arusha	28,000-36,000
Dodoma	20,000-27,000
Iringa	22,000-30,000
Kampala (Uganda)	100,000-115,000
Mbeya	32,000-49,000
Mwanza	43,000-65,000
Nairobi (Kenya)	55,000-75,000
Songea	40,000-56,000

Dar Express (Map p56; Libya St, Kisutu; ⊘6am-6pm) Has daily buses to Moshi (Tsh30,000 to Tsh36,000, 8½ hours) and Arusha (Tsh30,000 to Tsh36,000, 10 hours) departing between 5.30am and 8am from Ubungo bus station. There's also a daily bus to Nairobi (Tsh65,000, 15 hours) at 5.45am.

Kilimanjaro Express (Map p56; Libya St, Kisutu; ⊘4.30am-7pm) Runs two daily buses to Moshi (Tsh33,000 to Tsh36,000, 8½ hours) and Arusha (Tsh33,000 to Tsh36,000, 10 hours), departing at 6am and 7am from outside the Kilimanjaro Express office on Libya St, and then about 45 minutes later from Ubungo. Arriving in Dar es Salaam, the buses terminate at Ubungo-Sheikilango bus stop. From Ubungo-Sheikilango, catch a BRT bus into town (Tsh650, 20 minutes).

TRAIN

The train station for **Tazara** (Tanzanian-Zambia Railway Authority; Map p72; ☑ 0713 354648, 0732 998855, 022-286 5187; www.tazarasite. com; cnr Nyerere & Nelson Mandela Rds; ⊘ticket office 7.30am-noon & 2-4.30pm Mon-Fri, 9am-noon Sat) is 6km southwest of the city centre (Tsh15,000 to Tsh20,000 in a taxi). Dalla-dallas to the station leave from the New Posta transport stand, and are marked Vigunguti, U/Ndege or Buguruni. Train services run between Dar es Salaam, Mbeya and Kapiri Mposhi (Zambia).

The train station for **Tanzania Railways Limited 'Central Line' trains** (☑ 0754 460907, 022-211 6213, 022-211 7833; www.trl.co.tz; cnr Railway St & Sokoine Dr) is just southwest of the ferry terminal in the city centre. 'Central Line' services connect Dar es Salaam with Kigoma and Mwanza via Tabora.

 DAR RAPID TRANSIT

The Dar Rapid Transit (DART) project in Dar es Salaam is gradually taking over old dalla-dalla routes. The Kimara–Kivukoni line of the new system runs express buses between the city centre and Ubungo (Tsh650, about 20 minutes), stopping en route at both Ubungo Bus Terminal and Ubungo-Sheikilango, and in the city centre at Kisutu St, **Old Posta Transport Stand** (Posta ya zamani; Map p56; Sokoine Dr) and Kivukoni. Purchase your ticket at any station in advance of boarding.

❶ Getting Around

TO/FROM THE AIRPORT

Taxis to central Dar es Salaam cost Tsh35,000 to Tsh45,000 (30 to 90 minutes) and Tsh40,000 to Tsh50,000 to Msasani Peninsula (45 to 90 minutes).

CAR & MOTORCYCLE

Most car-rental agencies offer self-drive options in town; none offer unlimited kilometres. Another option is to negotiate a daily or half-day rate with a reliable taxi driver (p71).

First Car Rental (Map p56; ☑ 0754 451111, 022-211 5381; www.firstcarrental.co.tz; Amani Place, Ohio St; ⊘8.30am-5pm Mon-Fri, 8.30am-1pm Sat) Not the cheapest prices, but offers a professional service. Has desks at the Hyatt Regency and the airport, as well as branch offices in Arusha and Stone Town.

Green Car Rentals (Map p56; ☑ 0713 227788, 022-218 3718; www.greencarstz.com; Nyerere Rd; ⊘9am-5pm Mon-Fri, 9am-noon Sat) A reputable company with over 20 years of experience. It also has branch offices in Arusha and in Zanzibar Town. You'll find it next to Dar es Salaam Glassworks.

PUBLIC TRANSPORT

Dalla-dallas (minibuses and 30-seater buses) have long been the mainstay of Dar's public transport system, servicing many city destinations for an average price of Tsh400 per ride. They are invariably packed to overflowing, and are difficult to board with luggage. First and last stops are shown in the front window, but routes vary, so confirm with the conductor that the driver is going to your destination.

As DART buses take over, dalla-dallas are being gradually phased out, especially in the city centre, where their numbers have already been greatly reduced. City-centre dalla-dalla terminals still operational at the time of research include the following:

New Posta Transport Stand (Posta Mpya; Map p56; Azikiwe St) At the main post office.

Stesheni Transport Stand (Map p56; Algeria St) Near the Central Line Train Station. Dalla-dallas to Temeke also leave from here; ask for 'Temeke *mwisho*'.

TAXI

Taxis don't have meters. Short rides within the city centre cost from Tsh5000. Fares from the city centre to Msasani Peninsula start at Tsh15,000. Never get into a taxi that has other people already in it, and always use taxis affiliated with hotels, or operating from a fixed stand and known by the other drivers at the stand. A convenient **taxi stand** (Map p56; Ohio St) is the one opposite the Dar es Salaam Serena Hotel.

An option for longer trips is to negotiate a daily or half-day rate with a reliable taxi driver such as **Jumanne Mastoka** (Map p56; ☑ 0659 339735, 0784 339735; mjumanne@yahoo.com), who is highly recommended also for airport pick-ups and for travel elsewhere in Tanzania.

AROUND DAR ES SALAAM

Northern Beaches

The beaches, resorts and water parks 25km north of Dar es Salaam are popular weekend getaways for families. They are close enough to Dar es Salaam that you can also visit for the day (though leave early to avoid heavy traffic). The southern section of coast around Jangwani Beach is broken up by frequent stone jetties.

◉ Sights & Activities

Kunduchi Ruins   RUINS
(Map p72; adult/child Tsh10,000/5000) These overgrown but worthwhile ruins include the remnants of a late 15th-century mosque as well as Arabic graves from the 18th or 19th centuries, with some well-preserved pillar tombs plus some more recent graves. Fragments of Chinese pottery found here testify to ancient trading links between this part of Africa and Asia. Arrange a guide with your hotel, and expect to pay from about Tsh20,000 for the excursion including entry fee. It's not safe to go alone.

Kunduchi Wet 'n' Wild   WATER PARK
(Map p72; ☑ 0688 058365, 022-265 0050; www. wetnwild.co.tz; Kunduchi; weekday/weekend adult Tsh10,000/15,000, child 2-8yr Tsh8000/10,000;

☺9.30am-5.45pm) This large complex next to and affiliated with Kunduchi Beach Hotel has multiple pools and waterslides, video arcades, a jungle gym and an adjoining, sometimes functioning, go-kart track. Various meal and entry packages are also available.

Kunduchi Kite School   KITESURFING
(Map p72; ☑ 0787 802472; www.kunduchi-kite -school.com; Kunduchi; lessons per hour US$50-65) This place – one of the few kite-surfing schools on the mainland – takes advantage of northeasterly and southeasterly winds that blow between mid-December and February and from April to October. As well as lessons, the school provides the following to experienced kiters: assistance with take-off and landing, lockers, rigging and inflation air, a repair shop and showers.

🛏 Sleeping & Eating

Friendly Gecko Guesthouse   GUESTHOUSE $
(Map p72; ☑ 0759 941848; www.friendlygecko. com; Africana area; dm US$20, s/d from US$30/50; P❋🛜) If you want to stay in Dar a couple of days and connect with an interesting project, consider checking into Friendly Gecko Guesthouse, 20km north of the city centre off New Bagamoyo Rd. The guesthouse has a mixture of simple rooms in a large, private house with a garden and kitchen, and all profits go to support affiliated community programs. It's just inland from Jangwani Beach.

White Sands Hotel   RESORT $$$
(Map p72; ☑ 0758 818696; www.hotelwhitesands. com; Jangwani Beach; s/d/apt from US$180/200/ 230; P❋🛜🏊) This large resort has rooms in two-storey rondavels lined up along the waterfront, all with TV, minifridge and sea views. There are also 28 self-catering apartments – some directly overlooking the beach. There's also a gym and a business centre, and the restaurant serves popular weekend buffets.

Kunduchi Beach Hotel & Resort   HOTEL $$$
(Map p72; ☑ 0789 563726, 0688 058365; www.well worthcollection.co.tz; Kunduchi Beach; s/d US$180/ 210; P❋🛜🏊) This renovated former government hotel is set on a large stretch of white sand, with a long row of attractive beach-facing rooms and expansive landscaped grounds. All the rooms have floor-to-ceiling windows and balconies, and there's a restaurant.

❶ Getting There & Away

Hotels on Jangwani Beach are reached via the signposted White Sands turn-off from New

Around Dar es Salaam

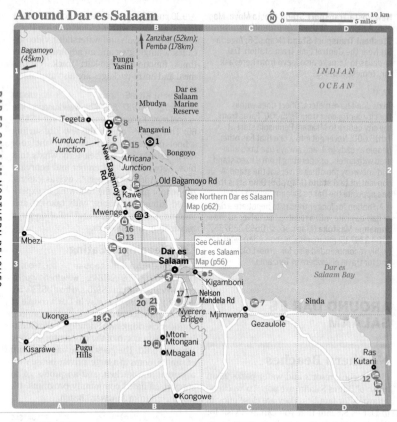

Around Dar es Salaam

Bagamoyo Rd. About 3km further north along New Bagamoyo Rd is the signposted turn-off for Kunduchi Beach.

Via public transport, take a dalla-dalla from New Posta Transport Stand (p71) in Dar es Salaam to Mwenge (Tsh400). Once at Mwenge, for Jangwani Beach, take a 'Tegeta' dalla-dalla to Africana Junction (Tsh200), and from there a *bajaji* (tuk-tuk; Tsh2000) or taxi (Tsh3000 to Tsh5000) the remaining couple of kilometres to the hotels. It's also possible to get a direct dalla-dalla from Kariakoo to Tegeta. For Kunduchi Beach, once at Mwenge, take a 'Bahari Beach' dalla-dalla to 'Njia Panda ya Silver Sands'. From here, take a motorcycle or *bajaji* the remaining distance. Don't walk, as there have been muggings along this road.

Taxis from Dar es Salaam cost from about Tsh60,000 one way. All hotels arrange airport pick-ups.

If you're driving, the fastest route is along Old Bagamoyo Rd via Kawe.

Offshore Islands

The uninhabited islands of Bongoyo, Mbudya, Pangavini and Fungu Yasini, just off the coastline north of Dar es Salaam, were gazetted in 1975 as part of the **Dar es Salaam Marine Reserve System** (Map p72; www.marineparks. go.tz; adult/child US$11.80/5.90). **Bongoyo** and **Mbudya** – the two most visited islands (especially on weekends, when they are often packed), and the only ones with tourist facilities – offer attractive beaches.

The islands are home to coconut crabs, and dolphins can sometimes be spotted in the surrounding waters. There are several nearby dive sites, most off the islands' eastern sides. **Fungu Yasini** is a large sandbank without vegetation, while **Pangavini** has only a tiny beach area. Much of its perimeter is low coral outcrops, making docking difficult, and it's seldom visited.

The admission fee to enter the reserve, including visiting any of the islands, is included in the price of excursions (p58), and collected before departure.

◉ Sights & Activities

Unlike on mainland beaches, swimming on the islands is not tide dependent. Bongoyo has a pretty stretch of beach offering snorkelling, swimming and walking trails. Mbudya has several beaches (the best runs along the island's western edge), walking trails and snorkelling. For both, arrange snorkel hire before leaving the mainland at the boat ticketing office (p58). Sea Breeze Marine (p58)

offers diving around the coral gardens near Bongoyo, Pangavini and Mbudya Islands, and PADI diving certification courses.

🛏 Sleeping & Eating

The only overnight options are prearranged camping (with your own tent) on **Bongoyo** (☑0786 143842; with own/rented tent US$20/50; ☺) and **Mbudya** (☑0713 645460; with own tent Tsh20,000). During the day, thatched shade umbrellas are available for rent (Tsh5000).

Simple meals of grilled fish and chips (Tsh12,000 to Tsh15,000), plus soft drinks, are available on Bongoyo and Mbudya, or bring your own food and drink from the mainland.

❶ Getting There & Away

A ferry (p58) for Bongoyo departs from Dar es Salaam roughly hourly from 9.30am to 3.30pm daily (except during the long rains) from Msasani Slipway, with a minimum of four passengers. The departure and ticketing point is opposite Waterfront restaurant (p65). Mbudya is best reached from the beaches north of Dar es Salaam; all the hotels organise excursions. Boat transfers are also possible from Msasani Slipway (same ticketing office as for the Bongoyo ferry) with a minimum of six people.

Southern Beaches

The coastline south of Dar es Salaam gets more attractive, tropical and rural the further south you go, and makes an easily accessible getaway, far removed – in ambience, if not in distance – from the city. The beach begins just south of Kigamboni, which is opposite Kivukoni Front and reached in five minutes by the Kigamboni ferry (p74) or with your own vehicle via Kilwa Rd and the Nyerere Bridge.

Kigamboni

POP 30,500

The long, white-sand beach ('South Beach') south of Kigamboni, around Mjimwema village, is the closest spot to Dar es Salaam for camping and chilling. It's an easy and worthwhile day trip if you're staying in the city and want some sand and surf, as well as a relaxing overnight spot.

🛶 Activities

Dekeza Dhows   SNORKELLING, KAYAKING
(Map p72; ☑0787 217040, 0754 276178; www.de kezadhows.com; Kipepeo Beach) Dekeza's daily dhow trips (US$35 per person) depart from Kipepeo Beach to Sinda Island. Boats set off

KIGAMBONI FERRY

The **Kigamboni (Magogoni) ferry** (Map p56; per person/vehicle Tsh200/ 2000; ⊙ 5am-midnight) makes a good excursion in itself. It runs throughout the day from Kivukoni Front. Although just a five- to 10-minute trip, it offers great views across the water to the rising modern cityscape, plus a slice of local life as vendors hawk snacks and accessories to city commuters. In rush hour, it can take more than an hour to get on board the ferry. To alleviate the pressure, the new six-lane, cable-stayed Nyerere Bridge has been built across Kurasini Creek further south, connecting Kilwa and Nelson Mandela Rds in Dar es Salaam with Kibada Rd in Kigamboni. It can save some time, and the evening laser display is impressive to watch, but it won't beat the fun of the ferry.

at 10am, tracing the edge of nearby coral reefs for an hour or so of snorkelling before setting up lunch on a deserted beach. Fishing trips aboard the dhows are also possible (US$250 for four people), as are sunset cruises.

The same outfit also operates kayak tours (US$15 per person) up the Siwatibe Creek, allowing for the exploration of the unspoilt mangrove forest behind Kipepeo Village. The 2½-hour sunset kayak tours set off in the late afternoon.

🛏 Sleeping & Eating

Kipepeo Beach & Village   LODGE **$$**
(Map p72; ☎ 0754 276178; www.kipepeobeach. com; Kipepeo Village; camping US$10, s/d/tr banda US$20/30/40, s/d/tr chalet US$65/85/115; P) Laid-back Kipepeo, 8km south of the ferry dock, has raised chalets with balconies just back from the beach. Closer to the water are thatched beach huts without windows, and a camping area. It's a sand-in-the-toes kind of place and has a beachside restaurant-bar. Dekeza Dhows tours depart from here. On weekends there's a Tsh5000 fee for day use of the beach (the cost can be redeemed at the bar or restaurant).

Sunrise Beach Resort   HOTEL **$$**
(Map p72; ☎ 0755 400900, 022-282 0222; www. sunrisebeachresort.co.tz; Mjimwema village; camping US$10, r US$80-140; P ❋ ☎ ❄) Sunrise has a decent beachfront location but rather average accommodation in closely spaced

rooms just in from the sand or air-con 'executive' rooms in two-storey brick rondavels to the back of the property. Renovations and expansion are planned, so this is likely to change. There is a per-person day-use fee on weekends of Tsh5000.

❶ Getting There & Away

Take the Kigamboni ferry from Kivukoni Front in Dar es Salaam. Once on the other side, take a *bajaji* (tuk-tuk) to the beaches (Tsh3000 to Tsh5000). Dalla-dallas from the ferry (Tsh400) will drop you at Mjimwema village, which is about 1km on foot from several beach lodges.

With your own car, an alternative route to/ from the city is the Nyerere Bridge (Tsh2000), which crosses over Kurasini Creek and is accessed from Kilwa Rd. Once over the bridge, stay left at the various forks to get onto the road to the beach lodges.

Ras Kutani

This secluded cape, about 30km south of Dar es Salaam, offers the chance for a tropical-island-style getaway without actually leaving the mainland. Snorkelling is good (there's no diving) and nesting sea turtles favour this section of coast.

🛏 Sleeping & Eating

Ras Kutani   RESORT **$$$**
(Map p72; ☎ 022-212 8485; www.selous.com; per person with full board bungalow/ste from US$390/ 440; ⊙ Jun–mid-Mar; ☎❄) Set between the sea and a small lagoon on a wonderful stretch of beach, this lovely, barefoot luxury resort has spacious natural-style bungalows with beach-facing verandas. On a rise away from the main lodge are several suites, each with their own plunge pool. Canoeing in the lagoon can be arranged.

Protea Hotel Dar es Salaam Amani Beach   BUNGALOW **$$$**
(Map p72; ☎ 0782 410033; www.marriott.com; s/d US$150/180; P ❋ @ ☎ ❄) Peaceful Amani Beach has 10 roomy, well-spaced cottages set on a low cliff directly above the beach. There's also a beachside swimming pool and horse riding can be arranged.

❶ Getting There & Away

The main ways to reach Ras Kutani are with your own vehicle or charter taxi. Expect to pay about Tsh100,000 from Dar es Salaam for a drop-off. The hotels can also help you to arrange transport. The Ras Kutani resort has its own airstrip for charter flights.

Zanzibar Archipelago

Best Places to Stay

➡ Emerson Spice (p90)

➡ Lost & Found Hostel (p88)

➡ Upendo (p108)

➡ Demani Lodge (p110)

Best Places to Eat

➡ Emerson on Hurumzi Rooftop Teahouse (p93)

➡ Mr Kahawa (p112)

➡ Zanzibar Coffee House (p91)

➡ Monsoon Restaurant (p92)

Why Go?

Step off the boat or plane onto the Zanzibar Archipelago and you're transported through time and place. This is one of the world's great cultural crossroads, where Africa meets Arabia meets the Indian Ocean.

In Zanzibar Town, the narrow alleys of historic Stone Town meander between ancient buildings decorated with balconies and gigantic carved doors. Meanwhile, on the coast, fishing boats set sail, and in the countryside farmers tend fields of rice or the clove plantations that give Zanzibar its 'Spice Islands' moniker.

Beyond these little-changed traditions, visitors see a very different landscape. The idyllic beaches are dotted with hotels, and the ocean becomes a playground for diving, snorkelling and kitesurfing.

With its tropical tableau and unique culture, plus an active beach-party scene for those that want it, the Zanzibar Archipelago offers a fascinating and highly enjoyable East African Indian Ocean experience.

When to Go
Zanzibar Town

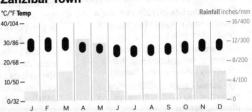

Dec–Feb Popular period, especially over Christmas and New Year when hotel rates can rocket.

Mar–May Rainy season; Zanzibar is crowd-free, some hotels close while others offer discount rates.

Jul–Aug High season; hotels and beaches can be busy.

Zanzibar Archipelago Highlights

1 **House of Wonders** (p79) Marvelling at the most famous building in Stone Town, Zanzibar Town's historic quarter.

2 **Darajani Market** (p85) Bargaining for spice, colourful cloth or live chickens at Zanzibar Town's traditional market.

3 **Menai Bay** (p117) Launching from Fumba and viewing the ocean from the deck of a traditional boat with Safari Blue.

4 **Chumbe Island** (p100) Visiting a classic desert island and seeing coral conservation in action.

5 **Nungwi** (p100) Sunbathing, swimming, relaxing, partying; there's something for everyone at Nungwi.

6 **Jozani Forest** (p99) Admiring butterflies, red colobus monkeys and other indigenous wildlife.

7 **Paje** (p111) Learning to fly over water with Airborne Kite Centre.

8 **Kigomasha Peninsula** (p125) Exploring underwater marvels in Pemba.

9 **Kiweni** (p122) Heading off the beaten track to remote Pemba Lodge.

History

The history of Zanzibar stretches back at least to the start of the first millennium, when Bantu-speaking peoples from the mainland ventured across to the archipelago's many islands. The *Periplus of the Erythraean Sea* (written for sailors by a Greek merchant around AD 60) makes reference to the island of Menouthias, which many historians believe to be Zanzibar. From around the 8th century, Shirazi traders from Persia also began to make their way to East Africa, where they established settlements on the islands of Pemba and Unguja (now generally called Zanzibar Island).

Between the 12th and 15th centuries trade links with Arabia and the Persian Gulf blossomed. Zanzibar became a powerful city-state, with Zanzibar Town its focal point, supplying slaves, gold, ivory and wood to places as distant as India and Asia, while importing spices, glassware and textiles. With the trade from the East also came Islam and the Arabic architecture that still characterises Stone Town, the historic quarter of Zanzibar Town.

Europeans & Omanis

During the 16th century Zanzibar came under Portuguese control, then at the end of the 17th century under the rule of the Sultan of Oman.

By the early 19th century Oman controlled trade across the archipelago, reaching such a high point that in the 1840s the Sultan of Oman relocated his court from the Persian Gulf to Zanzibar, establishing many of the buildings still seen today in the historic quarter of Stone Town. From the mid-19th century, with increasing European interest in East Africa and the end of the slave trade, Omani rule began to weaken, and in 1890 Zanzibar became part of the British Empire, as a 'protectorate', with Omani sultans ostensibly ruling, supervised by British colonial officials.

This arrangement lasted until 10 December 1963, when Zanzibar gained its independence. Just one month later, in January 1964, the sultans were overthrown in a bloody revolution instigated by the Afro-Shirazi Party (ASP), which then assumed power.

Union with the Mainland

On 12 April 1964 Abeid Karume, president of the ASP, signed a declaration of unity with Tanganyika (on the mainland), and the two countries came together as the United Republic of Tanzania. Karume was assassinated in 1972 and Aboud Jumbe assumed the

THE SLAVE TRADE

Slavery has been practised in Africa throughout recorded history, but its greatest expansion in East Africa came with the rise of Islam, which prohibits the enslavement of Muslims. Demands of European plantation holders on the islands of Réunion and Mauritius were another major catalyst, particularly during the second half of the 18th century.

At the outset, slaves were taken from the coastal regions of the African mainland and shipped to Arabia, Persia and the Indian Ocean islands. Kilwa Kisiwani was one of the major gateways. As demand increased, traders made their way further into Africa, ranging as far as Malawi and the Congo.

By the 19th century, with the rise of the Omani Arabs, Zanzibar had eclipsed Kilwa Kisiwani as East Africa's major slave-trading depot. According to some estimates, by the 1860s from 10,000 to as many as 50,000 slaves were passing through Zanzibar's market each year. Overall, close to 600,000 slaves were sold through Zanzibar between 1830 and 1873, when a treaty with Britain finally ended the regional trade.

presidency of Zanzibar until he resigned in 1984. A succession of leaders followed, culminating in 2000 with the highly controversial election of Aman Abeid Karume, son of the first president.

The Archipelago Today

For many years, the two major political parties on the Zanzibar Archipelago have been the Chama Cha Mapinduzi (CCM) and the opposition Civic United Front (CUF), which has its stronghold on Pemba. Tensions between the two peaked in the 1995, 2000 and 2005 elections, all marred by violence and allegations of fraud.

In 2010, after much wrangling, voters accepted proposals for the incumbent CCM government and the CUF to share power in a new Government of National Unity, allowing for a gradual rapprochement.

In 2015 the delicate relationship was again thrown off balance when initial balloting was declared invalid by the CCM. Many Zanzibaris boycotted the rerun election, held in March 2016 and won by the CCM.

For the present, it is likely that the peaceful but fragile stalemate will continue, at least until the next elections in 2020.

ZANZIBAR ISLAND

♪ 024 / POP 950,000

Zanzibar Island is a jewel in the ocean, surrounded by beaches that rate among the finest in the world. Here you can swim, snorkel or just lounge the hours away, while shoals of luminous fish graze over nearby coral gardens and pods of dolphins frolic offshore.

In the island's capital, Zanzibar Town, sits the historic quarter of Stone Town, with a mesmerising mix of influences from Africa, Arabia, India and Europe.

For these reasons and more, Zanzibar Island (officially called Unguja) is the archipelago's focal point, and the most popular destination for visitors, but choose your spot carefully. While it's easy to find tranquil beauty or party buzz (or both), increasing development threatens the island's ineluctable magic and fragile community resources.

Zanzibar Town

POP 400,000

For most visitors Zanzibar Town means Stone Town, the historic quarter where you can wander for hours through a maze of narrow streets, easily losing yourself in centuries of history. Each twist and turn brings something new – a former palace, a Persian bathhouse, a tumbledown ruin, a coral-stone mansion with carved doors and latticework balconies, or a school full of children chanting verses from the Quran.

Today Zanzibar Town (sometimes designated Zanzibar City) is the capital of the state of Zanzibar, and by far the biggest settlement on Zanzibar Island. It's divided into two unequal parts, separated by Creek Rd: to the west is Stone Town, while to the east are the more recently built areas known as Ng'ambo (literally, 'The Other Side'), with other suburbs such as Amaani, Mazizini, Magomeni and Mwanakwerekwe, an urban sprawl of shops, markets, offices, apartment blocks, crowded slums and middle-class neighbourhoods.

⊙ Sights

Shaped like a triangle, Stone Town is bounded on two sides by the sea, and along the

Zanzibar Island (Unguja)

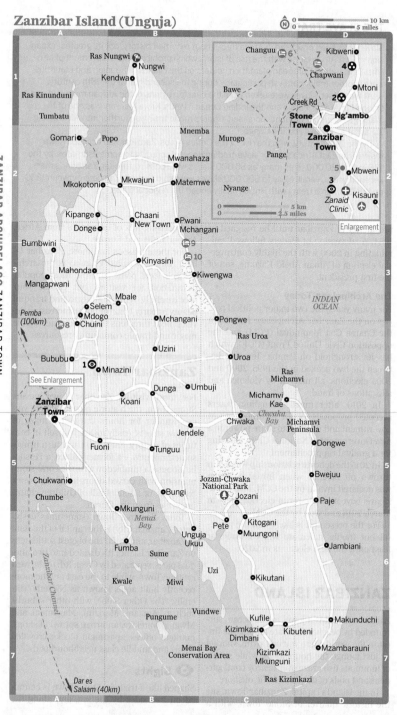

Zanzibar Island (Unguja)

third by Creek Rd (officially renamed Benjamin Mkapa Rd). Most sights are on the northern seafront (Mizingani Rd) or hidden away in the narrow streets.

Princess Salme Museum   MUSEUM

(Map p82; ☑ 0779 093066; selgpsm@gmail.com; Emerson on Hurumzi hotel, Hurumzi St; US$5; ⊙ 10am-5pm Mon-Sun) Carefully curated by the renowned historian Said al Gheithy, this delightful little museum tells the story of Princess Salme, a sultan's daughter who eloped with a German merchant in the late 19th century and later wrote *Memoirs of an Arabian Princess from Zanzibar*. If Said is on duty, his guided tour of the museum adds depth to the story.

House of Wonders   HISTORIC BUILDING

(Beit el-Ajaib; Map p82; Mizingani Rd) An icon of Stone Town, the House of Wonders rises in impressive tiers of slender steel pillars and balconies overlooking the waterfront. Its enormous carved doors are said to be the largest in East Africa, fronted by two bronze canons with Portuguese inscriptions dating them to the 16th century. Inside, the National Museum of History & Culture has exhibits on Swahili civilisation and the peoples of the Indian Ocean.

Built for ceremonial purposes by Sultan Barghash in 1883, in its heyday the House of Wonders boasted marble floors, panelled walls and never-before-seen electricity and running water – hence its name. But in 2012, after years of neglect, a large section of balcony collapsed, closing the building's interior to the public.

Restoration has since stalled, and at the time of research there was no date for re-opening, but you can still admire the House of Wonders from the outside. Even though the white paint continues to fade, it's still one of the grandest structures on Zanzibar.

Forodhani Gardens   GARDENS

(Jamituri Gardens; Map p82) One of the best ways to ease into Zanzibar life is to stop by this waterfront public space. It's a social hub for tourists and locals alike; there's a large restaurant jutting into the sea, two small cafes with outside seating, benches under shady trees, a children's play park, and food stalls in the evening. The gardens were originally laid out in 1936 to commemorate the Silver Jubilee of Sultan Khalifa (r 1911–60); you can still see the domed podium where a brass band would play, while the marooned ceremonial arch at the water's edge was built to welcome Britain's Princess Margaret on a state visit in 1956.

Old Dispensary   HISTORIC BUILDING

(Map p82; Mizingani Rd) With its peppermint-green latticework balconies and sculpted clock tower, this 19th-century charitable dispensary is one of the most attractive landmarks on the waterfront. It was built by Tharia Topan, a prominent Ismaili Indian merchant who also acted as financial adviser to the sultan and as banker to Tippu Tip, Zanzibar's most notorious slave trader. You're free to wander through the interior, which now accommodates offices. In the airy courtyard on the ground floor is the **Abyssinian's Steakhouse** (☑ 0772 940566; mains Tsh10,000-17,000; ⊙ 11am-10pm) restaurant.

Aga Khan Mosque   MOSQUE

(Kiponda Mosque; Map p82) In the Kiponda area of Stone Town, this mosque is one of the largest in Zanzibar, catering to the Ismaili community since 1905. The beautifully detailed building has pointed Arabesque windows, a large airy courtyard and an impressive Gujarati-style carved door.

Mtoni Palace   RUINS

(Map p78) Overlooking the coast, away from the heat and hustle of Zanzibar Town, Mtoni Palace was built for Sultan Seyyid Said in 1828. It was home to the sultan's only legitimate wife, many secondary wives and hundreds of children. According to contemporary descriptions, it was a beautiful building with a balconied exterior and a large garden courtyard complete with peacocks and gazelles. Now only a ruin remains with roofless halls and arabesque arches framing glimpses of tropical foliage and an azure sea. To get here, head north from Zanzibar Town on the main road towards Bububu for 6km, from where a dirt road leads west to the ruins.

Catholic Cathedral
CATHEDRAL

(St Joseph's Catholic Cathedral; Map p82; Cathedral St) One of the first sights travellers see when arriving by ferry are the twin spires of the Roman Catholic cathedral. Serving the local Catholic community, including Goans, Europeans and Tanzanians from Zanzibar and the mainland, it was designed by French architect Berange, whose other work includes the cathedral in Marseilles, and built by French missionaries between 1893 and 1897. Entrance is free but a donation is requested. Mass times are posted on the porch.

The main entrance is on Cathedral St, but this is often closed (although you can see the impressive front of the cathedral through the railings). The back gate is usually open, and reached via a small alley branching off the western end of Gizenga St. Look for the small catholic bookshop; the back gate is next to this.

Kidichi Persian Baths
HISTORIC SITE

(Map p78) Sultan Seyyid Said built this bathhouse at Kidichi (11km northeast of Zanzibar Town) in 1850 for his Persian wife, Scheherezade. The royal couple would come here after hunting to refresh themselves in the stylised stucco interiors. Although poorly maintained, you can still make out much of the carving and see the bathing pool and massage tables. Situated among some of Zanzibar's famous spice plantations, Kidichi Persian Baths is usually visited as part of a spice tour.

To get here under your own steam, take dalla-dalla 502 to the centre of Bububu (best landmark is the police station), from where it's a 3km walk eastwards along a dirt road. Look for the bathhouse to your right.

Maruhubi Palace
RUINS

(Map p78; Tsh5000) Maruhubi Palace was built outside Zanzibar Town in 1882 for Sultan Barghash to house his impressively large harem. A few years later, it was destroyed by fire, although the remaining walls and arches, and the large columns that once supported an upper balcony, hint at its previous scale. The entrance is 4km north of Zanzibar Town, on the left (west) of the main road towards Bububu.

Anglican Cathedral
CATHEDRAL

(Christ Church Anglican Cathedral; Map p82; www.zanzibaranglican.or.tz; New Mkunazini Rd; with guide, incl slave chambers & slavery exhibit US$5; ⊘9am-6pm Mon-Sat, noon-6pm Sun) The tall spire and grey-yellow walls of the Anglican cathedral dominate the surrounding streets in this part of Stone Town, while the dark-wood pews and stained-glass windows will remind British visitors of churches back home. This was the first Anglican cathedral in East Africa, constructed in the 1870s by the Universities Mission to Central Africa (UMCA) on the site of the former slave market after slavery was officially abolished.

STONE TOWN'S ARCHITECTURE

Stone Town's architecture is a fusion of Arabic, Indian, European and African influences. Arab buildings are often square, with two or three storeys. Rooms line the outer walls, allowing space for an inner courtyard and verandas, and cooling air circulation. Indian buildings, also several storeys high, generally include a shop on the ground floor and living quarters above, with ornate facades and balconies. A common feature is the *baraza*, a stone bench facing onto the street that serves as a focal point around which townspeople meet and chat.

The most famous feature of Zanzibari architecture is the carved wooden door, a symbol of wealth and status, and often the first part of a house to be built (or sometimes older than the house, having been moved from a previous location).

Some Zanzibari doors are centuries old, others simply decades old, while others are relatively recent; there's still a thriving door-carving industry today.

Generally, Arabian-styled doors have a square frame with a geometrical shape, and 'newer' doors – many of which were built towards the end of the 19th century and incorporate Indian influences – often have semicircular tops and intricate floral decorations.

Doors may be decorated with carvings of passages from the Quran, and other commonly seen motifs include images representing items desired in the household, such as a fish (expressing the hope for many children) or the date tree (a symbol of prosperity). Some doors have large brass spikes, which are a tradition from India, where spikes protected doors from being battered down by elephants.

Inside the cathedral, the **altar** reputedly marks the spot of the whipping tree where slaves were lashed with a stinging branch. It's a moving sight, remembered by a white marble circle surrounded by red to symbolise the blood of the slaves.

The driving force behind the construction of the cathedral was Bishop Edward Steere (1828–82), but the inspiration was David Livingstone, whose call to compassion the missionaries answered in 1864 when they settled on the island. One of the stained-glass windows is dedicated to his memory, while the cathedral's **crucifix** is made from the tree that grew where his heart was buried in the village of Chitambo in Zambia.

In the grounds outside the cathedral is the moving **Slave Memorial**, depicting five slaves standing in a pit below ground level. The poignant figures emerge from the rough-hewn rock and thus appear hopelessly trapped, shoulders slumped in despair. Around their necks they wear metal collars from which a chain binds them. Although nothing remains of the slave market today, the memorial is a sobering reminder of the not-so-distant past.

At the entrance to the cathedral compound is the **East Africa Slave Trade Exhibit**, a series of displays and informative panels. Also here are the former **slave chambers** where slaves were imprisoned before sale. In the same building is St Monica's Lodge (p88).

Services are held at the cathedral on Sunday mornings in English and Swahili. Times are posted on a notice in the porch.

The entrance to the cathedral compound is from New Mkunazini Rd. The entry fee gets you into the slave trade exhibit and the slave chambers as well as the cathedral and grounds.

Old Fort
HISTORIC BUILDING

(Ngome Kongwe; Map p82; Mzingani Rd; ⊙ 9am-10pm) **FREE** With its pale-orange ramparts overlooking Forodhani Gardens and the ocean beyond, the fort was built by Omani Arabs when they seized the island from the Portuguese in 1698, and over the centuries it's had various uses, from prison to tennis club. Today the scale of the fortifications is still impressive, although there has been some modernisation inside, notably a line of souvenir shops and a pleasant cafe that turns into a bar in the evening.

Another modern feature is the open-air **amphitheatre**, used for local shows and major events, such as the **Zanzibar**

WHAT'S IN A NAME?

For visitors today, it's worth noting that history has bequeathed the name 'Zanzibar' to various different entities: it's the name of the entire archipelago, a collection of over 50 islands; it's the name of the state, which together with the mainland (formerly Tanganyika) creates the United Republic of Tanzania; it's the common name of the main island, Zanzibar Island (also called Unguja); and it's the name of the main city, which despite its size is usually called Zanzibar Town.

International Film Festival (Festival of the Dhow Countries; www.ziff.or.tz; festival pass US$50; ⊙ Jul) and **Busara** (Voices of Wisdom; www.busaramusic.org; festival pass visitors/locals US$120/10; ⊙ early–mid-Feb); the tourist information desk (p96) at the fort entrance can advise on performance schedules. Also here (in one of the towers) is the **Cultural Arts Gallery**, connected to the Cultural Arts Centre Zanzibar (p94), where you can meet local artists at work or join a hands-on course.

Palace Museum
MUSEUM

(Beit el-Sahel; Map p82; Mizingani Rd; adult/child US$3/1, incl guide, additional tip optional; ⊙ 9am-6pm) Occupying several large buildings along the waterfront, this was the palace of Sultan Seyyid Said from 1828 until it was largely destroyed by the British bombardment of 1896. It was then rebuilt and used until the 1964 revolution when the last sultan was overthrown. Remarkably, much of the royal paraphernalia – banqueting tables, portraits, thrones and water closets – survives to now provide the human-interest story in this museum dedicated to the sultanate in the 19th century.

In its day the palace and adjacent harem, **Beit el-Hukm**, and some other nearby buildings, were a self-contained unit with raised walkways allowing royal personages to avoid city streets. One of these walkways can still be seen crossing above the street behind the Palace Museum.

Insights into the life of the palace can be gleaned from Princess Salme's fascinating book *Memoirs of an Arabian Princess from Zanzibar* (originally published in 1886, reprinted more recently), which you can buy in the museum and local bookshops, and from a visit to the separate Princess Salme Museum (p79). Getting to know the key players,

Stone Town

200 m
0.1 miles

A

Zanzibar Channel

B

C

Forodhani
Gardens

◎ 5

✕ 61

91 ⓘ

🏛 10

D

🏛 11

🏛 7

82

86

19 ●

Hurumzi St

77

14

Hurumzi St

41 34

Nyumba ya Moto St

Mizingani Rd

70

55

✕

Changa Bazaar

25 12

🏛

75

E

Passenger Ferry
Terminal

71

Big
Tree

◎ 8

🏛 9

52

33

Jamatini Rd

39

74

KIPONDA

68

1

26

F

Old Dhow
Harbour (100m)

Cargo
Port

Azam
Marine

Ferry
Ticket
Booths

Ferry
Ticket
Booths

Cine
Afrique

16

50

Malindi Rd

MALINDI

Malindi St

Kokoni St

Tropical
Air

13 ✚

Kiponda St

45

56

G

37

40

47

Funguni Rd

Malawi Rd

53 ✕

Kenya Airways (400m);
Precision Air (400m);
Mtoni (3.6km)

Creek Rd

Transport Stand
(destinations north)

Mlandege St

Darajani St

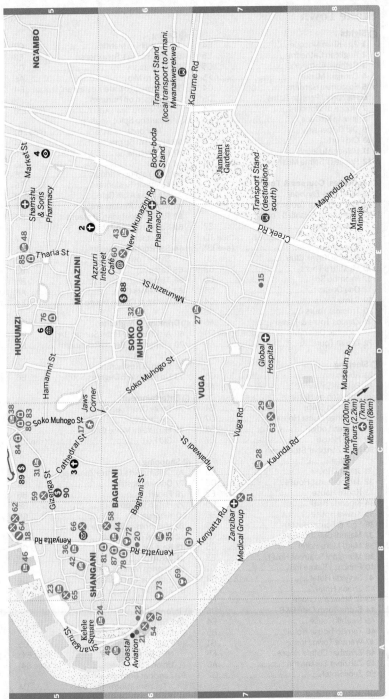

NG'AMBO

Transport Stand
(local transport to Amani,
Mwanakwerekwe)

Karume Rd

Boda-boda
Stand

Jamhuri
Gardens

Transport Stand
(destinations
south)

Mapinduzi Rd

Mnazi
Mmoja

Creek Rd

Market St 4

Shamshu
& Sons
Pharmacy

85 48

Tharia St

MKUNAZINI

2

Azzurri
Internet
Café 60

43

New Mkunazini Rd

Fahud
Pharmacy

57

88

Mkunazini St

HURUMZI

6 76

Hamamni St

SOKO
MUHOGO

32

27

15

Soko Muhogo St

VUGA

Global
Hospital

38
80 83

84

Soko Muhogo St

Jaws
Corner

Ppalwadi St

29

63

Museum Rd

89 $

31

Gizenga St

Cathedral St

3

90

59

BAGHANI

Baghani St

Vuga Rd

28

Kaunda Rd

Mnazi Moja Hospital (200m);
Zan Tours (2.2km);
Mbweni (7km);
Mbweni (8km)

62
64
18

Kenyatta Rd

36
66

58

44

72

20

35

79

Zanzibar
Medical Group

51

Kenyatta Rd

46

42

81

87

78

SHANGANI

Kenyatta Rd

69

73

23
65

24

Kelele
Square

49

Coastal
Aviation

21

22

54
67

Shangani St

Stone Town

◎ Sights
1 Aga Khan Mosque	E4
2 Anglican Cathedral	E5
3 Catholic Cathedral	C5
4 Darajani Market	F5
5 Forodhani Gardens	C4
6 Hamamni Persian Baths	D5
7 House of Wonders	C4
8 Ijumaa Mosque	E3
9 Old Dispensary	E2
10 Old Fort	C4
11 Palace Museum	D3
12 Princess Salme Museum	D4

✪ Activities, Courses & Tours
13 Bluebikes Zanzibar	F4
14 Eco + Culture Tours	D4
15 Institute of Swahili & Foreign Languages	E7
Jafferji Spa	(see 31)
Kawa Tours	(see 13)
Membe Kayak Club	(see 33)
16 Mr Mitu's Tours	G2
17 Mrembo Spa	C5
18 One Ocean	B5
19 Sama Tours	C4
20 Tropical Tours	B6
21 Zancos Tours & Travel	A6
Zanzibar Different	(see 17)
22 Zenith Tours	A6

🛏 Sleeping
23 Abuso Inn	B5
24 Beyt al-Salaam	A5
25 Emerson on Hurumzi	D4
26 Emerson Spice	E4
27 Flamingo Guest House	D7
28 Garden Lodge	C7
29 Hiliki House	C7
30 Ikala Zanzibar Stonetown Lodge	F2
31 Jafferji House	C5
32 Jambo Guest House	D6
33 Kholle House	E2
34 Kiponda B&B	D3
35 Kisiwa House	B6
36 Lost & Found Hostel	B5
37 Malindi Guesthouse	G1
38 Maru Maru Hotel	C5
39 Mizingani Seafront Hotel	E3
40 Princess Salme Inn	G1
41 Seyyida Hotel	D3
42 Shaba Hotel	B5
43 St Monica's Lodge	E6
44 Stone Town Café B&B	B6
45 Swahili House	E4
46 Tembo House Hotel	B5
47 Warere Town House	G1
48 Zanzibar Coffee House	E5
49 Zanzibar Serena Inn	A6
50 Zenji Hotel	G2

✕ Eating
51 Abyssinian Maritim	C7
52 Abyssinian's Steakhouse	E2
53 Al-Shabany	G2
54 Amore Mio	A6
55 Archipelago Café-Restaurant	B4
Emerson on Hurumzi Rooftop Teahouse	(see 25)
Emerson Spice Rooftop Teahouse	(see 26)
56 House of Spices	F4
57 La Taverna	F6
58 Lazuli	B6
59 Luis Yoghurt Parlour	C5
60 Lukmaan Restaurant	E6
Ma Shaa Allah Cafe	(see 60)
61 Monsoon Restaurant	B4
62 Radha Vegetarian Restaurant	B5
63 Sambusa Two Tables Restaurant	C7
64 Silk Route Restaurant	B5
Stone Town Café	(see 44)
65 Tamu	B5
66 Tapería	B5
67 Travellers Cafe	A6
68 Zanzibar Coffee House	E4

🍸 Drinking & Nightlife
69 Africa House Hotel Sunset Bar	B6
70 Livingstone Beach Restaurant	B4
71 Mercury's	E2
72 Sunrise Restaurant	B6
73 Up North @ 6 Degrees South	B6

✪ Entertainment
74 Dhow Countries Music Academy	D3
75 Hurumzini Movie Café	E4
Old Fort	(see 10)

🛍 Shopping
76 Cultural Arts Centre Zanzibar	D5
77 Doreen Mashika	D4
78 Fahari	B6
79 Hellen's Shop	B6
80 Kihanga	C5
81 Memories of Zanzibar	B6
82 Moto & Dada Shop	D4
83 Real Art	C5
84 Sasik	C5
85 Upendo Means Love	E5
86 Zanzibar Curio Shop	D4
87 Zanzibar Gallery	B6

ℹ Information
88 CRDB Bank	E6
89 Diamond Trust Bank	C5
90 Eagle Change Bureau	C5
NBC Bank	(see 64)
Union Forex Bureau	(see 84)
91 Zanzibar Commission for Tourism Information Desk	C4

such as Salme and her brothers Barghash and Majid, helps bring to life the now dusty displays. Outside the museum, you can still see the tombs of various sultans, including Barghash and Majid. Look out for the curious 'double tomb' – apparently this sultan's legs were amputated and buried first, to be joined by the rest of his body when the sultan died some years later.

Darajani Market MARKET
(Map p82; Creek Rd; ⊙6am-4pm) Zanzibar's main market is a hive of activity, with everything – from spices, fresh fish, slabs of meat and huge baskets full of live chickens to sandals, plastic buckets and mobile phones – all set out in a series of covered halls and overflowing into the surrounding streets. If you're buying food, come in the morning when stuff is fresh, although it's much busier then. For a slightly less crowded and chaotic experience come in the afternoon.

There are also several stalls catering for tourists selling packs of spice and other souvenirs. In the surrounding streets are shops and stalls selling clothes, shoes, DVDs, electrics and household goods. Especially worth a visit is the area known as Kanga St, where shops sell colourful local prints and fabrics of all kinds.

Ijumaa Mosque MOSQUE
(Map p82) This lovely Arabesque-style mosque is one of the largest in Stone Town. As an Ijumma (Friday) mosque, the faithful come to pray here, rather than at their local mosque, on Fridays, so it gets especially busy on this day.

Mbweni Ruins HISTORIC SITE
(Map p78; Tsh5000) The upmarket suburb of Mbweni, 5km south of Zanzibar Town, was a Universities Mission to Central Africa (UMCA) base and settlement for former slaves in the 19th century. The ruins of St Mary's School for Girls, built by missionaries for girls freed from slave ships, is now set amid the lush gardens of Mbweni Ruins Hotel (p91). It's an evocative spot, but a long trek from Stone Town, so best combined with a visit to the hotel's restaurant or private beach.

Hamamni Persian Baths HISTORIC BUILDING
(Map p82; Hamamni St; Tsh1500) Built by Sultan Barghash in the late 19th century, these were the first public baths on Zanzibar. The various rooms were renovated in 2017 and, although there's no longer water inside, it's easy to imagine them in use in bygone days.

If the entrance door is closed, ask at the Cultural Arts Centre opposite.

🏃 Activities

With numerous islands in easy reach of Stone Town, the most popular activity is going out on a boat for swimming, snorkelling or diving. Other energetic options include cycling or kayaking, which may then inspire you to go for a muscle-relaxing massage at one of Stone Town's numerous spas.

★Mrembo Spa SPA
(Map p82; ☎024-223 0004, 0777 430117; www.mrembospa.com; cnr Cathedral & Soko Muhogo Sts; massage & treatments per hour US$30; ⊙10am-6pm) 🖉 Don't come to Mrembo looking for clinical suites. This imaginative Swahili spa offers kanga-covered massage tables in colour-washed rooms with a friendly atmosphere, where softly spoken Zanzibari therapists provide massages, manicures and traditional treatments using handcrafted oils and scrubs – which you can also buy (along with local soaps and other products) in the excellent shop.

Bluebikes Zanzibar CYCLING
(Map p82; www.bluebikeszanzibar.com; bike per day/week US$15/75) Rent a bike or join an organised cycling tour around Stone Town or out to the surrounding rural area. Most popular is the Spice Tour by Bike. Personalised tours with a local guide are also available. Bluebikes is a social enterprise associated with Kawa Training Centre and all guides are trained and accredited.

Membe Kayak Club KAYAKING
(Map p82; ☎0774 228205; www.membekayak zanzibar.com; Kholle House Hotel, off Malindi Rd; kayak per hour/day US$10/30) Good-quality sea kayaks for rent; you can 'self-drive' (if you're familiar with kayaks on the open sea), or go with a local guide (if you're not). Popular destinations are the islands off Stone Town, or less demanding trips along the waterfront.

Jafferji Spa SPA
(Map p82; ☎0774 078441; www.jafferjihouse.net; Jafferji House, Gizenga St; ⊙9am-10pm Tue-Sun) Attached to the hotel of the same name, Jafferji Spa has a discreet rooftop treatment room, where you can enjoy massage, scrubs and traditional relaxation treatments.

One Ocean DIVING
(Map p82; ☎0774 310003, 0773 048828; www.zanzibaroneocean.com; cnr Shangani St & Kenyatta

Rd; single dive US$85, 8 dives US$395; ⊙8am-6pm) This PADI five-star dive operator has many years of experience, and caters for all abilities. From the main office in Stone Town, short dive trips go to nearby reefs and wrecks, while longer trips can be arranged to other sites around Zanzibar Island. One Ocean also has branches at a number of locations on the coast around the island.

Courses

Creative Solutions CRAFT
(☑0773 309092; www.creativesolutionszanzibar.co.tz; Mangapwani; per person incl lunch US$40; ⊙11am-3pm Mon-Thu) Join the locals at a practical workshop, upcycling glass bottles into jewellery and ornaments. Courses are held outside Zanzibar Town at Mangapwani and must be booked in advance. You can also buy Creative Solutions products, from delicate glass dragonflies to witty Tangawizi ashtrays, in the Cultural Arts Centre Zanzibar (p94) and other shops in Zanzibar Town.

Institute of Swahili & Foreign Languages LANGUAGE
(Map p82; ☑024-223 0724; www.suza.ac.tz; per week US$200) Zanzibar is regarded as the home of the Swahili language (known locally as Kiswahili), making this a great place to take some lessons. Courses at the institute, which is part of the State Univeristy of Zanzibar (SUZA), are aimed at different levels (beginner to advanced). They run for one week and need to be booked in advance.

☞ Tours

Guided tours can be organised with one of the many local tour companies in Zanzibar Town. Popular excursions include dhow cruises (especially popular at sunset), city walking tours (focusing on historical sites in Stone Town), boat trips (usually with snorkelling, swimming and lunch on an island) and spice tours (you guessed it, to nearby spice plantations). Spice tours usually include some out-of-town historical sites as well.

Longer excursions from Zanzibar Town include cruises in Menai Bay or to see dolphins at Kizimkazi. If you choose to take a dolphin tour, use a reputable tour operator that has ethical practices on viewing dolphins (and especially on swimming with dolphins – which we don't recommend).

Look out for guides belonging to the Heritage Guide Association; accredited members specialise in Stone Town history and culture.

Zenith Tours TOURS
(Map p82; ☑0774 413084, 024-223 2320; www.zenithtours.com) Very experienced company, catering for individuals and tour groups. Local tours of the city and island can be arranged, while other efficient services include hotel and flight reservations, plus car hire and safaris to the mainland.

Zancos Tours & Travel TOURS
(Map p82; ☑0777 232747, 024-2233 489; www.zancos.co.tz; Kelele Sq, Shangani; ⊙7am-7pm Mon-Fri, to 5pm Sat & Sun) This reliable company offers tours around Zanzibar Town and Zanzibar Island, and also to mainland Tanzania, including fly-in safaris to national parks operated with sister company Coastal Aviation.

Grassroots Traveller CULTURAL
(☑0772 821725; www.grassroots-traveller.com) ✎ Working closely with community-based projects, NGOs and organisations striving for sustainable development, this forward-thinking company helps travellers craft interesting itineraries blending adventure with community engagement to discover that there's more to Zanzibar than sun, sand and sea. It also helps volunteers hook up successful short- and long-term projects.

Kawa Tours CULTURAL
(Map p82; ☑0777 957995, 0773 795758; www.zanzibarkawatours.com; ⊕) This company covers unusual ground. For example, the Ghost Tour takes you to reputedly haunted locations as a way of understanding the history of the slave trade; the Cooking Workshop includes market shopping followed by hands-on learning in a local kitchen; and various Heritage Tours focus on Stone Town's history, culture, architecture, religious buildings and so on.

At the time of research, Kawa Tours was in the process of changing its name, although guides will still be drawn from the affiliated Kawa Training Center (which helps locals find employment in the tourism industry) and Heritage Guide Association (including, unusually for Zanzibar, several female guides).

Zanzibar Different CULTURAL
(Map p82; ☑024-223 0004, 0777 430117; www.zanzibardifferent.com; Mrembo Spa, Baghani St; ⊕) As the name implies, this company offers unusual excursions and well-known tours with a culturally engaging twist. Stone Town tours focus on marriage roles, children's education and mourning rituals, and a plethora of handicraft traditions. Options further afield include the Princess Salme Tour, retracing

SPICE TOURS

While spices no longer dominate the Zanzibar Archipelago's economy as in years past, plantations still dot the centre of Zanzibar Island. It's possible to visit them on 'spice tours' from Zanzibar Town arranged through hotels and local tour companies, usually with a day's notice.

Along the way you'll see (and taste) many of the spices, herbs and fruits that the island produces, including cloves, vanilla, black pepper, cardamom, cinnamon, nutmeg, breadfruit, jackfruit, vanilla and lemongrass.

Most spice tours follow a similar pattern: a half-day excursion visiting plantations plus some local ruins and other sights of historical interest, ending with lunch (included in the price). A few tour companies offer variations – visiting local schools or village cooperatives.

Longer tours are available, including to historic sites a little further from Zanzibar Town and often with a stop for a swim on the way home.

Half-day spice tours start at about US$10 to US$15 per person with budget operators, based on a group of 10 to 20 people. If you want something a little less crowded, expect to pay around US$20, or up to US$70 per person for a private tour.

the fascinating history of this Zanzibari princess by dhow and flower-fringed donkey chariot.

Mr Mitu's Tours TOURS
(Map p82; ☑ 0773 167620; Funguni Rd, off Malawi Rd; tours US$10-20) Mr Mitu's budget-priced spice tours have been famous for decades, so much that the company is now run by his son (also called Mr Mitu). Prices for a half-day tour cost US$10 to US$20 depending on group size, including lunch. Day trips are also available, including the caves and historic sites at Mangapwani, plus a swim at the beach.

Gallery Tours & Safaris TOURS
(Map p78; ☑ 0772 077090, 0774 305165; www.gallery tours.net; ☻9am-5pm) Specialising in top-of-the-line tours and excursions, Gallery Tours can also arrange Zanzibar weddings, honeymoon itineraries and exclusive dhow cruises.

Sama Tours TOURS
(Map p82; ☑ 024-223 3543; www.samatours.com; Hurumzi St; ☻8.30am-7pm) This long-standing and reputable tour company offers reasonably priced standard boat trips and spice tours, and can set you up with more off-the-beaten-track outings on request. Flights, hotel bookings and ferry tickets can also be arranged by the quietly efficient office staff, while multilingual guides are extremely helpful. The office is behind the House of Wonders.

Tropical Tours TOURS
(Map p82; ☑ 0777 413454, 024-223 6794; www.facebook.com/TropicalToursZanzibar; Kenyatta Rd; ☻8.30am-6.30pm) This reliable tour operator handles everything from ferry and plane

bookings to spice tours and boat trips. You'll find up-to-the-minute deals on its Facebook page.

ZanTours TOURS
(☑ 024-223 3042; www.zantours.com; Nyerere Rd) This large and professional outfit offers upmarket tourism services. It has its own fleet of vehicles and is affiliated with ZanAir, which facilitates easy transfers.

Eco + Culture Tours TOURS
(Map p82; ☑ 024-223 3731, 0755 873066; www.ecoculture-zanzibar.org; Hurumzi St; ☻10am-5pm)
🖉 Standard spice/city/dhow tours are offered, plus some longer excursions with an environmental and cultural focus. Guides speak English, French, Spanish, Italian and German. A speciality is the off-the-beaten-track trip to the village of Unguja Ukuu, with a dhow cruise in Menai Bay stopping at tiny remote islands for snorkelling and lunch (US$65 per person for four people).

🛏 Sleeping

From low-budget hostels to boutique hotels, nearly all accommodation options are in the historic quarter of Stone Town, while beyond the heat and bustle are a few out-of-town options.

🏠 Stone Town

★**Jambo Guest House** GUESTHOUSE $
(Map p82; ☑ 0776 686239, 024-223 3779; www.jamboguest.com; off Mkunazini St; s/d with shared bathroom US$30/40; ❄ 🖥 🛜) Probably the best-value budget accommodation in town and extremely popular with backpackers,

❶ ETIQUETTE

The people of Zanzibar are traditional, mostly rural, and overwhelmingly Muslim, and attitudes are often correspondingly conservative. Avoid getting off to a bad start by observing the following tips:

Clothing Dress appropriately in public: locals are deeply offended by revealing clothing. Keep swimwear to the beach. In towns and villages women should avoid sleeveless tops, plunging necklines and shorts, while men should keep shirts on and avoid shorts that come anywhere near skimpy.

Photography Always ask permission before photographing local people.

Mosques Do not enter mosques without permission, and then only without shoes.

Ramadan During Ramadan take particular care with dress, and show respect by not eating or drinking in public places during daylight hours.

Jambo runs as smooth as clockwork. Nine spick-and-span rooms with Zanzibari beds share four bathrooms, there's complimentary tea and coffee, and it's within easy reach of several good-value eateries. Local tours and transfers to the east-coast beaches can be arranged.

★ **Lost & Found Hostel**　　　HOSTEL $
(Map p82; ☑ 0684 320699; www.lost57.com; 57 Kenyatta Rd; dm from US$20; ❄ 🛜) Zanzibar's first dedicated backpackers hostel, Lost & Found is perfect for travellers on a tight budget. It's clean, modern, safe, friendly and well located. Guests sleep in comfortable 'pods' (single or double), with curtains for privacy, in two dorms (mixed gender and female only). The shared bathrooms are spotless. There's funky decor and a small balcony overlooking the street.

Kiponda B&B　　　HOTEL $
(Kiponda Hotel; Map p82; ☑ 0777 431665, 024-223 3052; www.kiponda.com; Nyumba ya Moto St; s/d US$30/50; ❄ 🛜) A long-standing and popular place with friendly and relaxed staff, the Kiponda has simple but clean rooms (all with fan, some with air-con) on three floors. Breakfast is served on the top-floor terrace, which is also a great place to relax during the day (it's got wi-fi too). Free transfers from the ferry or airport.

Malindi Guesthouse　　　GUESTHOUSE $
(Map p82; ☑ 024-223 0165; Makunazini Rd; d US$40, with shared bathroom US$30) This long-standing backpacker favourite is in the scruffy end of town near the dhow harbour. It's not especially clean, and downstairs rooms are dark and damp, but upstairs rooms are OK, and it's all offset by helpful staff, a friendly vibe, a rooftop restaurant and wacky upcycled furniture, such as tables made from bike wheels and lampshades from cassettes.

Princess Salme Inn　　　HOTEL $
(Map p82; ☑ 0777-435303; www.princesssalmeinn. com; off Funguni Rd; s/d from US$47/67, with shared bathroom US$35/50; ❄ @) In the scruffy but authentic part of town near the dhow harbour, this friendly place has clean and simple rooms with Zanzibar beds and mosquito nets, plus a rooftop breakfast room that catches the breeze. Some cheaper rooms have fan but no air-con. Transport to the east coast and no-hassle boat rides to the nearby islands can be arranged.

Flamingo Guest House　　　GUESTHOUSE $
(Map p82; ☑ 0777 491252, 024-223 2850; www. flamingoguesthouseznz.com; Mkunazini St; s/d US$17/34, with shared bathroom US$15/30) The total lack of decor and stark concrete stairwell may be off-putting, but the Flamingo offers perfectly adequate no-frills accommodation at rock-bottom prices. All rooms have fans and mosquito nets and there's a rooftop sitting/breakfast area.

Garden Lodge　　　GUESTHOUSE $
(Map p82; ☑ 0777 663843, 024-223 3298; www.garden.co.tz; Kaunda Rd, Vuga; s/d US$40/50; ❄ 🛜) This efficient, friendly, family-run place offers 18 rooms in a characterful house fringed with balconies and decorated with stained-glass windows. Rooms are slightly austere but clean, bright and spacious, especially on the upper floors. There's a rooftop breakfast terrace, and other meals available with advance order. Tours and bike hire can be arranged.

St Monica's Lodge　　　HOSTEL $
(Map p82; ☑ 024-223 0773; www.zanzibarhostel. com; New Mkunazini Rd; s/d US$40/50, with shared bathroom US$30/40; ❄ 🛜) Built in the late 19th century by UMCA missionairies, St Monica's is very near the Anglican cathedral and still has a somewhat historic ambience. As well as accommodating tourists, it's also used by visiting church and youth groups. Staff are friendly, while rooms (some with balcony) are simple but very clean and tidy.

Ikala Zanzibar Stonetown Lodge   HOTEL $$

(Map p82; ☑0628 001520; www.ikalalodges.com; s/d US$49/79; ☀︎🛜🅟) Bright and cheerful in an unashamed 'economy' model, the Ikala is ideal if all you need is a clean room, friendly staff and efficient service. Extras (breakfast, air-con, luxury linen, TV, bathroom amenities) are optional for a small fee. Another plus is the neat little bar-restaurant on the roof.

Kholle House   BOUTIQUE HOTEL $$

(Map p82; ☑0772 161033; www.khollehouse.com; off Malindi Rd, behind Old Dispensary; d US$100-140; ☀︎🛜🅟) This hotel was once a palace, built in 1860 for Princess Kholle, favoured daughter of Sultan Said. After meticulous renovation, it now offers bright and luxurious (if slightly compact) rooms, decorated with Zanzibari and art deco furniture. The staff are friendly, the small garden has a plunge pool and the rooftop 'teahouse' has great views over this part of Stone Town.

Shaba Hotel   BOUTIQUE HOTEL $$

(Map p82; ☑024-223 8021; www.shaba-zanzibar. com; s/d US$60/75) Hidden in the back streets in a quiet part of Stone Town, but within a short walk of busy Kenyatta Rd, this small hotel is well located, with welcoming staff and rooms combining contemporary design, dhow-wood furniture and African fabrics. There's no restaurant; breakfast is taken in the leafy garden, and there's also a rooftop terrace.

Hiliki House   GUESTHOUSE $$

(Map p82; ☑0777 410131; www.hilikihouse-zanzibar.com; Victoria St; d from US$90; ☀︎🛜) Covering two houses side by side – the original in colonial style, the other in 1950s retro – this small family-run hotel offers peaceful and elegant rooms on a quiet street on the edge of Stone Town, overlooking Victoria Gardens.

Zenji Hotel   HOTEL $$

(Map p82; ☑0774 276468; www.zenjihotel.com; Malawi Rd; d US$70-90, with shared bathroom US$50-60; ☀︎🛜) The Zenji offers clean rooms, efficient service and a friendly welcome. On Malawi Rd, near the port, it's in the heart of the action, or a bit noisy, depending on your attitude. Some rooms have balconies; the quieter ones are at the back. Breakfast is served on the rooftop terrace and there's the great little Zenji Cafe downstairs (open to nonguests).

Stone Town Café B&B   B&B $$

(Map p82; ☑0773 861313, 0778 373737; www. stonetowncafe.com; Kenyatta Rd; s/d from US$65/80; ☀︎@) Simple, unpretentious and uncluttered, the Stone Town Café has five rooms with Zanzibar beds dressed in pristine white linens. Black-and-white photos, decorative chests and rugs lend atmosphere. Some rooms have balconies overlooking Kenyatta Rd. Breakfast is served downstairs at the Stone Town Café (p92) – choose from inside seating or the palm-shaded patio.

Zanzibar Coffee House   BOUTIQUE HOTEL $$

(Map p82; ☑024-223 9319, 0773 061532; www. riftvalley-zanzibar.com; Tharia St, Mkunazini; d US$110-170; ☀︎@) Dating from 1885, this building once belonged to a minister to Sultan Barghash, and today it's a stylish hotel above a first-class coffeeshop (p91). Eight rooms (all named after types of coffee, naturally) are decorated with Zanzibari beds, vintage lamps, antique furniture, old prints and twirling fans, evoking the atmosphere of those bygone days.

Swahili House   HOTEL $$

(Map p82; ☑0777 510209; www.theswahilihouse zanzibar.com; Mchambawima St, off Kiponda St; d US$100-150; ☀︎🛜🅟) Over the years, this grand building has been home to an Indian merchant, the sultan's family and other Zanzibari dignitaries. Restored to its original state, it offers 22 vast rooms (some with open bathroom) over five floors, neatly furnished with Zanzibari beds and handcrafted furniture. The 5th-floor terrace offers stunning views, plunge pool and an excellent bar-restaurant (open to nonguests).

Seyyida Hotel   BOUTIQUE HOTEL $$

(Map p82; ☑024-223 8352; www.theseyyida -zanzibar.com; Nyumba Ya Moto St; d from US$110; ☀︎🛜🅟) Lighter and brighter than many Stone Town hotels, the Seyyida eschews dark wood in favour of white tiles. Rooms are modern and styled in neutral tones, reached off open corridors decorated with antique

---

EID AL-FITR

Eid al-Fitr, marking the end of Ramadan, is a fascinating time to be travelling on the Zanzibar Archipelago. In the towns across Pemba and the traditional villages on Zanzibar Island, there is a festive atmosphere, as families dress in their best clothes to visit friends and relatives or simply promenade. It's an especially enjoyable period in Stone Town, with lanterns lighting the narrow streets and passageways.

photos and arranged around a verdant courtyard; some have balconies but only one has sea views. There's also a rooftop restaurant, small swimming pool and spa.

Tembo House Hotel   HOTEL $$

(Map p82; ☑024-223 3005, 0779 413348; www. tembohotel.com; Shangani St; s/d from US$120/150; P ❄ 🕸 🛰 ⌂) This attractively restored building has a prime waterfront location, including a patch of private beach (separated from the sea and public beach by a small rope fence). There's around 40 rooms – some with ocean views – in new and old wings, plus a swimming pool, restaurant (no alcohol), and a buffet breakfast served on the seaside terrace. It's popular, especially with families.

Warere Town House   HOTEL $$

(Map p82; ☑0782 234564; www.warere.com; off Funguni Rd; s/d US$45/55; 🕸 🕷) Down by the old dhow harbour, in a restored former merchant's house, the Warere is a friendly and well-run budget hotel. Rooms are clean and tidy, with Zanzibari beds and nice decorative touches; some rooms also have small balconies bedecked with flowers. If you book ahead, staff will meet you at the ferry port.

Abuso Inn   HOTEL $$

(Map p82; ☑0777 425565, 024-223 5886; www. abusoinn.com; Shangani St; s/d from US$60/80; 🕸 🕷) Despite its unexciting appearance and dark wood interior, the family-run Abuso is a solid choice with spacious rooms and friendly staff. Triple and quad rooms are also available.

Beyt al-Salaam   BOUTIQUE HOTEL $$

(Map p82; ☑0773 000086; www.beytalsalaam. com; Kelele Sq, Shangani; d from US$80; 🕸 🕷) Set back from Kelele Sq (near several top-end hotels), this is a quiet and atmospheric choice, with 10 individually designed rooms, all with traditional decor and ornate bathrooms.

★Emerson Spice   BOUTIQUE HOTEL $$$

(Map p82; ☑0775 046395, 024-223 2776; www. emersonspice.com; Tharia St; d US$150-300; 🕸 🕷) With its stained-glass windows, wooden latticework balustrades, tinkling fountains and soft-hued colour scheme, Emerson Spice is one of the most stylish and atmospheric hotels in Stone Town. Created from a 19th-century mansion with wide steps leading down to a small square in the narrow street outside, it has 11 rooms filled with antiques, quirky decorations, rich textiles and deep bathtubs.

The set-course dinner in the rooftop teahouse (p93) is deeply memorable, as is the Secret Garden – with lush plants decorating the romantic ruins. Both are open to non-residents.

Kisiwa House   BOUTIQUE HOTEL $$$

(Map p82; ☑024-223 0685; www.kisiwahouse. com; off Kenyatta Rd; d from US$200; 🕸 🕷) The lovely Kisiwa House has nine spacious rooms and an excellent rooftop restaurant with sea views. Public areas have a traditional appearance, including the grand wooden staircase and large brass-studded front door, while rooms have Swahili-inspired contemporary decor, airy and uncluttered, with cream drapes, Persian rugs and dark-beamed ceilings.

Mizingani Seafront Hotel   HISTORIC HOTEL $$$

(Map p82; ☑024-223 5396, 0776 100111; www. mizinganiseafront.com; Mizingani Rd; s/d from US$100/150; 🕸 🕸 🕷 ⌂) In a renovated building between two Stone Town landmarks, the Big Tree and the Old Customs House, the Mizingani has a prime location. There's an attractive courtyard pool, while landings and stairways are decorated with antiques. Rooms have modern furniture built in traditional style, some with balconies overlooking the ocean, plus a flat-screen TV should you tire of the view.

Maru Maru Hotel   HISTORIC HOTEL $$$

(Map p82; ☑024-223 8516; www.marumaru zanzibar.com; Gizenga St; d from US$180; 🕸 🕷) In a grand old building just behind the Old Fort and House of Wonders, this hotel has historic credentials. Spaced over several floors around two courtyards, rooms combine traditional touches with modern facilities like flat-screen TV and minibar. For people with mobility problems, taxis can get to within a very short distance of the hotel, and it has a lift.

Jafferji House   BOUTIQUE HOTEL $$$

(Map p82; ☑0774 078441; www.jafferjihouse.net; 120 Gizenga St; d US$180-225; 🕸 🕷) The historic former home of the Jafferji family, this beautifully decorated hotel is packed with traditional, modern and colonial artefacts, plus stunning images by well-known photographer Javed Jafferji. You can choose standard or luxury rooms and enjoy the rooftop restaurant with uninterrupted 360-degree views across Stone Town. And if it all gets too much, you can relax in the spa.

Emerson on Hurumzi
BOUTIQUE HOTEL **$$$**

(Map p82; ☑0779 854225, 024-223 2784; www.emersononhurumzi.com; 236 Hurumzi St; r/ste US$175/225; 🖂) This hotel is simply brimming with character. Two adjacent historic buildings have been restored in a fantastical *Arabian Nights* style; each of the 15 rooms is uniquely and decadently decorated, with traditional Swahili and contemporary design combined perfectly (some might say outrageously). The popular rooftop teahouse restaurant (p93) is open to nonguests for lunch and dinner. Some rooms are reached by steep staircase, which might be a problem for those with limited mobility.

Zanzibar Serena Inn
HOTEL **$$$**

(Map p82; ☑024-223 2306, 024-223 3587; www.serenahotels.com; Kelele Sq, Shangani; s/d from US$210/350; 🅿🌐@🖂🏊💪) Serena is a chain with hotels and lodges all over East Africa, and its Zanzibar location is hard to beat: with a huge shady patio set above the beach and spectacular vistas across the ocean. All rooms have balcony and sea views too. Although well-appointed, it still has a charming air of colonial times with white-suited staff serving afternoon tea.

🏠 Outside Stone Town

★ Mangrove Lodge
LODGE **$$**

(Map p78; ☑0777 691790, 0773 516213; www.mangrovelodge.com; Chiuni; s US$40-60, d US$80-120; 🅿🖂💪) 🌿 The delightful Mangrove Lodge is owned by a Zanzibari-Italian couple; their gentle style imbues the whole place, from the palm-thatched lounge overlooking the bay to the spacious bungalow rooms in the lush garden. The lodge is at Chiuni, about 15km from Stone Town, so it's an ideal place to come to relax after a few days of arduous historical sightseeing.

The lodge is heavily invested in the locale; staff come from Chiuni village, where the lodge funds a dispensary. Using these neighbourly contacts, the lodge can set you up with village visits, traditional craft workshops, walks and bike rides to nearby spice plantations, and fishing trips with local fishers. Or you can just stroll hassle-free in the surrounding fields. If you fancy a dip, it's a very short walk from the lodge to Chiuni Beach (also known as Mawimbini Beach).

Near the lodge is Chiuni Bay and the ruins of Chuini Palace, where Sultan Barghash once spent his weekends. To get here, follow the main road north (via Bububu) for about 12km to reach Chuini village, then turn left (look for the Mangrove Lodge sign) and follow sandy tracks through the farmland for another 3km. If you book ahead, transfers can be arranged; to/from town is US$20.

Pili Pili House
RENTAL HOUSE **$$$**

(☑0777 410131; www.hilikihouse-zanzibar.com; house per night up to 6 people US$210; 🅿) Pili Pili House is a three-bedroom beach house on a beautiful stretch of sand at the village of Bumbwini, 20km from Stone Town, about 5km beyond the cultural and historic sites at Mangapwani. Housekeeping and a cook offer all the benefits of a hotel in a cosy home setting.

Mbweni Ruins Hotel
LODGE **$$$**

(Map p78; ☑024-223 5478; www.proteahotels.com; Mbweni; d US$200; 🅿🌐🖂🏊💪) Away from the hustle, 5km south of Zanzibar Town, trim and tranquil Mbweni Ruins Hotel (part of the Marriott-Protea chain) has light and airy rooms set in expansive botanical gardens. The eponymous ruin – a former mission school for freed slaves – is also in the hotel grounds. Other attractions include a private beach, excellent restaurant and bar with ocean views.

🍴 Eating

For traditional Zanzibari food, you can't beat Stone Town, where all of these listings are located. Being near the coast, seafood unsurprisingly features on most menus, often seasoned with flavours from around the Indian Ocean. For those with deep pockets, luxury rooftop restaurants are a must, while markets and street-food options abound for those on lower budgets.

Note that during low seasons (April to May and October to November) and Ramadan, many restaurants close or operate with reduced hours.

★ Lukmaan Restaurant
ZANZIBARI **$**

(Map p82; New Mkunazini Rd; meals Tsh5000-7000; ☺7am-9pm) Probably the best local restaurant for quality Zanzibari food. There's no menu: just make your way inside to the 1950s counter and see what's on offer. Servings are enormous and include various biryanis, fried fish, coconut curries and freshly made naan.

★ Zanzibar Coffee House
CAFE **$**

(Map p82; ☑024-223 9319; www.riftvalley-zanzibar.com; snacks Tsh5000-12,000; ☺8am-6pm; 🌐🖂) The top spot in Zanzibar for a serious cup of genuine East African Rift Valley coffee is undoubtedly this charming cafe. Alongside espressos and cappuccinos are milkshakes, crêpes, salads, sandwiches and toasted bruschetta. Tours of the roasting area can be arranged. Upstairs are eight guestrooms (p89), decorated in traditional Zanzibar style.

Ma Shaa Allah Cafe   INDIAN $

(Map p82; New Makunazini Rd; meals Tsh3000-9000; ⊙11am-8pm) A good no-frills option serving up various curries with rice or fresh naan cooked before your eyes in an oven on the terrace overlooking the street.

Luis Yoghurt Parlour   GOAN $

(Map p82; ☑0765 759579; 156 Gizenga St; meals Tsh12,000-15,000; ⊙10am-3pm & 6-9pm Mon-Sat; ☑) It's not just yoghurt here. As well as creamy *lassis* (yoghurt drinks) and snacks, Madam Blanche Luis cooks up Goan specialities such as coconut crab curry – all served with freshly made naan, fruit smoothies and spiced tea in small and understated surroundings. The restaurant is sometimes unexpectedly closed, so call in during the day if you're planning to come for dinner.

Tamu   ITALIAN $

(Map p82; ☑0772 459206; Shangani St; mains Tsh15,000, ice cream Tsh3000; ⊙10.30am-10.30pm; ☑) This genuine Italian place just off Shangani St serves pizza and homemade pasta, as well as cakes and ice cream in traditional and local flavours like baobab or tamarind.

Stone Town Café   CAFE $

(Map p82; Kenyatta Rd; meals Tsh10,000-15,000; ⊙8am-10pm) Great little place with seating inside or outside under potted palms overlooking the street. The menu includes all-day breakfasts, milkshakes, freshly baked cakes, veggie wraps and good coffee. Upstairs is the Stone Town Café B&B (p89).

Al-Shabany   ZANZIBARI $

(Map p82; off Malawi Rd; meals from Tsh3500; ⊙10am-2pm) For no-nonsense food at budget prices, it's worth searching out this place in the small side streets off Malawi Rd. Expect pilau and biryani, plus chicken and chips. Takeaway also available.

Radha Vegetarian Restaurant   VEGETARIAN $

(Radha Food House; Map p82; ☑024-223 4808; off Shangani St; thalis Tsh15,000; ⊙8am-9.30pm, thalis from 11am; ☑☑) This great little place is tucked away on the small street behind the NBC bank. The strictly vegetarian menu features thalis and other dishes from the Indian subcontinent. Radha also serves alcohol, so some people come to drink only.

Amore Mio   ITALIAN $

(Map p82; Shangani St; meals Tsh15,000-20,000; ⊙10am-10pm; ☑) Amore Mio has well-prepared pasta dishes and other light meals, paninis, good coffee and fantastic views of the ocean. At the time of research, new owners were adding Turkish specialities to the menu.

Archipelago Café-Restaurant   CAFE $

(Map p82; ☑024-223 5668; Shangani; mains Tsh10,000-17,000; ⊙8am-10pm; ☑) This local restaurant is tucked away on the lane that leads to the beach from the bottom of Kenyatta Rd, with a terrace next to the spot where traditional dhows are built. Tasty breakfasts are served until 11am, followed by an assortment of seafood curries, grills and pilaus. There's no alcohol, so fill up on excellent juices and smoothies.

Monsoon Restaurant   ZANZIBARI $$

(Map p82; ☑0777 410410; Forodhani; mains Tsh17,000-30,000; ⊙noon-10pm) Something slightly different: Monsoon has traditional-style dining, so you eat at low tables lounging on cushions (shoes off at the door, naturally). The menu is well-prepared Swahili cuisine with a modern twist. It's very atmospheric, further enhanced by the gentle backdrop of live *taarab* music on Wednesday and Saturday evenings. There's also conventional table seating on the terrace outside.

Travellers Cafe   CAFE $$

(Map p82; Shangani St; mains Tsh13,000-20,000; ⊙10am-11pm; ☑) This simple beachfront cafe-bar has rustic charm, friendly staff and good food, ideal for a long lunch or an evening meal with an ocean view. Choose from seafood dishes, steaks, burgers, salads and sandwiches, or check the specials board.

Tapería   TAPAS $$

(Map p82; ☑0773 226989; Kenyatta Rd; tapas Tsh8000-14,000, mains Tsh10,000-20,000; ⊙restaurant 10am-10pm, bar to midnight) Come to eat, drink or both. There are well-prepared tapas, pizzas and Spanish-favoured snacks, plus beers, a range of wines and other drinks, including some tempting nonalcoholic concoctions, and an open-air terrace overlooking busy Kenyatta Rd. The adjoining deli has freshly baked breads and gourmet sandwiches. Entry is off Gizenga St, around the back of the post office.

Abyssinian Maritim
ETHIOPIAN $$

(Map p82; ☑0772 940556; Vuga Rd; mains Tsh20,000-25,000; ☺noon-3pm & 6-10pm Wed-Mon) Sit on the airy terrace underneath the pergola of exuberant bougainvillea and wait for enormous platters of *tibs* (grilled meat), *injera* (flatbread) and other specialities at this great little Ethiopian place. Spectacular multi-coloured fruit smoothies, *tej* (honey beer) and freshly ground coffee complete the feast.

La Taverna
ITALIAN $$

(Map p82; ☑0776 650301; www.lataverna zanzibar.com; Creek Rd; mains Tsh10,000-20,000; ☺11am-11pm) Bringing a dash of Italian brio to Zanzibar Town, La Taverna has a warm terracotta-tiled interior with the requisite checked tablecloths and an outside terrace screened from the main road. Seafood takes pride of place with dishes like calamari *fritti* and grilled lobster, alongside regional dishes such as Milanese cutlets and ever-popular pasta and pizza standards.

House of Spices
MEDITERRANEAN $$

(Map p82; ☑0773 573727, 024-223 1264; www. houseofspiceszanzibar.com; Kiponda St; meals Tsh12,000-15,000; ☺10am-11pm Mon-Sat; ☎) With its lantern-lit rooftop terrace this Mediterranean has well-executed seafood and wood-fired pizzas. Fish dishes come with a choice of five spiced sauces, there's a good wine list and you can round off your meal with a special spiced digestif. For a lighter evening, there's also a tapas bar. A bonus is the attached small and stylish guesthouse.

Silk Route Restaurant
INDIAN $$

(Map p82; ☑0786 879696; Shangani St; mains Tsh15,000-20,000; ☺11am-10pm Mon-Sun; ✍) A classic Indian restaurant with staff in Raj outfits, serving contemporary and traditional Indian dishes, some with a Zanzibari twist. The restaurant rises over three storeys; to get a table on the covetable top floor book ahead or come early.

Lazuli
CAFE $$

(Map p82; off Kenyatta Rd; meals Tsh10,000-15,000; ☺noon-4pm & 6-10pm Mon-Sat) ✎ On a dusty courtyard just off Kenyatta Rd, this relaxed place serves lunch and dinner, offering curries, fresh juices, burgers, chapati wraps, salads, smoothies, pancakes and more – all freshly prepared with a healthy touch.

Sambusa Two
Tables Restaurant
ZANZIBARI $$

(Map p82; ☑024-223 1979, 0774 881921; Victoria St; meals Tsh25,000) This simple place did indeed start with just two small tables, but now caters for larger numbers – although it's still in the family house. Here's the routine: visit first, ask what's on offer, if you like it make a reservation, then come along later to sample numerous Zanzibari dishes.

There are no set opening hours; you can come for lunch or dinner, times by advance arrangement. To get here, turn off Victoria St, go past the second-hand plumbing yard, and round to the back of the house.

★Emerson Spice
Rooftop Teahouse
FUSION $$$

(Map p82; ☑024-223 2776; www.emersonspice. com; Tharia St; dinner set menu US$40; ☺7-11pm Fri-Wed) Perched on top of the Emerson Spice hotel (p90), the 'teahouse' (open-sided room) offers 360-degree views and some of the finest food in Stone Town. Many guests come for pre-dinner sundowner cocktails before enjoying five courses of Zanzibar specialities. Mains are mostly seafood-based, such as lemongrass calamari or prawns with grilled mango. Reservations are essential.

Emerson on Hurumzi
Rooftop Teahouse
ZANZIBARI $$$

(Map p82; ☑024-223 2784, 0779 854225; www. emersononhurumzi.com; Hurumzi St; set menu Tsh40,000; ☺noon-4pm & 5-11pm) Part of the well-known Emerson on Hurumzi hotel (p91), the rooftop teahouse restaurant is open to nonguests. The food is excellent, and the view simply stunning. Lunch is served from noon to 4pm, or come early for sunset drinks followed by three-course dinners that feature vintage Zanzibari recipes. There's often a live *taarab* music performance too. Reservations are usually required.

🍷 Drinking & Nightlife

Most bars in Zanzibar Town are connected to hotels, with a few notable stand-alone exceptions. They all serve local and international brands of beer and other drinks, and several offer cocktails or mocktails involving local fruits and spices. Many hotels also have a 'teahouse' (traditional open-sided room at the top of a building) where you can enjoy a drink with spectacular views.

Sunrise Restaurant
BAR

(Map p82; Kenyatta Rd, cnr Kenyatta Rd & Baghani St; ☺10am-10pm) The no-frills Sunrise is frequented by locals and budget travellers, and despite the name it's as much a bar as a restaurant, although basic meals (around

ZANZIBAR ARCHIPELAGO ZANZIBAR TOWN

LOCAL KNOWLEDGE

CATCHING THE SUNSET

One of the best ways to start an evening in Stone Town is sipping a drink while watching the sun set over the ocean. But if you want a genuine sundowner, choose your spot carefully as the sun's position changes through the year. Locations on the southwest side of Stone Town (eg Africa House Hotel) get the best sunset views from October to March, while for locations on the northwest side (eg Mercury's) it's best from April to September.

Tsh10,000) are available. Sit inside to watch TV or out in the garden to catch the breeze.

Up North @ 6 Degrees South   BAR
(Map p82; ☑062-064 4611; www.6degrees south.co.tz; Shangani St; ⊙5-11pm; ☜) Enjoy sundowners and sea views from this rooftop bar above 6 Degrees South restaurant on the southwest-facing side of Stone Town.

Mercury's   BAR
(Map p82; ☑024-223 3076; Mizingani Rd; ⊙noon-midnight) Named for Queen vocalist Freddie Mercury, this is a scruffy but popular waterside hang-out for daytime drinks, evening drinks or sundowners in-between. If you get bored of the view over the beach and port, there's usually football on TV, and live music most Saturdays. Food – in the pizza, pasta and curry vein (mains Tsh16,500 to Tsh25,000) – is also served.

Africa House Hotel Sunset Bar   BAR
(Map p82; www.africahousehotel.co.tz; Shangani St; ⊙5pm-midnight) With a front-row view of the ocean, the Sunset Bar at the Africa House Hotel – once the British Club – has a wide terrace and steady supply of cold beer, making it a perennially popular place for sundowners.

Livingstone Beach Restaurant   BAR
(Map p82; off Shangani St; ⊙10am-2am) This worn but popular place in the old British consulate building has seating inside and outside on a deck under trees directly on the beach. Food is available lunchtime and evening, but mainly this is the place to come for drinks, especially at sunset or after dark when the setting is delightful by candlelight. There's often live music too.

☆ Entertainment

Entertainment Zanzibar-style centres on traditional music and dance performances.

★ Dhow Countries
Music Academy   LIVE MUSIC
(Map p82; ☑0777 416529; www.zanzibarmusic. org; Old Customs House, Mizingani Rd; concerts Tsh10,000; ⊙9am-6pm) Many music genres are studied at this academy and regular evening concerts showcase students' work, from Afro-jazz and fusion to *taarab* – Zanzibar's celebrated sung poetry. For a more hands-on experience, workshops are also available. Check the notice board in the lobby for performance times here and at other venues around town.

Hurumzini Movie Café   CINEMA
(Hurumciné; Map p82; ☑0628 014454; www.face book.com/hurumzini; off Hurumzini St; ⊙10am-9pm) Come for coffee, a meal or a movie – or all three. With comfortable sofas, funky decor and an imaginative menu (snacks from Tsh3000, meals Tsh9000 to Tsh15,000), this is a great little place. Swing by during the day to see what's showing in the evening; between 10am and 5pm customers can choose the film, or just enjoy the food and friendly ambience.

Old Fort   DANCE
(Map p82; Tsh5000-10,000) Performances of local music, dance and drumming are often held at the Old Fort, but the schedule is variable. Stop by the information desk at the entrance during the day to check what's on in the evening.

🛍 Shopping

From casual browser to fine-art collector, there's something for everyone in Stone Town. Many stalls sell *tinga-tinga* paintings, wood carvings and other straightforward souvenirs, while dedicated shoppers can find historic antiques, contemporary jewellery, traditional handicrafts, designer fashion and artworks of astounding quality. Shopping here is also a great way to make a contribution to the local economy.

★ Cultural Arts Centre Zanzibar   ART
(Map p82; ☑0773 612551; hamadcac.z@gmail.com; Hamamni St; ⊙10am-6.30pm) Organised by the dedicated Hamad and other local artists, with an emphasis on quality and distinctiveness, this arts centre and shop provide a refreshing change to the wooden animals and *tinga-tinga* found elsewhere in Stone Town. On sale are stunning paintings in traditional and contemporary styles, plus jewellery, candles, soaps and craftware items, mostly made by local cooperatives around Zanzibar.

Zanzibar Curio Shop GIFTS & SOUVENIRS
(Map p82; Hurumzi St; ⊙10am-7pm) The phrase 'Aladdin's Cave' can be overused, but not here. Step inside for floor-to-ceiling displays of gifts and souvenirs, and browse with no pressure. Go into the next room and then the next to find antiques, ornaments, carvings and collectables. Need a clock? Or maybe a glass lantern, brass diving helmet or enamel cigarette advertisement? This is the place.

Memories of Zanzibar GIFTS & SOUVENIRS
(Map p82; Kenyatta Rd; ⊙8am-6pm Mon-Sun) This place calls itself an emporium, and it does indeed have a massive range of souvenirs: carvings, clothing, books, ornaments, furnishings, jewellery, fabrics, toys and more, all in a modern environment. Everything has a price label, so there's no haggling, and absolutely no pressure as you browse.

Real Art ART
(Map p82; Gizenga St; ⊙10am-6pm) As the name implies, a gallery of good-quality paintings and sculpture. A sign outside declares 'All our artists are featured in contemporary art books'.

Kihanga CLOTHING
(Map p82; Gizenga St; ⊙10am-6pm) Ready-to-wear and custom-made dresses and skirts from kanga fabric (the colourful wraps worn by women all over East Africa).

Hellen's Shop GIFTS & SOUVENIRS
(Map p82; Kenyatta Rd; ⊙9am-6pm Mon-Sun) The friendly Hellen has her shop slightly off the main track, down near the Africa House Hotel. Come here to buy kangas, clothing, basketware, postcards and straightforward souvenirs in a no-hassle environment.

Doreen Mashika FASHION & ACCESSORIES
(Map p82; www.doreenmashika.com; 267 Hurumzi St; ⊙10am-6pm) For Zanzibari high fashion head to this store on Hurumzi St. Trained in Switzerland, Doreen has a signature style that effortlessly combines African prints and materials with European designs, producing beaded collars and cuffs, printed pencil skirts, horn-and-silver necklaces and bags in loud African prints. Any outfit can be made to measure within two to three days.

Sasik ARTS & CRAFTS
(Map p82; ☑0773 132100; Gizenga St; ⊙10am-6pm) The cushions, coverlets and throws in Sasik are the work of self-taught Saada Abdullah Suleiman and her team of over 45 Zanzibari women. Their intricate vegetal designs in bright primary colours are influenced by typical Swahili and Arabian patterns, many of them originating in the carved doors around Stone Town. Buy off the shelf or order bespoke designs and colour schemes.

Fahari FASHION & ACCESSORIES
(Map p82; www.fahari-zanzibar.com; 62 Kenyatta Rd; ⊙10am-6pm) 🖊 Shop and social enterprise Fahari combines traditional Zanzibari skills with the cutting-edge expertise of accessories designer Julie Lawrence to produce eye-catching bags in leather and *ukili* (woven palm fonds), delicate oyster-shell jewellery and kaftans fit for a Spice Island honeymoon.

ZANZIBAR ARCHIPELAGO ZANZIBAR TOWN

TAARAB MUSIC

No visit to Zanzibar would be complete without spending an evening listening to the evocative strains of *taarab*, the archipelago's most famous musical export. *Taarab*, from the Arabic *tariba* (roughly, 'to be moved'), fuses African, Arabic and Indian influences, and is considered by many Zanzibaris to be a unifying force among the island's many cultures.

A traditional *taarab* orchestra consists of several dozen musicians using both Western and traditional instruments, including the violin, the *kanun* (similar to a zither), the accordion, the *nay* (an Arabic flute) and drums, plus a singer. There's generally no written music, and songs – often with themes centred on love – are full of puns and double meanings.

Taarab-style music was played in Zanzibar as early as the 1820s at the sultan's palace, where it had been introduced from Arabia. However, it wasn't until the 1900s, when Sultan Seyyid Hamoud bin Muhammed encouraged formation of the first *taarab* clubs, that it became more formalised.

One of the first clubs founded was Akhwan Safaa, established in 1905 in Zanzibar Town. Since then other clubs have sprung up, including the well-known Culture Musical Club. In traditional clubs, men and women sit separately, with the women decked out in their finest garb and elaborate hairstyles. Audience participation is key, and listeners frequently go up to the stage to give money to the singer.

All manufacture is carried out in the workshop, which you can see as you shop.

Upendo Means Love
CLOTHING

(Map p82; www.upendomeanslove.com; Tharia St; ⊙10am-6pm) This multifaith community project builds bridges between Zanzibar's minority Christians and the largely Muslim population through its sewing school and fashionable boutique. The result: stylish ladies' and children's summerwear in funky fabrics, plus cross-cultural friendships and economic independence. Danish fashion students help keep the line fresh and on-trend. The shop is opposite Zanzibar Coffee House (p91), or you can buy online.

Moto & Dada Shop
ARTS & CRAFTS

(Map p82; www.motozanzibar.wordpress.com; Hurumzi St; ⊙10am-6pm) 🖉 This shop sells products from Moto, a Zanzibar-wide handicraft cooperative that supports the island's rural economy by selling bags, sun hats, baskets, mats and other goods woven from *ukili* (palm leaves), and from Dada, a similar scheme helping local women sell cosmetics and foodstuffs made from natural local materials.

Zanzibar Gallery
GIFTS & SOUVENIRS

(Map p82; 📞024-223 2721; www.zanzibargallery. net; Kenyatta Rd; ⊙9am-6.30pm Mon-Sat, to 1pm Sun) This long-standing gallery has a huge collection of souvenirs, textiles, woodcarvings, antiques, contemporary art, framed photographs and more.

ℹ️ Information

DANGERS & ANNOYANCES

While Zanzibar is relatively safe, Zanzibar Town does see occasional robberies and muggings.
➡ Keep your money and valuables out of sight (and reach), especially in crowded areas like Darajani Market.
➡ Avoid isolated areas, such as the beaches to the north or south of Stone Town.
➡ At night in Stone Town, especially in the port area, take a taxi or walk in a group.
➡ If you leave Zanzibar Town on the night ferry, take care with your valuables, especially when arriving in Dar es Salaam.

INTERNET ACCESS

Most hotels in Stone Town (and many cafes and restaurants) offer wi-fi, either in the lobby/bar/restaurant or in all rooms – although this can be sketchy in historic buildings due to the thick walls.

Some hotels also have an internet-enabled computer for guest use.

Public internet is available at Shangani Post Office and **Azzurri Internet Café** (Map p82; New Mkunazini Rd; ⊙8.30am-8.30pm); both charge Tsh1000 per hour.

MEDICAL SERVICES

Zanzibar Town has the large state-run **Mnazi Moja Hospital** (Kaunda Rd), but most visitors (and most locals, if they can afford it) use a private facility. Options include **Zanzibar Medical Group** (Map p82; 📞024-223 3134; Kenyatta Rd), a small private clinic, and **Zanaid Clinic** (Map p78; 📞0777 777112; www.zanaid. org; Chukwani Rd, Mbweni; ⊙1-5pm Mon Fri), where the two European-trained doctors have experience in tropical illness and diving injuries. There's also **Global Hospital** (Tasakhtaa Global Hospital; Map p82; 📞024-223 2341; www. tasakhtaahospital.co.tz; Victoria St, Vuga), a large medical centre where facilities include casualty/emergency room (with ambulance), surgery, dentist, general physician/practitioner (GP) and pharmacy.

For small-scale medical problems, pharmacists can advise; reputable and well-stocked pharmacists include **Shamshu & Sons Pharmacy** (Map p82; 📞0715 411480, 024-223 2199; Market St; ⊙9am-8.30pm Mon-Thu & Sat, 9am-noon & 4-8.30pm Fri, 9am-1.30pm Sun) and **Fahud Pharmacy** (Map p82; New Mkunazini Rd).

MONEY

The most useful ATMs for travellers in Stone Town are attached to **CRDB** (Map p82; New Mkunazini Rd), **NBC** (Map p82; Shangani St) and **Diamond Trust Bank.** (Map p82; narrow street behind Old Fort)

The handiest place to change money is at one of the licensed bureaus on Gizenga St, including **Union Forex Bureau** (Map p82; Gizenga St; ⊙8am-4pm Mon-Sun) and **Eagle Change Bureau** (Map p82; Gizenga St). They will change US dollars, British pounds, euros and other hard currencies into Tanzanian shillings.

Officially, accommodation on Zanzibar must be paid for in US dollars, and so prices for hotel rooms, as well as various other tourist-related services, are often quoted in this currency. However, it's almost never a problem to pay the equivalent in Tanzanian shillings.

POST & TELEPHONE

Shangani Post Office (Map p82; Kenyatta Rd; ⊙8am-12.30pm & 2-4.30pm Mon-Fri, to 12.30pm Sat) offers international calls at Tsh2000 per minute and Skype at Tsh2000 per hour.

TOURIST INFORMATION

The official Zanzibar Commission for Tourism has a **tourist information desk** (ZCT; Map p82; Mzingani Rd; ⊙9am-6pm) just inside the entrance to the Old Fort. It's worth stopping to pick up leaflets or get information on upcoming festivals and events. For advice on anything else, the staff's knowledge is limited.

Also be aware that many local tour companies around Zanzibar Town display signs claiming to offer 'tourist information' – but mainly they want to sell you stuff.

TRAVEL AGENCIES & TOUR OPERATORS

Travel agencies sell plane and ferry tickets, while tour companies sell tours and excursions; many do both. You should make bookings only inside the official offices of travel agencies and tour companies, and not with anyone outside claiming to be staff.

ⓘ Getting There & Away

AIR

Airlines flying in and out of **Zanzibar International Airport** (ZNZ, Abeid Amani Karume International Airport; Map p78) include the following:
Coastal Aviation (Map p82; ☑ 024-223 3489, airport 024-223 3112; www.coastal.co.tz; Zancos Tours & Travel, Shangani St) Numerous daily flights connecting Zanzibar with Dar es Salaam, Arusha, Pemba, Tanga and elsewhere in Tanzania and East Africa.
Kenya Airways (☑ 0786 390 004, 024-223 4520/1; www.kenya-airways.com; Muzammil Centre, Malawi Rd) At least two flights daily to/from Nairobi (Kenya), with connections to other cities in Africa and beyond.
Precision Air (☑ 024-223 5126, 0786 300418; www.precisionairtz.com; Muzammil Centre, Malawi Rd, cnr Malawi & Mlandege Rds) Several flights to/from Dar es Salaam daily, with connections to Kilimanjaro and other destinations in Tanzania and East Africa.

Tropical Air (Map p82; ☑ 0777 431431, 024-223 2511; www.tropicalair.co.tz; Creek Rd) Daily flights connecting Zanzibar with Dar es Salaam, Pemba, Mafia and Arusha.
ZanAir (☑ 024-223 3678, 024-223 3670; www.zanair.com; Muzammil Centre, Malawi Rd) Daily flights to/from Dar es Salaam, Pemba and Arusha.

Costs of flights to destinations within Tanzania are similar on all the airlines, although departure days and times vary, and special offers are sometimes available. Some sample destinations and standard one-way fares:
➡ Arusha/Moshi/Kilimanjaro US$250
➡ Dar es Salaam US$75
➡ Pemba US$100

BOAT

Many visitors to Zanzibar travel on one of the regular and reliable services:
Zanzibar to/from Dar es Salaam Kilimanjaro Fast Ferries; high-speed passenger catamarans (standard adult fare US$35, two hours, four services each way daily).
Zanzibar to/from Pemba Sealink Ferries; roll-on, roll-off car and passenger ships (standard adult fare US$35, approximately six hours, two services each way weekly). This ferry also goes to/from Dar, and once weekly to/from Tanga.

Other ferries are *Mandeleo, Serengeti* and *Flying Horse,* but services are unreliable.

All ferries arrive in Zanzibar Town; the **passenger ferry terminal** (Map p82) gate is on Mizingani Rd. There is no reliable phone number for the public to use for ferry information; it is better to contact Azam Marine, the main ferry operator.

In Zanzibar Town, you can buy tickets for *Kilimanjaro* or *Sealink* ferries at the **Azam Marine**

ⓘ PAPASI

In Zanzibar Town you will undoubtedly come into contact with street touts, known as *papasi* (street touts; literally, ticks), offering to set you up with boat trips, spice tours or a hotel. Some carry false Zanzibar Tourist Corporation identification cards, and lurk around the ferry port, beach and main shopping streets. Some can be genuinely helpful, others can be downright irritating.

If you decide to use the services of a *papasi* to find a hotel, tell them where you want to go and your price range. Make it clear you won't pay, as you know they get commission from the hotel. If the *papasi* tells you your hotel of choice is full, they may be directing you to another hotel where they get a bigger kickback.

If you go for a *papasi*-arranged boat trip, it may be with an unregistered boat, which could mean compromised safety. Also, if anything goes wrong you won't get your money back.

If you want a reliable and knowledgable guide for a spice tour or to show you around Stone Town, it's better arranged via your hotel or a local tour agency.

If you're not interested in *papasi* services, explain this firmly and politely. You may have to do it several times.

booking office (Map p82; ☎ 024-223 1655; www.azammarine.com; cnr Malawi & Mizingani Rds), and for other ferries at ticket booths opposite the **passenger ferry terminal** (Map p82; Mizingani Rd) and near the roundabout at the junction of **Malawi and Mizingani Rds** (Map p82). For a less frenetic experience, you can also purchase ferry tickets through travel agents in Zanzibar Town.

BUS & DALLA-DALLA

Zanzibar Town is the hub for bus and dalla-dalla routes around Zanzibar Island. The main routes (and numbers) are between Zanzibar Town and the following destinations:

➡ Bwejuu (via Paje) 324
➡ Chwaka 206
➡ Jambiani (via Paje) 309
➡ Kiwengwa 117
➡ Kizimkazi 326
➡ Makunduchi 310
➡ Matemwe 118
➡ Nungwi 116
➡ Uroa 214

Fares on most of these routes cost Tsh2000 to Tsh3000, and trips take one to two hours.

At the time of research, long-distance bus and dalla-dalla transport from Zanzibar Town was in a state of flux after the long-distance transport stands along Creek Rd were closed.

➡ For destinations to the north (Mangapwani, Kiwengwa, Matemwe, Kendwa, Nungwi) the **transport stand** (Map p82) is on Creek Rd near the petrol station.

➡ For destinations to the south (Airport, Fumba) the **transport stand** (Map p82) is on Creek Rd just south of Jamhuri Gardens.

➡ For destinations to the east and southeast (Jozani, Paje, Bweju, Jambiani, Michamvi, Kizimkazi) the transport stand is at Mwanakwerekwe market in the suburb of the same name, about 5km east of Creek Rd.

➡ For destinations to the northeast (Chwaka, Uroa, Pongwe) the transport stand is at Mwembe Ladu, about 2km east of Creek Rd near Amani Stadium.

To reach Mwanakwerekwe or Amani Stadium, local transport leaves from the **stand** (Map p82) on Karume Rd to the east of Creek Rd. **Boda-boda** (Map p82; motorbike taxis) can be found at the cross-roads of Karume and Creek Rds.

CAR

For getting around Zanzibar Island, you can rent a car in Zanzibar Town via a travel agent or tour company. Self-drive is rare; most vehicles come with driver (and are in fact taxis). Expect to pay from US$50 per day for car and driver, plus fuel.

PRIVATE SHARED MINIBUS

The most common way for visitors to get from Zanzibar Town to Nungwi, Paje and other popular coast destinations around Zanzibar Island is by private shared minibus. It's fast and straightforward, and easily arranged. Hotels, tour companies and local guides cooperate to put groups together, so you'll find yourself sharing a minibus with several other passengers all going to the same destination.

Most minibuses leave in the morning (they'll pick you up from your hotel or a prearranged meeting point), although there are departures through the day at busy times. The fare is usually US$10 per person each way, and the journey takes one to 1½ hours. Coming back from the coast to Zanzibar Town it's the same deal.

TAXI

Taxis (usually four-seater cars, but sometimes six-seater people carriers) carry tourists from Zanzibar Town to destinations around Zanzibar Island, such as Nungwi or Paje. A one-way trip costs US$25 to US$50 (shared between passengers).

ℹ Getting Around

For getting around Stone Town, most people (locals and foreigners) simply walk. It's a compact area and many of the narrow streets are impassible for cars.

TO/FROM THE AIRPORT & FERRY TERMINAL

Zanzibar International Airport (7km southeast of Zanzibar Town) Taxis between the airport and Stone Town charge US$10 to US$20. It generally costs more going *from* the airport, especially at night (expect to pay US$30). Or you can take dalla-dalla 505 (Tsh300, 30 minutes).

Ferry Terminal (Stone Town) Taxis wait outside the gates of the passenger ferry terminal, and charge Tsh5000 to Stone Town hotels (recommended after dark), although nowhere is too far to walk in Stone Town (if you know where you're going).

Many hotels in Stone Town offer airport and ferry port pick-ups for confirmed bookings, sometimes free, sometimes for a small charge; arrange this in advance if required.

TAXI

Taxis around Zanzibar Town don't have meters, so you'll need to agree on a price with the driver before getting into the car. For short hops, expect to pay around Tsh5000, more at night. Longer trips, for example from the ferry port to Serena Hotel, cost around Tsh10,000. There are taxi ranks at the Big Tree, outside the House of Wonders, at the northern end of Kenyatta Rd, and in Kidele Sq in Shangani.

Zanzibar Town's Offshore Islands

For clean-water swimming, incredible snorkelling or hassle-free sunbathing, several islands sit within reach of Zanzibar Town, all with stunning beaches and surrounded by reefs.

Bawe, Changuu, Chapwani and Chumbe are 'proper' islands, while others such as Nyange, Pange and Murogo are just sandbanks that partially disappear at high tide.

Changuu

Commonly known as Prison Island and within easy reach of Zanzibar Town, Changuu has a delightful beach, plus clean water for swimming and snorkelling.

You can also admire the giant tortoises, whose ancestors were brought here from the Seychelles over a century ago. History fans may like to know the island was once used to detain slaves and later was the site of a prison and quarantine station. Also on the island is the former house of the British governor, General Lloyd Matthews.

Beyond the main beach, day visitors cannot explore at will, as much of the island is only for guests at Changuu Private Island Paradise (Map p78; ☑ central reservations 027-254 4595; www.hotelsandlodges-tanzania.com; ⊠), which was closed for renovation at the time of research.

Changuu Island lies about 5km northwest of Zanzibar Town. Trips by boat are organised by most hotels and tour companies in Zanzibar Town and cost around US$25 to US$30 per person.

Chapwani

This island has a fabulous beach and enviable location, so near and yet so far from Zanzibar Town, but you can visit only if you're staying at Chapwani Private Island Resort (Map p78; ☑ 0777 433102; www.chapwani-resort-zanzibar-hotel.com; half board per person from US$130; ☎⊠), in one of the five luxury cottages. There's a touch of history too – a small cemetery for colonial-era British seamen – so Chapwani is sometimes called Grave Island.

Chapwani Island is about 4km north of Zanzibar Town; guests at Chapwani Private Island Resort can arrange boat transfers when booking.

ZANZIBAR ARCHIPELAGO ZANZIBAR TOWN'S OFFSHORE ISLANDS

WORTH A TRIP

JOZANI-CHWAKA NATIONAL PARK

Jozani Forest is the largest area of indigenous forest on Zanzibar Island. Situated south of Chwaka Bay on low-lying land, the area is prone to flooding, which nurtures a lush swamp-like environment of moisture-loving trees and ferns. The whole area is protected as Jozani-Chwaka National Park (Map p78; adult/child with guide US$10/5; ⊗ 7.30am-5pm), and is famously home to populations of Zanzibar red colobus monkey (an endangered species found only on Zanzibar) as well as other monkey species, bushbabies, duikers and more than 40 species of birds.

The main activity is walking the forest nature trail (about 45 minutes) and a nearby boardwalk through the creek-side mangroves. When observing the monkeys, park staff recommend getting no closer than 3m, for your safety and that of the animals. In addition to the risk of being bitten, there's considerable concern that if the monkeys were to catch a human illness it could rapidly wipe out the already threatened population.

The park entrance gate and information centre is 35km southeast of Zanzibar Town, just off the road to Paje. The park makes a good day trip from Zanzibar Town and most people come on an organised tour. You can also get here on bus 309 or 310 from Paje or Zanzibar Town. While in the area, don't miss stopping at the nearby Jozani Sea Turtle Sanctuary (Uwemajo, Swahili Wonders; ☑ 0777 416213; www.uwemajo.org; adult Tsh10,000; ⊗ 9am-5pm), Zanzibar Butterfly Centre (☑ 0774 224472; www.zanzibarbutterflies.com; Pete; adult/child Tsh12,000/6000; ⊗ 10am-5pm) and ZALA Park (☑ 0777 850816; mohadayoub2@hotmail.com; tours per person per day from US$10). ZALA Park was founded as a project to help local people appreciate the value of wildlife, with funds raised by tourist visits. While the park itself is now forlorn, more energy is going into tours exploring local woodland, mangrove shoreline and nearby villages by foot, bike or kayak, plus tours of Makunduchi, taking in rarely visited caves, animist shrines and historical sites. Advance bookings are essential.

WORTH A TRIP

CHUMBE

The uninhabited island of Chumbe, about 12km south of Zanzibar Town, has an exceptional shallow-water coral reef along its western shore that abounds with life. The island and reef are protected as Chumbe Island Coral Park, a privately managed nature reserve and ecotourism project.

The reef is in such good condition mainly because it was part of a military zone, off-limits to locals and visitors, until becoming Chumbe Island Coral Park in the 1990s. There are nearly 200 species of coral and about 370 species of fish. The island is also a haven for hawksbill turtles, and dolphins are often seen. Meanwhile, more than 50 species of birds have been recorded here, including the endangered roseate tern.

Day visits cost US$90 per person and must be arranged in advance, via hotels and tour companies in Zanzibar Town. Boats to Chumbe leave from Mbweni Ruins Hotel; you can make your own way here by taxi or a combination of bus and walking, or have transport included in your tour for US$15 per person each way.

Overlooked by its landmark historic lighthouse, about 12km south of Zanzibar Town, **Chumbe Island Coral Park Lodge** (☑ 0777 413232, 024-223 1040; www.chumbeisland.com; Chumbe Island; full board per person US$280; ☎ 🏠) 🖉 is a real island getaway combining style, exclusivity and environmental benefits. Accommodation is in 'eco-bungalows' with local decor, solar power, rainwater collection, ocean views and a loft sleeping area that opens to the stars. Activities include forest walks, diving or snorkelling on the reef, and just lounging.

Bawe

Bawe's shallows are stunning for a snorkel, however, it's a private island so you can't land here unless you're a guest of **Bawe Tropical Island Lodge** (☑ central reservations 027-254 4595; www.hotelsandlodges-tanzania.com), which was closed indefinitely for renovations at the time of research.

Mangapwani

The small beach at Mangapwani, about 20km north of Zanzibar Town, is notable for its nearby historic sites, and is frequently included on spice tours. **Mangapwani Slave Chamber** (incl guide Tsh2000) is a dark cell cut into the coral rock that was used as a holding pen to hide slaves after the legal trade was abolished in the late 19th century. From here it's a short walk to a rock outcrop and small bay where slaves would be unloaded from boats. **Mangapwani Coral Cave** is a large natural cavern with a freshwater pool that was originally used as a source of drinking water for local people and is rumoured to have been used in connection with the slave trade. Meals are available at **Mangapwani Serena Beach Club** (☑ 024-223 3051; mains Tsh15,000-30,000; ⊙ 11am-3pm).

To get here, follow the main road north from Zanzibar Town past Bububu and Chuini. Fork left towards Bumbwini, then take another left to pass through Mangapwani village and reach Mangapwani beach. It's tarmac road all the way to the beach. The Slave Chamber is about 1.5km north along a dirt road; the Coral Cave and WWII bunkers are to the south. Dalla-dallas (route 102) run between Zanzibar Town and Bumbwini and usually go up the end of the tarmac road at Mangapwani beach, from where it's a short walk to the historic sites (all signposted).

Nungwi

POP 10,000

This large village at Zanzibar Island's northernmost tip was once best known as a dhow-building centre. Today it's a major tourist destination, thanks in part to the beautiful beach and stunning sunsets. The result: a place where traditional and modern knock against each other with full force. Fishing boats still launch from the beach – a scene unchanged for centuries – but they're overlooked by a long line of hotels. Some travellers say Nungwi is a definite highlight; others are happy giving it a miss.

Nungwi spreads over a large area. The main focal point is the roundabout at the end of the tarmac road from Zanzibar Town, from where dirt roads radiate northwards to the lighthouse on the headland (Ras Nungwi), eastwards to a few hotels on the quieter east side of the headland, and westwards through the village to the lively west side where most of the hotels are located.

◉ Sights & Activities

Mnarani Marine Turtle
Conservation Pond
ANIMAL SANCTUARY
(Mnarani Aquarium; www.mnarani.org; US$5; ⏱9am-6pm) In 1993 the villagers of Nungwi opened this turtle sanctuary in a large natural tidal pool near the lighthouse and since then these sea creatures have enjoyed a degree of protection from being hunted and eaten. You can see turtles of various species and sizes, and proceeds from entrance fees fund an education project for local children, hopefully demonstrating the benefits of turtle conservation.

Divine Diving
DIVING
(www.scubazanzibar.com; Amaan Bungalows Beach Resort) Divine Diving, on Nungwi's west beach, is a five-star PADI centre offering small-group dives, Mares equipment and (uniquely) courses in efficient breathing using yoga techniques.

Spanish Dancer Dive Centre
DIVING
(☑0777 417717; www.divinginzanzibar.com; 2/6 dives US$110/295) Based on Nungwi's west beach, Spanish Dancer Dive Centre is a large five-star PADI outfit with instructors teaching courses in a dedicated classroom, and speaking several languages. Boats include a traditional wooden dhow for nearby sites and a fast speedboat for more-distant sites.

Kiteboarding Zanzibar
KITESURFING
(☑0779 720259; www.kiteboardingzanzibar.com; ⏱lessons 3/9hr US$165/495, rental per day US$90) Kiteboarding Zanzibar is IKO certified and equipped with modern kit. Its Nungwi base is linked to its centre at Pwani Mchangani (where clients are taken if conditions aren't good at Nungwi). If you know what you're doing, and have certification, you can rent gear. For everyone else, lessons are available.

East Africa Diving &
Water Sport Centre
DIVING
(☑0777 420588; www.diving-zanzibar.com; 2/6 dives US$100/280) This is Nungwi's oldest diving outfit, located on the beach near Jambo Brothers Guesthouse. It's five-star PADI accredited, and has boats to carry clients to dive sites, as well as tanks, wetsuits and other kit in various sizes.

Zanzibar Watersports
DIVING
(☑0773 235030; www.zanzibarwatersports.com; Paradise Beach Bungalows; 2/6 dives US$115/310) This company is based at Kendwa with a branch at Paradise Beach Bungalows in west Nungwi. Snorkelling, kayaking, fishing, wakeboarding and dhow cruises are also offered, including an all-day 'seafari' (dhow cruise, snorkelling and lunch on a beach).

ZanziYoga
YOGA
(☑0776 310227; www.yogazanzibar.com; 6-day retreat with accommodation s/d US$1295/1970) Centre yourself with yoga under the skillful guidance of Marisa van Vuuren. On offer are six-day retreats, including morning and evening yoga sessions plus accommodation at Flame Tree Cottages (p102); budget and luxury retreats use other Nungwi hotels.

☞ Tours

Nungwi Cycling Adventures
CULTURAL
(☑0778 677662, 0777 560352; www.zanzibar cyclingadventures.com; per person US$25-40) Explore the world beyond Nungwi on bike tours to rural villages, ancient ruins, coral caves, traditional blacksmiths, farms and plantations or secret beaches. Trips are led by the mild-mannered and knowledgeable Machano; a Nungwi local and freelance guide, he can also be hired for any other local tours by bike, foot or car.

Cultural Village Tour
CULTURAL
(2hr per person US$15) At the Mnarani Marine Turtle Conservation Pond you can arrange village tours that are a great way to see local life beyond the hotel strip. Most fascinating are the dhow-builders; your guide will introduce you, so you can ask questions or simply observe their skills. Note, however, that the dhow-builders don't like being photographed so always ask permission first.

🛏 Sleeping & Eating

Most of Nungwi's hotels have restaurants open to nonguests, either in the hotel grounds or down on the beach. In the village there are several small shops selling a basic but sufficient range of groceries for picnics and simple self-catering.

> ### ⓘ NUNGWI ETIQUETTE
>
> Because of the large number of tourists in Nungwi, it's easy to overlook the fact that you're in a traditional, conservative environment. When walking in the village, be respectful, especially with your dress and your interactions with locals, and ask permission before snapping photos.

ZANZIBAR ARCHIPELAGO NUNGWI

West Nungwi

Nungwi Guest House GUESTHOUSE **$**
(☑ 0777 777708; www.nungwihouse.com; d US$50)
It's not on the beach, but this local-style
guesthouse is just a short walk away in the
village centre, and a good budget option. You
get simple and clean rooms, all with fans and
mosquito nets, in a small garden courtyard,
plus a friendly welcome.

Jambo Brothers Guesthouse GUESTHOUSE **$**
(d US$50) A simple budget option, right on
the beach. Rooms have mosquito nets, fans
(some also have have air-con) and a small veranda looking onto a sandy garden, although
where the garden stops and the beach starts
is a little unclear.

Safina Bungalows GUESTHOUSE **$**
(☑ 0777 415856; www.newsafina.com; s/d from
US$30/50) Safina has simply furnished no-
frills bungalows (some with air-con) set
around a scruffy garden, just in from the
beach.

Nungwi Inn Hotel HOTEL **$$**
(☑ 0777 418769; www.nungwiinnhotel.com; s/d
from US$55/80; ✳☎) At the far southern
(quieter) end of the west beach, Nungwi Inn
has rooms in spacious bungalows with palm-
thatched roofs. All have a small veranda, and
most have air-con. Six of the rooms look di-
rectly onto the beach; others are set in the
sandy garden. There's a small supermarket, a
restaurant and a beach bar where entertain-
ment is arranged some nights.

Amaan Bungalows Beach Resort HOTEL **$$**
(☑ 0777 318112; www.amaanbungalows.com; d
US$100-150; ✳☎🏊) Large, long-standing, ef-
ficient: Amaan (pronounced *amaani* by locals) has over 100 rooms, ranging from small
garden rooms to medium rooms around the
pool and villas with air-con and balcony
overlooking the sea. There's also a restaurant
on a deck above the beach, a sports bar and
a more relaxed bar, plus spa, dive centre and
tour office.

Flame Tree Cottages HOTEL **$$**
(☑ 0777 479429, 0737 202161; www.flametree
cottages.com; s/d US$130/170; ✳☎🏊🍴) The
small and welcoming Flame Tree offers un-
fussy and thoughtfully furnished rooms in
cottages surrounded by beautiful flowering
gardens. It's at the quieter end of Nungwi's
west beach, and is a perfect spot for families.

There's a swimming pool, and evening meals
are served on a patio overlooking the beach.

Baraka Beach Bungalows BUNGALOW **$$**
(☑ 0777 422910, 0777 415569; http://baraka
bungalow.atspace.com; s/d US$45/60) This
friendly place has simple bungalows around
a tiny well-kept garden. It's near the beach,
but the sea view is obscured by a two-storey
hotel at the front. At the time of research,
Baraka was building a *three*-storey block, so
expect more rooms and new prices (and possibly a view from the top floor).

Union Beach Bungalows BUNGALOW **$$**
(☑ 0773176923,0777128860;http://unionbungalow.
atspace.com; d US$50-70; ✳☎) With simple
bungalows and rooms with glass sliding
doors in a two-storey block, this is a no-frills
joint but makes up for it with its position
right on the beach. Next door is the affiliated
and equally no-frills Waves cafe-bar.

Langi-Langi Beach Bungalows HOTEL **$$**
(☑ 024-224 0470; www.langilangizanzibar.com; d
from US$100; ✳✳) This hotel has comfort-
ably furnished rooms in a neat multistorey
complex overlooking a swimming pool, with
a deck on high stilts above the beach. It's surrounded on three sides by other hotels, but
the view out to sea is uninterrupted.

Smiles Beach Hotel HOTEL **$$$**
(☑ 0773 444105; www.smilesbeachhotel.com; d
US$160; ✳☎🏊) At the quieter end of Nung-
wi's west beach, Smiles has well-appointed
rooms in colourful double-storey houses
with balconies and a spiral staircase, all set
in a spacious sandy garden. There's a pool
and restaurant, with sunloungers and para-
sols overlooking the sea.

Double Tree RESORT **$$$**
(Double Tree Resort by Hilton Hotel; ☑ 0779 000008;
www.doubletree.hilton.com; d US$220-280; ✳☎
🏊🍴) A luxurious hotel complex, with rooms
in several two- and three-storey buildings,
some with sea views, others overlooking the
large swimming pool and manicured gardens, and all with balconies and TV. There's
a restaurant, and a bar on a deck overlooking
the public beach, plus (should you overin-
dulge in the bar or restaurant) a fitness room.

East Nungwi

Mabwe Roots Bungalows BUNGALOW **$**
(s US$40) Rustic and relaxed with a reggae
vibe, this locally run place has a handful of

DIVING OFF ZANZIBAR ISLAND

With an abundance of reefs, islets and atolls, as well as water temperatures around 27°C (although reportedly rising) and clear visibility, Zanzibar Island is not surprisingly a very popular dive destination.

The reefs are home to hard and soft coral, and many species of colourful tropical fish, along with seahorses, barracudas, marlins and turtles.

At popular beach destinations like Nungwi, Kendwa, Matemwe and Paje, there's a host of dive companies to choose from. As a rough guide, introductory 'discover scuba' dives for beginners cost about US$100 each (about US$150 for two dives); a two-day 'scuba diver' course is US$300 to US$400; a four-dive 'open water' course around US$500. If you're already experienced, it costs about US$100 to US$120 for two dives or US$250 to US$350 for six.

Charges vary between companies, but bottom-line price shouldn't be your main decider. Instead, carefully consider the experience of the company and their attitude to training and safety (including medical forms and client-staff ratios), the personality and qualifications of the instructors, and the quality of the gear.

Other items to note:

➡ Do not touch live coral, and instruct dive boat captains not to drop anchor on live coral.

➡ Beware of fake 'PADI-registered' dive centres. Check the real ones at www.padi.com.

➡ Do not dive if you feel ill or dehydrated, eg especially after a night of partying.

➡ Even if holiday time is limited, don't dive too deep too quickly.

If you suffer a dive-related decompression illness (DCI, commonly known as 'the bends'), it's essential you seek medical help. Reputable dive companies will know the drill. Alternatively contact Zanaid Clinic (p96) in Zanzibar Town; the doctor here is experienced in dive illnesses, and will advise next steps (eg X-ray). The doctor can also be reached via the diving emergency number (☑0777 788500). Once the nature of your illness has been assessed, the doctor may call in other medics or technicians to assist. It may also be necessary for them to send you to the **hyperbaric chamber** (www.sssnetwork.com) in the village of Matemwe on the east coast of Zanzibar Island.

simple rooms with small bathrooms in a garden set back from the beach behind a couple of larger hotels. It's on Nungwi's quieter eastern side, about 2km from the village centre.

Mnarani Beach Cottages LODGE $$
(☑0777 415551, 024-224 0494; www.lighthousezanzibar.com; d US$80-200; ❋ 🕸 🛏 🐾) 🐾
On Nungwi's quieter eastern side, near the lighthouse, Mnarani is on a low cliff with a lovely waterside terrace with the beach just below. It's relaxed and efficient, with friendly staff and small rooms in ochre-painted cottages on spacious grounds overlooking the sea. Also available are large superior rooms, a honeymoon suite and apartments for families or groups of friends.

Warere Beach Hotel HOTEL $$
(☑0782 234564; www.warere.com; d US$80-110; ❋ 🕸) 🐾 Small, peaceful and relaxed, the Warere is 2.5km outside town on Nungwi's east beach. Two rows of cottages have an angular style but the design ensures all have a beautiful sea view (and also provides 'natural air-con'). Lush gardens, sandy pathways and an infinity pool complete the picture. There's a restaurant, and tours or activities can be arranged.

Sazani Beach Hotel HOTEL $$
(☑0774 633723, 0774 271033; www.sazanibeach.com; d US$130; 🕸) Sazani is a low-key place with a local ambience and 10 basic cottages on a small hillside leading down to the beach and overlooking the sea, about 2.5km from Nungwi's centre. Facilities are deliberately simple; there's no air-con or swimming pool, and the garden is somewhat overgrown. There's also a bar and restaurant, and very friendly staff.

❶ Information

There have been occasional robberies on quiet sections of the beach; don't walk here alone or with valuables, particularly at night.

Nearly all hotels, cafes and bars offer wi-fi, although at the budget places this tends to be very slow and patchy.

There's no ATM, but most hotels can help you change US dollars into local currency, and there's a forex desk at Amaan Bungalows Beach Resort (p102).

ⓘ Getting There & Away

Buses and dalla-dallas (route 116) run throughout the day between Nungwi and Zanzibar Town. It's tarmac road all the way. The public transport stand is near the roundabout in the town centre; taxis and private tourist minibuses will drop you at your hotel.

Kendwa

Kendwa Beach is a long stretch of sand extending down the west coast about 3km south of the tip of Zanzibar Island. Not surprisingly, this idyllic location means a string of resorts, hotels and guesthouses, but there is still lots of space on the beach. Other attractions include a range of water-based activities, and favourable tidal patterns that ensure swimming at all hours.

🏃 Activities

⭐ Scuba Do   DIVING
(☑ 0777 417157; www.scuba-do-zanzibar.com; 2/6 dives US$120/330) ⚑ Based at Sunset Kendwa, this long-standing and highly experienced Gold Palm and Green Star dive centre is one of the most professional outfits on Zanzibar. The owners, Tammy and Christian, and their well-trained crew of instructors offer excellent courses. Small groups are preferred, with families and kids a speciality. Popular and less well-known dive sites can be reached using high-speed boats.

TOP BEACHES

Kendwa Popular, wide, swimmable around the clock.

Matemwe (p105) Powdery sands, taste of village life.

Pongwe (p108) Tranquil atmosphere, lack of crowds.

Paje (p110) Kitesurfing mecca, lively buzz.

Jambiani (p113) Waters of otherworldly turquoise shades.

Zanzibar Parasailing   WATER SPORTS
(☑ 0779 073078; www.zanzibarparasailing.com; solo/tandem flights US$100/130) Solo and tandem flights along with other motor-powered activities, such as jet skiing, waterskiing, wakeboarding and banana-boating.

Kendwa Community Tours   TOURS
(☑ 0778 883306; http://kendwa-communitytours. com) This organisation is run by local people. On offer are tours to Stone Town and other parts of Zanzibar Island, but most interesting are the tours of Kendwa village itself, a chance for visitors to leave the beach for a while and see how Zanzibaris live day-to-day. Be prepared for arrangements to be a little relaxed.

🛏 Sleeping

Kendwa Beach Villa   GUESTHOUSE $
(d US$40-50) A no-frills joint with a few rooms in a building set back from the beach, and two other rooms overlooking the beach (well, the beach restaurants). Rooms have nets, fans and a basic bathroom. It's at the end of the dirt road at the far southern end of the beach.

Kendwa Rocks   BUNGALOW $$
(☑ 024-294 1113, 0777 415475; www.kendwarocks. com; s/d banda with shared bathroom US$40/50, d bungalow US$60-170; ❄ 🛜) This long-standing Kendwa classic has something for everyone, from basic *bandas* (thatched-roof huts) with shared bathrooms to luxurious bungalows with private plunge pool right on the beach, via several accommodation options in-between, all set in gardens covering a gently sloping cliff. Rooms set back from the sea may not have views, but they're quieter and more private.

Mocco Beach Villa   GUESTHOUSE $$
(☑ 0772 171777; www.moccobeachvilla.co.tz; s/d US$50/80; ❄ 🛜) A locally run guesthouse at the southern end of Kendwa beach, straightforward Mocco is set back slightly from the beach, although the affiliated restaurant is right down on the sand. Rooms are plain but fairly clean, with nets, fans and air-con. Three of the rooms have a sea view.

Sunset Kendwa   HOTEL $$
(☑ 0777 413818; www.sunsetkendwa.com; d US$98, without air-con US$60; ❄ 🛜) This long-standing place has bungalows on the beach (though no sea view) and rooms in two-storey blocks on the cliff top. Staff are friendly, but standards are a tad relaxed. On the upside, the restaurant overlooks the

ocean and the small beach bar is popular, and Scuba Do (p104) diving is based here.

Diamonds La Gemma dell'Est RESORT **$$$**
(☑ 024-224 0125; http://lagemmadellest.diamonds-resorts.com; s/d with full board from US$350/500; ❄ ☂ ⛱ 🏊) On the northern end of Kendwa beach, this is a very large and luxurious all-inclusive resort (called simply 'Gemma' by the locals) with around 130 rooms all with private veranda and sea view. Facilities include huge swimming pool, beautiful (maintained) beach, several restaurant-bars (including one on a jetty over the water), tennis courts, dive centre, gym and spa.

✕ Eating & Drinking

In addition to Kendwa's hotel restaurants, most of which are open to nonguests, there are several small places along the dirt road that runs behind the hotels at the southern end of the beach. These include **Kendwa Coffee House** (meals Tsh8000-10,000), with coffee and meals on a small garden terrace; **Fisherman Local Restaurant** (mains Tsh7000-10,000), featuring local-style seafood dishes and **Varadero Zanzibar House** (meals Tsh8000-10,000; ☎); serving Lebanese and Zanzibari meals.

Full-moon beach parties are a Kendwa staple; they take place at a few of the big hotels and nonguests are charged a small entrance fee.

ⓘ Getting There & Away

Kendwa can be reached via any bus or dalla-dalla (route 116) that runs between Zanzibar Town and Nungwi (Tsh3000). Get off at the main Kendwa turn-off, from where it's about 2km along a dirt road to the village and main cluster of hotels. If you're driving, this access road is passable in 2WD, with some care needed over the rocky patches.

Tumbatu

POP 10,000
The large and seldom-visited island of Tumbatu, just off the northwest coast of Zanzibar Island, is populated by the Tumbatu people, one of the three original tribal groups on the archipelago. Although Tumbatu's early history is unknown, ruins of a mosque have been found at the island's southern tip that may date from the early 11th century.

There are no tourist facilities, and no 'sights' or activities (other than simply walking around the villages and farmland), so tourists rarely visit. Perhaps because of this, residents of Tumbatu are generally very traditional and conservative, and expect visitors to behave accordingly.

The usual route is via Mkokotoni on Zanzibar Island, from where sailing boats ferry passengers across to Tumbatu. The fare is around Tsh500 and the trip takes 30 minutes to three hours, depending on the wind. More predictable motor boats cost around Tsh1000 each way.

Matemwe

POP 5000
The idyllic beach at Matemwe has some of the finest sand on Zanzibar and in this sleepy village life still moves at its own pace, despite the hotels and guesthouses nearby. Of all the coastal destinations on Zanzibar Island, this area seems to have the most 'local' atmosphere. For tourists, this tranquil unhurried ambience means Matemwe is definitely a place where it's easy to switch off.

🏃 Activities

As with many places along Zanzibar's coastline, diving is a popular activity here, but Matemwe has a special card to play: it's within easy reach of Mnemba Island and the surrounding conservation area, which is one of the most popular dive and snorkelling sites in the whole archipelago.

One Ocean DIVING
(www.zanzibaroneocean.com; Matemwe Beach Village; 2/6 dives US$110/305) One Ocean is an experienced five-star PADI dive outfit with bases in Zanzibar Town and on the east coast, including Matemwe Beach Village (p106) guesthouse. On offer are diving courses and trips to Mnemba Island and other local dive sites. Snorkelling trips are also available for US$45 per person.

Dada COOKING
(☑ 0777 466304; https://dadazanzibar.wordpress.com; per person around US$25, depending on group size) Bestir yourself from the sunbed and head out to meet local women and learn how they cook. On the menu could be baobab jam or coconut and cassava leaves. This activity is run by Dada, a local development project, just outside Matemwe village. You can book direct with Dada or via most Matemwe hotels.

🛏 Sleeping & Eating

Key's Bungalows BUNGALOW **$**
(☑ 0777 411797; www.allykeys.com; s/d US$30/50; ☎) This local-style place is near the fish

market and the effective centre of Matemwe village. It's an odd combination of simple rooms in a two-storey concrete block and a delightfully relaxed palm-thatched bar-lounge-restaurant on the beach. Meals may need to be ordered in advance, while boat rides, rental bikes and cars (and just about anything else) can be arranged.

★ Sele's Bungalows BUNGALOW $$
(☑0776 931690; www.selesbungalows.wix.com/zanzibar; d US$80-100; ☺May-Feb; ❄🕸) This is a great little place, with friendly owners and just seven impeccably maintained rooms. There's a small swimming pool and convivial bar-restaurant, all set in a lush garden just a few steps from the beach. Most rooms are large and with balcony, and there's a couple of smaller (and cheaper) ones tucked away downstairs.

Zanzibar Retreat Hotel BOUTIQUE HOTEL $$
(☑0776 108379; www.zanzibarretreat.com; d US$140-190; ❄🕸🞐) 🕊 This luxurious place has just 12 rooms in what was once a large private house. The polished hardwood floors and safari chairs give it a lovely old colonial feel, offset by the Zanzibar furniture in the rooms, and the bright and breezy bar-lounge area overlooking the beach. Everything is quiet and relaxing, and the food is excellent.

DIVING AT MNEMBA

Mnemba Island (also called Mnemba Atoll) is one of the best-known and most popular dive sites in Zanzibar, and on the whole coast of East Africa. Here you can see a wonderful variety of marine life, including tuna, barracuda, moray eels, reef sharks, turtles, dolphins, and shoals of batfish, trigger fish and humpback snappers. During the migration season, it's even possible to spot humpback whales.

While the island itself is privately owned, with access restricted to guests of Mnemba Lodge, the surrounding coral reef can be visited by anyone.

As Mnemba is so popular (it's been dubbed the 'Ngorongoro of Zanzibar'), in some areas the sheer number of boats and divers is causing damage to the reef. Experienced dive companies will be delighted to take you to quieter, less crowded sites.

★ Zanzibar Bandas BUNGALOW $$$
(☑0773 434113; www.zanzibarbandas.com; d US$150-300; 🕸🞐) 🕊 With a small collection of palm-thatched huts and bungalows in a garden on the beach, this place has a laid-back and welcoming atmosphere. Although simply built, accommodation is spotless and good quality. There's also a small swimming pool and bar-restaurant, and the management are keen musicians so performances or informal jamming sessions are common.

Green & Blue BOUTIQUE HOTEL $$$
(☑0774 411025; www.greenandblue-zanzibar.com; d US$270-450; ❄🕸🞐) This gorgeously designed place is nestled in luxuriant green gardens on a rocky bluff at the northern end of the village, almost opposite Mnemba Island. Fourteen independent cottages have bright colour schemes, private verandas and two showers (indoor or outdoor); most also have private plunge pool. The restaurant-bar serves excellent food, matched by spectacular views.

Matemwe Beach Village GUESTHOUSE $$$
(☑0777 417250; www.matemwebeach.net; d with half board US$220-300; 🕸🞐🞐) 🕊 This beachfront place has a very friendly and refreshingly low-key ambience. Guests can choose from two types of bungalow: small and simple, or spacious and more comfortable. Most are on the beach, with a few more set back in the garden. There's also a restaurant, a lounge area padded with colourful pillows, a swimming pool and One Ocean (p105) dive centre.

Sunshine Hotel HOTEL $$$
(☑0774 388662; www.sunshinezanzibar.com; d US$230; 🕸🞐) 🕊 Towards the southern end of Matemwe, this immaculate place has 12 rooms with louvre doors, soft furnishings and traditional-style in-room bathrooms. All overlook the garden or across the infinity pool to the beach. The hotel's dive centre is based at Sunshine Marine Lodge, a sister property at the north end of Matemwe village.

Matemwe Lodge LODGE $$$
(☑central reservations in Cape Town +27 21 418 0468; www.asiliaafrica.com/matemwe; d with full board US$720-790; 🕸🞐) Matemwe Lodge, at the northern edge of the village, is a luxurious hotel with a dozen spacious and impeccably decorated bungalows, all with sea views and set in verdant gardens. Nearby are two affiliated accommodation options: Matemwe Retreat (luxury villas) and Matemwe House (ideal for for families or small groups). Diving and all the usual activities can be arranged.

SEEAWEED FARMING IN ZANZIBAR

Wherever you go on the coast of Zanzibar Island, you'll often see local people (mainly women and children) tending crops of seaweed. It seems simple: in beach areas between the high and low water lines, small seaweed plants are attached to strings stretched between poles pushed into the sand. Then, once the plants have grown, the seaweed is harvested.

You may think that seaweed farming is a traditional island trade, but it was introduced only in the late 1980s, when commercial companies, in conjunction with Dar es Salaam University, promoted the activity as a means of employment and sustainable resource management.

The project was hugely successful. Seaweed contains a natural gelling agent used in products from toothpaste, perfume and shampoo to yoghurt, milkshakes and medicine. In 2013 an estimated 12,000 tonnes of seaweed was exported to countries such as China, Korea, Vietnam, Denmark, Spain, France and the USA, and was second only to tourism in terms of foreign-exchange earnings.

In recent years, Zanzibar's seaweed farmers have reported a decline in the trade thanks to increasing ocean temperatures, which slows the seaweed's growth, and a drop in prices in other parts of the world where seaweed is farmed.

❶ Getting There & Away

Matemwe village is on the northeast coast of Zanzibar Island. Dalla-dallas (route 118) travel daily to/from Zanzibar Town (Tsh2500). Early in the day the terminus is the fish market in the centre of the village at the northern end of the beach; later in the day the terminus is the main junction where the main tarmac road meets the dirt road that runs parallel to the coast.

Kiwengwa

POP 4000

The spectacular beach at Kiwengwa is popular with large hotels and resorts, mostly hidden behind high walls and mostly all-inclusive, with guests seldom leaving the lush grounds. By contrast, just back from the beach, Kiwengwa village appears poor and dusty, highlighting an uncomfortable contrast.

🛏 Sleeping & Eating

Zan View Hotel   HOTEL $$

(Map p78; ☑0774 141803; www.zan-view.com; d US$100-150, with sea view US$175-195; 🛜🍴) An unexpected find among the large resorts along this stretch of coast, Zan View is a friendly little place with spotless rooms in a house overlooking a small pool and two-storey Robinson Crusoe–style bar, with the ocean beyond. It's not on the beach; to get there is a short walk past a couple of beachfront properties.

Waikiki   RESORT $$

(☑0779 401603; www.waikikiafrica.com; d with half board US$100-130, family room per person US$50; ⊗mid-Jun–Apr; 🍴🛜) Waikiki is a fun and friendly resort where Italian ownership means good coffee, great food (including pizza and ice cream) and a legendary Friday party during summer. There are dozens of chill-out zones, an on-site kite school, a popular beach bar and a lovely stretch of beach where, even at low tide, you can wallow in deep tidal pools.

Bluebay Beach Resort   RESORT $$$

(☑0774 413321; www.bluebayzanzibar.com; d with half board US$250-320; 🍴🛜🍴🛏) The enormous luxury resort of Bluebay has around 100 rooms and suites, some in the gardens, others overlooking the ocean. There's a large swimming pool, a choice of restaurants and bars, a private beach, and a host of activities on offer from sailing and tennis to windsurfing. There's also a spa, fitness centre and dive base.

Shooting Star Lodge   BOUTIQUE HOTEL $$$

(Map p78; ☑0777 414166; www.shootingstarlodge.com; d US$200-315; 🍴@🛏) This small lodge has a beautiful location on a low cliff overlooking a quiet stretch of sand. It also has excellent service and cuisine. The impeccably decorated accommodation ranges from garden rooms to spacious sea-view cottages, and from beside the curved salt-water infinity pool steps lead straight down to the beach.

❶ Getting There & Away

Buses and dalla-dallas (route 117) run between Kiwengwa village and Zanzibar Town (Tsh 2500).

Pongwe

POP 1000

Pongwe's arc of sand is dotted with palm trees and about as close to the quintessential tropical paradise as you can get – it's at the far southern end of the more famous Kiwengwa beach.

★ **Pongwe Beach Hotel** HOTEL $$$
(☏ 0784 336181; www.pongwe.com; d US$210-230; P@☎≋♨) The unassuming Pongwe Beach Hotel has 20 bungalows among the palms on a deep arc of bleached white sand. Most rooms are sea facing (three are garden view), spacious and breezy, and deliberately have no air-con, no TV and not even glass in the windows to ensure you fully immerse yourself in this idyllic location.

Seasons Lodge LODGE $$$
(☏ 0776 107225; www.seasonszanzibar.com; s/d US$118/235; ☎≋) ✿ This delightful place has 10 rooms, with breezy coral stone bungalows set in a small patch of natural vegetation, each with louvre doors that open onto a deck overlooking the beach. The friendly (and slightly eccentric) owner ensures materials and supplies used are locally made, and only staff from the area are employed, which adds to the relaxed and welcoming atmosphere.

ⓘ Getting There & Away

Most buses and dalla-dallas between Zanzibar Town and Kiwengwa go via Pongwe. Dalla-dallas also run along the coast road between Matemwe and Chwaka via Pongwe and Kiwengwa.

Michamvi Peninsula

POP 2000

Lined with some of the most beautiful beaches on Zanzibar, this long bony finger of a peninsula stretches 10km north from the popular coastal villages of Paje and Bwejuu, separating the mangrove creeks of Chwaka Bay from the turquoise waters of the Indian Ocean.

🛏 Sleeping & Eating

Sagando Hostel HOSTEL $
(☏ 0773 193236; www.sagandohostel.com; s/d US$20/40) This amenable budget option has a handful of bungalows (some two-storey), most with a small veranda, set in a sandy garden. There's a Rastafarian vibe, friendly staff and a relaxed bar, and meals can be

JENGA

In Michamvi, watch for **Jenga** (www.jenga zanzibar.com), a social enterprise offering Zanzibari entrepreneurs a platform (both online and in-store) from which to sell handmade products. And what products they are: bags and clutches in colourful graphic fabrics, laptop cases made from kitesurfing sails, beaded bracelets, natural beauty products and more. The main Jenga shop is near Upendo and opposite The Rock.

arranged. The beach is a short walk away. Sagando is easily reached on foot from the bus stop at the end of the tarmac road in Michamvi village.

Kae Funk BUNGALOW $$
(☏ 0774 361768, 0777 021547; www.kaefunk. com; d US$70-100; @) This relaxed place has eight double rooms perched on a small cliff overlooking Chwaka Bay, with a breezy lounge-restaurant down on the sand below, imaginatively decorated with driftwood and flotsam. A large development next door means you can't see the sea, but Kae Funk's own beach bar a short walk away has excellent views, especially at sunset.

Ras Michamvi Beach Resort HOTEL $$
(☏ 0777 413434; www.rasmichamvi.com; d $120-140; ≋♨) Occupying one of the most scenic locations on the island at the tip of the peninsula, Ras Michamvi sits on a bluff with expansive views. Idyllic, deserted beaches flank both sides and can be accessed via steep staircases, although the views from the infinity pool are mesmerising enough.

★ **Upendo** HOTEL $$$
(☏ 0777 244492, 0777 770667; www.upendozanzibar. com; villa from US$250) Upendo offers luxurious villas and an excellent bar-restaurant (meals US$8 to US$25) that's also open to nonguests. Villas have between one and four bedrooms, with nice touches like coffee machines and fans inside large mosquito nets. Some villas are aimed at honeymooners, and there's an extra-large one for families. Also available are some simple *bandas* (thatched-roof huts).

Breezes Beach Club & Spa RESORT $$$
(☏ 0774 440883; www.breezes-zanzibar.com; d with half board US$250-450; ❋@☎≋) This luxurious hotel has well-appointed rooms,

some overlooking the sea, in traditionally styled two-storey buildings, surrounded by gardens. All rooms are the same size, but those upstairs have bigger balconies. Facilities include a library, gym and spa. Diving, boat trips and other activities can be arranged. Upgrade deals sometimes available to sister hotels Baraza (all-inclusive) and the Palms (luxury villas) next door.

Michamvi Sunset Bay RESORT $$$

(☑ 0777 878136; www.michamvi.com; d from US$240; ❋ 🖥 ☎) This small resort just north of Michamvi village has comfortable rooms in two-storey buildings set in gardens with direct access to the beach. There's also a pool, spa, restaurant and bar with a deck, which – unusually for Zanzibar's east coast – offers great sunset views over the water.

★ The Rock SEAFOOD $$$

(☑ 0776 591360; www.therockrestaurantzanzibar. com; meals Tsh15,000-30,000; ⊙10am-10pm) Zanzibar's most photogenic restaurant is perched on a coral outcrop in a stunning location surrounded by sea. At low tide you can walk to it; at other times (maybe after a long lunch) boats are provided. Of course, you're paying for the location, but the food is good and unsurprisingly includes prawns, lobster, crab, fish and other seafood.

The Rock is just off Kijiweni beach, opposite Upendo (villas and restaurant) about halfway between Michamvi and Bwejuu. Reservations recommended.

ⓘ Getting There & Away

Dalla-dallas and buses (route 340) travel regularly between Zanzibar Town and Michamvi Kae village (at the tip of the peninsula) via Paje and Bwejuu. There's also at least one dalla-dalla daily between Michamvi Kae and Makunduchi, via Jambiani.

Bwejuu

POP 2000

The elongated village of Bwejuu sits between the beach and the main tarmac road between Paje and Michamvi. It's generally a quiet place, nicely shaded by palms, with a classic east-coast vista of searing white sand and turquoise sea.

🛏 Sleeping & Eating

★ Mustapha's Place BUNGALOW $

(☑ 024-224 0069, 0772 099422; www.mustaphas place.com; d US$65, with shared bathroom US$45,

dm from US$20; ☎) Mustapha's has a relaxed Rastafarian atmosphere, creatively decorated rooms and a dorm, all in a large leafy compound, which also has a bar-restaurant, breezy upstairs chill area, and a swimming pool in the shape of Africa. Staff can assist with beach activities, bike rental, local walks, drumming lessons and other diversions.

Fontaine Garden Village BUNGALOW $

(☑ 0777 709353, 0714 902618; www.fontainegarden village.com; d bungalow US$40, with shared bathroom US$35, d hotel room US$45-55) In a garden compound set back about 200m from the beach, in a quiet part of the village (not that anywhere in Bwejuu is noisy), you can choose one of the palm-thatched bungalows with shared bathroom, or go for an en-suite hotel room. There's a circular bar-restaurant where strangely ornate chairs are a notable feature.

★ Bellevue Guesthouse GUESTHOUSE $$

(☑ 0777 209576; www.bellevuezanzibar.com; d from US$80; 🖥 ☎) Bellevue is deservedly popular for its efficient management and laid-back atmosphere. Set in lush gardens on high ground overlooking the sea, rooms are in bungalows decorated in local style, and have their own veranda (or try the open-sided jungle room). The food – including Swahili specials – is excellent. Also on offer are tours and excursions, ranging from kitesurfing to crab-catching.

Palm Beach Inn BUNGALOW $$

(www.facebook.com/PalmBeachInnZanzibar; s/d US$60/80; 🖥 ☎ 🛗) One of the Bwejuu originals, Palm Beach has seen some changes over the years, but it's still the same relaxed and friendly place with a great connection to the surrounding village. Simple bungalows sit in a shady garden that looks straight onto the beach. There's also a small swimming pool and a great little restaurant, and boat trips can be arranged.

Upepo Boutique Beach
Bungalows BUNGALOW $$

(☑ 0784 619579; www.zanzibarhotelbeach.com; d US$65-70; 🖥) This neat, friendly place has a homey feel and spacious rooms in simple two-storey bungalows. All have a small terrace or veranda and views over the garden to the glorious beach. The thatched restaurant-bar serves pasta, curries and fish, along with jugs of sangria.

Kilimani Kwetu BUNGALOW $$

(☑ 0777 465243, 024-224 0235; www.kilimani.de; s/d US$50/70) Conceived as a community development project between a group of Germans and Bwejuu villagers, this small place has four simple rooms in two bungalows in sandy gardens. Managed by Wadi and his friendly team, there's good Swahili food in the restaurant, and it's a short walk to the beach (where the hotel has a simple cafe and a couple of thatched parasols).

Robinson's Place GUESTHOUSE $$

(☑ 0777 413479; www.robinsonsplace.net; d US$80, with shared bathroom US$40-60, s with shared bathroom US$30) 🍴 Run by Ann and Ahmed, inspired by *Robinson Crusoe,* this delightful guesthouse has simple and brightly styled rooms (with shared bathrooms), plus a two-storey house with upstairs rooms opening to the sea and the palms. There's no restaurant, but guests eat at other nearby hotels. It's on the beach at the northern end of Bwejuu.

Evergreen Bungalows BUNGALOW $$

(☑ 0784 408953; zanzievergreen@yahoo.com; d US$80; 🛜) This low-key locally run place is right on the beach with a collection of rustic bungalows; some are two storey, with upstairs rooms hotter in the day but cooler at night. There's a bar-restaurant, and all the usual local excursions and activities can be arranged.

ℹ Getting There & Away

Buses and dalla-dallas (route 324) run a few times daily between Zanzibar Town and Bwejuu (Tsh2500), and will drop you on the road, from where it's about 500m down to the beach.

Paje

POP 3500

Thanks to its wonderful beach of white sand and shallow waters, Paje has changed from a sleepy fishing village to a busy resort town with plenty of places to stay and a lively atmosphere. In recent years it has become very popular as a kitesurfing destination, to such an extent that it's sometimes hard to go for a swim.

🛏 Sleeping

Paje's hotels cater primarily to budget and midrange travellers. Most of the hotels clustered together on the beach near the main junction are geared to those wanting to be in the centre of the action; as you go north and south from here, the ambience becomes more tranquil.

★ Demani Lodge LODGE $

(☑ 0772 263115; www.demanilodge.com; dm/s/d US$20/38/50; 🛜⊠) Demani Lodge is a delightful budget option with neatly constructed cabins and bungalows. There's a seven-bed dorm and double rooms; some have private bathroom, others share a spotless shower block. Friendly management, clean rooms, big garden, hammocks, laundry, small pool and sociable bar make for instant success. The beach is a short walk away along a footpath.

New Teddy's Place BUNGALOW $

(☑ 0773 096306; www.teddys-place.com; dm US$22, s/d banda US$36/42, bungalow US$42/56; 🛜) Next door to (you guessed it) Original Teddy's Place, there's a choice of seven-bed or four-bed dorms, small *bandas* (thatched-roof huts) or larger bungalows circled around an open sandy area with a volleyball net. Day and night, most activity occurs in the large bar-restaurant. It's 100m to the beach, or you can relax on hammocks and sunloungers in the garden.

Summer Dream Lodge HOSTEL $

(☑ 0777 294809; www.summerdreamlodge.com; dm US$16, d US$55, with shared bathroom US$40; 🛜) Palm thatched is the word at this backpackers place. It's the main ingredient of a large dorm, several bungalows, and the bar-restaurant with chill zone on stilts so you can see the sunset. The cheap rooms have sand floors, all beds have nets, and it's a two-minute walk to the beach.

Original Teddy's Place HOSTEL $

(☑ 0778670576; www.originalteddys-place.com; dm US$18, d banda US$40; 🛜) After a few years of service, the original Teddy's is looking a little tired and scruffy, but that means simple accommodation at low prices. There's a dorm, some basic *bandas* and a friendly reggae vibe in the bar. It's next door to the separate New Teddy's Place.

Jambo Beach Bungalows BUNGALOW $

(☑ 0774 529960; www.jambobeachbungalows.com; dm from US$20, d US$50) Jambo's enviable beachfront location and laid-back atmosphere make up for its rather frayed palm-thatched bungalows. There's a dorm and double rooms with rustic wooden furniture, a mix of sand and concrete floors, fans and mosquito nets, plus a simple restaurant and beach bar, which is often the site of lively parties.

★**Airborne Kite &**
Surf Village TENTED CAMP **$$**
(☑ 0715 548464, 0776 687357; www.airbornekite
centre.com; d from US$100, tented d from US$90;
🛰) Closely linked to Airborne Kite Centre,
this delightful place has rooms in a large
house and safari tents (with private bath-
room), plus a tree house, all in a large gar-
den under shady trees. There's a very friendly
atmosphere, and evening parties and barbe-
cues are frequently arranged to polish off a
hard day's kiting.

Hotel on the Rock HOTEL **$$**
(☑ 0629 987902; www.hotelontherockzanzibar.
com; d small/large bungalow US$85/110; ❄ @)
South of Paje, in a very spacious garden on
a small slope overlooking the sea, are a few
bungalows; those lower down are bigger. A
major draw is the bar-restaurant, splendidly
positioned to look along the beach and out
to the blue horizon, while the menu tempts
with seafood grills and pasta dishes with a
Zanzibari twist.

Not to be confused with The Rock (p109),
a restaurant north of Paje on the Michamvi
Peninsula.

Mahali HOTEL **$$**
(☑ 0778 382915; www.mahalizanzibar.com; d
US$100-125; ❄ ⛵) The Mahali is packed tight
between other hotels on the central section
of beach, but once inside it's spacious, relax-
ing and very good quality. Rooms are neat
and uncluttered with spotless bathrooms,
all in small double-storey blocks around the
pool and terrace; those upstairs have balcony
and sea views (and cost more). Also available
are family rooms.

Cristal Resort HOTEL **$$**
(☑ 0777 875515; www.cristalresorts.com; d US$110-
130; 🛰 ⛵ ⛵) In a spacious sandy garden just
a few steps from the beach, this place has 'de-
lux' rooms in a concrete block, beach bungalows and 'eco' (wood and thatch) bungalows.
All rooms are clean and comfortable, but get
very warm thanks to sliding glass doors. The

ZANZIBAR ARCHIPELAGO PAJE

KITESURFING IN PAJE

Paje is Zanzibar's main kitesurfing centre. In fact it's one of Africa's best spots, attracting enthusiasts and beginners from all around the world. Reasons for this include the
constant and predictable onshore winds, the large flat-water lagoon between the beach
and the reef, a shallow and sandy sea bed (ideal for beginners), big waves on the reef (for
experts), warm water and the relative lack of seaweed farming. Oh yes, and because it's
simply beautiful.

Most kite centres rent equipment from around US$15 per hour or US$50 to US$100
per day, and offer a wide range of courses from around US$100 for a half-day beginner's
intro to around US$300 for a full-day's advanced training. There are also freelancing
locals on the beach who rent out kit at bargain prices, which is fine if you know what
you're doing.

Recommended outfitters include:

Kite Centre Zanzibar (www.kitecentrezanzibar.com) This IKO-accredited outfit has been
operating in Paje since 2006, with experienced instructors offering excellent courses
catering to all abilities, as well as kite rental and sales. Also available are downwinders
and longer trips, plus week-long package deals combining kiting with accommodation
in a nearby hotel or the affiliated Bellevue Guesthouse (p109) 5km up the coast (free
transfers).

Airborne Kite Centre (☑ 0715 548464; www.airbornekitecentre.com) Friendly and professional outfit offering IKO-accredited courses and private tuition for beginners to would-
be instructors. Equipment sales and rental. Full-moon and sundowner trips (followed by
a beach party) and downwinders are also available. Guests can stay in the associated
Airborne Kite & Surf Village.

You can also try **Aquaholics** (☑ 0776 897978; www.aquaholics-zanzibar.com), who actually
focus on surfing, but do kite-surfing as well, and **Paje by Kite** (www.pajebykite.net), who
have a wide range of courses, plus rentals and sales. If the activity above the water gets
too much, you can head for the depths with **Buccaneer Diving** (☑ 0777 853403; www.
buccaneerdiving.com; 1 dive US$56, with equipment US$77), a PADI five-star centre.

ZANZIBAR ARCHIPELAGO PAJE

SEEAWEED CENTER

While in Paje, don't miss a stop at the Seaweed Center (📞 0777 107248; www.seaweedcenter.com; tour US$10) ✐, the HQ of a local social enterprise that enables the women of Paje to harvest seaweed and then make a living by transforming it into desirable organic soaps, scrubs and essential oils (also involving cloves, coconut and local honey). Come here to shop or arrange a fascinating tour of the seaweed farms and processing centre. It's in the village centre and signposted off the tarmac road just north of the main junction.

restaurant is excellent. Staff are friendly and helpful, although service is little haphazard.

Kilima Kidogo   GUESTHOUSE $$
(📞 reservations +447817124725; www.kilimakidogo. com; d with garden/sea view US$95/100; ❄ 🛜 ≋ 🐾) South of the village, where the beach is quieter (although the sea still busy with kiters), relaxed and friendly Kilima Kidogo has 10 straightforward but colourful rooms in a building with a central courtyard, overlooking the flower-filled garden or the pool with the beach beyond. The bar-restaurant is right on the beach and has good food with vistas to match.

Kitete Beach Bungalows   HOTEL $$
(📞 0772 361010; www.kitete.com; s/d US$60/90; ❄ 🛜 ≋ 🐾) In a perfect spot on the beach, Kitete has 18 spacious rooms in double-storey bungalows with balconies or verandas giving ocean views, all set around a swimming pool and patio with chairs, parasols and sunloungers.

There are also a few triple rooms that are handy for families.

Paje by Night   LODGE $$
(📞 0777 880925; www.pajebynight.net; d bungalow US$80-110, d concept US$120; 🛜 ≋) Located in the centre of Paje, at heart of the action, this long-standing and deservedly popular place has well-appointed bungalows in the slightly crowded garden, plus some 'concept rooms' with quirky (and very non-Zanzibari) decor. There's a lively bar, relaxed lounge, Mondrian-inspired pool and a good restaurant, with meals including Swahili and Italian specialities (thanks to the on-site pizza oven).

Paradise Beach Bungalows   BUNGALOW $$
(📞 0777 414129, 0785 340516; http://nakama.main. jp/paradisebeachbungalows; d US$80; 🛜) This long-standing Japanese-run place is hidden among the palm trees in a quiet beachside compound at the northern edge of Paje, slightly removed from the main cluster of hotels. Rooms are in small thatched bungalows, which are a little cramped, but they all have a private veranda overlooking the beach where you'll be spending most of your time anyway.

Dhow Inn   HOTEL $$$
(📞 0777 525828; www.dhowinn.com; d with half board from US$200; ❄ 🛜 ≋ 🐾) With bungalows clustered around three pools, set amid gardens and palms, Dhow Inn is neat and stylish. In the rooms, beige-and-white interiors soothe heat-weary travellers, while other facilities include a bar-restaurant, kite storage and wash down, and a spa. It's a 100m walk to the beach, which may be a disadvantage for some but makes for a more peaceful ambience.

🍴 Eating & Drinking

Most of Paje's hotels have restaurants open to nonguests. Paje has a lively nightlife, centred on the various hotel beach bars. They cooperate to ensure that on every night one of them puts on a party, usually with music and a small admission cost.

Patterns vary with the season, so simply ask around to find out where the night's action is happening.

★ Mr Kahawa   CAFE $$
(www.facebook.com/mr.kahawa; snacks & lunches Tsh8000-14,000; ☺ 8.30am-5pm; 🛜 ✐) After a hard morning's kitesurfing, or maybe after a hard night's partying, this is the place for a top-notch espresso or cappuccino, accompanied by a sweet pancake, savoury wrap, panini, juice or salad. It's cool, stylish and in a fantastic position on the beach, so is understandably popular, meaning service can be a little slow at busy times.

Kinazi Upepo   INTERNATIONAL $$
(📞 0776 087780; www.kinaziupepobeachhotel. com; mains Tsh12,000-25,000; ☺ 10am-11pm; 🛜) In a wooden cabin with great views of the beach and ocean, this local place offers all the favourites – pizza, burgers, curries, seafood grills – plus Thai and sushi specials, in a straightforward and slightly old-fashioned ambience.

❶ Getting There & Away

Paje is located at the junction of the main road along the southeast coast and the road to/from Zanzibar Town.

Dalla-dallas and buses (Tsh2500) run several times daily between Paje and Zanzibar Town. Those between Zanzibar Town and Jambiani or Bwejuu stop here, too. Paje is also on the bus route between Makunduchi and Michamvi.

Private taxis between Zanzibar Town and Paje cost about US$30, and it's around US$10 in a private shared minibus.

Jambiani

POP 8000

Jambiani is a long village stretching over several kilometres on a stunning stretch of coastline and one of the best places on the island to gain an insight into local life. The village itself (actually several villages grouped together as Jambiani) is a sunbaked collection of palm-thatched huts and the sea is an ethereal shade of turquoise – even by Zanzibar standards – dotted with fishing boats, while on the beach women tend seaweed farms.

🛏 Sleeping

★**Mango Beach House**   GUESTHOUSE $
(☑0773 498949, 0773 827617; www.mango-beach house.com; s/d from US$35/50; ☎📶🏊) With only three bedrooms and an open-plan living area like a lounge on the beach, Mango Beach House is a small and sociable place. Rooms are simple but neat with artful decor and colourful fabrics, while the garden has daybeds and driftwood furniture. The attached **Kiddo's Cafe** is excellent (though meals need advance ordering) and attracts nonguests from nearby hotels.

Jambiani Beach Hotel   HOTEL $
(☑0778 064891, 0629 224522; www.jambiani-beach.com; d US$70-90; ☎📶) In a great position overlooking the ocean, Jambiani Beach Hotel has rooms in bungalows set back slightly from the beach, while the bar and restaurant under large thatched roofs are just a few steps from the sand and sea. In some of the larger bungalows, extra beds can be added to make them family rooms.

Al Hapa Hotel   HOTEL $
(☑0773 048894, 0772 190901; www.alhapazanzi bar.com; s/d US$60/75) A simple place consisting of five beachside bungalows, a two-storey house and a large beach bar. Rooms have bright yellow walls, firm beds and kanga curtains, and all are equipped with mosquito nets, fans and hot water.

★**Zanzistar Guesthouse**   GUESTHOUSE $$
(☑0774 440792; www.zanzi-star.com; d US$70-80, family house US$220; ☎) A new addition to Jambiani's hotel scene, Zanzistar is simply delightful. Small size and attentive management makes it feel homey and exclusive at the same time. Rooms have cool and uncluttered decor, and some have their own small private garden shaded by palms and banana trees, while the cheerful restaurant-bar (with occasional live music) attracts guests from nearby hotels.

★**Red Monkey Lodge**   HOTEL $$
(☑0777 713366; www.redmonkeylodge.com; d US$95-130; ☎) ❂ At the far southern end of Jambiani village, Red Monkey is a small hotel with around 10 spacious rooms – some in bungalows, others in a two-storey building – overlooking the beautiful beach. If you're feeling lazy, there are hammocks dotted about and a shady outdoor bar-restaurant. If you're feeling energetic, bike hire, kitesurfing and other activities can be arranged.

Nur Beach Hotel   HOTEL $$
(www.nur-zanzibar.com; d US$85; ☎🏊) Relaxed, unfussy, cool, stylish. The Nur is this and more. Rooms are in two lines of thatched bungalows; they're straightforward and not massive but spotlessly clean, all with small private veranda overlooking the infinity pool just a few steps away from the beach. There's a large open-plan bar and restaurant area, with colourful sofas for lounging during the day.

JAMBIANI ECO INITIATIVES

Coastal erosion and declining fish populations in the Jambiani area have prompted cooperation between Jamabeco (Jambiani Marine & Beach Conservation) and Marine Cultures (www.marinecultures.org) to promote conservation, create an artificial reef, and explore new aquaculture projects such as sponge and sea-cucumber farms. With support and sustained education Jambiani will hopefully be able to pioneer more sustainable fishing and tourism practices, which will ultimately benefit the island as a whole.

MWAKA KOGWA

A four-day festival in Makunduchi, **Mwaka Kogwa** is usually held in late July. It's a distinctly Zanzibari event and thought to originate in Zoroastrianism. During the festivities villagers have mock battles, with men symbolically beating one another with banana leaves to settle old scores and start afresh.

The event's highlight is the ceremonial burning of a palm-thatched house (built for the occasion), and everything ends with a large feast accompanied by drumming, music and dancing.

Blue Oyster Hotel
HOTEL **$$**

(☎ 0779 883554, 0783 045796; www.blueoysterhotel.com; s US$50-125, d US$100-200; P 🛜 🛗) Personable and professional, Blue Oyster offers good-value and high-quality accommodation on the beach. Rooms are furnished in local style in two-storey villas; some overlook the garden, others overlook the sea (and tend to cost more). The open-air terrace restaurant serves excellent meals, including Swahili specials like coconut curry and mango kingfish.

Jambiani Guesthouse
GUESTHOUSE **$$**

(www.zanzibar-guesthouse.com; d US$50, house US$150-200) Blink and you might miss this tiny guesthouse with its sandy front yard and just five simple double rooms. There are two external bathrooms, and one of the rooms has its own private facilities. Rooms can be rented individually or you can have the entire house – ideal for groups (sleeps seven to 10 people).

Garden Beach Bungalows
BUNGALOW **$$**

(www.facebook.com/gardenbeachbungalow; d US$100-120; 🛜) A collection of thatched-roof bungalows with veranda located right on the beach, with a choice of compact ocean-view rooms or more spacious garden rooms. There is also a restaurant serving Turkish specialities.

Coral Rock
HOTEL **$$**

(☎ 0776 031955; www.coral-rock.com; r US$100-150; ❄ 🛜 🖥 🛗) This aptly named hotel sits on a low coral cliff jutting into the sea at the southern end of Jambiani. Spacious bungalows have smart furnishings, and there's a gorgeous swimming pool, while the cliff edge overlooking the beach is dotted with small decks, hammocks and sunloungers. A major plus is the hotel's affinity with the local village and natural surroundings.

Casa del Mar Hotel
HOTEL **$$**

(☎ 0777 455446; www.casadelmar-zanzibar.com; d US$100-130; 🖥 🛗) Casa del Mar brings a dash of colour and design to Jambiani with 14 rooms in two double-storey houses set amid tropical gardens just a few short steps from the beach. Hotel management aims to work closely with the local community: most furniture and artworks were made in Jambiani and many of the staff come from the village.

Sea View Lodge
BOUTIQUE HOTEL **$$$**

(☎ 0777 729393; www.seaviewlodgezanzibar.com; d US$170; ❄ 🛜 🖥 🛗) Small, neat and stylish, Sea View Lodge has just 10 rooms in bungalows (five facing the beach, five set back in the garden) and a calm professional air. Most rooms are doubles, and there are some larger family rooms. Decor combines Swahili and Italian aspects, as does the menu – so choose octopus in coconut or *spaghetti al granchio* (spaghetti with crab).

🍴 Eating

Most of the hotels and lodges have restaurants open to nonguests. Jambiani also has a lively local scene, with simple eating houses offering tasty dishes at very reasonable prices; these places tend to come and go, so the best way to see what's available is to stroll around during the day then make a booking for the evening.

Kim's Restaurant
ZANZIBARI **$**

(☎ 0777 457733; meals Tsh5000-15,000; ⏰ 11am-9pm) Dig your toes into the sandy floor of this palm-thatched local eatery and tuck into simple but tasty local meals like grilled fish and octopus curry. Everything runs in a leisurely manner, so order in advance and with time to spare. Kim's is signposted from the easily located Blue Oyster Hotel.

ℹ️ Getting There & Away

Dalla-dalla 309 runs several times daily between Zanzibar Town and Jambiani (Tsh2500). Buses between Makunduchi and Michamvi also stop here. Jambiani village sits between the tarmac road and the sea; all public transport uses the tarmac road, from where it's about 500m to 1km down to the beach.

Makunduchi

POP 10,000

Makunduchi is a small town at the far southeastern end of Zanzibar Island with a deep sense of history and culture. In the surrounding area are ancient shrines, coral caves, a lighthouse built in the colonial days and reputedly the largest baobab tree on the island.

On the scenic beach, local fishers launch boats and bring in the catch as they have for generations. Meanwhile, in the town centre, about 1km inland, the 1970s Soviet-style apartment blocks are not at all scenic but remind of Tanzania's post-independence socialist era.

To visit the various historic and cultural sites a local guide is recommended. This can be arranged though ZALA Park (p99) at the village of Muungoni about 20km from Makunduchi.

The only place to stay is **La Madrugada Beach Hotel** (☏ 0777 423331; www.sansibarurlaub.de; d US$98; ❋ 🛜 🚗).

Buses and dalla-dallas (route 310) run between Zanzibar Town and Makunduchi. Dalla-dallas also run between Makunduchi and Michamvi, along the east coast via Jambiani and Paje.

During the Mwaka Kogwa festival, there's plenty of additional transport from Zanzibar Town and many other parts of Zanzibar Island. Most tourists come to see the festival on a day trip organised by a hotel or tour company.

Kizimkazi

POP 5000

At the southern tip of Zanzibar Island, Kizimkazi would be just another sleepy fishing village if it weren't for the local dolphins that frolic offshore becoming a major tourist attraction. Most days visitors from all over Zanzibar come here to take a boat ride across the clear blue waters of Menai Bay to see the dolphins.

Arranged via local hotels, prices for dolphin-watching trips start from US$25 per person with reputable operators. Local beach boys and taxi drivers also organise boat trips, but use responsible operators who follow appropriate codes of conduct, both for your safety and the dolphins' well-being.

Kizimkazi's other claim to fame is its **old mosque**. Although it is thought to be one of the oldest Islamic buildings on the East African coast, the mosque has been extensively restored and appears relatively modern on the outside. However, on the inside are inscriptions (in Kufic and Arabic) dating from 1107 and 1770. The mosque is just north of the main beach area in Kizimkazi Dimbani. If you want to take a look, ask permission and (if you're non-Muslim) get a local to accompany you. As in all mosques, you should

---

WATCHING THE DOLPHINS

Dolphin-watching trips are a great way for local people to earn income from a natural resource, and help prevent dolphin hunting (an activity that used to occur here). But such is Kizimkazi's popularity that it can be very crowded out on the water sometimes, with a large number of boats literally chasing the animals at high speed (something that is not responsible or ethical behaviour).

Ramming and blocking is not uncommon, and some boats keep their propellers running, which can injure dolphins.

In addition, many operators encourage guests to jump in and 'swim with the dolphins', which may also injure or cause stress for the dolphins, and (more practically) mainly just scares them away.

If you want to enjoy Kizimkazi's dolphins, be happy with just seeing them, possibly at a distance. Ideally, go early or late in the day, with a reputable captain who will allow you to see the dolphins without disturbing them.

Be wary of tour operators claiming 'eco' credentials; many local boatmen flout any guidelines for responsible activity.

Consider the following points, based on advice from Whale & Dolphin Conservation (http://uk.whales.org/), and ensure your operator agrees to them before booking:

➡ Do not chase dolphins.

➡ Do not get too close to dolphins.

➡ Keep boat engines in neutral wherever possible.

➡ Never try to swim with or touch dolphins, for your safety and theirs.

take off your shoes and cover up bare shoulders or legs.

🛏 Sleeping & Eating

Kizimkazi consists of two separate settlements: Kizimkazi Mkunguni (also called Kizimkazi Mtendeni), where most of the boat trips depart, and smaller Kizimkazi Dimbani to the north. There's a couple of accommodation options here, with more hotels dotted down the coast to the southeast.

Little David Lodge
LODGE $

(0689 218217; www.littledavid-zanzibar.com; Kizimkazi Mkunguni; d US$40) This simple place has a few rooms in a small compound between the road and the beach in Kizimkazi Mkunguni. For those arriving by public transport it's the easiest place to reach. Good honest meals are available in the attached Mama Lucia Restaurant (Tsh12,000 to Tsh16,000).

Dolphin Safari Lodge
LODGE $$

(0774 007360; www.dolphin-safari-lodge.com; Kizimkazi Mkunguni; d from US$50; 🖥 🛜) Lowkey, peaceful, friendly and well-managed, this small lodge overlooks a quiet beach about 1km southeast of Kizimkazi Mkunguni. Rooms are in bungalows or palm-thatched huts with safari-tent-style zipped doors. There's a simple bar-restaurant with beautiful sea views. The owners hire and train local people to work in the hotel, and operate responsible dolphin- and whale-spotting trips.

Promised Land
LODGE $$

(0779 909168; www.promisedlandlodge.com; Kizimkazi Mkunguni; s/d US$38/60; 🛜 🖥 🛜) Tucked away on the coast, southeast of Kizimkazi Mkunguni, this is a little gem of a place, with a Caribbean vibe and rooms in simple thatched huts. The garden has hammocks but few big trees, so there isn't much shade, but it's no hardship to spend the day lounging under a parasol or in the airy bar-restaurant-lounge overlooking the sea.

Karamba
LODGE $$

(0773 166406; www.karambaresort.com; Kizimkazi Dimbani; d US$75-120; 🛜 🖥 🛜) Karamba, on the northern end of Kizimkazi Dimbani, has around 20 rooms of different sizes in whitewashed cottages along a small cliff overlooking the sea. Steps lead down to the beach, and the hotel has a pool. Diving, cycling, kayaking and other activities can be arranged, or you can simply relax and enjoy the ocean view from the bar-restaurant.

★ Unguja Lodge
LODGE $$$

(0774 477477; www.ungujalodge.com; Kizimkazi Mkunguni; s/d with half board from US$280/500; 🛜 🖥 🛜) 🌿 Set in a patch of forest, this secluded luxury lodge has 10 villas with high thatched roofs and curved walls reminiscent of seashells. They're impeccably decorated and many have sea views (including from the shower). Add the private beach, infinity pool, dive centre and excellent restaurant, and it's easy to see why this place is regularly booked out.

🛈 Getting There & Away

To reach Kizimkazi from Zanzibar Town take bus or dalla-dalla 326. The fare is Tsh2500.

Alternatively, take Makunduchi bus 310 as far as Kufile junction, then wait for another vehicle or walk to Kizimkazi (about 5km). At the next fork, go right to Kizimkazi Dimbani or left to Kizimkazi Mkunguni.

Fumba & Menai Bay

Fumba is a small village at the end of a long peninsula, about 15km south of Zanzibar Town. There's a beach, a few fishing boats and a spectacular view across Menai Bay towards the sleepy village of Unguja Ukuu. The main reason most visitors come to Fumba is to join one of the dhow trips operated by Safari Blue (p117).

Fumba Beach Lodge
HOTEL $$$

(0778 919525; www.fumbabeachlodge.com; Fumba; s/d from US$180/280; 🅿 🛜) Set on a secluded peninsula, Fumba Beach Lodge has 26 spacious cottages set in expansive grounds, with some overlooking the sea (about US$15 per person extra) producing an ambience that's a great mix of safari camp and beach hotel. There's a bar-restaurant area around a small swimming pool with a terrace overlooking the beach and Menai Bay beyond.

The beach itself isn't picture-perfect and has a considerable amount of coral rock, but the setting is beautiful and uncrowded. The hotel also has a spa and dive centre.

Menai Beach Bungalows
BUNGALOW $$

(0777 772660; www.visitzanzibar.se; Unguja Ukuu; d US$60; 🖥) On a broad beach among palms and mangroves, Menai Beach Bungalows offers a unique opportunity to see a corner of the island so far unaffected by tourism. Comfortable, whitewashed rooms open onto the sand, hammocks rock in the breeze and

MENAI BAY

Menai Bay lies on the southwest side of Zanzibar Island between the tip of the Fumba Peninsula and the southern tip of Zanzibar Island near Kizimkazi. Within this area, and extending out to sea beyond the bay itself to include many offshore islands and sandbanks, is the **Menai Bay Conservation Area**. At 470 sq km, this is Zanzibar's largest protected marine environment and is home to an impressive assortment of corals, mangroves, fish, dolphins and other marine wildlife. **Safari Blue** (☑ 0777 423162; www.safariblue.net; Fumba; adult/child $65/35) is a tour company that organises just one main activity: day trips on beautiful traditional dhows around Menai Bay. Each dhow carries about 20 people, and each trip includes swimming, snorkelling (equipment provided), seafood lunch on a remote island beach and time to relax on a sandbank. It's a great activity for families (kids under six years go free).

each evening seafood bought from the local fishers makes its way to the barbecue.

ℹ Getting There & Away

Fumba is easily reached by dalla-dalla from Zanzibar Town. The terminus is the end of the tarmac road just a few metres from the beach.

PEMBA

☑ 024 / POP 450,000

Pemba's terrain is hilly and lushly vegetated, while much of the coast is lined with mangroves and lagoons, interspersed with idyllic beaches and islets. Offshore, coral reefs offer some of East Africa's best diving.

Throughout, Pemba remains largely 'undiscovered', and you'll still have most things to yourself, which is a big part of the island's appeal.

For much of its history, Pemba has been overshadowed by Zanzibar Island, its larger neighbour to the south. Although the islands are separated by only 50km of sea, relatively few tourists cross the channel. Those who do, however, are seldom disappointed.

ℹ Information

OPENING HOURS

Shops & Businesses 8am to noon or 3pm Monday to Saturday; many shops and businesses close for a few minutes around 1pm so the men can visit the mosque for prayers. In towns and larger villages, some shops open again from 7pm–9pm. Outside Chake Chake there's not much open anywhere on Sundays.

ℹ Getting There & Away

AIR

Pemba's main airport is **Pemba-Karume Airport** (PMA), 6km east of Chake Chake. ZanAir (www.

zanair.com), Coastal Aviation (www.coastal.co.tz) and Auric Air (www.auricair.com) offer daily flights to/from Dar es Salaam (US$140) via Zanzibar Island (US$95). Flights to/from Tanga are also possible with Coastal (US$100) and Auric (US$65).

BOAT

Pemba's main port is at Mkoani, at the southern end of the island. All ferries to/from Zanzibar and Dar es Salaam dock here. Most reliable are the Sealink roll-on, roll-off car and passenger ferries, operated by Azam Marine (p97).

On Pemba, tickets can be purchased at Azam Marine's office at the port in Mkoani, as well as at various travel agents in Chake Chake and Wete.

Another option is the government-operated *Mapinduzi* ferry, which goes twice weekly in each direction between Pemba and Zanzibar. The fare is US$25, but the service is slow and unreliable.

Dhows sail between Wete (in the northwest of Pemba) and Tanga and Mombasa, but foreigners are prohibited.

If you come by boat from Zanzibar Island, mainland Tanzania or Kenya, you'll need to go to the immigration office at the port to get your passport and visa checked.

ℹ Getting Around

BICYCLE

Renting a bike makes sense on Pemba because several sights are off the main public transport routes, and the roads have relatively light motor traffic.

Many hotels on the coast have bikes for rent (around US$10 per day) so you can explore the surrounding area. For longer jaunts, don't forget that Pemba is a hilly place!

BUS & DALLA-DALLA

Buses and dalla-dallas (pick-up truck or minibus) cover the main routes between towns and villages. Over the past few years, many of Pemba's roads have been tarred, and some completely new roads constructed, which has

Pemba

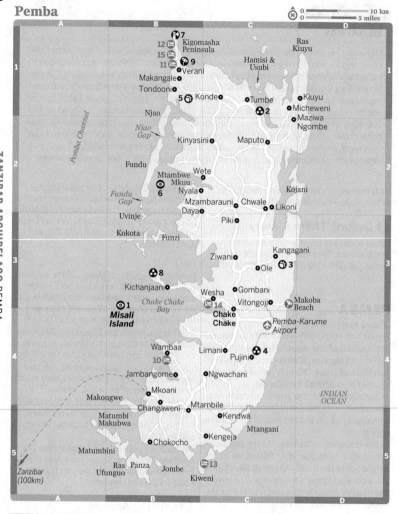

Pemba

improved comfort if not journey times. Sample routes, fares and durations include Chake Chake to Mkoani (Tsh2000, one to 1½ hours) and Chake Chake to Wete (Tsh2000, 1½ to two hours).

CAR & MOTORCYCLE

Renting a self-drive car to get around Pemba is unusual, but may be possible via hotels and tour companies in the main towns. Much easier is to hire a car with driver – also via hotels and tour companies, or ask around at a taxi rank. Expect to pay US$50 to US$70 per day; it's usually easier for both parties if you pay for fuel separately. All hotels across Pemba have parking.

Motorbikes can be hired via Coral Tours in Chake Chake (advance notice required).

Chake Chake

POP 30,000

Chake Chake is the capital of Pemba. Often called simply 'Chake', it's an appealingly scruffy place with a busy centre of shops and market stalls.

Sights are limited, and the nearest beach is at Makoba (7km to the east), so Chake Chake is mainly used by visitors as a transport hub and starting block for deeper exploration on Pemba.

◉ Sights & Activities

ZSTC Clove Oil Distillery   FACTORY
(tours Tsh5000; ⊙8am-3.30pm Mon-Fri) Pemba is well known for its clove industry, and this distillery is where the clove stems are turned into essential oil. It's operated by the Zanzibar State Trading Corporation (ZSTC) and also here on occasion are cinnamon leaves, eucalyptus leaves, lemongrass and sweet basil. The tour may be a little lackadaisical, but the process is fascinating. Go first to the office and small shop selling the finished product (yes, enter through the gift shop) and arrange a guide.

The distillery is in the suburb of Machomane, about 1km north of the town centre, east of the main road. You can take a dalla-

dalla to the junction then walk, or arrange a visit through a tour company.

Pemba Museum   MUSEUM
(US$3; ⊙8.30am-4.30pm Mon-Fri, 9am-4pm Sat & Sun) Filling an 18th-century Omani **fort**, which was probably built on the remains of a 16th-century Portuguese garrison, this small museum has well-organised (if a little dusty) displays on island history. You'll get a lot more out of your visit to the ruins at places like Ras Mkumbuu if you stop at the museum first.

Umoja Children's Park   AMUSEMENT PARK
(Tsh500; ⊙weekends & public holidays) This fairground was established in Pemba's socialist days, and completely renovated (a gift from China) in recent years. The gleaming big wheels and dodgem cars are an unexpected sight, but this place is understandably popular with the locals. It's open weekends, and on some religious festivals or public holidays. There's a small entry fee when the rides are operating, but at all other times wandering around is free. It's on the edge of town, on the road to Wesha.

Coral Tours   TOUR
(☑0777 437397; tours_travelpemba@yahoo.com; Main Rd; tours for 2 people half-/full-day from US$50/100; ⊙8am-5pm) Headed up by Nassor Haji, the charming and energetic manager, Coral Tours can fix you up with rental bikes (US$10 per day) or cars (US$50), or supply a vehicle and knowledgeable guide for tours (to nearby ruins, Misali Island, Ngezi Forest Reserve, or just about anywhere else on Pemba). Also on sale are ferry and plane tickets.

DON'T MISS

MISALI ISLAND

Surrounded by crystal waters and stunning coral reefs, **Misali** (US$5) offers some of the best diving in East Africa, while snorkelling is spectacular and easily reached from the beach. Around the island, nesting turtles favour beaches on the western side, while on the northeast coast is Baobab Beach, with fine sand and a small ranger centre.

The island is part of the **Pemba Channel Conservation Area** (PECCA; www. pembaprojects.org/pembachannel.html; US$5), which covers Pemba's entire west coast. All divers, snorkellers and beachgoers here must pay the admission fee. There are no permanent settlements, though the island is in active use by local fishers, and camping is not permitted for tourists. Inland from the beaches are caves, believed to be inhabited by the spirits of ancestors.

You can get to Misali by arranging a boat from Wesha, but it's easier, and not much more expensive, to arrange excursions through hotels or travel agencies. Expect to pay about US$50 per person (depending on group size), including lunch and entry fees.

Chake Chake

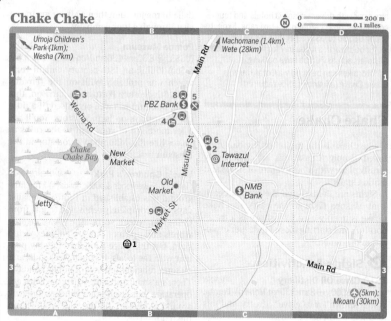

🛏 Sleeping & Eating

Hotel Archipelago HOTEL $$
(formerly Hifadhi Hotel; ☎0777 254777; www.
hotelarchipelagopemba.com; Wesha Rd; s/d
US$50/70; ❋🛜❄) With its austere stairwells
and utilitarian furniture (including inventory numbers) the Archipelago has the air of a
government rest house – which it was – but
now it's privately run and the best hotel in
town. Rooms are clean and tidy with fridge,
TV and tea-/coffee-making facilities, while
staff are friendly and efficient.

Pemba Misali Beach RESORT $$
(☎central reservations 0777 470278; www.ocean
grouphotel.com; Wesha Rd; s/d US$80/120;
❋@🛜) 🌊 Out amid the mangroves, 7km
from Chake Chake and reached by an impressively long jetty, this resort has functional rooms in a row of bungalows on a small
white-sand beach. On a small pier, the restaurant serves international and local food
(mains Tsh8000 to Tsh16,000), with a great
view over the water towards the eponymous
Misali Island in the distance.

Pemba Island Hotel HOTEL $$
(☎0777 490041; pembaisland@gmail.com; Wesha
Rd; s/d US$40/60; ❋🛜) Above a row of shops
on the main road, at first glance this hotel is
unappealing, but once inside the rooms are
clean with TV, mosquito nets and hot water.
Be sure to abide by the rules painted on the
wall by the entrance stairs.

Ahaabna TANZANIAN $
(Main Rd; meals Tsh5000-6000; ⊙6-8pm) Located on the top floor of a modern concrete
building, reached by an anonymous staircase, this no-frills restaurant serves evening
meals, usually with just one option on the

menu, such as rice with chicken or fish. If you plan to eat here, it's worth checking in advance during the day.

❶ Information

The main banks in Chake Chake are **NMB** (Main Rd) and **PBZ** (Main Rd); both have ATMs but these don't accept non-Tanzanian cards, and changing money inside the bank itself is a very slow process.

You can change US dollars into local currency at a large hotel, or ask at large shops selling imported (especially electrical) items.

To get on-line, try **Tawazul Internet** (Main Rd; per hour Tsh1000; ⊙8am-9pm).

For medical emergencies, the privately run **Dira Hospital** (☑ 0777 424418; Wete Rd; ⊙7am-9pm) is out in the suburb of Machomane.

❶ Getting There & Away

There's a transport stand near the old market, but most people go to the main junction near the petrol station and wait there for a dalla-dalla going in the right direction.

Dalla-dallas to Mkoani (Tsh2000, 1½ hours) leave from near Coral Tours. Dalla-dallas to Wete (Tsh1500, 1½ hours) and Konde (Tsh2000, two hours) depart from near PBZ bank, while to Wesha (Tsh500, 30 minutes) they go from the top of Wesha Rd.

A taxi between town and the airport costs about US$10. For longer trips, expect to pay around US$40 to Mkoani and US$70 to the hotels on the Kigomasha Peninsula.

Mkoani

POP 20,000

Although it's Pemba's major port, Mkoani has eschewed all attempts at development and remains a small and uneventful town. Many visitors arrive here on the boat from Zanzibar Island.

🛏 Sleeping & Eating

Lala Lodge   GUESTHOUSE $$
(☑0777 111624; www.lalalodgepemba.com; d US$60; ❋) This delightful place has an airy upstairs seating area with views across the bay, and just two rooms available. It's clean, neat and tidy, and right on the beach in the part of town by the fish market, which is either scruffy or authentic depending on your attitude. Kayaks are available for guests (free), and boat trips and diving can be arranged.

It's about 750m southwards from the port. To get here, turn right out of the port gates and follow the dirt road through the huts, keeping the sea on your right.

ZANZIBAR ARCHIPELAGO MKOANI

EXPLORING AROUND CHAKE CHAKE

If you're staying in Chake Chake, there are a number of interesting sights within easy reach by either bicycle or taxi. Coral Tours (p119) in Chake can help arrange the logistics.

Mkame Ndume Ruins The ruined palace of Mohammed bin Abdul Rahman, who ruled Pemba prior to the arrival of the Portuguese (late 15th to early 16th centuries), is an evocative spot. Rahman had a reputation for cruelty and was known as Mkame Ndume (Milker of Men). Today the ruins' primary feature is a large stone staircase that led from the kilometre-long channel (now dry) connecting this site to the ocean.

The ruins are 10km southeast of Chake Chake, near the village of Pujini. Dalla-dallas from Chake Chake to Pujini (Tsh1000, one hour) are infrequent and the ruins are poorly signposted. A taxi from Chake Chake costs about Tsh30,000 return. Or rent a bike; head south of Chake Chake, past the airport road then turn left (southeast) onto the dirt road by a sign that says 'Skuli Ya Chan Jaani'.

Ras Mkumbuu Ruins (adult/student US$5/3) Ras Mkumbuu is the headland at the end of the thin strip of land jutting into the sea northwest of Chake Chake. It's also the name given to the ruins of an ancient settlement, once called Qanbalu, dating from the 8th century, which by the early 10th century had become one of the major cities along the East African coast. The main ruins, consisting of a large mosque, some tombs and houses, date from around the 14th century, and several walls are still standing.

Ras Mkumbuu is about 10km from Chake Chake. Dalla-dallas run as far Wesha but after that transport is erratic, and you may have to walk. Other options are taxi or rented bike, or a boat from Wesha.

Zanzibar Ocean Panorama GUESTHOUSE $$

(⌂ 0777 870401; www.oceanpanorama-zanzibar. com; s/d US$35/70; ❄) The welcoming and aptly named Ocean Panorama is on a hill with great views over the sea. Rooms are basic but clean, with a small terrace. The manager, Mohammed (known as Eddie Prince), is a great source of local info and can set you up with tours, boat trips, snorkelling and diving at reasonable prices.

Meals are available (from Tsh10,000) if pre-booked. The guesthouse is in the area of Mkoani called Jondeni; when exiting the port, head north (keep the sea to your left) and walk 750m up the hill.

Emerald Bay Hotel HOTEL $$$

(⌂ 0789 759698; www.emeraldbay.co.tz; Chokocho village; d with full board US$200; ☎ ❄ ♨) ✈ About 9km south of Mkoani, the charming Emerald has seven comfortable rooms overlooking a neat garden and pool, with a view to the sea beyond. The low-key friendly atmosphere is enhanced by the relatively remote location. It's a short walk to the nearest beach, and boat trips to quieter locations on nearby islands and sandbanks are included in the rate.

Emerald takes great pride in its relationship with the local village, funding several community projects, and in return asks guests to behave and dress conservatively when outside the hotel grounds. There's no public transport, but transfers to/from Mkoani can be arranged.

Fundu Lagoon LODGE $$$

(⌂ reception 0774 438668, reservations +44 7561 366593; www.fundulagoon.com; d full board US$880-980; ☉ Jun-Apr; ☎ ✉) Luxurious and exclusive, Fundu has rooms in large tents under palm-thatched roofs to create a beach lodge with a safari feel. Rooms are on the hillside with a great view, or on the beach with a small private deck. The restaurant overlooks the infinity pool with the ocean beyond, and the jetty bar is the obvious place for sundowners.

ℹ Information

If you come by boat from Zanzibar Island, mainland Tanzania or Kenya, you'll need to go to the immigration office at the port to get your passport and visa checked.

There is a bank in Mkoani, but the ATM doesn't accept non-Tanzanian cards. To change US dollars into local currency, ask discreetly at any shop selling imported goods.

The best health centre in Mkoani, and indeed all Pemba, is **Abdalla Mzee Hospital** (⌂ 0778 161246; Chake Chake road, Uweleni).

ℹ Getting There & Away

Buses and dalla-dallas run regularly to Chake Chake (Tsh1500, one hour) from in front of the port. You can also get buses to Wete (Tsh3000, two hours) and Konde (Tsh3500, 2½ hours) via Chake Chake, but these run more occasionally. To save waiting you're usually better off getting something to Chake and changing there for your onward journey.

Kiweni

This remote and tranquil island just off Pemba's southeastern coast is surrounded by mangroves and long stretches of sand. At its southern end is **Pemba Lodge** (⌂ 0777 415551, reservations 024-224 0494; www.pembalodge.com; per person full board US$120; ☎ ❄) ✈, which provides a truly off-the-beaten-track experience. Overlooking the empty beach and ocean beyond are just five rooms in bungalows raised on wooden decks. There's also a restaurant-lounge where friendly staff serve meals, including seafood brought by local fishers. Activities include kayaking, snorkelling and walks to the village.

At the other end of the island is the village of Kiweni, separated from mainland Pemba by a 2km stretch of water.

The island is occasionally marked as Shamiani on some maps.

Locals reach Kiweni village by boat from a landing point about 2km south of the village of Kengeja, which is about 15km directly south of Chake Chake. Guests at Pemba Lodge are transferred by private boat from a tiny beach, hidden among the mangroves, about 1km south of Kengeja.

Wete

POP 20,000

The sleepy town of Wete is on the northwest coast of Pemba and is a good base for travellers to explore the north of the island. For locals, it's a port for boats to Kenya.

Hanging in trees just up from the port is a colony of Pemba flying foxes (a species of large bat usually found in forest areas). Despite their proximity to streets and houses, they remain undisturbed.

Wete

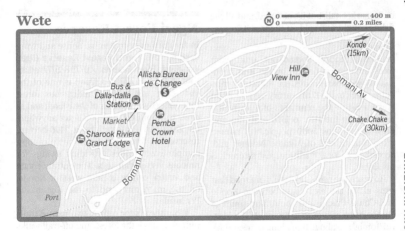

🛏 Sleeping & Eating

Hill View Inn GUESTHOUSE $
(📞0776 338366; hillviewinn@gmail.com; s/d US$20/35) This place is a little gem; simple but clean rooms with TV in the lounge, and a nice walled garden with banana trees and a couple of shaded seats. Meals and hot water are available, but both need to be arranged in advance. It's on the edge of the town centre, opposite the grim Soviet-style apartment blocks.

Pemba Crown Hotel HOTEL $
(📞0777 493667, 0773 336867; www.pembacrown. com; Bomani Ave; s/d from US$30/50; ❄️ 🛜) With balconies overlooking the main street, very near the market, mosque and bus station, you're certainly in the heart of things at the Crown. Rooms are fairly clean if dull, with mosquito nets. There's no restaurant, but a simple breakfast is provided.

Sharook Riviera Grand Lodge GUESTHOUSE $$
(📞0777 431012; www.pembaliving.com; s/d US$40/70; ❄️ 🛜) A long-time favourite for travellers in Wete, and now in an improved location, this place has simple rooms with mosquito nets. Mr Sharook the owner is friendly and can set you up with tours to Ngezi Forest Reserve and elsewhere on the island. Meals can be arranged, and there's a view of the bay from the rooftop restaurant.

ℹ Information

Wete has a bank, but the ATM does not accept non-Tanzanian cards. You can change money at **Allisha Bureau de Change** (Bomani Ave; ⏰8.30am-3.45pm Mon-Sat, 8.45am-12.30pm Sun).

ℹ Getting There & Away

There are two dalla-dalla routes between Wete and Chake Chake (Tsh1500, one to 1½ hours): route 606 uses the old road via Ziwani; route 607 uses the new road via Chwale. There are also frequent dalla-dallas between Wete and Konde (route 601; Tsh1500, one hour).

There's a direct bus from Wete via Chake to Mkoani (Tsh3000) timed to connect with the main ferry to/from Zanzibar Island. Departure times vary, so check in advance at the bus station.

All public transport leaves from the **bus and dalla-dalla station** next to the market in the town centre.

Tumbe

POP 4000

The large village of Tumbe lies on a sandy cove on the northern coast fringed by dense mangroves. On the edge of the village is a beach, but forget about parasols and pina coladas here; this is the site of Pemba's largest fish market, while nearby are the ancient Chwaka Ruins.

There's no accommodation in Tumbe or nearby Konde. Your nearest options are on the Kigomasha Peninsula or in Wete (from where Tumbe makes a good day-trip destination).

Tumbe Fish Market MARKET
Down on the beach beyond Tumbe village, the sands are covered in fishing boats and tackle, and lined with a motley collection of huts where fishers gather to pass the day or wait for the tides to turn. There is a newly

built market hall, but it's not used, and all the fish is bought and sold on the beach.

Chwaka Ruins   RUINS

(adult/child US$5/3) Spread out amid palm trees and cassava fields, Chwaka Ruins consist of two separate sites, the **Mazrui Tombs** dating back to the 17th century, and the main **Haruni Site** – the remnants of a town that existed from the 11th to 15th centuries and grew to perhaps 5000 people. It's named after Harun, son of Mkame Ndume and, according to local tradition, just as cruel as his father.

To reach the ruins, take the main road that runs along the east coast between Konde and Chake Chake, and about 3km south of Tumbe, turn east onto a dirt road. The Mazrui Tombs are about 1km along here, and it's another 1.5km to Haruni. The ruins alone may appeal only to keen historians, but this is also a lovely spot for a walk through the fields on a patch of high ground with views over the bay.

❶ Getting There & Away

Dalla-dallas travel on two routes between Chake Chake and Konde; those on the main road that runs up the east side of the island go past the junction for Tumbe (Tsh2000, two hours), from where it's a 1km walk through the village to the fish market.

If you're coming from Wete, get a dalla-dalla to Konde, then any vehicle heading west towards Chake, and get off at the Tumbe junction.

PEMBA FLYING FOXES

Commonly known as the flying fox, Pemba's only endemic mammal is a large and critically endangered bat (*Pteropus voeltzkowi*), called *popo* in Swahili.

Flying foxes spend their days in trees rather than caves, and places to most easily see them include a colony near the port in Wete. There are also several colonies in Ngezi Forest Reserve but they're all far from the trails. By far Pemba's biggest flying fox roosting site is **Kidike Flying Fox Sanctuary** (✆0777 472941; adult/student/child US$5/3/1; ⊙9am-6pm), near Kangagani village, 2km east of the new main road between Chake Chake and Wete. The turn-off from the main road is about 10km northeast of Chake.

Ngezi Forest Reserve

In far northeastern Pemba, dense and wonderfully lush **Ngezi Forest Reserve** (Ngezi Vumawimbi Forest Reserve; ✆0773 885777; adult/child US$5/2; ⊙7.30am-3.30pm) is one of the last remaining areas of indigenous forest that once covered much of the island, and as close to rainforest that you'll get anywhere on Zanzibar. Protected by a 1476-hectare reserve, the forest is a true double canopy, complete with vines providing swings for raucous vervet monkeys. The entrance gate and visitor centre is 5km west of Konde, on the main dirt road to the Kigomasha Peninsula.

From the visitor centre, two nature trails tunnel through the forest, and off-trail walks are allowed. All visits must be done with a naturalist guide, some of whom speak English. Most visitors follow the Joshi Trail (Tsh16,000 per person), which takes about an hour and is good for spotting birds, red colobus monkeys and Pemba flying foxes (especially in the early morning and late afternoon). A longer option is the Taufiki Trail (Tsh20,000), which heads north through the forest to reach Vumawimbi Beach (after three to four hours); from here you can retrace your steps, or walk back through the villages bordering the reserve, or arrange a lift in a local pick-up.

Also available are birdwatching and bat-watching walks, plus night walks (all Tsh20,000) to see bushbabies and for keen birdwatchers to spot the endemic Pemba scops owl (*Otus pembaensis*).

Vehicles pass through Ngezi Forest on the way to the beach hotels on the Kigomasha Peninsula. There's no transit fee unless you stop in the forest. To reach the visitor centre without your own wheels, you could walk from Konde or get an unofficial taxi or *boda-boda* (motorbike taxi) for around Tsh5000. Some hotels can provide tours or transfers, or you can rent a bike and cycle here.

Kigomasha Peninsula

Spectacular beaches sweep along the shores of the Kigomasha Peninsula and this, along with some of the best diving in the whole Zanzibar Archipelago, attracts adventurous visitors. The remote location, in the far northwest of Pemba Island, is another key draw.

Away from the sea and the sand, several traditional villages collectively known as Makangale are dotted along the peninsula's length. Some hotels arrange cultural visits here, although with a sense of exploration (and a sense of direction) you can easily take a stroll in this area and see a slice of local life.

Stretching along the east side of the Kigomasha Peninsula and north of Ngezi Forest Reserve is the idyllic **Vumawimbi Beach**. Not many outsiders come here, as all the hotels are on the west side, but it's sometimes visited if the wind is from the west, as it's more sheltered. It's an isolated spot, so come with company and a picnic.

Up on the headland (*ras*) at the far northern tip of the peninsula is **Ras Kigomasha Lighthouse** (US$5). Built by the British in 1900, it is still actively maintained by its keeper. Unlike many lighthouses on Zanzibar it's built of iron, rather than stone. Scale the tiny staircase (95 steps) for wonderful views out to sea and back across the island.

🏃 Activities

Spectacular dive sites include the Njao Gap, the Swiss Reef sea mountains and the sponge-covered Edge, which plunges into the Pemba Channel. As well as the spectacular coral and small marine life, dolphins, manta rays and whales are also regular visitors.

Swahili Divers   DIVING
(https://swahiligecko.com; 2 dives US$170) Located at Gecko Nature Lodge and run by the same friendly team, this five-star PADI Dive Centre offers dives for all levels at various sites off the Kigomasha Peninsula. Check the website for combined dive and accommodation deals.

🛏 Sleeping & Eating

Verani Beach Lodge   CABIN $
(cabins per person US$30) This very basic locally run place has a couple of simple cabins on the beach. The friendly staff can cook meals with enough advance notice, but most guests here come with their own stoves and supplies. There's no way to book in advance, so turn up and try your luck.

Pemba Paradise   HOTEL $$
(🖉 0777 800773; www.pembaparadise.com; d US$65-80) This low-key hotel has 16 rooms,

white-painted with minimal decor, in a row of double-storey buildings set back slightly from the beach; the upstairs rooms have a better view. The bar-restaurant is set further back, behind the rooms, although there are seats and parasols on the beach so you can still enjoy a sundowner.

You can order a couple of dishes or choose the set menu in the restaurant (three-course dinner US$15). Activities include walking tours to nearby villages or there are bikes for rent, and transfers to Ngezi Forest Reserve cost US$10. Diving can be arranged at other hotels nearby.

Gecko Nature Lodge   LODGE $$$
(formerly Kervan Saray; 🖉 0773 176737; https://swahiligecko.com; dm/s/d with full board US$80/180/220; 🖥🕸🛜) This lodge is a wonderfully relaxing place, under new management since 2016, with double rooms in high-roof bungalows, plus a six-bunk dorm. The restaurant serves a set menu (nonguests US$15) and the beach deck is perfect for a beer at sunset. The same team runs Swahili Divers; other activities include fishing, snorkelling and kayaking, and bike rental is available.

Manta Resort   RESORT $$$
(🖉 0776 718852; www.themantaresort.com; d with full board US$320-570; 🕸@🛜🏊) Superbly situated on the beach at the northern end of the Kigomasha Peninsula, this relaxed and well-appointed resort sits on a small escarpment with perfect ocean views. Accommodation is in spacious cottages, on the seafront or in the garden, all with uncluttered decor and private terrace. For total privacy – at least from humans – try the glass-walled offshore underwater room (US$1500).

ℹ Getting There & Away

Most of the hotels on the Kigomasha Peninsula arrange transfers for guests, usually from the airport at Chake Chake, but collection from Wete or Konde can also be arranged.

If you're on public transport, from Wete there are frequent dalla-dallas to Konde (a surprisingly lively junction village with a couple of shops and cafes), from where you can usually find local dalla-dallas heading up the peninsula as far as the village of Makangale, although you may need to wait several hours; if you're in a rush, you can use a *boda-boda* (motorbike taxi).

Northeastern Tanzania

Why Go?

Northeastern Tanzania's highlights are its coastline, its mountains and its cultures. These, combined with the area's long history, easy access and lack of crowds, make it an appealing focal point for a Tanzanian sojourn.

Visit the atmospheric ruins at Kaole and Tongoni, step back to the days of Livingstone in Bagamoyo, relax on palm- and baobab-fringed beaches north and south of Pangani, or explore Saadani National Park. Inland, hike forested footpaths in the Usambaras while following the cycle of market days of the local Sambaa people. Learn about the rich traditions of the Pare Mountains, and experience the bush in seldom-visited Mkomazi National Park.

Most of the northeast is within a half-day's drive or bus ride from both Dar es Salaam and Arusha, and there are good connections to the Zanzibar Archipelago. Main roads are in decent condition and there is a wide range of accommodation.

Best Places to Stay

➡ Tides (p134)

➡ Fish Eagle Point (p139)

➡ Tembo Kijani (p135)

➡ Maweni Farm (p144)

➡ Simply Saadani (p131)

Best Places to Eat

➡ Tides (p134)

➡ Capricorn Beach Cottages (p133)

➡ Tembo Kijani (p135)

➡ Irente Farm Lodge (p146)

➡ Lawns Hotel (p145)

When to Go
Lushoto

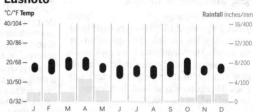

Mar–May The 'long rains' bring lovely green vistas and excellent birding but muddy, slippery hiking paths.

Jun–Nov Enjoy relaxing beaches, cool mountain air and optimal wildlife spotting.

Oct Drumming, dancing and other cultural displays are highlights at the Bagamoyo Arts Festival.

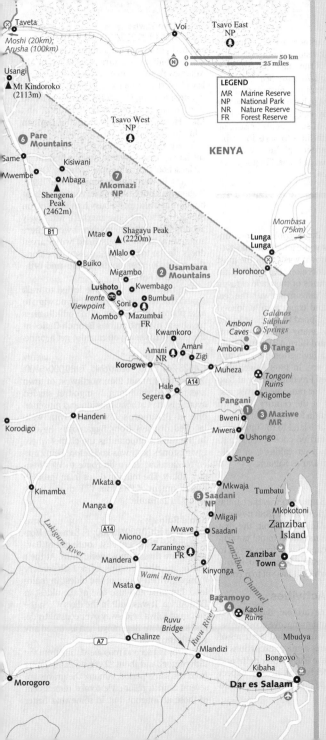

Northeastern Tanzania Highlights

1 **Pangani** (p132) Lazing on long white beaches while getting a taste of Swahili history and culture at this sleepy town.

2 **Usambara Mountains** (p141) Hiking along winding village footpaths and past scenic rolling-hill panoramas.

3 **Maziwe Marine Reserve** (p135) Snorkelling in crystal-clear waters amid colourful fish and corals.

4 **Bagamoyo** (p128) Stepping back into history in the former colonial capital.

5 **Saadani National Park** (p130) Watching wildlife and exploring the coastal wilderness.

6 **Pare Mountains** (p149) Getting acquainted with Pare traditions and culture.

7 **Mkomazi National Park** (p152) Spotting a wealth of birds and spending time in the bush.

8 **Tanga** (p136) Enjoying the relaxed vibe of this attractive coastal city.

History

For at least 2000 years northeastern Tanzania has been attracting visitors. In the 1st century AD the author of the mariners' chronicle *Periplus of the Erythraean Sea* mentions the existence of the trading outpost of Rhapta, which is thought to have been somewhere around present-day Pangani. Several centuries later, a string of settlements sprang up along the coast with links to ports in Arabia and Asia. Today, traces of this history are best seen along the coast at Kaole, Tongoni, Pangani and Bagamoyo.

Bagamoyo

📀 023 / POP 14,500

Strolling through Bagamoyo's narrow, unpaved streets takes you back to the mid-19th century, when the town was one of the most important settlements along the East African coast and the terminus of the trade caravan route linking Lake Tanganyika with the sea. Slaves, ivory, salt and copra were unloaded here before being shipped to Zanzibar Island and elsewhere, and many European explorers, including Richard Burton, Henry Morton Stanley and David Livingstone, began and ended their trips here. In 1868 French missionaries established Freedom Village at Bagamoyo as a shelter for ransomed slaves, and for the remainder of the century the town served as a way station for missionaries travelling from Zanzibar Island to the interior.

Bagamoyo's unhurried pace and fascinating history make it an agreeable day or weekend excursion from Dar es Salaam.

History

From 1887 to 1891 Bagamoyo was the capital of German East Africa, and in 1888 it was at the centre of the Abushiri Revolt, the first major uprising against the colonial government. In 1891 the capital was transferred to Dar es Salaam, sending Bagamoyo into a slow decline from which it has yet to recover.

⊙ Sights & Activities

The lovely coastline around Bagamoyo is full of waterbirds and mangrove ecosystems, and there are a few uncrowded stretches of sand. Most hotels can arrange excursions to **Mbegani lagoon**, the **Ruvu River delta** and **Mwambakuni sand bar**, all nearby. Expect to pay from US$25 to US$30 per person with four people.

Bagamoyo Town   HISTORIC SITE

(adult/child Tsh20,000/10,000) With its cob-webbed portals and crumbling German-era colonial buildings, central Bagamoyo, or Mji Mkongwe (Stone Town) as it's known locally, is well worth exploration. The most interesting area is along Ocean Rd. Here you'll find the old German **boma**, built in 1897, and **Liku House**, which served as the German administrative headquarters.

There is also a school, which dates from the late 19th century and was the first multiracial school in what is now Tanzania. On the beach is the German **customs house** (1895); Bagamoyo's **port**, where you can watch boat builders at work; and a busy **fish market** (on the site of the old slave market), with lively auctions most afternoons. Northwest of here are several small streets lined with carved doors similar to those found elsewhere along the coast. Further south is the mid-19th-century **Old Fort**.

The ridiculously steep fee levied to walk around the old town (required if you want to take photos or enter any of the buildings) is payable at the **Antiquities Branch Office** at the Old Fort, where you can also get a guide.

Catholic Museum   MUSEUM

(📀 023-244 0010; adult/child Tsh10,000/5000; ⊙ 10am-5pm) About 2km northwest of town and reached via a long, mango-tree-shaded avenue is the Catholic mission and museum, one of Bagamoyo's highlights, with well-labelled displays from Bagamoyo's heyday. In the same compound is the chapel where Livingstone's body was laid before being taken to Zanzibar Town en route to Westminster Abbey. The mission dates from the 1868 establishment of Freedom Village and is the oldest in Tanzania.

Kaole Ruins   RUINS

(adult/child Tsh20,000/10,000; ⊙ 8am-4pm Mon-Fri, 9am-5pm Sat & Sun) Just southeast of Bagamoyo are these atmospheric ruins. At their centre are the remains of a 13th-century mosque, which is one of the oldest in mainland Tanzania and also one of the oldest in East Africa. It was built in the days when the Sultan of Kilwa held sway over coastal trade, and long before Bagamoyo had assumed any significance.

Nearby is a second mosque, dating from the 15th century, and about 22 graves, many dating from the same period. Among the graves are several Shirazi pillar-style tombs reminiscent of those at Tongoni, but in somewhat better condition, and a small museum housing Chinese pottery fragments and other remnants. Just east of the ruins, past a dense stand of mangroves, is the old harbour, now silted, that was in use during Kaole's heyday.

The easiest way to reach the ruins on foot is by heading south for about 5km along the road running past Chuo cha Sanaa to the signposted Kaole turn-off at the southern end of Kaole village. A *bajaji* (tuk-tuk) from town costs around Tsh5000 (Tsh10,000 for a taxi).

College of Arts   ARTS CENTRE
(Chuo cha Sanaa; www.tasuba.ac.tz) Located about 500m southeast of Bagamoyo along the road to Dar es Salaam is this renowned theatre and arts college, home of the national dance company. When school is in session there are occasional performances, and it's usually possible to arrange drumming or dancing lessons.

The annual highlight is the **Bagamoyo Arts Festival**, usually held around late September or October. The festival features traditional dance and drumming performances, acrobatics displays, drumming workshops and much more.

The festival is not the most organised – advance information on schedules is rarely available – but it is a good way to meet Tanzania's up-and-coming artists and performers, and to get introduced to local talent and culture.

Caravan Serai Museum   MUSEUM
(Tsh20,000; ⊙9am-6pm) This undistinguished museum has a small display documenting the slave trade. It's at the town entrance, just past and diagonally opposite CRDB bank. More interesting than the present museum is the site at which it is built, which was formerly the starting point for slave and trade caravans to the interior.

🛏 Sleeping

Funky Squids B&B   B&B $
(☏0755 047802; the.funky.squids@gmail.com; s/d US$37/47; 🛜) This beachside place has a handful of modest rooms in a small house just back from the beach, plus a large beachfront bar-restaurant. It's at the southern end of town, next door to (and immediately south of) the College of Arts (Chuo cha Sanaa).

Travellers Lodge   LODGE $$
(☏023-244 0077, 0754 855485; www.travellers -lodge.com; camping US$8, cottages s US$60-70, d US$80-90; 🅿️🛜📶) With its relaxed atmosphere and reasonable prices, this is among the best value of the beach places. Accommoda-

tion is in clean, pleasant cottages, some with two large beds, scattered around expansive grounds. There's a restaurant and a children's play area. It's just south of the entrance to the Catholic mission and museum.

Firefly   HISTORIC HOTEL $$
(☏0759 177393; www.fireflybagamoyo.com; India St; camping US$10, dm/r US$15/60; 🛜📶📶) This is a fine choice, with camping on a large lawn sloping down towards the sea (although there's no beach access). Rooms – in an old Arab merchant's house – are no-frills but spacious and atmospheric. There's a small restaurant and an outdoor poolside lounge. The location on the edge of the old town is excellent. A *bajaji* here from the bus stand will cost Tsh2500.

🍴 Eating

Poa Poa   TANZANIAN $
(☏0768 300277; light meals Tsh5000-12,000; ⊙9am-10pm; 🛜) Coffees, spiced tea, milkshakes, chapati wraps, pizza and local-style meals are among the offerings at this small, popular place in the old town centre. It's several blocks back from the dhow port and customs house.

Nashe's Cafe   CAFE $
(☏0676 506705, 023-244 0171; mains Tsh6000-15,000; ⊙9am-10pm Mon-Sat, 10am-10pm Sun; 🛜) Tasty seafood and meat grills are served on a nice rooftop terrace in the centre of the old town. It also does good coffees.

Funky Squids
Beach Bar & Grill   TANZANIAN, EUROPEAN $$
(☏0755 047802; the.funky.squids@gmail.com; meals Tsh10,000-20,000; ⊙11am-10pm; 🛜) This bar-restaurant serves a good selection of appetising meat and seafood grills on a large beachfront terrace.

ℹ Information

MONEY
CRDB At the town entrance; has an ATM.
National Microfinance Bank At the town entrance; with ATM.
NBC At the petrol station 500m before town along the Dar es Salaam road; has an ATM.

TOURIST INFORMATION
The **Tourist Information Office** (⊙8.30am-4.30pm) at the town entrance can set you up with guides for walking tours of the old town, as well as for excursions to the Kaole Ruins and further afield. The Catholic Museum (p128) also offers tourist information.

❶ Getting There & Away

BOAT

Nonmotorised dhows to Zanzibar Island cost around Tsh5000 (around Tsh10,000 to Tsh15,000 for motorised boats) and take around four hours with a good wind. Foreigners are discouraged from taking these, however, and you'll need to register first with the immigration officer in the old customs building, which is also the departure point. Departure times vary, and are often around 1am, arriving at Zanzibar Island sometime the next morning if all goes well. There is no regular dhow traffic to Saadani or Pangani.

BUS

Dalla-dallas (minibuses) from Makumbusho (north of Dar es Salaam along the New Bagamoyo Rd, and accessed via dalla-dalla from New Posta; Tsh500) head to Bagamoyo (Tsh2000, two hours) throughout the day. The transport stand in Bagamoyo is about 700m from the town centre, just off the road heading to Dar es Salaam. Taxis to the beach hotels charge from Tsh3000, and *bajajis* (tuk-tuks) slightly less. There is also a daily dalla-dalla to Saadani village via Msata on the main Arusha highway, departing Bagamoyo at about 10am (Tsh10,000, three hours).

CAR

Bagamoyo is about 70km north of Dar es Salaam and an easy drive along good tarmac. The best route for self-drivers is via Old Bagamoyo Rd through Mikocheni and Kawe. It's also possible to reach Bagamoyo from Msata (65km west on the Dar es Salaam–Arusha highway, north of Chalinze) on a good, paved 64km road. The coastal road between Bagamoyo and Saadani National Park has been graded and is in good condition, although enquire first about the bridge over the Wami River if travelling during the rainy season.

Saadani National Park

About 70km north of Bagamoyo along a lovely stretch of coastline, and directly opposite Zanzibar Island, is tiny **Saadani National Park** (www.saadanipark.org; adult/child US$35.40/11.80), a 1000-sq-km patch of coastal wilderness. Unpretentious and relaxing, it bills itself as one of the few spots in the country where you can enjoy the beach and watch wildlife at the same time. While terrestrial wildlife-watching opportunities are modest, there is fine birding and animals are definitely present. In addition to hippos and crocodiles, it's quite likely that you'll see giraffes, and elephant sightings are increasingly common. With luck, you may also see Lichtenstein's hartebeests, and even lions, although these are more difficult to spot.

To the north, about 25km beyond Saadani's Madete gate is the long, mostly deserted and beautiful **Sange beach**, with several places to stay. To the south of the reserve is the languidly flowing **Wami River**, where you'll see hippos, crocodiles and many birds, including lesser flamingos (in the delta between July and October), fish eagles, hamerkops, kingfishers and bee-eaters. The best way to explore is on the boat safaris offered by most lodges.

Saadani is easily accessed from both Dar es Salaam and Zanzibar as an overnight or weekend excursion.

🏃 Activities

Boat trips along the Wami River, wildlife drives in open-sided vehicles, bush walks and village tours can be arranged through most camps and lodges.

Bush Walks

Bush walks (US$23.60 per person, plus a guide fee of US$23.60 per group) are a good way to get a taste of the bush and of Saadani's more subtle attractions. They are available in the dry season only.

Boat Safaris

Boat safaris are relaxing and enjoyable. There is a chance you may spot hippos, crocs and many birds, and it's interesting to watch the vegetation along the banks of the Wami River change with the decreasing salinity of the water as you move upstream. In some sections there are also marked variations between the two banks, with areas of date palms and lush foliage on one side, and whistling thorn acacias reminiscent of drier areas of the country on the other. Expect to pay about US$50 per person.

Wildlife Drives

All the lodges offer vehicle safaris. You'll need to explore off main routes for the best wildlife watching; during the rains, take care not to drive through Saadani's notorious black cotton soil when detouring. A park guide (optional) costs US$23.60 per group.

🛏 Sleeping & Eating

Saadani has several private tented camps (in and outside of the park), plus a park-run resthouse and campsite. The coastal lodges and camps north of Saadani in Sange (p135) also make good bases for exploring the park.

Inexpensive street food and local-style meals are available in Saadani village. Otherwise, the private tented camps have good restaurants for their guests. For self-caterers, a small selection of basics is available in Saadani village.

Inside the Park

Saadani Park Campsite CAMPGROUND $
(camping US$35.40) Saadani's main public campsite is in a good location directly on the beach just north of Saadani village, with basic ablution facilities but no food or drink available.

Saadani Park Resthouse & Bandas BANDA $$
(☑ 0785 555135, 0689 062346; saadani@tanzaniaparks.go.tz; banda & resthouse per person US$35.40) Saadani's nice park *bandas* (thatched-roofed huts) and resthouse are just back from the beach near Saadani village, in an area that elephants seem to like. The resthouse has three singles and a suite; the *bandas* have spacious single- and double-bed rooms. Both have cold-water showers and self-catering kitchens (for which you'll need to be self-sufficient with food and drink).

Outside the Park

Simply Saadani LODGE $$$
(☑ 0737 226398, 0713 323318; www.saadani.com; s/d full board from US$355/550, s/d incl full board & wildlife excursions US$475/790; P 🛜 🐾) This hideaway (formerly called Tent With A View) has raised tree-house-style *bandas* on a lovely stretch of deserted, driftwood-strewn beach, just northeast of the Saadani park boundary. All have verandas and hammocks. Excursions include safaris in the park and boat trips on the Wami River. The same management runs a lodge in Selous Game Reserve and another camp in Saadani, and combination itineraries can be arranged.

Kisampa TENTED CAMP $$$
(☑ 0679 443330; https://kisampa.com; per person full board US$180; 🛜) 🐾 For genuine bush adventure, it's difficult to beat this unique and warmly recommended camp. Set about a two-hour drive from Saadani in a private nature reserve, Kisampa is integrated with the surrounding community, and offers many ways for guests to get involved. Accommodation is in open-style bungalows. Saadani safaris, bush walks, beach camping and other activities fill the days.

Favourable package deals are also offered with children, making it an ideal destination for a family bush adventure.

Kuro Maringo TENTED CAMP $$$
(www.kuromaringo.com; per person incl half board & wildlife excursions US$290) 🐾 This very basic bush camp has three twin-bedded tents with bucket shower. It's near Buyuni village, and is normally only booked as a fly-camp experience in conjunction with a stay at the affiliated Tembo Kijani (p135), outside Saadani on the coast. No children below six years of age.

Ekocenter BAR
(☼ 8am-9pm) 🐾 This little place has a good selection of cold water, juice, beer and other drinks (Tsh500 to Tsh3000) from their solar-powered fridge. It's on the edge of Saadani village, and is unmissable with its bright red paint.

ℹ️ Information

Saadani Tourist Information (☑ 0689 062346; saadani.tourism@tanzaniaparks.go.tz;

ℹ️ PLANNING TIPS: SAADANI NATIONAL PARK

Why Go To enjoy the long, mostly deserted coastline plus some wildlife; ease of access from Dar es Salaam for those without much time.

When to Go June to February; black cotton soil is a problem in many areas during the heavy rains from March to May.

Practicalities Drive, bus or fly in from Dar es Salaam; bus from Bagamoyo; drive from Pangani. Entry points are Mvave gate (at the end of the Mandera road, for visitors from Dar es Salaam); Madete gate (for those coming from Pangani along the coastal road); and Wami gate (for those coming from Bagamoyo). Entry fees are valid for 24 hours, single entry only. All fees are paid with Visa or MasterCard only at the Saadani Tourist Information office at Mvave gate. All entry gates are open from 6am to 6pm; exiting the park is permitted up to 7pm. **Saadani National Park Headquarters** (www.tanzaniaparks.go.tz; ☼ 8am-5pm) are at Mkwaja, at the northern edge of the park.

Budget Tips There's no vehicle rental at the park. Your best budget bet is to get a group together and arrange a day safari with one of the lodges outside Saadani.

SAADANI VILLAGE

This tiny, scruffy village, just south of the main park entrance area, doesn't look like much today, but it was once a major local port. You can still see the crumbling walls of an Arab-built fort that was used as a holding cell for slaves before they were shipped to Zanzibar Island. During German colonial times the fort served as the customs house. Short walking tours with local guides can be arranged at the Saadani Tourist Information office (p131), just west of the village.

⊙ 6am-6pm) This office is the place to go to pay your Saadani National Park fees, book park-run accommodation and arrange guides for the park and tours of Saadani village.

🚹 Getting There & Away

AIR

There are airstrips in the north near Mkwaja headquarters and in the south near Saadani village. Flights from Dar es Salaam (one way US$150) and Zanzibar Island (one way US$75) can be booked with **Coastal Aviation** (🖉 0713 325673; www.coastal.co.tz).

BOAT

Local fishing boats sail regularly between Saadani and Zanzibar Island, but the journey is known for being rough and is not recommended. It's better to arrange a boat charter with one of the Saadani lodges or with lodges near Pangani.

BUS

There's a daily bus between Saadani and Dar es Salaam's Mbezi transport stand (west of Ubungo, along the Morogoro road), departing Dar between 11am and 1pm, and departing Saadani between 4.30am and 5am (Tsh10,000, five to six hours).

From Bagamoyo, there's a vehicle daily via Msata on the main Chalinze–Arusha road, departing Bagamoyo at about 10am and Saadani village at 6am (Tsh10,000, three hours).

If you've arrived in the park via public transport, there's no vehicle rental in the park for a safari, unless you have arranged something in advance with the lodges. The Saadani Tourist Information office (p131) can help you arrange a motorcycle or (sometimes) vehicle transfer from Saadani village to the nearby park campsite and park *bandas*.

CAR

Several lodges provide road transport to and from Dar es Salaam from about US$230 per vehicle, one way. Allow four to five hours for the journey.

From Dar es Salaam, the main route is via Chalinze on the Morogoro road, and then north to Mandera village (about 50km north of Chalinze on the Arusha highway). At Mandera bear east along a good gravel road and continue about 60km to Saadani. It's more relaxing and scenic to reach Saadani from Dar es Salaam via Bagamoyo. From Bagamoyo town, head west for about 15km along the tarmac road towards Msata and then north for 44km along an unpaved but reasonably smooth road to the Wami entry gate and the Wami River. Except during heavy rains, the river is bridged; check with park headquarters or the camps about the bridge's status before venturing up. Once at the bridge, it's 21km further to Saadani village.

Coming from Pangani, take the ferry across the Pangani River, then continue south along a reasonably good, scenic road past stands of cashew, sisal and teak to the reserve's northern Madete gate. (At the large signboard for Mkwaja, continue straight, then take the right fork at the next 'Y' junction.) Transfers can be arranged with Saadani or Pangani (Ushongo) lodges from about US$150 per vehicle each way (1½ to two hours).

Although Saadani officially stays open year-round, roads within the park get very muddy and difficult to pass during the rains and you'll probably be limited to the area around the beach and the camps. When driving away from the main park routes during the rains, be careful to avoid getting your vehicle stuck in the area's treacherous black cotton soil.

Pangani

📳 027 / POP 3000

About 55km south of Tanga is the small Swahili outpost of Pangani. It rose from obscure beginnings as just one of many coastal dhow ports to become a terminus of the caravan route from Lake Tanganyika, a major export point for slaves and ivory, and one of the largest ports between Bagamoyo and Mombasa. Sisal and copra plantations were established in the area, and several European missions and exploratory journeys to the interior began from here. By the end of the 19th century, the focus had shifted to Tanga and Dar es Salaam, and Pangani again faded into anonymity. Today, the sleepy, dilapidated town makes for an intriguing step back into history.

A walk back in time in Pangani is especially powerful about three blocks north of the river, where you'll see some carved doorways, buildings from the German colonial era and old houses of Indian traders. More of a draw for many travellers are the beaches running north and south of town, which are lovely, with stands of coconut palms alternating with dense coastal vegetation and the occasional baobab. The beaches, which get more beautiful the further south you go, are also the best places to base yourself.

History

Compared with Tongoni, Kaole and other settlements along the East African coast, Pangani is a relatively modern settlement. It rose to prominence during the mid-19th century, when it was a linchpin between the Zanzibar sultanate and the inland caravan routes, and it was during this era that the riverfront slave depot was built. Pangani's oldest building is the old *boma,* which dates from 1810 and was originally the private residence of a wealthy Omani trader. More recent is the customs house, built a decade later. Probably several centuries older is the settlement at Bweni, diagonally opposite Pangani on the southern bank of the river, where a 15th-century grave has been found. In September 1888, Pangani was the first town to rebel against the German colonial administration during the Abushiri Revolt (p134).

⊙ Sights & Activities

The Pangani Cultural Tourism Program Office (Pangani bus stand; ⊘8am-5pm) organises town tours (per person US$10), Pangani River cruises (US$70 for up to three people), bicycle tours and other excursions. Most hotels also organise Maziwe trips and other activities around Pangani.

Kasa Divers DIVING
(☑0786 427645; www.kasa-divers.com; Ushongo beach) A good outfitter for snorkelling, diving and excursions, including to Maziwe island. It's at the northern end of Ushongo beach.

Tanga Coelacanth Marine Park PARK
(www.marineparks.go.tz) The goal of this recently declared 'park' is to protect the local population of prehistoric coelacanth fish. The temporary headquarters are in Kigombe village, about 20km north of Pangani. At the

time of research, no fees were being collected and the park existed in name only.

🛏️ Sleeping & Eating

Decent sleeping options are limited in Pangani to one simple church-run guesthouse, but there are some great beach lodges north and south of town, including in Ushongo and Sange.

🛏️ Town Centre

Seaside Community Centre Hostel GUESTHOUSE $
(☑0755 276422, 0756 655308; s/d/tr Tsh30,000/ 40,000/75,000, with air-con Tsh40,000/60,000/ 85,000; P🔊) This church-run place has simple but spotless and pleasant rooms with fans and verandas, and meals on order. It's just back from the sea, and about 1km from the bus stand (Tsh2000 in a taxi). From the bus stand head straight towards the coast, cross the tarmac Pangani road and follow the signs, bearing right at the fork.

🛏️ North of Pangani

Capricorn Beach Cottages BOUTIQUE HOTEL $$
(☑0768 811551; www.capricornbeachcottages. com; s/d/tr/q US$75/114/171/228; P@🔊🐾) This lovely, tranquil place on the beach about 20km north of Pangani has several comfortable, spacious self-catering cottages with verandas and hammocks in beachside grounds dotted with baobab trees and overflowing with bougainvillea flowers. There's a clothing boutique, delicious pizza and a good restaurant. Another highlight: catered dinners under the stars on a terrace overlooking the sea. A pool is planned.

Peponi CAMPGROUND, BANDA $$
(☑0713 540139, 0784 202962; www.peponiresort. com; camping US$7.50, s/d half board US$75/130; P🔊🐾🐾) This place has a lovely dining-bar-lounge area, shady beachfront camping, breezy bungalows set in expansive, palm-studded grounds, a small pool, a kite-surfing centre, and a dhow for snorkelling excursions. The overall vibe is relaxed, and it's especially recommended for campers and families.

Peponi is about 20km north of Pangani and 30km south of Tanga. Buses running along the Tanga–Pangani road will drop you at the gate.

Bahari Pori LODGE $$
(☑0754 073573; www.baharipori.com; s/d/tr US$40/70/85, 6-person cottage US$150; P🔊) On a small cliff set well back from the water,

---

PANGANI RIVER BOAT TRIPS

Meandering along the southern edge of town, the muddy Pangani River attracts waterbirds, crocodiles and other animals. It's best explored on a cruise via local dhow, which can be arranged with any of the hotels. Expect to pay about US$70 for up to three people.

Bahari Pori has pleasant, Zanzibari-bedded safari-style tents set around manicured grounds overlooking the mangroves and the sea in the distance. It's good if you want peace and quiet, but is not geared to those seeking a beach holiday.

A footpath leads for about 10 minutes down the escarpment through the mangroves to the water, although the coast here is not good for swimming. It's about 7km north of the Pangani–Muheza road junction.

Mkoma Bay　　　　　　　　　　LODGE **$$$**
(☑ 0786 434001, 0682 002202; www.mkomabay. com; s/d luxury tents with half board from US$125/ 220, 4-8-person house from US$480; P 🛜 🛋 🛜) The highlights at this lodge are the fine views over Mkoma Bay and the subdued ambience. Accommodation is in raised tents of the sort you find in upmarket safari camps, all set in the vegetation around expansive grounds on a low cliff overlooking the beach. There's also a four-bedroom self-catering house, a family *banda* and a restaurant.

Activites include swimming in the bay, beach walking and kayaking. It's 3km north of the Pangani–Muheza road junction.

🏖 Ushongo Beach

Ushongo beach is a beautiful, long arc of fine white sand about 15km south of the Pangani River.

Beach Crab Resort　　CAMPGROUND, COTTAGES **$**
(☑ 0767 543700, 0784 543700; www.thebeach crab.com; camping US$6, s/d/tr beach huts US$25/ 40/60, s/d/tr bungalows US$80/120/150; P 🛜 🛋) This backpacker-friendly place is at the southern end of Ushongo beach. It has beachside camping, backpacker huts sharing ablution blocks with the campsite, and simple double and family bungalows. It also has a large beachside bar-restaurant, windsurfing, kayaks, beach volleyball, snorkelling excursions and a raised tree-house lounge. Pick-ups can be arranged from the Pangani ferry.

★**Tides**　　　　　　　　　　　　LODGE **$$$**
(☑ 0713 325812, 0756 328393; www.thetideslodge. com; s/d half board from US$265/380; P 🛜 🛋 🛜) The beautiful Tides has a prime beachside location, plus spacious upmarket cottages on the sand and excellent cuisine. The cottages have huge beds surrounded by billowing mosquito nets, large bathrooms and stylish decor. There are also several family cottages and a private honeymooners' luxury suite, plus a beachside bar and restaurant.

The lodge arranges honeymooners' snorkelling trips to Maziwe, complete with a waiter, cool box, champagne and all the trimmings.

Emayani Beach Lodge　　　　LODGE **$$$**
(☑ 0782 457668; www.emayanilodge.com; s/d half board US$115/180; P 🛜 🛋 🛜) On the northern end of Ushongo beach, Emayani has a row of pleasant rustic bungalows strung out along a fine stretch of sand. The ambience is very natural – all bungalows are made entirely of thatching and open to the breezes – and the cuisine is tasty. Kayaks and windsurfing equipment are available to rent. There's a nearby outfitter, Kasa Divers (p133), for snorkelling, diving and other excursions.

THE ABUSHIRI REVOLT

Although the Abushiri Revolt, one of East Africa's major colonial rebellions, is usually associated with Bagamoyo, Pangani was its birthplace. The catalyst came in 1884, when a young German, Carl Peters, founded the German East Africa Company (Deutsch-Ostafrikanische Gesellschaft or DOAG). Over the next few years, in an effort to tap into the lucrative inland caravan trade, Peters managed to extract agreement from the Sultan of Zanzibar that the DOAG could take over the administration of customs duties in the sultan's mainland domains. However, neither the sultan's representative in Pangani nor the majority of locals were amenable to the idea. When the DOAG raised its flag next to that of the sultan, simmering tensions exploded. Under the leadership of an Afro-Arab trader named Abushiri bin Salim al-Harth, a loosely organised army, including many of the sultan's own guards, ousted the Germans, igniting a series of fierce power struggles that continued in other port towns along the coast. The Germans didn't subdue the revolt until more than a year later, after the arrival of reinforcements, the imposition of a naval blockade and the hanging of Abushiri. In the wake of the revolt, the DOAG went bankrupt and the colonial capital was moved from Bagamoyo to Dar es Salaam.

📍 Sange Beach

Lovely, long and almost-deserted Sange beach is about midway between Pangani town and the northern border of Saadani National Park (p130).

★**Tembo Kijani** LODGE, BANDA **$$**
(☑0785 117098, 0687 027454; www.tembokijani.com; s/d tree-house banda US$105/160, s/d bungalow US$155/240, all incl half board; P🛜) 🍽
This small ecolodge on a wonderful stretch of beach has four open-sided tree-house *bandas* nestled into the bush just back from the sea, plus comfortable ground-level beach bungalows and tasty, healthy cuisine. The owners have made great efforts to minimise the lodge's footprint and maximise sustainability. The overall results are impressive, with the lodge running on solar and wind power.

Saadani safaris, bush walks and other cultural excursions can be arranged. A minimum two-night stay is required.

Kijongo Bay Resort LODGE **$$$**
(☑0787 055572; www.kijongobayresort.com; s/d half board in villas US$250/380; P🛜🏊🍽)
Kijongo Bay has spacious, airy two-storey villas overlooking a lovely stretch of beach. They're all set in a large, sandy compound, and each can sleep up to five. There's also a smaller family-style cottage ('Boma House'), a restaurant and a motorised boat for river trips and excursions.

ℹ Orientation

Pangani's centre, with the market and bus stand, is on the corner of land where the Pangani River meets the sea. About 2km north of here is the main junction where the road from Muheza joins the coastal road. This is where you should get off the bus if you're arriving from Muheza and staying at the beaches north of town.

ℹ Information

National Microfinance Bank (Boma Rd) ATM that accepts Visa and MasterCard.

ℹ Getting There & Away

AIR

Coastal Aviation (☑0713 325673; www.coastal.co.tz) has daily flights connecting Mashado airstrip (just south of Pangani town, on the south side of the river) with Dar es Salaam (US$185 one way), Zanzibar Island (US$110), Kilimanjaro airport (US$250) and Arusha (US$250).

MAZIWE MARINE RESERVE

About 10km offshore from Pangani is **Maziwe Marine Reserve** (adult/child US$11.80/5.90), a tiny and idyllic sand island with snorkelling in the surrounding crystal-clear waters. Dolphins favour the area and are frequently spotted. Most hotels and the Pangani Cultural Tourism Program Office organise excursions for about US$35 to US$45 per person with a minimum of two people. Maziwe can only be visited at low tide. There's no food or drink, but a picnic lunch is usually included in the excursions.

BOAT

Dhows sail regularly between Pangani and Mkokotoni, on the northwestern coast of Zanzibar, but these are officially off-limits for foreigners and not recommended. Better and safer is the faster **MV Ali Choba** (☑0782 457668, 0784 134056; ttozonc@gmail.com), which sails several times weekly between Ushongo (south of Pangani), Pangani and Zanzibar Island (Kendwa). The trip takes about two hours and costs US$335 per boat for up to five passengers, or US$65 per person for six or more passengers between Ushongo and Zanzibar Island (US$355 per boat or US$70 per person between Pangani and Zanzibar). Book directly with them, or through Emayani Beach Lodge (p134). Another option is to contact **Mr Wahidi** (☑0784 489193), who offers motorised dhow transfers between Pangani town and either Nungwi or Kendwa on Zanzibar Island for US$140 per boat for up to four people, or US$35 per person for five or more passengers. Allow about four hours for the trip.

BUS

The best connections between Pangani and Tanga are via the rehabilitated coastal road, with about five buses daily (Tsh2500, 1½ hours). The first departure from Pangani is at about 6.30am, so you can connect with a Tanga–Arusha bus. There's at least one daily direct bus between Pangani and Dar es Salaam (Tsh15,000). Pangani is also connected by dalla-dalla with Muheza (Tsh2500), from where there are connections to Tanga or Korogwe, but the road is worse than the coastal one and transport is sporadic.

There's also a daily bus between Tanga and Mkwaja (at the northern edge of Saadani National Park) that passes Mwera village (6km from Ushongo) daily at about 7am going north and 3.30pm going south. It's then usually possible to hire a motorcycle to take you from Mwera to Ushongo.

WORTH A TRIP

PLACE OF RUINS

About 20km south of Tanga and just off the coastal road, the **Tongoni ruins** (adult/child Tsh10,000/5000; ☉8am-5pm) are set picturesquely amidst the baobabs on a low rise overlooking stands of mangroves and the sea. They include the crumbling remains of a mosque and about 20 overgrown Shirazi pillar-style tombs, the largest collection of such tombs on the East African coast. Both the mosque and the tombs are estimated to date from the 14th or 15th century.

Tongoni's heyday was in the 15th century, when it had its own sultan and was an inadvertent port of call for Vasco da Gama, whose ship ran aground here. By the early 18th century, the settlement had declined to the point of nonexistence, due to Portuguese disruption of local trade networks and the fall of Mombasa. In the late 18th century, Shirazis fleeing Kilwa resettled here (renaming it Sitahabu, or 'Better Here Than There'), where it experienced a brief revival before completely declining shortly thereafter.

Although most of Tongoni's pillars have long since toppled to the ground, you can still see the recessed areas on some where decorative porcelain vases and offering bowls were placed. There are also about two dozen more recent, and largely unremarkable, tombs dating from the 18th or 19th century.

To get here, take any vehicle heading towards Pangani along the coastal road and get out at the turn-off (marked by a rusty signboard). The ruins are about 1km further east on foot, on the far edge of the village (ask for *magofu*). It's worth getting an early start, as finding a lift back in the afternoon can be difficult. Taxis from town charge from about Tsh50,000 for the round trip. The Tanga tourism office, Tanga Cultural Tourism Enterprise (p140), charges US$52 for car rental.

CAR & MOTORCYCLE

The vehicle ferry over the Pangani River from Pangani to Bweni village runs regularly between about 6am and 10pm daily (Tsh300/50 per adult/child, Tsh6000 per vehicle). From Bweni, you can arrange a taxi in advance with the Ushongo hotels (about Tsh30,000 per taxi for up to three passengers). Otherwise, motorcycle taxis charge about Tsh10,000 to the Ushongo hotels.

For the beaches south of Pangani, all the hotels do pick-ups from both Bweni (the village just across the river from Pangani town) and Tanga.

Tanga

☑ 027 / POP 273,300

Tanga, a major industrial centre until the collapse of the sisal market, is Tanzania's second-largest seaport and its fourth-largest town behind Dar es Salaam, Mwanza and Arusha. Despite its size, it's an agreeable place with a sleepy, semicolonial atmosphere, wide streets filled with cyclists and motorcycles, intriguing architecture and faded charm. It makes a pleasant stop en route to or from Mombasa, and is a springboard to the beaches around Pangani, about 50km south.

History

Although there has probably been a reasonably sized settlement at Tanga since at least the Shirazi era, the town first came into its own in the early to mid-19th century as a starting point for trade caravans to the interior. Ivory was the main commodity traded, with a turnover of about 70,000lb annually in the late 1850s, according to explorer Richard Burton who visited here. The real boom, however, came with the arrival of the Germans in the late 19th century. They built up the town and harbour as part of the construction of a railway line linking Moshi and the Kilimanjaro region with the sea. The Germans also introduced sisal to the area, and Tanzania soon became the world's leading producer and exporter of the crop, with sisal the centre of local economic life. In WWI, Tanga was the site of the Battle of Tanga (later memorialised in William Boyd's novel, *An Ice-Cream War*), in which poorly prepared British troops were soundly trounced by the Germans.

As the world sisal market began to collapse in the 1970s, Tanga's economy spiralled downward. Today, much of the town's infrastructure has been abandoned and the economy is just a shadow of its former self, although vast plantations still stretch westwards along the plains edging the Usambara Mountains.

◎ Sights & Activities

The most interesting areas for a stroll are around Jamhuri Park overlooking the harbour. Here you'll find the old German-built **clock tower**, and the park and cemetery surrounding the Askari Monument at the end of Market St.

Urithi Tanga Museum   MUSEUM
(☑ 0784 440068; Independence Ave; Tsh5000; ☺ 9am-5pm) Tanga's old *boma* has been rehabilitated, and now houses this small but worthwhile museum, with historical photos and artefacts from the area.

Toten Island   ISLAND, HISTORIC SITE
Directly offshore from Tanga is small, mangrove-ringed island Toten Island ('Island of the Dead'), with the overgrown ruins of a mosque dating from at least the 17th century and some 18th- and 19th-century gravestones. Pottery fragments from the 15th century have also been found, indicating that the island may have been settled during the Shirazi era. Toten Island's apparently long history ended in the late 19th century, when its inhabitants moved to the mainland.

While the ruins are less accessible and less atmospheric than those at nearby Tongoni, the island is worth a look if you have extra time. Excursions can be organised through the Tanga Cultural Tourism Enterprise (p140) for about US$60 per person including motorboat transfer and guided tour.

Tanga Yacht Club   SWIMMING
(☑ 027-264 4246; Hospital Rd, Ras Kazone; Tsh6000; ☺ 10am-2.30pm & 5.30-10pm Mon-Thu, 10am-11pm Fri-Sun) This place has a small, clean beach, showers and a restaurant-bar area overlooking the water. It's a pleasant place to relax and, especially on weekend afternoons, it's a good spot to meet resident expats and get the low-down on what's happening in town.

🛏 Sleeping

Tanga's hotels are divided between the city centre and the Ras Kazone residential area, 2km east of town and reached by following Hospital Rd (which runs parallel to the water) northeastwards. It's also well worth considering one of the relaxing beach hotels to the north or south of Tanga.

🛏 City Centre & Ras Kazone

New Raskazone Hotel   HOTEL $
(☑ 0745 643157, 0717 860058, 0756 444529; www.newraskazonehotel.com; Ras Kazone; r without/with air-con Tsh40,000/50,000; ❄) This reliable, good-value place has tidy gardens, quiet, spotless rooms with hot water, TV and window

screens, plus a restaurant (meals Tsh6000 to Tsh10,000). The air-con rooms are slightly larger, and worth the extra money. It's in the Ras Kazone residential section of town, and is Tsh5000 in a taxi from the bus stand.

Panori Hotel   HOTEL $
(☑ 027-264 6044, 0655 049260; www.panorihotel.com; Ras Kazone; s/d/tr Tsh65,000/95,000/120,000; P❄ ➹ ≋) This long-standing place has 18 straightforward rooms, all with fan and TV, a small garden and a large outdoor thatched-roof restaurant. It's in a quiet residential area about 3km from the town centre (Tsh5000 in a taxi from the bus stand). Take Hospital Rd east to Ras Kazone and follow the signposts. Rooms vary in size, so check a few.

CBA Hotel   HOTEL $
(☑ 0689 444000, 0753 419269; Ras Kazone; s/d Tsh50,000/55,000; P❄ ➹) CBA has a quiet setting in a large garden, and clean, modest rooms with mosquito nets that are reasonable value for money. It also has a restaurant. It's directly opposite the Tanga Yacht Club.

ELCT Mbuyukenda
Tumaini Hostel   GUESTHOUSE $
(☑ 0658 131557, 0763 410059; mbuyukendahostel@elct-ned.org; Hospital Rd; s/d Tsh25,000/30,000; P❄) Rather faded overall, but the newer rooms here (all doubles) are decent value for the price, and the compound is quiet, spacious and green, making this a decent budget choice. It's just southwest of Bombo Hospital, and diagonally opposite the easy-to-spot Katani House. Meals (Tsh7000) can be arranged with advance notice. Taxis charge Tsh5000 here from the bus stand.

Regal Naivera Hotel   HOTEL $
(☑ 027-264 5669, 0767 641464, 0712 996668; www.regalnaiverahotel.com; r Tsh50,000-120,000; P❄ ➹) This large pink edifice is in a quiet location two blocks in from Hospital Rd and behind the easy-to-spot Katani House. It has soulless but acceptable rooms in varying sizes, all with double bed, fan and minifridge. There's also a restaurant.

Motel Sea View   HOTEL $
(Bandarini Hotel; ☑ 027-264 5581, 0713 383868; Independence Ave; s/d US$20/30; P❄) In a colonial-era building opposite Jamhuri Park, this place is faded and very scruffy, with only the remotest whiff of character. The double-bed rooms have fans but no mosquito nets, and a few have verandas overlooking the harbour. The in-house restaurant serves breakfast and dinner only.

Tanga

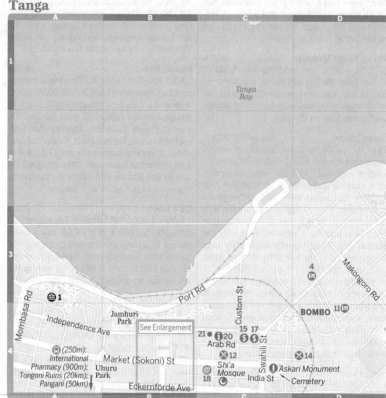

Tanga Bay

NORTHEASTERN TANZANIA TANGA

Tanga

Nyumbani Hotel HOTEL **$$**
(☏027-264 5411, 0759 463578; www.nyumbani hotels.com; Independence Ave; s/d US$70/90; P❋☞⩳) This modern high-rise has a convenient central location and a glitzy exterior, although rooms often fall short of initial expectations. There's a restaurant and a small pool.

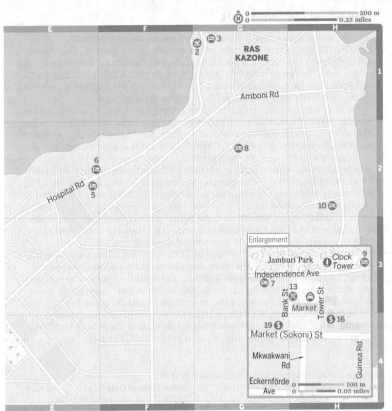

Majuba's B&B   B&B **$$**
(☎ 0784 395391, 0715 395391; graberh1@gmail.
com; Hospital Rd; r US$100; P ✳ ☎ ☎) This
B&B offers two quiet, spacious and beauti-
fully decorated luxury rooms, each with a
minifridge and satellite TV.

Mkonge Hotel   HOTEL **$$**
(☎ 0754 238611, 027-264 4446, 027-264 3440;
www.mkongehotel.com; Hospital Rd; s/d/tr US$80/
90/120, with sea view US$90/100/130; P ✳ ☎ ☎)
Mkonge Hotel has a lovely setting on a vast,
grassy lawn overlooking the sea, a restaurant and wonderful views, although rooms
and service often fall short of potential. It's
worth the extra money for a seaview room.

🛏 North of Tanga

★ **Fish Eagle Point**   LODGE **$$**
(☎ 0784 346006, 0687 680494; www.fisheagle
point.com; per person full board US$75-130;
P ☎ ☎ ✱) 🌿 This lovely lodge has spacious,
open-style beachfront cottages in varying siz-
es, all set around a mangrove-fringed cove.
There's a dhow, snorkelling, sea kayaking,
fishing and birding. It's ideal for families.
Follow the tarmac Horohoro road north
from Tanga for 38km to the signposted right-
hand turn-off, from where it's 10km further
along a dirt track.

🍴 Eating

Tanga Fresh   DAIRY **$**
(yoghurt & milk from Tsh500; ⏰ 6.30am-4pm) 🌿
Tanga is the home of Tanga Fresh, which pro-
duces delicious fresh yoghurt and milk that's
sold throughout the region. The outlet is at
the end of the small dirt road running east
from the Tanesco building; watch for the big
gate to the left.

Food Palace   INDIAN **$**
(☎ 027-264 6816; Market St; meals Tsh6000-10,000;
⏰ 7.30am-3.30pm Mon-Thu, 7.30am-3.30pm &
7-10pm Fri-Sun; 🌿) Tasty Indian snacks and

EXPLORING AROUND TANGA

Long the subject of local legend, the limestone **Amboni Caves** (adult/child Tsh20,000/10,000) are one of the most extensive subterranean systems in East Africa and an intriguing excursion for anyone with an interest in spelunking. Now home to thousands of bats, they were traditionally believed to house various spirits, and continue to be a place of worship and ritual. It's possible to visit a small portion of the cave network, which is quite interesting, once you get past the litter at the entrance.

The caves were originally thought to extend 200km or more, and are said to have been used by the Kenyan Mau Mau during the 1950s as a hideout from the British. Although a 1994 survey concluded that their extent was much smaller – with the largest of the studied caves only 900m long – rumours of them reaching all the way to Mombasa persist.

To reach the caves, which are about 8km northwest of Tanga off the Tanga–Mombasa road, the best option is via bicycle arranged through **Tanga Cultural Tourism Enterprise** (about Tsh65,000 per person including entry fee, bicycle rental and guide). Alternatively, take a dalla-dalla towards Amboni village (Tsh1000) and get off at the turn-off for the caves, near the forestry office. From here, it's 2.5km on foot to Kiomoni village; the caves stretch west of Kiomoni along the Mkulumuzi River. Bring along a torch and wear closed shoes to avoid picking bat droppings off your feet afterwards. Hiring a taxi from Tanga costs about Tsh50,000 return, including waiting time.

A visit to **Galanos Sulphur Springs** (Tsh5000), northwest of Tanga, is usually included with most Amboni tours. These green, odorous and rather underwhelming sulphur springs take their name from a Greek sisal planter who was the first to recognise their potential for relaxation after the rigours of a long day in the fields. Although still in use, they are rather unappealing despite their purportedly therapeutic properties.

The unsignposted turn-off for the springs is along the Tanga–Mombasa road, just after crossing the Sigi River. From here, it's about 2km further. Dalla-dallas from Tanga run as far as Amboni village, from where you'll need to continue on foot.

meals, including some vegetarian selections, and local ambience. Overall good value.

Pizzeria d'Amore   ITALIAN $$
(☑ 0715 395391, 0784 395391; Hospital Rd; meals Tsh15,000-20,000; ⊙ 11.30am-2pm & 6.30-10pm Tue-Sun) A small garden restaurant with tasty pizzas, pasta, seafood and continental fare. It has a breezy upstairs dining terrace and a bar.

Tanga Yacht Club   EUROPEAN $$
(☑ 027-264 4246; Hospital Rd, Ras Kazone; entry Tsh6000, meals Tsh12,000-20,000; ⊙ 10am-2.30pm & 5.30-10pm Mon-Thu, 10am-11pm Fri-Sun; ☎) Seafood and mixed-grill dishes in an attractive setting overlooking the water.

Self-Catering
SD Supermarket   SUPERMARKET $
(Bank St; ⊙ 9am-1.30pm & 3-6pm Mon-Fri, 9am-2pm Sat) A good stop for self-caterers; it's behind the market.

ℹ Information

DANGERS & ANNOYANCES
The harbour area is seedy and best avoided. In the evenings, take care around Port Rd and Independence Ave near Jamhuri Park.

INTERNET
Global Internet Cafe (Market St; per hour Tsh2000; ⊙ 8.30am-6pm Mon-Sat)

MEDICAL SERVICES
International Pharmacy (☑ 0686 108160, 0713 237137; cnr St No 7 & Mkwakwani Rd; ⊙ 9am-5pm Mon-Sat, 10am-1pm Sun) Well-stocked pharmacy.

MONEY
Barclays (Independence Ave) Has an ATM.
CRDB (Tower St) Also with ATM.
Exim (Independence Ave) Next to Barclays; ATM.
NBC (cnr Bank & Market Sts) Just west of the market.

TOURIST INFORMATION
Tanga Cultural Tourism Enterprise (☑ 027-264 5254, 0765 162875, 0713 375367; www.tangatourismcoalition.com; ⊙ 8.30am-4pm Mon-Fri, to 1pm Sat) The helpful staff here can assist with arranging excursions and booking accommodation.

ℹ Getting There & Away

AIR
There are daily flights on **Coastal Aviation** (☑ 0713 596075, 0713 325673; www.coastal.

co.tz; cnr Independence Ave & Usambara St; ⊙ 8am-4pm Mon-Sat) and **Auric Air** (🖉 0757 466648; www.auricair.com) between Tanga, Dar es Salaam, Zanzibar Island and Pemba (one way between Tanga and Pemba/Zanzibar Island/ Dar es Salaam approximately US$95/130/195). Auric Air's Tanga representative is at the airfield, which is about 3km west of the town centre, just off the Korogwe road (Tsh5000 by taxi).

BOAT

Azam Marine's Sealink ferry goes weekly between Tanga and Pemba (four hours, US$35), with connections to Zanzibar Island. Departures from Tanga are on Tuesday, and from Pemba on Sunday. Tickets can be bought online or at the **Azam Marine Booking Office** (www. azammarine.com; Custom St; ⊙ hrs vary).

BUS

Ratco and other buses for Dar es Salaam depart daily every few hours from 6am to 2pm in each direction (Tsh15,000 to Tsh17,000, six hours).

To Arusha, there are at least three departures daily between about 6am and 11am (Tsh17,000 to Tsh19,000, seven to eight hours). To Lushoto there are several direct buses departing daily from 7am (Tsh7000 to Tsh8000, four hours).

To Pangani (Tsh2500, 1½ hours), there are several larger buses and many dalla-dallas throughout the day along the coastal road.

All transport leaves from the main bus stand on Taifa Rd ('Double Rd'), at the corner of Street No 12. It's about 1.5km south of the town centre (Tsh5000 in a taxi), and south of the railway tracks in the Ngamiani section.

🛈 Getting Around

There are taxi ranks at the bus station and near the market at Market St. Occasional dalla-dallas run along Ocean Rd between the town centre and Ras Kazone.

Muheza
🖉 027

Muheza is a scrappy junction town where the roads to Amani Nature Reserve and to Pangani branch off the main Tanga highway. Although well inland, it's culturally very much part of the coastal Tanga region, with a humid climate, strong Swahili influences and surrounding landscapes marked by extensive sisal plantations broken by stands of palms. Muheza's main market and trading area, dominated by rows of rickety wooden market stalls and small corrugated metal-roofed houses, is about 1km uphill from the main highway.

If you get stuck overnighting in Muheza, try **Msangazi Guest House** (Amani Nature Reserve Rd; r Tsh20,000-30,000; 🅿), a simple but cheery place about 2.5km from the bus stand en route to Amani Nature Reserve. It's on the left (south) side of the road; watch for the pinkish-orange building. Meals can be arranged with advance notice.

Transport to Amani Nature Reserve leaves from the bus stand just off the Tanga road. There are two buses daily to and from Amani, departing Muheza about 2pm, and Amani at 6am (Tsh4000, two hours). There are connections between Muheza and Tanga throughout the day (Tsh1500, 45 minutes), and direct daily buses in the morning from Muheza to Lushoto (Tsh4000, three hours).

Korogwe
🖉 027 / POP 68,308

Korogwe – a scrappy town set in a beautiful area of open fields, rolling hills and low mountains – is primarily of interest as a transport junction. In the western part of town, known as 'new' Korogwe, are the bus stand and several accommodation options. To the east is 'old' Korogwe, with the now-defunct train station. Southwest of town, a rough road branches down to **Handeni**, known for its beekeeping and honey production, and its hospital.

If you must break your journey here, **Motel White Parrot** (🖉 027-264 5342; motel whiteparrot@gmail.com; Main Hwy; camping Tsh15,000, s/d from Tsh40,000/50,000; 🅿 ❋) is a roadside rest stop that has a collection of plastic animals at the entrance, decent, mostly clean rooms, an adjoining, rather bare campsite with hot-water showers and cooking area, and a buffet-style restaurant. It's a soulless but efficient place to stop.

All buses travelling along the main highway between Arusha and Tanga, or between Arusha and Dar es Salaam, will drop you at Korogwe. To catch onward transport, a good place to wait is Motel Blue Parrot, along the main highway about 2km southeast of central Korogwe, as many buses stop here.

USAMBARA MOUNTAINS

With their wide vistas, cool climate, winding paths and picturesque villages, the Usambaras are one of northeastern Tanzania's delights. Rural life revolves around a cycle of colourful, bustling market days that rotate from one village to the next, and is largely untouched by the booming safari scene and influx of 4WDs

WORTH A TRIP

LUTINDI CULTURAL TOURISM

Perched on the edge of the Usambara Mountains southeast of Lushoto is Lutindi and the **Lutindi Cultural Tourism Project** (☑027-264 1040, 0763 695541; lutindi-hospital@elct.org). Lutindi is the site of the first mental hospital in East Africa, and you can arrange a tour through the compound, visit the workshops where some residents are employed at craft-making, walk in the surrounding tea plantations and gain insights into a side of local life far removed from general tourism.

There's a simple guesthouse (per person Tsh30,000), with breakfast, lunch and dinner available (Tsh5000 to Tsh7000). Lutindi is reached via Msambiazi village, which is about 20km northwest of the town of Korogwe (which in turn is along the main Dar es Salaam–Arusha highway). To get here, take a dalla-dalla from Korogwe for about 6km to Msambiazi village (Tsh600), from where you can catch a motorcycle taxi for the remaining 8km or so to the hospital (Tsh5000 to Tsh8000). Taxis from Korogwe to Lutindi charge between Tsh35,000 and Tsh50,000. With an early start from either Moshi or Tanga, you should be in Lutindi by mid-afternoon.

in nearby Arusha. It's easily possible to spend at least a week trekking from village to village or exploring with day walks.

The Usambaras, which are part of the ancient Eastern Arc chain, are divided into two ranges separated by a 4km-wide valley. The western Usambaras, around Lushoto, are the most accessible. The eastern Usambaras, around Amani, are less developed. Both ranges are densely populated, with an average of more than 300 people per sq km. The main tribes are the Sambaa, Kilindi, Zigua and Mbugu. Although the climate is comfortable year-round, paths get too muddy for trekking during the rainy season from March through May. The best time to visit is from June to November, after the rains and when the air is clearest.

For cycling tours to and through the Usambaras, contact the Moshi-based **Summit Expeditions & Nomadic Experience** (☑0787 740282; www.nomadicexperience.com) 🖉.

Amani Nature Reserve

The Amani Nature Reserve (per visit adult/child US$10/5, per visit Tanzania-registered/foreign vehicle Tsh10,000/US$25) is located west of Tanga in the heart of the eastern Usambaras. Often overlooked, it's a peaceful, lush patch of montane forest humming with the sounds of rushing water, chirping insects and singing birds. It is also exceptionally rich in unique plant and bird species – a highly worthwhile detour for those ornithologically or botanically inclined. Among the unique bird species you may see are Amani sunbirds, banded green sunbirds and the green-headed oriole.

History

Although Amani was only gazetted as a nature reserve in 1997, research in the area began a century earlier when the Germans established a research station and botanical gardens here. Large areas of forest were cleared and numerous new species introduced. Within a few years the gardens were the largest in Africa, totalling 304 hectares and containing between 600 and 1000 different species of plants, including many endemic species. Soon thereafter, exploitation of the surrounding forest began and the gardens began to decline. A sawmill was started and a railway link was built connecting Zigi, about 12km below Amani, with the main Tanga–Moshi line to transport timber to the coast.

During the British era, research shifted to Nairobi, and the railway was replaced by a road linking Amani with Muheza. Many of the facilities at Amani were taken over by the nearby government-run malaria research centre and the gardens fell into neglect.

More recently, thanks to funding from the Tanzanian and Finnish governments and the EU, projects have been under way to promote sustainable resource use by local communities. Local guides have been trained and visitor access to the eastern Usambaras has improved thanks to Amani's trail network.

◉ Sights & Activities

The **Zigi Information Centre** (◷8am-5pm) at the old Station Master's House opposite the Zigi entrance gate has information about the area's history, animals and medicinal plants. Entry and guide fees are also payable here. There's a network of short walks along shaded forest paths that can be done alone or with a guide (per person per day US$15). They are detailed in the booklet *A Guide to Trails and Drive Routes in Amani Nature Reserve,* which is sometimes available at the Zigi Information Centre.

🛏 Sleeping & Eating

Amani Conservation
Centre Rest House   CAMPGROUND, GUESTHOUSE **$**
(☑ 027-264 0313, 0784 587805; camping US$15, s/d incl full board US$22.50/45; **P**) This reserve-run resthouse has a forested setting and simple, clean rooms. There's also a small area to pitch a tent, a supply of hot water and basic meals. Continue straight past the main fork in Amani to the signposted reserve office. The guesthouse is next to the office.

Zigi Rest House   CAMPGROUND, GUESTHOUSE **$**
(☑ 027-264 0313, 0784 587805; camping US$15, s/d incl full board US$22.50/45) Rooms at this reserve-run resthouse have bathrooms, three twin beds and a rustic mountain feel. There is hot water for bathing and meals are available, though it's a good idea to bring fruit or snacks as supplements. Camping is also possible; bring all supplies. Ongoing repair work at the time of writing meant some rooms were a bit noisy. It's at the main reserve gate.

Amani Forest Camp   CAMPGROUND, COTTAGES **$$**
(Emau Hill; ☑ 0693 119690; www.amaniforestcamp. com; camping US$10, s/d safari tent US$100/156, s/d cottage US$112/176; ☺ mid-Jun–Mar; **P** 🛜 🛗) 🌿 This rustic place has camping, plus pleasant tents and cottages, all in a wooded setting with fine birding and nature walks. There's also a restaurant. Continue 1.5km past Amani on the Kwamkoro road to the signposted turn-off, from where it's 3km further along a narrow bush track. Half- and full-board options are also available.

ℹ Getting There & Away
Amani is 32km northwest of Muheza along a dirt road, which is in fair to good condition the entire way, except for the last 7km, where the road is rocky and in bad shape (4WD only). There's at least one truck daily between Muheza and Amani (Tsh3500, two hours), continuing on to Kwamkoro, 9km beyond Amani. Departures from Muheza are between about 1pm and 2pm. Going in the other direction, transport passes Amani (stopping near the conservation centre office) from about 6am.

In the dry season, you can make it in a 2WD as far as Zigi (25km from Muheza), after which you'll need a 4WD. Allow 1½ to two hours between Muheza and Amani, less in a good car with high clearance. There's also a walking trail from Zigi up to Amani (2½ to three hours). Driving from Muheza, the route is straightforward and signposted until the final junction, where you'll see Bulwa signposted to the right; Amani is 2km further to the left.

Soni
☑ 027 / POP 12,840
Tiny Soni is ideal for those seeking a quieter alternative in the Usambaras than the increasingly crowded base of nearby Lushoto (p144). While there is no tourist infrastructure, there is plenty of local character and activity, especially in the market area at the main junction.

The best place to base yourself and organise hikes is at Maweni Farm (p144), from where you can explore Soni's many attractions. These include **Kwa Mungu Mountain**, about 30 minutes on foot from Soni village centre, and **Ndelemai Forest**. Soni is also the starting point for several wonderful walks, including a two- to three-day hike to the **Mazumbai Forest Reserve** and Bumbuli town, and a three- to five-hour return walk to pine-clad **Sakharani**, a Benedictine mission that sells locally produced wine. There's also a lovely longer walk from Maweni Farm up to Gare Mission and on to Lushoto. The area around Gare (one of the first missions in the area) was reforested as part of erosion-control efforts, and it's interesting to see the contrast with some of the treeless, more eroded surrounding areas. After Gare, and as a detour en route to Lushoto, stop at the village of **Kwai**, where there's a women's pottery

---

LOCAL KNOWLEDGE

MARKET DAYS

Local villages are especially colourful on market days, when traders come on foot from miles around to peddle their wares:

Bumbuli Saturday, with a smaller market on Tuesday

Lushoto Sunday, with a smaller market on Thursday

Mlalo Wednesday

Soni Tuesday, with a smaller market on Friday

Sunga Wednesday, very colourful

project. Kwai was also an early research post for soil science and erosion control.

Maweni Farm   LODGE **$$**
(☑ 0713 417858, 0713 565056, 0787 279371; www.maweni.com; s US$30, d US$50-80, f US$80; P 🛜) This atmospheric old farmhouse is set in lovely rambling grounds against a backdrop of twittering birds, flowering gardens and a water-lily-covered pond, with Kwa Mungu mountain rising up behind. Rooms are straightforward and spacious, and meals are healthy and excellent. Knowledgable guides are available, and the property makes a wonderful and quiet base for exploring the Usambaras. To reach Maweni, follow the signposted dirt road from Soni junction past the weekly market for 2.9km.

❶ Getting There & Away

Soni is about 20km uphill from Mombo along the road to Lushoto (which is 12km further on). It's easy to reach via dalla-dalla from either destination (Tsh1500 from either Lushoto or Mombo).

Lushoto

☑ 027 / POP 500,000

This leafy highland town is nestled in a fertile valley at about 1200m, surrounded by pines and eucalyptus mixed with banana plants and other tropical foliage. It's the centre of the western Usambaras and makes a convenient base for hikes into the surrounding hills.

Lushoto is also the heartland of the Wasambaa people (the name 'Usambara' is a corruption of Wasambaa or Washambala, meaning 'scattered'). Local culture is strong. In Muheza and parts of the Tanga region closer to the coast, Swahili is used almost exclusively. Here, however, Kisambaa is the language of choice for most residents.

History

During the German era Lushoto (then known as Wilhelmstal) was a favoured holiday spot for colonial administrators, a local administrative centre and a mission station. It was even slated at one point to become the colonial capital. Today, thanks to a temperate climate, it's best known for its bustling market – liveliest on Sundays – and its fine walking opportunities. In addition to a handful of colonial-era buildings – notably the German-built churches, the prison and various old country estates – and the paved road from Mombo, the Germans left a legacy of home-made bread and cheeses, now produced by several missions in the area.

Due in part to the high population density of the surrounding area and the resulting deforestation, erosion has long been a serious concern for this region. Erosion-control efforts were first initiated during the British era and today various projects are under way.

🏃 Activities

The western Usambaras around Lushoto offer wonderful walking. Routes follow well-worn footpaths that weave among villages, cornfields and banana plantations, and range from a few hours to several days. It's possible to hike on your own but you'll need to master basic Swahili phrases, carry a GPS, get a map of the area and plan your route via the handful of villages where local guesthouses are available. However, occasional robberies of solo hikers means that hiking with a guide is recommended.

Most Lushoto hotels can recommend guides and routes, and the tourist information centres also organise hikes. Don't go with freelancers who aren't associated with an office or a reliable hotel. Rates vary depending on the hike and have become very costly. Expect to pay Tsh35,000 per person for a half-day hike to Irente Viewpoint. You'll pay up to Tsh120,000 per person per day on multiday hikes, including camping or accommodation in very basic guesthouses, guide fees, forest fees for any hikes that enter forest reserves (which includes most hikes from Lushoto) and food. Most of the set stages for the popular hikes are quite short and, if you're fit and keen on covering some distance, it's easy to do two or three stages in a day. However, most guides will want to charge you the full price for the additional days, so you'll need to negotiate an amicable solution. A basic selection of vegetables and fruits is available along most routes and bottled water is sold in several of the larger villages. If you're hiking on your own, carry a filter.

Lushoto can get chilly and wet at any time of year, so bring a waterproof jacket.

🛏 Sleeping

Lushoto has a good range of budget places, with some midrange choices as well. Most are in or near the town centre, although a few are up in the hills and require your own transport.

Lushoto

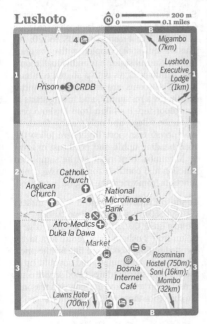

Lushoto

Lushoto, on the left coming from Soni. Ask to get dropped at the Montessori Centre.

Tumaini Hostel   HOSTEL $
(☑ 027-266 0094; Main Rd; s/d/ste/tr Tsh30,000/30,000/40,000/50,000, s with shared bathroom Tsh20,000-25,000; ℗) This good-value place run by the Lutheran church offers clean twin-bed rooms and hot-water showers in a two-storey compound overlooking tiny gardens. A restaurant is attached. It's directly in the town centre, near the Telecom building. Profits support church-run community projects in the area.

Rosminian Hostel   GUESTHOUSE $
(☑ 0785776348, 0684116688; rosminihostellushoto@yahoo.co.uk; s Tsh30,000, d Tsh35,000-40,000; ℗) This small church-run place has straightforward double-bed rooms overlooking a tiny compound. All have hot-water showers, mosquito nets and TVs; meals are available with advance order. It's 1.8km before town, and about 300m off the main road to the left when coming from Soni. Ask the bus driver to drop you at the turn-off.

Lushoto Highland Park   HOTEL $
(☑ 0789 428911; lushotohighlandparkhotel@yahoo.com; s/d/ste Tsh40,000/50,000/60,000; ℗ 🖤) Just uphill from the post office, and just below the old district commissioner's residence, this modern-looking place has reasonable although somewhat cluttered and overfurnished rooms. Some have a balcony, all come with mosquito nets, and there's a restaurant.

Midtown A Guesthouse   GUESTHOUSE $
(s/d Tsh15,000/20,000) This is a reasonable shoestring choice with no-frills rooms, but

🛏 In & Near Town

Lawns Hotel   LODGE $
(☑ 0652 315914, 0759 914144; www.lawnshotel.com; camping Tsh15,000, s Tsh30,000, d Tsh50,000-130,000, f from Tsh185,000; ℗ 🖤 🖤) This Lushoto institution has changed ownership and is warmly recommended. It's full of charm, with vine-covered buildings, extensive gardens and fireplaces in some rooms. There's good camping, a restaurant with tasty home-style meals, a lovely terrace and plenty to do for children. It's in a small patch of pine forest, conveniently located at the entrance to town and signposted.

Go left at the roundabout at the town entrance, following the unpaved road up and around to the right through the pine trees to the hotel.

St Eugene's Lodge   GUESTHOUSE $
(☑ 027-264 0055, 0784 523710; www.s243760778.onlinehome.us/lushoto; s/tw/tr/ste US$25/45/54/60; 🖤) Run by an order of sisters, unpretentious St Eugene's has pleasant rooms with balconies and views over the surrounding gardens. Tasty meals are served, and homemade cheese and jam are for sale. St Eugene's is along the main road, about 3.5km before

no food available. It's up the hill behind the bus stand (about seven minutes' walk).

View Point Guest House
GUESTHOUSE $
(s/d Tsh15,000/20,000; P) This budget place is on the hill behind the bus stand. No food is served and the rooms are basic.

🛏 Outside Town

Irente Farm Lodge
GUESTHOUSE $
(Irente Farm; ☎0783 685888, 0788 503002; www.irentefarmlodge.com; camping Tsh15,000, d with half board Tsh95,000-150,000, tr with half board Tsh180,000, s/d with shared bathroom Tsh35,000/70,000; P 🛜 🛖) 🍴 This lovely, rustic church-run place in a quiet setting 4.5km from Lushoto town has camping, a variety of rooms and several self-catering cottages. The gardens and views are beautiful, and meals include fresh produce from Irente Farm.

Staff will also prepare picnic lunches (Tsh12,000) with advance order, and homemade cheese, jams and bread are for sale.

Swiss Farm Cottage
COTTAGE $$
(☎0715 700813; www.swiss-farm-cottage.co.tz; s/d US$60/95, 2- to 4-room cottage US$95-220; P) This tranquil spot, complete with cows grazing on the hillsides, has individual rooms in separate cottages with a shared common area. The rooms are reasonably comfortable, there's a restaurant, and hiking starts at your doorstep. It's 15km from Lushoto past Migambo village, and only feasible for those with private transport. To get here, follow the road heading uphill and northeast of town to Magamba, turn right at the signposted junction and continue for 7km to Migambo junction, from where the lodge is signposted.

Lushoto Executive Lodge
LODGE $$
(☎0784 360624; www.lushotoexecutivelodge.co.tz; s/d from Tsh90,000/120,000; P 🛜) This lodge is 3.5km from Lushoto town centre in a lovely forested setting. Rooms are fine for the price, albeit somewhat cramped and not quite up to the beautiful surroundings. Good service compensates, however, and the lodge is a reasonable choice for those with their own transport.

HIKES FROM LUSHOTO

An easy walk to get started is to **Irente Viewpoint** (6km, allow two to three hours return). It begins on the road running southwest from the Anglican church and leads gradually uphill to the viewpoint, with wide views on clear days. It's impressive to see how abruptly the Usambaras rise up from the plains below. En route is Irente Farm Lodge, where you can get accommodation or buy fresh cheese, yoghurt and granola. Once near the viewpoint, there are two paths; the better one goes through Irente Cliff View Lodge (p147) and costs Tsh3000 to the viewpoint, including a soft drink. The adjoining 'container' route costs Tsh2000.

For another easy walk, head north out of Lushoto along the road running between the Catholic and Anglican churches. After about five minutes, bear sharply left and start climbing, following the road past scattered houses and small farm plots. About 35 minutes further is the royal village of **Kwembago**, the traditional seat of the local Sambaa chief and notable for its large open field and handful of old double-storey, balconied houses. Continue uphill, bear right at the junction, and follow the path around and then down again to the other side of the Lushoto valley, where it joins with the tarmac road leading to Migambo. For a longer variant, head left at the large junction after Kwembago, and follow footpaths steeply down to the former mission hospital station of **Bumbuli**, where you can find transport back to Lushoto via Soni. From Bumbuli, it's a scenic, gentle climb up and into the cool **Mazumbai Forest Reserve**, which at its higher levels protects patches of dense upper montane forest.

There's also a lovely three- to four-day hike – ideal for scenery and local culture – from Lushoto to **Mtae** or **Mambo** through stands of pine, patches of wild asters, cornfields and villages. Alternatively, try the rugged and challenging six-day walk to Amani Nature Reserve. The tourist information centres have wall maps detailing some of the routes. Nearby villages with accommodation include Bumbuli (with rooms at the old Lutheran mission hospital guesthouse), Lukozi (local guesthouse rooms), Rangwi (basic rooms in a lovely setting at the local convent), Mtae (local guesthouse) and Mambo – Mambo Viewpoint Eco Lodge (p148) and Mambo Cliff Inn (p148). In Mazumbai Forest Reserve, there is accommodation in the middle of the forest at university-run guesthouses.

At the small roundabout at the entrance to town take the right fork (leading uphill towards Migambo) and follow the well-signposted route to the gate.

Irente Cliff View Lodge LODGE $$
(☑027-264 0026, 0784 866877, 0653 479981; www.irenteview.com; camping US$5, s/d from US$50/60; Ⓟ) Stunning views over the plains below on clear days from all the rooms compensate for the somewhat overfurnished interior at this lodge, which is built on the edge of a cliff about 1.5km beyond Irente Farm at Irente Viewpoint. Just below is a grassy campground with hot-water showers.

✗ Eating

Tumaini Cafe & Makuti African Restaurant TANZANIAN, EUROPEAN $
(☑027-266 0094; Main Rd; meals Tsh6000-12,000; ⊙7am-9.30pm) Tumaini Cafe – on the main road next to the Telecom building – offers cheap snacks, breakfasts and meals, including banana milkshakes, freshly baked rolls and continental fare. In the same compound and under the same management, is Makuti African Restaurant, which is open for lunch and dinner only and serves tasty local food.

Mamma Mia Pizza PIZZA $$
(Main Rd; mains Tsh14,000-17,000; ⊙11am-9pm Tue-Sat, 2.30-9pm Sun & Mon) Tasty pizzas, pastas, ciabattas, brownies, shakes, smoothies and more in this slick eatery on the main road, just up from the market.

ℹ Information

INTERNET ACCESS
Bosnia Internet Café (Main Rd; per hr Tsh2000; ⊙8.30am-6pm Mon-Fri, 9am-2pm Sat) At the southern end of town.

MEDICAL SERVICES
Afro-Medics Duka la Dawa (Main Rd; ⊙8am-1pm & 2-8pm Mon-Sat) Pharmacy near the market.

MONEY
CRDB (Main Rd) Visa and MasterCard; at the Western Union building, diagonally opposite the prison, at the northern (uphill) end of the main road.

National Microfinance Bank (Main Rd; ⊙8.30am-3.30pm Mon-Fri) ATM accepting Visa and MasterCard.

TOURIST INFORMATION
Tupande (☑0783 908596, 0783 908597; www.tupandeusambara.wordpress.com) In the

GREETINGS IN KISAMBAA

As you're hiking in the Usambaras, you'll likely hear more of the local Sambaa language spoken than Swahili. The following are a few phrases in Kisambaa to get you started:

➡ *Onga maundo* Good morning

➡ *Onga mshee* Good afternoon

➡ *Niwedi* I'm fine (in response to *Onga maundo* or *Onga mshee*)

➡ *Hongea (sana)* Thank you (very much)

southwestern corner of the bus station, with a good range of hikes and cultural tours.

SED Tours (☑0784 689848; www.sedadventures.com; 1st fl, Super Hongera Bldg, Main Rd) Hikes and cultural tours; on the main road opposite National Microfinance Bank.

Friends of Usambara Society (☑027-266 0132; www.usambaratravels.com) Just down the small road running next to National Microfinance Bank, with hikes and cycling tours (bring your own bicycle).

ℹ Getting There & Away

Dalla-dallas go throughout the day between Lushoto and Mombo (Tsh4000, one hour), the junction town on the main highway.

Daily direct buses travel from Lushoto to Tanga (Tsh7000, four hours), Dar es Salaam (Tsh15,000 to Tsh17,000, six to seven hours) and Arusha (Tsh15,000, six hours), with most departures from 7am.

The main bus stand is near the market, with some lines also beginning about 2km below town along the main road opposite the hospital turnoff.

About 1.5km before town on the Mombo road, **Rosmini Garage** is worth a try if you need vehicle repairs.

Mlalo
☑027 / POP 8100
Set in a valley cut by the Umba River, Mlalo is an incongruous place with a Wild West feel, intriguing double-storey houses and a modest selection of basics. Nearby is Kitala Hill, home of one of the Usambara subchiefs. The walk between Mlalo and Mtae (five to six hours, 21km) is beautiful, passing terraced hillsides, picturesque villages and patches of forest.

CHIEF KIMWERI

Kimweri, chief of the powerful Kilindi (Shambaa) kingdom during the first half of the 19th century, is one of the Usambara region's most legendary figures. From his capital at Vuga (on the main road between Mombo and Lushoto), he ruled over an area stretching from Kilimanjaro in the north to the Indian Ocean in the east, levying tributes on towns as distant as Pangani. The extent of his dominion in the coastal regions soon brought him into conflict with Sultan Seyyid Said of Zanzibar, who also claimed sovereignty over the same areas. Ultimately, the two leaders reached an agreement for joint governance of the northeastern coast. This arrangement lasted until Kimweri's death in 1869, after which the sultan assumed full authority.

Tradition holds that Kimweri had magical powers, including control of the rain and the ability to call down famines upon his enemies. His kingdom was highly organised, divided into subchiefdoms ruled by his sons and districts ruled by governors, prime ministers and local army commanders. It was Kimweri to whom the missionary Johann Ludwig Krapf went to request land to build his first church for the Anglican Church Missionary Society.

Following the death of Kimweri, interclan rivalries caused the kingdom to break up, and fighting over who was to succeed him continued until the Germans arrived in the region.

The old Mlalo mission has a **guesthouse** (per person Tsh15,000) with basic rooms (some of which have lovely views), and meals available with advance notice. It's on the edge of town; anyone will be able to point you in the right direction.

Buses run daily between Dar es Salaam and Mlalo via Lushoto, departing Lushoto by about 1pm, and Mlalo by about 5am (Tsh3000, 1½ hours between Mlalo and Lushoto). There are also sporadic dalla-dallas.

Mtae

☑ 027 / POP 12,850

Tiny Mtae is perched on a cliff about 55km northwest of Lushoto, with fantastic 270-degree views over the Tsavo Plains and down to Mkomazi National Park. The area makes a fine destination if you only have time for one hike from Lushoto. En route is Sunga village, with a colourful market on Wednesdays. Just to the southeast is **Shagayu Peak** (2220m), one of the highest in the Usambara Mountains. In addition to its many walking paths, the area is also known for its traditional healers.

🛏 Sleeping & Eating

Mambo Cliff Inn   COTTAGE $

(☑ 0784 734545; www.mambocliffinn.com; camping US$15, dm US$25, d US$35-70) This good place perched at 1900m has wonderful views, plus camping, dorm rooms and cottages. Tasty local-style meals are available,

and guides can be arranged for hikes and other excursions. It's a fine budget base for exploring the Usambaras.

Muivano II   GUESTHOUSE $

(r Tsh6000) This very basic place offers bucket baths and dark, no-frills rooms. It's along the main road in Mtae. Meals are available nearby.

Mambo Viewpoint Eco Lodge   LODGE, CAMPGROUND $$

(☑ 0769 522420, 0785 272150; www.mamboview point.org; camping US$8-10, s US$50-90, d US$75-130; ☁ ☎) ◆ This place, set at about 1900m and reached via the signposted left-hand fork at the junction 3km before Mtae, has stunning views, plus pleasant cottages and permanent tents. The owners offer information on the area, and can organise hikes, village stays and more. It's a recommended base for exploring the Usambaras.

ℹ Getting There & Away

The road between Lushoto and Mtae is full of turns and hills, and is particularly beautiful as it winds its way up the final 7km to Mtae. Buses depart Lushoto (Tsh5000, three hours) about 10am. There are also direct daily buses to Mtae from Arusha (Tsh17,000, nine hours), Dar es Salaam (Tsh17,000, nine hours) and Tanga (Tsh15,000, six to seven hours). Taxis from Lushoto charge from about Tsh70,000. For those staying in Mambo, negotiate with the driver to take you all the way or ask to get dropped at the Mtae–Mambo junction, from where it's about 2km further on foot to Mambo village, Mambo Cliff Inn and Mambo Viewpoint Eco Lodge.

PARE MOUNTAINS

The seldom-visited Pare Mountains, divided into northern and southern ranges, lie southeast of Kilimanjaro and northwest of the Usambara range. With the Usambaras, they form part of the ancient Eastern Arc chain, and their steep cliffs and forested slopes host a number of unique birds and plants. The Pares are densely populated, with many small villages linked by a network of paths and tracks. The main ethnic group here is the Pare (also called the Asu). While there are some historical and linguistic differences among various Pare groups, socially they are considered to be a single ethnic entity.

The Pare Mountains are not well developed for tourism. There is no major base from where you can take a series of hikes, and you'll be mostly on your own when exploring. Yet, thanks to the relative isolation, the traditions and folklore of the Pare have remained largely untouched.

The best way to begin exploration is to head to Same and then up to Mbaga (for the south Pares) or to Usangi (for the north Pares). From both Usangi and Mbaga there are hikes ranging from half a day to three days or more, and English-speaking guides can be arranged.

Same

📞 027 / POP 9000

Same (*sah*-may) is a lively market town and the largest settlement in the southern Pares. You'll need to pass through here to get to Mkomazi National Park and Mbaga, a centre for hikes in this area. Same has only minimal tourist infrastructure and the town is more suitable as a starting point for excursions into the Pares rather than as a base. If you want to stay a few days before heading into the villages, there are walks into the hills behind town, although for most of the better destinations you will need to take local transport at least part of the way. Sunday is the main market day, when traders from all over the Pares come to trade their wares.

Guides for hikes can be arranged with the Amani Lutheran Centre and Elephant Motel. The **Same District Catchment Office** (Main Rd; ⊙ 7.30am-4pm) – for paying forest reserve fees – is at the end of town, on the main road past the market.

National Microfinance Bank (⊙ 8.30am-4.30pm) has an ATM. Go left out of the bus stand, up one block, then left again.

🛏 Sleeping & Eating

Elephant Motel   MOTEL **$**
(📞 027-275 8193, 0754 839545; www.elephant motel.com; camping US$10, s/tw/tr US$40/45/55; 🅿🌫🛜♿) Elephant Motel has simple, pleasant rooms, a restaurant serving up decent meals, a children's playground and a campground. It's on the main highway 1.5km southeast of town, and is a popular overnight stop for self-drivers between the coast and points west. It can also help with car hire for Mkomazi safaris and hikes in the southern Pare mountains.

Amani Lutheran Centre   GUESTHOUSE **$**
(📞 027-275 8107, 0784 894140, 0657 172708; s Tsh15,000-35,000, d Tsh25,000-35,000; 🅿) This

---

ℹ EXPLORING THE PARE MOUNTAINS

Lodging in the Pares is, for the most part, very basic. With the exception of Tona Lodge (p150) in Mbaga and Mhako Hostel (p151) in Usangi, most accommodation is with villagers or camping. Prices for both average Tsh10,000 to Tsh20,000 per person per night. For all destinations except Mbaga and Usangi it's a good idea to bring a portable stove.

The best places to arrange guides are Lomwe Secondary School (p151) in Usangi and Tona Lodge in Mbaga. For organised hikes, expect to pay per person about Tsh40,000 per day for guide fees, Tsh4000 per day for village fees and about Tsh5000 per meal. There's also a forest fee of US$30 per person per visit (Tsh5000 for Tanzania residents) for any hikes that go into forest reserves. This includes hikes to Shengena Peak and most other routes. The forest fees can be paid at the Same District Catchment Office or through your guide. For any hikes with guides, the stages are generally short (two or three can usually be easily combined if you are reasonably fit) although your guide will still expect you to pay for the same number of days.

The Pares can be visited comfortably at any time of year, except during the long rains from March through May, when paths become too muddy.

good-value place offers a handful of clean, renovated and pleasant rooms in a quiet compound, plus meals on order. It's about 300m north of the highway, about five minutes' walk uphill from the bus stand. Staff can help arrange vehicle rental for Mkomazi safaris through the nearby Lutheran diocese offices.

ℹ️ Getting There & Away

Buses on the Dar es Salaam–Arusha highway stop at Same on request. There's also a direct bus from Arusha to Same, departing Arusha at around 8am (Tsh5000 to Tsh6000, 2½ hours). To Mbaga, there are one or two vehicles daily, departing Same between 11am and 2pm (Tsh5000, two to three hours). The bus station is just north of the main road near the large roundabout.

Mbaga

📱 027

Mbaga (also known as Mbaga-Manka), in the hills southeast of Same at about 1350m, is a good base for hikes deeper into the surrounding southern Pare mountains. You can walk from here in two or three days to the top of Shengena Peak (2462m), the highest point in the Pares. Mbaga, an old Lutheran

mission station, has long been an influential town because of its location near the centre of the Pares, and even today it is in many respects a more important local centre than Same.

A popular three-day circular route is from Mbaga to Chome village, where you can spend a night before ascending Shengena Peak on the second day and then returning to Mbaga.

Guides for hiking can be arranged with Tona Lodge from US$10 per day. For hikes to Shengena Peak, you will also need to pay nature reserve fees of US$30 per person per visit, plus camping fees of US$30 per person per night.

Tona Lodge   LODGE $

(📱 0754 852010; http://tonalodge.org; camping US$15, s US$15-40, d US$30-70, village development fee per person per day US$5; 🅿️) The rustic Tona Lodge is the former mission house of Jakob Dannholz. It is an amenable base with views, camping and serviceable, albeit overpriced, rooms in the original complex and in a newer annex. Meals are also available (US$10). It provides guides for hiking (from US$10 per day), and traditional dancing performances can be arranged.

PARE CULTURE

The Pare (locally, Wapare) hail from the Taita Hills area of southern Kenya, where they were herders, hunters and farmers. It was the Maasai, according to Pare oral tradition, who pursued them into the mountains, capturing and stealing their cattle. Today, many Pare are farmers, cultivating plots of vegetables, maize, bananas, cassava and cardamom. Thanks to significant missionary activity, the Pare distinguish themselves as being among Tanzania's most educated groups. During the 1940s, leading Pares formed the Wapare Union, which played an important role in the independence drive.

Traditional Pare society is patrilineal. Fathers are considered to have great authority during their lifetime as well as after death, and all those descended from a single man through male links share a sense of common fate. Once a man dies, his ghost influences all male descendants for as long as the ghost's name is remembered. After this, the dead man's spirit joins a collectively influential body of ancestors. Daughters are also dependent on the goodwill of their father. Yet, since property and status are transmitted through the male line, a father's ghost only has influence over his daughter's descendants until her death.

The Pare believe that deceased persons possess great powers, and thus have developed elaborate rituals centred on the dead. Near most villages are sacred areas where the skulls of tribal chiefs are kept, although you're unlikely to see these unless you spend an extended period in the mountains. When people die, they are believed to inhabit a netherworld between the land of the living and the spirit world. If they are allowed to remain in this state, ill fate will befall their descendants. The prescribed rituals allowing the deceased to pass into the world of the ancestors are of great importance.

For more about Pare culture, read *The Shambaa Kingdom* by Steven Feierman (1974) and *Lute: The Curse and the Blessing* by Jakob Janssen Dannholz, who established the first mission station at Mbaga.

Transport from Same to the lodge can be organised with the owner from about Tsh100,000 per vehicle (worth negotiating for smaller groups).

❶ Getting There & Away

There are one or two vehicles daily around noon from Same to Mbaga, departing Same between about noon and 2pm (Tsh5000, two to three hours, 40km). Coming from Moshi, you'll need to get a bus by 8am in order to reach Mbaga the same day. Coming from Dar es Salaam, you'll probably need to stay overnight in Same. From Mbaga to Same, departures are between 4am and 5am. It's also possible to catch one of several daily dalla-dallas from Same to Kisiwani, and then walk about 5km uphill to Mbaga.

If you're driving to Mbaga, there is an alternate route via Mwembe, which can be reached by following the Dar es Salaam–Arusha highway about 5km south to the dirt road leading off to the left.

Mwanga

☑ 027 / POP 15,780

This district capital sprawls across the plains at the foot of the Pare mountains, 50km northwest of Same on the Dar es Salaam–Arusha highway. Away from the scruffy central junction and old market area, it's a shady, pleasant town with wide, unpaved roads, swaths of green and stands of palm. It's of interest primarily as a transport junction for changing vehicles to reach Usangi, the starting point for excursions into the northern Pares.

About 10km south of Mwanga is Nyumba ya Mungu (House of God) Reservoir, home to Luo fishing communities that originally migrated here from the Lake Victoria area.

If you start your travels to Usangi early, you shouldn't need to overnight in Mwanga; it's easily possible to reach Usangi by afternoon from Arusha or Moshi. Otherwise, there's the basic but reasonable Anjela Inn (d Tsh15,000, in newer annex Tsh30,000; ⓟ ❀).

Buses run daily between Moshi and Mwanga (Tsh4000, one hour), departing in the morning. From Mwanga, there are several dalla-dallas to Usangi (Tsh1500), with the last departure at about 2pm.

Usangi

☑ 027

Usangi lies in a valley ringed by mountains about 25km southeast of the low-lying town of Mwanga. It is the centre of the northern Pares and a convenient base for starting your explorations of the area, particularly if you're here for hiking.

Guides for hikes can be arranged at Lomwe Secondary School; ask for the school director. Even if school isn't in session, someone will be around to help. Expect to pay Tsh40,000 for the guide, plus a Tsh4000 village development fee, a Tsh4000 forest fee and a Tsh6000 coordinator's fee. All fees are per person per day.

In addition to short walks, a long day-hike is possible into Kindoroko Forest Reserve (which begins about 7km south of Usangi village) to the top of Mt Kindoroko (2113m), the highest peak in the northern Pares. From the upper slopes of Mt Kindoroko you can see over the Maasai Steppe to the west and to Lake Jipe and into Kenya to the northeast.

🛏 Sleeping & Eating

Mhako Hostel & Restaurant GUESTHOUSE $
(☑ 027-275 7642; s/ste Tsh25,000/65,000, s/d with shared bathroom Tsh15,000/25,000) This cheery place has clean, pleasant rooms and inexpensive meals. Some of the non-self-contained rooms only have interior windows; it's worth paying a little more for the nicer ones with toilets and balconies. Mhako is along the main road to the right as you enter Usangi.

Lomwe Secondary School CAMPGROUND $
(lomwesec@googlemail.com; camping Tsh4000, r per person Tsh7000; ⓟ) There's a basic guesthouse and camping at this local secondary school at the top end of Usangi. If you sleep at the school, you can prepare your own meals (bring your own stove, equipment and ingredients), or you can arrange to eat meals prepared by school staff (Tsh3000/5000/3000 for breakfast/lunch/dinner). To get here, follow the main road, bearing right at the fork.

❶ Getting There & Away

Dalla-dallas run several times daily along the unpaved but good road winding up from Mwanga (which is on the main Tanga–Arusha highway) to Usangi (Tsh2500, 1½ hours), from around 8am. Hiring a taxi costs from Tsh35,000. From both Arusha (Tsh7000, four hours) and Moshi (Tsh5000, two hours), there are several direct buses daily to Usangi, departing in the morning. Ask to get dropped at Lomwe Secondary School. Allow at least two to three days for an excursion to Usangi, including time to get here and organise things.

MKOMAZI NATIONAL PARK

Wild and undeveloped **Mkomazi National Park** (☑0689 062336, 0767 536132, 027-275 8249; adult/child US$35.40/11.80) spreads along the Kenyan border in the shadow of the Pare Mountains, its dry savannah lands contrasting sharply with the moist forests of the Pares. The reserve, which is contiguous with Kenya's Tsavo West National Park, is known for its black-rhino conservation project, as well as for its marvellous birding.

Apart from birding, the main reason to visit is to appreciate the evocative nyika bush landscapes studded with baobab and thorn acacia and broken by low, rocky hills. Despite its relative ease of access, Mkomazi is still well off the beaten track, and you will often have it completely to yourself.

☉ Sights & Activities

Multihour bush walks can be arranged at Zange gate (US$23.60 guide fee, plus US$23.60 to US$29.50 walking tour fee, ages 12 years and older only).

Wildlife Watching

Animals that you're likely to spot include oryx, eland, dik-dik, the rarely seen gerenuk, kudu and Coke's hartebeest. The huge seasonal elephant herds that once crossed regularly between Tsavo and Mkomazi are

---

ⓘ MKOMAZI NATIONAL PARK

Why Go Excellent birding; dry, savannah wilderness scenery; eland, oryx and gerenuk.

When to Go June until February for wildlife, year-round for birding. Much of Mkomazi's secondary road network is impassable during the rains; main routes are all-weather, although be aware of sections of black cotton soil, especially north of Babu's Camp.

Practicalities Drive in from Same on the Dar es Salaam–Arusha highway to Zange main entry gate (open 7am to 6pm). Park entry, guide and walking-safari fees are payable with Visa or MasterCard only. There's another exit point at Njiro gate to the southeast, which makes a circuit drive possible.

Budget Tips Take a dalla-dalla or taxi from Same to Zange gate; camp and do a walking safari.

---

beginning to come back, after reaching a low point of just a dozen elephants in the area in 1989, although elephants still are not commonly spotted in Mkomazi.

The reserve is also known for its black rhinos, which were introduced into the area from South Africa for breeding in a project spearheaded by Tony Fitzjohn. The rhinos are within a heavily protected 45-sq-km enclosure in northcentral Mkomazi, and are not viewable as part of general tourism. There are also wild dogs (reintroduced too, and, as part of a special endangered species program, also not viewable to general tourists).

Birding

With more than 400 species, Mkomazi is a birder's delight. Species to watch for include various weaver birds, secretary birds, crowned and bateleur eagles, helmeted guinea fowl, various hornbills, storks and the pygmy falcon.

⌯ Sleeping & Eating

Zange Gate Public Campsite CAMPGROUND $$
(☑0689 062336, 027-275 8249; per adult/child US$35.40/5.90) Located about 1.5km from Zange gate and Mkomazi National Park headquarters, this pleasant campsite has toilets, shower and – sometimes (when the key is available) – a dining/cooking area.

Dindira Special Campsite CAMPGROUND $$
(☑0767 536132, 027-275 8249; per adult/child US$59/11.80) This attractive special campsite, 20km from Zange gate and overlooking Dindira Dam, is ideally situated for birding and wildlife watching. There are no facilities.

Babu's Camp TENTED CAMP $$$
(☑0784 402266, 027-254 8840; www.anasasafari. com; per person full board from US$227) This classic safari-style camp is the only permanent camp in Mkomazi National Park. Its five tents are set in the northern part of the reserve looking towards the Gulela Hills. The cuisine is tasty, staff are attentive and the surrounding landscapes are wide and lovely. Wildlife drives, walks and night drives can be arranged.

ⓘ Getting There & Away

Dalla-dallas between Same and Mbaga can drop you about 2km from Zange gate, from where you will need to walk in to the gate. Once at the gate, you can arrange guides and begin a walking safari. Vehicles for Mkomazi safaris can be arranged in Same at Elephant Motel (p149) and through Amani Lutheran Centre (p149) for about US$150 per vehicle per day. There is no vehicle rental at the park.

Northern Tanzania

Best Places to Stay

➜ Lamai Serengeti (p198)

➜ Ngorongoro Crater Lodge (p183)

➜ Lake Manyara Tree Lodge (p177)

➜ Shu'mata Camp (p236)

Best Places to Eat

➜ Blue Heron (p162)

➜ Khan's Barbecue (p161)

➜ Hot Plate (p161)

➜ Onsea House (p161)

Why Go?

To paraphrase that well-known quote about Africa, those of you who've never been to northern Tanzania are to be envied, because you still have so much to look forward to. Northern Tanzania is a land of superlatives, from Africa's highest mountain to one of the greatest wildlife spectacles on the planet. But Kilimanjaro and the Serengeti are mere starting points to so many journeys of a lifetime. Mt Meru is Kilimanjaro's rival in both beauty and the challenge of climbing it, while the Crater Highlands could be Africa's most haunting landscape. When it comes to wildlife, there's Tarangire's baobab-and-elephant kingdom, Lake Manyara's tree-climbing lions and the flamingos of Lake Natron. And venturing down into Ngorongoro's crater can feel like returning to earth's first morning.

But this is also a journey among the Maasai, the Hadzabe, and others whose presence here makes this one of Africa's most stirring and soulful destinations.

When to Go
Arusha

Jan–Mar The wildebeest migration is in the southern Serengeti.

Apr & May Rains can turn some roads muddy, but there are fewer visitors.

Jun & Jul The migration streams north through the Serengeti towards Kenya.

Northern Tanzania Highlights

1 Serengeti National Park (p191) Witnessing one of the most epic wildlife shows ever.

2 Ngorongoro Crater (p181) Descending into a lost world of wildlife.

3 Lake Natron (p188) Experiencing stunning views of Ol Doinyo Lengai volcano.

4 Mt Kilimanjaro (p233) Standing on the top of Africa with views that go on forever.

5 Lake Manyara National Park (p176) Looking for tree-climbing lions.

6 Crater Highlands (p186) Venturing through the dramatic world of the Rift highlands.

7 Tarangire National Park (p172) Watching elephants amid the baobabs.

8 Arusha (p156) Learning about local life on a Cultural Tourism Program tour.

9 Lake Eyasi (p180) Visiting the nomadic Hadzabe.

10 West Kilimanjaro (p235) Leaving well-trodden trails for wildlife and Kili views.

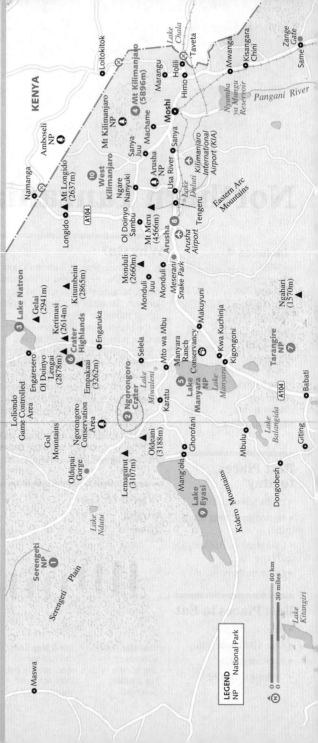

LEGEND
NP National Park

0 ────── 60 km
0 ────── 30 miles

NORTHERN SAFARI CIRCUIT

Ngorongoro, Serengeti, Tarangire, Lake Manyara – Tanzania's northern safari circuit offers some of the best wildlife watching anywhere on the continent.

Arusha

⊿027 / POP 416,500

Arusha is Tanzania's gateway to the northern circuit of stellar national parks and the starting point of many a memorable safari. It's also a large, sprawling city with all the contradictions that brings.

The town offers a nice break from the rigours of life on the African road – it has excellent places to stay and eat and, for the most part, it's lush and green and enjoys a temperate climate throughout the year, thanks to its altitude (about 1300m) and its location near the foot of Mt Meru.

As the safari capital of northern Tanzania, though, Arusha is also where you're most likely to encounter touts offering safaris, souvenirs and all manner of deals, some genuine, many of them not. Their main haunts are the bus stations and along Boma Rd. The city's downtown area and the main road towards Dodoma are noisy and packed with people and traffic.

◉ Sights & Activities

The best thing to do in Arusha, besides arrange your safari and/or trek, is join a Cultural Tourism Program (p156) in the surrounding countryside.

Natural History Museum MUSEUM
(⊿027-250 7540; Boma Rd; adult/student Tsh10,500/6300; ⊙9am-6pm) This museum inside the old German *boma* (fortified compound), completed in 1900, has three parts. The best is the wing dedicated to human evolution, since much of what we know about the topic came from fossils unearthed in Tanzania. There are also displays on insects, the history of Arusha during the German colonial era, and wildlife photos and mounts.

Arusha Declaration Museum MUSEUM
(⊿027-254 5380; www.facebook.com/Arusha Declaration; Makongoro Rd; adult/child Tsh8000/4000; ⊙9am-5.30pm) Despite the promising subject matter – the museum celebrates the groundbreaking 1967 declaration by then-president Julius Nyerere calling for

African self-reliance, socialism and *ujamaa* (familyhood) – you'd have to be pretty bored to come to this unfocused little museum. Half the space is filled with photos of government officials. It improves slightly after that, with some photos from the colonial era and a handful of ethnographic artefacts.

★**Weaving & Walking Tour** CULTURAL, WALKING
(⊿0624 235886; per person Tsh10,000) A wonderful way to get under the skin of local life, these tours run by Reda and Flora take you into the heart of Arusha as locals experience it, ending up at Flora's weaving workshop, where she uses recycled textiles to create innovative new fabrics. Tours last between two and four hours. Ring ahead to be picked up from your hotel.

★**Via Via Cultural Tours** CULTURAL
(⊿0767 562651; www.viaviacafe.com; Boma Rd; 1hr/day drum lesson US$20/50, city/market tour US$30/30, cooking class US$30; ⊙9am-4pm) Run out of the Via Via cafe (p162) just off the back of the Natural History Museum, this place offers drum lessons (including an all-day version in which you learn to make your own drum), two-hour city tours, three-hour 'Maasai Market Tours', and cooking classes.

🛏 Sleeping

The best budget area in Arusha is generally the Kaloleni neighbourhood, north of Stadium St and east of Colonel Middleton Rd (a 10-minute walk from the bus stand), followed by the busy central market area south of the stadium. Things are slightly quieter in the Clock Tower area. For midrange and top-end places, head to leafy eastern Arusha.

The places outside the city combine a semi-rural setting with easy transport into town, and most do cultural walks. Lodges within Arusha National Park are an easy drive from town; these are another option, especially if you're arriving in Arusha from Kilimanjaro International Airport.

🛏 City Centre & Clock Tower

Raha Leo GUESTHOUSE $
(⊿0784 822999, 0753 600002; Stadium St; s/d Tsh30,000/40,000; 🖥) This bright, welcoming place has simple but adequate double and twin rooms, some along the corridor, others around an open-air lounge. With hot water and cable TV, it's one of the best-value budget options in town. The location is central, but it's quieter than most.

CULTURAL TOURISM PROGRAMS

Numerous villages around Arusha (and elsewhere in the country) run 'Cultural Tourism Programs' that offer an alternative to the safari scene. Most centre on light hikes and village activities. Although the line is sometimes blurred in these programs between community empowerment and empowering the enterprising individuals who run them, they nevertheless provide employment for locals and offer an excellent chance to experience Tanzania at the local level. Most have various 'modules' available, from half a day to several nights. Transport, sometimes by dalla-dalla and sometimes by private vehicle, is extra. Overnight tours involve camping or homestays; expect conditions to be basic. Payment should be made on-site; always ask for a receipt.

All tours in the Arusha area (and elsewhere) can be booked through the Tanzania Tourist Board Tourist Information Centre (p165), which has detailed information, including prices and transport options. Most tours should be booked a day in advance, but some guides wait at the TTB office on standby each morning. If you have further questions, the Cultural Tourism Program office at the back of the Natural History Museum in Arusha may be able to assist. You can also contact many of the places directly to make arrangements.

Ilkiding'a (☎ 0732 978570, 0713 520264; www.ilkidinga.com) Walks (ranging from half-day strolls to a three-day 'cultural hike' that allows you to sleep in homes along the way) and the chance to experience the traditional culture of the local Maasai and Wa-arusha people are the main attractions of this well-organised program around Ilkiding'a, 7km north of Arusha.

Ilkurot (☎ 0713 332005, 0784 459296; www.tanzaniaculturaltourism.com/ilkurot.htm) A good choice for those interested in Maasai culture. Stops on the village tours and treks (using donkeys or camels, if you wish) include a *boma* (fortified compound), a herbal doctor, a midwife and other community members. Overnighters can camp, or sleep in a guesthouse or *boma*. The village is 25km north of Arusha off the Nairobi Rd.

Longido (☎ 0787 855185, 0715 855185; www.tanzaniaculturaltourism.com/longido.htm) This program centres on the 2637m-high Mt Longido and the large Maasai village of the same name. In addition to the climb itself (eight to 10 hours return), Longido makes a good introduction to Maasai life, including a visit to some *bomas* and the Wednesday cattle market. The village is easily reached by dalla-dalla.

Flamingo Inn GUESTHOUSE $
(☎ 0754 260309; flamingoarusha@yahoo.com; Kikuyu St; s/tw US$20/25; ☎) This low-key place has sparse but spotlessly clean rooms with fans and nets, a convenient central location, decent breakfasts and friendly staff.

Arusha Centre Tourist Inn HOTEL $
(☎ 0764 294384, 0767 277577; atihotel@habari.co.tz; Livingstone Rd; s/d US$30/35; @ ☎) Unremarkable but clean and fairly spacious rooms are on offer here – they're just about fine for the price (ask for a discount anyway), but be prepared for an early-morning wake-up call from the neighbouring mosque. The three storeys ring a courtyard, and there's a restaurant at the front with OK food and plenty of Maasai men staring at the TV.

Arusha Backpackers HOSTEL $
(☎ 0773 377795; www.arushabackpackers.co.tz; Sokoine Rd; dm/s/d with shared bathroom US$10/12/22; ☎) There's a buzz about this place in more ways than one – it's popular for those looking to hook up with other travellers, but the absence of mosquito nets may deter some. Shared bathrooms have an institutional feel, but, considering the price, it's a fair enough deal overall. There's free wi-fi in the common areas.

Centre House Hostel GUESTHOUSE $
(☎ 0767 820203, 0762 169910; cathcenterhouse@yahoo.com; Kanisa Rd; s Tsh15,000-40,000, d Tsh30,000-40,000; P) Run by the Catholic diocese, this no-frills place hosts long-term volunteers and short-term budget travellers. Rooms vary, and several of the self-contained rooms have been recently renovated. All have hot water. Meals (Tsh10,000) are available with advance order. The gate shuts at 11pm unless you've made previous arrangements.

New Safari Hotel HOTEL $$
(☎ 027-254 5940, 0787 326122; www.newsafarihotel.com; Boma Rd; s/d/tr US$100/125/180; ❄ @) Once the favourite of white hunters and their tall tales from the African bush,

Mkuru (☑ 0784 724498, 0784 472475; www.mkurucamelsafari.com) The Maasai village of Mkuru, 14km off the Nairobi road north of Mt Meru and 60km from Arusha, hosts the region's pioneering camel camp. You can take a short camel ride around the village or a multi-day safari as far away as Mt Kilimanjaro and Lake Natron. There's a simple tented camp in the village or you can pitch your own tent.

Monduli Juu (☑ 0787 756299, 0786 799688; www.tanzaniaculturaltourism.com/monduli.htm) Monduli Juu (Upper Monduli) comprises four small villages along the Monduli Mountains, northwest of Arusha in Maasai country. You can visit traditional doctors, see a school or eat a meaty meal in a bush *orpul* (Maasai camp where men go to eat meat). Many people come to trek along the escarpment for views over the Rift Valley plains.

Mulala (☑ 0784 499044, 0784 747433; www.tanzaniaculturaltourism.com/mulala.htm) Set on the southern slope of Mt Meru about 30km northeast of Arusha, this program is completely run by women. Tours focus on farming and daily life and include visits to a women's cooperative and cheesemakers. Camping is possible if you have camping gear, though with an early start you could do this tour as a day trip from Arusha.

Ng'iresi (☑ 0754 320966, 0754 476079; www.arusha-ngiresi.com) The popular program at Ng'iresi village (about 7km northeast of Arusha on the slopes of Mt Meru) includes visits to Wa-arusha farms, houses and a school. There's also a traditional-medicine tour, along with trips to several waterfalls and a hike up a small volcano. There's no public transport here; arrange it as part of your booking.

Oldonyo Sambu (☑ 0784 694790, 0784 663381; www.tanzaniaculturaltourism.com/sambu. htm) Oldonyo Sambu's trekking/camping trips include the option to ride donkeys, horses or camels. Cultural activities in the village are also on offer. The village is 35km north of Arusha off the Nairobi road and can be easily reached by dalla-dalla.

Tengeru (☑ 0756 981602, 0754 960176; www.tengeruculturaltourism.org) Site of the biweekly Tengeru Market, about 10km east of Arusha and signposted off the main highway, Tengeru offers a program including visits to a coffee farm and a local school, and an introduction to the life of the Meru people. Homestays can be arranged.

the New Safari was reborn in 2004 and is the pick of the central midrange options. Rooms are generally large, have tiled floors, and boast a touch of class in the decor. The hotel's also within walking distance of just about anything in the centre.

Arusha Naaz Hotel HOTEL **$$**
(☑ 0755 785276, 027-257 2087; www.arushanaaz. net; Sokoine Rd; s/tw/tr from US$45/60/75; ❇ 🛜) Naaz is short on atmosphere but otherwise OK value, with comfortable 1st-floor rooms in a convenient central location by the Clock Tower. Rooms aren't all the same, so check out a few before committing; those around the triangular courtyard are best.

Arusha Hotel HOTEL **$$$**
(☑ 027-250 7777; www.thearushahotel.com; Clock Tower roundabout; s/d from US$230/260; ❇ @ 🛜 ❇) One of the first hotels in town (though it barely resembles its former incarnation) and now one of the best, the Arusha's smack in the city centre, but its large, lush and beautiful gardens give it a countryside feel. Though the rooms should be larger considering the price, service and facilities (including gym, casino and 24-hour room service) are top-notch.

🏨 Eastern Arusha

Eight Boutique Hotel BOUTIQUE HOTEL **$$**
(Bay Leaf Hotel; ☑ 027-254 3055; www.bayleaftz. com; Vijana Rd; r/ste from US$120/130) Upstairs from the elegant restaurant (p163) of the same name, this place has classy, large rooms and even better suites for prices that you don't often see in Arusha these days. Some have zany contemporary splashes of colour that are rarely overdone, others wear a more sedate, old-fashioned style that works equally well. It's on a quiet side street.

Themi Suites Hotel APARTMENT **$$**
(☑ 0732 979621, 0732 979617; www.themisuiteshotel. com; Njiro Hill Rd; 2/3-bedroom apt US$150/180; ❇ 🛜 🏠) This excellent place is ideal for families

Arusha

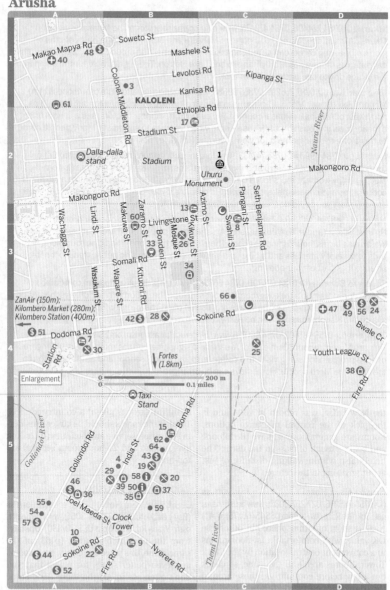

or those who want their own spacious serviced apartment with kitchen, dining and lounge area. Apartments have attractive wrought-iron furnishings, as well as flat-screen TVs, microwaves and washing machines. The two-bedroom apartments sleep four, and the three-bedroom ones can accommodate six. There's also a good on-site restaurant.

Spices & Herbs GUESTHOUSE $$
(☏ 0685 313162, 0754 313162; axum_spices@hotmail.com; Simeon Rd; s/d/tr US$50/55/85; @ 🛜)

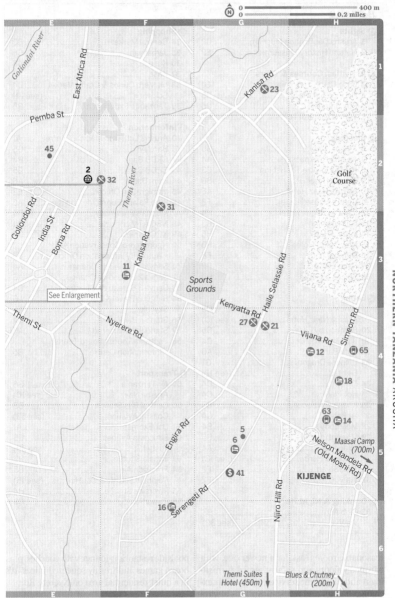

N
0 — 400 m
0 — 0.2 miles

The 19 rooms behind this popular Ethiopian restaurant (p163) are simple but warm, with woven-grass mats and wooden wardrobes adding character not often found at this price level. There's an internal patio and it's cheaper than most in eastern Arusha – excellent value.

Impala Hotel   HOTEL **$$**

(☏027-254 3082; www.impalahotel.com; Simeon Rd; s/d/tr US$100/130/160; ▣✳@🛜🏊🐾) Filling a gap between the small family-run guesthouses and the big luxury hotels, the Impala offers a convenient location,

Arusha

reasonable rooms (ask for a newer one, with parquetry floors and safari-themed furnishings) and abundant services, such as an exchange bureau and a restaurant. It's always worth asking for discounts.

Outpost Lodge LODGE **$$**
(☏0754 318523; www.outpost-lodge.com; Serengeti Rd; s/d/tr/q US$65/85/102/136; @🅿🛜🏊) This popular place has a mix of rooms, with the nicest ones in a newer, two-storey building set in lush gardens. There's also a communal poolside restaurant-lounge with couches, plus board games and freshly squeezed juices. It's in a quiet residential area off Nyerere Rd.

★ **Blues & Chutney** B&B **$$$**
(☏0658 127380, 0732 971668; www.bluesandchutney.com; House No 2 Olorien, Lower Kijenge; s/d US$130/175; 🛜) An intimate and sophisticated boutique B&B on a quiet street southeast of the centre, this place has the feel of a tranquil enclave for people in the know. The decor is white wood and classy, the

atmosphere refined, and four of the six light and airy rooms have large private balconies. The restaurant serves home-style cooking and there's a small bar.

★**African Tulip** BOUTIQUE HOTEL **$$$**
(☏0783 714104, 027-254 3004; www.theafrican tulip.com; Serengeti Rd; s/d/tr US$190/250/330, ste US$350-550; P❋@🛜☷) 🏊 The deservedly popular African Tulip inhabits a quiet green side street and successfully combines a safari theme with a genteel ambience. The large rooms are supremely comfortable havens from Arusha's noise. There's a whimsical baobab tree in the restaurant, carved wood in the common areas and a small garden around the swimming pool at the back.

Outside Arusha

Meserani Snake Park CAMPGROUND **$**
(☏027-253 8282; www.meseranisnakepark.com; Arusha-Dodoma Rd; camping incl snake-park admission US$15; P) This overlander-oriented place has good facilities, including hot showers, a bar-restaurant with cheap meals and a vehicle-repair shop. It's 25km west of Arusha along the Dodoma road.

★**Karama Lodge** LODGE **$$**
(☏0754 475188; www.karama-lodge.com; s/d/tr US$115/150/215; P@🛜☷) Truly something different, off Onsea–Moivaro Rd on a forested hillside in the Suye Hill area just southeast of town, Karama offers 22 rustic and rather lovely stilt bungalows, each with a veranda and views to both Kilimanjaro and Meru on clear days. It's signposted north of Old Moshi Rd.

Mvuli Hotels Arusha HOTEL **$$**
(☏0786 287761; www.mvulihotels.co.tz; Kundayo Rd; r from US$65; P❋🛜) Not far from the centre, but set in quiet and pretty gardens, Mvuli offers some of Arusha's best midrange accommodation. Rooms are large and comfortable and come with mosquito nets. There's nothing too remarkable afoot here; it's just that the price-to-quality ratio is rare in these parts for midrange places.

★**Mt Meru Game Lodge** LODGE **$$$**
(☏0689 706760; www.mtmerugamelodge.com; Arusha-Himo Rd; per person from US$275; P❋🛜) East of Arusha in Usa River and bordering a private wildlife sanctuary that has zebras, ostriches and colobus monkeys, Mt Meru Game Lodge is a wonderful place to stay. Stunning rooms decked out in soothing wood and white linen are some of the most

pleasing in Arusha, while public areas have ample African art without being overdone.

★**Arusha Coffee Lodge** LODGE **$$$**
(☏027-250 0630; www.elewana.com; Dodoma Rd; s US$193-413, d US$386-550, ste US$325-770; P@🛜☷) Set smack in the middle of a shade-grown coffee plantation and elegant through and through, this is one of the most talked-about properties in Arusha. The gorgeous standard rooms have split-level floors, making them feel like suites, and the restaurant has few peers. The only downside is that traffic noise is loud. It's along the highway just west of town.

★**Onsea House** B&B **$$$**
(☏0787 112498; www.onseahouse.com; Onsea Rd; s/d US$275/350; P🛜☷) This tranquil, classy B&B is run by a Belgian chef whose eye for detail is what makes this such a great place. Rooms each have their own themes, plus there's the Machweo Wellness Retreat and Fine Dining, a fabulous spa and yoga centre with a top-notch restaurant. It's about 1km off the Moshi road on the edge of town.

Kigongoni LODGE **$$$**
(☏0732 978876; www.kigongoni.net; s/d/tr incl guided walks from US$195/220/350; P@🛜☷) 🏊 Kigongoni's tranquil hilltop perch about 5km past Arusha gives it an almost wilderness feel. Spacious cottages, all with porches, fireplaces and wide views, are scattered around the forest, some quite a hilly walk from the cosy common areas. It's about 5km beyond Arusha towards Moshi.

✖ Eating

City Centre & Clock Tower

★**Hot Plate** INDIAN **$**
(☏0783 030730, 0715 030730; Navrat St; mains Tsh6000-12,000; ⊗7.30am-10pm Tue-Sun; 🛜☏) Delicious Indian food – including southern Indian specialities, plus some Punjabi and other dishes, both vegetarian and non-vegetarian – is on offer here in a shady, streetside setting. It's off Sokoine Rd, down the small side street just next to Manji's petrol station, tucked away behind a leafy stand of bamboo.

★**Khan's Barbecue** BARBECUE **$**
(Mosque St; meals Tsh9000-10,000, mixed grill Tsh13,000; ⊗6.30-11pm Mon-Fri, 5-11pm Sat & Sun) This Arusha institution is an auto-spares store by day (look for the Zubeda Auto Spares sign) and the best known of many earthy roadside

barbecues around the market area by night. It lays out a heaped spread of grilled, skewered meat and salad. If you want to experience Arusha like a local, this is a fine place to begin.

Cafe Barrista
CAFE $

(☑ 027-254 5677, 0754 288771; www.cafebarrista. com; Sokoine Rd; meals Tsh9000-14,000; ⊙ 7am-6.30pm Mon-Sat, to 2.30pm Sun; 🛜🍴) Great coffee is why this place exists, but try the chocolate croissant, or fill up with sandwiches, salads and wraps. There's also an internet cafe (Tsh2000 per hour) and wi-fi (free with meal purchases).

Bamboo by Fifi's
INTERNATIONAL $

(Boma Rd; mains Tsh7000-22,000; ⊙ 6.30am-10pm; 🛜🍴) Tasty baked goods, shakes and smoothies, salads and baguette sandwiches, plus an intriguing array of main dishes – all served in a bright, clean dining area – make this a recommended meal choice.

Arusha Naaz Hotel
TANZANIAN $

(☑ 027-257 2087; Sokoine Rd; snacks Tsh1000-5000, lunch buffet Tsh12,000; ⊙ 6.45am-6.30pm Mon-Sat, to 3pm Sun, buffet 11.30am-3pm Mon-Sat) This unassuming place has a good-value all-you-can-eat lunch buffet and a large snack counter.

McMoody's
BURGERS $

(☑ 0735 303030; Sokoine Rd; mains Tsh6000-16,000; ⊙ 10am-9.30pm; 🛜) A perennial favourite for burgers of all sorts, as well as pizzas, kebabs and other light meals.

Shanghai
CHINESE $

(☑ 027-250 3224, 0756 659247; Sokoine Rd; meals Tsh5000-17,000; ⊙ noon-3pm & 6-10.30pm; 🍴) Passable Chinese-owned restaurant with fast service and 'Far East meets the Wild West' decor – let's face it, when did a Chinese restaurant in Africa ever win a style award? It's hidden behind the post office.

Mirapot
TANZANIAN $

(India St; meals Tsh6000-12,000; ⊙ 7am-6.30pm Mon-Sat) Mirapot serves local fish dishes, traditional beef stew, and chicken in coconut sauce, as well as burgers, sandwiches and decent local coffee.

★ Fifi's
INTERNATIONAL, BAKERY $$

(☑ 027-254 4021; www.fifistanzania.com; Themi St; breakfast Tsh8500-18,500, mains Tsh11,000-21,500; ⊙ 7.30am-9.30pm Mon-Fri, 8.30am-9.30pm Sat & Sun; 🛜) Good for breakfast or a quiet afternoon coffee as well as for a more substantial meal, this chic bakery also serves up exciting dishes such as beef fillet with blue-cheese sauce or Swahili beef stew. Free wi-fi.

Via Via
CAFE $$

(☑ 0782 434845, 0767 562651; www.viaviacafe. com; Boma Rd; mains Tsh10,000-18,000; ⊙ 9am-10pm Mon-Sat) Cultured and laid-back, with the best soundtrack of any restaurant in Arusha, this place along the river behind the Natural History Museum (p155) is a popular meeting spot. It serves coffee, salads and sandwiches, plus more substantial meals like pastas and grilled fish. There's a decent bar and live music.

TapaSafari
SEAFOOD $$

(☑ 0757 009037; Kanisa Rd; small/large tapas from Tsh4500/7000, mains Tsh12,000-38,000; ⊙ 11am-10pm; 🛜🍴) With a semi-outdoor setting, this restaurant and wine bar ticks many boxes. There are snacks, grills, pizza and pasta, but the real stars are the Spanish tapas and extensive list of South African wines. Sundays are especially popular, with a four-course set menu (Tsh26,000) on offer.

Chinese Dragon
CHINESE $$

(☑ 027-254 4107; Kanisa Rd; mains Tsh9500-19,500; ⊙ noon-3pm & 6-10.30pm) This place at the Gymkhana Club northeast of the centre is in the same family as the wonderful Shanghai. Service and decor are no-nonsense, and the food is excellent – try the shredded beef with chilli and basil.

Africafé
CAFE $$

(Boma Rd; breakfast Tsh7000-12,000, mains Tsh14,000-24,000; ⊙ 7.30am-9pm Mon-Fri, 8am-9pm Sat & Sun; 🛜) A fine refuge from the Boma Rd touts, this place has European-cafe vibes with prices to match. The menu is heavy on sandwiches, with other dishes such as grilled meats, burgers and grilled Nile perch with garlic and butter. There's also a bakery.

🍴 Eastern Arusha

★ Blue Heron
INTERNATIONAL $$

(☑ 0785 555127; www.facebook.com/pizzaheron; Haile Selassie Rd; mains Tsh12,000-25,000; ⊙ 9am-5pm Mon-Thu, to 10pm Fri & Sat; 🍴) The pick of the garden restaurants that are a recurring theme in Arusha's east, the Blue Heron gets the tricky combination of lounge bar and family restaurant just right. Sit on the leafy veranda or out on the lawn tables to enjoy a menu ranging from paninis and soups to beef tenderloin and various creative specials. The smoothies are divine.

Chinese Whispers
ASIAN $$

(☑0688 969669; www.facebook.com/chinesewhis persarusha; 1st fl, Njiro Shopping Complex, Njiro Hill Rd; mains Tsh15,000-26,000; ⊙11am-3pm & 6-10.30pm Mon-Thu, 11am-10.30pm Fri-Sun) Consistently ranked among Arusha's best restaurants, this place is beloved by the local expat community for its extensive, predominantly Chinese menu with dim sum and all the staples you'd expect, but cooked better than anywhere else in northern Tanzania.

Spices & Herbs
ETHIOPIAN, EUROPEAN $$

(☑0685 313162, 0754 313162; Simeon Rd; mains Tsh14,000-21,000; ⊙11am-10.30pm; 🐾☑) Unpretentious al fresco spot serving two menus: Ethiopian and Continental – ignore the latter and order *injera* (Ethiopian bread) soaked in beef, chicken or lamb sauce, and *yegbeg tibs* (fried lamb with Ethiopian butter, onion, green peppers and rosemary). The service is good and there's plenty of art on the walls.

Le Patio
FRENCH $$$

(☑0783-701704; www.facebook.com/LePatio Arusha; Kenyatta Rd; mains Tsh15,000-34,000; ⊙8.30am-11pm) Le Patio follows a tried-and-tested eastern-Arusha template: a large garden beneath shady trees, an open fire at its heart, a lounge bar and outdoor tables, all a world away from the clamour of the city centre. The food is mainly French, but there are also the usual salads, grills, pizza, sandwiches and moussaka.

Eight
EUROPEAN $$$

(Bay Leaf; ☑0758 777333, 027-254 3055; www. bayleaftz.com; Vijana Rd; mains Tsh16,000-40,000, Sun brunch Tsh39,000; ⊙8am-11pm, brunch 11am-4pm Sun; 🐾) Arusha's poshest menu features fresh ingredients and creative dishes such as slow-cooked West Kili lamb shanks. Seating is in the quiet dining room or in the shaded, walled garden.

It also offers a great wine list (choices by the glass and bottle), as well as separate lunch and dinner menus. It does a popular Sunday brunch.

Self-Catering

Village Supermarket
SUPERMARKET $

(Njiro Hill Rd; ⊙9am-9pm) Part of the Njiro Hill Shopping Complex southeast of the centre, this place is one of Arusha's best-stocked supermarkets. There's a decent open-air food court outside the door and a cinema complex in the same building.

Food Lover's Market
SUPERMARKET $

(Sable Square Shopping Village, Dodoma Rd; ⊙9am-7pm; 🅿) A well-stocked, South African-run supermarket, conveniently located west of Arusha, just past Arusha Airport, en route to the national parks.

🍷 Drinking & Nightlife

⭐Fig & Olive
BAR

(☑0784 532717; www.facebook.com/thefigand olivearusha; Dodoma Rd; ⊙9am-5pm Sun-Wed, to 10pm Thu-Sat) On the terrace of the large Cultural Heritage complex on Arusha's western outskirts, Fig & Olive has a Thursday cocktail night, and mellow live jazz and soul at 2pm on the first and third Sundays of the month.

Club AQ
CLUB

(Aqualine Hotel, Zaramo St; Tsh5000; ⊙9pm-late Fri & Sat) Nightclubs come and go in Arusha with a lot of noise but not much staying power, to the extent that Club AQ is almost a veteran. It has music you can dance to, a mixed crowd tending towards 30-somethings and DJs eager for you to have a good time.

Via Via
CAFE

(Boma Rd; ⊙9am-10pm Fri-Wed, to midnight Thu) This cafe is a good spot for a drink, and one of the best places to find out about upcoming cultural events, many of which are held here. On Thursday night there's karaoke and a live band (admission Tsh10,000), while Saturday is a barbecue buffet with African music. Things get started at 9pm.

🛍 Shopping

⭐Schwari
ARTS & CRAFTS

(☑0783 885833; www.schwari.com; Blue Heron, Haile Selassie Rd; ⊙9am-5pm Mon-Thu, to 8pm Fri & Sat) Quality handicrafts and classy homewares, children's toys and national-park maps – Schwari has picked the best of local crafts to create a fine collection. Combine your visit with lunch at Blue Heron (p162).

⭐Shanga
ARTS & CRAFTS

(☑0689 759067; www.shanga.org; Arusha Coffee Lodge, Dodoma Rd; ⊙9am-4.30pm) 🌿 What started as a small enterprise making beaded necklaces has branched into furniture, paper, clothing and many other products, mostly using recycled materials and made by workers with disabilities. The products are sold around the world, and a visit to the workshop and store, based at Arusha Coffee Lodge (p161), is quite inspiring.

DON'T MISS

ARUSHA MARKETS

The **Central Market** (Soko Kuu; Somali Rd; ⊙7am-6pm) in the heart of the city and the larger **Kilombero Market** (Dodoma Rd; ⊙7am-6pm) just west are worth an hour or two of strolling time. There are many more colourful local markets around the region, including **Ngaramtoni Market**, 12km northwest of town on the Nairobi road, on Thursday and Sunday, which draws Maasai from miles around, and the **Tengeru Market**, 10km east towards Moshi, on Wednesday and Saturday. Mind your pockets and bags at all of them.

Cultural Heritage   GIFTS & SOUVENIRS
(⊠027-250 7496; www.culturalheritage.co.tz; Dodoma Rd; ⊙9am-5pm Mon-Sat, to 2pm Sun) The large and unmissable Cultural Heritage craft mall on the western edge of Arusha has all the usual souvenirs as well as some less common items. Shopping is hassle-free, but prices are higher. There's a DHL office here, as well as the lovely Fig & Olive (p163) bar.

Mt Meru Curios & Crafts Market   MARKET
(Fire Rd; ⊙7am-7pm) Souvenirs (and a few high-quality items) are here at Mt Meru Curios & Crafts Market, often incorrectly called the Maasai Market. Hard bargaining is required, but it's worth persisting, as the market has the widest selection in central Arusha.

Jamaliyah   HOMEWARES
(⊠0754 592721; Boma Rd; ⊙9am-12.30pm & 2-6pm Mon-Sat, 9am-2pm Sun) This original little Aladdin's cave of a place makes and sells picture frames made of dhow wood. Step inside and start fossicking or talk with the friendly owner and you're bound to find something you like.

Tanzanite Experience   JEWELLERY
(⊠0767 600990; www.tanzaniteexperience.com; 3rd fl, Blue Plaza, India St; ⊙8.30am-5.30pm Mon-Sat, 10am-3pm Sun) One of many shops selling tanzanite; this one has set up a little museum about the rare gem, which is mined almost exclusively in the Kilimanjaro area.

Kase   BOOKS
(⊠027-250 2640; Boma Rd; ⊙9am-5.30pm Mon-Fri, to 2pm Sat) Your best bet for national-park books and maps. If the Boma Rd shop doesn't have what you want, try the other branch

(⊠027-250 2441; Joel Maeda St; ⊙9am-5pm Mon-Fri, to 2pm Sat) around the corner.

ⓘ Orientation

Central Arusha is divided by the small Naura River valley. To the west are the bus stations, the main market and many budget hotels. To the east are most of the airline offices, craft shops, midrange and upmarket hotels, and other facilities aimed at tourists; many are clustered around Clock Tower roundabout (a 20-minute walk from the central bus stand), where the two main roads (Sokoine Rd to the west and Old Moshi Rd to the east) meet.

ⓘ Information

DANGERS & ANNOYANCES

At night, take a taxi if you go out. It's not safe to walk after dusk except around the market, where the streets remain crowded for a few hours after dark. But even here be wary and don't carry anything valuable.

GARAGES

Fortes (⊠027-254 4887, 027-250 6094; www.fortes-safaris.com; ⊙8am-6pm) Reliable vehicle repairs. Located off the Nairobi–Arusha Hwy in the Sakina area.

Meserani Snake Park (⊠0754 440800, 0754 445911; www.meseranisnakepark.com) The mechanic of choice for overland trucks, 25 kilometres west of town on Dodoma Rd.

Puma Petrol Station (Sokoine Rd; ⊙24hr) In the centre of town.

IMMIGRATION

Immigration Office (East Africa Rd; ⊙7.30am-3.30pm Mon-Fri)

INTERNET ACCESS

There are numerous internet cafes around the market and Clock Tower areas. The normal rate is Tsh2000 per hour. Cafe Barrista (p162) has computers and wi-fi (the latter is free if you buy a meal). New Safari Hotel (p156) has internet access in the hotel lobby (Tsh3000, per hour).

MEDICAL SERVICES

Akaal Pharmacy (⊠0715 821700, 0718 444222; Sable Square Shopping Village, Dodoma Rd; ⊙9am-5.30pm Mon-Sat, 11am-4pm Sun) Well-stocked pharmacy en route to the northern parks.

Arusha Lutheran Medical Centre (⊠027-254 8030; www.selianlh.habari.co.tz; Makao Mapya Rd; ⊙24hr) This is one of the better medical facilities in the region, but for anything truly serious, go to Nairobi (Kenya).

Moona's Pharmacy (⊠027-254 5909, 0754 309052; moonas_pharmacy@cybernet.com; Sokoine Rd; ⊙8.45am-5.30pm Mon-Fri, to 2pm Sat) Well-stocked pharmacy west of NBC bank.

NORTHERN TANZANIA ARUSHA

MONEY

Forex bureaus are clustered along Joel Maeda St, India St, and Sokoine Rd near the Clock Tower. Most are open 8am to 6pm, including public holidays. ATMs are scattered around the city centre and easy to find, but be prepared for long waits, especially on Friday afternoon.

Foreign-exchange offices include **Kibo Palace** (Joel Maeda St; ☉7am-5pm), and **Sanya 1** (Dodoma Rd; ☉7am-7pm), **Sanya 2** (Sokoine Rd; ☉7am-7pm) and **Sanya 3** (Sokoine Rd; ☉7am-7pm).

Barclays (Sopa Lodges Bldg, Serengeti Rd; ☉9.30am-4pm Mon-Fri, 9am-noon Sat)

CRDB Bank (Boma Rd; ☉8am-4pm Mon-Fri)

CRDB Bank (Sokoine Rd; ☉8am-4pm Mon-Fri)

Exim Bank (cnr Sokoine & Goliondoi Rds)

NBC ATM (Father Babu Rd; ☉24hr)

NBC Bank (Sokoine Rd; ☉8.30am-4pm Mon-Fri, 9am-noon Sat)

Stanbic Bank (Sokoine Rd; ☉8.30am-3.30pm Mon-Fri)

Standard Chartered (Goliondoi Rd; ☉24hr)

TOURIST INFORMATION

The bulletin boards at the tourist-board info centre and at Cafe Barrista (p162) are good spots to find safari mates.

Ngorongoro Conservation Area Authority (NCAA) Information Office (☑027-254 4625; www.ngorongorocrater.go.tz; Boma Rd; ☉8am-4pm Mon-Fri, 9am-1pm Sat, 10am-1pm Sun) Has free Ngorongoro booklets and a relief map of the conservation area. If you're not paying by credit card at the gate, you'll need to stop here to arrange payment of your entry fees prior to heading out to the crater.

Tanzania National Parks Authority (Tanapa; ☑027-250 3471; www.tanzaniaparks.go.tz; Dodoma Rd; ☉8am-4pm Mon-Fri) Just west of town, this office has info on Tanzania's national parks and can help with general information and bookings for park accommodation.

Tanzania Tourist Board Tourist Information Centre (TTB; ☑027-250 3842, 027-250 3843; www.tanzaniatouristboard.com; Boma Rd; ☉8am-4pm Mon-Fri, 8.30am-1pm Sat) Knowledgeable and helpful staff have information on Arusha, northern-circuit parks and other area attractions. They can book Cultural Tourism Program tours (p156) and provide a good free map of Arusha and Moshi. The office also keeps a 'blacklist' of tour operators and a list of registered tour companies.

TRAVEL AGENCIES

Satguru Travel & Tours (☑0732 979980; www.satguruun.com; Goliondoi Rd) Excellent travel agency selling air tickets with a vast network across Africa.

Skylink (☑027-250 9108, 0755 351111; www.skylinktanzania.com; Goliondoi Rd; ☉8.30am-5.30pm) Domestic and international flight bookings.

❶ Getting There & Away

AIR

Most flights use Kilimanjaro International Airport, about halfway between Moshi and Arusha, while small planes, mostly to the national parks, leave from Arusha Airport, 8km west of town along the Dodoma Rd.

Confirm whether your flight will leave from Kilimanjaro International Airport or Arusha Airport when you buy your ticket.

Air Excel (☑027-297 0248, 027-297 0249; www.airexcelonline.com; Arusha Airport) Flights from Arusha Airport to various Serengeti airstrips and Lake Manyara National Park.

Air Tanzania (☑0784 275384, 0754 282727; www.airtanzania.co.tz; Boma Rd; ☉8.30am-5pm Mon-Sat) Flights five times weekly between Arusha Airport, Dar es Salaam and Zanzibar Island.

Coastal Aviation (☑027-250 0343; www.coastal.co.tz; Boma Rd; ☉7am-6pm) Arusha to Lake Manyara, Serengeti and Ruaha National Parks, West Kilimanjaro and Zanzibar.

Ethiopian Airlines (☑027-250 4231; www.ethiopianairlines.com; Boma Rd; ☉8.30am-12.30pm & 2-5pm Mon-Fri, 8.30am-1pm Sat) International services to Kilimanjaro International Airport from Addis Ababa (Ethiopia).

Fastjet (☑0783 540540; www.fastjet.com; 2nd fl, Blue Plaza, India St; ☉8am-6pm Mon-Sat) Good for low-cost flights to domestic and other African destinations, with direct Kilimanjaro International Airport to Dar es Salaam flights and onward connections.

Precision Air (☑0756 979490; www.precisionairtz.com; Boma Rd) Flies to Dar es Salaam, Mwanza and Zanzibar Island from Kili International and Arusha Airports. Also handles Kenya Airways bookings.

NORTHERN TANZANIA ARUSHA

---

❶ THE NAIROBI SHUTTLE

The fastest, most comfortable and most reliable services between Arusha and Nairobi (Kenya) are the minibus shuttles. The following companies are among the most reliable operators:

Impala Shuttle (☑027-254 3082; Impala Hotel, Simeon Rd; ☉8am & 2pm)

Rainbow Shuttle (☑0784 204025; www.facebook.com/rainbowshuttle; New Safari Hotel, Boma Rd)

Riverside Shuttle (www.riverside-shuttle.com; Simeon Rd; ☉8am & 2pm)

Regional Air ([☎] 0754 285754, 0784 285753; www.regionaltanzania.com; Sable Square Shopping Village, Dodoma Rd) Connects Arusha Airport with Serengeti and Lake Manyara airstrips, as well as Zanzibar Island.

RwandAir ([☎] 0732 978558; www.rwandair. com; Swahili St) Twice-weekly Kigali to Kili International service.

ZanAir ([☎] 027-254 8877; www.zanair.com; Summit Centre, Dodoma Rd) Connects Arusha Airport with Dar es Salaam, Pemba and Zanzibar Island.

BUS

Arusha has several bus stations, but if you want to avoid them, most buses make a stop on the edge of town before going to the stations. Taxis will be waiting at that location.

Most buses leave early to mid-morning. When leaving Arusha, the best thing to do is book your ticket the day before, so that in the morning when you arrive with your luggage you can get straight on your bus. For pre-dawn buses, take a taxi to the station and ask the driver to drop you directly at your bus.

Despite what you may hear, there are no luggage fees (unless you have an *extraordinarily* large pack).

Central Bus Station (cnr Somali Rd & Zaramo St) Arusha's biggest bus station is intimidatingly chaotic in the morning and popular with touts. If you get overwhelmed, head straight for a taxi, or duck into the lobby of one of the hotels across the street to get your bearings.

Dar Express Bus Station (Makao Mapya Bus Station; Wachagga St) Most of the luxury buses to Dar es Salaam depart from here, including Dar Express and Kilimanjaro Express.

Kilombero Station (Makao Mapya Rd) Several companies serving Babati, Singida, Mwanza and other points generally west, including Mtei Express, have their offices and departure points here, near Kilombero market.

Buses to Musoma & Mwanza

Buses from Arusha to Musoma and Mwanza pass through Serengeti National Park and Ngorongoro Conservation Area. Foreigners must pay entry fees for both Serengeti and Ngorongoro to ride this route.

Buses to Lushoto

Buses to Lushoto depart daily from 6am at the Central Bus Station, but it's more comfortable overall, and often works out just as fast (although more expensive), to take an express bus heading for Dar es Salaam as far as Mombo, and then get local transport from there to Lushoto.

Buses to Moshi

Buses and minibuses from Arusha to Moshi run up to 8pm, departing from the Central Bus Station. It's pricier (Tsh5000 or US$10, depending on your negotiating skills) but more comfortable to take one of the Arusha–Nairobi shuttles.

Buses to Dar es Salaam

The best companies (all with relatively new, air-conditioned buses with four-across seating) to/from Dar es Salaam (eight to 10 hours), are listed in the table below. If you take an early departure, with luck you *might* be able to catch the last ferry to Zanzibar Island. Super luxury means there's a toilet on board. Less reliable options depart early morning from the Central Bus Station. They're sometimes cheaper, but you get what you pay for.

BUSES FROM ARUSHA

DESTINATION	DURATION (HR)	FARE (TSH)	BUS COMPANY
Babati	3	6500	Mtei Express
Dar es Salaam	8-10	28,000-36,000	Kilimanjaro Express; Dar Express; Metro Express
Dodoma	9	25,000	Mtei Express; several (Central Bus Station)
Kigoma	20	64,000	several (Central Bus Station)
Kolo	6½	12,000	Mtei Express
Kondoa	7	13,000	Mtei Express
Lushoto	6	12,000-13,000	several (Central Bus Station)
Morogoro	10	32,000	Kilimanjaro Express
Moshi	2	3000	several (Central Bus Station)
Musoma	12	35,000-40,000	several (Central Bus Station)
Mwanza	13-14	35,000	several (Central Bus Station)
Singida	6-7	15,000	Mtei Express
Tabora	12	32,000	several (Central Bus Station)
Tanga	7	16,000-20,000	several (Central Bus Station)

ⓘ Getting Around

TO/FROM KILIMANJARO INTERNATIONAL AIRPORT

The starting price for taxis from town is Tsh50,000. Some drivers will go for less, but many others will only go for more.

TO/FROM ARUSHA AIRPORT

Taxis from town charge from Tsh20,000. Any dalla-dalla heading out along Dodoma Rd can drop you at the junction, from where you'll have to walk about 1.5km.

CAR

Parking anywhere in the city centre costs Tsh1000 per day – an attendant with tickets is likely to be lurking not far from where you park.

For any serious safari, you'll need a large 4WD (ie Toyota Landcruiser) with a pop-top roof for wildlife viewing. It's worth shopping around, as quoted prices can vary significantly. Do your sums carefully, particularly in regard to included kilometres, as extra kilometres are charged steeply – between US$0.50 and US$1 per kilometre.

You can get smaller and cheaper RAV4-style 4WDs, but they're not ideal for wildlife viewing, although they're generally fine during the dry season. Expect to pay around US$600 per week with around 100km free per day.

Drivers are almost always included in the price. Book as early as possible because demand is high.

Arusha Naaz (☑ 027-257 2087, 0786 239771; www.arushanaaz.net; Sokoine Rd; ⊙9am-5pm)
Fortes (p164) Excellent and experienced operator that also allows self-drive.

LOCAL TRANSPORT

Dalla-dallas (minibuses; Tsh400) run along major roads from early until late; there's a big dalla-dalla stand west of the stadium, off Stadium St. There are taxi stands all around the city centre, including on **Makongoro Rd** (⊙24hr), and some park in front of most hotels, even many budget ones. A ride across town, from the Clock Tower to Makao Mapya bus station, for example, shouldn't cost more than Tsh5000. The usual asking price for both motorcycle taxis and *bajajis* (tuk-tuks) is Tsh2000 for a ride in the city centre.

Arusha National Park

The transition between unappealing urban chaos and pristine mountain hiking trails is rarely so abrupt as it is in **Arusha National Park** (☑ 027-255 3995, 0767 536136; www.tanzaniaparks.go.tz; adult/child US$53.10/17.70; ⊙6.30am-6.30pm). One of Tanzania's most beautiful and topographically varied protected areas, the park is dominated by **Mt Meru**,

---

ⓘ ARUSHA NATIONAL PARK

Why Go Climbing Mt Meru; canoe and walking safaris; fine birding; easy access (even a day trip) from Arusha.

When to Go Year-round.

Practicalities Drive in from Arusha or Moshi. The main park entrance is at the southern Ngongongare gate. The northern Momella gate is 12km further north near the **park headquarters** (www.tanzaniaparks.go.tz), which is the main contact for making campsite reservations. Entrance fees can be paid by credit card at the main Ngongongare gate.

Budget Tips Join a pre-arranged safari or charter a dalla-dalla for the day with other travellers in Arusha; if you're not climbing Mt Meru, visit on a day trip to avoid camping fees.

---

an almost perfect volcanic cone with a spectacular crater. It also shelters **Ngurdoto Crater** (often dubbed Little Ngorongoro), with its swamp-filled floor and lost-world feel.

At 552 sq km, it's a small park and, while there is wildlife here, it's nothing compared to that of other northern-circuit parks. But these minor details can be quickly forgotten when you're walking amid the soul-stirring scenery and exploring the meaningful trekking possibilities.

⊙ Sights & Activities

Wildlife Drives

Just north of Ngongongare gate is Serengeti Ndogo (Little Serengeti), a small patch of open grassland that almost always has zebras and other plains animals. Here the road divides: Outer Rd, to the west, has great Meru views, but the eastern Park Rd is the better route for wildlife. Both are good all-year roads passable in 2WD cars, as are most other tracks through the park. Park Rd leads past the road up Ngurdoto Crater and then to Momella Lakes, both beautiful attractions as well as good wildlife-spotting areas.

The park's altitude varies from 1400m to more than 4500m, and there's a variety of vegetation zones, but most of the park is forested (watch for blue monkeys) and the dense vegetation reduces visibility. Nevertheless, you can be fairly certain of sighting zebras, giraffes, waterbucks, bushbucks, klipspringers,

TREKKING MT MERU

At 4566m, Mt Meru is Tanzania's second-highest mountain. Although overshadowed by Kilimanjaro in the eyes of trekkers, it's a spectacular volcanic cone with one of East Africa's most scenic and rewarding climbs, involving a dramatic walk along the knife edge of the crater rim.

Mt Meru starts its steep rise from a circular base some 20km across at 2000m. At about 2500m some of the wall has broken away, so the top half of the mountain is shaped like a giant horseshoe. The cliffs of the inner wall below the summit are more than 1500m high, making them among the tallest in Africa. Inside the crater, more recent volcanic eruptions have created a subsidiary peak called the Ash Cone that adds to the scenic splendour.

Momella Route

The Momella route is the only route up Mt Meru. It starts at Momella gate on the eastern side of the mountain and goes to the summit along the northern arm of the horseshoe crater. The route can be done comfortably in four days (three nights). Trekkers aren't allowed to begin after 3pm, which means that if you travel to the park by bus you'll almost certainly have to camp and wait until the next day to start climbing.

While Meru is small compared to Kilimanjaro, don't underestimate it: because of the steepness, many have found that Meru is almost as difficult a climb. And it's still high enough for you to feel the effects of altitude, so don't try to rush up if you're not properly acclimatised.

Stage 1: Momella gate to Miriakamba Hut (10km, four to five hours, 1000m ascent)
There are two routes, one long and one short, at the start of the climb. Most people prefer taking the mostly forested long route up and the short route down, so that's how the trek is described here. And do watch out for buffaloes…

From Momella gate, the road winds uphill for an hour to **Fig Tree Arch**, a parasitic wild fig that originally grew around two other trees, eventually strangling them. Now only the fig tree remains, with its distinctive arch large enough to drive a car through. After another hour the track crosses a large stream, just above Maio Falls, and one hour further you'll reach Kitoto Camp, with excellent views over the Momella Lakes and out to Kilimanjaro in the distance. It's then one final hour to Miriakamba Hut (2514m). From Miriakamba you can walk to the **Meru Crater floor** (a two- to three-hour return trip) either in the afternoon of Stage 1 or during Stage 4 (there is time to do it on the morning of Stage 2, but this is a bad idea as it reduces your time for acclimatisation), but you need to let your guide know you want to do this before starting the climb. The path across the floor leads to Njeku Viewpoint on a high cliff overlooking a waterfall, with excellent views of the Ash Cone and the entire extent of the crater.

Stage 2: Miriakamba Hut to Saddle Hut (4km, three to five hours, 1250m ascent)
From Miriakamba the path climbs steeply up through pleasant glades to reach **Topela Mbogo** (Buffalo Swamp) after 45 minutes and **Mgongo Wa Tembo** (Elephant Ridge) after another 30 minutes. From the top of Mgongo Wa Tembo there are great views down into the crater and up to the main cliffs below the summit. Continue through some open grassy clearings and over several stream beds (usually dry) to **Saddle Hut** (3570m).

From Saddle Hut a side trip to the summit of **Little Meru** (3820m) takes about an hour and gives impressive views of Meru's summit, the horseshoe crater, the top of the Ash Cone and the sheer cliffs of the crater's inner wall. As the sun sets behind Meru, casting huge jagged shadows across the clouds, the snows on Kili turn orange and then pink as the light fades.

Stage 3: Saddle Hut to Meru Summit and return (5km, four to five hours, 816m ascent, plus 5km, two to three hours, 816m descent) This stage, along a very narrow ridge between the outer slopes of the mountain and the sheer cliffs of the inner crater, promises some of the most dramatic and exhilarating trekking anywhere in East Africa. During the

dik-diks, buffaloes and hippos. There are also elephants, red duikers, black-and-white colobuses (most often sighted near the Ngurdoto Museum) and rarely seen leopards. There are no lions or rhinos.

Birdwatching

Bird life is abundant, with around 400 species recorded in the park. Raptors are common at higher altitudes. Like many in the Rift Valley, the seven spring-fed Momella

rainy season, ice and snow can occur on this section of the route, so take care. If there's no mist, the views from the summit are spectacular.

If you're looking forward to watching the sun rise behind Kilimanjaro, but you're not keen on attempting this section in the dark, the views at dawn are just as impressive from **Rhino Point** (3814m), about an hour from Saddle Hut, as they are from the summit, perhaps even more so because you'll also see the main cliffs of the crater's inner wall being illuminated by the rising sun.

Stage 4: Saddle Hut to Momella gate (5km, three to five hours, 2250m descent)
From Saddle Hut, retrace the Stage 2 route to Miriakamba. From Miriakamba, the short path descends gradually down the ridge directly to Momella gate. It goes through forest some of the way, then open grassland, where giraffes and zebras are often seen.

Practicalities

Costs Trekking companies in both Arusha and Moshi organise treks on Mt Meru. Most charge from US$450 to US$800 for four days. That said, you can do things quite easily on your own for around US$400 for a four-day, three-night trek. You'll also need to add in the costs of food (which you should get in Arusha, as there's nowhere to stock up near the park), and of transport to and from the park.

The following are the minimum per-person costs:

➡ park entrance fee: US$53.10 per day

➡ hut fees: US$35.40 per day

➡ rescue fee: US$23.60 per trip

➡ guide fees: US$17.70 per day

Tipping Park rangers receive a fixed monthly salary for their work and get no additional payment from the park for guiding, which means that tips are much appreciated. It happens rarely, but rangers and porters here occasionally expect the big tips demanded by their Kilimanjaro counterparts. If this happens and you're already on the trail, work out an arrangement to keep going, and then report them to headquarters when you get down the mountain.

For a good guide who has completed the full trek with you, plan on a tip of about US$50 per group. Cook and porter tips should be around US$30 and US$20 respectively. Tip more with top-end companies.

Guides and porters A ranger-guide is mandatory and can be arranged at Momella gate. Unlike on Kilimanjaro, guides on Meru are regular park rangers whose purpose is to assist (and protect) you in case you meet some of the park's buffaloes or elephants, rather than to show you the way, although they do know the route. If there's a shortage of rangers, which is often, you may end up in a larger group than you hoped for.

Optional porters are also available at Momella gate. The charge is US$11.80 per porter per day and this is paid directly to them at the end of the trek. They come from one of the nearby villages and are not park employees, so you'll also need to pay their park-entrance (Tsh1500 per day) and hut (Tsh2000 per night) fees at Momella gate before starting to trek. Porters will carry rucksacks weighing up to 20kg (excluding their own food and clothing).

Accommodation There are two blocks of four-bed bunkhouses ('huts') spaced for a four-day trek. Especially during the July–August and December–January high seasons, they're often full, so book ahead. It's also a good idea to carry a tent (though if you camp, you'll still need to pay hut fees). Each bunkhouse has a cooking and eating area; bring your own stove and fuel.

Lakes are shallow and alkaline and attract a wide variety of wading birds, including year-round flamingos. Due to their varying mineral content, each lake supports a different type of algal growth, which gives them different colours. Bird life varies quite distinctly from one lake to another, even when they're only separated by a narrow strip of land. Watch for raptors such as the Augur buzzard and Verreaux's eagle soaring on the

Arusha National Park

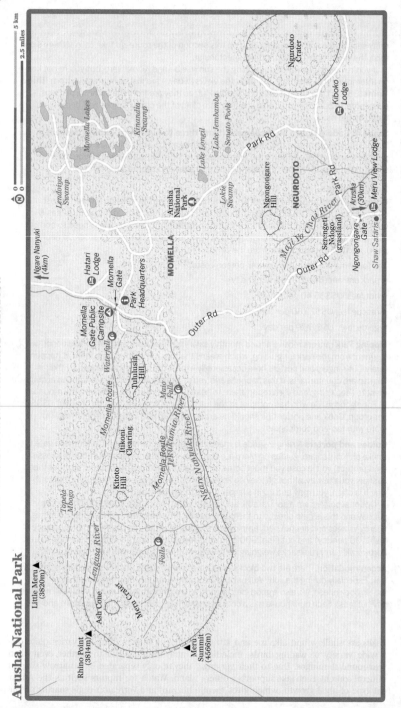

Little Meru (3820m)

Rhino Point (3514m)

Ngare Nanyuki (4km)

Hatari Lodge

Momella Gate

Momella Gate Public Campsite

Waterfall

Park Headquarters

Tululusia Hill

Maio Falls

Itikoni Clearing

Kitoto Hill

Topela Mbogo

Momella Route

Ngare Nanyuki River

Tekukumia River

Lengusa River

Ash Cone

Meru Crater

Meru Summit (4566m)

Falls

Lembnya Swamp

Momella Lakes

Kimandia Swamp

Ngurdoto Crater

Kiboko Lodge

Lake Longil

Lake Jembamba
Senato Pools

Park Rd

Arusha National Park

Lokie Swamp

NGURDOTO

Ngongongare Hill

Maji Ya Chai River

Serengeti Ndogo (grassland)

Ngongongare Gate

Park Rd

Arusha (30km)

Meru View Lodge

Shaw Safaris

Outer Rd

MOMELLA

Outer Rd

N

0   5 km
0   2.5 miles

thermals above Ngurdoto. The park's bird population increases dramatically when migratory birds arrive around November; they usually stay until April. In the forests, highlights include turacos and trogons.

Canoeing

Wayo Africa (Green Footprint Adventures; ☑0784 203000, 0783 141119; www.wayoafrica. com) offers 2½-hour Momella Lakes canoe safaris (US$60 per person plus a US$20 canoeing fee paid at the park gate) in the morning and afternoon.

Walking Safaris

Walking safaris (US$25 per person per half-day) are popular. Several trails pass below Mt Meru and another follows the Ngurdoto Crater rim trail (descending into the crater is not permitted). The walk to Njeku Viewpoint in the Meru Crater floor, which follows Stage 1 (p172) of the climb up Mt Meru, is an excellent day hike.

🛏 Sleeping & Eating

In the vicinity of Momella gate are three areas of **public campsites** (camping US$35.40), including one with a shower. There are pretty views from here, but the sites can get very busy at weekends.

Kiboko Lodge　　　　　　　　LODGE $$
(☑0765 688550; www.kibokolodge.nl; s/d with half board from US$83/146; 🐾) 🐾 Most employees at this nonprofit, charity-run lodge are former street kids who received training at the Watoto Foundation's vocational training school, and a stay here supports the project. The slightly worn but spacious stone cottages have fireplaces, hot water and safes, and the thatched-roof lounge is almost homey. It's 5km down a 4WD-only road east of Ngongongare gate.

Meru View Lodge　　　　　　　LODGE $$
(☑0784529636; www.meru-view-lodge.com; s/d with half board US$105/140; @🐾🐾) This unassuming place has a mix of large and small cottages (all priced the same) set in quiet grounds just 1km south of Ngongongare gate. The proprietors also run the nearby **Ngurdoto Lodge**, which has the same prices and similar facilities.

★Hatari Lodge　　　　　　　　LODGE $$$
(☑027-255 3456/7, 0752 553456; www.hatari lodge.com; s/d with full board & incl all activities US$558/944; 🅿🐾) The most atmospheric and upmarket of the park lodges has tasteful 'modern-retro' rooms filled with personality, a prime location on large lawns frequented by giraffes, and views of Meru and Kilimanjaro on clear days. Rooms are spacious, boasting large windows, and there's a fireplace and top-notch cuisine. It's on the edge of the park, about 2km north of Momella gate.

The property was originally owned by Hardy Kruger, of *Hatari!* film fame, and the current owners, Jörg and Marlies, are welcoming and knowledgeable hosts. They offer cheaper packages if you stay at both of their properties, here and Shu'mata Camp (p236) at West Kilimanjaro.

Rivertrees Country Inn　　　　LODGE $$$
(☑0732 971667, 0713 339873; www.rivertrees. com; s/d from US$199/262, 2-room River House US$1000; 🅿@🐾🐾) With a genteel old-world ambience and excellent cuisine served family style around a large wooden table, Rivertrees is a perfect post-national-park stop. A variety of rooms and cottages, some wheelchair accessible, are spread throughout vast natural gardens with huge trees along the Usa River. It's east of Usa River Village, set back off the Moshi Hwy.

African View Lodge　　　　　　LODGE $$$
(☑0784 419232; www.african-view.com; s/d with full board US$125/190; 🐾🐾) This good-value place features prime views of Mt Meru, an infinity pool, a good restaurant and accommodation in stylishly furnished bungalows dotted around lovely gardens. The in-house tour operator also organises northern-circuit safaris, Meru and Kilimanjaro climbs, and add-on excursions to Zanzibar and other coastal destinations.

❶ Getting There & Away

The entrance to Arusha National Park is about 35km northeast of Arusha. Take the main road between Arusha and Moshi to the signposted turn-off, from where it's about 10km north to Ngongongare gate, where you pay your entry fees. Momella gate – the location of the park headquarters – is about 14km further on. From Momella gate, it's possible to continue along a rough track to Lariboro, on the main Nairobi highway, passing Ngare Nanyuki village (6km north of Momella gate) en route.

There are several buses daily between Arusha and Ngare Nanyuki village, departing Arusha between 1.30pm and 4pm and Ngare Nanyuki between 7am and 8am. Buses stop at Ngongongare gate (Tsh6000, 1½ hours). A taxi from Arusha should cost from Tsh50,000.

Tarangire National Park

Welcome to one of Africa's most underrated parks. Thanks to its proximity to Serengeti National Park and Ngorongoro Crater, **Tarangire National Park** (✆ 0767 536139, 0689 062248; www.tanzaniaparks.go.tz; adult/child US$53.10/17.70; ◷ 6am-6.30pm) is usually assigned only a day visit as part of a larger northern-circuit itinerary. Yet it deserves much more, at least in the dry season (July to October). It's a place where elephants dot the plains like cattle, and where lion roars and zebra barks fill the night, all set against a backdrop of constantly changing scenery.

Tarangire has the second-highest concentration of wildlife of any Tanzanian national park (after the Serengeti) and reportedly the largest concentration of elephants in the world. The Tarangire ecosystem, with the park as its heart, also has more than 700 resident lions, and sightings are common. Less visible, but nonetheless present, are leopards and cheetahs. Sustaining them are large herds of zebras, wildebeest, hartebeests, elands, oryx, waterbucks, lesser kudus, giraffes and buffaloes. With more than 450 species, including many rare ones, Tarangire is among the best birdwatching destinations in Tanzania.

But this is one place where the wildlife tells only half the story. Dominating the park's 2850 sq km are some of Northern Tanzania's most varied landscapes. The great stands of epic baobabs should be reason enough to come, but there are also sun-blistered termite mounds in abundance, as well as grassy savannah plains and vast swamps. Cleaving the park in two is the Tarangire River, its meandering course and (in some places) steep riverbanks providing a dry-season lure for

> ### ⓘ TARANGIRE NATIONAL PARK
>
> **Why Go** Excellent dry-season wildlife watching, especially elephants and lions; evocative baobab-studded landscapes.
>
> **When to Go** June to October.
>
> **Practicalities** Drive in from Arusha; entrance fees (valid for 24 hours, single entry only) can be paid by credit card at both the main gate and the Boundary Hill gate.
>
> **Budget Tips** Join a pre-arranged safari or charter a dalla-dalla with other travellers; stay outside the park to avoid camping fees.

animals and thus many stirring wildlife encounters for visitors.

Come the short rainy season, the park changes completely, as its wild inhabitants disperse across the Maasai Steppe over an area 10 times larger than the park. This, too, is a Tarangire speciality: one of the park's greatest rewards is the chance to discern and tune into the seasonal rhythms of wild Africa.

◉ Sights & Activities

The **northern triangle**, bordered by the park boundaries to the northeast and west, and by the Tarangire River and Tarangire Safari Lodge to the south, offers the most easily accessible as well as some of the most rewarding wildlife areas of the park. Amid a varied habitat of open plains and light woodland, you'll find elephants, zebras and wildebeest in abundance in this baobab-rich region, with predators, particularly lions, also a possibility.

Further south, wildlife draws near to the water all along the **Tarangire River valley** that cuts the park in two, while the swamps of **Silale**, **Lormakau** and **Ngusero Oloirobi** are alive with possibility, as predators lie in wait in the shallows whenever herbivores come to drink. This chain of swamps runs north-south through the park, beginning just west of the Tarangire Sopa Lodge. **Gurusi Swamp**, in the park's southwestern bulge, is another area rich in wildlife.

Southwest of Tarangire Hill, a couple of hundred metres west of the main north-south track through the park, **Poacher's Hide** is a marvellous old baobab with a slightly concealed entrance and an internal cavern once used as a hideout by poachers. Beware of bees, which had taken a liking to the hide at the time of research. Also check for lions in these parts before getting out of your vehicle.

Night Drives

Inside the park, Tarangire Safari Lodge (p173) can arrange night drives for guests for US$80 per person, plus a US$23.60 ranger fee per group; expect other lodges to follow suit in the not-too-distant future. All of the camps and lodges outside the park boundaries offer night drives in the conservancies and range lands beyond the park. Ask at the gate about the park's own night drives (adult/child US$59/29.50).

Walking Safaris

Three-hour walking safaris (US$23.60 per person plus US$23.60 per group) can be organised from the park gate (though the armed rangers are simply security and haven't had much training about wildlife). Most of the lodges can organise walks with their own trained guides, but only for their guests.

🍴 Sleeping & Eating

Staying in the park gets you into the heart of the action from the moment you wake up. Besides the many mostly upmarket lodges (some of which also offer fly camping), there are several park-run campsites.

There are midrange and upmarket camps outside Tarangire. Remember that the closer you are to the park gate the better, so as not to miss the crucial first hour or two for wildlife watching inside the park.

A further option is the Tarangire Conservation Area (TCA), a remote region outside the park to the northeast with animals aplenty from November to March, fewer in other months. If you're staying in the TCA, park access is through the Boundary Hill gate.

🛏 Inside the Park

Public Campsite   CAMPGROUND **$**
(tarangire@tanzaniaparks.go.tz; camping US$35.40) Tarangire's public campsite is just a short drive into the park near the northwestern tip. It has a good bush location and simple cold-water facilities. Bring supplies from Arusha. Bookings can be made in advance via email or on arrival at the park gate.

★Oliver's Camp   TENTED CAMP **$$$**
(www.asiliaafrica.com; per person all-inclusive Jul & Aug US$959, rest of year US$689-889; ☺ closed Apr & May; ℗) Oliver's is notable for its fine location near Silale Swamp deep in the park's heart. The 10 comfortable, spacious tents have an agreeably rustic style and the whole camp has an intimate ambience. Excellent guides lead walking safaris, night drives (sometimes using night-vision equipment) and fly camping, making this place ideal for adventurous travellers. Tents have leather armchairs and mahogany headboards.

★Tarangire Safari Lodge   LODGE **$$$**
(☏027-254 4752, 0756 914663; www.tarangire safarilodge.com; s/d with full board US$270/440; ℗ 🛜 🐾 🛝) A fabulous location high above the Tarangire River, good food and service, and well-priced accommodation make this lodge the pick of the in-park options. The sweeping vistas mean that there's no need to go elsewhere for a sundowner. Accommodation

Tarangire National Park

Tarangire National Park

includes stone bungalows and standard ensuite safari tents; the latter have good views from their doorsteps. It's 10km inside the park gate.

Sanctuary Swala
TENTED CAMP $$$

(☏027-250 9817; www.sanctuaryretreats.com; per person with full board & incl all activities Jun-Oct US$775, rest of year rates vary; ☻Jun-Mar; ℗@ 🛜⛵) Arguably the most refined safari experience inside Tarangire, this premier-class camp nestles in a grove of acacia trees and overlooks a busy waterhole in the southwestern part of the park near Gurusi Swamp. Each of the 12 lovely tents has a big deck and its own butler. The camp's in a great wildlife-watching location with lots of lions.

🛏 Before the Park Gate

Zion Campsite
CAMPGROUND $

(☏0754 460539; camping US$10; ℗) A bare and unkempt compound 6km before the park gate it may be cheaper than camping inside the park, and the showers are warm. Bring your own food.

Maramboi Tented Lodge
TENTED CAMP $$$

(☏0784 207727; www.twctanzania.com; s/d/tr with full board US$250/375/510; ℗@🛜⛵) Unlike any other lodge around Tarangire, Maramboi sits amid palms and savannah on Lake Manyara's southeastern shore, 17km from Tarangire's entrance. The 20 large, airy tents with wooden floors all have decks looking out towards the lake, Rift Valley Escarpment and sunset. The staff are friendly. The turn-off to the lodge is 6km south of Kigongoni village.

Tarangire River Camp
LODGE $$$

(☏0737 206420, 0732 978879; www.mbalimbali. com; s/d with full board US$375/660; ☻closed Apr; ℗) With terrific views from its hilltop perch overlooking a river valley and lovely open-sided thatched huts, Tarangire River Camp is a fine choice set away in a private, Maasai-run concession northwest of the park – it's around 30 minutes by road from the lodge to the main park gate.

Roika Tarangire Tented Lodge
TENTED CAMP $$$

(☏0754 001444, 027-250 9994; www.tarangireroika tentedlodge.com; camping US$30, s/d US$250/ 380; ℗@🛜⛵) Though it's set off from the park southwest of the gate, Roika sits in the bush and is visited by lots of wildlife, especially elephants. The 21 widely spaced tents sit on elevated platforms under thatched roofs and have bizarre concrete animal-shaped bathtubs. Maasai-village visits and night drives are available. The campsite has hot showers and a kitchen is planned.

🛏 In the Tarangire Conservation Area

★ Tarangire Treetops Lodge
TENTED CAMP $$$

(☏027-250 0630; www.elewana.com; s/d with full board Jun-Oct US$1268/1690, rest of year rates vary; ℗@🛜⛵) Not your ordinary tented camp, this pampered place has 20 huge suites set on stilts or built treehouse style around the baobabs. It's almost an hour's drive from here to the Boundary Hill gate, but it's ideal if you're looking for more of a luxury-in-the-wilderness experience.

Boundary Hill Lodge
LODGE $$$

(☏0787 293727; www.tarangireconservation.com; per person with full board US$575; ℗@⛵) 🌿 Widely praised for its commitment to the environment and the Maasai community (the community owns a 50% stake in the lodge), Boundary Hill has eight large, individually designed hilltop rooms with balconies peering out over Silale Swamp in the park.

ℹ Getting There & Away

Tarangire is 130km from Arusha via Makuyuni (which is the last place for petrol and basic supplies). At Kigongoni village, there's a signposted turn-off to the main park gate, which is 7km further down a good dirt access road. The only other entrance is Boundary Hill gate along the northeastern border, which provides access to some lodges located in the area. The park doesn't rent vehicles.

Coastal Aviation (p165) and Air Excel (p165) sometimes stop at Tarangire's Kuro airstrip on request on their flights between Arusha and Lake Manyara.

Manyara Ranch Conservancy

Occupying an important wildlife-dispersal area northwest of Tarangire National Park, the privately run, 140-sq-km **Manyara Ranch Conservancy** (☏027-254 5284, 0683 918888; www.manyararanch.com) is a critical cog in the ecosystem of northern Tanzania's Maasai Steppe.

The conservancy began life as a colonial cattle ranch, which later fell into disuse. Thanks to the **African Wildlife Foundation** (AWF; ☏0711063000; www.awf.org), vegetation is recovering and wildlife is returning to the area. Already there are fairly reliable year-round populations of elephants, lions (two small resident prides), leopards, hyenas (striped and spotted), giraffes, zebras and other herbivores. More than 300 bird species have also been recorded here.

True to the conservancy model, the project is not just about protecting wildlife: the AWF works closely with neighbouring Maasai communities to ensure that they receive some benefits from the wildlife that lives in their midst.

Walking safaris and day or night **wildlife drives** (watch for lions, leopards, striped hyenas and aardwolfs on the latter) are all possible and are usually included as part of accommodation packages. Other activities include **cultural visits** to nearby Maasai villages.

Manyara Ranch Tented Camp (☑027-254 5284; www.manyararanch.com; all-inclusive s US$730-990, d US$1230-1680), between Lake Manyara and Tarangire National Parks, is the only one on the Manyara Ranch Conservancy, ensuring a quiet stay far from the parks' crowded trails. Tents are classic safari style but delightfully uncluttered and supremely comfortable. Activities include nature walks with an armed guide, day or night wildlife drives, birdwatching and Maasai village and/ or school visits.

ⓘ Getting There & Away

There's no public transport to the conservancy. If you're self-driving, from Makuyuni head south along the road towards Tarangire. After 10km, opposite a building with red and blue walls, a stone sign on the right-hand (western) side of the road says 'Manyara Ranch Conservancy'. Take the turn, veering right, then follow the dirt road and the signs for 6.6km into the camp.

Mto wa Mbu
☑027 / POP 11,400

Mto wa Mbu is the busy gateway to Lake Manyara, which is fed by the town's eponymous 'River of Mosquitoes', and you'll pass through here en route between Arusha and Ngorongoro. Over the years, this diverse place – by some estimates, all of Tanzania's 120 tribal groups are present here – has evolved into something of a travellers centre, with plenty of lodges, campsites, hole-in-the-wall eateries, petrol stations, money changers, souvenir stalls and just about anything else that could tempt a passing safari vehicle to disgorge its inhabitants.

The well-organised **Mto wa Mbu Cultural Tourism Program** (☑027-253 9303, 0784 606654; http://mtoculturalprogramme.tripod.com; day trip from US$30; ⊙8am-6.30pm) 🌾 offers walking and cycling tours to surrounding

LOCAL MARKETS

Consider timing your arrival in the area around the Crater Highlands, Lake Natron and Mto wa Mbu to coincide with one of the region's weekly markets. They're social as well as commercial events, and, with the partial exception of the market in Mto wa Mbu, almost entirely local affairs. Market days:

Monday Engaruka Juu

Wednesday Selela

Thursday Engaresero, Engaruka Chini and Mto wa Mbu

---

villages, markets and a nearby waterfall, with an emphasis on farming, and hiking along the escarpment. Homestays and meals with local families can also be arranged. The office is at the back of the Red Banana Cafe, close to the bus stop on the main road.

CRDB (⊙8am-4pm Mon-Fri, to noon Sat) on the main road has a sometimes-functional ATM.

🛏 Sleeping & Eating

The best area to look for budget guesthouses is south of the main road behind the market.

Maryland Resort   GUESTHOUSE **$**
(☑0756 740948; www.facebook.com/Maryland hotel; camping Tsh10,000, s/d from Tsh40,000/ 50,000, d with shared bathroom Tsh28,000; ℗) Signposted off the main road just before the Lake Manyara National Park gate, this bright-peach building is meticulously maintained by the friendly owner, who lives on-site. Most of the nine rooms are on the small side, but with hot water and cable TV they're priced right. Meals are available by request, and there's a kitchen.

Twiga Campsite & Lodge   HOSTEL **$$**
(☑0784 901479, 0758 510000; www.twigalodge campsite.com; Arusha-Karatu Rd; camping US$10, r US$50-100; ℗@⊜) This popular place is a real travellers hub, with simple but well-kept standard rooms, bungalows and a decent campsite. It's a good place to hook up with other safari-goers, and bike and vehicle hire is available.

Njake Jambo Lodge & Campsite   CAMPGROUND **$$**
(☑027-250 5553; www.njake.com; Arusha-Karatu Rd; camping US$10, s/d US$95/130; 🕾⊜) A base for both independent travellers and large overland trucks, Njake Jambo has a shaded and

well-maintained grassy camping area, plus 16 good rooms in double-storey chalet blocks.

Blue Turaco Pizza Point   PIZZA **$$**
(Arusha-Karatu Rd; pizzas Tsh12,000-16,000; ☺noon-9pm) The Blue Turaco Pizza Point, unmissable along the south side of the main road, makes good wood-fired pizzas. Seating is in a small courtyard area just behind.

🛈 Getting There & Away

Buses and dalla-dallas run all day from Arusha (Tsh7000, two hours) and Karatu (Tsh2500, one hour) to Mto wa Mbu. You can also come from Arusha on the minibuses that run to Karatu. All vehicles stop along the main road in the town centre.

Car hire for trips to Lake Manyara and Tarangire National Parks (including fuel and driver US$150 to US$200) and to Ngorongoro Crater (US$200 to US$250) is available in Mto wa Mbu through the Cultural Tourism Program office (p175) and Twiga (p175) and Njake Jambo (p175) campsites.

The track north to Lake Natron begins here.

Lake Manyara National Park

One of Tanzania's smaller and most underrated parks, **Lake Manyara National Park** (☑027-253 9112, 0767 536137; www.tanzaniaparks.go.tz; adult/child US$53.10/17.70; ☺6am-6pm) has a wide range of ecosystems – 11 in all. While it may lack the size and variety of other northern-circuit destinations (there's pretty much one main north–south route through the park), its vegetation is diverse, ranging from savannah to marsh to evergreen forest, and it supports one of the highest biomass densities of large mammals in the world. The chance to see elephant families moving through the forest or Lake Manyara's famous population of tree-climbing lions (although sighting them is becoming increasingly rare) are alone reason enough to come.

The dramatic western escarpment of the Rift Valley forms the park's western border. To the east is the alkaline Lake Manyara, which covers one-third of the park but shrinks considerably in the dry season. During the rains, the lake hosts millions of flamingos and other bird life.

◉ Sights & Activities

The park is also notable for its raised **treetop walkway** (☑0756 977384; www.wayoafrica.com/treetop-walkway; US$35.40, plus treetop park fee US$17.70; ☺6.30am-5pm), Tanzania's first.

Entry fees are valid for 24 hours, for a single entry only – worth remembering if you're thinking of returning to your hotel outside the park for lunch; bring a picnic lunch instead.

Wildlife Drives

Just inside the park's main gate, the northern woodland is dense, green and overrun by baboon troops; sightings of blue monkeys are also possible. There's a hippo pool at the lake's northernmost tip. Between the water's edge and the steep Rift Valley walls, the floodplains host wildebeest, buffaloes, zebras and Lake Manyara's much-studied elephants, while the thin acacia belt that shadows the lakeshore is where you're most likely to see arboreal lions.

Lake Manyara is the only northern-circuit park where *anybody* (not just guests at certain hotels) can do **night drives**. They're run by Wayo Africa (p171) from 8pm to roughly 11pm (US$50 per person, plus the park fee of US$59/23.60 per adult/child). Park fees must be paid directly to the park before 5pm. Advance booking (and usually advance payment) is required.

Walking Safaris

The park allows two- to three-hour walking safaris (US$23.60 per person, plus US$23.60 per group of up to eight) with an armed ranger along three trails. Reservations are required and the park has no vehicles to take hikers to the trailheads.

The **Msara Trail**, the nearest path to the gate (11km away), follows its namesake river along the Rift Valley Escarpment through great birdwatching territory up to a viewpoint. The **Lake Shore Trail** starts 38km into the park near the *maji moto* (hot springs). It crosses acacia woodland and savannah and is the path where walkers are most likely to meet large mammals and find flamingos. The **Iyambi River Trail**, 50km from the gate, is wooded and rocky with good birdwatching and a chance to see mammals.

Wayo Africa (p171) has three walking options (US$18 to US$35 per person) in the area: a nature walk along the escarpment, a forest walk down the escarpment, and a village walk in Mto wa Mbu (p175). All start from the Lake Manyara Serena Safari Lodge (p177) or a pre-arranged point in Mto wa Mbu.

🛏 Sleeping & Eating

There are several mostly upmarket options within park boundaries, plus cheaper park-run accommodation. The latter includes **park bandas** (www.tanzaniaparks.go.tz; bandas per person US$35.40) and a **public campsite** (www.tanzaniaparks.go.tz; camping US$35.40) just inside the gate, as well as another **public campsite** (www.tanzaniaparks.go.tz; camping US$35.40) near the Endabash River, about an hour's drive from the park gate. There are also several good midrange and top-end places atop the escarpment, outside park boundaries; most have sweeping views over the lake. Mto wa Mbu is another good base, especially for budget travellers.

In the Park

★Lake Manyara Tree Lodge   LODGE $$$

(☑028-262 1267; www.andbeyond.com; per person with full board & incl all activities Jun-Sep US$1340, rest of year rates vary; ☉closed Apr; P🖥🏊) This lovely, luxurious place is one of the most exclusive lodges in all of Tanzania. The gorgeous stilted tree-house suites with private decks and views from the bathtubs and outdoor showers are set in a mahogany forest at the remote southern end of the park. The food is excellent and the rooms have butler service.

On the Escarpment

Panorama Safari Campsite   CAMPGROUND $

(☑0763 075130; www.panoramasafaricamp.com; camping per tent US$10, permanent tents/igloos per person US$12/25) Located near the top of the escarpment is this hot, sometimes dusty place with camping and faded warm-water ablutions. The price is great, however, and the views are as wonderful as those at any of the nearby luxury lodges. There's also a restaurant. Dalla-dallas running between Mto wa Mbu and Karatu will drop you at the entrance.

★Escarpment Luxury Lodge   LODGE $$$

(☑0767 804864; www.escarpmentluxurylodge.com; s/d with full board & incl all activities US$850/1100; P@🏊) The wood-floored chalets at this attractive place are the height of luxury – plenty of space, wonderfully deep bathtubs, leather sofas, tasteful recycled furnishings, wide verandas, the finest linens and big windows. Views of the lake are as expansive as you'd expect from up here on the escarpment.

Lake Manyara Serena Safari Lodge   LODGE $$$

(☑027-254 5555; www.serenahotels.com; s/d with full board Jul-Oct US$301/509, Nov-Jun s US$114-256, d US$228-433; P@🖥🏊) The 67 well-appointed rooms in this large complex occupy appealing two-storey conical thatched bungalows in shady grounds. Nature walks and village visits are available, as is massage. There's no extra cost for the fine views (the best are from the swimming pool). It lacks the intimacy and naturalness of other escarpment properties but is nevertheless a justifiably popular choice.

Kirurumu Manyara Lodge   TENTED CAMP $$$

(☑027-250 7011; www.kirurumu.net; s/d with full board US$275/475) A unpretentious ambience, closeness to nature and memorable cuisine are the hallmarks of this well-regarded camp. It's about 6km down a rough road from the main road, with views of Lake Manyara in the distance and a bush feel up close. Tents are well spaced amid the vegetation. Maasai-guided ethno-botanical and sunset walks are free, and fly camping can be organised.

Below the Escarpment

Manyara Wildlife Safari Camp   LODGE $$$

(☑0712 332211; www.wildlifecamp.co.tz; s/d with full board US$275/350; P🏊) Tastefully furnished safari tents and stilted cottages with tiled floors and four-poster beds, all on the plains close to Lake Manyara, make this a good choice if being close to the lake is a priority. It's a 15-minute drive to the park gate, and signposted off the main road.

Migunga Tented Camp   TENTED CAMP $$$

(☑0754 324193; www.moivaro.com; camping US$10, s/d/tr with full board US$247/348/450; P@) The main attraction of this place (still often known by its previous name, Lake Manyara Tented Camp) is its setting in a grove of enormous fever trees (*migunga* in Swahili) that echoes with bird calls. The 21 tents ringing large, grassy grounds are small but adequate, and they're fairly priced. The camp is 2km south of the main road.

Ol Mesera Tented Camp   TENTED CAMP $$$

(☑0784 428332; www.ol-mesera.com; s/d with full board US$120/200; P@) Run by a sprightly

---

TREE-CLIMBING LIONS

Lions climb trees in other parks, too, but it's a real speciality of Manyara's lions – scientists speculate that they may have developed the habit to escape a nasty biting fly that devastated the Ngorongoro Crater lion populations back in the 1960s. Tracking the lions down can be tricky, but it's worth the effort.

🛈 LAKE MANYARA NATIONAL PARK

Why Go Excellent birding; tree-climbing lions; dramatic Rift Valley Escarpment scenery.

When to Go Year-round. June to October is best for large mammals; November to June is best for birds.

Practicalities Stay in Mto wa Mbu, atop the escarpment or inside the park; bring binoculars, as flamingos can be distant, depending on the day. Entrance fees are paid by credit card at the main gate.

Budget Tips Stay in Mto wa Mbu to avoid camping fees; charter a dalla-dalla for the day.

Slovenian pensioner, this personalised place, in a bush setting amid baobab and euphorbia trees, has four straightforward safari tents and is an ideal spot to do cultural walks or cooking classes, or just relax for a few days. It's 14km up the Lake Natron road, and hence a long way from the lake, but lovely and quiet.

Public transport towards Engaruka or Lake Natron can drop you at the turn-off, from where it's an easy 1.5km walk.

🛈 Information

The hand-drawn *New Map of Lake Manyara National Park,* available in Arusha and elsewhere, has different versions for wet and dry seasons but doesn't include the Marang Forest Reserve that has recently been added to the park.

🛈 Getting There & Away

Air Excel (p165), Coastal Aviation (p165) and Regional Air (p166) offer daily flights between Arusha and Lake Manyara.

Buses and dalla-dallas run frequently from Arusha (Tsh7500, two hours) and Karatu (Tsh3500, one hour) to Mto wa Mbu, the gateway village for Lake Manyara National Park. Once you're at Mto wa Mbu, it's straightforward to get onward transport to Lake Manyara lodges and camps or to hire a vehicle (from US$150 including fuel and driver) to explore the park.

Karatu

📞 027 / POP 26,600

Roughly halfway between Lake Manyara National Park and Ngorongoro (it's 14km southeast of Lodoare gate), this charmless town set in a beautiful surrounding area makes a convenient base for visiting both. Indeed, many camping safaris out of Arusha overnight here to avoid paying the camping fees in Ngorongoro. Services are basic but include banks that change cash and have ATMs, petrol stations, and several mini supermarkets (although it's better to stock up in Arusha).

The **Ganako-Karatu Cultural Tourism Program** (📞 0787 451162, 0767 612980; www.facebook.com/www.kcecho.org) offers trips to nearby coffee plantations and Iraqw (Mbulu) villages. Many of its half- and full-day trips are done by mountain bike, while others include hiking.

The seventh day of each month is Karatu's **market** (*mnada*) day; it's worth making some time for if you happen to be passing through.

🛏 Sleeping & Eating

Karatu has some excellent accommodation to suit a range of budgets. Most options lie just beyond the main road, which makes for a quieter stay, but for most you'll need a vehicle to get anywhere. The Bawani neighbourhood, south of the Bamprass petrol station and supermarket, has many good, reasonably priced guesthouses, plus several local restaurants and bars.

Vera Inn   GUESTHOUSE $
(📞 0767 578145, 0754 578145; Milano Rd; r Tsh40,000) This is one of many local guesthouses lining the dusty streets of the busy Bawani area of Karatu, just south of the main road behind the Bamprass petrol station. Rooms are clean, and have hot-water showers and cable TV.

ELCT Karatu Lutheran Hostel   HOSTEL $
(📞 0755 742315, 0787 458856; www.karatuhotel. com; s/d/tr Tsh55,000/65,000/90,000; 🅿) The Lutheran Hostel has simple, clean rooms with hot water, and good meals (Tsh10,000). Hostel proceeds go towards a vocational training centre for local unemployed young people. It's just off the main road at the western end of town.

Eileen's Trees Inn   LODGE $$
(📞 0783 379526, 0754 834725; www.eileenstrees. com; s/d with half board from US$75/110; 🅿 🛜 ❄) This consistently popular place offers accommodation in comfortable adjoining cottages. The rooms are large and come with wooden four-poster beds with mosquito nets, and wrought-iron furnishings in some bathrooms, and the food in the restaurant is well prepared and tasty. The real highlight is the lovely garden – wonderfully silent at night, and filled with birdsong by day.

Octagon Safari Lodge & Irish Bar LODGE $$
(📞 0765 473564, 0784 650324; www.octagonlodge.com; camping with own/hired tents US$25/40, s/d with half board US$90/160; @ 🛜) The lush and lovely gardens at this Irish-Tanzanian-owned lodge mean you'll soon feel far away from Karatu. The cottages are small but comfortable, and by Karatu standards the rates are reasonable. The restaurant and Irish pub round out the vibe. It's about 1km south of the main road on the western side of town.

St Catherine's Monastery GUESTHOUSE $$
(📞 0753 497886, 0754 882284; www.tanzaniarelax.com; d with full board US$90; P) This quiet, church-run place offers simple rooms around a flower-filled courtyard, and local-style meals. It's just outside Ngorongoro Conservation Area's Lodoare gate, and north of the main road. Turn off at the Kambi ya Nyoka school sign.

Ngorongoro Camp & Lodge HOSTEL $$
(📞 0763 258167; www.ngorongorocampandlodge.weebly.com; camping US$10, s/d/tr US$95/150/170; @ 🛏) This place on the main road at the eastern end of town is often busy with overland trucks. Camping facilities are fine, and the rooms are, too, with their tiled floors and pine furnishings, although they should be half the price.

★ Country Lodge LODGE $$$
(📞 027-253 4622, 0789 582982; www.countrylodgekaratu.com; s/d/tr with full board US$122/214/285; P @ 🛜 🛏) Signposted off the main road just north of Karatu, this excellent place offers 22 simple but quiet and tidy rooms in 11 cottages arrayed around 2 hectares of greenery. The cottages have verandas, and there's a restaurant serving good food made from locally sourced ingredients.

★ Plantation Lodge LODGE $$$
(📞 0784 397444, 0784 260799; www.plantation-lodge.com; s/d with half board US$345/530, ste from US$750; P @ 🛜 🛏) A place that makes you feel special, this relaxing lodge fills a renovated colonial farmstead and the decor is gorgeous down to the last detail. The uniquely decorated rooms spaced around the gardens have large verandas and crackling fireplaces to enhance the highland ambience. There's excellent home-grown food, too. It's west of Karatu and about 2.5km north of the highway.

★ Gibb's Farm LODGE $$$
(📞 027-253 4397; www.gibbsfarm.net; s/d/tr with half board US$580/925/1275; P 🛜 🛜) 🍴 The long-standing Gibb's Farm, filling a 1920s farmstead, has a rustic highland ambience, a wonderful setting with views over the nearby coffee plantations, a spa, and beautiful cottages (and a few standard rooms) set around the gardens. The cuisine is made with home-grown organic produce. It's about 5km north of the main road.

Ngorongoro Farm House LODGE $$$
(📞 0784 207727, 0736 502471; www.twctanzania.com; s/d/tr with full board US$275/425/575; P @ 🛜 🛏) This atmospheric place, 4km from Ngorongoro Conservation Area's Lodoare gate, is set in the grounds of a 202-hectare working farm that provides coffee, wheat and vegetables for this and the company's other lodges. The 50 well-appointed rooms, some a long walk from the restaurant and other public areas, are huge. Farm tours and coffee demonstrations are available, as is massage.

Bougainvillea Safari Lodge LODGE $$$
(📞 027-253 4083; www.bougainvilleasafarilodge.com; s/d/tr with full board US$140/255/350; P 🛜 🛏) A lovely place just north of the main road about 2km west of Karatu with two dozen spacious attached stone bungalows – all with fireplaces and small verandas – plus attractive gardens and a good restaurant.

Kudu Lodge & Campsite LODGE $$$
(📞 027-253 4055, 0754 474792; www.kuducamp.com; camping US$10, s/d/tr US$160/189/283; P 🛜 🛏 🛝) Kudu – signposted to the south of the main road at the southern end of town – has large, comfortable rooms in individual cottages scattered around the green grounds. There's also a pleasant, grassy camping area with hot-water showers and a cooking area, plus two swimming pools. Pool use is free for lodge guests and costs US$10 for campers.

ℹ Information

CRDB, **Exim** and **NBC** banks on the main road have 24-hour ATMs.

The **Ngorongoro Conservation Area Authority Information Office** (www.ngorongorocrater.go.tz; ⊘ 7.30am-4.30pm Mon-Fri, to 12.30pm Sat & Sun) – about 2km west of Karatu centre in the small complex of shops next to the Bougainvillea petrol station – is the place to go to make arrangements to visit Ngorongoro Crater or elsewhere in the Ngorongoro Conservation Area (NCA), if you don't have a credit card to pay for your entry into the NCA 14km up the road.

ℹ Getting There & Away

There are several morning buses between Karatu and Arusha (Tsh7500, three hours), some continuing to Moshi (Tsh11,000, 4½ hours). There are also more comfortable nine-seater minivans to/from Arusha (Tsh8500, three hours) that depart throughout the day. Transport leaves from several spots along the main road.

Lake Eyasi

Uniquely beautiful Lake Eyasi lies at 1030m between the Eyasi escarpment in the north and the Kidero Mountains in the south. Like Lake Natron far to the northeast, Eyasi makes a rewarding detour on a Ngorongoro trip for anyone looking for something remote and different. The lake itself varies considerably in size depending on the rains and supports a mix of waterbirds, including huge breeding-season (June to November) populations of flamingos and pelicans. In the dry season, it's little more than a parched lake bed, adding to the rather other-worldly, primeval ambience of the area.

The traditional Hadzabe lend a soulful human presence to the region. Also in the area are the Iraqw (Mbulu), a people of Cushitic origin who arrived about 2000 years ago, and the Datoga, noted metalsmiths whose dress and culture is quite similar to those of the Maasai.

◉ Sights & Activities

Ghorofani, Lake Eyasi's main village, lies a few kilometres from the lake's northeastern end. Its mnada **market** (village tax US$10), held on the fifth day of the month, attracts shoppers and traders from around the lake region.

The **Lake Eyasi Cultural Tourism Program** (☏0764 295280; www.tanzaniacultural tourism.com/dumbe.htm; ⊗8am-6pm), centred on Lake Eyasi, is at the entrance to Ghorofani. Here you can hire English-speaking guides (US$30 per group of up to 10) to visit nearby Hadzabe (an extra US$20 per group) and Datoga communities or the lake. One option is to join the Hadzabe on a hunting trip, for which you'll need to depart before dawn. All foreigners must also pay the US$10 village tax here.

🛏 Sleeping & Eating

Basic supplies are sold in the village, but it's better to stock up in Karatu.

Eyasi-Nyika Campsite   CAMPGROUND $
(☏0762 766040; www.facebook.com/NyikaCamp site; camping US$10; 🅿) One of Eyasi's best campgrounds, Eyasi-Nyika has seven widely spaced grassy sites, each under an acacia tree, and you can cook for yourself. It's in the bush, 3km outside Ghorofani, signposted only at the main road; after that, just stick to the most travelled roads and you'll get there.

★**Kisima Ngeda**   TENTED CAMP $$$
(☏027-254 8715; www.anasasafari.com/kisima -ngeda; camping US$10, s/d with half board US$350/ 475; 🅿🞖) Kisima Ngeda roughly translates as 'spring surrounded by trees': there's a natural spring at the heart of this lakeside property, creating an unexpectedly green and lush oasis of fever trees and doum palms. The seven tents are very comfortable and the cuisine (much of it locally produced, including dairy

---

THE HADZABE

The area close to Lake Eyasi is home to the Hadzabe (also known as the Hadzapi, Hadza or Tindiga) people, who are believed to have lived here for nearly 10,000 years. The Hadzabe are often said to be the last true hunter-gatherers in East Africa and, of the around 1000 who remain, between one-quarter and one-third still live according to traditional ways.

Traditional Hadzabe live a subsistence existence, usually in bands or camps of 20 to 30 people, and there are no tribal or hierarchical structures within their society. Families engage in communal child rearing, and food and all other resources are shared throughout the camp. Camps are often moved, sometimes due to illness, death or the need to resolve conflicts; they may even relocate to the site of a large kill such as a giraffe. An enduring characteristic of Hadzabe society is that their possessions are so few that each person can carry everything they own on their backs when they travel.

The Hadzabe language is characterised by clicks and may be distantly related to that of Southern Africa's San. However, it shows only a few connections to Sandawe, the other click language spoken in Tanzania, and genetic studies have shown no close link between the Hadzabe and any other East African people.

Academic studies of the Hadzabe abound, but there is no finer treatment of the group than in the final chapter ('At Gidabembe') of Peter Matthiessen's *The Tree Where Man Was Born* (1972).

from the camp's own cows) is excellent. It's signposted 7.5km from Ghorofani. There's basic camping (the only camping on the lakeshore) 2km past the main lodge, with a toilet and shower and the same awesome scenery.

★**Ziwani Lodge**   LODGE $$$
(☑0784 400507; www.ziwanilodge.com; 🅿 🛜 ⚟) Worth every one of its four stars, Ziwani combines faux-Moroccan style with local building materials and the results are stunning. The seven stone-built cottages are stylish, with whitewashed walls, perfectly placed wooden chests and wall decorations. With strong community roots, the lodge offers plenty of opportunities to spend time with the Hadzabe, whether out hunting or on a nature walk.

Tindiga Tented Camp   TENTED CAMP $$$
(☑0754 324193, 027-250 6315; www.moivaro.com; s/d with full board US$258/360) Just under 2km from the lakeshore, Tindiga Tented Camp has rustic tents that fit nicely with the overall Lake Eyasi experience – comfortable, but with a sense of being far away from it all.

ℹ️ **Getting There & Away**

Two daily buses connect Arusha to Barazani, passing Ghorofani (Tsh13,000, 4½ to five hours) on the way. They leave Arusha about 5am and head back about 2pm; you can also catch them in Karatu (Tsh5000, 1½ hours to Ghorofani). There are several passenger-carrying 4WDs to Karatu (Tsh6500; they park at Mbulu junction), departing Ghorofani and other lake towns during the morning and returning throughout the afternoon.

Ngorongoro Conservation Area

Ngorongoro is one of the true wonders of Africa, a lost world of wildlife and singular beauty in the near-perfect crater of a long-extinct volcano. This is one of the most extraordinary places in northern Tanzania and should on no account be missed. Apart from Ngorongoro Crater, lying within the boundaries of the 8292-sq-km **Ngorongoro Conservation Area** (NCA; ☑027-253 7046, 027-253 7019; www.ngorongorocrater.go.tz; adult/child US$70.80/23.60, crater services fee per vehicle per 24hr US$295; ⏱6am-6pm) are some of northern Tanzania's greatest sights, including Oldupai (Olduvai) Gorge and much of the Crater Highlands (although not Ol Doinyo Lengai and Lake Natron).

ℹ️ **BLACK KITES**

Just about everyone who heads down into Ngorongoro Crater for the day takes a packed lunch and stops for a picnic at Ngoitoktok Springs picnic site. In recent years, however, black kites (large birds of prey) have worked out that such picnics offer easy pickings and have begun to brazenly swoop down and grab food, sometimes right out of people's hands and occasionally causing injuries and scratches to those under attack. So, by all means get out and go for a walk, but eat your food inside your vehicle.

Ngorongoro Crater

Pick a superlative: amazing, incredible, breathtaking...they all apply to the stunning, ethereal blue-green vistas of the **Ngorongoro Crater** (☑027-253 7046, 027-253 7019; www.ngorongorocrater.go.tz; adult/child US$70.80/23.60, crater service fee per vehicle US$295). But as wonderful as the views are from above, the real magic happens when you get down inside and drive among an unparalleled concentration of wildlife, including the highest density of both lions and overall predators in Africa. One of the continent's premier attractions, this renowned natural wonder is deservedly a Unesco World Heritage Site.

CRATER FLOOR

At 19km wide and with a surface of 264 sq km, Ngorongoro is one of the largest unbroken calderas in the world that isn't a lake. Its steep walls soar 400m to 610m and provide the setting for an incredible natural drama, as prey and predators graze and stalk their way around the open grasslands, swamps and acacia woodland on the crater floor.

There are plenty of hippos around the lovely Ngoitoktok Springs picnic site, and Lake Magadi attracts flocks of flamingos to its shallows in the rainy season. Lereal Forest (which has a less appealing picnic site, and is the starting point for the Lereal or Lerai ascent road) is good for elephants, of which there are 200 to 300 in the crater. Predators include around 600 spotted hyenas, 55 lions (at last count), and both golden and black-backed jackals. These predators are sustained by large numbers of resident herbivores, with wildebeest, zebras, buffaloes and Grant's gazelles the most common. Less commonly seen are elands, warthogs, hartebeests, bushbucks, waterbucks and bohor reedbucks. Around 20% of the wildebeest and zebras migrate annually between the crater and the Serengeti. Another huge drawcard is the chance to see the critically endangered black rhino – around 30 inhabit the crater floor, and they're most often seen between the Lereal Forest and the Lemala ascent-descent road.

The reason for all this abundance is the presence of water, both from the permanent springs that sustain the swamps, and the permanent streams and rivers fed by run-off from the crater-rim forests.

The main route into the crater is the Seneto descent road, which enters the crater on its western side. To come out, use the Lerai ascent road, which starts south of Lake Magadi and leads to the rim near park headquarters. The Lemala road is on the northeastern side of the crater near Ngorongoro Sopa Lodge and is used for both ascent and descent.

CRATER RIM

A sealed road encircles all but the northern section of the crater rim, and there are stunning views through the trees at various places along the way. Apart from the vantage points offered by the lodges, the best views are from the head of the Seneto descent road above the crater's western end, and where the road reaches the rim after climbing up from Lodoare gate.

Unlike national parks where human residents were evicted, the NCA remains part of the Maasai homeland, and over 40,000 Maasai live here with grazing rights. You're sure to see them out tending their cattle and goats, as well as selling necklaces and knives alongside the road. Many children wait along the road to pose for photos, but note that most of them are skipping school or shirking their chores, so it's best not to stop. There are cultural *bomas* (compounds), too, which charge US$50 per vehicle.

There's wildlife outside the crater, but not the abundance found in most other parks. Still, you might see elephants and leopards along the rim road, and the western plains are full of wildebeest, eland, topi, gazelle and zebra herds on the southern stretch of their endless migration between January and March. Trekking here at this time, before the long rains begin, can be awesome. Good easy day-trek spots are Markarot, Little Oldupai and Lake Ndutu.

🛏 Sleeping & Eating

Ngorongoro's only public campsite is **Simba A** (🖉 027-253 7019; www.ngorongorocrater.go.tz; camping US$47.20), up on the crater rim not far from headquarters. It has basic facilities and can get very crowded, so the hot water sometimes runs out. Even so, it's a fine location and by

---

ℹ ESSENTIAL NGORONGORO INFORMATION & FEES

Ngorongoro Conservation Area (NCA), which includes Ngorongoro Crater and much of the Crater Highlands, is administered by the Ngorongoro Conservation Area Authority (NCAA), with its **headquarters** (🖉 027-253 7019, 027-253 7006, Lodoare Gate 027-253 7031; www.ngorongorocrater.go.tz; ⊙ 8am-4pm) at Park Village at Ngorongoro Crater and information centres in Arusha (p165) and Karatu (p179). The two entry points for the NCA are Lodoare gate, just south of Ngorongoro Crater on the road from Arusha and about 14km west of Karatu, and Naabi Hill gate, on the border with Serengeti National Park.

Payment of all fees for visiting Ngorongoro Crater and anywhere else within the NCA can be made at either Lodoare or Naabi Hill gate by credit card only (no cash). Should you wish to add days or activities to your visit, you can pay fees (cash only) at NCAA headquarters.

Visiting here can be an expensive (if infinitely rewarding) proposition. If you're here as part of a pre-paid organised tour, the costs will likely be absorbed into the fees you paid for the overall trip. For non-resident independent travellers, you'll need to budget for the following:

NCA admission fee adult/child US$70.80/23.60

Crater service fee (to descend into the crater per day) per vehicle US$295

Vehicle permit Tsh23,600 (Tanzania-registered vehicle) or US$47.20 (foreign-registered vehicle)

Camping fees for public/special campsite US$47.20/70.80. Note that most tented camps are located on special campsites.

All fees are valid for 24 hours, single entry only. Note that if you're transiting through Ngorongoro en route to the Serengeti, you still have to pay the NCA entrance fee.

far the cheapest place to stay up on the rim. If you're not self-catering, try **Mwahingo Canteen** (mains from Tsh2500; ⊙11am-9pm) at park headquarters; there are also several small restaurants and bars in nearby Kimba village.

Kitoi Guesthouse　　　　GUESTHOUSE **$**
(📱0754 334834; r without bathroom Tsh10,000; ℗) This unsigned place is the best of four guesthouses in Kimba village, near the crater – it's well known in the village, so ask around. The ablutions block is out the back, as are awesome views of Oldeani. On request, someone will cook food or heat water for bucket showers. Officials at the park gate may insist you pay the camping fee, even if you plan to sleep in this village.

★**Highlands**　　　　TENTED CAMP **$$$**
(www.asiliaafrica.com; per person with full board US$359-824) Claiming to be the highest tented camp in the region and with some of the most original tented accommodation in Tanzania, the Highlands is a real treat, combining sweeping Crater Highlands views with blissful isolation. It's a luxurious variation of the dome tent and sits high above Olmoti Crater.

★**Ngorongoro Crater Lodge**　　LODGE **$$$**
(📱028-262 1267; www.andbeyond.com; r per person all-inclusive Dec-Feb & Jun-Sep US$1715, rates vary rest of year; ℗ @ 🛜) Self-described as 'Versailles meets Maasai', this eclectic rim-top lodge (actually three separate lodges) has every luxury you could want. Few spaces lack crater views (even the toilets have them), and the rooms are sophisticated and intimate, with abundant use of wood. This is the place to go for the full Ngorongoro experience of knock-out views and no-expense-spared indulgence.

Entamanu Ngorongoro　　TENTED CAMP **$$$**
(📱0787 595908; www.nomad-tanzania.com; per person with full board US$690-875; ℗ 🛜) Part of the excellent Nomad Tanzania portfolio, this lovely place opened in 2016. Lying as it does beyond the main Serengeti–Ngorongoro thoroughfare on the crater's northwestern side, it's blissfully quiet, close to the Seneto descent road and filled with attractive tents that face the crater.

Ngorongoro Serena Safari Lodge　LODGE **$$$**
(📱027-254 5555; www.serenahotels.com; s/d with full board Jul-Oct US$433/725, rates vary rest of year; ℗ @ 🛜) The popular Serena sits unobtrusively in a fine location on the southwestern crater rim near the main descent route. It's comfortable and attractive (though the

ℹ NGORONGORO CRATER

Why Go Extraordinary scenery and fabulous wildlife watching.

When to Go Year-round.

Practicalities Usually visited en route to the Serengeti from Arusha via Karatu. It can get *very* cold on the crater rim, so come prepared.

Budget Tips Stay outside the park to avoid camping fees: visit as part of a larger group to reduce your portion of the crater services fee. Even though the US$295 fee to enter the crater is per vehicle, the guards check the number of passengers against the permit, so it's not possible to join up with people you meet at your campsite or lodge once you're inside the Ngorongoro Conservation Area.

cave motif in the rooms is kind of kitschy), with good service and outstanding views (from the upper-floor rooms), though it's also big and busy.

Ngorongoro Wild Camp　　TENTED CAMP **$$$**
(📱0746 034057; www.tanzaniawildcamps.com; s/d with full board US$510/720) In an area on the crater rim where few travellers pass, Ngorongoro Wild Camp has a sense of wilderness that you just don't get elsewhere on the rim – don't be surprised if a giraffe wanders up to your tent. Tents are large and nicely turned out, a mix of simplicity and wood floors with wrought-iron four-poster beds.

Ngorongoro Sopa Lodge　　LODGE **$$$**
(📱027-250 0630; www.sopalodges.com; s/d with full board Jan, Feb & Jun-Oct US$385/680, rest of year prices vary; ℗ @ 🛜 ⛳) This 98-room lodge is well located on the eastern crater rim (the sunset-watching side) – it's convenient for Empakaai and the Crater Highlands, less so if you're heading to the Serengeti. The rooms are spacious but plain, and many lack views or have only limited sight lines: request the top floor. There's hot water only in the morning and evening.

Olduvai Camp　　　　TENTED CAMP **$$$**
(📱0782 993854; www.olduvai-camp.com; per person with full board US$250-395; ℗) An intimate, remote camp in wonderful opposition to the large corporate lodges on the crater rim, Olduvai is built around a kopje with postcard views of Makarot, and it makes a fine spot to watch wildebeest during the rainy season.

NORTHERN TANZANIA NGORONGORO CONSERVATION AREA

Ngorongoro Conservation Area

NORTHERN TANZANIA NGORONGORO CONSERVATION AREA

The 17 tents are attractive if sparse, but the dining room and lounge are lovely. It's 3.5km off the Serengeti road (unsigned). All accommodation bookings must be made through a safari company; direct bookings are not encouraged.

Rhino Lodge   LODGE $$$

(☎0785 500005; www.ngorongoro.cc; s/d with half board US$145/260; ☎) This small, friendly lodge, run by Italians in conjunction with the Maasai community, is one of the cheapest places in the Ngorongoro Conservation

NORTHERN TANZANIA NGORONGORO CONSERVATION AREA

Area. The rooms are simple and tidy, and the balconies have fine forest views, often with bushbucks or elephants wandering past. It's arguably the best-value place up here, as long as you don't need a crater view.

Ngorongoro Wildlife Lodge LODGE $$$
(☏ 027-254 4595; www.hotelsandlodges-tanzania. com; r per person with full board US$240/480; ℗@🛜) The rooms here are tired and in desperate need of an overhaul, and the service can be dysfunctional. But (and it's a big

TREKKING THE CRATER HIGHLANDS

The best way to explore the Crater Highlands is on foot, although because of the logistics and multiple fees involved, trekking here is expensive: from US$350 per person and up (less if you have a large group) for overnight trips. Treks range from short day jaunts to excursions of two weeks or more. For all routes, you'll need to be accompanied by a guide, and for anything except day hikes, most people use donkeys or vehicle support to carry water and supplies (though vehicles can't go everywhere the donkeys can).

Nearly all visitors arrange treks through a tour company. Many Arusha-based companies can take you up Ol Doinyo Lengai, just outside the Ngorongoro Conservation Area (NCA) boundaries, as can the accommodation places in Lake Natron or Engaruka.

There are no set routes, and the possibilities are numerous. Good two-day trips include the **Ngorongoro Crater rim**, **Olmoti to Empakaai**, and **Empakaai to Lake Natron**. These three can be strung together into an excellent four-day trip: start at Nainokanoka ranger post to make it three days or extend it one day to climb **Ol Doinyo Lengai**.

If you base yourself at Ngorongoro Crater or Karatu, there are some good day hikes that let you experience the area on a lower budget, such as climbing **Makarot** or **Oldeani**, or walking along the **Empakaai** or **Olmoti** craters. Apart from transport costs, these involve only the US$70.80 NCA entry fee and US$23.60-per-group guide fee. Oldeani is the least complicated option, since the climb starts at the Ngorongoro Conservation Area Authority headquarters. From Oldeani, it's possible to camp and continue on down to Lake Eyasi, where there's public transport.

but), the crater views (from the rooms, from the bar...) are the best on the rim. In fact, the views are so good that they may just outweigh all of the lodge's shortcomings.

Ndutu Safari Lodge
LODGE $$$

(☑ 027-253 7015; www.ndutu.com; s/d with full board Jul, Aug & Dec-Apr US$430/640, rates vary rest of year) This good-value place has a lovely setting in the far-western part of the Ngorongoro Conservation Area, just outside the Serengeti. It's well located for observing the enormous herds of wildebeest during the rainy season; also watch for genets lounging in the dining-room rafters. The 34 Lake Ndutu–facing cottages lack character, but the lounge is attractive and the atmosphere relaxed and rustic.

❶ Getting There & Away

There's no public transport to the crater. If you aren't travelling on an organised safari and don't have your own vehicle, the easiest thing to do is hire one in Karatu, where most lodges charge from US$160 per day for a 4WD with a pop-up top, including fuel and driver but excluding entry and vehicle fees. Vehicle rental from Mto wa Mbu costs from US$220 per day, including fuel and driver. Note that vehicles with a pop-up top or safari companies without an official licence will not be permitted to enter the Ngorongoro Conservation Area; this usually affects Kenyan companies in particular. Be sure to verify this before making any payments.

Crater access roads:

Seneto Descent only (at the western end of the crater)

Lerai Ascent only (along the southern rim)

Lemala (Sopa) Descent and ascent (eastern end of crater rim)

The gates open at 6am and close for descent at 4pm; all vehicles must be out of the crater before 6pm. Officially, you're only allowed to stay down in the crater for a maximum of six hours, but this is rarely enforced. Self-drivers are supposed to hire a park ranger (US$23.60 per vehicle) for the crater – note that this rule is being more strictly enforced than it used to be and it's a long way back to the park gate to hire a ranger if they don't let you go down without one. Petrol is sold at headquarters, but it's cheaper in Karatu.

Crater Highlands

The hauntingly beautiful Crater Highlands is where the Rift Valley really gets interesting. The highlands warp along numerous extinct volcanoes, calderas (collapsed volcanoes) and the dramatic Rift Valley Escarpment on the park's eastern side. The peaks include Oldeani (3188m), Makarot (Lemagurut; 3107m), Olmoti (3100m), Loolmalasin (3648m), Empakaai (also spelled Embagai; 3262m), Ngorongoro (2400m) and the still-active Ol Doinyo Lengai (2878m). The different peaks were created over millions of years by a series of eruptions connected with the birth of the Great Rift Valley, and the older volcanoes have since collapsed, forming the striking 'craters' (really, they're calderas) that give the range its name.

◉ Sights & Activities

★ Empakaai Crater   VOLCANO
Lake-filled Empakaai Crater, 23km northeast of Olmoti Crater, may not be as famous as Ngorongoro (p181), but many travellers consider it to be its match in beauty. The lake, which draws flamingos and other waterbirds, fills most of the crater floor, which is surrounded by steep-sided, forested cliffs at least 300m high. The view from the crater rim is one of the most appealing in northern Tanzania, but hiking down into the crater is a wonderful experience as well.

The road from Ol Doinyo Lengai (p190) runs along part of the eastern crater rim, which varies in altitude from 2700m to 3200m, and a steep, well-kept trail descends from the road through montane forest rich in bird life; also keep an eye out for hyenas, buffaloes, blue monkeys and even elephants. En route to the crater floor, watch for views of the turquoise lake down below and the perfect volcanic cone of Ol Doinyo Lengai away to the northeast. Count on around 30 minutes down to the lakeshore, and an hour for the climb back up. It's possible to circumnavigate the lake on foot, which will take at least four hours.

If you're planning on hiking, you are, in theory, required to pick up an armed ranger (US$23.60) from the ranger post at Nainokanoka (next to Olmoti Crater) en route to Empakaai. To get here, count on a 90-minute drive from the Lemala ascent-descent road.

Engaruka   RUINS
(adult/child Tsh10,000/5000) Halfway to Lake Natron, on the eastern edge of the Ngorongoro Conservation Area, lies this 300- to 500-year-old ruin of a farming town that developed a complex irrigation system with terraced stone housing sites. Although the ruins are historically significant, casual visitors are likely to be more impressed with the up-close views of the escarpment than the vaguely house-shaped piles of rocks.

Archaeologists are unsure of Engaruka's origins, although some speculate that the town was built by ancestors of the Iraqw (Mbulu) people, who once populated the area and now live around Lake Eyasi. Others propose it was the Sonjo, a Bantu-speaking people.

Knowledgeable English-speaking guides (no set prices) for the ruins or other walks in the area, including a one-day climb of nearby Kerimasi, can be found at Engaruka Ruins Campsite (p188), or they can be arranged in advance through the Tanzania Tourist Board Tourist Information Centre (p165) in Arusha. It's also worth contacting the **Engaruka Cultural Tourism Program** (☑ 0754 507939, 0787 228653; www.tanzaniaculturaltourism.com/engaruka.htm), which arranges visits to Maasai villages and other local attractions, as well as climbs up Kerimasi and Ol Doinyo Lengai (p190).

The ruins are unsigned above the village of Engaruka Juu. Turn west at Engaruka Chini, a smaller village along the Lake Natron road, and follow the rough track 4.5km until you reach Engaruka Juu Primary Boarding School.

THE MAASAI

The Maasai are pastoral nomads who have actively resisted change, and many still follow the same lifestyle they have pursued for centuries. Their traditional culture centres on their cattle, which, along with their land, are considered sacred. Cows provide many of their needs: milk, blood and meat for their diet, and hides and skins for clothing, although sheep and goats also play an important dietary role, especially during the dry season.

Maasai society is patriarchal and highly decentralised. Maasai boys pass through a number of transitions during their life, the first of which is marked by the circumcision rite. Successive stages include junior warriors, senior warriors, junior elders and senior elders; each level is distinguished by its own unique rights, responsibilities and dress. Junior elders, for example, are expected to marry and settle down sometime between the ages of 30 and 40. Senior elders assume the responsibility of making wise and moderate decisions for the community. The most important group is that of the *moran* (newly initiated warriors), who are charged with defending the cattle herds.

Maasai women play a markedly subservient role and have no inheritance rights. Polygyny is widespread and marriages are arranged by the elders, without consulting the bride or her mother. Since most women are significantly younger than men at the time of marriage, they often become widows; remarriage is rare.

Olmoti Crater
VOLCANO

Though lacking the drama of Ngorongoro (p181) and Empakaai (p187), Olmoti Crater, 13km north of the Lemala ascent-descent road, is worth visiting on your way north into the highlands. It's also the starting point for a two-day trek to Empakaai. Olmoti's crater floor is shallow, haired with grass and crossed by the Munge River. To reach the rim, it's a one-hour return walk from where the 4WD track ends on the crater's eastern side. From here, a short trail leads to the Munge Waterfall.

🛏 Sleeping & Eating

Apart from a few rudimentary campsites out here and options around Lake Natron, there's no formal accommodation in these parts. There are two campsites around the rim of Empakaai Crater and a further 15 out on the western plains. Camping at each costs US$70.80/35.40 per adult/child; reservations should be made through the Ngorongoro Conservation Area Authority as far ahead as possible. There's a very basic **guesthouse** (s/d with shared bathroom Tsh7500/14,000) in Engaruka. You'll need to carry in your own supplies of food and water, as very little is available in the villages out on the trail.

Engaruka Ruins Campsite (Engaruka Juu; camping US$10; 🅿) is dusty but shady, with acceptable ablutions. You can use its tents for free and meals are available on request.

ℹ Getting There & Away

A daily bus to Arusha (Tsh12,000, four to five hours) via Mto wa Mbu (Tsh5000, 1½ hours) leaves Engaruka at 6am, turning around for the return trip shortly after arrival. There's no public transport between here and Ngorongoro Crater.

Village fees (ie tourist taxes) must be paid at three gates along the way: Engaruka Chini (US$10), 7km before Engaresero (US$10), and just outside Engaresero (US$15). Note that if you're coming from Lake Natron and you're heading for Arusha, you can avoid the fees at Engaruka Chini and the one between Engaruka and Engaresero by taking the graded track that runs east to the Arusha–Namanga Rd soon after leaving Engaresero.

Lake Natron

Shimmering amid the sun-scorched Kenyan border northeast of Ngorongoro Conservation Area, this 58km-long but just 50cm-deep alkaline lake should be on every adventurer's itinerary. The drives from Mto wa Mbu

ℹ INDEPENDENT TRAVEL TO LAKE NATRON

Independent exploration of the southern reaches of the lake isn't really encouraged: it's the community's way of ensuring that they receive some benefits from travellers passing through their town. This means that, although there's nothing to stop you from driving down to the lakeshore, you can expect someone from the local community-run tourism operative to turn up at your accommodation and ask politely for payment. It's recommended that you pay or, better still, contact them in advance so that you can take a local guide with you to make the most of your visit.

or the northern Serengeti are remote, with a desolate, other-worldly beauty and an incomparable feeling of space and antiquity. The roads pass through untrammelled Maasai land, with small *bomas* (fortified compounds) and big mountains often in view in a wild, cauterised landscape. From June to November at the lake itself, upwards of three million flamingos gather here – it's one of East Africa's most stirring wildlife spectacles. And close to the southern end of the lake, the views of Ol Doinyo Lengai volcano are splendid.

The base for visits is the small oasis of Engaresero (also spelled Ngare Sero; 'impermanent water' in Maasai) on the lake's southwestern shore.

🏃 Activities

Drawing together a host of activities around Engaresero and Lake Natron, the Maasai-run **Engaresero Cultural Tourism Program** (☑0784 769795, 027-205 0025; www.engaresero.org) ✐ offers guided walking trips to the lake, hot springs, a nearby waterfall or a set of recently discovered 120,000-year-old human footprints preserved in volcanic ash; biking tours; village visits; 'ethno-botanical' tours; and trekking to the summit of Ol Doinyo Lengai volcano (US$60 to US$100). Most tours (except the Ol Doinyo Lengai climb) cost US$25 per person. The program is affiliated (and shares a website and premises) with the **Engaresero Tourism Office** (☑0784 769795; www.engaresero.org; ⊙6am-6.30pm), located near the southern entrance to town.

🛏 Sleeping & Eating

There are several budget campsites clustered around the southwestern end of the lake, and Engaresero village has a couple of basic grocery shops.

Waterfall Campsite   CAMPGROUND $
(camping US$10) Where the road ends and the walking trail to the waterfall begins, this campground has simple amenities but a nice, shady location. There are no cooking facilities.

Maasai Giraffe Eco Lodge   LODGE $$
(🖉 0762 922221; www.maasaigiraffe.com; camping US$10, s/d US$84/118; 🛜) There's not much shade to be had in this large fenced compound, but the views of Ol Doinyo Lengai volcano are superb. Rooms, in thatched bands, are simple but fine, but you'll want to spend most of your time on the terrace gazing at the mountain. Meals are available and there's a kitchen for self-caterers.

Halisi Camp   TENTED CAMP $$$
(🖉 027-275 4295, 0682 303848; www.halisicamps.com; per person with full board US$450) 🍴 With safari tents that look as though they could be removed without leaving a trace, Halisi has an appealing bush-camp feel to it without compromising on comfort. There are good views of Ol Doinyo Lengai volcano, and the camp is away from the town and close to the lake; it can become unpleasant when winds blow sand across the plains.

**Ngare Sero Lake
Natron Camp**   TENTED CAMP $$$
(www.lake-natron-camp.com; per person with full board from US$275; 🅿) 🍴 As close as you can sleep to the lake, Lake Natron Camp is wonderfully sited, with tents just back from the shore. The tents are excellent and often strategically placed around natural plunge pools,

and there's a range of activities on offer. The place is at its best when the sun goes down and silence envelopes the lake.

Natron River Camp   TENTED CAMP $$$
(🖉 0765 941778; www.wildlandssafaris.com; per person with half board US$250; 🅿 🛜 🍴) A simple but nicely turned-out camp in Engaresero, Natron River Camp has eight safari tents with concrete floors and a pleasant, shady location alongside the riverbed. Tents are a nice mix of comfort and simplicity, while the public areas have a quiet sophistication.

Lake Natron Tented Camp   TENTED CAMP $$$
(🖉 0754 324193; www.moivaro.com; camping US$10, with half board s US$140-250, d US$200-350; 🅿 🍴) At the southern end of Engaresero in a grove of trees, this tented camp is a little rundown and the tents are a tad dated, but it's comfortable enough. There's a large and sometimes busy campground with good facilities next door. Strangely, given the proximity, you'll need to step beyond the property for a view of Ol Doinyo Lengai volcano.

Lengai Safari Lodge   LODGE $$$
(🖉 0768 210091, 0754 550542; www.lengaisafari lodge.com; camping US$10, per person with full board US$120; 🅿 🛜 🍴) A few kilometres south of town along the escarpment, this lodge offers unbeatable views of Ol Doinyo Lengai, and good ones of the lake, too, including from some rooms. The newly constructed rooms and tents are comfortable rather than luxurious; more were being built at the time of research. It's easily the best location of any of the area's accommodation options.

ℹ Getting There & Away

The road from Mto wa Mbu is partly sandy and partly rocky. During the rainy season you may

---

FLAMINGOS & THE ART OF STANDING ON ONE LEG

From Lake Natron to Lake Bogoria in Kenya, it's the classic Rift Valley image: the flamingo – or, rather, massed ranks of flamingos – standing completely still on one leg. Why they do so has baffled scientists for decades.

Finally a 2017 study found that this pose has a very strong scientific reason: flamingos, it seems, expend less energy by standing on one leg than they do standing on two. More specifically, flamingos do not actively use their muscles in any way in this one-legged position. Closer examination of the pose revealed that the standing foot sits directly beneath the body, meaning that the leg angles inwards, enabling the bird to assume the position and remain almost entirely motionless for significant periods.

So easy and perfectly balanced is the pose that flamingos can sleep while standing like this. And the scientists who carried out the study discovered that even dead flamingos could remain on one leg (but not two) without any means of support!

have to wait a few hours at some of the seasonal rivers before you're able to cross. The road past the lake to Loliondo and into the Serengeti is in better shape because it's used far less. Those continuing this way should carry extra supplies of petrol, since the last proper station is in Mto wa Mbu, though some people sell (expensive) petrol from their homes.

A rickety, crowded bus runs between Arusha and Loliondo, stopping in Engaresero (Tsh27,000, nine hours). It departs Arusha at 6.30am on Sunday and passes back through Engaresero on Thursday around 10am. Trucks (and sometimes 4WDs operating as public transport) run between Mto wa Mbu and Engaresero pretty much daily, but it's not unheard of to have to wait two days to find a ride, especially in the rainy season.

If you're driving from Ngorongoro, you'll need to set out early and count on an entire day to reach Lake Natron – ask at the Ngorongoro Conservation Area Authority headquarters (p182) and Nainokanoka ranger post about track conditions.

Oldupai Gorge & Western Ngorongoro

Standing near the western rim of the Ngorongoro Crater and looking out towards the west is like contemplating eternity. Table-flat plains stretch towards the Serengeti, with the forbidding Gol Mountains away to the north. Within this landscape, Maasai eke out an existence from the dust of plains where

wildlife is wary but present nonetheless – wildebeest, eland, topi, gazelle and zebra herds come here between January and March on the southern stretch of their migration.

But there's more to these plains than meets the eye. Slicing its way through up to 90m of rock and two million years of history, Oldupai (Olduvai) Gorge on the plains northwest of Ngorongoro Crater is a dusty, 48km-long ravine sometimes referred to as the cradle of humankind.

Its unique geological history provides remarkable documentation of ancient life, allowing us to look back to the days of our earliest ancestors.

There's nowhere to sleep at Oldupai Gorge, with the nearest places a few hours' drive away in Ngorongoro and the Serengeti – everyone who visits does so en route between the two. Safari lodges in Ngorongoro and the Serengeti will pack a lunchbox for those departing – whether you pay extra for one will depend on how many meals you've had at the lodge/camp in question.

Oldupai Museum   MUSEUM
(adult/child US$20/10; ⏰ 7.30am-4.30pm) The small Oldupai Museum on the rim of Oldupai Gorge stands on one of the most significant archaeological sites on earth. It was here in 1959 that Mary Leakey discovered a 1.8-million-year-old ape-like skull from an early hominin (human-like being) now

---

CLIMBING OL DOINYO LENGAI

The northernmost (and youngest) volcano in the Crater Highlands, **Ol Doinyo Lengai** (www.oldoinyolengai.pbworks.com), 'Mountain of God' in the Maasai language, is an almost perfect cone with steep sides rising to a small, flat-topped peak (2878m). It's still active, last erupting in 2008. At the peak, you can see hot steam vents and growing ash cones in the north crater. Climbing the mountain is possible – at once challenging and extremely beautiful – but it's a serious undertaking: you'll need a guide, stamina and a head for heights.

With a midnight start, a trek from the base village of Engaresero at Lake Natron is possible in one long day. You'll usually be back down by mid-morning. The climb is not for the faint-hearted, but the rewards are considerable: the sunrise views out over Lake Natron, the escarpment and beyond are among the best in Tanzania.

There are, however, some things to take into account when preparing your ascent. It's strongly recommended that you take a helmet – there are often baboons on the higher slopes and they frequently dislodge gravel and sometimes larger stones; other wildlife to watch out for includes leopards and klipspringers. It's also extremely steep near the summit – although it's a trek rather than a technical climb, in places you'll be close to vertical. And throughout the climb, the loose ash along most of the path makes it difficult going when ascending, and it can be an even tougher, often painful, descent.

Climbing Ol Doinyo Lengai costs between US$60 and US$100 per person, depending on how many are in the party. Guides can be arranged through your lodging or through the community-run Engaresero Tourism Office (p188) at the southeastern entrance to Engaresero.

LAETOLI & THE GOL MOUNTAINS

About 45km south of Oldupai (Olduvai) Gorge at remote **Laetoli** (adult/child US$23.60/ 11.80; ⊘7.30am-4.30pm) is a 27m-long trail of 3.7-million-year-old hominid footprints, probably made by *Australopithecus afarensis*. Discovered by Mary Leakey's team in 1976 and excavated two years later, it's an extraordinarily evocative and remote site. An EU-funded museum (still under construction) is planned, but there's a small temporary museum on the site, with only copies of the prints currently visible. Cast copies of the prints are in Oldupai Museum (p190).

An extremely rough, 4WD-only track connects Oldupai Museum with Laetoli via Noorkisaruni Kopje and Endulen. A far better road runs to Endulen from Kimba on the Ngorongoro Crater rim along the southern side of Makarot. Via either route, Laetoli lies 9km from Endulen.

Some places are so far off well-travelled routes that there are no tracks other than those left by wildlife and traditional herders. The remote and rarely visited **Gol Mountains** area, northwest of Ngorongoro but still within the boundaries of the Ngorongoro Conservation Area, is just such a place. This remains one of the most traditional corners of Tanzania, home to Maasai who still kill lions as their rite of passage into warriorhood, and who still live outside cash society.

Travelling out here is a major, multiday undertaking that is best organised through a professional Arusha-based safari company.

known as *Australopithecus boisei*. This discovery, along with that of fossils of over 60 early hominids (including *Homo habilis* and *Homo erectus*) forever changed the way we understand the dawn of human history. Sadly, the museum is a work in progress.

An EU-funded museum has been under construction at the site for years, but work seems to have stalled – 2018 is the latest official estimate of when the new museum will open. Despite this, admission fees have risen massively in recent years, prompting some safari companies to encourage their guests to boycott the museum until the new museum is completed. Don't join the boycott, though: admission is indeed overpriced for what you get, but the site is still hugely significant and, unless you're likely to have the chance to return, it's a must-see.

In its unrenovated form, the small, two-room museum documents the foundation of the gorge, fossil finds and the legacy of Mary Leakey and her husband, Louis. One room is dedicated to Oldupai, the other to Laetoli. It's a fascinating collection, if poorly presented. You can then walk (or drive) into the gorge (where a small stone signpost marks the place where the fossils were discovered). You can also head out to the **shifting sands**, a 9m-high, 100m-long black dune of volcanic ash that has blown across the plain from Ol Doinyo Lengai. If you wish to take a guide it will, naturally, cost extra.

The turn-off to the museum is 27km northwest of Ngorongoro Crater's Seneto descent road, and from the turn-off it's a further 5.5km along a rutted track to the museum.

❶ Getting There & Away

There's no public transport to the site – indeed, you'll often see locals hitchhiking in the area due to the dearth of reliable transport. The gorge is 27km from Ngorongoro Crater's Seneto descent road and 141km from the Serengeti.

Serengeti National Park

Few people forget their first encounter with the **Serengeti** (☑028-262 1515, 0767 536125, 0689 062243; www.tanzaniaparks.go.tz; adult/child US$70.80/23.60; ⊘6am-6pm). Perhaps it's the view from Naabi Hill at the park's entrance, from where the grasslands appear to stretch to the ends of the earth. Or maybe it's a coalition of lions stalking across open plains, their manes catching the breeze. Or it could be wildebeest and zebra migrating in their millions, following the ancient rhythm of Africa's seasons. Whatever it is, welcome to one of the greatest wildlife-watching destinations on earth.

◉ Sights

On the vast plains of the Serengeti, nature's mystery, power and beauty surround you as they do in few other places. It's here that one

THE SERENGETI LION PROJECT

The Serengeti Lion Project is widely considered to be the second-longest-running continuous scientific study of a species in Africa; Jane Goodall's study of chimpanzees in Gombe Stream National Park is the only study to have lasted longer.

And it is from the Serengeti Lion Project that we have learned much of what we know about lions – why they form prides, why they roar, and so on. It all began back in 1966 with Dr George Schaller, now one of the world's most respected wildlife scientists, who wrote what remains the seminal text on lion behaviour: *The Serengeti Lion*.

All the subsequent heads of the project have written books, and it is one of these, Craig Packer's *Lions in the Balance*, that almost sounded the project's death knell. Packer's ongoing criticism of the relationship between the Tanzanian government and the trophy-hunting industry would ultimately lead to Packer's expulsion from the country. For three years, the Serengeti Lion Project barely functioned, and there were fears that the project would fall into the wrong hands or perhaps even come under the aegis of the trophy-hunting industry itself. In the end, in June 2017 responsibility for the project was handed to respected lion scientists Bernard Kissui and Mike Anderson. It now appears likely that the project will continue, at least for the foreseeable future.

The heads of the project and the books they wrote about their experiences are as follows:

George Schaller (1966–69) *The Serengeti Lion* (1972)

Brian Bertram (1969–74) *Pride of Lions* (1978)

Jeannette Hanby and David Bygott (1974–78) *Lion's Share: The Story of a Serengeti Pride* (1982)

Craig Packer (1978–2014) *Into Africa* (1994) and *Lions in the Balance: Man-Eaters, Manes, and Men With Guns* (2015)

Although not specifically relating to lions, Anthony Sinclair's *Serengeti Story: Life and Science in the World's Greatest Wildlife Region* (2012) is also worth tracking down.

of earth's most impressive natural cycles has played itself out for aeons as hundreds of thousands of hoofed animals, driven by primeval rhythms of survival, move constantly in search of fresh grasslands. The most famous, and numerous, are the wildebeest (of which there are some 1.5 million) and their annual migration is one of the Serengeti's biggest draws. Besides the migrating wildebeest, there are also resident populations in the park and you'll see these smaller but still impressive herds year-round. In February more than 8000 wildebeest calves are born per day, although about 40% of these die before reaching four months old. A few black rhinos in the Moru Kopjes area give you a chance to glimpse all of the Big Five (lion, elephant, rhino, leopard and buffalo), although the rhinos are very rarely seen.

The 14,763-sq-km national park is also renowned for its predators, especially its lions. Hunting alongside them are cheetahs, leopards, hyenas, jackals and more. These feast on zebras, giraffes, buffaloes, Thomson's and Grant's gazelles, topis, elands, hartebeests, impalas, klipspringers, duikers and so many more. The Serengeti is an incredible birdwatching destination also, with over 500 species. Entry fees are valid for 24 hours, with a single entry only.

Seronera & the South

Visiting or staying in Seronera, in the heart of the park and readily accessed from both Arusha and Mwanza, involves something of a trade-off. On the one hand, this is wildlife central, with sightings of lions (around 300 live in the park's south alone), leopards and cheetahs almost guaranteed. On the other, such abundance comes at a price: you may find yourself among a pack of 20 vehicles jostling in unlovely fashion to look at a single lion.

Southeast of Seronera is a prime base for wildlife watching during the December–April wet season, when it's full of wildebeest. This corner of the Serengeti also has year-round water and a good mix of habitats. Most Seronera safaris concentrate on the **Seronera River** and with good reason: the trees along the riverbank are home to one of the world's densest concentrations of leopards, while lion sightings are common. Lion sightings are also probable around the **Maasai Kopjes**, **Simba Kopjes**, **Moru Kopjes**, **Gol Kopjes** and **Barafu Kopjes**, and around **Makoma Hill**. The vast plains south of the Seronera River, often known simply as the **Serengeti Plains**, are particularly good for cheetahs. The plains that rise towards the **Kamuyo Hills** west of the Seronera River (draw a line west of the Seronera Wildlife Lodge) are particularly good for elephants, spotted hyenas and cheetahs.

Grumeti & the Western Corridor

The herd migration usually passes through the Serengeti's Western Corridor, and the contiguous **Grumeti Game Reserve**, sometime between late May and early July. The crossing of the **Grumeti River** may not rival that of the Mara River further north – there are few vantage points and the river is much narrower and easy to cross here – but it's still one of the migration's great spectacles.

During the rest of the year, lions and leopards are prevalent along the forest-fringed Grumeti River, which also has hippos and giant crocodiles. North of the river, try the **Kitunge Hills**, **Ruana Plain** and just about anywhere in the Grumeti Game Reserve, while south of the river concentrate on the **Ndabaka Plains**, **Simiti Hills**, **Dutwa Plains**, **Varicho Hills** and down to the **Mbalageti River**.

These western reaches of the Serengeti are most easily reached from Mwanza. If driving from the Ndabaka gate, count on at least half a day to reach Seronera, at the centre of the park, more if you stop along the way.

Central Plains

Except when the herd migration passes through (usually in November and December), this is not the Serengeti's most prolific corner when it comes to wildlife. Its mix of light woodland, acacia thorn and open plains can also be dispiriting during the heat of the day, which, given the lack of lodges in the area, is when most people pass through as they travel between the north and south of the Serengeti. This is also one area of the park experiencing a growing problem with local communities encroaching into the park, with a concomitant effect on wildlife numbers. In other words, you're more likely to visit here on your way elsewhere, rather than for its own sake.

Even so, there are some fine vistas along this north–south route through the park, not to mention a blissfully remote feel to much of the countryside around here. If nothing else, the park's central area is worth passing through to gain a deeper appreciation of just how vast the Serengeti's ecosystem really is.

Mara River & the North

Compared with Seronera and the south, the Serengeti's north receives relatively few visitors. It begins with acacia woodlands, where elephants congregate in the dry season, then north of Lobo stretches into vast open plains. The herd migration usually passes through

THE SERENGETI KOPJES

Some of the Serengeti's most distinctive land forms are its kopjes: strange bouldered hills in a landscape where the horizon seems to continue to infinity. They're also important wildlife refuges, sheltering leopards, lion prides and a host of reptile species. But how were they formed?

Kopjes began life as bubbles of molten rock that, billions of years ago, forced themselves up into the layers that form the substrata of the earth. Around 500 million years ago, shifts in the surface of the earth forced up low hills across the Serengeti; over the millions of years that followed, these hills slowly eroded, leaving behind only the kopjes, which are made of hard, crystalline rock. In other words, kopjes are the summits of ancient mountains that long ago eroded away. The most obvious example of a mountain at an earlier stage of erosion is Naabi Hill. And it's not just erosion that plays a role in shaping the kopjes. The eruption of the volcanoes of the Crater Highlands over the past five million years blanketed the land here in ash, creating the Serengeti's plains and further submerging the hills that the kopjes once crowned.

Even now, the process of geological change continues as extremes of climate stretch and shrink the outer layers of the rocks that form the kopjes, causing pieces to break off and changing the shape of what remains.

the western side during August and September and comes down the eastern flank in November.

North of the Grumeti River, the Bologonya Hills, Bologonya River, Nyamalumbwa Hills and Mara River are all outstanding.

If you're driving from the Mara River to Seronera, allow the best part of a day. Outside the park, the little-visited Ikorongo Game Reserve, which shadows the northwestern boundary of the park, is wild and worth visiting. Away to the east, the Loliondo Game

Serengeti National Park

lands or Ngorongoro is a wonderfully remote alternative to driving back through the park.

🏃 Activities

Wildlife drives are the main activity here – some would say they're the reason to come to the Serengeti in the first place. Walking safaris are a relatively new activity here, but with luck they'll catch on.

Wildlife Drives

A wildlife drive in the Serengeti – whether self-drive, as part of an organised safari or as operated by your Serengeti lodge – is one of the most enjoyable things you can do in Africa. Exploring the Serengeti's four major areas – Seronera and the South, Grumeti and the Western Corridor, Central Serengeti and Northern Serengeti – requires careful planning; understanding what each area has to offer and at what time of year will determine how you experience this wonderful place.

Walking Safaris

A new development in the Serengeti is the introduction of walking safaris. Led by Wayo

Controlled Area, just outside the Serengeti's northeastern boundary, offers the chance for Maasai cultural activities, walking safaris, night drives and off-road drives. A loop (p200) east across Loliondo and then down through to Lake Natron and the Crater High-

Africa (p171), multiday camping trips are available in the Moru Kopjes, at Kogatende (by the Mara River) and in other areas of the park, and they can be as relaxing or as adventurous as clients prefer. Prices start at US$1650 per person per day for a two-day, two-night expedition; expeditions can also be combined with other safaris.

Balloon Safaris

Serengeti Balloon Safaris SAFARI
(☑ 0784 308494, 027-254 8077; www.balloon safaris.com; per person incl park ballooning fee US$546.20) There's no better way to see the Serengeti than by spending an hour floating over the plains at dawn, followed by an 'Out of Africa' full English breakfast in the bush under an acacia tree. You'll rise to 1000m for a vast view, then drop to treetop level. To be sure of a spot, reserve well in advance.

🛏 Sleeping & Eating

There are nine public campsites (US$35.40/5.90 per adult/child) in the Serengeti: six around Seronera, one at Lobo and one each at Ndabaka and Fort Ikoma gates. All have flush toilets, and two (Pimbi and Nyani, both in the Seronera area) have kitchens, showers and solar lighting.

There are dozens of special campsites (US$59/11.80 per adult/child) scattered throughout the Serengeti, although many are occupied on a semi-permanent basis by mobile or more sedentary camps. The others

---

> ### ℹ SERENGETI NATIONAL PARK
>
> **Why Go** Wildebeest migration; excellent chance of seeing predators; overall high wildlife density; fine birdwatching; stunning savannah scenery.
>
> **When to Go** Year-round; July and August for wildebeest migration across the Mara River; February for wildebeest calving; February–May for birdwatching.
>
> **Practicalities** Drive in from Arusha or Mwanza, or fly in. To avoid congestion, spend some time outside the central Serengeti/Seronera area. Entrance fees can be paid in cash or by credit card at the Naabi Hill, Ndabaka and Klein's gates.
>
> **Budget Tips** Catch the Arusha–Musoma bus and hope to see something along the way; stay in the public campsites; book a budget safari from Arusha.

---

should be booked well in advance through Tanapa at serengeti@tanzaniaparks.go.tz.

If you're camping and don't want to cook for yourself, there are two local restaurants (meals Tsh6000 to Tsh15,000) and three little grocery shops at national-park staff quarters. Anyone can also dine at the park's Twiga Resthouse. Self-caterers should stock up in Arusha or Mwanza.

🛏 Seronera & the South

Twiga Resthouse GUESTHOUSE $$
(☑ 028-262 1510; www.tanzaniaparks.go.tz; Central Serengeti; r per person US$35.40; ℗) Twiga offers simple but decent rooms with electricity and hot showers, and satellite TV in the lounge. Guests can use the kitchen, or meals can be cooked for you if you order way in advance. There's a well-stocked little bar and a bonfire at night.

Dunia Camp TENTED CAMP $$$
(www.asiliaafrica.com; Southern Serengeti; per person with full board Jan, Feb & Jun-Oct US$834, rest of year US$369-699; ℗) Unlike the large, impersonal lodges that predominate in Seronera, this intimate eight-tent camp has a classic safari ambience. Comfortable, with great service, it's essentially a mobile camp that stays put. Set below the Nyaraboro Hills, but at the end of a long rise, Dunia has both distant views and up-close encounters with wildlife. Highly recommended if you want a bush atmosphere.

Serengeti Sopa Lodge LODGE $$$
(☑ 027-250 0630; www.sopalodges.com; Southern Serengeti; s/d/tr with full board Jan, Feb & Jun-Oct US$385/680/867, rest of year rates vary; ℗ @ 🛜 ⛲) Though architecturally unappealing and with less inspired rooms than you might expect for the price, the Sopa Lodge is removed from the Seronera scrum in a valley of yellow acacia trees. The 73 rooms are spacious, with small sitting rooms and two double beds, and some even have views. It's 45 minutes south of Seronera.

Serengeti Serena Safari Lodge LODGE $$$
(☑ 027-254 5555; www.serenahotels.com; Central Serengeti; s/d with full board Jan, Feb & Jul-Oct US$426/711, rest of year rates vary; ℗ @ 🛜 ⛲) Serena's Maasai-style bungalows boast well-appointed rooms with lovely furnishings and views. The top-floor rooms are best. Guides lead short nature walks, and the Maasai stage an evening dance show. It's a good location for those who want to explore several parts of the park but not switch accommodation,

FOLLOW THE MIGRATION

You've come to see the wildebeest migration, but how can you be sure to be there when it happens? The short answer is that you can't, and making the decision of when to go where always involves some element of risk. What follows is a general overview of what usually happens, but it's a guide only:

January–March During the rains, the wildebeest are widely scattered over the southern and southwestern section of the Serengeti and the western side of Ngorongoro Conservation Area.

April Most streams dry out quickly when the rains cease, nudging the wildebeest to concentrate on the few remaining green areas, and to form thousands-strong herds that begin to migrate northwest in search of food.

May–early July In early May, the herds cross northwest towards the Western Corridor, and the crossing of the crocodile-filled Grumeti River usually takes place between late May and early July, and lasts only about a week.

Mid-July–August By the second half of July, the herds are moving north and northwest into the northern Serengeti and Kenya's Masai Mara. As part of this northwards push, they make an even more incredible crossing of the Mara River.

September & October In early September, the last stragglers leave the Serengeti and most will remain in the Masai Mara throughout October.

November & December The herds usually begin moving south again in November in anticipation of the rains, crossing down through the heart of the Serengeti and to the south in December.

Exceptions to these general guidelines are common, and it's becoming increasingly rare for the herd to remain in one group. In 2017, for example, the herds were still in the far south well into April. When they did finally move north, one group headed all the way up to Kenya and were already crossing the Sand River into Kenya's Masai Mara in early June. The remainder followed a more traditional path into the Western Corridor, but even this group was beginning to gather in the Serengeti's north by late June.

and the hilltop site offers fine views when the herd migration's in town.

Grumeti & the Western Corridor

Serengeti Stop-Over CAMPGROUND $
(☑ 0757 327294, 028-262 2273; www.serengetistop overlodge.com; Western Serengeti; camping US$10, s/d US$55/80; 🅿) Just 1km from Ndabaka gate along the Mwanza–Musoma road, this sociable place has camping with hot showers and a cooking area, plus 14 simple rondavels and a restaurant-bar. Safari-vehicle rental is available with notice and Serengeti day trips are feasible. It also offers trips on Lake Victoria with local fishers, visits to a traditional healer and other Sukuma cultural excursions.

Balili Mountain Resort TENTED CAMP $$
(☑ 0754 710113, 0764 824814; www.bmr.co.tz; Western Serengeti; camping with own/hired tents US$15/20, s/d/tr US$50/80/105, day entry US$5; 🅿) It's neither a mountain nor a resort, but 'no-frills tented lodge on a big rocky hill'

doesn't have the same ring to it. It's perfectly comfortable, but Balili's main draws are the views of Lake Victoria and the Serengeti. It's up above Bunda, north of Ndabaka gate, reached by a roller-coaster of a road.

★**Grumeti Serengeti Tented Camp** TENTED CAMP $$$
(☑ 028-262 1267; www.andbeyond.com; Western Serengeti; per person with full board & incl all activities US$740-1340; ⊘ closed Apr; 🅿 🛜 🏊) This is one of the best and most luxurious camps in the Serengeti. It mixes its wild location with chic pan-Africa decor and the 10 tents are super-luxe. Only three tents have unobstructed views of the Kanyanja River, a prime spot during the herd migration; at other times watch hippos while you lounge in the swimming pool.

Sasakwa Lodge LODGE $$$
(www.singita.com; Western Serengeti; r per person with full board & incl all activities US$1995; 🅿 🛜 🏊) 🌿 Sasakwa is one of three exclusive lodges in a private concession in the Grumeti Game Reserve. In addition to its tourism focus,

conservation dominates much of what the lodge does, from running a private anti-poaching unit to facilitating the reintroduction of the black rhino to the Serengeti's Western Corridor. Rooms are all about old-world elegance. Horseback rides are available.

Kirawira Camp
TENTED CAMP $$$

(☑027-254 5555; www.serenahotels.com; Western Serengeti; s/d with full board Jul-Oct US$636/916, rest of year rates vary; P@☎☀) A rare foray by Serena into the world of tented camps, Kirawira makes you wonder why it doesn't do it more often. The camp, ringing a low hill, works a colonial theme with plenty of antiques and polished-wood floors. The tents have big porches and very un-tent-like bathrooms. Guests rave about the food.

Ikoma Tented Camp
TENTED CAMP $$$

(☑0754 324193, 027-250 6315; www.moivaro. com; Western Serengeti; s/d with full board from US$230/345; P) Just outside Fort Ikoma gate and handy for just about anywhere in the park, this relatively simple tented camp combines closeness to the local community with excellent prices and high levels of comfort.

Robanda Safari Camp
TENTED CAMP $$$

(☑027-250 6315; www.moivaro.com; Western Serengeti; s/d with full board from US$230/345; P) This refreshingly small budget (by Serengeti standards) camp on the plains near Robanda village just outside Fort Ikoma gate has seven no-frills tents covered by a thatched roof. You can do guided walks, and night drives if you have your own vehicle.

Mara River & the North

★Serengeti Bushtops Camp
TENTED CAMP $$$

(www.bushtopscamps.com; Northern Serengeti; s/d with full board & incl all activities US$1250/1800; P@☎☀) In a remote corner of the northern Serengeti, close to the boundary with the Ikorongo Game Reserve, this remarkable camp has large permanent tents with expansive wooden floors, decks with a spa bath, perfectly placed sofas and fabulous views. Many Serengeti lodges are luxurious, but this place is simply magnificent. The food is similarly excellent.

★Lamai Serengeti
LODGE $$$

(☑0784 208343; www.nomad-tanzania.com; Northern Serengeti; s/d with full board & incl all activities US$1570/2150; ⊙Jun–mid-Mar; P☎☀) Built on a kopje near the Mara River in the far-northern Serengeti, Lamai blends into its surroundings so well it's nearly invisible. There are two lodges, one with eight rooms and another with four, each with its own dining areas and swimming pools. All rooms have African-themed decor and soothing earth tones and are open-fronted, with great views.

SERENGETI: BATTLES ON THE FRINGE

For a number of years the Serengeti authorities have been struggling to protect the park's boundaries from encroachment by Maasai herders and their cattle, particularly along the Serengeti's eastern border. But it's a movement the other way by park authorities and government agents that may prove to be a much bigger flashpoint.

Since at least 2009, and after a similar failed effort caused a minor international outcry around Lake Eyasi, the Tanzanian government has been seeking to set aside land for foreign hunters in an area known as the Loliondo Game Controlled Area, just outside the eastern border of the northern Serengeti. More specifically, the government has sought to create a 1500-sq-km wildlife corridor for the exclusive use of a Dubai-based company that sells trophy-hunting packages for wealthy tourists from the United Arab Emirates. The plan would displace an estimated 30,000 Maasai and would restrict access to dry-season grazing lands for local communities.

The dispute took a nasty turn in August 2017 when park authorities burned more than 100 Maasai huts, leaving many homeless and at least one protester critically injured. Food was destroyed and livestock killed. It all took place close to Ololosokwan, a small village not far from the Serengeti's Klein's gate; Ololosokwan lies along the popular tourist route between the Serengeti and Lake Natron.

The escalation occurred despite a promise in 2014 by then-president Jakaya Kikwete, responding to a two-million-signature petition against the trophy-hunting corridor, that the government had no plans 'to evict the Maasai from their ancestral lands'. Earlier in 2017, the Tanzanian government commissioned a report on the dispute, although the findings were yet to be made public at the time of writing.

★ **Serengeti**

Migration Camp   TENTED CAMP $$$
(☏027-250 0630; www.elewanacollection.com; Northern Serengeti; s/d with full board Jul-Oct US$1268/1690, rest of year rates vary; P ☎ ☀)
One of the most highly regarded places in the Serengeti, this camp has 20 large, stunning tents with decks, set around a kopje by the Grumeti River where it passes through the north (not the Western Corridor). A tent's immersion in its surroundings is perfectly blended with the luxury of permanence here. You'll have front-row seats when the herd migration passes through.

Klein's Camp   LODGE $$$
(☏028-262 1267; www.andbeyond.com; Northern Serengeti; per person with full board & incl all activities US$840-1340; P ☎ ☀) This classic Serengeti lodge is exclusive and strikingly situated (the views are awesome) on a private concession just outside the northeastern park boundary. There are 10 luxurious stone-and-thatched cottages, and the chance to enjoy bushwalks, night wildlife drives or a relaxing massage.

🏕 **Mobile Camps**

Mobile camps are a great idea, but the name's somewhat misleading. They do move (though never when guests are in residence), following the wildebeest migration so as to stay in always in good wildlife-watching territory. But with all the amenities people expect on a luxury safari, relocating is a huge chore and most camps only move two or three times a year.

★ **Wayo Green Camp**   TENTED CAMP $$$
(☏0784 203000; www.wayoafrica.com; Northern Serengeti; per person with full board from US$300-350) 🖉 These 'private mobile camps' combine the best aspects of tented camps and budget camping safaris and are the best way to get a deep bush experience in the Serengeti. They use 3m-by-3m dome tents and actual mattresses (off the ground), and move from site to site every couple of days, usually sticking to the Serengeti's north.

★ **Olakira Camp**   TENTED CAMP $$$
(☏0736 500156; www.asiliaafrica.com; Northern Serengeti; per person with full board & incl all activities Jul & Aug US$929, rest of year rates vary; ☽ Jun–mid-Nov; P ☎) 🖉 Olakira's northern location is one of the Serengeti's finest, with long-distance views down towards Mara River crossing 8, 500m away – one of the busiest during the herd migration – and close to the lively junction between the Mara and

THE PICK OF THE MOBILE CAMPS

Numerous companies operate mobile camps that move with the wildebeest herds and the seasons. The better ones:

Ubuntu Western Corridor (May to July) and northern Serengeti (July to November)

Lemala Serengeti Ndutu (December to March) and Mara River (July to October)

Serengeti Safari Camp Moves four or five times a year

Serengeti Savannah Camp (p200) Ndutu (December to March), Mara River (late May to October) and Seronera (year-round)

Bologonya Rivers. The nine tents are large and beautifully set up and the whole place runs on solar power.

A match for many of the more permanent camps dotted around the Serengeti, Olakira moves between the far south (roughly December to March) and far north of the park.

Ubuntu Tented Camp   TENTED CAMP $$$
(www.asiliaafrica.com; per person with full board & incl all activities US$369-784) This tented camp moves twice a year but feels as comfortable and permanent as any of the year-round camps. With just seven tents, all nicely spaced, there's a feeling of intimacy that you just don't get elsewhere, helped by a friendly staff that has worked together as a team for a while.

Lemala Serengeti   TENTED CAMP $$$
(www.lemalacamp.com; s/d with full board & incl all activities US$1110/1700) Another leader in mobile-camp comforts in the Serengeti, Lemala has a camp in Ndutu from December to March and one close to the Mara River from July to October. Its formula is simple and compelling – make the camps look as permanent as possible, but with the flexibility to move them when the time is right. Expect luxury and high service standards.

Serengeti Safari Camp   TENTED CAMP $$$
(☏0784 208343; www.nomad-tanzania.com; s/d with full board & incl all activities US$1150/1600) One of the original mobile camps and now one of the most exclusive, Nomad Tanzania's mobile camp has six tents and some of the best guides in the Serengeti. Unlike the

SERENGETI TO LAKE NATRON

If you're in the northern Serengeti, to really get off the beaten track – not to mention avoid the long and expensive route back through the Serengeti and Ngorongoro Conservation Area – it's possible to drive from Klein's gate all the way to Lake Natron in around five hours. Although the road is unpaved all the way, it's generally in good condition and passable in most vehicles, except after rain.

After leaving Klein's gate, drive 13km to Ololosokwan, where you should stop to buy honey from **Maasai Honey** (☎ 0767 889684, 0684 155793; www.maasaihoney.org; ⊙ 9am-4pm Mon-Fri, 1-5pm Sun). The road roughly shadows the Kenyan border and passes through the barren, stony country that forms part of the Loliondo Game Controlled Area. After 10km, you'll reach Soitsambu; at the time of research, the roads at the western approach to Soitsambu were some of the worst along the whole route. From Soitsambu, the road continues southeast and then south to the large town of Waso. Some 17km south of Waso, take the road branch that heads left (southeast); if you take the right branch, you'll reach the town of Loliondo and, eventually, the Ngorongoro Conservation Area, close to Oldupai (Olduvai) Gorge.

After the road branches, you begin the long, slow descent from the Rift Valley Escarpment to the valley floor. Watch for views of Gelai (2941m) and, later, Lake Natron and Ol Doinyo Lengai (2962m) before you make the final descent. It's 81km from the turn-off to the village of Engaresero, the town with most of the tourist infrastructure near Lake Natron's southern shore, with the last 20km or so along the Rift Valley floor and the lakeshore.

other camps, which move just twice a year, this place moves four or five times, trying to keep pace with the herd migration.

Serengeti Savannah Camp   TENTED CAMP $$$ (☎ 027-254 7066; www.serengetisavannahcamps. com; s/d/tr with full board US$375/580/840) It's a little less luxurious than others of its kind, but Serengeti Savannah Camp is a lot more reasonably priced. It moves three times a year between Ndutu in the south, Seronera in the centre and the Mara River in the north.

ℹ Information

Serengeti Visitor Centre (serengeti@tanzania parks.go.tz; ⊙ 8am-5pm) This office at Seronera has a self-guided walk through the Serengeti's history and ecosystems, and it's well worth spending time here before exploring the park. The gift shop sells various basic booklets and maps, and there's a coffee shop with snacks and cold drinks. A new media centre was under construction in mid-2017.

ℹ Getting There & Away

The park has three main entry and exit points, plus two lesser-used gates at Handajega and Fort Ikoma, and the disused Bologonya gate; this gate would be on the route to/from Kenya's Masai Mara National Reserve, but the border is closed and unlikely to open any time soon.

Naabi Hill gate The main (and most heavily trafficked) access gate if you're coming from Arusha; 45km from Seronera, in the central Serengeti.

Ndabaka gate Main gate for the Western Corridor; a 1½-hour drive from Mwanza and 145km from Seronera. Last entry at 4pm.

Klein's gate In the far northeast, Klein's gate allows a loop trip combining the Serengeti, Ngorongoro and Lake Natron, the latter just two to three hours from the park. Last entry at 4pm.

AIR

Air Excel (p165), Coastal Aviation (p165) and Regional Air (p166) have daily flights from Arusha to the park's seven airstrips, including Seronera and Grumeti.

BUS

Although it's not ideal, shoestring travellers can do their wildlife watching through the window of the Arusha–Musoma buses that cross the park, but you'll need to pay entrance fees for Serengeti and Ngorongoro. The buses stop at the staff village at Seronera, but you're not allowed to walk or hitchhike to the campsites or rest houses, and the park has no vehicles for hire, so unless you've made prior transport arrangements it's nearly pointless to get off here.

CAR

Driving is not permitted in the park after 7pm, except in the visitor-centre area, where the cut-off is 9pm. Petrol is sold at Seronera. Almost everyone explores the park in a 4WD, but except during the heaviest rains 2WDs will have no problems on the main roads and can even manage some of the secondary ones.

continued on page 225

Zebras

Wildlife & Habitat

Think of East Africa and the word 'safari' comes to mind – and Tanzania offers the finest safari experiences and wildlife spectacles found anywhere on the planet. This is a land where predators and prey still live in timeless rhythm. You will never forget the shimmering carpets of wildebeest and zebras, the explosion of cheetahs springing from cover, or the spine-tingling roars of lions at night when you visit the Serengeti or Ngorongoro Crater. With more than 40 national parks and game reserves, there is plenty of room to get off the beaten path and craft the safari of your dreams.

– *David Lukas*

1. Lioness **2.** Lion **3.** Leopard **4.** Cheetah

DAVID LAZAR / GETTY IMAGES ©

Big Cats

The three big cats – leopard, lion and cheetah – provide the high point for so many memorable safaris. The presence of these apex predators, even the mere suggestion that they may be nearby, is enough to draw the savannah taut with attention. It's the lion's gravitas, roaring at night, stalking at sunset. It's the elusive leopard that remains hidden while in plain view. And it's the cheetah in a fluid blur of hunting perfection.

Lion

Weight 120–150kg (female), 150–225kg (male); length 210–275cm (female), 240–350cm (male) Those lions sprawled out lazily in the shade are actually Africa's most feared predators. Equipped with teeth that tear effortlessly through bone and tendon they can take down an animal as large as a bull giraffe. Each group of adults (a pride) is based around generations of females that do the majority of the hunting; swaggering males typically fight among themselves and eat what the females catch. Best seen in Serengeti National Park and Ngorongoro Crater.

Leopard

Weight 30–60kg (female), 40–90kg (male); length 170–300cm More common than you realise, the leopard relies on expert camouflage to stay hidden. During the day you might only spot one reclining in a tree after it twitches its tail, but at night there is no mistaking their bone-chilling groans. Best seen in Serengeti, Ruaha and Tarangire National Parks.

Cheetah

Weight 40–60kg; length 200–220cm Less cat than greyhound, the cheetah is a world-class sprinter. Although it reaches speeds of 112km/h, the cheetah runs out of steam after 300m and must cool down for 30 minutes before hunting again. This speed comes at another cost – the cheetah is so well adapted for running that it lacks the strength and teeth to defend its food or cubs from attack by other large predators. Best seen in Serengeti National Park.

1. Serval 2. Caracal 3. Wildcat

Small Cats

While big cats get the lion's share of attention from tourists, Tanzania's small cats are equally interesting though much harder to spot. You won't find these cats chasing down gazelles or wildebeest; instead look for them slinking around in search of rodents or making incredible leaps to snatch birds out of the air.

Caracal

Weight 8–19kg; length 80–120cm
The caracal is a gorgeous tawny cat with extremely long, pointy ears. This African version of the northern lynx has jacked-up hind legs like a feline dragster. These beanpole kickers enable this slender cat to make vertical leaps of 3m and swat birds out of the air. Widespread in Tanzania's parks, although difficult to spot.

Serval

Weight 6–18kg; length 90–130cm Twice as large as a house cat, but with towering legs and very large ears, the beautifully spotted serval is highly adapted for walking in tall grass and making prodigious leaps to catch rodents and birds. More diurnal than most cats, it may be seen tossing food in the air and playing with it. Best seen in Serengeti National Park.

Wildcat

Weight 3–6.5kg; length 65–100cm If you see what looks like a tabby wandering the plains of Tanzania you're probably seeing a wildcat, the direct ancestor of our domesticated house cats. Occurring wherever there are abundant mice and rats, the wildcat is readily found on the outskirts of villages, where it can be identified by its unmarked rufous ears and longish legs.

Ground Primates

East Africa is widely considered the evolutionary cradle of primate diversity, giving rise to more than 30 species of monkeys, apes and prosimians (the 'primitive' ancestors of modern primates), all of which have dextrous hands and feet. If you think primates hang out in trees, you'll be surprised to see several species that have evolved to ground-living where they are vulnerable to predators.

HENNER DAMKE / SHUTTERSTOCK ©

1. Chimpanzees 2. Olive baboons 3. Vervet monkey

Chimpanzee

Weight 25–40kg; length 60–90cm Like humans, chimpanzees live in highly social groups built around complex hierarchies with mutually understood rules. It doesn't take a brain surgeon to perceive the deep intelligence and emotion lurking behind such eerily familiar deep-set eyes, and researchers at Gombe Stream and Mahale Mountains National Parks are making startling discoveries about chimp behaviour – you deserve to see it for yourself.

Olive Baboon

Weight 11–30kg (female), 22–50kg (male); length 95–180cm Although the olive baboon has 5cm-long fangs and can kill a leopard, its best defence consists of running up trees and showering intruders with liquid excrement. Intelligent and opportunistic, troops of these greenish baboons are becoming increasingly abundant over northern Tanzania, while the much paler yellow baboon ranges over the rest of the country. Best seen in Lake Manyara National Park.

Vervet Monkey

Weight 4–8kg; length 90–140cm If any monkey epitomised East Africa, it would be the vervet monkey. Each troop of vervets is composed of females that defend a home range passed down from generation to generation, while males fight each other for bragging rights and access to females. If you think their appearance drab, check out the extraordinary blue and scarlet colours of their sexual organs when aroused.

Arboreal Primates

Forest primates are a diverse group that live entirely in trees. These agile, long-limbed primates generally stay in the upper canopy where they are well-hidden as they climb and swing among branches in search of leaves and arboreal fruits. It might take the expert eyes of a professional guide to help you find some of these species.

Black-and-White Colobus

Weight 10–23kg; length 115–165cm The black-and-white colobus is one of about seven colobus species found in Tanzania, but it's the mantled colobus that gets the lion's share of attention due to its flowing white frills. Like all colobus, this agile primate has a hook-shaped hand so it can swing through the trees with the greatest of ease. When two troops run into each other, it's a real show. This black-and-white beauty is best seen in Arusha National Park.

1. Black-and-white colobus 2. Blue monkey 3. Greater galago

Blue Monkey

Weight 4–12kg; length 100–170cm These long-tailed monkeys are widespread primates that have adapted to many forested habitats throughout sub-Saharan Africa, including some of the forested parks in Tanzania where they are among the easiest monkeys to spot. These versatile monkeys live in large social groups that spend their entire lives among trees. Best seen in Arusha and Lake Manyara National Parks.

Greater Galago

Weight 550–2000g; length 55–100cm A cat-sized nocturnal creature with a dog-like face, the greater galago belongs to a group of prosimians that have changed little in 60 million years. Best known for its frequent bawling cries (hence the common name 'bushbaby'), the galago would be rarely seen except that it readily visits feeding stations at many popular safari lodges. Living in a world of darkness, galagos communicate with each other through scent and sound. Widespread throughout Tanzania.

ALEKSEI ROMANOV / SHUTTERSTOCK ®

1. Gerenuk 2. Wildebeest 3. African buffalo 4. Greater kudu

DAVID LAZAR / GETTY IMAGES ©

Cud-Chewing Mammals

Hoofed mammals often live in immense herds to protect themselves from predators. Among this family, antelopes are particularly numerous, with 40 species in East Africa alone.

Greater Kudu

Weight 120–315kg; length 215–300cm
The kudu's white pinstripes conceal it in brushy thickets, while the long spiralling horns of the male are used in ritualised combat. Best seen in Ruaha National Park.

Wildebeest

Weight 140–290kg; length 230–340cm
On the Serengeti, wildebeest form vast herds accompanied by predators and jeeps of wide-eyed spectators. Best seen in Serengeti National Park, Ngorongoro Crater and Tarangire National Park.

Thomson's Gazelle

Weight 15–35kg; length 95–150cm Lanky and exceptionally alert, the Thomson's gazelle is built for speed. They migrate in great herds with zebras and wildebeest. Best seen in Serengeti National Park and Ngorongoro Crater.

African Buffalo

Weight 250–850kg; length 220–420cm
Imagine a big cow with curling horns, and you have the African buffalo (Cape Buffalo). Best seen in Katavi National Park, Mikumi National Park and Ngorongoro Crater.

Gerenuk

Weight 30–50kg; length 160–200cm
Adapted for life in the semi-arid brush of northeastern Tanzania, the gerenuk stands on its hind legs to reach 2m-high branches. Best seen in Tarangire National Park.

Waterbuck

Weight 160-300kg; length 210-275cm If you see any antelope it's likely to be the big, shaggy waterbuck. Dependent on waterside vegetation, numbers fluctuate dramatically between wet and dry years. Best seen in Selous Game Reserve and Lake Manyara National Park.

Hoofed Mammals

A full stable of Africa's most charismatic animals can be found in this group of ungulates. Other than the giraffe, these ungulates are not cud-chewers and can be found over a much broader range of habitats than the cud-chewing animals. They have made their home in Africa for millions of years and are among the most successful mammals to have ever wandered the continent. Without human intervention, Africa would be ruled by elephants, zebras, hippos and warthogs.

Giraffe

Weight 450–1200kg (female), 1800–2000kg (male) The 5m-tall giraffe does such a good job with upward activity – towering above the competition and reaching up to grab mouthfuls of leaves on high branches – that stretching down to get a simple drink of water is a difficult task. Though giraffes usually stroll along casually, they can outrun most predators. Widely sighted, especially in northern safari circuit parks.

African Elephant

Weight 2200–3500kg (female), 4000–6300kg (male); height 2.4–3.4m (female), 3–4m (male) No one, not even a human or lion, stands around to argue when a towering bull elephant rumbles out of the brush. Commonly referred to as 'the king of beasts', elephant society is actually ruled by a lineage of elder females who lead each group along traditional migration routes. Best seen in Ruaha National Park, Selous Game Reserve, Ngorongoro Crater and Tarangire National Park.

Plains Zebra

Weight 175–320kg; length 260–300cm My oh my, those zebras sure have some wicked stripes. Scientists first thought the stripes, each distinct as a human fingerprint, were to confuse predators by making it difficult to distinguish the outline of individual zebras in a herd. However, new studies suggest the stripes help combat disease-carrying horseflies. Best seen in Serengeti and Tarangire National Parks.

1. Giraffes **2.** African elephants **3.** Plains zebras

1. Black rhinoceros 2. Rock hyraxes
3. Warthog 4. Hippopotamus

MANOJ SHAH / GETTY IMAGES ©

More Hoofed Mammals

This sampling of miscellaneous hoofed animals highlights the astonishing diversity in this major group of African wildlife. Every visitor wants to see elephants and giraffes, but don't pass up a chance to watch hippos or warthogs.

Black Rhinoceros

Weight 700–1400kg; length 350–450cm Pity the black rhinoceros for having a horn that is worth more than gold. Once widespread and abundant south of the Sahara, the rhino has been poached to the brink of extinction. Unfortunately, females may only give birth every five years. Best seen in Ngorongoro Crater.

Rock Hyrax

Weight 1.8–5.5kg; length 40–60cm It doesn't seem like it, but those funny tail-less squirrels you see lounging around on rocks are actually an ancient cousin to the elephant. Look for their tiny tusks when one yawns. Best seen in Serengeti National Park.

Warthog

Weight 45–75kg (female), 60–150kg (male); length 140–200cm Despite their fearsome appearance and sinister tusks, only the big males are safe from lions, cheetahs and hyenas. To protect themselves when attacked, warthogs run for burrows and reverse in while slashing wildly with their tusks. Easily spotted in many of Tanzania's parks.

Hippopotamus

Weight 510–3200kg; length 320–400cm The hippopotamus is one strange creature. Designed like a floating beanbag with tiny legs, the 3000kg hippo spends its time in or very near water chowing down on aquatic plants. Placid? No way! Hippos have tremendous ferocity and strength when provoked. Best seen in Selous Game Reserve and Katavi National Park.

1. Golden jackal 2. Spotted hyena
3. Banded mongooses 4. Wild dog

MARC GUITARD / GETTY IMAGES ©

Carnivores

It is a sign of Africa's ecological richness that the continent supports a remarkable variety of predators. When it comes to predators, expect the unexpected and you'll return home with a lifetime of memories!

Banded Mongoose

Weight 1.5–2kg; length 45–75cm Bounding across the savannah on their morning foraging excursions, family groups seek out delicious snacks like toads, scorpions and slugs. Widespread in Tanzania.

Wild Dog

Weight 20–35kg; length 100–150cm Organised in complex hierarchies maintained by rules of conduct, packs of these efficient hunters (also known as the hunting dog) chase down antelope and other animals. Best seen in Selous Game Reserve and Ruaha National Park.

Honey Badger

Weight 7–16kg; length 75–100cm Africans say they would rather face a lion than a honey badger, and even lions relinquish their kill when one shows up. It finds its favourite food by following honey guide birds to bee hives. It's also known as a 'ratel'. Best seen in Mikumi National Park.

Spotted Hyena

Weight 40–90kg; length 125–215cm Living in groups that are ruled by females (who grow penis-like sexual organs), hyenas use bone-crushing jaws to disembowel terrified prey on the run. Best seen in Ngorongoro Crater.

Golden Jackal

Weight 6–15kg; length 85–130cm Through a combination of sheer fierceness and bluff the trim little jackal manages to fill its belly while holding hungry vultures and much stronger hyenas at bay. Best seen in Serengeti National Park and Ngorongoro Crater.

218

1. African fish eagle 2. White-backed vultures
3. Secretary bird 4. Bateleur

DMUSSMAN / SHUTTERSTOCK ©

Birds of Prey

Tanzania has nearly 100 species of hawks, eagles, vultures and owls. More than 40 have been seen at Lake Manyara National Park alone, making this one of the best places in the world to see an incredible variety of birds of prey.

Secretary Bird

Length 100cm With the body of an eagle and legs of a crane, the bizarre secretary bird towers 1.3m tall and walks up to 20km a day in search of vipers, cobras and other snakes. Best seen in Serengeti National Park.

Bateleur

Length 60cm French for 'tightrope-walker', bateleur refers to this bird's distinctive low-flying aerial acrobatics. At close hand, look for its bold colour pattern and scarlet face. Best seen in Katavi and Tarangire National Parks.

African Fish Eagle

Length 75cm This replica of the American bald eagle presents an imposing appearance, but it is most familiar for its loud, ringing vocalisations that have become known as 'the voice of Africa'. Best seen in Rubondo Island National Park.

Augur Buzzard

Length 55cm Perhaps Tanzania's most common raptor, the augur buzzard occupies a wide range of wild and cultivated habitats, where they hunt by floating motionlessly in the air then stooping down to catch unwary critters.

White-Backed Vulture

Length 80cm Mingling with lions, hyenas and jackals around carcasses, vultures use their sheer numbers to compete for scraps of flesh and bone. Easily spotted in most of Tanzania's parks.

GASCHWALD / SHUTTERSTOCK ©

1. Superb starling 2. Lesser flamingos
3. Lilac-breasted roller 4. Ostrich

ANTONIO JORGE NUNES / SHUTTERSTOCK ©

Other Birds

Birdwatchers from all over the world travel to Tanzania in search of the country's 1100 species of birds – an astounding number by any measure – including birds of every shape and in every colour imaginable.

Saddle-Billed Stork

Height 150cm; wingspan 270cm The saddle-billed stork is the most stunning of Tanzania's eight stork species. As if a 2.7m wingspan isn't impressive enough, check out its brilliant-red-coloured kneecaps and bill. Best seen in Serengeti National Park.

Lesser Flamingo

Length 100cm When they gather by the hundreds of thousands on shimmering salt lakes, lesser flamingos create unforgettable wildlife images. Best seen in Lake Manyara National Park.

Lilac-Breasted Roller

Length 40cm Nearly everyone on safari gets to know the gorgeous lilac-breasted roller. Rollers get their name from the tendency to 'roll' from side to side in flight as a way of showing off their iridescent blues, purples and greens. Easily spotted in many of Tanzania's parks.

Ostrich

Height 200–270cm Standing 2.7m high and weighing upwards of 130kg, these ancient birds escape predators by running away at 70km/h or lying flat on the ground to resemble a pile of dirt. Best seen in Serengeti National Park.

Superb Starling

Length 18cm With a black face, yellow eyes and metallic blue-green upperparts that contrast sharply with their red-orange belly, superb starlings seem like a rare find, but are actually surprisingly abundant. Best seen in Tanzania's northern safari circuit parks.

Habitats

Nearly all of Tanzania's birds and animals spend most of their lives in specific types of habitat, and you will hear rangers and fellow travellers refer to these habitats repeatedly as if they were code words. If this is your first time in East Africa, some of these habitats and their seasonal rhythms take some getting used to, but your wildlife-viewing experiences will be greatly enhanced when you learn how to recognise these habitats and which animals you might expect in each one.

Semi-Arid Desert

Parts of northeastern Tanzania see so little rainfall that shrubs and hardy grasses, rather than trees, are the dominant vegetation. This is not the Tanzania that many visitors come to see and it doesn't seem like a great place for wildlife, but the patient observer will be richly rewarded. While it's true that the lack of water restricts larger animals such as zebras, gazelles and antelope to areas around waterholes, this habitat explodes with plant and animal life whenever it rains. During the dry season, many plants shed their leaves to conserve water and grazing animals move on in search of food and water. Mkomazi Game Refuge is one of the best places in Tanzania to experience this unique habitat.

Savannah

Savannah is the classic East African landscape – broad rolling grasslands dotted with lone acacia trees. The openness and vastness of this landscape

1. Mt Kilimanjaro (p233) **2.** Baobab trees, Ruaha National Park (p297)

make it a perfect home for large herds of grazing zebras and wildebeest, in addition to fast-sprinting predators such as cheetahs, and it's a perfect place for seeing large numbers of animals. Savannah develops in areas where there are long wet seasons alternating with long dry seasons, creating ideal conditions for the growth of dense, nutritious grasses. Shaped by fire and grazing animals, savannah is a dynamic habitat in constant flux with its adjacent woodlands. One of the best places in the world for exploring the African savannah is found at Serengeti National Park.

Woodland

Tanzania is the only place in East Africa to find the woodland habitat, locally known as *miombo* (moist woodland), which is more characteristic of south-central Africa. Here the trees form a continuous canopy cover that offers shelter from predators and shade from the harsh sunlight. This important habitat provides homes for many birds, small mammals and insects, and is a fantastic place to search for wildlife. In places where fingers of woodland mingle with savannah, animals such as leopards and antelope often gather to find shade or places to rest during the day. During the dry season, fires and elephants can wreak havoc on these woodlands, fragmenting large tracts of forest habitat. Ruaha National Park is a fantastic place to see both pure *miombo* forests and the ecological mix of savannah and *miombo*.

Lionesses, Ngorongoro Conservation Area

continued from page 200

KILIMANJARO AREA

Moshi

☑ 027 / POP 184,300

The noticeably clean capital of the densely populated Kilimanjaro region sits at the foot of Mt Kilimanjaro and makes a good introduction to the splendours of the north. It's a low-key place with an appealing blend of African and Asian influences and a self-sufficient, prosperous feel, due in large part to its being the centre of one of Tanzania's major coffee-growing regions. Virtually all visitors are here to climb Mt Kilimanjaro or to recover after having done so. Yet there's much more to do, including cultural tours and hikes on the mountain's lower slopes.

Even inside the city, Mt Kilimanjaro is the main attraction and you'll probably be continually gazing north trying to catch a glimpse of it. Most of the time it will be hidden behind a wall of clouds, but nearly every evening after 6pm it emerges from the mist to whet your appetite for altitude. From December to June it's usually visible during the morning, too, and generally topped by much more snow.

🛏 Sleeping

Most budget places are in or near the town centre; midrange options are spread between the centre and the Shanty Town neighbourhood, about 3km northwest.

Central Moshi

★ Haria Hotel   HOTEL $
(☑ 0656 318841; www.hariahotel.com; Mawenzi Rd; r US$35, dm/d with shared bathroom US$10/25; 🛰) 🍴 This laid-back, switched-on place has simple, spacious rooms and a friendly overall feel. The rooftop restaurant-bar serves a good menu of local meals at fair prices with Kili views. It's run by Team Vista (www.teamvista.com.au), and profits go to support its work in the community.

Nyota Bed & Breakfast   B&B $
(☑ 0754 481672; www.nyotabedandbreakfast.com; Rengua Rd; tw/tr with shared bathroom US$40/60) This small place has spacious, spotless rooms with fans and some with verandas, plus carefully prepared breakfasts and a convenient central location. Overall, it's a highly recommended budget choice.

Lutheran Umoja Hostel   GUESTHOUSE $
(☑ 0769 239860, 027-275 0902; Market St; s/d Tsh30,000/40,000, with shared bathroom Tsh15,000/25,000; 🅿 @ 🛰) The cheapest place in the city centre has clean, no-frills rooms around a small, (mostly) quiet courtyard. It's popular with volunteers.

AA Hill Street Accommodation   GUESTHOUSE $
(☑ 0754461469,0784461469;azim_omar@hotmail.com; Kilima St; s/d/tr Tsh20,000/25,000/35,000) Walk past the seamstresses plying their trade just off Kilima St, and climb the stairs to this quiet, friendly place with simple, tidy rooms. It's ideal for those looking for an alternative to the busy backpacker scene. Don't be put off by the list of restrictions (no alcohol, no shared rooms for non-married couples) – if those things matter, go elsewhere.

Buffalo Hotel   HOTEL $
(☑ 0752 401346, 0756 508501; New St; s/d/tr/ste US$40/45/55/65; 🌐) The long-popular Buffalo Hotel has straightforward rooms, all with private bathroom. Avoid the ground-floor rooms and head up the stairs; there's no elevator. The lack of wi-fi lets it down a little, but there's an internet cafe next door and it's generally a good deal.

Kindoroko Hotel   HOTEL $
(☑ 0753 377795; www.kindorokohotels.com; Mawenzi Rd; s/d/tr US$20/30/45; @) Rooms here are small and sit somewhere between basic and simple, but they have cable TV and hot water. The main reason to stay is the guests-only rooftop bar, an excellent meeting place with fine Kilimanjaro views.

Bristol Cottages   HOTEL $$
(☑ 027-275 5083; www.bristolcottages.com; 98 Rindi Lane; s/d US$60/90, s/d/tr cottages US$70/100/130, s/d/tr ste US$80/110/140; 🅿 🌐 🛰) This place exudes a sense of peace upon entering – the leafy compound is an attractive counterpoint to the busy Moshi streets – and the rooms are well presented; the suites are particularly spacious. For all this talk of peace, however, early-morning noise can be a problem. Even so, it's the midrange pick in the downtown area.

Nyumbani Hotel   HOTEL $$
(☑ 027-275 4432, 0767 123487; www.nyumbanihotels.com; Rengua Rd; s/d from US$85/100; 🌐 🛰) A good midrange choice in the heart of town, with a modern business feel. Rooms are fairly large and some have balconies. There's not a huge amount of charm, but it's a reasonably good deal nonetheless.

Kilimanjaro Crane Hotel   HOTEL $$

(☑ 027-275 1114, 0763 399503; www.kilimanjaro
cranehotel.com; Kaunda St; s/d US$50/60; ❄ @
☏ ☀) This long-standing midrange option
has tired but adequate rooms with safari
colours of the kind you'll see fading in the
sun at roadside furniture showrooms. It's a
touch cheaper than others in this category,
and rooms have cable TV and large beds
backing a small garden. There are great Kili
views from the rooftop.

🛏 Outside the City Centre

★ Hibiscus   B&B $

(☑ 0766-312516; www.thehibiscusmoshi.com; Paris
St; s/tw US$30/40; ☏) This cosy B&B has spot-
less, nicely decorated rooms, all with fan and
most with private bathroom, plus a pleasant
garden and meals on request. It's in a quiet
residential area just northwest of the town
centre off Arusha Rd.

★ AMEG Lodge   LODGE $$

(☑ 027-275 0175, 0754 058268; www.ameglodge.
com; s/d from US$82/106, s/d ste US$135/159;
🅿 ❄ ☏ ☀) This friendly place wins plaudits
from travellers for its lovely setting in 2 hectares of manicured gardens with palm trees
and frangipanis, 4km northwest of the centre,
off Lema Rd. Attractive rooms with broad verandas and plenty of space lie dotted around
the compound, service is friendly, and the feel
is that of a rural oasis on the city fringe.

Lutheran Uhuru Hotel   LODGE $$

(☑ 0753 037216, 027-275 4512; www.uhuruhotel.org;
Sekou Toure Rd; s/d with fan from US$45/55, with air-
con from US$50/60; ❄ @ ☏) This alcohol-free
place has clean, good-value rooms in leafy,
expansive grounds, and a restaurant serving
tasty, simple meals (Tsh6000 to Tsh15,000).
Some rooms are wheelchair accessible and
many have Kili views. It's 3km northwest of
the town centre (Tsh5000 in a taxi). Wi-fi
costs a steep Tsh2000 per hour.

Honey Badger   GUESTHOUSE $$

(☑ 0787 730235, 0767 551190; www.honeybadger
lodge.com; s/d from US$55/80; 🅿 @ ☏ ☀) This
large, family-run place has shady gardens,
and a pool for guests as well as day visitors
(US$6). It offers a variety of tours and lessons
(drumming, cooking), and volunteer opportunities can be arranged. The restaurant
serves gourmet pizzas from its stone oven
at weekends. It's 7km from town off the Marangu road. Dorm-style rooms are available
for larger groups.

Altezza Lodge   HOTEL $$

(☑ 0786 350414; www.altezza-lodge.com; Sekou
Toure Way; s/d US$85/95; 🅿 ❄ ☏ ☀) One of
Moshi's best midrange hotels, Altezza is in a
quiet area just north of the centre, and has
attractive if simple rooms in a green setting.
In other words, it gets the important things
right and doesn't charge over the odds for
them, which may be reason enough to stay.

🍴 Eating & Drinking

The Coffee Shop   CAFE $

(☑ 027-275 2707; Kilima St; mains Tsh5000-7000;
🕐 7.30am-9.30pm Mon-Sat; ☏) 🌿 Garden seating, good coffee, and homemade bread, cakes,
yoghurt, breakfast, soups and low-priced
light meals. Of the latter, the local dishes
(choose a sauce with ugali or chapati) are
generally preferable to the Chinese-inspired
selections. Proceeds go to a church project,
and there's an interesting noticeboard.

Milan's   INDIAN $

(Makinga St; meals Tsh6000-10,000; 🕐 11am-
9.30pm; 🍴) This colourful all-vegetarian spot
is the town's most appealing Indian restaurant, and not only because the prices are so
low; the food's also really delicious.

Story Lounge   TANZANIAN $

(☑ 0745 333491; Kibo Rd; mains Tsh6000-14,000;
🕐 8am-1am) This smooth place does good
coffee and everything from burgers to biryani; Tuesday is biryani day. In the evening it
morphs into a very cool lounge space.

Pamoja Cafe   TANZANIAN, INTERNATIONAL $

(☑ 0755 246485; New St; mains Tsh4500-10,000;
🕐 8am-10pm Mon-Sat, 10am-9pm Sun; ☏)
Following a time-honoured tradition of
budget-traveller hang-outs the world over,
basic Pamoja Cafe gives the punters what
they want with free wi-fi, a funky soundtrack,
Western snacks (burgers, sandwiches) and
cheap local cuisine, such as *nyami mchuzi*
(beef stew with rice, ugali or chapati). There's
also a nightly barbecue from 5.30pm. It's not
what it was, but it's still cool.

★ Peppers   INDIAN $$

(☑ 0754 058268, 027-275 2473; Ghala St; mains
Tsh12,000-16,000; 🕐 noon-3pm & 6-10pm Tue-Sun;
🍴) Changes of ownership and name (it used
to be called the Sikh Club) have done this
place the world of good. It's part restaurant
serving excellent Indian food (which gets the
nod from the local Indian community) and
part sports bar for those who like their action

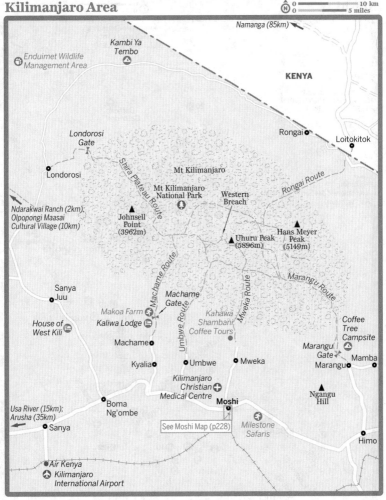

N 0 — 10 km
0 — 5 miles

Namanga (85km)

KENYA

Enduimet Wildlife Management Area

Kambi Ya Tembo

Londorosi Gate

Rongai

Loitokitok

Londorosi

Shira Plateau Route

Mt Kilimanjaro

Rongai Route

Mt Kilimanjaro National Park

Western Breach

Ndarakwai Ranch (2km); Olpopongi Maasai Cultural Village (10km)

Johnsell Point (3962m)

Uhuru Peak (5896m)

Hans Meyer Peak (5149m)

Machame Route

Marangu Route

Sanya Juu

Mweka Route

Makoa Farm

Machame Gate

House of West Kili

Kaliwa Lodge

Kahawa Shambani Coffee Tours

Umbwe Route

Coffee Tree Campsite

Machame

Marangu Gate

Mamba

Kyalia

Umbwe

Mweka

Marangu

Kilimanjaro Christian Medical Centre

Ngangu Hill

Usa River (15km); Arusha (35km)

Boma Ng'ombe

Moshi

Sanya

See Moshi Map (p228)

Milestone Safaris

Himo

Air Kenya

Kilimanjaro International Airport

on the high screen. There's a pleasant terrace overlooking the football pitch.

★ **Kilimanjaro Coffee Lounge**   CAFE **$$**
(☎ 0754 610892; Station Rd; meals Tsh8000-16,000; ⊙ 8am-9pm Mon-Sat, 10am-8pm Sun; ☎) This cafe's semi-garden setting is back a bit from the road, bringing a semblance of peace, and the food ranges from pizza and Mexican dishes to salads, sandwiches, burgers and steaks, alongside excellent milkshakes and juices. There are the makings of a travellers' classic here, although hopefully it's stopped charging for wi-fi by the time you arrive.

Mr Feng Chinese Restaurant   CHINESE **$$**
(☎ 0768 565656; meals Tsh8000-17,000; ⊙ noon-3pm & 6.30-10pm Mon-Fri, 11am-10pm Sat & Sun; ☎) Delicious Chinese food, including many veg options, plus tranquil garden seating and a friendly, helpful proprietor make this a recommended spot for a meal in Moshi.

Jay's Kitchen   KOREAN **$$**
(☎ 0768 607456, 0765 311618; www.facebook.com/JaysAdventureTanzania; Boma Rd; meals Tsh8000-20,000; ⊙ 11am-9pm Wed-Mon) Jay's boasts tasty Korean food and sushi, a central location, and good garden seating. Also offers takeaway.

Moshi

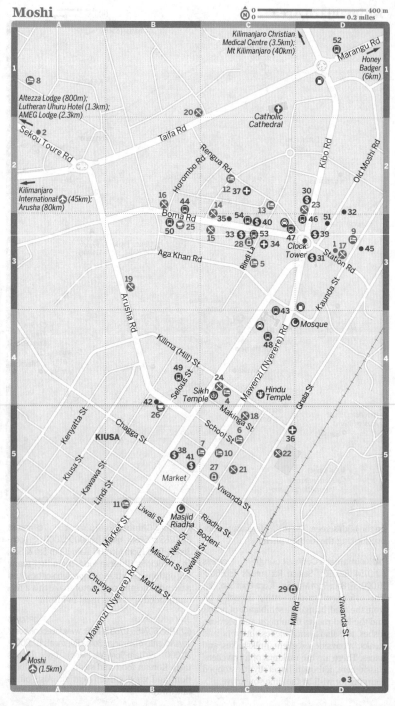

Kilimanjaro Christian
Medical Centre (3.5km);
Mt Kilimanjaro (40km)

Honey
Badger
(6km)

Altezza Lodge (800m);
Lutheran Uhuru Hotel (1.3km);
AMEG Lodge (2.3km)

Kilimanjaro
International (45km);
Arusha (80km)

Catholic
Cathedral

Taifa Rd

Rengua Rd

Horombo Rd

Boma Rd

Aga Khan Rd

Arusha Rd

Kilima (Hill) St

Selous St

Sikh
Temple

Hindu
Temple

Makinga St

School St

Mawenzi (Nyerere) Rd

Ghala St

Kaunda St

Clock
Tower

Station Rd

Mosque

KIUSA

Chagga St

Kenyatta St

Kiusa St

Kawawa St

Lindi St

Market St

Market

Liwali St

Masjid
Riadha

New St

Mission St

Swahili St

Bodeni St

Riadha St

Viwanda St

Chunya St

Mafuta St

Mawenzi (Nyerere) Rd

Moshi
(1.5km)

Mill Rd

Viwanda St

Moshi

**Mimosa
Restaurant-Bar-Cafe** INTERNATIONAL $$
(☑ 0765 352826; www.facebook.com/mimosa
moshi; Arusha Rd; mains Tsh10,000-20,000;
⊙9am-10.30pm; 🛜) This popular place sits at
the southwestern end of Uhuru Park, with
a comfortable, green outdoor eating area. It
serves up tasty beef and chicken dishes, a few
Thai offerings and a kids' menu, plus good
smoothies, milkshakes and desserts. There's
a daily happy hour (4pm to 7pm).

★**Union Café** CAFE
(☑ 027-275 2785, 0784 590184; Arusha Rd;
⊙7.30am-8.30pm; 🛜) 🥗 The Kilimanjaro Na-
tive Cooperative Union, representing tens of
thousands of coffee smallholders, runs this
stylish shop. Although it also serves good
pizzas, pastas and burgers (meals Tsh8000
to Tsh18,000), it's all about the coffee – the
cooperative's own beans are roasted on-site.
It also has a generator, reliable wi-fi and an
atmosphere that's trendy but carries echoes
of colonial Africa.

Arusha Coffee Lounge CAFE
(☑ 0755 763700; Boma Rd; ⊙6am-6pm; 🛜) If
you're craving a coffee in the busy Boma Rd
area, Arusha Coffee Lounge is a cool, quiet
hang-out, with good wi-fi, better coffee and
a range of pastries and snacks.

Self-Catering

Abbas Ali's Hot Bread Shop BAKERY $
(Boma Rd; ⊙9am-6pm Mon-Fri, to 5pm Sat)
Moshi's best bakery, with fresh bread, samo-
sas, yoghurt and other snacks.

Aleem's SUPERMARKET $
(Boma Rd; ⊙8.45am-1pm & 2-5pm Mon-Fri, 8.45am-
1pm & 2-4pm Sat) Small, reasonably well-
stocked grocery store.

🛍 Shopping

Moshi Mamas ARTS & CRAFTS
(☑ 0757 151992; Boma Rd; ⊙10am-5pm Tue-Sat,
noon-5pm Sun) A local craft cooperative run
by, as the name suggests, a handful of friend-
ly local mamas, this place sells beadwork,

COFFEE TOURS

With the most popular coffee tour in town, **Kahawa Shambani Coffee Tours** (☎ 0782 324121; www.kiliman culturaltourism.com/coffee-tour; per person Tsh40,000, transport from Moshi Tsh60,000) is a laudable community-run venture that not only shows you how beans are grown, picked and roasted but offers insight into the lives of the Chagga coffee farmers who live on Kilimanjaro's lower slopes. Meals with local families can be arranged, as can additional village and waterfall walks.

It's easiest to book at Union Café or contact them directly to, as they say on their website, 'avoid irrelevant people'.

kitenge cloth and a small collection of other craft items made by the cooperative's members. It's signposted on Boma Rd but about 100m up an arcade, past Riverside Shuttle.

I Curio ARTS & CRAFTS
(Viwanda St; ⊗ 8am-6.30pm) Better than the ordinary craft shops, and with fixed prices. Also stocks a small selection of national-park maps and books.

Shah Industries GIFTS & SOUVENIRS
(☎ 0754 260348; www.kiliweb.com/shah; Mill Rd; ⊗ 9am-5pm Mon-Fri, to 2pm Sat) 🖉 Lots of interesting leatherwork, some of it made by people with disabilities.

ℹ Information

IMMIGRATION
Immigration Office (Boma Rd; ⊗ 7.30am-3.30pm Mon-Fri) For visa extensions.

MEDICAL SERVICES
First Health CRCT Hospital (☎ 027-54051; Rindi Lane) City-centre hospital; no emergency department.

Jaffery Charitable Medical Services (☎ 027-275 1843; Ghala St; ⊗ 8am-7pm Mon-Fri, to 6pm Sat, 9am-noon Sun) Medical clinic with Moshi's most reliable laboratory.

Kemi Pharmacy (☎ 027-275 1560; Rengua Rd; ⊗ 7.30am-7.30pm Mon-Sat, 11am-4pm Sun) One of numerous pharmacies dotted around the city centre.

Kilimanjaro Christian Medical Centre (☎ 027-275 4377/80; www.kcmc.ac.tz; ⊗ 24hr) Around 4.5km north of the centre, off Sokoine Rd.

MONEY
There are numerous ATMs scattered around the central part of Moshi, including several along Boma Rd. **Exim Bank** and **Stanbic Bank** (⊗ 8.30am-3.30pm Mon-Fri, to noon Sat) both have ATMs on Boma Rd; NBC Bank has 24-hour ATMs, including on Market St and the Clock Tower roundabout.

CRDB (⊗ 8.30am-4pm Mon-Fri, to 1pm Sat), also on the roundabout, has an efficient exchange counter. Private exchange bureaus include **Classic** (Kibo Rd; ⊗ 8am-4pm) and **Trast** (Chagga St; ⊗ 9am-5pm Mon-Sat, to 2pm Sun).

TOURIST INFORMATION
There's no tourist office in Moshi. The Coffee Shop (p226), Kilimanjaro Coffee Lounge (p227) and Union Café (p229) have message boards, and people seeking climbing partners sometimes post requests on them. **Kiliweb** (www. kiliweb.com) is another info option.

TRAVEL AGENCIES
Emslies Global (☎ 027-275 2701, 0689 772379; www.emsliesglobal.com; Old Moshi Rd; ⊗ 8.30am-5pm Mon-Fri, to noon Sat) Domestic and international flight bookings.

ℹ Getting There & Away

AIR
Kilimanjaro International Airport (KIA) is 50km west of town, halfway to Arusha. The standard taxi fare to/from Moshi is Tsh50,000, although drivers will often request more. There's also the small Moshi airport just southwest of town along the extension of Market St (Tsh5000 by taxi to central hotels), which handles Coastal Aviation flights and occasional charters.

Coastal Aviation (☎ 0785 500729, 0785 500445; www.coastal.co.tz; Arusha Rd; ⊗ 8.30am-5pm Mon-Fri, to noon Sat) Flies daily to and from Moshi airport (if there are enough passengers) on the Arusha–Tanga–Pangani–Pemba–Zanzibar–Dar es Salaam circuit, with links also possible to the northern national parks.

Fastjet (☎ 0784 108900; www.fastjet.com; Kaunda St) Daily flights between KIA and Dar es Salaam, with onward connections across Tanzania and East Africa.

Precision Air (☎ 027-275 3495, 0787 800820; www.precisionairtz.com; Old Moshi Rd; ⊗ 8am-5pm Mon-Fri, 9am-1pm Sat & Sun) Flies from KIA to Dar es Salaam, Zanzibar Island and Mwanza.

BUS
Buses and minibuses run throughout the day to Arusha (Tsh3000, two hours) and Marangu (Tsh1500 to Tsh2200, 1½ hours).

The **bus station** (Market St) is conveniently located in the middle of the city. There are many touts, and arrivals can be quite annoying if you're new to this sort of thing. This is one good reason to travel with bus companies that have their own offices (many are located along Boma Rd and near the Clock Tower roundabout). It's best to buy tickets the day before you plan to travel.

All of the following buses use their own offices rather than the bus station. Ordinary buses and a few less-reliable luxury companies use the bus station.

Dar Express (Boma Rd) Daily departures to Dar es Salaam (Tsh36,000, seven to eight hours) from 7am to noon aboard full luxury buses (with air-con and toilets). The 7am bus sometimes arrives early enough for you to catch the afternoon ferry to Zanzibar, but don't count on it.

Kilimanjaro Express (Rengua Rd) Morning luxury departures to Dar (from Tsh33,000).

Metro Express (📱0715 113344; Selous St) Two daily departures (luxury/full luxury Tsh33,000/36,000) for Dar at 8am.

Mtei Express (Boma Rd) Buses to Babati (Tsh10,000, four to five hours), Singida (Tsh20,000, nine hours) and Dodoma (Tsh28,000, 12 to 14 hours) via Arusha.

Tahmeed Coach (www.tahmeedcoach. co.ke; Boma Rd) One bus daily to Mombasa (Tsh20,000, eight hours).

There are also several shuttle companies with daily services to and from Nairobi (Kenya) via Arusha for around US$40 per person. These include the reliable **Impala Shuttle** (📱0754 293119, 0754 360658; Kibo Rd; ⊙6.30am & 11.30am), as well as **Riverside Shuttle** (📱027-275 0093; www.riverside-shuttle.com; YWCA Bldg, Boma Rd; ⊙6am & 11.30am) and **Rainbow Shuttle** (📱0784 204025; ⊙6am & 11am).

ⓘ Getting Around

TO/FROM THE AIRPORT

Taxis charge Tsh50,000 between Kilimanjaro International Airport and Moshi, although first quotes are often higher.

TAXI & DALLA-DALLA

There are taxi stands near the Clock Tower and at the bus station, plus you can find taxis by most hotels. From the bus station to a city-centre hotel costs about Tsh3500; to Shanty Town, it's Tsh6000. *Boda-bodas* (motorcycle taxis) are everywhere; expect to pay Tsh1000, even for a very short ride, and from Tsh2000 for anything longer. Dalla-dallas run down main roads from next to the bus station, and there's a dalla-dalla stand at the northern end of the bus station.

There are taxi stands on Rengua Rd, just up from the Clock Tower roundabout, and on Market St, next to the bus station.

CAR & MOTORCYCLE

Parking your vehicle anywhere in the city centre costs Tsh500 per day – an attendant with ticket machine is sure to be lurking not far from where you park.

There are a number of petrol stations along the main thoroughfares, including along **Nyerere Rd** (⊙24hr) and on Taifa Rd, on the main roundabout where Kibo Rd meets the main highway.

Machame

📱027 / POP 23,300

The rather ill-defined and spread-out village of Machame lies 25km northwest of Moshi on Mt Kilimanjaro's lower slopes, surrounded by dense vegetation and stands of banana. Most visitors only pass through briefly on their way to the trailhead for the popular Machame route up the mountain. As such, it's a last outpost of clamour before your ascent into the clouds.

There aren't many places to stay in Machame, but **Kaliwa Lodge** (📱0762 620707; www.kaliwalodge.com; s/d US$99/198; P) is so good as to almost be a destination in its own right. At an altitude of 1300m and close to Kilimanjaro's Machame gate, this German-run place opened in 2012 and has a refreshingly contemporary Bauhaus architectural style, comprising restful grey cube-like structures. Rooms have abundant glass, the colour scheme is muted but very modern, and the setting amid palm trees and lush gardens is as lovely as the rest of the place.

A handful of daily minibuses connect Machame and Moshi (Tsh2500, two hours).

Marangu

📱027 / POP 23,000

Nestled on the lower slopes of Mt Kilimanjaro, 40km northeast of Moshi amid dense stands of banana and coffee plants, is the lively, leafy market town of Marangu. It has an agreeable highland ambience, a cool climate and a good selection of hotels, all of which organise treks. While you'll sometimes get slightly better budget deals in Moshi, Marangu makes a convenient launch pad for Kili climbs using the Marangu or Rongai routes, and it's an enjoyable stop in its own right. Apart from anything else, there's a real sense of being up in the foothills here, which adds to the pre-Kili excitement and aids psychological preparation.

Marangu is also the heartland of the Chagga people, and there are many possibilities for walks and cultural activities. *Marangu* means 'place of water', and the surrounding area is laced with small streams and waterfalls (most with a small entry charge for visitors).

◉ Sights & Activities

There are authentic scale models of traditional Chagga houses at Banana Jungle Lodge (☑ 0713 780464, 027-275 6565; Ⓟ) and Kilimanjaro Mountain Resort (☑ 0754 693461; www.kilimountresort.com; Ⓟ @ ☲). About 6km southwest of Marangu is Ngangu Hill, with views and the small, old Kilema mission church nearby.

There are ATMs near the main Marangu junction. Most hotels can provide English-speaking guides (US$10 to US$15 per person per day) to area attractions, including rather claustrophobic 'caves' (actually dugout holes and tunnels) that were used as hiding places by the Chagga during the era of Maasai raids about 200 years ago, a sacred tree, local blacksmiths' workshops, and waterfalls. Day hikes as far as Mandara Hut (10km one way; allow around three hours up and 1½ hours back) in Mt Kilimanjaro National Park can be arranged with Marangu-area hotels and trekking operators.

🛏 Sleeping & Eating

Coffee Tree Campsite   CAMPGROUND $
(☑ 027-275 6604, 0754 691433; kilimanjaro@iwayafrica.com; camping/chalets per person US$8/15; @) 🖉 This place has expansive, trim grounds, hot-water showers, tents for hire and chalets of varying sizes. It's about 5km north of Marangu and 700m east of the main road, and signposted. There's no food, but there are several eateries nearby. The owner is committed to slowing the environmental destruction of Kilimanjaro, and is a good source of information on local conservation efforts.

Kibo Hotel   LODGE $$
(☑ 0754 038747; kibohotel@myway.com; camping US$5, s/d/tr US$50/65/85; Ⓟ) Kibo is where Hans Meyer stayed before he began his famous ascent of Kilimanjaro. (Another prominent guest in more recent times was US president Jimmy Carter.) Now the hotel is well past its prime, but the wooden flooring, large-paned windows and surrounding gardens lend atmosphere.

It's 1.5km west of Marangu's main junction. Meals are available.

Babylon Lodge   LODGE $$
(☑ 0762 016016, 027-275 6355; www.babylonlodge.com; s/d/tr US$50/70/80; Ⓟ @ ☎) Friendly Babylon has straightforward, clean twin- and double-bedded rooms clustered around small, attractive gardens. It's often somewhat more flexible than other properties about negotiating Kilimanjaro trek packages, and staff are very helpful as you sort out arrivals and departures via public transport. It's 700m east of the town's main junction.

Lake Chala Safari
Lodge & Campsite   CAMPGROUND, LODGE $$$
(☑ 0753 641087, 0786 111177; www.lakechalasafarilodge.com; camping with own/hired tents US$10/30, s/d with half board US$140/200, day visit US$5; Ⓟ ☎) If you're looking for something remote and relaxing, this eco-camp overlooking its namesake caldera lake by the Kenyan border could be perfect. It has attractive facilities (including a restaurant and cooking area) and a lovely location, ideal for walks, bird-watching or just chilling. The roomy tents are warm and luxurious, and the vantage point on a rise above the lake is ideal.

Lake Chala lies about 30km southeast of Marangu; continue east past the Marangu turn-off, then go left at the Lake Chala signpost.

Marangu Hotel   LODGE $$$
(☑ 0754 886092, 027-275 6594; www.maranguhotel.com; camping US$10, s/d/tr with half board US$120/200/275; ☎ ☲) This long-standing hotel is the first place you reach as you come from Moshi. It has a cosy and appealing old-world ambience, pleasant rooms in expansive, flowering grounds, lovely gardens, and a campground with hot-water showers. Room prices are discounted if you join one of the hotel's fully equipped climbs.

❶ Getting There & Away

Minibuses run throughout the day between Moshi and Marangu's main junction (Marangu Mtoni; Tsh1500 to Tsh2200, 1½ hours). Once you're in Marangu, there are sporadic pick-ups from the main junction to the Kilimanjaro park gate (Tsh1600), 5km further. For the Holili border crossing to Kenya, change at Himo junction.

If you're travelling to Marangu via public bus from Arusha or Dar es Salaam, ask the driver to drop you at Himo junction, from where frequent dalla-dallas go to Marangu junction (Tsh1200).

Mt Kilimanjaro National Park

Whether you come to climb it or simply to gaze in awe at this remarkable, snowcapped equatorial mountain, drawing near to Mt Kilimanjaro is one of *the* great experiences of African travel. And for once in Tanzania, visiting **Mt Kilimanjaro National Park** (027-275 6602; www.tanzaniaparks.go.tz; adult/child US$82.60/23.60; ⊙ gates 6.30am-6.30pm, headquarters 8am-5pm), the protected area that surrounds the mountain, is not about the wildlife.

At the heart of the park is the 5896m Mt Kilimanjaro, Africa's highest mountain and one of the continent's most magnificent sights. It's also one of the world's highest volcanoes, and the highest free-standing mountain on earth, rising from cultivated farmlands on the lower slopes, through lush rainforest to alpine meadows, and finally across a lunar landscape to the twin summits of Kibo and Mawenzi.

Kilimanjaro's third volcanic cone, Shira, is on the mountain's western side. The lower rainforest is home to many animals, including buffaloes, elephants, leopards and monkeys, and elands are occasionally seen in the saddle area between Kibo and Mawenzi.

A hike up Kili lures around 25,000 trekkers each year, in part because it's possible to walk to the summit without ropes or technical climbing experience. Non-technical, however, does not mean easy. The climb is a serious (and expensive) undertaking, and only worth doing with the right preparation.

There are also many opportunities to explore the mountain's lower slopes and to learn about the Maasai and the Chagga, two of the main tribes in the area.

🏃 Activities

There are seven main trekking routes to the summit. Trekkers on all but the Marangu route must use tents.

Officially, a limit of 60 climbers per route per day is in effect on Kilimanjaro. It's not always enforced, except on the Marangu route, which is self-limiting because of maximum hut capacities.

Marangu Route

A trek on this route is typically sold as a four-night, five-day return package, although at least one extra night is highly recommended to help you acclimatise, especially if you've just flown into Tanzania or arrived from the lowlands.

Machame Route

This increasingly popular route has a gradual ascent, including a spectacular day contouring the southern slopes before approaching the summit via the top section of the Mweka route. Usually a six- or seven-day return.

Umbwe Route

Steeper and with a more direct way to the summit than the other routes; very enjoyable if you can resist the temptation to gain altitude too quickly (aim for at least a six-day return). Although this route is direct, the top,

---

ⓘ WARNING: PARK-FEE SCAMS & DISREPUTABLE GUIDES

Paying park fees For anyone paying directly at the gate, all entry, hut, camping and other park fees must be paid with Visa or MasterCard and your PIN. One scam involves the relevant officer billing you for less than you owe (eg Tsh100 instead of US$100). As you exit the park after your trek, they point this out to you and ask you to pay the difference in cash. The cash, of course, goes into the pocket of whoever is collecting it. Carefully check the amount (*and* currency) before entering your PIN and keep all receipts at least until after you've left the park.

Disreputable guides While most guides are dedicated, professional, properly trained and genuinely concerned to make your trip safe and successful, there are exceptions. Although it doesn't happen often, some guides leave the last hut deliberately late on the summit day to avoid going all the way to the top. Going with a reputable company – preferably one that hires full-time guides (most don't) – is one way to avoid a bad experience. Insist on meeting the guide before you sign up for a trip, familiarise yourself with all aspects of the route, and when on the mountain have morning and evening briefings so you know what to expect each day. The night before summitting, talk to other climbers to be sure your departure time seems realistic (though note that not everyone leaves at the same time); if it doesn't, get an explanation from your guide. Should problems arise, be polite but firm.

TREKKING MT KILIMANJARO

When to Climb

Mt Kilimanjaro can be climbed at any time of year, though weather patterns are notoriously erratic and difficult to predict. Overall, the best time for climbing the mountain is in the dry season, from late June to October, and from late December to February or early March, just after the short rains and before the long rains. During November and March/April, it's more likely that paths through the forest will be slippery, and that routes up to the summit, especially the Western Breach, will be covered by snow. That said, you can also have a streak of beautiful sunny days during these times.

Climbing Conditions & Equipment

Conditions on the mountain are frequently very cold and wet, and you'll need a full range of waterproof cold-weather clothing and gear, including a good-quality sleeping bag. It's also worth carrying some additional sturdy water bottles. No matter what the time of year, waterproof everything, especially your sleeping bag, as things rarely dry on the mountain. It's often possible to rent sleeping bags and gear from trekking operators. For the Marangu route, you can also rent gear from the Kilimanjaro Guides Cooperative Society stand just inside Marangu gate, or from a small no-name shop just before the gate. However, especially at the budget level, quality and availability can't be counted on, and it's best to bring your own.

Apart from a small shop at Marangu gate selling a limited range of chocolate bars and tinned items, there are no shops inside the park. You can buy (steeply priced) beer and soft drinks at huts on the Marangu route.

Costs

Kilimanjaro can only be climbed with a licensed guide, and it's recommended that you organise your climb through a tour company. No-frills four-night/five-day treks up the Marangu route start at about US$1500, including park fees and taxes, and no-frills six-day budget treks on the Machame route start at around US$1900. Prices start at about US$1500 on the Rongai route, and about US$2000 for a seven-day trek on the Shira Plateau route. For other routes, the starting points are further from Moshi and transport costs can be significant, so clarify whether they're included in the price.

Most of the better companies provide dining tents, decent-to-good cuisine and various other extras to make the experience more enjoyable and to maximise your chances of getting to the top. If you choose a really cheap trip, you risk inadequate meals, mediocre guides, few comforts, and problems with hut bookings and park fees. Try not to skimp on supplies and other essential elements, as this may compromise your safety. Also remember that an environmentally responsible trek usually costs more. Whatever you pay for your trek, remember that the following park fees are not negotiable and should be part of any quote from your operator:

very steep section up the Western Breach is often covered in ice or snow, which makes it impassable or extremely dangerous. Many trekkers who attempt it without proper acclimatisation are forced to turn back. An indication of its seriousness is that until fairly recently the Western Breach was considered a technical mountaineering route. Only consider this route if you're experienced, properly equipped and travelling with a reputable operator.

Rongai Route

This popular route starts near the Kenyan border and goes up the northern side of the mountain.

Shira Plateau route

This route is scenic and good for avoiding crowds, but can be challenging for acclimatisation as it begins at 3600m at the Shira Track trailhead. To counteract this, an extra day at Shira Hut is recommended. Better – choose the Lemosho Route, which is essentially the same, but with the advantage that it starts lower at Londorosi gate and is normally done in eight days (rather than six or seven for Shira Plateau).

Lemosho Route

On the western side of the mountain, this is arguably the best all-round route for scenery and acclimatisation. It starts with two days

National Park entry fees US$82.60 per adult per day

Hut/camping fees US$70.80/59 per person per night

Rescue fee US$23.60 per person per trip

Other costs vary depending on the company, which should handle food, tents (if required), guides and porters, and transport to/from the trailhead; tips are additional.

Practicalities

Park entry gates include Machame, Marangu (the site of park headquarters), Londorosi and several other points; trekkers using the Rongai route should pay their fees at Marangu gate. You must pay at least six days' worth of park fees for all routes except Marangu (five-day minimum).

Tipping

Most guides and porters receive only minimal wages from the trekking companies and depend on tips as their major source of income. As a guideline, plan on tipping about 10% of the total amount you've paid for the trek, divided up among the guides and porters. Common tips for satisfactory service are from about US$10 to US$15 per group per day for the guide, US$8 to US$10 per group per day for the cook and US$5 to US$10 per group per day for each porter.

Guides & Porters

Guides, and at least one porter (for the guide), are obligatory and are provided by your trekking company. You can carry your own gear on the Marangu route, although porters are generally used, but one or two porters per trekker are essential on all other routes.

All guides must be registered with the national-park authorities. If in doubt, check that your guide's permit is up to date. On Kili, the guide's job is to show you the way and that's it. Only the best guides, working for reputable companies, will be able to tell you about wildlife, flowers or other features on the mountain.

Porters will carry bags weighing up to 15kg (not including their own food and clothing, which they strap to the outside of your bag), and your bags will be weighed before you set off.

Maps

Topographical maps include *Map & Guide to Kilimanjaro* by Andrew Wielochowski and *Kilimanjaro Map & Guide* by Mark Savage. The hand-drawn *New Map of the Kilimanjaro National Park* is evocative for an overview but no real use for trekking detail.

in the forest before crossing the Shira Plateau and then joining up with the Machame route.

Northern Circuit Route

This route – the longest (eight to 10 days) – initially follows the same path as the Shira Plateau route before turning north near Lava Tower and then continuing around the northern ('back') side of Kilimanjaro before tackling the summit via Gilman's Point.

West Kilimanjaro

In a remote corner of northern Tanzania, West Kilimanjaro is a gem. With a couple of terrific tented camps, a fabulous pre-Kilimanjaro world of Amboseli-like plains, and a sprinkling of Maasai manyattas, it's difficult to understand why so few travellers make it out here. You have to work a little harder for your wildlife, it's true, but this is an important dispersal area for lions from southern Kenya, and it's part of an elephant corridor linking Kenya's Amboseli National Park with Mt Kilimanjaro National Park. Climb any hill out here, too, and the views are extraordinary.

A destination in its own right, West Kilimanjaro (from Sanya Juu village to the Kenyan border, from the Arusha–Namanga road to Mt Kilimanjaro) is also the missing link on the northern safari circuit, enabling you to travel from Lake Natron to Kilimanjaro

International Airport without ever having to see Arusha.

You may never even be aware of its existence (there are no signs or entry fees), but **Enduimet Wildlife Management Area** (☑ 0787 903715; www.enduimet.org) is a quiet success story in protecting the wildlife corridors of West Kilimanjaro, including the Kitenden Corridor, an elephant 'highway' that reaches down into Kenya. Big cats, elands and other plains wildlife are increasingly plentiful. Wildlife drives from most of the West Kilimanjaro camps pass through the WMA – ask at your camp for more information.

◉ Sights & Activities

Wildlife watching on foot, on horseback and in traditional 4WD vehicles are all options, as are cultural encounters with local Maasai.

Wildlife drives out here sometimes stray into Kenya (shh...), but elephant sightings are pretty reliable. Elephants, zebras, cheetahs, warthogs and lesser kudus are either resident or pass through on a regular basis, while lions and buffaloes are rare but increasing. Night drives are also possible.

Olpopongi Maasai
Cultural Village   CULTURAL CENTRE
(☑ 0756 718455; www.olpopongi-maasai.com; per person per day/overnight visit US$59/95, with pick-up & transport from Moshi US$139/169, from Arusha US$169/190; ℗) Olpopongi Maasai Cultural Village is a good stop for anyone wanting to spend a night in an authentically constructed Maasai *boma* (a fortified living compound) or learn about Maasai traditions. There's a small, informative museum, medicinal walks, lessons in spear-throwing techniques, and more. It's an excellent destination for families with children. There's a booking office in Moshi.

🛏 Sleeping & Eating

House of West Kili   LODGE $$
(☑ 0753 462788; www.houseofwestkili.com; r US$99-180; ℗ 🛜) This pleasing white lodge house set in leafy grounds is a fine place to rest for a few days and an equally fine waystation en route between Moshi and West Kilimanjaro. The rooms are large and lovely, with whitewashed walls, zebra-print chairs, four-poster beds and straw mats, and it's never overdone. There's a good on-site restaurant and bar.

★ Shu'mata Camp   TENTED CAMP $$$
(☑ 0752 553456; www.shumatacamp.de; s/d with full board & incl all activities US$666/1160) This tented camp is a wonderful escape from the

safari circuit. Set on a steep hillside, the seven tents have splendid views of Kilimanjaro and down into the Amboseli ecosystem of southern Kenya. The camp's decor is inspired by Hemingway's love for a classic safari camp, and the sense of luxury and blissful isolation make this a fabulous experience.

From the sundowner spot above the camp, the views are some of the best in northern Tanzania, taking in Kilimanjaro, Mt Meru, Mt Longido, a distant glimpse of the Crater Highlands and numerous Maasai manyattas – pure magic. There's a lovely writing desk with full cognac bottle on one side, and massive outdoor showers enclosed within ochre-walled luxury. Throughout the camp the decor is warm and eclectic, featuring Maasai colours, chandeliers, dhow-wood furnishings and creatively deployed calabashes. The wildlife here is a little more sparse than elsewhere on the northern safari circuit, but there's an important elephant corridor close by, and lions and other big cats, though elusive, may be seen.

Pick-ups can be arranged from Moshi and elsewhere. The camp offers cheaper packages if you also stay at sister property Hatari Lodge (p171) in Arusha National Park.

★ Ndarakwai Ranch   TENTED CAMP $$$
(☑ 027-250 2713, 0754 333550, 0784 550331; www.ndarakwai.com; s/d with half board & incl wildlife drives US$600/850; ℗ 🛜) 🌿 Ndarakwai Ranch, a lovely 15-tent camp run by the Kili Conservancy, makes a comfortable base for safaris and walks. The sophisticated and spacious permanent tents occupy a lovely woodland area close to the banks of the Ngare Nairobi River amid stands of yellow-barked acacias. Accommodation rates include US$35 per person per night in conservancy fees.

Kambi Ya Tembo   TENTED CAMP $$$
(www.twctanzania.com; s/d with full board US$275/450) A fine tented camp in the narrow sliver of land between Mt Kilimanjaro and the Kenyan border, Kambi Ya Tembo has 14 comfortable safari tents and views that seem to extend forever into Kenya or high into the clouds of Kilimanjaro. Elephants are a real highlight here, sitting as it does along an important cross-border elephant corridor.

❶ Getting There & Away

There's no public transport to anywhere out here, although Shu'mata Camp, Ndarakwai Ranch and Olpopongi Maasai Cultural Village can all arrange pick-ups from Moshi and elsewhere (for a fee, of course).

Central Tanzania

Best Places to Stay

➡ New Dodoma Hotel (p239)

➡ Kahembe's Modern Guest House (p243)

➡ Kidia Vision Hotel (p239)

Best Places to Eat

➡ New Dodoma Hotel (p241)

➡ Rose's Café (p240)

➡ Ango Bar & Restaurant (p244)

Why Go?

Central Tanzania lies well off most tourist itineraries, and that's just the way we like it. Exceptional and enigmatic, the Unesco World Heritage–listed Kondoa Rock-Art Sites, scattered across remote hills along the Rift Valley Escarpment, are the region's premier attraction. Not far away, Mt Hanang soars to 3417m and is a worthy climb, both for its own sake and for the chance to summit with no one else around. Both attractions also serve as gateways to the world of the colourful Barabaig and other tribes whose traditional lifestyles remain little touched by the modern world.

And then there's Dodoma, Tanzania's legislative capital, an intriguing planned city with interesting architecture and the region's best facilities. Travel here isn't always easy – transport and accommodation can be a little rough around the edges – but it's a window on a Tanzania few visitors ever get to see.

When to Go
Dodoma

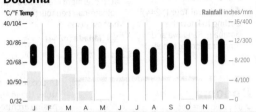

Apr–Aug Flamingos reside in some lakes.

Apr–Nov During the dry season, it's dusty but temperatures are refreshingly cool.

Dec–Mar During the rainy season, many roads are difficult to travel.

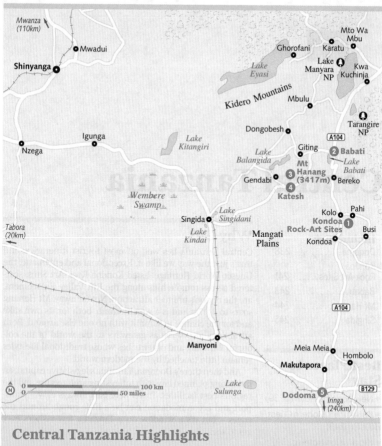

Mwanza
(110km)

Mwadui

Shinyanga

Mto Wa
Mbu

Ghorofani   Karatu

Lake
Eyasi

Lake
Manyara
NP

Kwa
Kuchinja

Kidero Mountains

Mbulu

Igunga

Nzega

Lake
Kitangiri

Dongobesh

A104

Tarangire
NP

Lake
Balangida

Giting

Babati
Lake
Babati

Gendabi

Mt
Hanang
(3417m)

Bereko

Katesh

Wembere
Swamp

Singida

Lake
Singidani

Kolo   Pahi

Kondoa
Rock-Art Sites

Busi

Tabora
(20km)

Lake
Kindai

Mangati
Plains

Kondoa

A104

Manyoni

Meia Meia

Hombolo

Makutapora

N   0   100 km
     0   50 miles

Lake
Sulunga

Dodoma

B129

Iringa
(240km)

Central Tanzania Highlights

1 Kondoa Rock-Art Sites
(p241) Visiting a mysterious
Unesco World Heritage–
listed attraction and having
it all to yourself.

2 Cultural Tour (p244)
Getting to know the
Barabaig, Sandawe and
other traditional tribes of

Central Tanzania on a tour
out of Babati.

3 Mt Hanang (p244)
Summiting (and sleeping
atop overnight) Tanzania's
seldom-climbed fourth-
highest peak.

4 Mnada (p244)

Experiencing a colourful
mnada (market), especially
the one at Katesh, where
people converge from miles
around to trade cattle.

5 Dodoma Admiring
the ambitious religious and
political architecture of the
nation's capital.

Dodoma

♪ 026 / POP 465,000

Dodoma was a nice idea at the time. Like
all custom-built capitals – think Abuja or
Yamoussoukro in Africa, Brasília or Canberra
elsewhere – Dodoma never really caught on
and lacks a certain authenticity and the atmosphere that goes with it, though that may
be set to change as President Magufuli is keen

to accelerate the capital's role. In the meantime, the grandiose street layout and the imposing architecture of many places of worship
and government buildings sharply contrasts
with the humdrum reality of daily life, and
makes Dodoma feel as though it's dressed in
clothes that are several sizes too big.

Because Dodoma has so many government buildings, be careful taking photos.

History

Although Dodoma was located along the old caravan route connecting Lake Tanganyika and Central Africa with the sea, it was of little consequence until 1973 when it was named Tanzania's official capital. According to the original plan, the entire government was to move to Dodoma by the mid-1980s and its population was to live in smaller independent communities set up along the lines of Nyerere's *ujamaa* (familyhood) program. The plans proved unrealistic for a variety of reasons, and although the legislature meets here, Dar es Salaam remains the unrivalled economic and political centre. As of September 2016, though, President Magufuli has been implementing measures to enhance Dodoma's role and shift government ministries from Dar to the capital. Whether this puts more of a spring in Dodoma's step remains to be seen.

Sights & Activities

Bunge NOTABLE BUILDING
(Dar es Salaam Rd) The home of Tanzania's parliament is an African-influenced round building. It's only open to visitors during sessions (bring your passport), but is well worth a look from the outside at other times. Photography is strictly prohibited.

Anglican Church CHURCH
(Hospital Rd) In an interesting swapping of styles, the domed Anglican church in the town centre looks like something straight out of the Middle East.

Catholic Cathedral CHURCH
(Mirembe Rd) West of the centre, the enormous Catholic cathedral has Roman-style mosaics showing some saints, including the Ugandan Martyrs.

Gaddhaffi Mosque MOSQUE
(Jamhuri Rd) Funded by the toppled Libyan dictator and opened in 2010, the pink Gaddhaffi Mosque north of the centre is one of East Africa's largest mosques. It can hold 4500 worshippers.

Jamatkhana (Ismaili) Mosque MOSQUE
(cnr Mahakama St & Jamatin Ave) This mosque sits across the road from the Anglican church. Built in 1954 and used exclusively by Dodoma's Ismaili Muslim community, it has a distinctly British neoclassical design.

Lutheran Cathedral CHURCH
(Mahakama St) Next door to the Jamatkhana (Ismaili) Mosque, the Lutheran Cathedral is Dodoma's finest example of modernist architecture.

Sunni Mosque MOSQUE
(Hatibu Ave) The latticed facade and tall green-domed towers of the mosque make it one of Dodoma's most imposing religious buildings.

Cetawico WINE
(Central Tanzania Wine Company; ☎0786 799010; www.cetawico.com) If you're willing to make a day of it, you can visit the vineyards at the Italian-owned Cetawico, which bottled its first product in 2005 and is now one of Dodoma's most successful vintners. It's 50km northeast of Dodoma at Hombolo.

Sleeping

Dodoma's hotels fill up fast whenever parliament is in session, so you may need to try several before finding a room.

Kidia Vision Hotel HOTEL $
(☎0784 210766; Ninth St; d Tsh30,000-45,000, ste Tsh70,000-80,000; P 📶) Well managed and, unlike most other hotels in its class, well maintained, this is a very solid choice at this level. Rooms are comfy and clean, though you don't get much extra as the price rises. Located on a dusty unpaved section of the street, but don't be put off by that.

Kilondoma Inn GUESTHOUSE $
(☎0745 477399; www.kilondoma.blogspot.com; off Ndovu Rd; d Tsh20,000; P ❄) An appealing and welcoming little guesthouse with a small garden and a porch flanked by statues of tribesmen. Rooms have nets, TV and hot water, but double beds are barely big enough for two.

★ **New Dodoma Hotel** HOTEL $$
(☎026-232 1641; www.newdodomahotel.com; Railway Rd; s/d with fan US$50/70, with air-con from US$70/95; P ❄ @ 📶 🏊) The former Railway Hotel's tree-filled courtyard is a lovely oasis and the rooms have some style. Suites face the main street and are noisier than the standard rooms. It has a gym, a small swimming pool and three restaurants. Visitors can pay Tsh5000 to use the pool and gym.

Eating

Dodoma Wimpy FAST FOOD $
(Jamatin Ave; snacks from Tsh350, mains Tsh2000-5000; ⏰7am-10pm) Not a real Wimpy, but it does have greasy burgers along with the usual assortment of local meals and snacks, most of them of Indian origin like *bhaji* and chicken *biryani*.

Dodoma

N 0 — 400 m
0 — 0.2 miles

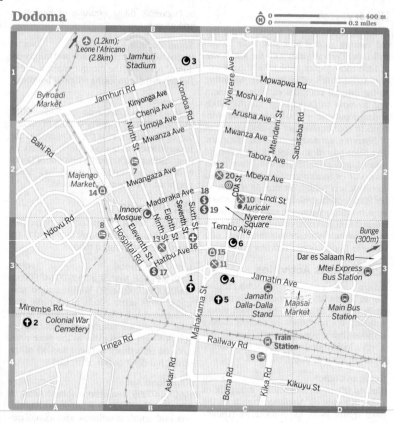

Dodoma

◎ Sights
1 Anglican Church		B3
2 Catholic Cathedral		A4
3 Gaddhaffi Mosque		B1
4 Jamatkhana (Ismaili) Mosque		C3
5 Lutheran Cathedral		C3
6 Sunni Mosque		C3

🛏 Sleeping
7 Kidia Vision Hotel		B2
8 Kilondoma Inn		A3
9 New Dodoma Hotel		C4

⊗ Eating
10 Aladdin's Cave		C2

11 Dodoma Wimpy		C3
12 Mama King		C2
New Dodoma Hotel		(see 9)
13 Rose's Café		B3

🛍 Shopping
14 Majengo Market		A2
15 Two Sisters		C3

ℹ Information
16 Aga Khan Health Centre		B3
17 Barclays		B3
18 CRDB		C2
19 DTC Bureau de Change		C2
20 Internet Café		C2

Rose's Café INDIAN **$**
(Ninth St; mains Tsh3000-7000; ⊗ 8am-7pm Mon-Sat; ⍩) A barebones cafe near Innoor Mosque serving good, cheap Indian food, including a vegetarian *thali*.

Aladdin's Cave SWEETS, EUROPEAN **$**
(CDA St; snacks from Tsh350, mains Tsh2500-8000; ⊗ 9.30am-1pm daily & 3.30-5.30pm Tue-Sat; ⍩) This little wood-panelled place is Dodoma's version of an old-fashioned candy store and

soda fountain. It also serves veggie burgers and pizzas.

Leone l'Africano — ITALIAN $$
(☑ 0788 629797, 0754 073573; Mlimwa Rd; mains Tsh8500-14,000; ☺ 5-10pm Tue-Fri, noon-3pm & 5-10pm Sat & Sun) Tasty Italian food, including one of Tanzania's better pizzas, served in the shadow of Lion Rock. You can try local wines or play it safe with a European vintage. It has a playground and a 12-hole minigolf course.

New Dodoma Hotel — INTERNATIONAL $$
(Railway Rd; mains Tsh5000-16,000; ☺ 7am-11pm; ☎) The menu here goes global with choices such as pizza, fish and chips, *dhal tadka* and fajitas. There are three separate menus and options: Italian, Indian/local and Chinese, with Indian dishes being the most reliable. The Chinese-owned restaurant within the hotel is a lucky dip, since dishes can be both good and awful.

Self-catering

Mama King — SUPERMARKET $
(Nyerere St; ☺ 8.30am-9pm Mon-Sat, 2-9pm Sun) Small supermarket for self-caterers.

🛍 Shopping

Majengo Market — MARKET
(Ndovu Road; ☺ 8am–5pm) You can't miss the city's high-energy street market, where you'll be assailed by vendors selling phone chargers, plastic shoes and clothing. There are a few more choice items, including local cloth, classic wicker baskets and handmade wooden utensils.

Two Sisters — FOOD & DRINKS
(Hatibu Ave; ☺ 9am-6pm Mon-Sat, to 1pm Sun) Grocery store with a good selection of cheese.

ℹ Information

INTERNET ACCESS
Dodoma Guide (www.dodoma-guide.com) Moderately useful privately run website.
Internet Café (per hr Tsh2000; ☺ 8am-8pm) An efficient place on Nyerere Sq.

MEDICAL SERVICES
Aga Khan Health Centre (☑ 026-232 1789; Sixth St; ☺ 8am-8pm Mon-Sat) First destination for illnesses. Has a good pharmacy.

MONEY
Barclays (Hatibu Ave; ☺ 9am-5pm Mon-Fri) The branch has an ATM and does currency exchange.
CRDB (Nyerere St; ☺ 8.30am-4pm Mon-Fri, to 1pm Sat, 10am-2pm Sun) Has an ATM and

changes US dollars, euro and British pounds plus regional African currencies.
DTC Bureau de Change (Nyerere St; ☺ 9am-5pm Mon-Sat) Next door to CRDB. Shorter queues, but not necessarily better rates.

ℹ Getting There & Away

AIR
The airport is just north of the city centre (Tsh4000 in a taxi).
Auricair (☑ 0783 233334; www.auricair.com; Nyerere Sq; ☺ 8am-6pm) Eight flights weekly between Dodoma and Dar es Salaam (around US$225).

BUS
The following bus services leave from the main bus station unless otherwise stated. For local destinations, use the Jamatini dalla-dalla stand west of the bus stand.
Arusha and Moshi Shabiby and Mtei Express have the best buses to Arusha (from Ts25,000, seven hours) and Moshi (Tsh30,000, 10 to 12 hours). All leave at 6am. Mtei buses leave from their terminal by the main bus station.
Dar es Salaam Shabiby has 'full luxury' buses (Tsh26,000, six to seven hours), which means four-across seating and toilets; they leave from the main bus terminal. Other buses (Tsh12,000 to Tsh20,000) depart Dodoma frequently from 6am to 1pm. Buses that started their trip to Dar in Mwanza pass through in the afternoon, and you can usually get a seat on them.
Iringa The route to Iringa (Tsh12,000, three hours) is now paved.
Kondoa and Babati Buses (Tsh7000/12,000, 2½ hours/four hours) depart 6am, 6.30am, 10.30am and noon.
Mwanza Buses (Tsh38,000, eight hours) via Singida (Tsh18,000, three hours) leave Dodoma between 6am and 7.30am, and Mwanza-bound buses from Dar es Salaam pass through around midday.

Kondoa Rock-Art Sites

The district of Kondoa, especially around the tiny village of Kolo, lies at the centre of one of the most impressive collections of ancient rock art on the African continent. The overhanging rocks in the surrounding hills shelter two thousand years' worth of artistic expression, with some sites being still actively in use for animist worship. It's one of Tanzania's least-known and most underrated attractions and, if you can tolerate a bit of rugged travel, makes an intriguing and worthwhile detour.

To visit independently, stop at the **Antiquities Department Office** (☑ 0752 575096;

Kolo; ⊙7.30am-6pm) along Kolo's main road to arrange a permit (Tsh27,000/13,000 per adult/child) and mandatory guide (free, but tips expected), some of whom speak English. There's a good little museum here covering not only archaeology, but also the culture of the Irangi people.

While very few safari operators have Kondoa on their itineraries, some will tack a day in Kondoa onto their longer safaris. The Kondoa Irangi Cultural Tourism Program (p244) in Kondoa regularly brings people here (US$60 per person, minimum two people), or try Kahembe's Culture & Wildlife Safaris (p244) in Babati.

⊙ Sights

There are 186 known rock-art sites (but perhaps as many as 450 in total), of which only a portion have been properly documented. If you base yourself in Kolo or Kondoa, you can comfortably see three of the best sites in a day, four if you really rush.

Fenga Rock-Art Complex ROCK ART
One of the most impressive of the Kondoa Rock-Art Sites is the excellent Fenga complex, with its dense and lively images. The dominant feature is a painting of people with wild headdresses who appear to be trapping an elephant. It's around 20km north of Kolo and just west off the Arusha–Dodoma Rd, followed by a hilly 1km walk.

Thawi Rock-Art Site ROCK ART
The most varied, and thus the best, overall collection of rock paintings in the Kondoa area is at Thawi, about 15km northwest of Kolo and reachable only by 4WD.

Kolo Rock-Art Site ROCK ART
The most visited, though not the best, Kolo sites (B1, B2 and B3) are 9km east of Kolo village and a 4WD is required. You'll need to climb a steep hill at the end of the road to see them. The most interesting images here are the elongated human figures with what are either wild hairstyles or masks; one scene has been interpreted as the abduction of a woman. You'll also see depictions of rhinos, giraffes and leopards.

Pahi Rock-Art Site ROCK ART
East of the Kolo Rock-Art Sites, on the back side of the same mountain east of Kolo, are the simpler, mostly white (ie relatively modern) Pahi sites. These can be reached by 2WD

KONDOA ROCK ART

Although several archaeologists, most prominently Mary Leakey, have studied these sites, the history of most remains shrouded in mystery, with little known about either their artists or even their age. Some sites are still used by local rainmakers and medicine men.

Rock-art experts divide the Kondoa paintings into two distinct styles or eras. The oldest are the so-called **Red Paintings**, which are also the most sophisticated. Some experts maintain that the oldest paintings date back around 7000 years, perhaps even further. The Red Paintings (often ochre or orange) usually contain stylised depictions of humans, sometimes hunting with bows and arrows or dancing and playing musical instruments, while many are drawn with skirts, strange hairstyles and body decoration. Large animals, notably giraffes and antelopes, are also common, and geometric shapes also appear. Intriguingly, the depictions of animals tend to be naturalistic, while the humans have a stick-figure abstraction.

The Red Paintings are thought to have been made by the Sandawe who, linguistically, are distantly related to South Africa's San a group also renowned for its rock art, or the Hadza people, who now live around Lake Eyasi in northern Tanzania. Whoever they were, the makers sometimes used hands and fingers, but also brushes made of reeds or sticks. Some of the colours were probably made by mixing various pigments with animal fat to form crayons.

The second category is known as the **Late White Paintings**. Far simpler (even crude) when compared to the Red Paintings, the Late White Paintings mostly date from the last 1500 years and were painted by Bantu-speaking peoples who migrated into the area. The better ones resemble wild or mythical animals, human figures and patterns using dots, circles and rectangles, but many of these more recent works take on unintelligible form, largely because most were painted using fingers rather than brushes. For more information, contact the **Trust for African Rock Art** (www.africanrockart.org) or pick up a copy of the excellent *African Rock Art* by David Coulson and Alec Campbell.

vehicles. Buses from Arusha and Babati going to Busi pass the nearby village of Pahi.

🛏 Sleeping & Eating

Plain guesthouses and a couple of basic campsites comprise the accommodation options, or you can arrange a homestay through the Kondoa Irangi Cultural Tourism Program (p244).

Amarula Campsite   CAMPGROUND $
(☑0754 672256; www.racctz.org; camping with own/hired tent US$8/20, cottage $25) Located 6km east of Kolo on the road to Pahi, this site has beautiful scenery and simple facilities – drop toilets and solar showers. It features a self-catering option in a small mud cottage, as well as safari tents. There's an attractive thatched dining area, and firewood is provided. A lovely spot, but a little expensive given the facilities.

Mary Leakey Campsite   CAMPGROUND $
(camping Tsh7500) Managed by the Department of Antiquities, there's nothing here but quiet isolation and year-round water. It's along the Kolo (Hembe) River halfway to the Kolo Rock-Art Sites.

Kondoa Climax Hotel   HOTEL $
(☑026-236 0389; Kondoa; d Tsh25,000; 🖥) The bizarrely named hotel is a cheery yellow-painted place with clean rooms, hot water, mosquito nets and en-suite bathrooms.

ℹ Information

A few guesthouses in Kondoa have internet access. There are no banking services for travellers.

ℹ Getting There & Away

Kolo is 80km south of Babati. Buses to Kolo (Tsh7500, 2½ hours) depart Babati at 7am and 8.30am. From Arusha, Mtei Express buses to Kondoa, leaving at 6am, pass Kolo (Tsh11,500, five hours). The last bus north from Kondoa leaves at 9am. There are only buses to Dodoma (Tsh8500, three hours) from Kondoa, not Kolo. They leave at 6am, 10am and 12.30pm. Catching a north-bound bus in Kondoa means you'll get a seat; wait for it to pass Kolo and you'll need to stand.

It could be possible to visit as a day trip from Babati (or as a stop en route to Dodoma) using public transport if you're willing to hitch-hike after visiting the Kolo sites; there are usually some trucks travelling this road in the afternoon.

ℹ Getting Around

It is possible to hire motorcycles in Kolo; these can reach all the sites detailed earlier, but you'll have to get off and walk up some hills. Hiring motorcycles is very expensive if done through the Antiquities Department (Tsh25,000 just to the Kolo sites, for example), but you can try to get a better price with locals or hire a vehicle in Kondoa, 25km south of Kolo.

Babati

☑027 / POP 105,000

The scruffy market town of Babati, about 175km southwest of Arusha in a fertile spot along the edge of the Rift Valley Escarpment, has a frontier feel despite the construction of a smooth new road. It's notable as a jumping-off point for Mt Hanang, 75km southwest, and for a long-running programme of cultural tours, but otherwise it has little to detain you. Stretching south from the city is tranquil Lake Babati, fringed by tall reeds and home to hippos and water birds. You can explore by dugout with Kahembe's Culture & Wildlife Safaris (p244) or the folk at the Royal Beach Hotel. If you're here on the 17th of the month, don't miss Babati's monthly *mnada*, about 5km south of town.

🛏 Sleeping & Eating

Royal Beach Hotel   CAMPGROUND, BANDAS $
(☑0785 125070; camping with own/hired tent Tsh15,000/18,000, bandas Tsh35,000; 🅿) On a peninsula in Lake Babati, the grandly named Royal Beach Hotel, 3km south of Babati, has an attractive bar/restaurant area and a thatched disco (Friday and Saturday). Boat trips to see hippos can be arranged. It's recommended for camping: the rock *bandas* (thatched-roof huts) are quite ordinary inside.

Kahembe's Modern Guest House   GUESTHOUSE $
(☑0784 397477; www.kahembeculturalsafaris. com; Sokoine Rd; s/d incl full breakfast Tsh25,000/ 30,000; 🖥) Home of Kahembe's Culture & Wildlife Safaris, this plain and friendly place just northwest of the bus stand has decent twin- and double-bedded rooms with TVs and hot-water showers. The breakfast with sausages, cornflakes, fruit, toast and eggs is included in the price. Pop next door to book a cultural tour with owner Joas.

White Rose Lodge   GUESTHOUSE $
(☑0784 392577; www.manyarawhiterose.blogspot. com; Ziwani Rd; d Tsh25,000; 🅿🖥) A good-value spot set somewhat inconveniently (unless you're driving) off the Singida Rd south of town. Rooms are similar in standard to other Babati cheapies, only much newer. Loud music from the bar can be an issue.

CENTRAL TANZANIA BABATI

Ango Bar & Restaurant TANZANIAN **$**
(Arusha-Dodoma Rd; buffet breakfast Tsh6000, lunch or dinner Tsh8000; ⊙7am-9.30pm) Behind a small petrol station opposite the exit from the bus station, this unexpectedly attractive place offers local fare, always including a veggie dish. It's also the best spot for an evening beer.

ℹ Information

There are internet connections at a couple of places around town.

Manyara Internet Café (Mandela Rd; per hour Tsh2000; ⊙7.30am-7pm Mon-Sat, 10am-2pm Sun)

Rainbow Communication (Mandela Rd; per hour Tsh2000; ⊙8am-6.30pm Mon-Sat)

NBC (Arusha-Dodoma Rd) Changes cash and has an ATM.

ℹ Getting There & Away

The football-pitch-sized bus station is packed with buses, travellers and touts from dawn to dusk. If travelling from Babati to Arusha (Tsh9000, four hours), the first departures in both directions are at 5.30am and the last leave at 4pm, though dalla-dallas go until 6pm. Other destinations include Dodoma (Tsh12,000, four hours), Kondoa (Tsh8500, three hours), Mwanza (Tsh29,000 to Tsh36,000, eight hours) and Singida (Tsh9000, three hours, last departure from Babati around 10am). The Shabiby 'full luxury' buses serving these routes cost Tsh5000 to Tsh10,000 more than the prices quoted, but are well worth it for increased comfort and safety.

Mt Hanang

One of Tanzania's most rewarding mountain treks is also one of its least known. The volcanic Mt Hanang (3417m), Tanzania's fourth-highest mountain, rises steeply above the surrounding plains between Babati and Singida, and you probably won't see anyone else on the satisfying trek to the summit. The mountain is a great option for climbers on a budget as it's not located in a national park, so you'll save on fees. The trail head town for the main route is Katesh, which is also known for its large *mnada* held on the 9th, 10th and 28th of each month. Maasai, Barabaig, Iraqw and other peoples from a wide surrounding area converge to buy and sell cattle and trade their wares, including baskets, jewellery and Maasai *shuka* fabric. The real highlight though is the sight of the brightly dressed participants and the chance to experience a local event.

🛏 Sleeping & Eating

There are a handful of basic guesthouses in Katesh; on the mountain itself you'll be staying in a tented camp.

Summit Hotel GUESTHOUSE **$**
(☏0787 242424; Katesh; r from Tsh20,000; 🅿) This bright-green place up the hill just east of the municipality office is Katesh's best lodging, and the most convenient for climbing Mt Hanang.

OFF THE BEATEN TRACK

CULTURAL TOURISM IN CENTRAL TANZANIA

Babati and Kondoa districts are home to a colourful array of tribes, many of whom have changed their lifestyle little over the past century. Many villages welcome visitors, but, unlike those around Arusha, none are geared towards tourism. The most famous (and most visited) tribe is the cattle-trading Barabaig, who still follow a traditional semi-nomadic lifestyle and are recognisable by the goatskin garments still worn daily by many women. Unrelated to the tribes around them, the diminutive Sandawe are one of the oldest peoples of Tanzania, and they may have been the ones who painted the early rock art around Kondoa. They speak a click language and still hunt with bow and arrow.

Kahembe's Culture & Wildlife Safaris (☏0784 397477; www.kahembeculturalsafaris. com; Sokoine Rd) This reliable and knowledgeable outfit in Babati have been offering cultural tours in the region since 1992. Besides cycling trips and village visits where you might join in with honey harvesting or maize pounding, it's the main operator organising Mt Hanang climbs. The volunteer programmes incorporate game viewing and cultural exchange with school-building projects.

Kondoa Irangi Cultural Tourism Program (☏0784 948858, 0715 948858; www. tanzaniaculturaltours.com; Kondoa; per person US$80, minimum 2 people) The Kondoa Rock-Art Sites are the bread and butter of this recommended company in Kondoa town, but director Moshi Changai also leads Barabaig, Sandawe and Irangi village visits by bicycle or car. Overnights in local homes are possible.

TREKKING MT HANANG

The principal path to the top is the Jorodom Route, which begins in the town of Katesh on the mountain's southern side. Although overnighting at the top is more enjoyable, it can be done in one long day (usually 10 hours) – with an additional day necessary for making arrangements. While a guide isn't strictly essential, the trail can be hard to follow, so we definitely recommend hiring one. This is best arranged through Kahembe's Cultural & Wildlife Safaris in Babati. With a group of two, the climb costs up to US$128 per person, including food, guide, lodging in Katesh the nights before and after the climb, and the US$40 per person forest reserve fee and Tsh2800 per person village fee. Transport is extra. If you're trekking independently, register and pay at the **forest cachement office** (✆ 0784 456590) in Room 15 of the Katesh municipality building (Idara ya Mkuu wa Wilaya) on the hill above Katesh. It's best to call ahead since the staff are sometimes out of the office. Guides can be hired here for Tsh12,000 per day, but you'll be responsible for your own food and water. Don't go with any freelancers who hang around Katesh (many of whom will say they're with Kahembe's). Some are legit, but there have been instances of these guides taking climbers part way up the mountain and then robbing them. Regardless of how you do the trip, carry plenty of water since there's none to be found during the climb.

Colt Guesthouse GUESTHOUSE $
(✆ 027-253 0030; Katesh; s/d Tsh15,000/20,000, without bathroom Tsh8000/10,000; P) A long-established guesthouse northwest of the bus stand by the market. It's simple but clean, with hot water.

ℹ Getting There & Away

Buses between Singida (Tsh7000, 1½ hours) and Babati (Tsh8000, 2½ hours), including all Arusha–Mwanza buses, pass through Katesh all morning, stopping at a stand at the main T-junction. After lunch, you'll probably need to hitch.

Singida

✆ 026 / POP 155,000

There's no compelling reason to do more than pass through Singida en route between Mwanza and Dodoma. If you find yourself with an hour or two to kill, **Lake Singidani** is one of three saline lakes just west of town. With green waters and plenty of rocky spots along the shore, it's quite beautiful even when it's completely dried up, which happens during some dry seasons. The lake attracts plenty of water birds, including pelicans and sometimes flamingos. Singidani begins 600m past the post office.

The **Regional Museum** (Makumbusho ya Mkoa; ⏰ 9am-5pm) FREE at the Open University of Tanzania is mostly lacking labels, but the little collection of weapons, jewellery and other items from the region's tribes is enough to detain you for an hour or so.

ATMs are located along Boma Rd (aka Sokoine Rd and Arusha Rd).

🛏 Sleeping & Eating

Regency Resort Singida HOTEL $
(✆ 026-250 2141; www.regencyresortsingida.co.tz; d US$35; 🛜 ❄) The fanciest option in town, the modern Regency has a decent-sized pool, a good restaurant and a view of Lake Singidani. The poolside bar hosts live music.

Stanley Motel Annex HOTEL $
(✆ 0754 476785; www.stanleygroupofhotels.com; camping US$5, s/d/ste US$20/25/30) Spread over three properties, this well-run place with 'executive suites' has pretensions to grandeur, but is really just a simple good-value establishment.

Razaki Munch Corner TANZANIAN $
(mains Tsh2500-6000; ⏰ 7am-9pm Mon-Sat, to 3pm Sun) This brilliantly named restaurant has a big menu of local foods, from goat pilau to chicken and chips. It's alongside the market, just west of the Ismaili Mosque's onion-shaped minaret clocktower.

ℹ Getting There & Away

Singida's bus stand is 2.5km outside town (Tsh3000 in a taxi). Buses depart to Arusha (Tsh17,000, six hours, between 6am and 9am) and Mwanza (Tsh16,000, 4½ hours, between 6am and 8am); Mtei Express is the best company for Arusha. Buses running between Arusha and Mwanza arrive in Singida later in the morning, but there may not be seats available. The Arusha-bound buses stop at Katesh (Tsh7000, 1½ hours) and Babati (Tsh9000, four hours). There are also several buses and coastals going to Dodoma (Tsh16,000, three hours) throughout the morning and two buses, originating in Arusha, going to Tabora (Tsh21,000, six hours).

Lake Victoria

Best Places to Stay

➡ New Mwanza Hotel (p252)

➡ Gold Crest Hotel (p252)

➡ Isamilo Lodge & Spa (p252)

➡ Rubondo Island Camp (p257)

➡ Matvilla Beach & Lodge (p248)

Best Places to Eat

➡ Hotel Tilapia (p254)

➡ Ryan's Bay (p252)

➡ Sizzlers Restaurant (p254)

➡ Isamilo Lodge & Spa (p252)

➡ Yun Long (p254)

Why Go?

Tanzania's half of Africa's largest lake sees few visitors, but the region holds many attractions for those with a bent for the offbeat and a desire to immerse themselves in the rhythms of local life beyond the tourist trail. The cities of Musoma and Bukoba have a quiet waterside charm, while most villagers on Ukerewe Island follow a subsistence lifestyle with little connection to the world beyond the shore.

Mwanza, Tanzania's second-largest city, is appealing in its own way and is the perfect launching pad for a Serengeti–Lake Natron–Ngorongoro loop. Add the forests of idyllic Rubondo Island National Park, deep in the lake's southwest reaches, for a well-rounded safari experience.

When to Go
Mwanza

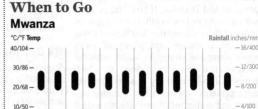

Jun Move with the groove at the Bulabo Dance Festival near Mwanza.

Jun–Sep During dry season there are clear days and high temperatures.

Dec This is the best time to catch and eat *senene* (grasshoppers). You've always wanted to, right?

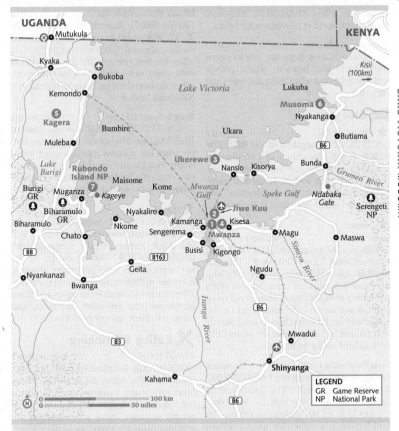

Lake Victoria Highlights

1 Mwanza (p249) Soaking up the sights, sounds and smells as you stroll Temple St and Makoroboi.

2 Jiwe Kuu (p249) Pondering the strange forces of nature that balanced these awesome boulders.

3 Ukerewe Island (p256) Biking through the villages, fields and farms, seeing wildlife and smiles,

and learning about hidden cultures.

4 Sukuma Museum (p253) Watching traditions defy time at the frenetic and exciting Bulabo Dance Festival in June.

5 Kagera (p260) Exploring waterfalls, cave paintings and rural homesteads of the Haya heartland in the seldom-

travelled Kagera region on a cultural tour from Bukoba.

6 Musoma Enjoying a crisp beer as the sun sets over Lake Victoria.

7 Rubondo Island National Park (p257) Seeing forest elephants, giraffes, hippos, crocodiles and birds in a jungle setting that seems pulled from a Hollywood set.

Musoma

☏ 028 / POP 134,000

Little Musoma, capital of the Mara region, sits serenely on a Lake Victoria peninsula with both sunrise and sunset views over the water. It's one of those African towns with nothing special on offer other than an addictive appeal.

◉ Sights

★ **Matvilla Beach**　　　　BEACH
The best thing to do in Musoma is visit Matvilla Beach at the tip of the peninsula, with its pinky-grey granite boulders. It's prime sunset-watching-with-a-beer territory – and there are bars here to help you with that.

To get here, follow Mukendo Rd, Musoma's main street, north of downtown for 1.5km.

Mwigobero Market   MARKET
Mwigobero Market is on the city's eastern shore. Small lake boats to nearby islands and villages load and unload passengers and cargo here.

🛏️ Sleeping

⭐Afrilux Hotel   HOTEL $
(☑️028-262 0031; Mwigobero Rd; s/d Tsh60,000/80,000; 🅿️❄️📶) Something of a Musoma institution, the Afrilux has decent hot showers, helpful staff, good wi-fi and a relaxed courtyard bar-restaurant. On the negative side there's zero sound insulation in the rooms.

⭐Tembo
Beach Club   CAMPGROUND, GUESTHOUSE $
(☑️028-262 2887; camping Tsh23,000, r Tsh66,000; 🕐bar-restaurant 6.30am-10pm; 🅿️📶) There's a sociable bar-restaurant (mains Tsh6500) here and a reasonable camping area that's often busy with the clients of overland truck tours. Some rooms have African art on the walls; they are far enough away from the bar that you can be lulled to sleep by waves rather than kept awake by music.

New Peninsula Hotel   HOTEL $
(☑️0756 505081; Mwisenge Rd; r Tsh45,000-75,000, ste Tsh110,000; 🅿️❄️📶) The long-standing Peninsula, about 1.5km from the town centre, has 15 faded but reasonable rooms. The best feature is a somewhat quieter setting than the other more central hotels in this category, and nice proximity to the lake.

WORTH A TRIP

LUKUBA ISLAND LODGE

An awesome island getaway available only as part of tour-operator-arranged visits, **Lukuba Island Lodge Resort** (tr incl all meals US$386; ❄️❄️📶) is a lovely remote resort with a laid-back ambience. There are cosy stone-and-thatched bungalows and safari tents with outdoor baths along the pretty beach. It's 17km from Musoma and one hour in the boat. Advance bookings are required – Bukoba Cultural Tours (p260) is one of many operators who can get you there.

Mlima Mukendo Hotel   HOTEL $
(☑️0768 065003; Mukendo Rd; s/d Tsh20,000/30,000; 🅿️❄️) A bright-green tower of a hotel on the main road (take a room at the back). It offers the best town-centre accommodation with smart, well-cared-for rooms with wardrobes, desks and big bathrooms. It's near the NBC bank branch.

King's Sport Lodge   GUESTHOUSE $
(☑️028-262 0531; Kusaga St; r without breakfast Tsh15,000) Near Mwigobero Market, this simple place has spotless rooms, a quiet town-centre location and low prices, making it an easy choice for backpackers. The rooms have school desks instead of normal tables.

⭐Matvilla
Beach & Lodge   CAMPGROUND, BUNGALOW $$
(☑️0684 964654; www.matvillabeach.co.tz; Matvilla Beach; camping US$20, bungalows s/d/t US$25/50/80; 🅿️📶) Out at the tip of the peninsula, 1.5km from the centre, this is a gorgeous multipurpose spot amid the rocks. There are hot showers for campers and stone bungalows that are calm and quiet, and blend into giant, granite boulders.

🍴 Eating & Drinking

Afrilux Hotel   TANZANIAN, EUROPEAN $
(☑️028-262 0031; Mwigobero Rd; mains Tsh10,000; 🕐7am-11pm) The restaurant at this four-storey hotel with round windows serves the usual hotel dishes, including grilled tilapia (Nile perch), vegetable curry and something resembling pizza. It's a good social place to eat.

Matvilla Beach & Lodge   TANZANIAN $
(☑️0684 964654; www.matvillabeach.co.tz; meals Tsh5000-7000; 🕐6am-11pm) With its lakeside setting, Matvilla Beach is everyone's favourite place for fried fish or chicken and a beer. Staff will arrange taxis to take you back to town.

Mara Dishes   BUFFET $
(☑️0787 505991; Kivukoni St; buffet Tsh5000; 🕐7am-9pm) Mara Dishes, east of CRDB bank, has a relatively large buffet and masses of locals piling in for a good feed.

ℹ️ Information

There are banks and internet cafes along and just off Mukendo Rd.

ℹ️ Getting There & Away

AIR
The airport is a five-minute walk from the city centre. **Precision Air** (☑️028-262 0713; www.

MWALIMU JULIUS K NYERERE MUSEUM

Julius Nyerere, the first president of Tanzania, was born in the otherwise insignificant little town of Butiama. The Mwalimu Julius K Nyerere Museum (☎0768 872205, 0769 363590; museum Tsh6500, homes Tsh4000; ☺8am-5.30pm) inside the family compound celebrates his life and work. It contains a few stools, shields and other gifts he was given. Boxes of Nyerere's personal effects, including his diaries, a handwritten Swahili translation of part of Plato's Republic and collections of his poetry are also here. Although these are not on display, you can ask the staff to see them.

In the family compound next to the museum you can see his two homes, still occupied by his wife and son; his father's house; and the graves of Nyerere and his parents. His mother's house, where he was born, along with the houses of his father's 21 other wives no longer exist. There are frequent dalla-dallas to Butiama (Tsh2500, two hours) from Musoma.

precisionairtz.com; Kivukoni St; ☺8am-4.30pm Mon-Fri, to noon Sat) flies four times weekly from Dar es Salaam (Tsh126,000) via Mwanza. The booking office is in the town centre.

BUS

The bus terminal is 6km out of town at Bweri, though booking offices remain in the town centre. Dalla-dallas go frequently to/from the city centre (Tsh4000, 20 minutes) and a taxi costs Tsh10,000. Frequent buses connect Musoma and Mwanza (Tsh10,000, four hours).

To get to Ukerewe Island, take a dalla-dalla to Bunda (Tsh4000, one hour, 5.30am to 4pm) and from there take a bus or dalla-dalla to Kisorya. A ferry (Tsh6000) connects Kisorya and Ukerewe; once on the island, it's another 20 minutes by bus or dalla-dalla to Nansio (the island's largest town).

There's a direct bus to Arusha daily (Tsh35,000, 11 to 12 hours) at 6am, passing through Serengeti National Park (using Ikoma gate) and Ngorongoro Conservation Area. However, you have to pay US$110 in park fees to ride this route, as it enters the park. The drive is pretty and can offer nice animal viewing on the way, but you'll not get the chance to stop for photos. Some people find it's better value to fly.

Mwanza

☎028 / POP 706,500

Tanzania's second-largest city, and the lake region's economic heart, Mwanza is set on Lake Victoria's shore, surrounded by hills strewn with enormous boulders. It is notable for its strong Indian influences, as well as for being a major industrial centre and a busy port. Yet, despite its rapidly rising skyline, Mwanza manages to retain a casual feel. In addition to being a stop on the way to Rubondo Island National Park, Mwanza is a great starting or finishing point for safaris through Ngorongoro and the Serengeti, ideally as a loop by adding in Lake Natron.

⊙ Sights

Central Mwanza along Temple St and west to Station Rd has an oriental feel due to its many temples (both Hindu and Sikh) and mosques, as well as Indian trading houses lining the streets. The streetside market and ambience continue west through the Makoroboi area, where the namesake scrap-metal workshop is hidden away in the rocks. Kerosene lamps (*makoroboi* in Swahili), ladles and other household goods are fashioned from old cans and other trash. East of Temple St, the huge and confusing Central Market is fun to explore.

Jiwe Kuu   LANDMARK

One of the more interesting rock formations around Mwanza is Jiwe Kuu (Big Rock), which some people call the Dancing Rocks. Many round boulders sit atop this rocky outcrop north of town and have managed to last for aeons without rolling off. Dalla-dallas to Bwiru run west down Nyerere Rd; their final stop leaves you within a 1.5km walk of the rocks.

Bismarck Rock   LANDMARK

Mwanza's icon, Bismarck Rock, is a precariously balanced boulder atop the lovely jumble of rocks in the lake next to the Kamanga ferry pier. The little park here is a brilliant sunset spot.

Mwaloni Market   MARKET

(☺6am-3pm) Mwaloni Market, under the roof with the giant Balimi ad, is quite a spectacle. The city's main fish market, it also has lots of fruits and vegetables, most shipped in on small boats from surrounding villages, and there are almost as many marabou storks as vendors. Photography is currently prohibited because some scenes in the controversial

Mwanza

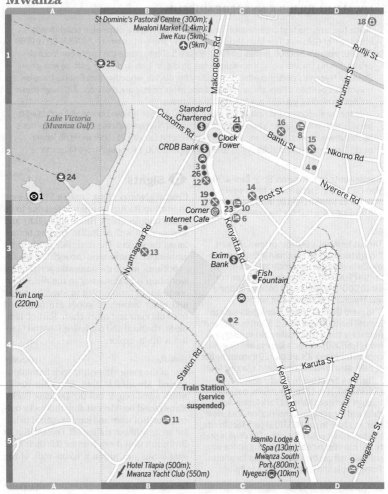

St Dominic's Pastoral Centre (300m);
Mwaloni Market (1.4km);
Jiwe Kuu (5km);
(9km)

Rufiji St

Makongoro Rd

Nkrumah St

Lake Victoria
(Mwanza Gulf)

Standard
Chartered

Customs Rd

CRDB Bank

Clock
Tower

Bantu St

Nkomo Rd

Nyerere Rd

Post St

Corner @
Internet Cafe

Kenyatta Rd

Nyamagana Rd

Exim
Bank

Fish
Fountain

Yun Long
(220m)

Station Rd

Kenyatta Rd

Karuta St

Lumumba Rd

Train Station
(service
suspended)

Isamilo Lodge &
Spa (130m);
Mwanza South
Port (800m);
Nyegezi (10km)

Rwagasore St

Hotel Tilapia (500m);
Mwanza Yacht Club (550m)

documentary film *Darwin's Nightmare* (2004) were shot here.

Saa Nane National Park   PARK
(028-254 0713; www.tanzaniaparks.go.tz; Capri Point; adult/child US$35.40/17.70; 6am-6pm) The rocky island 500m off Capri Point is Saa Nane National Park. Even though it's just 0.76 sq km and home to only monkeys and impalas, visiting costs more than some huge wildlife-filled national parks. Although with 70 bird species it does make a worthwhile short excursion for birders. Last entry is at 5pm.

In addition to the entry fees add US$41.30 for the return boat trip (which can seat 20).

You can check out the old bones and some rather sorry looking stuffed animals in the office (Capri Point Rd) for free.

Tours

Several travel agencies in town hire 4WDs and can organise complete safaris to Serengeti and Rubondo Island National Parks. It's not easy to meet other travellers in Mwanza, but you can ask the agencies whether they have other clients interested in combining groups to save money, or try posting a notice at Kuleana Pizzeria.

Fortes Africa SAFARI
(☎028-250 0561; www.fortes-africa.com; Station Rd) A reputable, reliable and professional company.

Masumin Tours & Safaris SAFARI
(☎0784 505786, 028-250 3295; www.masumin safaris.com; Kenyatta Rd) Vehicle hire, Serengeti safaris and other excursions, plus flight bookings.

Serengeti Services SAFARI
(☎028-250 0061; www.serengetiservices.com; Post St; ☺8am-5pm Mon-Fri, to 1pm Sat) Serengeti Services has merged with the similarly named Serengeti Passages, offering safaris and other excursions around Mwanza. Prices vary, but one-day excursions start at about US$400 plus park fees (up to eight people); multiday trips can be as low as US$250 per person per day. Direct deposit or cash only; however, park fees must be paid separately by credit card.

Serengeti Expedition SAFARI
(☎028-254 2222, 0684 123654; www.serengeti expedition.com; Nkrumah St; ☺8am-5.30pm Mon-Fri, to 1pm Sat) One of the cheaper operators in Mwanza. Also books plane tickets on Precision (p255), Fastjet (p255), Emirates, Auric (p255) and other Tanzanian airlines. Serengeti tours start at US$400 per person per day.

Mindful Adventures `SAFARI`

(☑ 0756 838008; http://mindfuladventure.nl/en) A Dutch-based operator, Mindful Adventures offers safaris designed to not only take you on a beautiful tour of the landscape, but to refresh your spirit as well, and some proceeds benefit a variety of Tanzanian causes. There is no office in Mwanza, but Rama, a local expert, can arrange details and guide. Most of its tours are multiday excursions.

🛏 Sleeping

Lenana Hotel `HOTEL $`

(☑ 0763 555774; Makongoro Rd; s/d Tsh40,000/50,000; ⓟ ✴ 🛜) The Lenana Hotel sits about halfway between central Mwanza and the airport (p255), with great hot water, a full breakfast, friendly staff, and clean, spick-and-span rooms. There's also a bar and restaurant, so if you're looking for somewhere outside town (perhaps just after arriving or on your last night before you leave), this is a great option.

Isamo Hotel `HOTEL $`

(☑ 028-254 1616; Rwagasore St; r Tsh40,000-50,000; ⓟ ✴ 🛜) There's a lot of street noise seeping into the rooms here but grab a pair of ear plugs and enjoy one of the cheapest and best deals in town. The well-kept rooms are a good size and some have little balconies overlooking the chaos.

Kantima Hotel `HOTEL $`

(☑ 0754 093048; Kenyatta Rd; s/d Tsh20,000/25,000; ⓟ ✴) This cheery and friendly place has bright and clean rooms, but the hot-water bathrooms, which are very small and not all that inviting, really let the side down. The hotel has world maps so you can plan your next adventure.

Mwanza Yacht Club `CAMPGROUND $`

(☑ 0762 891280; www.facebook.com/Mwanza YachtClub; Capri Point Rd; camping Tsh15,000; ⓟ 🛜) This is where the big, overland tourist trucks stop. It has a great lakeside location, hot showers and security.

St Dominic's Pastoral Centre `HOSTEL $`

(Nyakahoja Hostel; ☑ 028-250 0830, 0689 413159, 0788 556532; off Balewa Rd; s/d Tsh30,000/40,000, r with air-con Tsh50,000-60,000) This centrally located church-run hostel offers simple rooms plus meals on order (Tsh7000). It's about five minutes' walk north of the Clock Tower roundabout, and good value. Despite the church connection, there's also a bar replete with disco ball.

Kishamapanda Guesthouse `GUESTHOUSE $`

(☑ 0755 083218; Kishamapanda St, off Uhuru St; s/d Tsh20,000/30,000) This tidy little place down a tiny alley in the town centre offers clean, reliable budget rooms, some with shared bathrooms (Tsh15,000) and most with fans. There is no food.

⭐ Isamilo Lodge & Spa `HOTEL $$`

(☑ 0756 771111, 0736 200903; www.isamilolodge. com; 402 Block D, Isamilo; s/d new wing from US$60/80, old wing US$40/70; ⓟ ✴ 🛜 🏊 🐾) This hotel has been renovated, and is very good value, especially if you like being away from the town centre. Rooms in the new wing are spacious, and many have wonderful views down to the lake. There's also a spa, large pool and a good Indian restaurant. Travellers usually get the lower resident rates, which makes it much more tempting.

It's located high on a hillside in the Isamilo neighbourhood, about 2.5km from the town centre.

New Mwanza Hotel `HOTEL $$`

(☑ 028-250 1070, 028-252 1071; www.new mwanzahotel.com; Post St; s/d/ste Tsh123,050/179,000/223,745; ⓟ ✴ 🛜 🏊) This centrally located three-star place with five-star pretensions offers a variety of rooms (some with all-glass showers). If you want a one-stop shop this is it, with a long list of extras including a gym, valet parking, a casino and restaurants. Things get loud on weekends, as the attached nightclub plays dance tunes almost until breakfast.

Ryan's Bay `RESORT $$`

(☑ 0784 699393, 028-254 1702; www.ryansbay. com; Station Rd, Capri Point; s/d from US$110/140; ⓟ ✴ 🛜 🏊 🐾) The flashiest place in Mwanza has lake views and large, well-appointed rooms with acacia-tree murals on the walls. There's a good pool, and one of the best Indian restaurants in town (mains Tsh12,000 to Tsh20,000). Larger groups or families can ask about the adjoining rooms that make suites. Smoking allowed on the balconies only.

Gold Crest Hotel `HOTEL $$`

(☑ 028-250 6058; www.goldcresthotel.com; Post St; s/d from US$95/125; ⓟ ✴ 🛜 🏊) A solid business-class standard in the heart of town with noisy but reasonably comfortable rooms, all with balconies. Some of the upper-floor north-facing rooms have lake views. It's especially noisy on nights when a band at a neighbouring hotel rocks the city till late.

SUKUMA MUSEUM

A worthwhile day excursion from Mwanza is to Bujora village to visit the open-air Sukuma Museum (📞0765 667661; www.sukumamuseum.org; Tsh15,000, video Tsh200,000; ⏲9am-6pm Mon-Sat, 10am-6pm Sun). Here you'll see traditional Sukuma dwellings, the grass house of a traditional healer, blacksmith's tools and a rotating cylinder illustrating different Sukuma words for counting from one to 10. It is also the site of the Bulabo Dance Festival in June, where dancers compete using animals as props. Also on the grounds is the royal drum pavilion, built in the shape of a king's stool and holding a collection of royal drums that are still played on special occasions, and a round church with traditional Sukuma stylings. The church was built in 1958 by David Fumbuka Clement, the Québecois missionary priest who founded the museum. English-speaking guides are available.

The museum can organise performances of traditional drumming and dancing for Tsh130,000 (for up to nine people) per performance. It's also possible to take Sukuma drumming lessons. You'll need to negotiate a price with the instructors, but don't expect it to be cheap. Expect a little flexibility with Sunday opening times as it depends on 'when mass finishes'.

The museum has no-frills *bandas* (per person with meals Tsh30,000) in the style of Sukuma traditional houses and a campground (camping Tsh15,000). The accommodation is rarely used so you'll need to give advance notice. There's a little bar and you can use the kitchen.

Bujora is 18km east of Mwanza off the Musoma road. Take a dalla-dalla (Tsh500, 30 minutes) to Kisesa from Uhuru Rd north of the market in Mwanza. From Kisesa, motorcycle taxis cost Tsh1000. Or, walk a short way along the main road and turn left at the sign, following the small dirt road for 1.7km along some twists and turns. A taxi from Mwanza, with waiting time, will cost Tsh60,000 to Tsh70,000. En route from Mwanza, just past Igoma on the left-hand side of the road, is a graveyard for victims of the 1996 sinking of the Lake Victoria ferry MV *Bukoba*.

Midland Hotel
HOTEL $$
(📞0718 431255; Rwagasore St; s/d non-resident US$50/60, resident Tsh50,000/60,000; P❄🛜) This eye-catching blue tower is solid all-round with well-equipped rooms (free wi-fi reaches most), good service, a rooftop bar and a proper breakfast buffet. Best of all, it will sometimes discount to a much more reasonable tourist rate. There are no mosquito nets, but the rooms are sprayed daily.

Hotel Tilapia
HOTEL $$
(📞028-250 0617, 0784 700500; www.hoteltilapia. com; Capri Point Rd; s/d/ste US$100/120/150; P❄🛜🏊) The ever-popular Tilapia, on the city side of Capri Point, has a variety of rooms, most of which are dated but decent and look out at the lake. It also has rooms on a historic boat; though these are smaller and a little off-kilter, their special character makes them fun, and the two end ones have prime lake views.

Wag Hill Lodge
LODGE $$$
(📞0773 284084; www.waghill.co.tz; s/d bungalow US$105/150, tent US$154/220, villa US$700; P🏊🚣) The intimate and beautiful Wag Hill, on a small wooded peninsula outside Mwanza, is an excellent post-safari cool down. It has bungalows with screened walls and great wooden furniture, luxury tents and villas; almost all have great lake views. Note that some of the rooms require walking up rock stairs. There's even activities for kids and a special playground.

🍴 Eating & Drinking

DVN Restaurant
TANZANIAN $
(Nyamagana Rd; meals Tsh4000-5000; ⏲7am-5pm Mon-Sat) Excellent local fare is served fast and cheap in this church-run place with an old-fashioned cafe look and feel. There's no menu, just a daily special like fish and side dishes. It's behind the post office and the St Nicholas Anglican Church – quite hidden with just a small sign above a tucked-away door.

Salma Cone
STREET FOOD $
(📞0752 661939; Bantu St; ice cream Tsh2000-4000, kebabs Tsh4000; ⏲9am-10pm) *Sambusas* (Indian pastry snacks stuffed with curried meat or vegetables), soft-serve ice cream and juice are all pleasers here, but it's the smell of barbecuing meat that will draw you in for

a kebab. With plastic outdoor tables, this is a fun corner to lounge during the evening.

Shahensha Restaurant INDIAN $$
(☑0769 552299; Bantu St; meals Tsh10,000-12,000; ☺10am-midnight; ☑) Tasty samosas and other snacks, a daily menu featuring Pakistani and Tanzanian dishes, plus pleasant, casual indoor seating.

Sizzlers Restaurant INDIAN $$
(☑0766 424872; Kenyatta Rd; mains Tsh8000-12,000; ☺noon-3pm & 6-11.30pm) Quiet during the day, this cheap Indian joint transforms into a hive of buzzing activity in the evenings. This is when people grab a streetside table and tuck into the chicken tikka, which sizzles on the hot coals of the outdoor barbecue. It also does a range of other Indian and Chinese meals.

Kuleana Pizzeria INTERNATIONAL $$
(☑028-250 0955; Post St; snacks Tsh3000-6000, pizzas Tsh14,200-17,700; ☺7am-9pm; ☑) 🍃 Don't expect Italian-class fare, but this is a relaxed and popular place for pizzas and snack-style food (omelettes, sandwiches and breads) with a good mix of locals and expats. The friendly owner feeds many street children.

Diners INDIAN $$
(☑028-250 0682; Kenyatta Rd; meals Tsh6000-15,000; ☺noon-3pm & 6-11pm; ❄☑) This odd time warp serves some of Mwanza's best Indian food, though Chinese decorations and menu items are holdovers from its previous incarnation as a Chinese restaurant.

Hotel Tilapia INTERNATIONAL $$$
(☑028-250 0617; www.hoteltilapia.com; Capri Point; meals Tsh19,000-22,000; ☺7am-11pm; P�) The hub of Mwanza's expat population and a magnet to passing tourists, the restaurant of the Hotel Tilapia (p253) has an attractive terrace overlooking the lake. Pied kingfishers chatter and squabble as you

choose anything from Japanese teppanyaki and Indian to continental. The kitchen is slow, so expect to take your time.

Yun Long BAR
(☑0759 901986; Capri Point; ☺7am-10pm) While a dinner here (mains Tsh15,000 to Tsh20,000) is worth it for the waterside view and the leafy lakeside garden overlooking Bismarck Rock (p249), the best reason to come is to enjoy a relaxing drink and watch the sunset front row. It's a low-key place to relax, and billiard aficionados will want to play a game or two on the pool tables.

Self-Catering

U-Turn FOOD & DRINKS $
(Nkrumah St; ☺8am-8pm Mon-Sat, 10am-2pm Sun) One of Mwanza's best-stocked supermarkets, U-Turn also has many small gift items, such as teas, canned coffee and so on that make good souvenirs.

ℹ Information

DANGERS & ANNOYANCES
Mwanza is generally a fairly safe city to stroll about with few touts or security issues, but be as aware as you would at home. Street begging can be aggressive at times and after 9pm dark side streets should be walked with caution. Bantu St, with its *mishikaki* grills, is loud and boisterous, and gets dicey in the wee hours when many people – often drunk – are heading home.

INTERNET ACCESS
Corner Internet Cafe (Kenyatta Rd; per hour Tsh1500; ☺8am-5pm Mon-Sat) Centrally located and offers the usual services (internet, faxing, copies). Other net cafes are peppered along Post St.

MEDICAL SERVICES
Aga Khan Health Centre (☑0686 364540, 028-250 2474; www.agakhanhospitals.org; Miti Mrefu St; ☺24hr) For minor illnesses.

SUKUMA DANCING

The Sukuma, Tanzania's largest tribal group with nearly 15% of the country's population, are renowned nationwide for their dancing. Dancers are divided into two competing dance societies, the Bagika and the Bagulu, that compete throughout Sukumaland (the Sukuma homeland around Mwanza and southern Lake Victoria). The culmination is the annual **Bulabo Dance Festival** held at the Sukuma Museum (p253) in June. The most famous of the dozens of dances are those using animals, including the Bagulu's *banungule* (hyena and porcupine dance) and the Bagika's *bazwilili bayeye* (snake dance). Before beginning, the dancers are treated with traditional medicines to protect themselves from injury. The animals, too, are given a spot of something to calm their tempers.

Bugando Hospital (☑ 028-250 0513; www.bugandomedicalcentre.go.tz; Wurzburg Rd) The government hospital has a 24-hour casualty department.

MONEY

Access Bank (www.accessbank.co.tz; Pamba Rd; ⊗ 8am-7pm Mon-Fri, to 3pm Sat), CRDB Bank (Kenyatta Rd; ⊗ 9am-3pm Mon-Fri, to 12.30pm Sat), Exim Bank (www.eximbank-tz.com; Kenyatta Rd; ⊗ 9am-5pm Mon-Fri), NBC Bank (Liberty St; ⊗ 8am-7pm Mon-Fri, to 3pm Sat), Stanbic Bank (www.stanbicbank.co.tz; Nyerere Rd; ⊗ 8.30am-3.30pm Mon-Fri, to 12.30pm Sat), Standard Chartered (www.sc.com; Makongoro Rd; ⊗ 9am-5pm Mon-Fri) and other major banks have 24-hour ATMs, with branches scattered throughout the city centre. Most branches also change cash for major currencies.

TRAVEL AGENCIES

Global Travel (☑ 0762 738639; ⊗ 8am-6pm), at Mwanza Airport, can make a variety of local and international plane reservations.

❶ Getting There & Away

AIR

The airport (MWZ; ☑ 022-284 2402) is 10km north of the centre; taxis should cost between Tsh15,000 and Tsh20,000.

Auric Air (☑ 0783 233334; www.auricair.com; Mwanza Airport) and Air Tanzania (☑ 0756 067783; www.airtanzania.co.tz; Kenyatta Rd) fly daily to Bukoba. Air Tanzania also has at least five flights weekly to Dar es Salaam.

Coastal Aviation (☑ 0736 200840; www.coastal.co.tz; Mwanza Airport) has a daily flight to Arusha airport stopping at various Serengeti National Park airfields. It also flies to Dar es Salaam and Zanzibar.

Fastjet (☑ 0784 108900; www.fastjet.com; Kenyatta Rd) flies daily to Dar. One-way fares to Bukoba/Dar average Tsh140,000/200,000.

Precision Air (☑ 028-250 0819; www.precisionairtz.com; Kenyatta Rd) flies daily to Dar es Salaam, Zanzibar and Kilimanjaro.

Flight schedules and destinations constantly change so it pays to check each airline's website for the latest. There are instances when a flight is cancelled due to lack of customers, so be prepared to make alternative plans at inconvenient times.

BOAT

At the time of writing, the MV Victoria, which formerly connected Mwanza with Bukoba via its port in Kemondo, was not operating. Meanwhile, service on the Mwanza to Bukoba route began in January 2018 on the smaller MV Bluebird. For updates, check at Mwanza's north port. There

is a daily ferry service connecting Mwanza with Ukerewe Island.

BUS

About 10km south of town, Nyegezi Bus Station (Sirari-Mbeya Rd) handles buses to all points east, south and west including to Dar es Salaam (Tsh45,000, 15 to 17 hours), Arusha (Tsh35,000, 12 to 13 hours) and Moshi (Tsh45,000, 14 to 15 hours). The Arusha and Moshi buses go via Singida (Tsh25,000, six hours). There are no buses between Mwanza and Arusha via the Serengeti – you will need to catch these in Musoma. Buses also go to Babati (Tsh35,000, nine to 10 hours), Dodoma (Tsh30,000, 10 hours) and Iringa (Tsh60,000, 14 hours).

Buses to Bukoba (Tsh20,000, six to seven hours) via Chato (Tsh10,000) depart between 6am and 1pm and mostly use the Busisi Ferry (p256), but if they're redirected to the Kamanga Ferry (p256) in central Mwanza, you can meet them there.

Adventure is probably the best of several companies departing daily at 5.30am to Kigoma (Tsh40,000, 12 hours) via Tabora (Tsh15,000, six hours). You can also find buses to Kigoma taking the route via Kasulu. Both take about the same amount of time, but at the time of research, there was more tarmac going via Tabora than via Kasulu.

Buses for Musoma (Tsh10,000, three to four hours, last bus 4pm) and other destinations en route to the Kenyan border depart from Buzuruga Bus Station (Nyakato), 4km east of the centre.

There's no need to travel to the bus stations to buy tickets since numerous ticket agencies are stationed near the old City-Centre Bus Terminal in a converted multistorey parking garage, where the various companies have agents in numbered shops spread over two floors. Before arriving, ask staff at your hotel to recommend the current best company for your route and to verify current prices. It's also recommended to go with a Tanzanian to purchase your ticket, to avoid the inevitable haggling.

TRAIN
Mwanza is the terminus of a branch of the **Central Line** (Tanzania Railways Limited; ☑ 022-211 6213, 0754 460907; www.trl.co.tz; cnr Railway St & Sokoine Dr, Dar es Salaam) and trains run to Tabora (1st-/2nd-class sleeping/economy Tsh29,600/22,700/11,800, 12 hours) on Sunday, Tuesday and Thursday at 5pm. From Tabora, you can connect to Kigoma (Tsh31,700/24,200/12,500 from Tabora) or continue on to Dar es Salaam (Tsh76,100/54,800/25,000 from Mwanza). If travelling to Kigoma, you'll need to disembark in Tabora (arrivals are in the morning) and spend the day there before boarding the train to Kigoma in the evening. For Dar es Salaam, just stay on the same train.

❶ Getting Around
Dalla-dallas (labelled Buhongwa) to **Nyegezi Bus Station** (Tsh400) run south down Kenyatta and Pamba roads. The most convenient place to find a dalla-dalla (labelled Igoma) to **Buzuruga Bus Station** (Tsh400) is just northeast of the **clock tower**, where they park before running down Uhuru St. Dalla-dallas to the **airport** (Tsh400) follow Kenyatta and Makongoro roads.

There are taxi stands all around the city centre, such as near the **Fish Fountain** (Station Rd) and **Clock Tower** (Kenyatta Rd) roundabouts, with prices averaging Tsh4000 to Tsh6000 within the centre. Taxis to Buzuruga cost from Tsh800, and to Nyegezi about Tsh18,000. Taxis to the airport cost between Tsh15,000 and Tsh20,000. Motorcycle taxis are everywhere and charge Tsh1500 within the centre.

Ukerewe Island
With its simple lifestyle and rocky terrain broken up by lake vistas and tiny patches of forest, Ukerewe Island, 50km north of Mwanza, makes an intriguing, offbeat diversion. **Ikulu** ('White House') is the modest 1928 European-style palace of the island's former king, signposted just behind the market in Bukindo. The real attraction, however, is the deeply rural life of the island. Ukerewe is unusual in its highly successful farming techniques, centuries of stable population, and the fact that every patch of land and every tree is individually owned. There's a fascinating account of how this all works in John Reader's brilliant book *Africa: A Biography of the Continent*.

Nansio, the main town, has internet access (when the electricity is working) and one internationally linked ATM. Shared taxis and dalla-dallas connect Ukerewe's few sizeable villages.

La Bima Hotel   GUESTHOUSE $
(☑ 0752 179055; Nansio; s/tw Tsh18,000/20,000; **P**) Despite cramped rooms (some with hot water) and peeling paint, this place is Nansio's best lodging. It has the top restaurant, too.

❶ Getting There & Away
The passenger ferry MV *Clarius* has been undergoing repairs but usually sails daily from Mwanza North Port to Nansio (adult/child Tsh5000/3050, 3½ hours) at 8am; it leaves Nansio for Mwanza at 2pm.

Two other ferries dock at Kirumba, north of Mwanza's centre near the giant Balimi ad. The MV *Nyehunge I* (1st/2nd/3rd class Tsh15,000/7000/6000) departs Mwanza at 9am and Nansio at 2pm for a 3½-hour journey. Its sister, the MV *Nyehunge II* (2nd/3rd class Tsh7000/6000), leaves from Mwanza at 2pm,

---

❶ CROSSING THE MWANZA GULF

Until completion of the planned Busisi–Kigongo bridge (years in the future), travelling west from Mwanza along the southern part of Lake Victoria entails crossing the Mwanza Gulf by ferry. There are two ferries, each with advantages.

The **Kamanga Ferry** (Nasser Rd; per person/vehicle Tsh1000/7200) docks in town, near the post office. It departs Mwanza hourly between 6am and 6.30pm, except Sunday when departures are every two hours from 8am to 6pm. If you're travelling to Bukoba or anywhere along that highway, ask which ferry the bus will use; you may be able to save a trip to the bus station by boarding the bus here.

The government-run **Busisi Ferry** (per person/vehicle Tsh400/6500; ☎), also known as the Kigongo ferry, 30km south of Mwanza, has the advantage of the road west being paved. It also sails more often (every 30 minutes, 24 hours), but there are frequent delays, especially at peak commuting times. Many trucks also use this boat.

VISITING UKEREWE

What could be better than taking in the sights of gorgeous Ukerewe Island on a private bicycle tour? Join local guide Paschal Phares with **Visit Ukerewe Island** (☏0763 480134; www.facebook. com/visitukereweisland; half-/full-day bike tour Tsh40,000/60,000; ☉7am-7pm) for a trip around the island. Stops are tailored to your interests, but can include scenic viewing spots, a sunset photo op, the Chief's Palace, caves and more. Phares can also arrange walking or canoeing/ kayaking expeditions.

arriving at 6pm, and leaves Nansio at 7.30am the next morning.

It's also possible to reach Nansio from Bunda, a town on the Mwanza–Musoma road, which means that you can go from Mwanza to Ukerewe and then on towards Musoma or the Serengeti without backtracking. If using public transport, take a Mwanza–Musoma bus and disembark at Bunda. Here buses (and sometimes dalla-dallas) head to Nansio (Tsh6000, five to six hours) at 10am and 1pm daily using the Kisorya ferry (passenger/car Tsh400/6000, 40 minutes), which crosses five times daily between 9am and 5pm in each direction. After the buses depart there are no vehicles direct to Nansio, but you can take a dalla-dalla to Kisorya and catch another on the island. The last ferry to Ukerewe sails at 5pm. The last ferry leaving Ukerewe is at 3pm, but don't use it unless you have your own vehicle or are willing to try hitching part of the way to Bunda. Be aware that the ferry can be delayed at times or not even run at all.

Rubondo Island National Park

Alluring for its tranquillity and sublime lakeshore scenery, **Rubondo Island National Park** (adult/child US$35.40/11.80) is one of Tanzania's best-kept secrets. There may be days when you're the only guests on the 256-sq-km island. Elephants, giraffes, black and white colobus, and chimpanzees were long ago introduced alongside the island's native hippo, bushbuck and sitatunga, an amphibious antelope that hides among the marshes and reeds along the shoreline (Rubondo is the best place in Tanzania to see it).

🏃 Activities

Birdwatching, particularly for shore birds, brings the most visitors, but walking safaris

(from US$23.60 per adult, no under 12s) and boat rides (from US$23.60 per person) can also be rewarding.

Rubondo's **chimps** are not yet habituated, but at the time of research experts were still working on the long process of getting them used to human company. This could take up to four or five years but sightings will probably increase as the chimps lose their fear of us. In the meantime fascinating chimp-tracking walks can take you in search of their presence.

Though the beaches look inviting, there are enough **crocodiles and hippos** for swimming to be prohibited. Heed any cautions the rangers give, as attacks do occur.

🛌 Sleeping & Eating

Rubondo Park

Bandas & Resthouse   CAMPGROUND, BANDA $
(camping US$35.40, r per person US$35.40) The *bandas* facing the beach at Kageye on Rubondo's eastern shore are some of the better national-park-run *bandas* in Tanzania. Each has a comfortable double and single bed, hot-water bathroom, and privacy afforded by surrounding jungle trees. There's also a resthouse in the same location with similar quality rooms, but with TVs.

All rooms have electricity in the mornings and evenings, but not throughout the night. There are fully equipped kitchens for cooking, and staff can be hired to cook for you; a free meal for them should be payment enough. A tiny shop 10 minutes' walk north of the *bandas* sells a few basics such as rice, eggs and potatoes, and there's a cool little bar on the shore right by the *bandas*.

⭐**Rubondo Island Camp**   TENTED CAMP $$$
(☏0736 500515; www.rubondo.asiliaafrica.com; s/d all-inclusive US$884/1351; ☉closed Apr & May; 🛜🐾🍴) 🏆 Run by the very upmarket Asilia group, this is a wonderful lakeside perch with stunning safari tents. Well, we say tents, but these 'tents' have three solid walls, fine furnishings, bathrooms to splash in and deliciously comfortable beds. There's a restaurant area hanging onto a low cliff with lake views.

Activities on offer include chimp walks (for the moment you're very, very unlikely to see the chimps but you'll certainly see their night nests and other clues to their presence), birdwatching trips and fishing. Game drives can also be arranged, but they're not the best way to see the island.

ⓘ RUBONDO ISLAND NATIONAL PARK

Why Go The island has a Hollywood movie-set feel about it, with thick jungle, tall forests, and a wide variety of plants, animals and birds to see. It's easy to get close to wildlife and you'll likely have it all to yourself, too, making for a quiet, peaceful getaway.

When to Go June through early November.

Practicalities Start from Bukoba or Mwanza, travel to the nearest port (Muganza or Nkome) and continue by park boat. Alternatively, arrive by charter flight. Book accommodation and transport through the Saa Nane/Tanapa office (p250) in Mwanza.

Budget Tips This is generally a good park for budget travellers. Taking a boat ride from Muganza or Nkome costs only US$118. Once there the park *bandas* offer excellent cheap accommodation and self-catering possibilities. Safaris are taken on foot.

ⓘ Getting There & Away

AIR

Auric Air (p255) makes a Rubondo diversion on its Mwanza–Bukoba flights (one way US$72). This requires a two-night stay if flying return out of Mwanza since arrival is in the late afternoon and departure in the early morning. **Coastal Aviation** (☑ 0752 627825; www.coastal.co.tz) also flies to the park by request. A charter flight with Auric costs around US$3000.

BOAT

There are two ways to reach Rubondo by park boat (up to seven passengers); both should be arranged in advance. Fishers are prohibited from delivering people to the island.

The park recommends using Kasenda, a small port about 5km from Muganza (Tsh1500 on a motorcycle taxi or Tsh5000 in a taxi). From here it's 20 to 30 minutes by boat to Rubondo Island and another 15 minutes by park vehicle to drive across the island to Kageye. This costs US$118 return per boat. Muganza is just off the main Mwanza–Bukoba road. Public transport is frequent but buses normally drop you at the junction on the main road where the turn-off for Muganza is. There are plenty of motorbikes willing to whizz you into the town or Kasenda. All buses between Bukoba (Tsh12,000, two hours) and Mwanza (Tsh12,000, four hours) pass through, as do Bukoba–Dar es Salaam buses. Dalla-dallas run to nearby destinations such as Biharamulo (Tsh5000, two hours).

The second option is Nkome, at the end of a rough road north of Geita, where the boat costs US$118 to Kageye and takes about two hours. Expect choppy water on this crossing. The warden's office, where you get the boat, is located outside Nkome, Tsh1000 by *piki-piki* (motorbike) or Tsh5000 by taxi from where the final dalla-dalla stops. Two buses go direct from Mwanza to Nkome (Tsh12,000, four to five hours). They leave Mwanza at 10am, but you can meet them at the Kamanga ferry. Alternatively, it is possible to take a bus to Geita, from where there are frequent dalla-dallas to Nkome (Tsh5000, two hours).

Biharamulo

☑ 028 / POP 25,000

The old German administrative centre of Biharamulo is a small nowhere town that some travellers find inexplicably appealing. It certainly has a remote 'lost in Africa' feel.

Heading north from Biharamulo, the road passes between the 1300-sq-km **Biharamulo Game Reserve** and the 2200-sq-km **Burigi Game Reserve**, the latter long discussed as a new national park, but so far nothing has come of it. Neither has particularly significant tourist facilities, although animal populations, particularly in swampy Burigi, have revived after suffering severely from the refugee influxes during the 1990s. Roan and sable antelopes, eland, sitatungas, elephants, giraffes, zebras, lions and more are present. Arrangements to visit can be made with Bukoba Tours (p260).

🛏 Sleeping & Eating

★**New Aspen Hotel**   MOTEL $
(☑ 0753 349114; r Tsh30,000; 🅿 ❄ 🛜) Excellent value here, though the water heater needs time to warm up. Rooms are spick and span, with tiled floors, starched linens and mosquito nets in good condition. The on-site bar is open into the wee hours and is sometimes used for wedding receptions, as there's a restaurant and open-air nightclub/dance space as well. The restaurant's goat stew is popular.

German Boma   HISTORIC HOTEL $
(☑ 0766 477065; r per person Tsh10,000; 🅿) The 1902–05 German *boma* on the hill above town has a good guesthouse with well-kept rooms in little rondavels (circular African buildings) in the courtyard. They have hot water but no fans. There's no food, so you'll

need to eat down near the bus station. You can also camp here.

ⓘ Getting There & Away

There are two or three dalla-dallas and a bus (6am) that depart early each morning direct to Mwanza (Tsh12,000, six hours) and Bukoba (Tsh10,000, two hours). The Bukoba bus leaves at 8am. There's one dalla-dalla a day to the Rwandan border (Tsh12,000, two hours, 8am). To travel to Mwanza later in the day, take one of the frequent shared taxis to Nyankanazi (Tsh5000, one hour) and wait for a bus there. For Bukoba, catch a connection in Muleba (Tsh8000, 1½ hours). Coming into Tanzania from Rwanda, be aware that the little office at the border does not change Rwandan francs.

Bukoba

♪ 028 / POP 128,800

Bustling, green-leafed Bukoba has an attractive waterside setting and a pleasing small-town feel. Everyone who comes to visit here seems to like it, even though it's a little hard to put your finger on exactly why. The town traces its roots to 1890, when Emin Pasha (Eduard Schnitzer), a German doctor and inveterate wanderer, arrived on the western shores of Lake Victoria as part of efforts to establish a German foothold in the region. Since then, the second-largest port on the Tanzanian lakeshore has quietly prospered, thanks to the income generated by coffee, tea and vanilla farming.

In September 2016, the area was hit by a magnitude 5.7 earthquake, which levelled many of the earthen-brick dwellings. Shortly afterwards, extremely heavy rains caused floods and more devastation. The city has now bounced back from these disasters though, and has returned to being a great spot to visit any time of year.

◉ Sights

Kagera Museum MUSEUM
(📞 0713 568276; Tsh2000; ⊙ 9.30am-6pm) This small but worthwhile museum mixes a collection of local tribal items with photographs of wildlife from the Kagera region; drums, handbags and other crafted items are on display. A guide (which is more or less compulsory) charges Tsh3000.

The museum is across from Bukoba's airport (p262) in the Nyamukazi area. If taxi drivers or motorcycle-taxi drivers don't know the museum, tell them 'Peter Mulim' and they'll know the area. You can also walk along the lakeshore to the museum. Bukoba Tours (p260) can make arrangements if you need assistance.

Musira Island ISLAND
(Tsh3000) The big chunk of rock in front of Bukoba was a prison island in the days of the kings and now it offers an intriguing getaway. Upon arrival introduce yourself to the chairman and pay the island fee. Ask him to show you the path to the summit, which passes the Orthodox church and several homes made from elephant grass.

Crowded passenger boats (Tsh2000) depart Nyamukazi, near the museum, but with these you don't get the chance to see the cliffs and caves (where traditional healers used to be buried) on the backside, so it makes sense to hire a boat for the trip or take a tour. Bukoba Tours (p260) charges US$60 for a boat for one person and US$100 for two.

Bunena Church CHURCH
The town's original cathedral, the 1914 Bunena Church is the oldest church in Bukoba. It paints a pretty picture when seen from Bukoba Beach, but isn't much up close. The rocky cliff below it, however, is very attractive.

OFF THE BEATEN TRACK

ANCIENT KATURUKA

A stop on the Bukoba Tours (p260) circuit, the **Katuruka Heritage Site** (adult/child Tsh10,000/3000; ⊙ 9am-5pm) preserves the oldest-known iron-smelting furnace in East, Central and Southern Africa (from 500 BC; long before equivalent techniques were known in Europe). While the site itself is essentially just old bricks and some small nuggets, there are interesting shrines to King Rugomora (r AD 1650–75) and Mugasha, the god of storms and water. Your guide will tell you some fascinating legends about them. A replica of the king's thatched burial house holds a small **archaeological museum**.

The trip here is a chance to see deeply rural Tanzania. From Bukoba, take a Maruka-bound dalla-dalla to Katuruka (Tsh1500, 45 minutes). The ticket booth is 200m off the road.

Bukoba

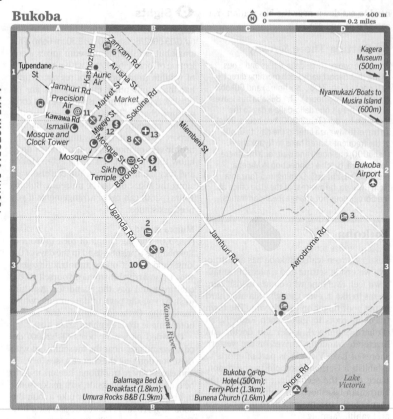

☞ Tours

★ Bukoba Cultural Tours TOURS
(☎0713 568276; www.bukobaculturaltours.co.tz; Lake Hotel; ⊙8.30am-6pm Mon-Fri, 9am-4pm Sat & Sun) Bukoba Tours is the new venture of William 'Willy' Rutta, a guide with years of experience in the Bukoba area. Offering wisdom, wit and expertise, Rutta operates from an office at the Lake Hotel (p261) and his business offers a wide variety of cultural and island tours, and can arrange safaris on Rubondo Island, in the Serengeti and beyond.

Kiroyera Tours CULTURAL
(☎0759 424933, 0713 526649, 0757 868974; www.kiroyeratours.com; Shore Rd) The established Kiroyera Tours offers half- and full-day tours of the area's local attractions. It has been in business for years and can arrange a variety of tours, including bike, bus, boat and plane adventures.

🛏 Sleeping

★ Umura Rocks B&B B&B $
(☎0783 828583; www.umurarocks.com; Umura Rocks, Busimbe A; s/d Tsh70,000/85,000; P 🕸 🛜) This is a lovely B&B with views of Lake Victoria and Musira Island (p259), located just outside Bukoba proper on a high hill. Getting here requires a 4WD vehicle, so call ahead if you don't have one to arrange for pick-up. In addition to serving breakfast, staff can also cook any fish you catch during your stay.

CMK Lodge HOTEL $
(☎0682 265028; off Uganda Rd; r Tsh25,000-35,000; P) Plain but sparkling rooms and a quiet side-road location make this near-downtown hotel one of Bukoba's best in terms of value. Rooms come with a simple breakfast, hot water and mosquito nets on the beds. On top of that you get a warm welcome for free!

Bukoba

Bukoba Co-Op Hotel   HOTEL $
(📞028-222 1251; Shore Rd; d/tw Tsh25,000/ 30,000; 🅿🛜) Fair value, but slightly aged rooms with TVs, ceiling fans and minifridge, but the best feature is its location at the end of Bukoba Beach. Rooms on the 2nd floor have tree and lake views and the restaurant is one of Bukoba's best. Smoking outside only.

Balamaga Bed & Breakfast   B&B $
(📞0754 760192, 0744 760192; www.balamagabb. com; Plot 27/28, Maruku Rd; s/d Tsh80,000/110,000, with shared bathroom Tsh70,000/100,000; 🅿) High up in the hills overlooking the lake and Musira Island (p259), this homey place has four spacious, comfortable rooms (two have a shared bathroom) decorated with artistic photographs. The garden is gorgeous and full of birds. Apart from breakfast, there is no food.

ELCT Bukoba Hotel   HOTEL $
(📞0754 415404, 028-222 3121; www.elctbukoba hotel.com; Aerodrome Rd; s/tw/ste US$40/45/60; 🅿🛜) This Lutheran conference centre between the lake and the city centre is a very good choice. The rooms in the rambling complex have a slight institutional feel, but it's impeccably maintained and well-run by friendly staff. The hotel sign promises 'tranquillity' and it delivers. Breakfast is included and the restaurant serves dinner as well. The gardens are a real treat.

Kiroyera Campsite   CAMPGROUND $
(📞0759 424933, 0766 262695; www.kiroyera tours.com; Shore Rd; camping/banda US$10/29; 🅿🛜) This backpackers' spot on the beach has camping, plus a handful of Haya-type *msonge* (grass huts), some with electricity and private bathroom. It's a basic spot, but to get closer to the water you'd need to be swimming in it. The (highly flammable!) grass huts are nonsmoking only. There's also a shack-restaurant that's got decent drinks and meals.

New Banana Hotel   HOTEL $
(📞0753 028636; Zamzam Rd; r Tsh20,000) Perhaps better called the 'Not-So-New Banana Hotel', this time-worn spot is in a good location and is bright and cheery. There's hot water, and fresh flowers in the rooms show that management cares. Outside there is a pleasing little bar-cafe.

Lake Hotel   HOTEL $
(📞0754 407860; r Tsh25,000, with shared bathroom Tsh10,000; 🅿) This historic hotel once hosted Frank Sinatra, among the many celebs who stayed here. It's within walking distance of the lake, but has little elegance at this point and in fact, some rooms are downright shabby. Come here for the faded historical charm.

🍴 Eating & Drinking

ELCT Tea Room   TANZANIAN $
(📞0754 415404; Market St; breakfast Tsh5000, lunch Tsh5000-8000; ⊙8am-5pm Mon-Sat) Popular all-you-can-eat buffet, right in the town centre, serving all your Tanzanian favourites at low prices.

New Rose Café   TANZANIAN $
(📞0754 761610; Jamhuri Rd; meals Tsh5000-6000; ⊙8am-7pm Mon-Sat) A wonderful and unassuming Bukoba institution that feels like a cross between a grocer and a little cafe-restaurant.

Bukoba Co-Op Hotel   INTERNATIONAL $$
(📞028-222 1251; Shore Rd; meals Tsh12,000; ⊙7am-11pm) The beach seating makes this a popular gathering spot. The grilled tilapia, pizzas and curries are good, but it's the view that makes it worth it. If there's no breeze, bring insect repellent.

Victorius Perch   INTERNATIONAL $$
(📞0754 603515; Uganda Rd; meals Tsh10,000-16,000; ⊙6am-midnight) The most ambitious menu in town features Chinese, Indian,

THE HAYA

Bukoba is the heartland of the Haya people, one of Tanzania's largest tribes and a prominent player in the country's history. The Haya had one of the most highly developed early societies on the continent and by the 18th or 19th century were organised into eight different states/kingdoms. Each was headed by a powerful and often despotic *mukama* (king) who ruled in part by divine right. It was the *mukama* who controlled all trade and who, at least nominally, owned all property, while land usage was shared among small, patrilineal communes. Order was maintained through a system of appointed chiefs and officials, assisted by an age-based army. With the arrival of the colonial authorities, this political organisation began to erode. The various Haya groups splintered and many chiefs were replaced by people considered more malleable and sympathetic to colonial interests.

In the 1920s, in the wake of growing resentment towards these propped-up leaders and the colonial government, the Haya began to regroup and in 1924 founded the Bukoba Bahaya Union. This association was initially directed towards local political reform but soon developed into the more influential and broad-based African Association. Together with similar groups established elsewhere in the country, notably in the Kilimanjaro region and Dar es Salaam, it constituted one of Tanzania's earliest political movements and was an important force in the drive towards independence.

Today the Haya receive as much attention for their dancing (characterised by complicated foot rhythms, and traditionally performed by dancers wearing grass skirts and ankle rattles) and singing as for their history. Saida Karoli, a popular female singer in the East African music scene, comes from Bukoba.

European and even tries for Italian, though many items aren't always available.

Lina's Night Club   CLUB
(☑ 0689 664559; Uganda Rd; ⊙ 24hr) *The* nightclub in Bukoba is open 24 hours but the bar only gets busy in the evening, and the club from Friday to Sunday. It's bright yellow, and so vast most of the city could dance inside it... there's even a gym!

❶ Information

INTERNET ACCESS

For internet access try **4 Ways** (☑ 0767 453362; Kashozi Rd; per hour Tsh1500; ⊙ 8am-7pm Mon-Sat, 10am-3pm Sun) or the **main post office** (Barongo St; internet per hour Tsh1000; ⊙ 8.30am-5pm Mon-Fri).

MEDICAL SERVICES

MK Pharmacy (☑ 0713 302140, 028-222 0582; Jamhuri Rd; ⊙ 8am-8pm Mon-Sat, 9am-2pm Sun)

MONEY

Bukoba has several main bank branches and 24-hour ATMs.
CRDB Bank (Sokoine Rd; ⊙ 8.30am-4pm Mon-Fri, to 1pm Sat) Has a branch and 24-hour ATM (Visa and MasterCard).

NBC (Jamhuri Rd; ⊙ 8.30am-4pm Mon-Fri, to noon Sat) Changes cash and has a 24-hour ATM (Visa and MasterCard).

❶ Getting There & Away

AIR

The Bukoba **airport** (BKZ) offers daily flights to and from Mwanza (US$72 one way) on **Auric Air** (☑ 0688 233335; www.auricair.com; Rwabizi Plaza, Kashozi Rd; ⊙ 8.30am-4.30pm Mon-Sat), and to and from Dar es Salaam (from Tsh360,000) via Mwanza (Tsh165,000) with **Precision Air** (☑ 028-222 0545, 0782 351136; www.precisionairtz.com; Kawawa Rd).

BOAT

At the time of writing, there was no ferry service between Bukoba and Mwanza.

BUS

All bus companies have ticket offices at or near the **bus station** (Tupendane St; ⊙ 5am-6pm). If you prefer to leave the haggling to an expert, the staff at Bukoba Cultural Tours (p260) can also buy tickets for you, for a US$3 fee.

Among the options are buses to the following:
Kampala, Uganda (Tsh20,000, six to eight hours) Two departures daily at 6am and 12.30pm. Visas can be issued at the border.
Kigoma (Tsh28,000, 13 to 14 hours) Every Monday, Wednesday and Friday at 6am.
Mwanza (Tsh20,000, eight hours) Frequent departures between 6am and 12.30pm.

Western Tanzania

Why Go?

Western Tanzania is rough, remote frontier land, with vast trackless expanses, minimal infrastructure and few visitors: not much different to when Stanley found Livingstone here. The west offers a sense of adventure now missing elsewhere in the country. This is precisely what attracts a trickle of travellers, many of whom plan their itineraries around the schedules of the MV *Liemba*, which sails down Lake Tanganyika, and the Central Line train, which crosses the country.

But it's wildlife watching that brings most people. Gombe, Jane Goodall's former stamping ground, and Mahale Mountains National Park are two of the world's best places for chimpanzee encounters, while the vast flood plains of Katavi National Park offer an almost primeval safari experience.

Unless you charter a plane as part of a tour, you'll need plenty of time and patience to travel here. But, for that certain sort of traveller, Tanzania's west is Tanzania's best.

Best Places to Stay

➡ Lake Shore Lodge (p276)

➡ Kigoma Hilltop Hotel (p268)

➡ Gombe Forest Lodge (p272)

➡ Jakobsen's Guesthouse (p268)

Best Places to Eat

➡ Lake Shore Lodge (p276)

➡ Coast View Resort (p268)

➡ Orion Tabora Hotel (p266)

➡ Kalambo Falls Lodge (p280)

When to Go
Kigoma

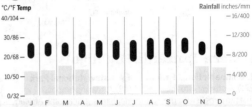

Dec–Apr Rains bring washed-out roads along with brilliant lightning displays.

May–Nov Dry-season travel is easiest, but the forests turn leafless.

May–Jun This is when chimpanzees are most likely to be seen in large groups.

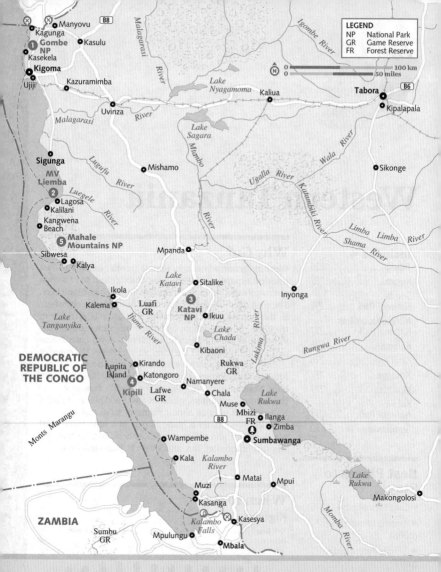

Western Tanzania Highlights

1 Gombe National Park (p271) Venturing into the forests to mingle with the chimps made famous by Jane Goodall's studies.

2 MV Liemba (p270) Sailing from port to port down Lake Tanganyika aboard the historic ferry that inspired the movie *The African Queen*.

3 Katavi National Park (p277) Staring hippos, elephants, giraffes and African buffaloes in the eye within one of the country's wildest parks.

4 Kipili (p276) Wading into the waters of Lake Tanganyka – and its Red Sea–like aquatic riches – to dive and snorkel amid the kaleidoscopic cichlids.

5 Mahale Mountains National Park (p272) Discovering this ultimate get-away-from-it-all destination, complete with chimpanzees, hikes and blissful beaches.

Tabora

📶 026 / POP 227,000

Leafy Tabora was once the most important trading centre along the old caravan route connecting Lake Tanganyika with Bagamoyo and the sea, and several other minor slave-trading routes converged here. The region, known in those days as Kazeh, was the headquarters of many slave traders, including the infamous Tippu Tib. A string of European explorers passed through Tabora's portals, most notably Livingstone and Stanley, who both spent many months here. Stanley estimated the population in 1871 to be about 5000 people. By the turn of the 19th century the Germans had made Tabora an administration and mission centre, and following construction of the Central Line railway Tabora became the largest town in German East Africa. It also became a regional education centre and many large schools are still located here.

Today, it's primarily of interest to history buffs and rail fans, who'll have to wait here if taking a branch line to Mpanda or Mwanza.

⊙ Sights

There are many buildings dating back to the German era, notably the **Catholic Cathedral**, which has concrete inner walls painted to look like wood and marble, and the old *boma* (compound), now an army base (photography forbidden).

Livingstone's Tembe   HISTORIC SITE
(📶 0787 281960, 0754 619627; Kwihara; Tsh10,000, guide Tsh5000; ⊙ 8am-4pm) This deep-maroon-coloured, flat-roofed Arabic-style home, built in 1857, is the main attraction in these parts. It was Livingstone's residence for part of 1871. Later that year, Stanley waited three months here hoping that the Arabs would defeat Mirambo, famed king of the Nyamwezi (People of the Moon) tribe, and reopen the trail to Lake Tanganyika. When Mirambo was victorious, Stanley had to travel to Ujiji via Mpanda. Stanley and Livingstone returned here together the next year.

It is now a museum and has some original Zanzibar carved doors, a few Livingstone letters and some slave-trading information. It's 8km southwest of town in Kwihara. Occasional dalla-dallas (Tsh1000 to Tsh1500) heading to Kipalapala from a stop just southwest of the new bus stand (near the public toilet) can drop you at Etetemia. From there it's a 2.5km walk straight down the road:

if in doubt, just ask for 'Livingstone'. Taxis from town should cost about Tsh20,000 return and motorbikes Tsh10,000, but there is a good chance you'll pay more. Still, there are enough English captions to make it worth the trip.

🛏 Sleeping

John Paul II Hostel   GUESTHOUSE $
(📶 0758 317020, 0789 812224, 0717 728515; Jamhuri St; s/d/ste Tsh15,000/20,000/50,000; P) Spotless, quiet, secure and cheap. You can't really go wrong at this church-run place where the foundation stone was laid by John Paul II himself. The entrance to the compound is in the back. If the cathedral gate is closed, walk around to the east; it's at the back of the big yellow building. Enter through the attached Nazareth Canteen.

Frankman Palace Hotel   HOTEL $
(📶 0768 778504; d Tsh75,000-85,000; P❄🛜) With glitter walls and mood lighting the rooms here are certainly eye-catching, but it's also one of the town's smarter offerings. It has wi-fi, but the manager describes it as 'too slow'. It's the green-roofed building behind the bus station next to the stadium, at the end of a small side street.

Golden Eagle Hotel   GUESTHOUSE $
(📶 026-260 4623; Market St; d Tsh25,000, s/d with shared bathroom Tsh15,000/20,000; P) Thanks to the friendly owner, plus the central location and good, cheap restaurant, this 1st-floor place is the most traveller-friendly spot in town. Rooms are old, but tidy, and have TVs, hot water and ceiling fans. It can be a bit noisy.

★ Orion Tabora Hotel   HISTORIC HOTEL $$
(📶 026-260 4369; oriontbrhotel@yahoo.com; Station Rd; camping Tsh5,000, s Tsh65,000-150,000, d Tsh80,000-175,000; P🛜) The old railway hotel, originally built in 1914 by a German baron as a hunting lodge, has been restored and provides unexpected class in this out-of-the-way region. Ask for a room in the Kaiser Wing, with screened porches looking out onto the gardens. The Orion also has the town's best restaurant (p266) and a well-stocked bar. It can be loud when a live band plays in the outdoor bar. Camping can also be arranged.

🍴 Eating & Drinking

Golden Eagle Hotel   INDIAN, TANZANIAN $
(📶 026-260 4623; Market St; meals Tsh8500-15,000; ⊙ 6am-midnight; 🍴) Good food and low prices; the Jeera chicken and veggie curry are

Tabora

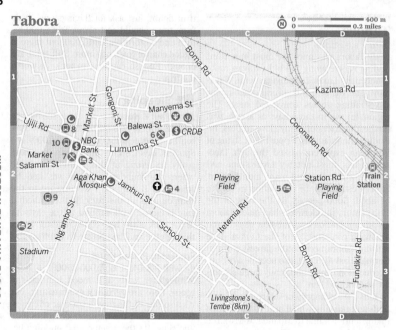

Tabora

◎ Sights
1 Catholic Cathedral B2

🛏 Sleeping
2 Frankman Palace Hotel A3
3 Golden Eagle Hotel A2
4 John Paul II Hostel B2
5 Orion Tabora Hotel C2

⊗ Eating
Golden Eagle Hotel .... (see 3)
6 Mayor's Fast Food B2
7 Mayor's Hotel A2
Orion Tabora Hotel .... (see 5)

ⓘ Transport
8 NBS Office A2
9 New Bus Stand A2
10 Old Bus Stand A2

just Tsh5000. Fish and chips is Tsh14,000. It also serves mocktails, beer and wine.

Mayor's Hotel   TANZANIAN $
(📞0784 341747, 0757 201656; snacks & meals Tsh1000-6000; ⊗7.30am-5pm) Next to the market; inexpensive samosas and other snacks plus local-style meals, including rice and beans. It's on the unnamed alley behind the Grand Penta hotel (which is at the corner of Salamini and Market Sts).

Mayor's Fast Food   TANZANIAN $
(📞0784 341747, 0757 201656; Lumumba St; snacks from Tsh300, buffet per plate from Tsh2500; ⊗7.30am-10pm) This popular local hang-out offers samosas and other snacks, plus a good-value buffet. The price depends on the meat you choose.

★**Orion Tabora Hotel**   TANZANIAN, EUROPEAN $$
(📞026-260 4369, ext 117; Station Rd; meals Tsh6000-15,000; ⊗6am-midnight) Tabora's top dining spot has a mix of local and continental food, with pizza and Indian available during dinner. There's dining indoors and in the outside bar area, which has a pool table, and live bands play on Friday, Saturday and Sunday. Even more vital, the bar has the skills, technology and ingredients to make a margarita!

ⓘ Information

There are ATMs at **CRDB** (Lumumba St; ⊗8am-4.30pm Mon-Fri) and **NBC** (cnr Market St & Ujiji Rd; ⊗8.30am-4pm Mon-Fri, to noon Sat).

ⓘ Getting There & Away

AIR

Air Tanzania (📞026-260 4401; www.air tanzania.co.tz) flies to both Kigoma (Tsh140,000, Wednesday) and Dar es Salaam (Tsh285,000, Sunday).

BUS

NBS (Ujiji Rd), mostly offering four-across seating, is the top company operating out of Tabora. Some NBS buses depart from its office at the **old bus stand**. All other buses use the nearby **new bus stand**. Several buses depart daily between 6am and 10am to Mwanza (Tsh15,000, six hours). Buses also go to the following:

Arusha (Tsh30,000, 10 to 11 hours, 6am) Goes via Singida (Tsh20,000, four hours) and Babati (Tsh25,000, six to seven hours).

Dodoma (Tsh30,000, 10 hours, 6am)

Kigoma (Tsh15,000, seven hours, 7am)

Mbeya (Tsh45,000, 14 hours, 6am) Sasebossa and Sabena have departures several times a week.

Mpanda (Tsh23,000, 12 hours, 7am)

For all buses, arrive 30 minutes before departure.

TRAIN

Tabora is an important train junction. Trains go to:

Dar es Salaam (1st/2nd sleeping/economy class Tsh56,500/33,900/25,400, 24 hours, 6.40am Monday, Wednesday and Friday for ordinary trains)

Kigoma (1st/2nd/3rd class Tsh35,700/21,400/16,100, nine to 10 hours, 5.30pm Monday, Wednesday and Saturday)

Mpanda (1st/2nd/3rd class Tsh27,500/21,200/11,100, 10 hours, 5pm Monday, Wednesday and Saturday)

Mwanza (1st/2nd/economy class Tsh29,600/22,700/11,800, nine to 10 hours, 7pm Monday, Wednesday and Saturday)

A deluxe train also runs to Dar es Salaam (Tsh56,500/33,900/25,400, 24 hours, 7.20pm Saturday) and Kigoma (Tsh35,700/21,400/16,100, nine to 10 hours, 6am Saturday).

Kigoma

028 / POP 135,000

This agreeable little town is the regional capital and only large Tanzanian port on Lake Tanganyika. It's also the end of the line for the Central Line train and a starting point for the MV *Liemba* and visits to Gombe National Park. It's hardly a bustling metropolis, but it feels that way if you've spent any time in other parts of western Tanzania.

Other than a few scattered buildings dating from the German colonial era, including the train station and what some call Kaiser House (now the home of the regional commissioner), Kigoma has no real attractions, but the pleasant ambience, some good restaurants and a lively market, plus nearby villages and beaches, make it a nice spot to spend a few days.

◉ Sights

Katonga VILLAGE

This large and colourful fishing village is quite a spectacle when the 200-plus wooden boats pull in with their catch. During the darkest half of the moon's cycle they come back around 8am after they've spent the night on the lake fishing by the light of lanterns. Dalla-dallas (Tsh400) come here frequently.

Jakobsen's (Mwamahunga) Beach BEACH

(Tsh7000) Jakobsen's is actually two tiny, beautiful sandy coves below a wooded hillside. The overall setting is idyllic, especially if you visit during the week when few people are around. There are some *bandas* for shade, and soft drinks and water are sold at the guesthouse (p268). Watch your belongings, as kleptomaniac baboons roam freely.

It's 5km southwest of town, signposted off the road to Katonga. Dalla-dallas to Katonga can drop you at the turn-off, from where it's about a 20-minute walk. A taxi is about Tsh10,000.

Kibirizi VILLAGE

There are many fishers at Kibirizi, 2km north of town by the oil depots. The early afternoon loading of the lake taxis is impressive in a noisy, colourful and rather chaotic kind of way. You can walk here by following the railway tracks or the road around the bay.

Kaiser House HISTORIC BUILDING

(Bangwe Rd) This colonial-era building was constructed in the early years of the 20th century for German emperor Wilhelm II, who was planning a hunting expedition to western Tanzania. He never made the journey, but the building still bears his title. Today it is the home of the regional commissioner.

⛵ Tours

Gombe Track Safaris & Tours Tanzania TOURS

(☏0756 086577; www.gombesafari.com; Lumumba St; 1-day tour US$395; ⊙9am-5pm Mon-Fri, to 1pm Sat) If taking a lake taxi for four hours to reach Gombe (p271) strikes you as inconvenient, contact Gombe Track Safaris for alternative (albeit more expensive) options. Though an overnight stay is highly recommended, it can even put together a one-day excursion that includes pick-up (at 6am!) right from your hotel.

Mbali Mbali SAFARI

(☏0739 313125, 0732 978879; www.mbalimbali.com; ⊙9am-5pm Mon-Fri, to 1pm Sat) This western

Tanzania–focused safari operator is based at Kigoma Hilltop Hotel. It does boat and air charters on and around Lake Tanganyika, and operates a network of lodges.

🛏 Sleeping

★ Jakobsen's Guesthouse   GUESTHOUSE $

(☑0789 231215, 0753 768434; www.kigomabeach. com; camping per person Tsh20,000, tent or r per person without breakfast Tsh30,000-75,000; 🅿🐾) This comfortable place has a guesthouse with a lovely clifftop perch above Jakobsen's Beach, two cottages and some standing tents, plus two shady campsites with bathrooms, lanterns and grills closer down near the lake. It's good value and a wonderful spot for a respite, but there is no food available so you'll need to self-cater.

You can rent kayaks, sailboats and snorkelling gear. Water and soft drinks are available. It's 5km southwest of town, signposted off the road to Katonga. Dalla-dallas to Katonga can drop you at the turn-off, from where it's about a 20-minute walk. Ever curious and thieving baboons will take what they can, so campers should be extra careful with valuables.

★ Green View Hotel   HOTEL $

(☑028-280 4055, 0744 969681; www.greenview hotel.co.tz; s/d/ste Tsh50,000/70,000/80,000; 🅿✳🛜🐾) Despite the lack of a view, Green View offers everything a traveller could need: spotless rooms, good air-con, hot showers and friendly, English-speaking staff, all in a rather Escher-esque building with odd stairs that lead up then down, and a variety of life-sized African animals as decor (fun for kids!). It's up a hill away from the town centre.

Aqualodge   GUESTHOUSE $

(☑0622 820998; Bangwe Rd; r Tsh50,000; 🅿🛜) You can't get closer to the lakeshore than at Aqualodge, where you're mere steps away from the lapping waters. While the rooms are basic, they have fridges and mosquito nets and are a steal if you consider the sunsets are part of the deal.

Gombe Executive Lodge   GUESTHOUSE $

(☑0758 891740; r Tsh25,000; 🅿✳) This is the standout cheapie in town. It's on a quiet and dusty side road and has a real homely feel to it, with spotless rooms, attached hot-water bathrooms and air-con. Breakfast is Tsh3000 extra.

Coast View Resort   HOTEL $

(☑0752 103029, 028-280 3434; r Tsh50,000-60,000; 🅿✳🛜) The highest hotel in town doesn't have rooms with views, but you can see everything from the restaurant's gazebo tower. It has a nice courtyard (alas, without views), a restaurant and friendly staff.

New Mapinduzi Guest House   GUESTHOUSE $

(☑0753 744336; pharmblue@gmail.com; Lumumba St; s/d Tsh15,000/20,000, without bathroom Tsh8000/12,000) This simple guesthouse down a tiny alley is a good choice if you want to be right in the centre of town, but it is as no-frills as it gets. The basic, self-contained rooms have TVs and fans. There is no food available.

Kigoma Hilltop Hotel   HOTEL $$

(☑0757 349187; www.mbalimbali.com; s/d/ste US$92/143/225; ✳🛜🐾) This hotel is atop an escarpment overlooking the lake. The double and twin cottages are within a large walled compound roamed by zebras. Rooms are reasonably well-appointed, there are lovely views from the gardens and there's an expensive restaurant. The pool (nonguests Tsh10,000) is large and well-maintained.

Lake Tanganyika Hotel   HOTEL $$

(☑0757 349187; www.laketanganyikahotel.com; s/d from US$85/105; 🅿✳🛜) A large place right on the lake, with lovely views, but rooms are on the small side and the staff are rather lacklustre. The gardens are pretty and nonguests can use the pool (Tsh10,000). Despite a full range of liquors on display at the well-stocked bar, the only drinks served are beer and wine.

🍴 Eating

Kigoma Catering   INTERNATIONAL $

(☑0713 492381; Lumumba St; mains Tsh3000-6000; ⏲8am-5pm) The biggest and broadest menu in town, with primarily local dishes. Though it won't wow you, the food is pretty good.

Sun City   TANZANIAN $

(Lumumba St; meals Tsh4000-6000; ⏲7am-9pm) This long-standing establishment is a clean and almost artistic spot for *wali maharagwe* (rice and beans) and other local meals. There's also chicken biryani on Sunday. Take-out is available.

★ Coast View Resort   TANZANIAN, ITALIAN $$

(mains Tsh10,000-13,000; ⏲7am-9pm, bar to 11pm) Assuming you can score a table with a view (up on the gazebo), it's worth the trip up here for dinner or sundowners. The menu is mostly local, but has some Italian too.

Kigoma

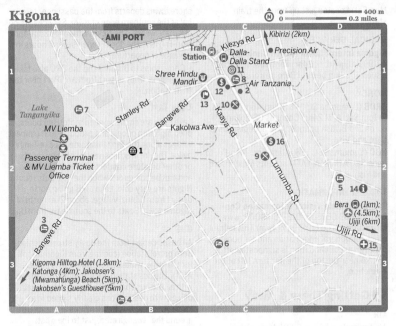

Kigoma

⊚ Sights
1 Kaiser House...B2

✪ Activities, Courses & Tours
2 Gombe Track Safaris & Tours
  Tanzania...C1

🛏 Sleeping
3 Aqualodge..A3
4 Coast View Resort....................................B3
5 Gombe Executive Lodge.........................D2
6 Green View Hotel.....................................C3
7 Lake Tanganyika Hotel............................A1
8 New Mapinduzi Guest House.................C1

✗ Eating
Coast View Resort..........................(see 4)
9 Kigoma Catering.....................................C2
10 Sun City..C1

ℹ Information
11 Baby Come & C@ll.................................C1
12 CRDB...C1
13 Democratic Republic of the Congo
  Consulate..C1
14 Gombe/Mahale Visitor Information
  Centre..D2
15 Kigoma International Health Clinic......D3
16 NBC...C2

ℹ Information

CONSULATES

Burundian Consulate (☎ 028-280 2865, 0659 876464; road to Kibirizi; ⊗ 8am-3pm Mon-Thu, 8am-1pm Fri) A one-month single-entry tourist visa for most Western nationalities costs US$90 (it only accepts US dollars), plus one passport photograph and a letter of invitation. The application fee is Tsh10,000. Allow up to two weeks for processing. It is often easier to apply for a visa in Dar es Salaam.

Democratic Republic of the Congo Consulate (☎ 028-280 2401, 0765 947249; Bangwe Rd; ⊗ 9am-4pm Mon-Fri) Congolese tourist visas must be obtained in advance from your home country. If you're just planning on visiting Virunga National Park and Goma then so-called Virunga Visas are easily issued via the Visit Virunga website (www.visitvirunga.org).

IMMIGRATION

Immigration formalities for those riding the MV *Liemba* are handled by an officer who boards the boat in Kasanga. If you're headed to Burundi or the DRC, there are immigration offices at Ami Port and Kibirizi.

INTERNET ACCESS

Baby Come & C@ll (☎ 028-280 4702; Lumumba St; per hour Tsh1500; ⊗ 7.30am-8pm

Mon-Sat) Located just up from the train station.

MEDICAL SERVICES

Kigoma International Health Clinic (☑ 0715 491995; Ujiji Rd; ⊙ 24hr) For minor medical issues. It's 1km beyond Bero petrol station.

MONEY

CRDB (Lumumba St; ⊙ 8.30am-4pm Mon-Fri, to 1pm Sat, ATM 24hr) Changes US dollars, euros and British pounds. ATM accepts Master-Card and Visa.

NBC (Lumumba St; ⊙ 8.30am-4pm Mon-Fri, to noon Sat, ATM 24hr) ATM accepts MasterCard and Visa.

TOURIST INFORMATION

Gombe/Mahale Visitor Information Centre (☑ 0689 062303, 028-280 4009; www. tanzaniaparks.co.tz; ⊙ 9am-4pm) This helpful office for general information and for booking park-run accommodation is signposted off Ujiji Rd near the top of the hill; turn left at the T-junction.

ⓘ Getting There & Away

AIR

Air Tanzania (☑ 0756 530154; www.air tanzania.co.tz; CRDB Bldg, Lumumba St; ⊙ 8am-5pm Mon-Fri, 9am-2pm Sat & Sun) flies four times weekly between Kigoma and Dar es Salaam (US$200). **Precision Air** (☑ 0784 298929; www.precisionairtz.com; Kibirizi road; ⊙ 9am-4pm Mon-Fri, to 2pm Sat) flies five times weekly between Kigoma and Dar es Salaam via Tabora (US$226). Both airlines accept cash only. Air travel to Kigoma is in a constant state of flux, so expect this information to change.

The **airport** (TKQ) is about 5km east of the town centre (about Tsh5000 in a taxi).

BOAT
Ferry

The **MV Liemba** (☑ 0766 633830, 028-280 2811; ⊙ office 8am-4pm Mon-Fri) between Kigoma and Mpulungu (Zambia) via Lagosa (for Mahale Mountains National Park) and other lake-shore towns departs from the passenger terminal at the southern edge of town. Services are on alternate weeks. The **ticket office** (⊙ 8am-4pm Mon-Fri) near the dock is open several hours in advance of departure.

Cargo ships to Burundi and the DRC also take passengers. They depart from Ami Port near the train station.

Lake Taxi

Lake taxis are small, wooden motorised boats, piled high with people and produce, that connect villages along the Tanzanian side of Lake Tanganyika. They're inexpensive, but offer no toilets or other creature comforts, little if any shade, and can be dangerous when the lake gets rough. Nights are very cold. Lake taxis going north depart from Kibirizi village, about 2km north of Kigoma town. Boats to the south leave from Ujiji.

BUS

All buses depart from the dusty streets behind Bero petrol station (coming from Kigoma, look for the large, white petrol station with an NBC ATM). The bus station is surprisingly organised with all the bus companies having little ticket offices with destinations clearly signed in a long row. Other bus ticket offices are scattered around the Mwanga area, just to the west.

Buses go to the following places:

Arusha (Tsh60,000, 20 hours)

Bukoba (Tsh30,000, 12 hours, 6am), via Biharamulo (Tsh27,000, eight hours)

Burundi (Tsh15,000, seven hours)

Mpanda (Tsh23,000, eight hours, 6am)

Mwanza (Tsh40,000, 10 to 12 hours, 6am), via Nyakanazi (Tsh22,000, seven hours)

Tabora (Tsh23,000, eight hours, 6am)

Uvinza (Tsh5000, four hours) All buses to Tabora or Mpanda pass through Uvinza.

TRAIN

Kigoma station is the final stop for the Tanzania Railways Limited **Central Line Train** (www.trl.co.tz) from Dar es Salaam and from Mwanza. Trains depart from Kigoma to Tabora (1st/2nd/3rd class Tsh31,700/24,200/12,500)

ⓘ TRAVELLING IN THE WEST

Travelling in western Tanzania has long been the preserve of the determined. In the past you had to put up with atrocious roads and be ready to rough it on the backs of trucks.

Today things are changing fast and almost all the main routes are being upgraded and paved. This is reducing journey times and allowing buses to replace trucks. In fact, if you stick to the main routes it's very unlikely you will need to ride in anything other than a bus.

Despite this, road conditions are more challenging here than in much of Tanzania and journey times are often long. The rainy season or a truck breakdown in the perfectly wrong place may mean delays of hours...or days. Many people take to the skies instead; there is an increasing range of internal flights linking towns and parks in western Tanzania.

and Dar es Salaam (Tsh76,100/55,600/27,000) at 4pm on Tuesday, Thursday and Sunday. There is also a weekly express train to Dar departing Kigoma at 8am on Saturday (Tsh79,400/47,600/35,700), stopping at Tabora (Tsh35,700/21,400/16,100).

ℹ Getting Around

Dalla-dallas (Tsh400) park in front of the train station and run along the main roads to Bera bus stand, Kibirizi, Katonga and Ujiji. Taxis between the town centre and Bera bus stand or Kibirizi charge Tsh3000 to Tsh4000. Don't pay more than Tsh1000 for a motorcycle taxi anywhere within the city.

Ujiji

🎵 028 / POP 4000

Tiny Ujiji, one of Africa's oldest market villages, earned its place in travel lore as the spot where explorer-journalist Henry Morton Stanley uttered his famously casual 'Dr Livingstone, I presume?'. Regardless of whether these were the actual words or not, the two certainly did meet in this small village, ending Stanley's search.

As a terminus of the old caravan route to the coast, Ujiji grew prosperous on the back of the slave and ivory trade and during Livingstone's time it was the main settlement in the region, a status it lost after the train station was built at Kigoma. Burton and Speke also stopped here in 1858 before setting out to explore Lake Tanganyika. Despite its distinguished past, little remains today of Ujiji's former significance except that some buildings away from the main road show Swahili traits.

Ujiji's beach and small **dhow port** are a step back into centuries past. They don't use power tools to build the boats, so the construction methods have been the same for generations. You may also suddenly be surrounded by herds of cattle that come to the water's edge to drink.

Livingstone
Memorial Museum   MUSEUM, MONUMENT
(🎵 0715 383878; Tsh20,000; ⊙ 8am-6pm) The site where the immortal words, 'Dr Livingstone, I presume?' were uttered by Stanley on meeting Livingstone in 1871 is commemorated by a stark grey monument inside a chain-link fence. The two mango trees here (two others died) are said to have been grafted from the original tree that shaded the two men during their encounter. Below, and

part of the same complex, the Livingstone Memorial Museum holds some artefacts and printed placards about the East African slave trade.

There are also a few paintings by local artists and papier-mâché replicas of Stanley and Livingstone. The admission fee may seem steep but the Livingstone and Stanley story is worth knowing and the humble museum's effort to recount the horrors of the slave trade makes it an interesting stop.

ℹ Getting There & Away

Ujiji is 8km south of central Kigoma and is easily visited as a day trip. Dalla-dallas (Tsh500, 20 minutes) run between the two towns throughout the day. The Livingstone site is down a cobblestone street about 1km off the main road. The port and the beach are 300m further on from there. Just ask for Livingstone and the dalla-dalla driver will drop you off at the right place.

Gombe National Park

With an area of only 56 sq km, **Gombe National Park** (🎵 0689 062303; www.tanzaniaparks.go.tz; adult/child US$118/23.60, trekking fee US$23.60; ⊙ 6.30am-6.30pm, chimp viewing 8am-4pm) is Tanzania's smallest national park, but its famous primate inhabitants and its connection to Jane Goodall have given it worldwide renown. Many of Gombe's 100-plus chimps are well habituated, and though it can be difficult, sweaty work traversing steep hills and valleys, if you head out early in the morning sightings are nearly guaranteed.

As well as chimp tracking, you can take walks along the lakeshore, and go and see Jane's old chimp-feeding station, the viewpoint on Jane's Peak and Kakombe Waterfall.

🛏 Sleeping & Eating

If you're planning on staying in park-run accommodation, it's best to book rooms in advance through the visitor information centre (p270) in Kigoma or directly with the park at gombe@tanzaniaparks.go.tz.

Tanapa Resthouse   GUESTHOUSE $
(🎵 0689 062303; r per person US$23.60, special tent with shower US$59) Next to the visitor centre at Kasekela, this amenable place has six simple rooms with electricity mornings and evenings. Two overflow facilities have rooms of lesser quality, and toilets at the back. There are also four 'special' glamping-style tents. Breakfast/lunch/dinner costs US$5/10/10,

🛈 GOMBE NATIONAL PARK

Why Go Thanks to the work of Dr Jane Goodall, this is arguably the most famous chimpanzee reserve in the world – and one of the best places to see chimps up close.

When to Go Plan your visit for any time other than March and April, when the lodge is closed and rains can make walking the trails hard work. June through October are the easiest (driest) months for chimpanzee tracking.

Practicalities The chimps can be a long walk from the two accommodation options, so be aware you may need to hike for more than an hour depending on where they happen to be. All activities are organised and paid for at Kasekela, on the beach near the centre of the park (this is where lake taxis drop you).

Budget Tips Apart from the high entry fees, it is possible to visit Gombe on a budget: take a lake taxi to and from the park, stay in the Tanapa Resthouse (p271) and self-cater. The clock on your entry fee starts the moment you arrive, so wise chimp trekkers arrive at noon on day one, with time for an afternoon trek, then leave by noon the following day after an additional morning trek. This enables two chimp-trekking trips while paying only one 24-hour park-entry fee; however, you will need to pay a guiding fee for each trek. If you stay past the 24-hour mark you will be charged for another full 24 hours even if you only stay a few hours...or minutes.

but you can bring your own food and use the kitchen for a modest fee.

Gombe Forest Lodge　　TENTED CAMP **$$$**
(📞0732 978879; www.mbalimbali.com; s/d all-inclusive except drinks US$875/1350; ☺May-Feb) Gombe's only private lodge has a shady, waterside location with just seven tents that offer a certain class and sophistication in the jungle. The tents are luxurious without being ostentatious, and staff do their best to meet your needs during your stay.

🛈 Information

Visitors at Gombe are limited to one hour with each group of chimps but you are allowed to go and find another group after your hour is up for no extra cost. A guide costs US$23.60 per group. Children under age 15 are not permitted to enter the forest, although they can stay at the resthouse.

🛈 Getting There & Away

Gombe is 26km north of Kigoma and the only way there is by boat.

At least one lake taxi to the park (Tsh4000, three to four hours) departs from Kibirizi village, just north of Kigoma, around noon. Returning, it passes Kasekela as early as 7am.

You can also hire boats at Kibirizi; hiring requires hard bargaining, but the price will be a little cheaper than the charter options (around US$250 return to charter a fishing or cargo boat). You may have to pay in advance for petrol, but don't pay the full amount until you've arrived back in Kigoma. Some boat owners may try to

tell you there are no lake taxis in an effort to get business.

It's safer and more comfortable (in part because there will be sun shade) to arrange a charter with an established company. Chartering the Tanapa boat costs US$354 return plus US$20 for each night you spend at Gombe. Organise it through the visitor information centre (p270) in Kigoma. Mbali Mbali, also in Kigoma, charges US$773 return for those not staying at the lodge in Gombe and US$413 return for lodge guests (there's no overnight charge). These boats take 1½ to two hours.

Day trips are possible on a chartered boat, but you should leave very early, as late starts reduce your chances of meeting the chimps. Gombe Track Safaris & Tours (p267) can set this up for US$395.

Mahale Mountains National Park

Plain breathtaking is the only way to describe **Mahale Mountains National Park** (www.mahalepark.org; per day adult/child US$94.40/23.60, guiding fee US$23.60; ☺6am-6pm), with its clear blue waters and white-sand beaches backed by lushly forested mountains soaring straight out of Lake Tanganyika, plus some of the continent's most intriguing wildlife. And, because of its unrivalled remoteness, visitor numbers are low, adding to the allure.

The rainforest blanketing Mahale's western half is, in essence, a small strip of the Congo that got orphaned by the rift that became Lake Tanganyika. It's most notable as a chimpanzee sanctuary, and there are around 900 of our primate relatives residing in and around the park, along with leopards, blue duikers, red-tailed monkeys, red colobus monkeys, giant pangolins and many Rift Valley bird species not found elsewhere in Tanzania. There are also hippos, crocodiles and otters in the lake, and lions, elephants, buffaloes and giraffes roaming the savannah of the mountains' difficult-to-reach eastern side.

🏃 Activities

In addition to its chimpanzees, Mahale also has hiking, snorkelling and chances for seeing other wildlife. Whether or not you look for chimps, guide fees are US$23.60/29.50 per group (up to six people; the higher fee is for full-day excursions).

Chimpanzee Tracking

The main reason most people make the considerable effort to visit Mahale is to see chimps. Kyoto University researchers have been studying chimps here since 1965 and their 'M' group is well habituated to people. Mahale's size and terrain mean chimp tracking can take time, and it requires steep, strenuous walking, but almost everyone who visits has a successful sighting. Mahale is widely regarded as one of the best places in the world to see wild chimpanzees.

Only one group of up to six people are allowed with the chimps at any one time. This means that you might have to wait several hundred metres back from the chimps before you get a turn. Each group is allowed only one hour a day with the chimps and this is strictly enforced (with calls of '10 minutes remaining', 'five minutes remaining'). If one hour is not enough (and most people find it is) then it's possible to pay an extra US$100 for a 'photographer's experience' and get three hours with the chimps. You'll also have to pay a negotiable extra fee to your guide.

Face masks (provided) must be worn at all times when in the presence of the chimps. Children under the age of 12 and anyone suffering from a cold, flu or other illness are not allowed to visit the chimps, as some have died in the past after they caught the flu from a park visitor.

During June and July the chimps come down to feed around the lodges almost daily.

Hiking

Climbs of **Mt Nkungwe** (2462m), Mahale's highest peak, must be accompanied by an armed ranger. The usual arrangement is two days up and one down, camping midway and again near the peak. Trekkers must bring their own camping gear and food. The climb requires a reasonable degree of fitness, but the trail is in decent shape. A two-day option requires a willingness to scramble and hack your way through the bush.

Swimming

Mahale has fine snorkelling and swimming off its powder-white beaches, but unfortunately humans aren't the only ones to enjoy such beachside beauty – a large crocodile population here means that swimming and snorkelling are only allowed in certain places, and may be banned at times.

🛏 Sleeping & Eating

Mango Tree Bandas   BUNGALOW $
(sokwe@tanzaniaparks.go.tz; Kasiha; bandas per person US$47.20) The cosy Mango Tree *bandas* are set in the forest about 100m from the shore in Kasiha, about 10km south of park headquarters (p274). While they lack lake views, the night sounds are wonderful. You will need to be completely self-sufficient with food and drink, and bring everything you might need with you. The kitchen is well-equipped.

Boat transfers with the Tanapa boat to/from park headquarters in Bilenge cost US$64.50 return.

Kungwe Beach Lodge   TENTED CAMP $$$
(📱 0737 206420; www.mbalimbali.com; s/d incl full board & chimpanzee tracking US$1052/1764; ⊗ mid-May–mid-Feb; 🐾) This is a low-key and

WESTERN TANZANIA MAHALE MOUNTAINS NATIONAL PARK

ℹ️ SPENDING TIME WITH THE CHIMPS

Both Gombe and Mahale Mountains National Parks have chimpanzee communities that are fully habituated to humans and visiting them is an awesome experience. Remember that chimpanzees are susceptible to human diseases, so if you have a cold, you won't be allowed to track them. Additionally, don't eat, drink, smoke, shout, point, use a camera flash or wear perfume anywhere near the chimps. Tracking is possible year-round, but during rainy season the mud makes the trails treacherous at both parks, and the chimps spend much of their time in trees.

enjoyable luxury camp with well-appointed safari tents that boast big four-poster beds, weathered storage chests and piping-hot showers, all hidden under the trees fringing a lovely beach. The centrepiece of the camp is the dhow-shaped dining area. The price includes daily chimp tracking and a boat safari.

Greystoke Mahale
LODGE $$$

(☑ 0787 595908; www.nomad-tanzania.com; s/d all-inclusive US$1885/2730; ☺ Jun-Mar) Situated on a beautiful sandy bay, this is a real Robinson-Crusoe-in-his-hippie-years kind of place where all the rooms are made of knocked-together, weathered, old ship timber. There's a gorgeous multilevel clifftop bar for the essential evening drinks and a tame pelican.

ⓘ Getting There & Away

There are many ways to reach Mahale, most either expensive or time-consuming. One of the best ways is on a five-day, six-night boat and camping safari organised by Lake Shore Lodge & Campsite (p276) in Kipili.

AIR

Zantas Air (☑ 0688 434343; www.zantasair. com) flies to Mahale twice weekly (assuming there are enough passengers to cover costs, normally four) on Mondays and Thursdays. Usually these are Mbali Mbali customers but nonguests are accepted to fill the plane. Flights may start from Arusha, Dar es Salaam or Zanzibar (via Dar). Flights sometimes also stop in Kigoma.

All flights stop at Katavi National Park (p277) en route, and thus the parks are frequently visited as a combination package. Expect to pay more than US$970 one way from Arusha, US$770 one way from Ruaha and US$450 to US$530 one way between Mahale and Katavi National Parks.

If you've booked with one of the lodges, a boat will meet your flight. Otherwise, arrange a boat in advance with park headquarters.

BOAT

Charter Boat

In Kigoma, Mbali Mbali (p267) charges about US$3500 return for a speedboat (four to five hours from Kigoma to Mahale).

Lake Taxi

Lake taxis head south from Ujiji to Kalilani (Tsh12,000), 2km north of park headquarters, on most days anytime from 5pm to 6pm (sometimes later). The trip often takes more than a day. Generally they depart from Kalilani around noon. Park staff know what's happening with the boats, so they can advise you on days and times.

One option to make the journey more bearable is to take a Saratoga bus from Kigoma to Sigunga (Tsh15,000, six to seven hours, 11am) and wait for the lake taxi there. Sigunga to Kalilani usually takes seven to eight hours. You could also have the park boat pick you up in Sigunga; it's two hours to headquarters. Sigunga has a basic guesthouse.

A couple of weekly boats head north from Kalema (Tsh25,000 or more) or nearby Ikola each evening for an even choppier journey than the one from Kigoma. It can take anywhere from 12 to 36 hours depending on the winds. They head south from Kalilani at around 3pm.

ⓘ MAHALE MOUNTAINS NATIONAL PARK

Why Go Up-close encounters with chimpanzees; stunning scenery with mountains rising up from the lakeshore.

When to Go Open year-round, but March to mid-May is too wet to enjoy it. June through October are the easiest (driest) months for hiking up the steep slopes.

Practicalities There are no roads to the park. Most visitors fly here, but a variety of boats, including the historic MV *Liemba* (p270), go from Kigoma, Kipili and other lakeshore towns. **Park headquarters** (www.tanzaniaparks.go.tz; ☺ 7am-6pm) are at Bilenge in the park's northwestern corner, about 10 minutes by boat south of the airstrip and 20 minutes north of Kasiha, site of the park *bandas* and guides' residences. Unless you have made other arrangements with one of the lodges, you will need to stop here to pay your park fees. Another park office, next to the airstrip and where fly-in guests can pay their entry fees, is open to coincide with flight arrivals.

Budget Tips By catching the MV *Liemba* ferry to Mahale, staying in the park *bandas* and self-catering you can have a cheap and fun chimpanzee experience. If your schedule doesn't match the *Liemba*'s you can also get there via lake taxis. Keep in mind that these are very slow, very uncomfortable and not all that safe.

TANZANIA'S CHIMPANZEES

Western Tanzania is the easternmost limit of chimpanzee habitat and their most famous residence due to the work of Jane Goodall. Hired in 1957 as Louis Leakey's secretary, Goodall had no formal scientific training, but Leakey was impressed by her detailed work habits in the field and love of animals. In 1960 he chose her to study wild chimp behaviour at Gombe Stream Chimpanzee Reserve, now Gombe National Park.

Her research was so groundbreaking that it redefined the relationship between humans and other animals. During her first year she was the first person to see chimps make and use tools (they stripped leaves off a stem and used these to fish termites out of their mounds) and hunt and eat meat. She also documented their elaborate social behaviour showing that they sometimes kill (and sometimes eat) each other, engage in long-term warfare, adopt orphans, form family bonds that last a lifetime and practise occasional monogamy. Goodall not only expanded our knowledge of primates, she revolutionised the entire field of ethology (animal behaviour). She gave the animals she observed names (David Greybeard, Mike, Frodo, Fifi etc) instead of numbers and insisted that they had personalities, minds and feelings. This seems logical to a layperson, but defied scientific convention. The research continues today, making it one of the longest-running studies of a wild animal population. Less famous, but also important, Toshisada Nishida of Kyoto University began research at Mahale the following year. That work also continues.

While *Pan troglodytes schweinfurthii* (Eastern chimpanzee), one of four chimp subspecies, was once common across western Tanzania, it's now endangered. Around 2800 remain, all along Lake Tanganyika and Rubondo Island where some were released in the 1960s and 1970s after being rescued from zoos and circuses. Many organisations are working to protect Tanzania's chimps, but three-quarters of them live outside protected areas. Also, loss of habitat (due to logging for wood and charcoal, and expanding farming) is accelerating.

Ferry

It's hard to beat the satisfyingly relaxing journey to Mahale via ferry. The **MV Liemba** (☑ 028-280 2811) stops at Lagosa (also called Mugambo) to the north of the park (1st/2nd/economy class US$40/35/30), about 10 hours from Kigoma. Under normal scheduling, it reaches Lagosa around 3am whether coming from the north (Thursday) or south (Sunday), but with the frequent delays, southern arrivals present a good chance of passing the park during daylight, which makes for a very beautiful trip. Services are on alternate weeks, but keep in mind the ferry is undergoing major restoration in 2017/18 and may be out of service for some time.

You can arrange in advance at the Gombe/Mahale Visitor Information Centre (p270) in Kigoma or through Mahale park headquarters (p274) for a park boat (holding eight people with luggage) to meet the *Liemba*. It's one hour from the MV *Liemba* to the *bandas,* including a stop to register and pay at Mahale's park headquarters, and costs US$192 return. Lagosa has a basic guesthouse where you can wait for the *Liemba* after leaving the park.

Tanapa Boat

With a bit of luck you can travel for free on the park boat. Park staff travel to Kigoma several times a month and if space is available they'll take passengers. This is usually only possible when leaving the park as on the return trip from Kigoma the boat carries supplies. The Gombe/Mahale Visitor Information Centre (p270) in Kigoma knows when boats are travelling.

ROAD

Saying you can get to Mahale by 'road' is a bit misleading, because there is no road and certainly no public transport – for the moment. However it is possible to get to Lagosa and the park airstrip by private 4WD (and it has to be a serious 4WD) from both Kigoma and Katavi National Park. The easier route is from Kigoma. A reasonable road runs from Kigoma to Sigunga, leading to a very bumpy track on to Lagosa. Allow six to seven hours for this journey. The route from Katavi is one of the roughest, slowest and most jarringly painful you can make in East Africa. Allow 10 to 12 hours. If you arrive in Lagosa after dark you'll have to overnight there. A jeep hired in either Kigoma or Katavi area will cost around US$300 with fuel per day (and remember it will take the driver a day to get back home again).

At the time of research, both routes were under construction. In the future, overland access might become easier and cheaper.

Kalema

📕 028 / POP 12,600

Kalema (Karema) is the first almost-major lakeshore centre south of Mahale Mountains. It's probably what Ujiji once was, back in the days of Livingstone: remote, quiet, calm and oddly captivating, if only for the remoteness and the beauty of its Tanganyika shore. Boys laze around, kids play with palm fronds, fishing boats rest haphazardly on the white sand.

It is a functioning Catholic mission station, originally established in 1885. Parts of the main compound – with brick arches that give it an Italian ambience – were originally a Belgian fort. The church built the following year is still in use, but it feels modern after extensive changes.

There are only a few simple ('simple' meaning no name, no telephone) guesthouses (Tsh8000 to Tsh10,000) in town. It's worth enquiring at the mission to see if it has rooms available. Buses connect Kalema with Mpanda (Tsh8000, four to five hours, one to two daily).

Kipili

POP 1500

Kipili, snoozing on the shores of Lake Tanganyika, is an old mission station. It is reached by a beautiful road through the Lafwe Game Reserve. The hilltop ruins of the 1880s church, 3km north of town, are very evocative and surrounded by dreamy lake views of the many islands just offshore. The islands have many rocky points, ideal for snorkelling with clouds of cichlids. The experience is akin to snorkelling in a coral reef in the Red Sea, only without the salt.

There are simple rooms with cold-water showers and meals at **St Bernard Kipili House** (📞0762 714375, 0786 213434; s/d without meals Tsh15,000/20,000; 🅿), just past the village along the lakeshore. However, most visitors come to experience the wonderful Lake Shore Lodge & Campsite.

⭐**Lake Shore Lodge & Campsite** LODGE $$
(📞0752 540792, 0684 540792, 0783 993166; www.lakeshoretz.com; camping US$14, banda s/d full board US$165/250, chalet s/d full board US$350/500; 🅿❄🛜🏊) 🏖 The universally praised Lake Shore Lodge & Campsite has beach chalets with a lovely open 'African Zen' design incorporating shells, sand, ropes, flowers and sun-bleached wood – it's an oasis of barefoot luxury. If this is outside your budget it also has garden *bandas,* which are a low-key version of the chalets, and camping with spotless bathrooms – something, indeed, for everyone.

There are enough activities to keep you busy for days: kayaking on the lake, quad biking, mountain biking, diving, snorkelling, village tours, island dinners, massages, yoga deck, jacuzzi and more. It's great to combine a trip to the lodge with a trip to Katavi and/or Mahale Mountains National Parks. Staff can take you to both using their own vehicles and boats. Best of all, the hosts are fantastic at making you feel right at home. You won't want to leave.

LAKE TANGANYIKA

Lake Tanganyika is the world's longest (660km), second-deepest (more than 1436m) and second-largest (by volume) freshwater lake. At somewhere between nine and 13 million years old, it's also one of the oldest. Thanks to its age and ecological isolation it's home to an exceptional number of endemic fish, including 98% of the 250-plus known species of cichlids. Cichlids are popular aquarium fish due to their bright colours, and they make Tanganyika an outstanding snorkelling and diving destination. Not all of the lake is bilharzia free, so it's best to check locally before diving in.

Kigoma is the only proper town, with the rest of the Tanzanian shoreline dotted by small, rarely visited settlements and a lovely ecolodge. Travelling here offers a fascinating look at local life. The rolling countryside around the villages is beautiful, and inviting for hiking.

Besides the services of the historic MV *Liemba,* lake taxis travel the shoreline at least every two or three days. Getting around can be difficult, and sometimes expensive, but with perseverance you can, eventually, get to all lakeside towns and villages overland by a mix of some of the world's most overcrowded buses and trucks, or along the lake via a variety of boats.

ℹ Getting There & Away

From Sumbawanga get a bus towards Kirando and get off at Katongolo (Tsh10,000, three to five hours, noon Monday to Saturday); arrive one hour early for the bus. Katongolo is 5km from Kipili. Next either walk, wait for a passing vehicle or ride on a motorbike (Tsh7000). Lake Shore Lodge can pick up its guests at Katongolo for US$5 per person (minimum US$10 per ride). From Mpanda go to Namanyere (Tsh15,000, four hours), where you can catch a passing vehicle heading to Kipili.

Kasanga

POP 800

The sprawling village of Kasanga is the MV *Liemba's* last (or first) stop in Tanzania, and the port is being upgraded to serve as an export-import hub for the DRC. The Germans founded it as Bismarckburg and the ruins of the old *boma* sit at the tip of the peninsula, 2km from the town, just behind the jetty (note that you can't visit or photograph it as it's now a military base). Kalambo Falls is within striking distance.

Atupenda Guest House (☑ 0764 044137; r Tsh10,000; P) has basic rooms with pit toilets and bucket baths.

Hekma Coach runs one bus per day between Sumbawanga and Kasanga (Tsh7000, five to six hours) via Matai, leaving each place at 6am and arriving at or before noon. The MV *Liemba* usually arrives from the north first thing on a Friday morning (every second week, if it's on schedule).

Mpanda

☑ 028 / POP 102,000

This small and somewhat scruffy town is a major transit point. Historically it was a significant trade hub and there are still many Arab businessmen living here.

🛏 Sleeping & Eating

Moravian Hostel GUESTHOUSE $
(☑ 0785 006944; s/tw without bathroom or breakfast Tsh7000/9000; P) Tucked behind the bright white Moravian church, this church-run place is friendly and good enough for the price, quieter than the competition (most other cheapies have attached bars) and convenient for early morning buses. The common bathrooms won't win any awards, but are functional.

Baraka Guesthouse GUESTHOUSE $
(☑ 025-282 0485; r Tsh25,000, with shared bathroom Tsh10,000; P) This quiet place west of the centre has tidy rooms with TV and occasional hot water. It's nothing special, but Mpanda being what it is, Baraka's rooms are up there with the best. The bright-blue gate is much easier to spot than the sign.

New Super City Hotel HOTEL $
(☑ 0764 370960; d & tw Tsh10,000-15,000; P) Some rooms here have sofas, all have wear and tear. Showers may or may not be hot, but there's a bar and in-house restaurant, and the staff are friendly. It's at the southern end of town heading to Sitalike. Breakfast costs Tsh5000.

ℹ Information

The post office has reliable internet and CRDB has an internationally linked ATM.

ℹ Getting There & Away

AIR

Auric Air (www.auricair.com) flies on Thursday afternoons to Mwanza.

BUS

Mpanda's bus station is east of the Sumbawanga road near the southern roundabout. Most companies have ticket offices near the half-built Moravian church in the town centre, and their buses actually start there before going to the station.

Sumry serves Sumbawanga (Tsh14,000, five to six hours, 6am, 8am and 2pm) via Sitalike (Tsh3000, 45 minutes). If you're going to Sitalike the company may try to charge you the full fare to Sumbawanga. Whether or not you pay the lower fare depends on the mood of the people in the ticket office.

NBS and Air Bus go to Tabora (Tsh23,000, eight hours, 6am).

Adventure goes to Kigoma (Tsh23,000, eight to 10 hours, 6am and 3pm) via Uvinza (Tsh20,000, four to five hours).

TRAIN

A branch of the Central Line connects Mpanda with Tabora (2nd/economy class Tsh21,200/11,100, 12 hours) via Kaliua at 3pm on Tuesdays and Sundays.

Katavi National Park

Katavi National Park (☑ 025-282 9213, 0689 062314; www.tanzaniaparks.go.tz; per day adult/child US$35.40/11.80; ⊙ 6am-6pm), 35km southwest of Mpanda, is Tanzania's third-largest national park (together with two contiguous game reserves the conservation area encompasses 12,500 sq km) and one of its most unspoiled wilderness areas. Though it's an isolated alternative to more popular destinations elsewhere in Tanzania (Serengeti National Park receives more visitors per day than Katavi does all year), the lodges are just as luxurious as anywhere else. For backpackers it's one of the cheapest and easiest parks to visit, if you're willing to take the time and effort to get there.

Katavi's dominant feature is the 425-sq-km **Katisunga Plain**, a vast grassy expanse at the heart of the park. This and other flood plains yield to vast tracts of brush and woodland (more southern African than eastern), which are the best areas for sighting roan and sable antelopes (together with Ruaha National Park, Katavi is one of the few places you have a decent chance of spotting both). Small rivers and large swamps that last all year support huge populations of hippos and crocodiles and Katavi has more than 400 bird species.

The park really comes to life in the dry season, when the flood plains dry up and elephants, lions, zebras, giraffes, elands, topis and many more gather at the remaining waters. Katavi stands out for its hippos – up to a thousand at a time gather in a single, muddy pool at the end of the dry season (late September to early October is the best time) – and its buffaloes. It has some of the largest remaining buffalo herds in Africa and it's not unusual to see over a thousand of these steroid-fuelled bovines at any one time.

🏃 Activities

Walking safaris with an armed ranger and bush camping (US$59 per person, plus a guided walking fee per group of US$23.60 for a short walk, US$29.50 for a long walk) are permitted throughout the park. This makes it a great park for budget travellers. The road to Lake Katavi, a seasonal flood plain, is a good walking route; it begins at the headquarters so a vehicle is not needed.

Some top-end camps no longer allow their guests to go on walking safaris. In part that's because your chance of seeing the park's variety of wildlife is greatly reduced. But there have been reports of some serious incidents involving under-trained park staff leading walking safaris resulting in injury to the tourists. This is also one of the most tsetse-fly-infested parks in Africa.

🛏️ Sleeping & Eating

Sleeping options run either top-end or budget here. You can stay in the ultra-luxury tented camps or the super-basic *bandas*. Both are good value for what they offer. Anyone staying in the park has to pay the camping fee, but this will be included in the overall package if staying at one of the top-end camps.

🛏️ In the Park

Besides bush camping, there are two public campsites (US$35.40): one at Ikuu near Katisunga Plain and the other 2km south of Sitalike. Both have a lot of wildlife passing through. Bring all your food and drink with you. All park lodges are located around the Katisunga Plain in the vicinity of the Ikuu Airstrip.

Katavi Park Bandas   BUNGALOW $

(☑ 025-282 9213; www.tanzaniaparks.go.tz; r per person US$35.40; ℗) This is 2km south of the village and within park boundaries (so you need to pay park entry fees when staying here). The rooms are big, bright and surprisingly good. Zebras, giraffes and other animals are frequent visitors.

★ Katavi Wildlife Camp   TENTED CAMP $$$

(Foxes; ☑ 0754 237422; www.kataviwildlifecamp.com; s/d all-inclusive except drinks US$685/1170; ☺ Jun-Feb; ℗) 🌿 This comfortable, well-run camp has a prime setting overlooking Katisunga making it the best place for in-camp wildlife watching. The six tents have large porches with hammocks and are down-to-earth comfortable without being over the top. The quality guides round out the experience. It's owned by Foxes African Safaris, which offers some excellent combination itineraries with southern parks.

Chada Katavi   TENTED CAMP $$$

(☑ 0787 595908; www.nomad-tanzania.com; s/d all-inclusive US$1260/1800; ☺ Jun-Jan; ℗) Set under big trees in a prime location overlooking the Chada flood plain, this place promotes a classic safari ambience. It's at its most Hemingway-esque in the dining tent. This is a good spot for walking safaris – it has excellent guides – and fly camping can be arranged with advance notice. The price includes a wildlife drive.

Katuma Bush Lodge   TENTED CAMP $$$

(☑ 0732 978879; www.mbalimbali.com; s/d all-inclusive except drinks US$767/1184; ☺ mid-May–

ⓘ KATAVI NATIONAL PARK

Why Go Outstanding dry-season wildlife watching. Rugged and remote wilderness ambience.

When to Go August through October is best for seeing large herds of wildlife. From February to May it's very wet, so getting around the park can be almost impossible and all the top-end camps close. It's a good time for birdwatching though.

Practicalities Drive in or bus from Mpanda or Sumbawanga; fly in from Ruaha National Park or Arusha. All park payments must be made with a credit card (no cash!) at the **park headquarters** (☑ 025-282 9213, 025-282 0213; katavi@tananiaparks.go.tz) located 1km south of Sitalike or the Ikuu Ranger Post near the main airstrip.

Budget Tips Katavi is one of the more budget-friendly parks. By taking a bus to Sitalike, staying in one of the cheap options there and then setting out on a walking safari you can see Katavi cheaply, though walking safaris often don't see much wildlife. You can also camp in the park.

mid-Feb; ℗ 🛜 🏊) With stunning views over the grasslands, the large safari tents here have four-poster beds, carved wooden showers and plenty of privacy. The defining feature is the relaxing lounge fronted by a deck with a small swimming pool. The price includes a wildlife drive.

🛏 Sitalike

Most backpackers stay at this little village on the northern edge of the park. You can get basic groceries here and there are a couple of local-style eateries.

Riverside Camp   BUNGALOW, CAMPGROUND $
(☑ 0767 754740, 0784 754740, 0785 860981; camping US$10, s/d US$25/50; ℗) Riverside Camp has a prime setting just above a hippo-filled river. The *bandas* are simple, but the location is worth it. Mr Juma, the owner, is very helpful with arranging vehicle rental for a Katavi safari. Meals can be arranged (dinner/breakfast per person US$10/5). Vervet monkeys and a host of birds are easy to see here.

Katavi Hippo Garden Resort   BUNGALOW $
(☑ 0784 405423; camping US$10, bungalow per person US$30; ℗) These no-frills rooms have a good setting on a green lawn sloping down to a hippo-filled river. Check first to be sure the showers and lights are working. Flora the owner speaks English.

Kitanewa Guesthouse   GUESTHOUSE $
(☑ 0767 837132; d Tsh15,000; ℗) This fair-value spot by the bus-truck stop has adequate concrete-cube rooms with bucket showers and squat toilets. It only has electricity at night for the first few hours.

ⓘ Getting There & Away

Safari Airlink (☑ 0783 397235, 0777 723274; www.flysal.com; Julius Nyerere International Airport, Dar es Salaam, Terminal 1) and Zantas Air (www.zantasair.com) fly twice a week to Ikuu Airstrip and the lodges will often let nonguests fly on their planes if space is available. All lodges provide free pick-up at Ikuu Airstrip for their guests. If you aren't staying at a lodge, arrange a vehicle or a ranger for walking *before* you arrive. If you are flying in, it is good to combine a trip to Katavi with a trip to Mahale Mountains National Park. Rangers will be waiting at the airstrip to collect park admission fees from those flying in.

Buses and trucks between Mpanda (Tsh3000, 45 minutes) and Sumbawanga (Tsh15,000, four hours) can pick you up and drop you off in Sitalike or at park headquarters. Transport is frequent in the mornings, but after lunch you may have to wait several hours for a vehicle to pass.

Dalla-dallas and taxis depart Sitalike for Mpanda (Tsh3000, 45 minutes) from 7am to 8pm once they have enough people to make it worth the ride. You can hire one directly for Tsh90,000 if there's an emergency.

If you're driving, the only petrol stations are in Mpanda and Sumbawanga.

Vehicle safaris including transport to Katavi and a safari inside the park can be arranged with Riverside Camp in Sitalike and Lake Shore Lodge & Campsite (p276) in Kipili.

ⓘ Getting Around

The park no longer hires vehicles but Riverside Camp in Sitalike charges US$200 per day for a 4WD, some with a pop-up roof. A guide or driver (US$20) is highly recommended, both for safety and to make the most of your viewing experience.

Sumbawanga

☎ 025 / POP 210,000

Sumbawanga is small and scruffy and not much of a tourist destination in itself, but it provides a great hub for beautiful day trips and overnights around the region, so it's well worth spending a couple of days here. It's large enough to have a solid variety of hotels, restaurants and shops, and is the last stocking-up spot for those headed north to Katavi National Park.

The surrounding Ufipa Plateau, which lies at an invigorating 2000m, is home to many important endemic plants. It has also been declared an 'Important Bird Area' by BirdLife International. The **Mbizi Forest Reserve** (US$10), a couple of hours' walk from Sumbawanga, is a closer place to meet feathered friends.

Also nearby is the shallow **Lake Rukwa**, a birding paradise, which is accessed from many villages near its meandering shoreline. Ilanga, served by frequent 4WDs (Tsh5000, two hours) throughout the day, provides the easiest access.

Charles at **Rukaki Adventure Tours and Safaris** (☎ 0784 704343; Mbeya Rd; walking tours US$10, hiking US$20, Kalambo Falls Tsh20,000 plus US$20; ☺ 7am-10pm) can help you organise excursions to these and other destinations in the region, and can also assist with arranging safaris to Katavi National Park.

🛏 Sleeping & Eating

There are many unexciting but adequate budget guesthouses in the lively neighbourhood around the bus station. About 2.5km away from here, uphill from the easy-to-find TRA office at the southeastern end of town, are a few quieter options.

Kalambo Falls Lodge
HOTEL $

(☎ 0757 381400, 0754 931336; Katandala St; r Tsh70,000-120,000; 🅿 🛜) Kalambo Falls Lodge has spacious rooms with large tubs, fridges and in-room wi-fi. It's also got a professional chef and a full bar, making an all-in-one stop if you're staying overnight in Sumbawanga. An additional plus is that it's a fair way from the noisy town centre.

Libori Centre
HOTEL $

(☎ 0744 396910, 0769 204443; Msakila St; r Tsh15,000-25,000; 🅿) This church-run place has rooms that are essentially clean, and very quiet and secure. Besides the addition

of a chair, we couldn't see any discernible difference between the cheapest and most expensive rooms. A very basic breakfast is included. It's close to the bus station. Look for the radio tower on top of the building.

Ikuwo Lodge
HOTEL $

(☎ 025-280 2393, 0754 647479; Mazwi Rd; r Tsh30,000-40,000) If all you want is a place to crash in the centre of the market district, then this aquarium-blue, all-glass block will do nicely. There are instant hot showers and plenty of street noise. The rooms have fridges and include bottled water. No English is spoken, though.

Moravian Church Conference Centre Hotel
HOTEL $

(☎ 025-280 2853; Nyerere Rd; r Tsh35,000-45,000, s/d without bathroom or breakfast Tsh15,000/25,000; 🅿 @ 🛜 ✉) A beautiful trumpet vine colours the outer walls here. Rooms are spare but pleasant and spacious (it's worth the extra Tsh10,000 for a larger one), and African art and bright paint liven up the rest of this concrete compound about 1km southeast of the bus station.

Forestway Country Club
HOTEL $

(☎ 025-280 2746, 0785 902940, 0764 966215; Nyerere Rd; s/d Tsh30,000/48,000; 🅿) The rooms could use some new paint, but are quite cosy overall, and the restaurant, one of the town's nicer places to dine, is a bonus. It's in a quiet, nondescript neighbourhood on the southeastern end of town, reached by heading uphill from NBC bank.

ℹ Information

There are some internet cafes on Fisi St, including **Dot.com** (☎ 0762 898373; Fisi St; per hour Tsh1000; ☺ 7.30am-9.30pm Mon-Sat, 11am-9.30pm Sun).

You'll find a couple of banks and 24-hour ATMs on the main road.

ℹ Getting There & Away

Numerous bus companies operate out of Sumbawanga and most ticket offices are located just outside the bus stand. Most buses depart between 7am and 9.30am. Buses go to:

Mbeya (Tsh15,000 to Tsh20,000, seven hours) via Tunduma (Tsh10,000)

Mpanda (Tsh14,000, four to six hours)

Kasesya (Tsh 6000, four to five hours)

To get to Kasesya on the Zambian border there's also a dalla-dalla (Tsh3000, four to five hours) at 8am and 4pm.

Southern Highlands

Why Go?

Tanzania's Southern Highlands officially begin at Makambako Gap, about halfway between Iringa and Mbeya, and extend southwards into Malawi. Here, the term encompasses the entire region along the mountainous chain running between Morogoro in the east and Lake Nyasa and the Zambian border in the west.

The highlands are a major transit route for travellers to Malawi or Zambia, and an important agricultural area. They are also wonderfully scenic and a delight to explore, with rolling hills, lively markets, jacaranda-lined streets, lovely lodges and plenty of wildlife. Hike in the Udzungwa Mountains, watch wildlife in Mikumi or Ruaha National Parks, get to know the matrilineal Luguru people in the Uluguru Mountains, or head well off the beaten track to the heart of the Southern Highlands in Tanzania's southwesternmost corner. Here, wild orchids carpet sections of Kitulo National Park and verdant mountains cascade down to the idyllic shores of Lake Nyasa.

Best Places to Stay

➡ Camp Bastian Mikumi (p287)

➡ Kisolanza – The Old Farm House (p296)

➡ Blue Canoe Safari Camp (p310)

Best Places to Eat

➡ Neema Crafts Centre Cafe (p294)

➡ Mufindi Highlands Lodge (p296)

➡ Maua Café & Tours (p305)

When to Go
Mbeya

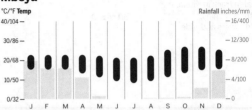

Jul–Sep Ruaha National Park is at its best, with 'sand rivers' and elephants.

Oct–Nov Jacarandas everywhere; wonderful wildlife viewing and hiking.

Dec–Mar Kitulo National Park's flower display is in full bloom; peak birding season in Ruaha.

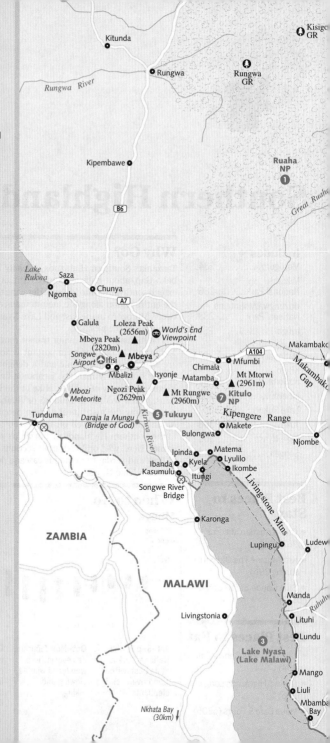

Southern Highlands Highlights

1 **Ruaha National Park** (p297) Spotting elephants amid the baobabs in this wild and rugged park.

2 **Mikumi National Park** (p286) Tracking snorting wildebeest, grazing buffaloes and skittish impalas in this lovely and easy-to-access spot.

3 **Lake Nyasa** (p309) Relaxing on the tranquil shores, where verdant mountains cascade down to quiet coves.

4 **Iringa** (p291) Getting acquainted with local life in and around this colourful and bustling city.

5 **Tukuyu** (p308) Enjoying lush rolling hill panoramas dotted with orchards and stands of bananas around tiny Tukuyu.

6 **Udzungwa Mountains National Park** (p288) Hiking past waterfalls and spotting birds and monkeys.

7 **Kitulo National Park** (p302) Exploring off the beaten track in Kitulo, with its orchids, wildflowers and wide vistas.

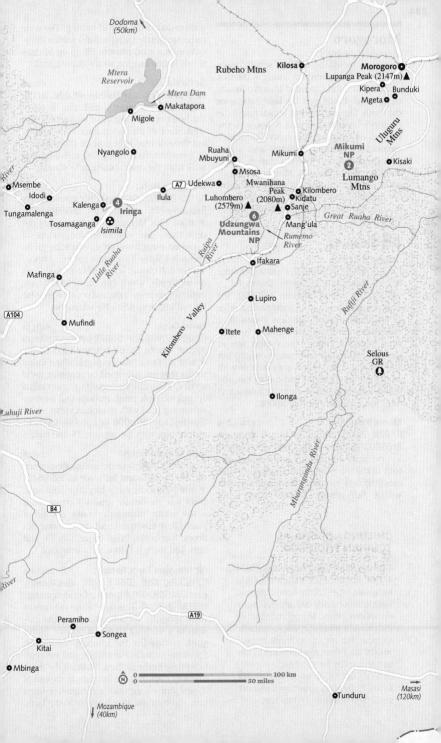

Morogoro

📞 223 / POP 315,000

Morogoro would be a fairly scruffy town were it not for its verdant setting at the foot of the often cloud-shrouded Uluguru Mountains, which brood over the landscape from the south. The surrounding area is one of the country's breadbaskets and is home to the prestigious Sokoine University (Tanzania's national agricultural institute) and a major educational and mission station. While there are few attractions, Morogoro offers a good and warm introduction to Tanzanian life outside Dar es Salaam, plus the chance for cultural tours and hikes in the nearby Ulugurus.

🛏 Sleeping

Amabilis Centre   HOSTEL $
(📞 0719 348959, 0716 880717; amabilis.conference centre@yahoo.com; Old Dar es Salaam Rd; s Tsh25,000, tw without bathroom Tsh20,000; P) This church place on the northeastern edge of town offers small, spotless rooms in a multistorey building surrounded by gardens; kindly Catholic sisters meet you at the gate. All rooms have fan, mosquito net and hot water, and meals are available with advance order. Dalla-dallas heading towards Bigwa will drop you in front, or take a taxi from Msamvu bus stand (Tsh6000).

Mama Pierina's   GUESTHOUSE $
(📞 0786 786913; Station St; tw with fan/air-con Tsh35,000/45,000; P❄) A warm welcome and a convenient central location: rooms to the back of the compound have four-poster-style mosquito nets, mountain views and a garden setting. Self-catering facilities were being

---

CHILUNGA CULTURAL TOURISM PROGRAM

Chilunga Cultural Tourism (📞 0754 477582, 023-261 3323; www.chilunga.or.tz; Rwegasore Rd; ⊙7.30am-6pm) organises flexible, tailor-made day and overnight excursions around Morogoro, including village visits, hikes and Mikumi safaris. Its programs are a good introduction to local life. Prices run from US$25 per person per day for short excursions up to about US$75 per person per day for multiday hikes, including transport, guide, and village and forest fees.

---

constructed at the time of writing. The wide restaurant terrace, wrapped in a golden shower vine, is a good place to fill up on Mama's Greek/Italian lasagne, moussaka or tzatziki.

Sofia Hotel   HOTEL $
(📞 0754 996664; John Mahenge Rd; d Tsh35,000-45,000; ❄🛜) A cheerful and basic hotel in the heart of town, with hot water, fans and wi-fi. Some of the rooms have no windows, but these do tend to be quieter. It's one block in from the main road, and a five-minute walk from the central dalla-dalla stand.

Morogoro Hotel   HOTEL $$
(📞 023-261 3270/1/2; www.morogorohotel.com; Rwegasore Rd; s/d/ste from US$59/84/183; P❄🏊) This Morogoro institution has decent twin- and double-bedded rooms in detached bungalows set in spacious green grounds 1.5km off the main road and opposite the golf course. It's popular for weddings on weekends, which can mean loud music until late. Its restaurant and pool are popular for whiling away a Sunday afternoon.

Hotel Oasis   HOTEL $$
(📞 0754 377602, 023-261 4178; hoteloasistz@moro goro.net; Station St; s/d/tr from US$50/60/80; P❄🛜🏊) Oasis has acceptable albeit faded rooms that are redeemed by generally good service, a decent restaurant, a convenient central location, small gardens and a pretty swimming pool with mountain views and a thatched bar (Tsh5000 for hotel visitors). All rooms come with fan, air-con, TV and fridge.

New Acropol Hotel   B&B $$
(📞 0754 309410; newacropolhotel@morogoro. net; Old Dar es Salaam Rd; s/d/tr US$55/65/75; P❄🛜) This enjoyably eccentric B&B-style hotel has six mostly spacious rooms in a 1940s estate manager's house around a plant-filled courtyard. All have terracotta floors, four-poster beds, fridge, fan, TV and nets, and there is a good restaurant-bar.

★ Mbuyuni Farm Retreat   B&B $$$
(📞 023-260 1220, 0784 601220; www.kimango. com; s/d US$90/180, 4-person self-catering cottage US$130; P🏊) 🍃 This quiet place consists of three spacious, elegant cottages in the gardens of a working farm just outside Morogoro, overlooking the Uluguru Mountains. Excellent meals are available, and two cottages have kitchens. Turn north off the main highway 12km east of Morogoro at the end of Kingolwira village onto a mango-tree-lined lane and continue over a bridge to the farm.

Morogoro

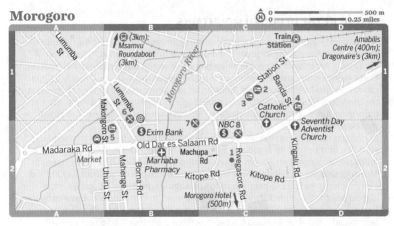

🍴 Eating & Drinking

Red Chilli Restaurant INDIAN, CHINESE $

(New Green Restaurant; ☏0784 498874; Station St; mains Tsh7000-10,000; ⊙9am-11pm; 🅟) This long-standing place features functional decor but great grub. The menu has a large selection of Indian dishes, plus Chinese options and grilled chicken or fish and chips.

Ricky's Café CAFE $

(Old Dar es Salaam Rd; snacks from Tsh5000; ⊙8am-4pm Mon-Sat) A great, simple lunchtime option in the heart of town opposite the Rwegasore Rd turn-off. It dishes up salads, soup, fried chicken, fish curry, cakes and shakes, which you can enjoy at red-painted tables on the palm-edged terrace.

Dragonaire's CHINESE, INTERNATIONAL $$

(☏0713 622262; mains from Tsh6000; ⊙3pm-midnight Tue-Sun; 🅟🛜) Green grounds, a small children's play area, sports TV, pizzas on weekends and huge portions make this a popular choice. The rest of the menu covers Chinese dishes, seafood and beef, with some vegetarian choices; allow plenty of time for orders. It's 3km east of town, signposted about 700m off the Old Dar es Salaam Rd.

Salon at Acropol VEGETARIAN $$

(☏0754 309410; Old Dar es Salaam Rd; mains from Tsh9000; ⊙7am-10pm; 🅟🛜) The Acropol has tasty soups, sandwiches, fish and meat platters, some vegetarian options, all-day breakfasts featuring steak, eggs and chips, and good local coffee. Sit on the covered porch or in the darkly atmospheric and well-stocked bar, which overflows with safari memorabilia and heavy, wooden furniture.

Rock Garden BAR

(☏0715 953 234; Boma Rd; ⊙9am-late) A simple open-air bar serving curry and beer, Rock Garden enjoys a gorgeous rocky setting with a stream running by. On weekends it's packed and is a great place to sink a drink, hear some live bands and see traditional dance. Located 4km from the centre of town – head down Rwegasore Rd and you'll get there.

Self-Catering

Pira's Supermarket SUPERMARKET $

(Lumumba St; ⊙10am-6pm) For self-catering, try this well-stocked supermarket.

ℹ Information

Exim Bank (Lumumba St; ⊙9am-5pm Mon-Fri) ATM.

Internet Cafe (off Lumumba St; per hour Tsh2000; ⊙8am-10pm Sun-Fri, 7am-10pm Sat)

HIKING IN THE ULUGURU MOUNTAINS

The verdant Uluguru Mountains – home to the matrilineal Luguru people – rise up majestically from the plains just south of Morogoro, dominating vistas from town. Part of the Eastern Arc chain, the mountains are home to a wealth of birds, plants and insects. These include many unique species, such as the Uluguru bush shrike. The only comparable mountain-forest area in East Africa, as far as age and endemism are concerned, is the Usambara Mountains. Sadly, due to the Uluguru's high population density, most of the original forest cover has been depleted, although small protected patches remain on the upper slopes.

Hiking is the best way to explore and to get acquainted with the life of the local Luguru. The best contact for organising things is the excellent Chilunga Cultural Tourism (p284) in Morogoro town. Routes include a half-day return hike (US$27 per person) to **Morningside**, an old German mountain hut to the south of town at about 1000m; and a day's return hike (US$45 per person) to **Lupanga Peak** (2147m). Lupanga is the highest point in the immediate vicinity, although views from the top are obscured by the forest. A recommended cultural walk is to **Choma** village, about an hour's walk beyond Morningside, and often included in a two-day, three-night tour (US$85 per person).

Mikumi Eco & Cultural Tourism Enterprise (☏ 0784 218113; ecofootprintltd@gmail.com; ⊘ 8am-6pm Mon-Sat) Ask for Pira's Supermarket; this tiny internet cafe is just around the corner.

Marhaba Pharmacy (☏ 023-261 3304; Old Dar es Salaam Rd; ⊘ 7.30am-5pm Mon-Sat) Morogoro's best-stocked pharmacy is just east of the dalla-dalla stand and just west of the small footbridge.

NBC (Old Dar es Salaam Rd; ⊘ 9am-5pm Mon-Fri) ATM.

ⓘ Getting There & Away

AIR

Due to increasing road congestion getting out of Dar es Salaam, the five weekly flights to/from Morogoro (US$160 one-way) by **Auric Air** (www.auricair.com) are an increasingly attractive alternative to the bus for travellers in a hurry.

BUS

The main **bus station** is 3km north of town on the main Dar es Salaam road, about 300m east of Msamvu roundabout (Tsh6000 in a taxi and Tsh400 in a dalla-dalla; look for vehicles marked 'Kihonda', and confirm that they are going to Msamvu). It's chaotic, with no real order to things; you'll need to ask where to find buses to your destination. Allow at least an hour to catch a dalla-dalla and get yourself sorted at Msamvu.

For all destinations, no larger buses originate in Morogoro. It's best to wait for buses from Dar es Salaam (Tsh7000 to Tsh8000, four hours) or Iringa (Tsh14,000 to Tsh15000, three to four hours), both of which begin passing Morogoro from about 9am. To Tanga, there's a direct bus (Tsh7000, five hours, daily) departing by 8am. Buses also go from Dar via Morogoro to Dodoma

(Tsh14,000 to Tsh17,000, four hours). For Kisaki (the closest village to Selous Game Reserve's Matambwe Gate), buses go at least once daily from Msamvu (Tsh9000, five to six hours), departing between 9am and 11am.

The main **dalla-dalla stand** is in front of the market, where there is also a taxi rank.

TRAIN

Morogoro is on the Central Line (p70), which links Dar es Salaam with Kigoma. The once-patchy service is being upgraded, and there's now a deluxe service once a week.

Mikumi National Park

This is Tanzania's fourth-largest national park, with a landscape of baobabs, black hardwood trees and grassy plains, and the most accessible from Dar es Salaam. With almost guaranteed year-round wildlife sightings, **Mikumi** (www.tanzaniaparks.go.tz; adult/child US$35.40/11.80) makes an ideal safari destination for those without much time. Within its 3230 sq km – set between the Uluguru Mountains to the northeast, the Rubeho Mountains to the northwest and the Lumango Mountains to the southeast – Mikumi hosts buffaloes, wildebeest, giraffes, elephants, lions, zebras, leopards, crocodiles and endangered wild dogs, and chances are high that you'll see a respectable sampling of these within a short time of entering the park.

Mikumi is an important educational and research centre. Among the various projects being carried out is an ongoing field study of yellow baboons, which is one of just a handful of such long-term primate studies on the continent.

To the south, Mikumi is contiguous with Selous Game Reserve.

 Activities

The most reliable wildlife watching is around the Mkata floodplain, to the northwest of the main road, with the open vistas of the small but lovely Millennium ('Little Serengeti') area a highlight. This area is especially good for spotting buffaloes – often quite near the roadside – as well as giraffes, elephants and zebras. Another attraction: the Hippo Pools, just northwest of the main entry gate, where you can watch hippos wallowing and snorting at close range, plus do some fine birding.

Throughout the park there are wonderful birding opportunities: look out for marabou storks and malachite kingfishers.

🛏️ Sleeping & Eating

Of the park's four **ordinary campsites** (☑ 0767 536135, 0689 062334; mikumi@tanzania parks.go.tz; camping adult/child US$35.40/5.90), the one closest to park headquarters is reasonably well-equipped with toilet facilities and a shower. There is also a **special campsite** (☑ 0689 062334, 0767 536135; mikumi@tanzania parks.go.tz; camping adult/child US$59/11.80) near Choga Wale in the north of the park. For all camping, be careful eating and storing food, due to the presence of yellow baboons.

★**Camp Bastian Mikumi**   LODGE $$
(☑ 0718 244 507, 0782 547 448; www.campbastian. com; b&b s from US$40, d US$60-150, camping US$10-15; 🛜) 🍴 Located 10km west of the main gate, Camp Bastian is a harmoniously beautiful and good-value choice, with quality food and good drivers/guides on hand. There are six stone-floored cottages with wide verandas, decorated with local fabric and furniture, as well as a campsite. There are options for half or full board too, also available to campers.

Mikumi Park
Cottages & Resthouse   COTTAGE $$
(☑ 0689 062334, 0767 536135; mikumi@tanzania-parks.go.tz; s/d/tr US$59/88.50/106.20; P❄️) About 3km from the gate, the park cottages and resthouse offer rooms in attached brick bungalows, all with bathroom, fan and aircon, and meals on order (Tsh10,000 per plate) at the nearby dining hall. The resthouse, which consists of two double rooms sharing an entrance, also has a kitchen

(bring your own gas). Animals frequently wander just in front.

Vuma Hills   TENTED CAMP $$$
(☑ 0754 237422; www.vumahills.com; s/d incl full board & wildlife drives from US$365/570; P🏊) This pleasant camp is set on a rise about 7km south of the main road, with views over the distant plains. The 16 elegant tented en-suite cottages each have a double and a single bed. The mood is relaxed, the cuisine good and the pool makes a nice post-safari treat. The turn-off is diagonally opposite the park entry gate.

Mikumi Wildlife Camp   LODGE $$$
(Kikoboga, ☑ 0684 886306, 022-260 0252/3/4; www.mikumiwildlifecamp.com; s/d half board US$230/390; P🏊) This camp, about 500m northeast of the park gate, has attractive stone cottages with shaded verandas and views over a grassy field frequented by grazing zebras and impalas. Given its proximity to the highway, it's not a wilderness experience, but the animals don't seem to mind and you'll probably see plenty from your porch. Vehicle rental possible with advance notice.

ℹ️ **MIKUMI NATIONAL PARK**

Why Go Easy access from Dar es Salaam; rewarding year-round wildlife watching and birding; giraffes, zebras, buffaloes, wild dogs and sometimes honey badgers.

When to Go Year-round.

Practicalities Drive or bus from Dar es Salaam. Entry fees (valid for 24 hours, single entry only) are payable only with Visa or MasterCard. Driving hours inside the park (off the main highway) are 6.30am to 6.30pm.

Budget Tips Any bus along the highway will drop you at the gate. The park doesn't hire vehicles, but staff sometimes rent their own. Arrange at the gate and be prepared to bargain. For sleeping, the park cottages are cheap and pleasant, with a dining room for meals. Post-safari: flag down an Iringa- or Dar-bound bus to continue your travels.

More reliable: hire a safari vehicle through one of the hotels listed under Mikumi town (about US$200 per five-person vehicle for a full-day safari); bring your own lunch and drinks.

❶ Getting There & Away

BUS

All through buses on the Dar–Mbeya highway will drop you at the park gate. Pick-ups can also be arranged from here to continue your onward journey. While vehicle rental can sometimes be arranged privately with park staff, it's better to arrive with your own vehicle or hire one through a Mikumi town hotel.

CAR

The park gate is about a five-hour drive from Dar es Salaam; speed limits on the section of main highway inside the park are controlled (70km/h during the day and 50km/h at night). A network of generally well-maintained roads in the park's northern section are accessible with a 2WD during most of the year; the south is strictly 4WD, except the road to Vuma Hills Tented Camp.

For combining Mikumi with Selous, the 145km road linking Mikumi's main gate with Kisaki village (21km west of Selous' Matambwe Gate) is now open year-round except during the heavy rains, and makes a scenic 4WD alternative; allow about five hours between the two. Alternatively, you can go via Morogoro (140km and five to six hours between Morogoro and Kisaki).

Mikumi Town

📞 223 / POP 18,000

Mikumi is the last of the lowland towns along the Dar es Salaam–Mbeya highway before it starts its climb through the Ruaha River gorge up into the hills of the Southern Highlands. Stretched out along a few kilometres of highway, it has an unmistakable truck-stop feel. It is of interest almost exclusively as a transit point for visits to the Mikumi or Udzungwa Mountains National Parks, although it's quite possible to visit both without overnighting here. If you do find yourself here for longer, there are good excursions with the local cultural tourism program.

🛏 Sleeping & Eating

Tan-Swiss Hotel & Restaurant   LODGE $$
(📞 0787 191827, 0755 191827; www.tan-swiss.com; Main Rd; camping US$10, s/d/tr US$70/80/100, f bungalow from US$110; 🅿️✳️🛜🏊) This place makes a good stop, with a camping area with hot-water showers, plus spacious grounds, comfortable rooms with private bathroom, and several double and family bungalows, some with small terraces. All are tidy, with fans and surrounding greenery. It has a large, spotless pool and a good

restaurant-bar, also selling takeaway sandwiches. Vehicle rental to Udzungwa/Mikumi parks costs US$150/260 per day.

It's about 2km east of the junction with the road to Udzungwa Mountains National Park.

Genesis Motel   GUESTHOUSE $$
(📞 0653 692127, 0716 757707; udzungwamountain viewhotel@yahoo.com; camping US$5, r per person with/without air-con US$40/30; 🅿️✳️) The functional Genesis, on the highway 2.5km east of the Ifakara junction, has small, closely spaced rooms (ask for a newer one), a restaurant and an attached snake park (admission US$5). One room has air-con. There's also a small, walled-in camping area with hot-water showers and nearby kitchen. Vehicle rental costs US$150/180 per day for Udzungwa/Mikumi parks; advance notice is required.

Angalia Tented Camp   TENTED CAMP $$$
(📞 0652 999019, 0787 518911; www.angaliacamp. com; Main Rd; s/d/tr full board US$180/300/425; 🅿️) Angalia Camp is about 1.5km off the main road, just west of the Mikumi National Park boundary, en route towards Mikumi town. It has five large safari-style tents set in a patch of forest, alongside a terrific restaurant and bar. It makes a reasonably priced alternative to the park-based lodges.

❶ Getting There & Away

Mikumi's bus stand is at the western end of town on the main highway. Minibuses go frequently towards Udzungwa Mountains National Park, but you'll need to change vehicles at Kilombero. It's better to wait for one of the larger Dar to Ifakara buses, which begin passing Mikumi about 11am, going directly to Udzungwa's Mang'ula headquarters (Tsh7000, two hours) and on to Ifakara (Tsh15,000, 3½ hours).

Going west, buses from Dar es Salaam begin passing Mikumi en route to Iringa (Tsh9000, three hours) from about 9.30am. There's also a direct bus from Kilombero to Iringa, passing Mikumi about 5.30am. Going east, there are large buses to Dar es Salaam (about Tsh15,000, five hours) departing at 6.30am and 7.30am.

Udzungwa Mountains National Park

Towering over the Kilombero Plains 350km southwest of Dar es Salaam are the wild, lushly forested slopes of the Udzungwa Mountains, portions of which are protected as part of the 1900-sq-km **Udzungwa Mountains National Park** (www.tanzaniaparks.go.tz; adult/child US$35.40/11.80) – an intriguingly offbeat destination for anyone botanically inclined or interested in remote hiking. In addition to unique plants, the park has an important population of primates (10 species – more than any of Tanzania's other parks) as well as the grey-faced sengi (a species of elephant shrew). There are also elephants, buffaloes, leopards, hippos and crocodiles, although these – particularly hippos and crocodiles – are primarily in the park's southwest and seldom seen.

Birding is excellent, especially on the surrounding Kilombero floodplains. A good place to start is the wetlands bordering the main road about 2km north of Mang'ula town, below Hondo Hondo (p290) camp. Behind here, at the forest's edge, colobus and other primates are frequently spotted.

🏃 Activities

There are no roads in Udzungwa; instead, there are about eight major and several lesser hiking trails winding through various sections of the park. Most trails are on the eastern side of the park, although several are now open in the west as well, including some shorter day trails in the baobab-studded northwestern corner of the park around Msosa Ranger Post. Bring a water filter for longer hikes.

The going can be tough in parts: the trail network is limited and those trails that do exist are often muddy, steep, humid and densely overgrown. Infrastructure is rudimentary and you'll need to have your own tent and do your hiking accompanied by a guide (US$23.60 per group per day). In wildlife areas you'll also need to be accompanied by an armed ranger (US$23.60 per group per day). Porter fees range between Tsh5000 and Tsh15,000 per day, depending on the trail.

But the night-time symphony of forest insects, the rushing of streams and waterfalls and the views down over the plains more than compensate for the logistical challenges. Plus, because the Udzungwas are well off the main road, relatively few travellers come this way and you'll often have trails to yourself.

For supplies there's a tiny market in Mang'ula near the train station, and another small one in town to the north of the station, both with limited selections. Stock up on major items in Dar es Salaam or Morogoro. For longer hikes, bring a supply of dried fruit and nuts to supplement the bland locally available offerings. You can find bottled water near the markets (bring a water filter for longer hikes).

Sanje Falls   HIKING
The most popular route is a short (three to five hours), steep circuit from Sanje village, 10km north of Mang'ula, through the forest to the wonderful 170m Sanje Falls, where swimming and camping are possible. The park charges a steep US$23.60 one-way for transfers between Mang'ula and the Sanje Falls trailhead.

Mwanihana Peak   HIKING
Very satisfying, and a good introduction to the Udzungwas, is the three-day, two-night (or two long days if you're fit) hike up to Mwanihana Peak (2080m), the park's second-highest point.

Luhombero Peak   HIKING
This challenging six-day trail goes from Udekwa (on the park's western side) to Luhombero Peak (2579m), the highest point in the Udzungwas. The trail should be booked well in advance to ensure it is cleared.

It is closed during the March through May rainy season.

Lumemo (Rumemo) Trail   HIKING
A five-day trail from Mang'ula along the Rumemo River to Rumemo Ranger Post, which is connected by a dirt track to Ifakara, about 25km further south.

🛏 Sleeping & Eating

There are three rudimentary campsites near park headquarters, as well as several other

---

UDZUNGWA MOUNTAINS BIODIVERSITY

The Udzungwas' high degree of endemism and biodiversity is due, in large part, to the area's constant climate over millions of years, which has given species a chance to evolve. Another factor is the Udzungwas' altitudinal range. From the low-lying Kilombero Valley south of the park (at approximately 200m) to Luhombero Peak (the park's highest point at 2579m), there is continuous forest, making this one of the few places in Africa with uninterrupted rainforest over such a great span.

ℹ️ UDZUNGWA MOUNTAINS NATIONAL PARK

Why Go Rugged hiking; 10 species of primates (including red colobus and mangabeys); waterfalls; endemic plants; newly discovered bird species, including the Udzungwa forest partridge.

When to Go Late June through January; avoid the March through May rainy season as many trails are not cleared (and hence not hikeable).

Practicalities Drive or bus from the Tanzam Hwy to Mang'ula town or take the ordinary train from Dar es Salaam to Mang'ula. Bring in all equipment (including trail snacks and waterproof gear). For now, park fees must be paid at Mang'ula headquarters (currently cash only) unless you make advance arrangements with headquarters for fees to be processed elsewhere.

Budget Tips You'll pay entry and guide fees per 24 hours, whether you take a short stroll or an eight-hour hike. It's best to arrive in Mang'ula, use the afternoon to plan, then set out early the next morning for a full day of hiking. The Udzungwa day trips offered by Mikumi town hotels aren't worth it.

One overnight or multi-night hike in the park is probably enough. Save on fees and spend the rest of your stay exploring the surrounding area. Activities outside park boundaries include village cycling from Hondo Hondo or hiking from Msosa Campsite (p291) or Crocodile Camp.

(similarly priced) campsites along the longer trails, and a couple of basic but decent hotels.

🛏️ Eastern Udzungwas

Udzungwa Mountains Park Headquarters Campsite CAMPGROUND $
(☑️0689 062291, 0767 536131; udzungwa@tanzaniaparks.com; camping US$35.40) The park has three rudimentary campsites near headquarters, one with a shower and the others near a stream. However, visitors rarely stay at them as prices are high for only the most basic facilities. Bring all supplies. There are also several other similarly priced park-run campsites along the longer trails.

Udzungwa Twiga Hotel HOTEL $$
(☑️023-262 0223/4; udzungwatwiga@gmail.com; s/d/tr US$45/65/85; 🅿️❄️) The Tanapa-run Twiga is set in expansive green grounds under the mountains and surrounded by forest, about 700m east of park headquarters. Rooms – overlooking a small courtyard garden – are clean and tidy. All have double bed (married couples only), fan and TV, and there's a restaurant serving local fare.

Udzungwa Mountain View Hotel HOTEL $$
(☑️0653 692127, 023-262 0218; udzungwamountainviewhotel@yahoo.com; camping US$8, r per person US$35; 🅿️) This straightforward hotel, under the same management as Genesis Motel in Mikumi, has 16 simple, somewhat cramped rooms in a shady compound, and a

restaurant (meals Tsh12,000 to Tsh20,000). It's about 800m south of the park entrance along the main road. Staff can help arrange treks.

Hondo Hondo TENTED CAMP $$$
(Udzungwa Forest Camp; ☑️0758 844228, 0712 304475; www.udzungwaforestcamp.com; s/d/tr hut US$38/64/120, s/d luxury tent US$136/216/282, camping US$10; 🅿️ 🌿) This camp has six safari-style tents with bathroom, a grassy camping area and five basic mud-and-thatched bungalows sharing solar-heated ablutions with the campsite. Prices are a little high, but the tasty cuisine and well-organised excursions compensate, and it's a good base for exploring the Udzungwas. Breakfast/lunch/dinner cost US$10/20/20. It's 2km north of park headquarters on the Mang'ula road.

It also offers also bike rental and many excursions, including day trips to Kilombero and hiking in nearby forest reserve areas.

🛏️ Western Udzungwas

Crocodile Camp CAMPGROUND, BANDAS $
(☑️0784 706835, satellite +882-1645-550267; www.crocodilecamp.de; camping Tsh20,000, d Tsh60-70,000, tr/f Tsh105,000/120,000; 🅿️) This friendly place is 300m off the main highway 12km east of Ruaha Mbuyuni, with a restaurant, camping and simple bungalows. Staff can organise guides for excursions, including crossing the river behind the camp via canoe and then hiking a rugged 14km to

Msosa village, from where you can explore the western Udzungwas. (Advance notice to park headquarters is essential.)

Msosa Campsite CAMPGROUND $
(📞0784 414514; camping US$6; 🅿) This bush campsite offers nothing but a shower, a toilet, firewood and wilderness walks. It's on the Msosa River, and is a good contact for arranging excursions in the western Udzungwas. Bring food and drink (or rely on the basic provisions available at Msosa village, 2km away), and call in advance to let staff know you're coming.

Take any bus along the highway to Al-Jazeera rest stop, where you can hire a motorcycle (Tsh5000) for the remaining 10km to the campsite; it's down the signposted Udzungwa park road diagonally opposite Al-Jazeera. Sporadic dalla-dallas go from Iringa via Al-Jazeera to Msosa village.

ℹ Information

The closest ATM is in Kilombero, 30km north of Mang'ula en route to Mikumi.

ℹ Getting There & Away

The main entrance gate and park headquarters are in Mang'ula village, 60km south of Mikumi town along the Ifakara road. There are entry posts at Msosa, about 10km off the main highway south of Ruaha Mbuyuni, and Udekwa, 60km off the main highway and accessed via a turn-off at Ilula. These are useful for those coming from Iringa or wanting to hike in the western Udzungwas.

BUS

Minibuses and pick-ups run daily between Mikumi town (from the dalla-dalla stand on the Ifakara road just south of the main highway) and Kilombero, where you'll need to wait for onward transport towards Mang'ula. However, it's faster to wait for one of the larger direct buses coming from Dar es Salaam to Ifakara via Mang'ula. These depart Dar between 6.30am and 10am, and pass Mikumi any time from about 10.30am to 2pm. Going in the other direction, there are several departures each morning from Ifakara, passing Mang'ula between 6am and 10am. The fare between Mang'ula and Mikumi (two hours) is Tsh5000, and is the same between Ifakara and Mang'ula (two hours).

From Iringa to Kilombero (Tsh10,000, five hours), there are one or two buses daily in each direction, departing by around midday from Iringa and between 5am and 7am from Kilombero.

There are sporadic minibuses between Mang'ula and Sanje (Tsh500), the trailhead for the Sanje Falls hike. Entering the park from the west, there's no reliable public transport to the Msosa or Udekwa entry gates, so you'll need to walk (feasible for Msosa, as it's only 10km off the highway) or hire your own transport.

TRAIN

Tazara ordinary trains stop at Mang'ula (currently arriving from Dar es Salaam at about 3am). The station is about a 30-minute walk from park headquarters; if you make advance arrangements, staff from the hotels will meet you. Express trains stop at Ifakara, 50km further south.

Iringa

🔲 026 / POP 175,000

Perched at a cool 1600m on a cliff overlooking the valley of the Little Ruaha River, Iringa was initially built up by the Germans in the late 19th century as a bastion against the local Hehe people. Now it's a district capital, an important agricultural centre and the gateway for visiting Ruaha National Park. Once away from the main street, with its congestion and hustlers, it's also an extremely likeable place, with an attractive bluff-top setting, healthy climate and bracing highland feel.

The new Boma museum of local culture and the Neema Crafts centre are enticing, and there are a couple of outstanding historical sites within easy reach: ancient rock art at Igeleke, and even more ancient Isimila, where you can see Stone Age flints and hammerstones, as well as an extraordinary landscape of earth pillars.

◉ Sights

⭐**Iringa Boma** MUSEUM
(📞026-270 2160, 0762 424642; www.fahariyetu. net; Tsh10,000; ⊙9.30am-5pm) This excellent EU-funded museum is a great new development, as is its small cafe (p295) and quality gift shop (p295). Located between Uhuru Park and Neema, Boma is housed in a 1900 German colonial building. Artfully displayed objects, including an embroidered chief's robe, wooden ceremonial stool and gleaming calabashes, are illuminated by extended captions exploring the ancient and colonial history of the area, tribal traditions and clothing and nearby attractions. It's the perfect place to start your explorations of the town.

⭐**Neema Crafts** ARTS CENTRE
(📞0783 760945; www.neemacrafts.com; Hakimu St; ⊙8.30am-6.30pm Mon-Sat) 🖉 This acclaimed

Iringa

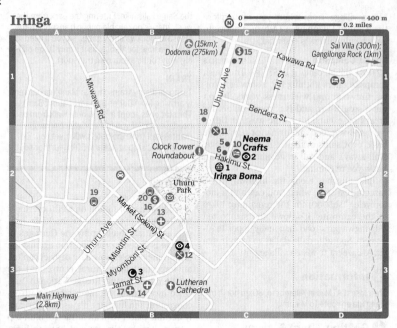

Iringa

vocational training centre for young deaf and disabled people sits just southeast of the Clock Tower roundabout. Operated by the Anglican church, it sells paper and cards made from elephant dung, jewellery, quilts, clothing, batiks and more. Behind the craft shop is a weaving workshop, and adjoining is a popular cafe (p294) and guesthouse (p293). Free workshop tours form part of the centre's remit to change perceptions of people with disabilities. Volunteer opportunities are occasionally available.

Ismaili Mosque　　　　　　　　　MOSQUE
(Jamatkhana) This unique German-built mosque is a visual highlight of Iringa's colonial centre – it was built in 1932 but, with

its clock tower and arcaded galleries, has the look of medieval European town hall.

Gangilonga Rock
HISTORIC SITE

(Tsh5000) This large rock northeast of town is where Chief Mkwawa meditated and where he learned that the Germans were after him. Its name, *gangilonga,* means 'talking stone' in Hehe, possibly because the chief's scouts communicated the movement of German troops from here. It's an easy climb to the top, with views over town. Staff at Neema Crafts Centre Internet Cafe (p295) can provide directions and a guide. Don't approach it on your own, as muggings are frequent.

Market Area
MARKET

(☉sunrise-sunset) Iringa's atmospheric covered market is piled high with fruit and vegetables, plus other wares, including large-weave, locally made baskets.

☞ Tours

★ Bateleur Safaris & Tours
SAFARI

(☑0765 735261, 0762 921825; www.bateleursafaris. co.tz; ☉8am-7pm) An efficient and welcoming locally run operation located round the corner from Neema Crafts centre. Staff create tailormade trips to Ruaha (including night safaris) and Mikumi National Parks, as well as short excursions to Igeleke Rock and other local attractions. Bike tours and wildlife are specialities, and it will book accommodation according to your budget.

Chabo Africa
SAFARI

(☑0784 893717, 0754 893717; www.chaboafrica safari.com; Hakimu St; ☉8.30am-5pm Mon-Fri, to 2pm Sat) Offers Ruaha safaris (from about US$450 for a one-night safari), visits to the Igeleke Rock Art and other excursions in and around Iringa.

Tatanca Safaris & Tours
SAFARI

(☑026-270 0610, 0766 338334; www.tatanca safaris.co.tz; Uhuru Ave; ☉8.30am-5pm Mon-Fri, to noon Sat) Organises Ruaha safaris and excursions elsewhere in the country.

🛏 Sleeping

★ Neema Umaki Guest House
GUESTHOUSE $

(☑0768 027991, 0683 380492; www.neemacrafts. com; Hakimu St; s/d/f Tsh25,000/45,000/65,000; ☎) ✐ This centrally located guesthouse has an array of clean, comfortable rooms, all with nets and TV. It adjoins Neema Crafts centre, but rooms are in a quieter section towards the back of the complex. Turn east off Uhuru Ave at the Clock Tower and go down about 100m. The guesthouse entrance is around the corner.

Staff can help with general Iringa information and with arranging guides for walking tours of town and excursions. Profits go to support the work of the craft centre.

Iringa Sunset Hotel
HOTEL $

(☑0754 469 854; Gangilonga Hills; d Tsh60,000-100,000; ☀☎) This new hotel enjoys one of the best locations in Iringa, with an eagle-eye view of the town and surrounding plains. There's a wonderful central dining hall with an open fire in the evenings, and accommodation is in an attractive cluster of stone *bandas* and wooden chalets. The chalets with a view are recommended, and are less expensive.

WORTH A TRIP

IGELEKE ROCK ART

A large prehistoric frieze, the **Igeleke Rock Art** (off Dodoma road; adult/student/child Tsh10,000/5000/5000; ☉8am-5.30pm) is similar in style to the Kondoa rock paintings, located at a spectacular site on the edge of town just west of the Dodoma road. The ochre drawings depict human figures, an elephant, jumping eland and giraffe hiding in long grass. It's an easy and worthwhile excursion from town involving a short but steep walk from the car park. A guide can be arranged on-site (about Tsh10,000 per group) or in advance with Iringa-based tour operators.

Take any dalla-dalla heading north along Uhuru Ave for about 6km to Kihesa Kilolo ('K/Kilolo') and ask it to drop you at the turn-off (marked by a tiny sign reading 'Igeleke Rock Arts'). From there, it's about 1km on foot to the base of the large rock where the paintings are: follow the dirt track west off the highway, going left at the fork and then right after the football pitch. Taxis charge Tsh20,000 return, including waiting time – be clear with the driver about how much time you will spend at the site, as drivers have been known to leave.

WORTH A TRIP

KILOMBERO VALLEY

The Kilombero Valley's extensive wetlands offer fine birding and wildlife watching, and a glimpse into local life. Hondo Hondo (p290) and **Wild Things Safaris** (www.wildthing safaris.com) organise day canoe trips beginning at the Ifakara ferry. With more time, you can extend your exploration to include Ifakara town, Mahenge (a picturesque mission station) or Idete, another old mission station.

In Ifakara, there's accommodation at **Mbega Resort** (Ifakara Rd, d Tsh40,000; ﷯), which offers simple, clean rooms and meals with a garden setting. It's along the main road before the tarmac begins. In Idete, there's a simple mission guesthouse.

There's a direct bus service between Dar es Salaam and Ifakara, running in both directions between 6.30am and 10am (Tsh15,000, seven hours). A couple of buses daily in each direction link Iringa and Kilombero (Tsh10,000, five hours), departing around midday from Iringa and between 5am and 7am from Kilombero. Express trains from Dar stop at Ifakara.

Alizeti Hostel   HOSTEL $

(☑ 0742 346 686; http://alizetihosteliringa.com; dm Tsh15,000, d Tsh35,000, camping Tsh8000; ﷯) A popular and sociable budget option with self-catering facilities near the centre of town. It offers board games, hammocks, an honesty bar and mountain views.

Mama Iringa B&B   B&B $

(☑ 0753 757007; mama.iringa@yahoo.com; Don Bosco area; tw/f Tsh40,000/60,000, s without bathroom Tsh15,000-20,000; ℗) Clean, simple rooms in an old convent: all have nets, and there's a great Italian restaurant (p295). It's 3.5km from town, in the Don Bosco area. Follow Mkwawa Rd downhill to the Danish School junction, turn left, then take the first (signposted) right. Continue to the end of the graveyards. Turn left. Mama Iringa is 1km further on your right, and signposted.

Iringa Lutheran Centre   GUESTHOUSE $

(☑ 026-270 0722, 0755 517445; www.iringalutheran centre.com; Kawawa Rd; s/d/tr incl full breakfast US$25/45/55; ℗ ﷯) This long-standing place has clean, quiet and pleasant twin and double-bedded rooms with bathrooms and hot water, a tranquil garden and a restaurant. It's on the northeastern edge of town, about 700m southeast of the main road.

Rivervalley Campsite   CAMPGROUND $

(Riverside Campsite; ☑ 0787 111663, 0684 009812; www.rivervalleycampsites.com; camping US$6, s/d US$35/53, with shared bathroom US$30/48; ℗ ﷯) The expansive Rivervalley Campsite has a lovely setting on the Little Ruaha River. Breakfast and lunch can be arranged. Children between three and 11 years of age pay half of the adult rate. Call in advance rather than turning up to ensure the place is open;

there were rumours of closure at the time of writing.

It's 13km east of Iringa; take an Ilula dalla-dalla to the signposted right-hand turn-off (Tsh1000), from where it's 1.5km further down a dirt lane. Taxis charge about Tsh20,000 from town or Ipogoro bus stand.

Sai Villa   GUESTHOUSE $$

(☑ 0684 062017, 0786 757757, 0783 767767; www. saivilla.co.tz; off Kawawa Rd, Gangilonga area; s/d from US$80/100; ℗ ﷯) This private residence has 10 comfortable modern, if uninspired, guest rooms and a good restaurant serving excellent Indian food. A sociable weekend spot for a drink.

🍴 Eating

★ Neema Crafts Centre Cafe   CAFE $

(☑ 0783 760945; www.neemacrafts.com; Hakimu St; mains Tsh3000-13,000; ⊙8am-6.30pm Mon-Fri; ﷯) Located upstairs at Neema Crafts (p291), this cafe is justifiably popular, with local coffees and teas, homemade cookies, excellent cinnamon buns, cakes, soups, and a selection of sandwiches and light meals. The noticeboard is great for finding out about safaris and Swahili classes, and the breezy terrace hung with bunting is one of the town's best hang-outs.

★ Hasty Tasty Too   TANZANIAN, INTERNATIONAL $

(☑ 026-270 2061; Uhuru Ave; mains Tsh6000-13,000; ⊙8.30am-8pm Mon-Sat; ℗) This long-standing Iringa classic has good breakfasts, yoghurt, samosas, shakes and reasonably priced main dishes, including a divine chickpea curry. It's popular with local and expat clientele. You can get toasted sandwiches packed to go and arrange food for Ruaha camping safaris.

Boma Café
INTERNATIONAL $

(www.fahariyetu.net; mains Tsh8000-10,000; ⊘9.30am-5pm) The Boma museum cafe makes a great daytime spot for a speciality coffee, and it serves filling European mains and snacks: pizza, quiches, meatballs and chilli con carne.

★Mama Iringa Pizzeria & Italian Restaurant
ITALIAN $$

(☑0753 757007; mama.iringa@yahoo.com; Don Bosco area; mains Tsh9000-15,000; ⊘noon-2.30pm & 5-9pm Tue-Sun; P) Delicious Italian food – pizzas, gnocchi, lasagne and more, plus salads – served in the quiet courtyard of a former convent. It's about 3km from the town centre (Tsh5000 in a taxi). Take Mkwawa Rd to the Danish School junction and follow the signposts.

Sai Villa
INDIAN, INTERNATIONAL $$

(☑0684 062017, 0759 945416; www.saivilla.co.tz; off Kawawa Rd, Gangilonga area; mains Tsh10,000-20,000; ⊘6.30am-9pm; P🛜🍴) A popular spot, especially in the evenings, with a large menu featuring Indian and continental cuisine. Follow Kawawa Rd past the Lutheran Hostel for about 500m to Mama Siyovelwa pub. Continue past the pub for 300m, taking the second right (just after the road merges with Kenyatta Dr). Sai Villa is the first gate on your right.

Self-Catering

Ng'owo Supermarket
SUPERMARKET $

(Jamat St; ⊘8.30am-8pm Mon-Sat, 10am-4pm Sun) This small but well-stocked supermarket is near the southeastern corner of the market.

🛍 Shopping

★Boma
ARTS & CRAFTS

(www.fahariyetu.net; ⊘9.30am-5pm) The craft store at the Boma museum has a terrific selection of gifts and crafts, with a specialism in quality handwoven fabrics. This is the place to buy special scarves and wraps; it also sells kids' clothes and soft toys, fabric-hanging storage, notepads and books.

ℹ Information

INTERNET ACCESS
Neema Crafts Centre Internet Cafe (Hakimu St; per hour Tsh2000; ⊘8am-6.30pm Mon-Sat) Wi-fi only.

SOUTHERN HIGHLANDS IRINGA

WORTH A TRIP

ISIMILA STONE AGE SITE

In the late 1950s here at the Isimila Stone Age Site (adult/child Tsh20,000/10,000, plus guide fee per group Tsh10,000; ⊘8am-6pm), amid a dramatic landscape of eroded sandstone pillars, archaeologists unearthed one of the most significant Stone Age finds ever identified. Tools found at the site – hammerstones, axeheads, flints and scrapers – are estimated to be between 60,000 and 100,000 years old. There's a museum with small, well-captioned displays highlighting some of the discoveries. Isimila is signposted off the Mbeya road to the left, about 21km southwest of Iringa.

The main pillar area is accessed via a walk down into a steep valley (about one hour round-trip), for which you'll need a guide. Visits are best in the morning or late afternoon, when the sun is not at its zenith. There's also a covered picnic area (bring your own food). Unexpectedly, the dusty museum has an excellent small shop selling colourful men's shirts and a few other items.

With a bit of endurance for heat and traffic, the site is straightforward to reach by bicycle from Iringa. Via public transport, take an Ifunda or Mafinga dalla-dalla from the Iringa town bus station and ask the driver to drop you at the Isimila junction (Tsh1500), from where it's a 15-minute walk to the site. Taxis charge from about Tsh25,000 for the return trip.

A possible detour on bicycle or with private vehicle is to nearby Tosamaganga, a pretty hilltop mission station established by Italian missionaries in the early 20th century. It's reached via the unsignposted 'Njia Panda ya Tosamaganga' turn-off from the main road, 4km northeast of the Kalenga turn-off. Follow the wide, unpaved road for about 5km, first past cornfields and then along a eucalyptus-lined lane to the red-tile roofs and imposing church of the mission.

Post office (⊙7.30am-4.30pm Mon-Fri, 8am-noon Sat) Has an attached internet cafe.

MEDICAL SERVICES

Aga Khan Health Centre (☑026-270 2277; Jamat St; ⊙8am-6pm Mon-Fri, to 2pm Sat & Sun) Next to the Lutheran cathedral and near the market.

Acacia Pharmacy (☑026-270 2335, 0754 943243; cnr Market & Myomboni Sts; ⊙7.30am-7.30pm Mon-Sat, 9am-7pm Sun) Near the market.

Myomboni Pharmacy (☑026-270 2617, 026-270 2277; Jamat St; ⊙7.30am-7.30pm) Just downhill from the Aga Khan Health Centre.

MONEY

Barclays (Uhuru Ave; ⊙9am-5pm Mon-Fri) Money changing and an ATM.

CRDB (Uhuru Ave; ⊙8.30am-4.30pm Mon-Fri, to 12.30pm Sat) Offers currency exchange and an ATM.

TOURIST INFORMATION

The bulletin boards at Hasty Tasty Too (p294), Neema Crafts Centre Cafe (p294) and Iringa Lutheran Centre (p294) are well worth checking, especially to find travel companions for sharing costs on Ruaha safaris. These places can also help you find reliable guides for local excursions and tours.

❶ Getting There & Away

AIR

Auric Air (☑0755 413090; www.auricair.com; Uhuru Ave; ⊙7.30am-4pm Mon-Fri, 8.30am-1pm Sat) Has daily flights connecting Iringa with Dar es Salaam (US$180 one-way). Iringa's Nduli Airfield is about 12km out of town along the Dodoma road.

BUS

Most buses arrive and depart from the hectic **bus station** just west of the main street. Ticket offices for all companies can be found here. Book ahead for Shabiby luxury buses to be sure of getting a seat.

If you're arriving on a bus continuing towards Morogoro or Mbeya, you may be dropped off at Ipogoro, 3km southeast of town below the escarpment where the Morogoro–Mbeya highway bypasses Iringa (Tsh5000 for a taxi to/from town, though initial quotes are usually much higher).

Numerous lines go daily to Dar es Salaam (Tsh19,000 to Tsh28,000, nine to 10 hours), leaving from 6am onwards. To Mbeya (Tsh14,000 to Tsh18,000, five to eight hours), Shabiby, Chaula Express and others depart daily between 6am and 10am; Shabiby is recommended for this route, which can otherwise be very slow. Otherwise, you can try to get a seat on one of the through buses from Dar es Salaam that pass Iringa (Ipogoro bus station) from about 1pm. To Njombe (Tsh11,000, 3½ hours) and Songea (Tsh19,000, nine hours),

---

WORTH A TRIP

IRINGA TO MAKAMBAKO

From Iringa, the Tanzam Hwy continues southwest, past dense stands of pine, before reaching the junction town of Makambako. En route are some lovely possibilities for detours.

Kisolanza – The Old Farm House (☑0754 306144; www.kisolanza.com; Ifunda; camping from US$9, s/d/tr cottages with half board from US$100/160/200, tw without bathroom US$50; P ⊞) This gracious 1930s farm homestead 50km southwest of Iringa is fringed by stands of pine and rolling hill country and recommended for its accommodation and outstanding cuisine. There are two campgrounds (overlanders and private vehicles), twin-bedded rooms, cosy wooden chalets, family cottages with fireplace, two luxury garden cottages and a spa. All are spotless, impeccably furnished and excellent value.

The farmhouse also features a bar and a shop selling home-grown vegetables and other produce, and there are many beautiful walks in the area. Buses will drop you at the Kisolanza turn-off, from where it's a 1.5km walk to the lodge. Advance bookings are advisable for accommodation, but there's always room for campers.

Mufindi Highlands Lodge (☑0754 237422; www.mufindihighlandlodge.com; s/d with full board US$210/300; P ⊞) This lovely lodge, set amid landscaped gardens in the forested hills and tea plantations around Mufindi, offers cool highland air and the chance to recharge, plus walking trails, cycling, horse riding and fishing. The cosy wooden cabins have sunset views, and family-style meals are prepared with farm produce. It's 45km south of Mafinga; pick-ups can be arranged.

CHIEF MKWAWA

Mtwa (Chief) Mkwawa, chief of the Hehe and one of German colonialism's most vociferous resisters, is a legendary figure in Tanzanian history. He is particularly revered in Iringa, near which he had his headquarters. Under Mkwawa's leadership during the second half of the 19th century, the Hehe became one of the most powerful tribes in central Tanzania. They overpowered one group after another until, by the late 1880s, they were threatening trade traffic along the caravan route from western Tanzania to Bagamoyo. In 1891, after several negotiation attempts by Mkwawa with the Germans were rejected, his men trounced the colonial troops in the infamous battle of Lugalo, just outside Iringa on the Mikumi road. The next year, Mkwawa's troops launched a damaging attack on a German fort at Kilosa, further to the east.

The Germans placed a bounty on Mkwawa's head and, once they had regrouped, initiated a counterattack in which Mkwawa's headquarters at Kalenga was taken. Mkwawa escaped, but later, in 1898, committed suicide rather than surrender to a contingent that had been sent after him. His head was cut off and the skull sent to Germany, where it sat almost forgotten (though not by the Hehe) until it was returned to Kalenga in 1954. The return of Mkwawa's remains was due, in large part, to the efforts of Sir Edward Twining, then the British governor of Tanganyika. Today, the skull of Mkwawa and some old weapons are on display at the Kalenga Historical Museum.

Super Feo departs at 6am from the town bus station. To Dodoma (Tsh14,000, four hours), Kimotco and several other companies depart daily from 6am, going via Nyangolo and Makatapora. Some Dodoma buses continue on to Singida (Tsh24,000, seven hours) and Arusha (Tsh40,000, 13 hours).

❶ Getting Around

The **Myomboni dalla-dalla stand** is the main one and is a short walk from the market and the bus station on the edge of Uhuru Park. **Taxi** ranks include those by the bus station, along the small road between the bus station and the market and at the Ipogoro bus station. Fares from the town bus station to central hotels average Tsh3000.

Kalenga

About 15km from Iringa on the road to Ruaha National Park is the former Hehe capital of Kalenga. It was here that Chief Mkwawa had his headquarters until Kalenga fell to the Germans in the 1890s, and it was here that he committed suicide rather than succumb to the German forces.

The tiny **Kalenga Historical Museum** (adult/child Tsh20,000/10,000; ⊙8am-5.30pm) contains the skull, personal effects and other relics of Chief Mkwawa. The admission price includes a historical explanation by the caretaker, though he also appreciates a tip. It's also possible to arrange with the caretaker to visit other nearby historical sites, including a cemetery with the graves of some of Mkwawa's 62 wives, and the site of part of Kalenga's old defensive wall (the ruins themselves are now nonexistent).

Dalla-dallas go regularly to Kalenga (Tsh500) from Iringa's post office, also stopping at Mlandege bus stand near the roundabout at the start of the Ruaha road. Ask to be dropped at the signposted turn-off, from where it's an 800m walk through the village to the museum.

Ruaha National Park

At approximately 22,000 sq km, **Ruaha** (www.tanzaniaparks.go.tz; adult/child US$35.40/11.80) is Tanzania's largest park. It forms the core of a wild and extended ecosystem covering about 40,000 sq km and provides home to Tanzania's largest elephant population, estimated at 12,000. In addition, Tanzania's largest national park hosts buffaloes, greater and lesser kudus, Grant's gazelles, wild dogs, ostriches, cheetahs, roan and sable antelope, and more than 400 types of birds.

Ruaha is notable for its wild and striking topography, especially around the Great Ruaha River, which is its heart, and which is home to crocodiles, hippos and wading birds. Much of it is undulating plateau averaging about 900m in height with occasional rocky outcrops and stands of baobabs. Mountains in the south and west reach to about 1600m and 1900m, respectively. Running through the park are several 'sand' rivers, most of which dry up during the dry season, when they are used by wildlife as corridors to reach areas where water remains.

Ruaha is also notable as it straddles a transition zone between East African savannah lands and the miombo woodlands more common further south, thus offering a mix of plant and animal species from both regions.

Although the area around the camps on the eastern side of the park fills up during the August to October high (dry) season, Ruaha receives relatively few visitors in comparison with the northern parks. Large sections are unexplored, and for much of the year, you're likely to have things to yourself. Whenever you visit, set aside as much time as you can spare; it's not a place to be discovered on a quick in-and-out trip.

Sights & Activities

The best place to experience the park is along the river, especially the circuit that runs northeast, following the riverbanks, before turning inwards towards the area around Mwagusi Safari Camp. Birding here is especially fine and sightings of hippos, crocodiles and elephants are almost guaranteed. Try not to miss sunrise and sunset, when the large rocks dotting the river's channel are illuminated and the bordering vegetation and flatlands come alive. Bat-eared foxes and jackals are common around the Msembe area. Lions aren't as readily seen as in the Serengeti, but they are definitely present, with the area just north of the river towards Mwagusi a good bet.

Besides wildlife drives, it's possible to organise two- to three-hour walking safaris (park walking fee US$23.60 per group) from June to January. Bateleur (p293), based in Iringa, organises thrilling night safaris here.

Ruaha Cultural Tourism Program   CULTURAL
(☑ 0752 142195, 0788 354286; www.ruahacultural tours.com; half-/full-day tour US$20/40, per person with full board in Maasai village US$27) 🌾 Cultural tours of a Maasai village, known as a *boma* (including the chance to spend the night), traditional cooking lessons, nature walks and more. Recommended stop en route to or from Ruaha.

Sleeping & Eating

The closest place to properly stock up for self-catering is Iringa. Inside the park, soft drinks and a few basics are for sale at park

headquarters, and it's sometimes possible to arrange to eat at the staff canteen. Local-style meals are also available at the 'new' park *bandas*. Otherwise, you'll need your own supplies.

Inside the Park

Inside the park there are both public and special campsites, as well as park *bandas*. The special campsites have no facilities, and are scattered in the bush well away from park headquarters. All park-run accommodation can be booked at the gate on arrival, or through tour operators in Iringa (p291). Payment must be made at the park gate with Visa or MasterCard.

Ruaha Park Bandas & Cottages   COTTAGE $$
(☑ 0756 144400; ruaha@tanzaniaparks.go.tz; s/d bandas with shared bathroom US$35.40/70.80, s/d/f cottages US$59/118/118; 🏠) Ruaha's 'old' park *bandas,* in a fine setting directly on the river near park headquarters, have been partially upgraded. Several have private bathroom, and meals can be arranged or cooked yourself. About 3km beyond here, on a rise overlooking the river in the distance, are the 'new' tidy cement cottages (all with private bathroom). There's a dining hall next door with inexpensive meals.

Accommodation must be paid for at the entry gate with credit card.

Ruaha Park Main Public Campsite   CAMPGROUND $$
(☑ 0756 144400; ruaha@tanzaniaparks.go.tz; camping public/special US$35.40/59) The park's main campsite (with a cooking area and basic ablutions) is in a lovely setting, directly on the river near Msembe park headquarters, but with plenty of wildlife around. The park has several other public campsites.

★ **Mwagusi Safari Camp**   TENTED CAMP $$$
(☑ UK +44 18226 15721; www.mwagusicamp.com; s/d all-inclusive US$700/1225; ☺ Jun-Mar; 🅿) This highly regarded 16-bed owner-managed camp is set in a prime wildlife-viewing location on the Mwagusi Sand River 20km inside the park gate – animals are more prolific at this spot once the rains have started. The atmosphere is intimate and the guiding is top-notch. Highlights are the spacious tented *bandas,* the rustic, natural feel and the romantic evening ambience.

★ **Ruaha River Lodge**   LODGE $$$
(☑ 0754 237422; www.tanzaniasafaris.info; s/d incl full board & wildlife drives US$425/660; 🅿) This

unpretentious, beautifully situated 28-room lodge was the first in the park and is the only place on the river. It's divided into two separate sections, each with its own dining area. The stone cottages directly overlook the river – sit on your veranda and look out for elephants and hippos – and there's a treetop-level bar-terrace with stunning riverine panoramas. It's about 15km inside the gate, southwest of park headquarters.

★ **Mdonya Old River Camp**   TENTED CAMP **$$$**
(☑ 022-260 1747; www.ed.co.tz; per person incl full board & excursions from US$390; ☺ Jun-Mar; ℗) The relaxed Mdonya Old River Camp, about 1½ hours' drive from park headquarters, has 12 tents on the banks of the Mdonya Sand River, with elephants occasionally wandering through camp. It's a straightforward, unpretentious place with the necessary comforts tempered by a bush feel. If you take advantage of Coastal Travel's special fly-in offers, it offers good value for a Ruaha safari.

🛏 Outside the Park

There are several lodges and campsites just outside Ruaha park boundaries along the Tungamalenga village road (take the left fork at the junction when coming from Iringa). If staying here, remember that park entry fees are valid for a single entry only per 24-hour period.

Chogela Campsite   CAMPGROUND **$**
(☑ 0782 032025, 0757 151349; www.chogelasafari camp.wix.com/chogelasafaricamp; off Tungamalen-

ga village road; camping US$10, s/d safari tents US$30/50; ℗) Shaded grounds, a large cooking-dining area and hot-water showers make this a popular budget choice. There are also twin-bedded safari-style tents. Vehicle rental can be arranged (US$250 for a full-day safari, advance notice required; US$350 including pick-up and drop-off in Iringa), as can meals. The camp is about 34km from the park gate along the Tungamalenga road.

Ruaha Cultural Tourism Program (p298) also has a base here, for arranging nature walks, village tours and day or overnight visits to a nearby Maasai community.

Tungamalenga Lodge & Campsite   LODGE **$**
(☑ 0787 859369, 026-278 2196; www.ruahatunga camp.com; Tungamalenga Rd; camping US$15, r per person with breakfast/full board US$45/70; ℗) This long-standing place, about 15km from the park gate and close to the bus stand, has a small garden for camping, basic but tidy rooms in double-storey wooden bungalows, and a restaurant. Village tours can be arranged.

Vehicle rental is possible with advance arrangement only.

Ruaha Hilltop Lodge   LODGE **$$**
(☑ 0784 726709, 026-270 1806; www.ruahahilltop lodge.com; off Tungamalenga village road; r per person full board US$90; ℗) This friendly no-frills lodge has a fine hilltop perch 1.5km off the Tungamalenga road, with wide views over the plains from the raised restaurant-bar area. Behind this are simple two-person cement *bandas*. During the dry season, it's

---

ⓘ RUAHA NATIONAL PARK

Why Go Outstanding dry-season wildlife watching, especially elephants, hippos, lions and endangered wild dogs; excellent birding; rugged scenery.

When to Go The driest season is between June and November, and this is when it's easiest to spot wildlife along the river beds. During the rainy season, some areas become impassable and wildlife is difficult to locate, but green panoramas, lavender-coloured flowers and rewarding birding compensate.

Practicalities Drive in from Iringa; fly in from Arusha or Dar es Salaam. Entry fees are per 24-hour period, single-entry only, and are payable with Visa or MasterCard only. The main gate (open 7am to 6pm) is about 8km inside the park boundary on its eastern side, near the park's Msembe headquarters. Driving is permitted within the park from 6am to 6.30pm.

Budget Tips Ruaha has no true budget options. Your best bet: get a group of four or five, hire a vehicle in Iringa for an overnight safari and sleep at the old park *bandas*. Meals are available, but bring your own drinks. It's also possible to take the bus from Iringa to Tungamalenga, and arrange car hire there for a safari (about US$250 per day). But confirm vehicle availability in advance, and remember park fees are single-entry only. Car hire from Iringa and sleeping inside the park usually works out to be better value.

THE TREE OF LIFE

One of the most distinctive sights in this region is that of receding panoramas of mighty baobab trees, with their swollen trunks, spindly branches reaching skyward and venerable, almost prehistoric air. Many baobabs live to be 400 to 500 years old, but they can survive for well over 1000 years. The tree's short-lived white blossoms are large and showy.

These gentle giants are sometimes called the tree of life, providing edible fruit, nutritious oil, fibre for clothing and rope, and storage for hundreds of litres of water. In markets you'll see packets of baobab fruit pulp candies (rolled with sugar and usually coloured red), and look out too for baobab powder, which is rich in vitamin C and calcium. The fat trunks of mature trees are often hollow, giving shelter to people and animals. Ruaha is a great place to get up close and personal with these wonderful trees.

common to see wildlife passing by down below. Cultural walks in the area can be arranged, as can vehicle rental for Ruaha safaris.

Tandala Tented Camp TENTED CAMP $$$
(☑ 0757 183420, 0755 680220; www.tandalacamp. com; off Tungamalenga village road; s/d full board US$250/440; ☺ Jun-Mar; ᴘ☀) Lovely Tandala sits just outside the park boundary, 12km from the gate. Eleven raised tents are scattered around shaded grounds with a bush feel (elephants and other animals are frequent visitors). Staff can organise vehicle rental to Ruaha, and guided walks and night drives in park border areas. The swimming pool and low-key ambience make it a good family choice.

❶ Getting There & Away

AIR
There is an airstrip at Msembe. **Coastal Aviation** (☑ 022-284 2700, 0713 325673; www. coastal.co.tz; Julius Nyerere International Airport, Dar es Salaam, Terminal 1) flies from Dar es Salaam and Zanzibar to Ruaha via Selous Game Reserve (one-way US$365 from Dar es Salaam, US$425 from Zanzibar) and between Ruaha and Arusha (US$365). **Safari Airlink** (www.flysal. com) has similarly priced flights connecting

Ruaha with Dar es Salaam, Selous and Arusha, and also with Katavi and Mikumi.

BUS
There's a daily bus between Iringa and Tungamalenga village (Tsh7000, five hours), departing Iringa's Mwangata bus stand (on the southwestern edge of town at the start of the Ruaha road) at 1pm. Look for the vehicle marked 'Idodi-Tungamalenga'. Departures from Tungamalenga's village bus stand (along the Tungamalenga road, just before Tungamalenga Camp) are at 6am. From Tungamalenga, there's no onward transport to the park, other than rental vehicles arranged in advance through the Tungamalenga road camps (prices start at US$250 per day). There's no vehicle rental once at Ruaha, except what you've arranged in advance with the lodges.

CAR
Ruaha is 115km from Iringa along an unsealed road. About 58km before the park, the road forks; both sides go to Ruaha and the distance is about the same each way, but it's best to take the more travelled and more populated Tungamalenga road (left fork). The closest petrol is in Iringa. Ask at Neema Umaki Guest House (p293) in Iringa about vehicle rental to Ruaha for around US$300 per vehicle for the first day, then US$200 per vehicle for each subsequent day. Neema is a good contact for finding other travellers interested in joining a group.

Makambako

☑ 026 / POP 120,000

Makambako (a stop on the Tazara railway line) is a windy highland town where the road from Songea and Njombe meets the Dar es Salaam–Mbeya highway. Geographically, the area marks the end of the Eastern Arc mountain range and the start of the Southern Highlands. Makambako, dominated by Bena people, is also notable for its large market, which includes an extensive used-clothes section. Otherwise, there's no real reason to stop here other than as a lunch stop if you are driving, or to get off the train and onto the bus to head south to Njombe and Songea.

NBC (Njombe road) has an ATM.

🛏 Sleeping & Eating

Shinkansen Lodge HOTEL $
(Njombe road; s/d Tsh35,000/45,000; ᴘ) This small compound has double- and twin-bedded rooms (some with interior windows only) accessed via an imposing Japanese-style entry gate and a well-fortified parking com-

pound. Inside, the rooms are clean, albeit slightly gloomy. There's no food. It's conveniently located, about 1km south of the main junction, and about 500m north of the bus stand.

Kondoa
AFRICAN $
(Njombe road; mains Tsh5000-8000) This busy local eatery is as good a spot as any to get a meal in Makambako. It's just south of the main highway.

ℹ Getting There & Away
The bus stand is about 1.5km south of the main junction along the Njombe road. The first bus to Mbeya (Tsh9000, three hours) leaves at 6am, with another bus at 7am. The first buses (all smaller Coastals) to Njombe (Tsh4000, one hour) and Songea (Tsh14,000, five hours) depart about 6.30am, and there's a larger bus departing at 6.30am for Iringa (Tsh9000, three to four hours), continuing on to Dar es Salaam (around Tsh30,000).

Njombe
📞 026 / POP 150,200

Njombe, about 60km south of Makambako and 235km north of Songea, is a district capital, regional agricultural centre and home of the Bena people. It would be unmemorable but for its highly scenic setting on the eastern edge of the Kipengere Range at almost 2000m. The town hosts a good market, selling wicker baskets coloured with natural dyes.

In addition to giving it the reputation of being Tanzania's coldest town, this perch provides wide vistas over hills that seem to roll endlessly to the horizon. The surrounding area, dotted with tea plantations and fields of wildflowers, is ideal for walking and cycling. As there is no tourism infrastructure, anything you undertake will need to be under your own steam. At the northern edge of town, visible from the main road and an easy walk, are the **Luhuji Falls**.

🛏 Sleeping & Eating

Hill Side Hotel
HOTEL $
(Chani Motel; 📞 0752 910068, 026-278 2357; chani hotel@yahoo.com; r Tsh30,000-55,000; 🅿) This cosy place has modest twin- and double-bedded rooms, hot water (usually), small but lovely poinsettia-studded gardens, and a good restaurant with TV and filling meals. Turn off the main road onto the dirt lane next to the courthouse (Mahakamani); it's

just downhill and diagonally opposite the police station.

FM Hotel
HOTEL $
(📞 0786 513321; Main St; s Tsh35,000-45,000, d Tsh55,000, ste Tsh75,000; 🅿) This large, soulless multistorey place bills itself as Njombe's sleekest option, with modern rooms boasting nets and TV. Some face the highway, with views over Njombe, others overlook an interior courtyard. There's a restaurant. It's on the main road 1km south of and diagonally opposite the bus stand.

Mwambasa Lodge
GUESTHOUSE $
(📞 026-278 2301; Main St; r Tsh25,000; @) Mwambasa is a local-style guesthouse that is slated to be knocked down when the road is expanded. Until this happens (and it probably won't happen for some time), it remains a reliable shoestring option. It is diagonally opposite (and just north of) the bus stand, on the main road. There's no food.

Duka la Maziwa
SUPERMARKET
(Cefa Njombe Milk Factory; 📞 026-278 2851; ⊘ 7am-6pm Mon-Sat, 10am-2pm Sun) Fresh milk, yoghurt and delicious Italian cheeses. It's just off the main road; turn in by the TFA building and go down about two blocks. The shop is to the left.

ℹ Information
The following banks are on the main street at the southern end of town.
CRDB (⊘ 8.30am-4pm Mon-Fri, to 1pm Sat) Currency exchange and an ATM.
NBC (Main St; ⊘ 9am-5pm Mon-Fri) ATM at the southern end of town.

ℹ Getting There & Away
It's possible to go from Njombe via public transport or private vehicle along scenic highland backroads to the Kitulo Plateau, and down to the shores of Lake Nyasa.

The bus stand (Main St) is on the west side of the main road, about 600m south of the large grey-water tank.

Buses go daily to Songea (Tsh10000 to Tsh13,000, four hours), Makambako (Tsh4000, one hour), Iringa (Tsh9000, 3½ hours) and Mbeya (Tsh10,000, four hours), with the first departures at 6.30am.

For hikers, there are daily vehicles to Bulongwa (departing Njombe about 10am) and Ludewa (departing by 8am), from where you can walk down to Matema and Lupingu respectively, both on the Lake Nyasa shoreline. You can also catch transport towards Bulongwa at the start of the Makete Rd at the northern end of town, just downhill from the Chani Motel turn-off. This road, which continues past Kitulo National Park and on to Isyonje and the junction with the Tukuyu road, is easily passable during the dry season, though somewhat slower during the rains. A small section near Makete is tarmac.

Kitulo National Park

This **national park** (www.tanzaniaparks.go.tz; adult/child US$35.40/11.80) protects the flower-clad Kitulo Plateau, together with sections of the former Livingstone Forest Reserve, which runs south from the plateau paralleling the Lake Nyasa shoreline. The area, much of which lies between 2600m and 3000m in the highlands northeast of Tukuyu, is a paradise for hikers, although tourism infrastructure is minimal.

The park reaches its prime during the rainy season from December until April, when it explodes in a profusion of colour, with orchids (over 40 species have been identified so far), irises, aloes, geraniums and many more flowers carpeting its grassy expanses. Orchids are at their peak in February. Look out too for zebra, which have been reintroduced here, and the rare and recently discovered kipunji monkey, with its long coat and 'honk-bark' call.

Rising up from the plateau is **Mt Mtorwi** (2961m), which is 1m higher than Mt Rungwe and southern Tanzania's highest peak.

🛏 Sleeping & Eating

The only accommodation inside the park is camping (US$35.40). At the time of writing, a planned campground with toilets and showers was about to open.

Outside the park there are several basic guesthouses in Matamba village, near park headquarters, and all within less than 10 minutes' walk of the bus stand.

You'll find some basic places to eat in Matamba, including the Super Eden Motel, but within the park you'll need to be self-sufficient.

Bustani ya Mungu GUESTHOUSE $
(God's Garden; ☏ 0752 251976; Matamba; s/d Tsh30,000/35,000) This small place has clean rooms overlooking a tiny garden, and meals on order. Go uphill (south) from the bus stand for about 100m to the signposted turn-off for 'Super Eden Motel'; after passing the Super Eden, continue for 150m further down the dirt lane. The unsignposted Bustani ya Mungu will be to your right; look for the red-brick, blue-roofed building.

Super Eden Motel GUESTHOUSE $
(☏ 0763 654441; Matamba; s/d/f Tsh20,000/ 25,000/35,000) This local guesthouse has small double-bedded rooms and a larger family room with one double and two twin beds. Meals can be arranged, as can buckets of hot water for bathing. It's at the southern end of Matamba village. Go uphill (south) from the bus stand for about 100m to the signposted right-hand turn-off, from where it's 50m further.

ℹ Getting There & Away

The best access is via Mfumbi village, about 90km east of Mbeya along the main highway, from where an all-weather road climbs 32km up to Matamba village and the Tanapa temporary headquarters, with some spectacular views en route. From Matamba, it's about 12km further via 4WD with high clearance (or a couple of hours on foot) along a rough road, which is sometimes impassable in the rains, upto the plateau itself.

It's also possible to reach Kitulo via the signposted park turn-off 2km west of Chimala town and about 80km east of Mbeya along the main

---

ℹ EXPLORING THE SOUTHERN HIGHLANDS

Before visiting Kitulo National Park or hiking elsewhere in the Southern Highlands, get a copy of Liz de Leyser's excellent *A Guide to the Southern Highlands of Tanzania*, available at many bookshops and hotels in and around Mbeya and Iringa. For more on Kitulo's wonderful flowers, see *Orchids and Wildflowers of Kitulo Plateau* by Rosalind Salter and Tim Davenport.

When planning hikes, keep in mind that you'll need to be completely self-sufficient (including tent and water filter) and carry a GPS.

Contact Maua Café & Tours (p305) in Mbeya to find out about its exciting horse-riding expeditions from Kitulo to the lakeshore at Matema, on a back route via the Livingstone Mountains. UK-based Greentours (www.greentours.co.uk) offers upmarket flora and fauna tours combining Kitulo and Udzungwa Mountains National Parks.

ℹ️ KITULO NATIONAL PARK

Why Go Stunning terrain with flowers and high waterfalls; excellent wilderness hiking for well-equipped hikers; horse riding; rare monkeys

When to Go June through October for drier hiking; December through March for wild-flowers

Practicalities At the time of research, the owner of Maua Café & Tours (p305) in Mbeya was about to open a campsite in the park, with bookable horse-riding safaris and treks. Otherwise, drive in from Mbeya or Iringa. Fees must be paid by a card system. Guides are not required, but can be arranged (US$20 per day) at Tanapa's temporary headquarters at Matamba village, which is also where you pay your park fees. For any hiking you'll need to be self-sufficient, with food, water (bring a filter or purifying tablets) and a GPS (if hiking independently).

Budget Tips There's a daily bus from Mbeya to Matamba village, where you can sleep in a local guesthouse. Next morning, pay park fees, hire a motorbike or pick-up to cover the 12km from town to the park gate, hike southwards through the park, camping overnight, and catch transport the next day along the Makete road on Kitulo's southern boundary to Isyonje village (for Tukuyu) or to Makete (for Njombe). Note: this route is for hardy, fully equipped hikers only. Alternatively, explore Kitulo by vehicle. Rentals from Mbeya are reasonably priced if you are in a group.

highway. From here, a rough and rocky road (4WD only) winds its way for 9km up the escarpment via 50-plus hairpin turns, offering wide vistas over the Usangi Plains below. From the top, it's a further 12km or so to Matamba, along a wonderfully scenic route across the Chimala River, past fields of sunflowers and the occasional small house. If you use this road, do so with extreme caution, as accidents are frequent.

Another option is via Isyonje village, just east of the Tukuyu road, following a mostly well-maintained dirt track for about 35km to the junction with the park road, from where it is 32km further through the park to Matamba. From Njombe, a good dirt road traverses 155km to the park via Makete and Bulongwa, joining the route from Isyonje.

Using public transport, a bus goes daily between Mbeya and Matamba via Mfumbi village on the main Tanzam Hwy, departing Matamba at 6am and Mbeya between noon and 1pm (Tsh7000, four hours).

Maua Café & Tours (p305) in Mbeya organises Kitulo excursions, as does Kisolanza – The Old Farm House (p296), near Iringa.

Mbeya

☑ 025 / POP 450,000

The thriving town of Mbeya sprawls at about 1700m in the shadow of Loleza Peak (2656m), in a gap between the verdant Mbeya Range to the north and the Poroto Mountains to the southeast. It was founded in 1927 as a supply centre for the gold rush at Lupa, to the north, but today owes its existence to its position on the Tazara railway line and the Tanzam Hwy, and its status as a major trade and transit junction between Tanzania, Zambia and Malawi.

The surrounding area is lush, mountainous and scenic. It's also a major farming region for coffee, tea, bananas and cocoa. While central Mbeya is on the scruffy side (especially around the bus station), the cool climate, jacaranda trees and views of the hills compensate, and there are many nearby excursions.

◉ Sights & Activities

Amelia at Maua Café & Tours (p305) arranges safaris, horseriding and hikes in the area (from US$70 per day, and US$200 per day with accommodation). She also leads trips to Ngozi Peak and Crater (p308) and many other destinations.

Mbeya Peak   MOUNTAIN
Just northwest of Mbeya is Mbeya Peak (2820m). It's the highest point in the Mbeya Range and makes an enjoyable day hike, best done by arranging a local guide through your hotel or a Mbeya travel agency.

There are several possible routes. One goes from Mbalizi junction, 12km west of town on the Tunduma road. Take a dalla-dalla to Mbalizi, get out at the sign for Utengule Coffee Lodge, head right and follow the dirt road for 1km to a sign for St Mary's Seminary. Turn right here and follow the road up past the seminary to Lunji Farm and then

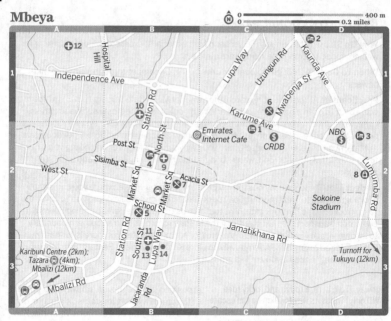

Mbeya

on to the peak. With a vehicle, you can park at Lunji Farm and continue on foot. Allow five hours for the return trip, and only climb accompanied by a guide, which you can arrange at Mbeya travel agencies or through most hotels.

🛏 Sleeping

Catholic Youth Centre   GUESTHOUSE $
(Karume Ave; ☉ dm/s/d Tsh15,000/25,000/ 30,000) Recommended budget accommodation in Mbeya – the spacious terracotta-floored rooms are set in tranquil gardens. Bathrooms are basic but perfectly adequate, with hot water. There's no breakfast, but

you'll find a bakery directly opposite, or head to nearby Maua Café (p305).

Ifisi Community Centre   HOTEL, GUESTHOUSE $
(☎ 025-256 1021, 0753 011622; www.mec-tanzania. ch; s Tsh30,000, guesthouse r Tsh50,000-60,000, hotel r Tsh60,000-80,000, camping Tsh10,000; 🅿 🛜 👪) A very good option for self-drivers en route to/from the Zambian border or points west. There are smallish but spotless guesthouse rooms in this church-run place, plus lovely, spacious, good-value hotel rooms, most with verandas overlooking a private wildlife sanctuary. It has an inexpensive restaurant and a children's playground.

On the north side of the main highway, 18km west of Mbeya.

Mbeya Hotel   HOTEL $
(☑025-250 2224, 025-250 2575, 0788 760818; www.mbeyahotel.com; Kaunda Ave; s/d/tw/ste Tsh60,000/80,000/90,000/120,000; P❋ ☎) The former East African Railways & Harbours Hotel has a faded colonial charm – check out the marble floor – and African art on the walls. Rooms are straightforward twins and doubles. The better ones (all doubles) are in an extension attached to the main building. More cramped rooms are in separate bungalows out back. Small shaded gardens and a restaurant.

Sombrero Hotel   HOTEL $
(☑0766 755227; Post St; s/d/ste Tsh40,000/60,000/75,000; ☎) Tidy, good-value, no-frills rooms in a convenient, central location, with a small restaurant downstairs. Offers a gentle welcome to the colonial centre of Mbeya.

Karibuni Centre   GUESTHOUSE $
(☑025-250 3035, 0754 510174; www.mec-tanzania.ch; camping Tsh10,000, s/d from Tsh35,000/50,000; P) This quiet mission-run place is in a small, enclosed compound where you can also pitch a tent. Most rooms have bathrooms, and there's a restaurant. Karibuni is 3km south of the town centre. Take a taxi from the bus stand (Tsh4000).

If you are driving, go 1.2km west along the highway from the big airport junction at the entrance to Mbeya, to the tiny signpost on Lehner St. Turn right, continue 300m to the T-junction, turn right again. The compound is 200m up on the left.

★Utengule Coffee Lodge   LODGE $$
(☑0786 481902, 0753 020901; www.riftvalley-zanzibar.com; camping US$11.50, s US$70-145, d US$110-195, f from US$180; P ☎ ❄) This lovely lodge is set in expansive grounds on a hilly coffee plantation 20km west of Mbeya. Tasteful accommodation includes spacious standard rooms, nicer two-storey balconied suites, and a large, rustic family room. The cafe and restaurant are excellent. From Mbeya, follow the highway 12km west to Mbalizi junction. Turn right and continue 8.5km to the entrance, on your right. It has tennis courts, and a grassy lawn for campers.

Hill View Hotel   HOTEL $$
(☑0767 502767, 025-250 2766; www.hillview-hotel.com; Kaunda Ave; s $38, r US$78-94, 4- to 6-person ste US$162-240; P❋ ☎) This friendly and flashy 25-room establishment has a quiet location and modern, comfortable rooms. The more expensive ones have Jacuzzi-like bathtubs, and many are apartment-style with a shared kitchen and TV sitting room. Some 'standard' rooms are not en-suite, so check when booking. There's a restaurant on-site.

✖ Eating & Drinking

★Maua Café & Tours   CAFE $
(☑0786 248199; 13 Mwabenja St; mains Tsh7000; ☺8am-5pm Mon, Wed & Thu, to 9pm Tue, Fri & Sat) A brick homestead turned cafe serving big breakfasts, including granola and fresh coffee (Tsh10,000); wraps, burgers and toasties for lunch (from Tsh5000); and pizza, fish and salads for dinner. Sit outside by the hibiscus bush on benches with bright fabric cushions. It has an excellent ethical craft shop, a small backyard campground (US$10) and owner Amelia organises a range of tours.

Amelia is a fount of knowledge on nearby sights and national parks, and arranges many safaris and other activities. At the time of research she was about to open a campsite in Kitulo Park (p302).

★Ridge Cafe   CAFE $
(1st fl, Business Centre Bldg, cnr Market Sq & Acacia St; drinks & snacks Tsh3000-5000; ☺7am-8pm Mon-Fri, 9am-9pm Sat, to 3pm Sun; ☎) If you're missing Western culture, stop by this sleek place, stylishly hung with local fabrics, for smoothies, fresh juices, locally sourced gourmet coffees, great baking and other delicacies. It also sells a few crafts and Mbeya coffee beans. It's a good place to connect with travellers and volunteers.

Sombrero Restaurant   TANZANIAN $
(North St; mains Tsh7000-8000; ☺7am-9pm Mon-Sat, to 8pm Sun) This hotel restaurant serves a small selection of local-style dishes. It's nothing special, but the food is decent, service is efficient and it offers a quiet place to sit in the town centre.

Mbeya Hotel   INDIAN $
(☑025-250 2224/2575; mbeyahotel@hotmail.com; Kaunda Ave; mains Tsh6000-10,000; ☺7am-9pm; ✍) This popular hotel restaurant has a large menu featuring good Indian cuisine, including vegetarian selections and naan bread, plus Chinese and continental fare. Non-Indian meals tend to be on the heavy side (lots of extra oil), but portions are large and it remains one of the better dining options in the town centre.

★ Utengule Coffee Lodge
EUROPEAN $$$
(☑0753 020901, 025-256 0100; www.riftvalley-zanzibar.com; mains Tsh15,000-25,000; ☺7am-10pm; ☏) If you have your own transport, this spot, 20km west of Mbeya, is the place to go for fine dining, with both a daily set menu and à la carte, and a bar. Speciality coffees (including to take home) are a feature. It also has a swimming pool and a pool table, meaning you can spend a good chunk of your day here.

New City Pub
CLUB
(☑0759 901229; Mafiati; ☺7pm-2am) This nightclub at the eastern end of town hosts regular concerts out in the parking lot, featuring bongo flava stars from Dar es Salaam. Call in advance to see what's on. There's a pool table, and a restaurant serves Tanzanian food.

Self-Catering
Azra Supermarket SUPERMARKET $
(School St) Small but well stocked; just up from the Tanesco building.

🛍 Shopping

African Movement Art and Crafts
ARTS & CRAFTS
(Karume Ave; ☺7am-6.30pm) One of a cluster of brightly painted and appealing local businesses, this store sells souvenirs with soul: bright fabric earrings made by the owner, quality wood and soapstone carvings, basketware, wooden bowls and batik wall hangings. It's unsigned, to the left of the 'hair saloon'.

ℹ Information

DANGERS & ANNOYANCES
As a major transport junction, Mbeya attracts many transients, particularly in the area around the bus station. Watch your luggage, don't change money with anyone, and only buy bus tickets in the bus-company offices. Also be very wary of anyone presenting themselves as a tourist guide and don't make tourist arrangements with anyone outside of an office. Bus ticketing scams abound, especially for cross-border connections. Ignore all touts, no matter how apparently legitimate, trying to sell you through-tickets to Malawi (especially) or Zambia. Pay the fare only to the border, and then arrange onward transport from there.

Due to road building and spurious police checks, at the time of writing trips to the airport were suffering severe delays. Allow at least an hour.

INTERNET ACCESS
Emirates Internet Cafe (Jacaranda Rd; per hour Tsh2000; ☺8am-8pm Mon-Sat, 9am-3pm Sun) Near the post office.

MEDICAL SERVICES
Aga Khan Medical Centre (☑025-250 2043; cnr North & Post Sts; ☺8am-8pm Mon-Sat, 9am-2pm Sun) Just north of the market.

Babito Pharmacy (☑0754 376808, 025-250 0965; Station Rd; ☺7.30am-6.30pm Mon-Fri, 8am-5pm Sat) Located at the north end of Station Rd.

Bhojani Chemists (☑0715 622999, 0688 617999; Jacaranda Rd; ☺8.30am-5.30pm Mon-Sat) Well-stocked pharmacy.

General Hospital (☑025-250 3456) Serves Mbeya and the surrounding region.

MONEY
CRDB (Karume Ave; ☺9am-5pm Mon-Sat) ATM.
NBC (cnr Karume & Kaunda Aves; ☺9am-5pm Mon-Fri, to noon Sat) Changes cash; ATM.

ℹ Getting There & Away

AIR
Air Tanzania (☑0782 737730, 0782 782732; www.airtanzania.co.tz) and **Fastjet** (☑0784 108900; www.fastjet.com) fly around five times weekly between Mbeya and Dar es Salaam (from about Tsh180,000 one-way). Air Tanzania is cheaper if you're booking with little notice, while Fastjet have some bargains if you're booking ahead. If you can't get online, book Air Tanzania through **Fastlink Safaris** (☑0752 111102, 0746 650750; Lupa Way; ☺8.30am-5.30pm Mon-Fri, to noon Sat), and Fastjet through **Kipunji Heritage** (☑0754 457760; www.kipunjiheritage-tours.org; Lupa Way).

Songwe Airport (MBI) lies 22km southwest of Mbeya, just north of the Tanzam Hwy (about Tsh25,000 in a taxi); allow at least an hour, and don't rely on the appearance of the 'shuttle service'.

BUS
Arriving in Mbeya, your bus may pull in at the hectic **Nane Nane** terminal on the edge of town (about 10km east along the main highway), in which case you'll need to switch to a dalla-dalla (Tsh400) to get to the centre.

Rungwe Express and other lines depart daily from Mbeya's main bus station to Dar es Salaam (Tsh45,000, 12 to 14 hours) from 6am, via Iringa (Tsh22,000, five to seven hours) and Morogoro (Tsh35,000, eight to nine hours).

Njombe (Tsh10,000, four hours) and **Songea** (Tsh17,500 to Tsh25,000, eight hours) Super Feo departs daily at 6am, with one to two later departures as well.

SOUTHERN HIGHLANDS MBEYA

Tukuyu (Tsh2500, one to 1½ hours), **Kyela**
(Tsh5000, two to 2½ hours) and the **Malawi
border** (Tsh5000, two to 2½ hours; take the
Kyela bus) There are several smaller Coastal
buses daily leaving from the Nane Nane bus
station. It's also possible to get to the Malawi
border via dalla-dalla, but you'll need to change
vehicles in Tukuyu. Note that there are no
direct buses from Malawi into Malawi, though
touts at the Mbeya bus station may try to
convince you otherwise. Dalla-dallas marked
Igawilo or Uyole will drop you at Nane Nane bus
station (Tsh400); taxis from town charge about
Tsh10,000.

Matema (Tsh12,000, six hours) There are two
direct buses daily, departing Mbeya's Nane
Nane bus station between 9am and 10am.
Otherwise, you'll need to take transport via
Tukuyu to Kyela, from there to Ipinda, and then
on to Matema.

Tunduma (Tsh5000, two hours) There are daily
minibuses to the Zambian border. Once across,
there's Zambian transport.

Sumbawanga (Tsh18,000, five to six hours)
Sumry goes daily beginning at 6am, with the
last bus at 3pm, with some of the early buses
continuing on to Mpanda (Tsh32,000, 12 to 14
hours).

Tabora (Tsh37,000, 13 to 15 hours) There are
a few vehicles weekly during the dry season,
going via Chunya, and departing from the main
Tanzam Hwy just east of central Mbeya.

Moshi (Tsh55,000, 16 hours) and **Arusha**
(Tsh58,000, 18 hours) Sumry departs daily
at 5am.

Dodoma (Tsh28,000, 10 hours) and **Singida**
(Tsh40,000, 13 hours) There is at least one bus
daily via Iringa (Tsh14,000 to Tsh18,000, five to
eight hours).

TRAIN
Book tickets at least several days in advance
(although sometimes cabins are available last
minute) at **Tazara train station** (☉8am-noon &
2-5pm Mon-Fri, 10am-noon Sat). It's about 4km
west of town just off the main highway.

❶ Getting Around

Taxis park at the **bus station** and near **Market
Sq**. Fares from the bus station to central hotels
start at Tsh3000. The Tazara train station
(Tsh8000 in a taxi) is 4km out of town on the
Tanzam Hwy. Dalla-dallas from the road in front
of New Millennium Hotel run to the train station
and to Mbalizi, but the ones to the train station
often don't have room for luggage; taxis are a
safer option.

Lake Rukwa

The large, alkaline Lake Rukwa is notable
for its many water birds and its enormous
crocodile population. The northern section
is part of Rukwa Game Reserve, which is
contiguous with Katavi National Park. As
the lake has no outlet, its water level varies
greatly between the wet and dry seasons.
It rarely exceeds about 3m in depth, and
sometimes splits into two lakes separated by
swamplands.

OFF THE BEATEN TRACK

MBOZI METEORITE

About 65km southwest of Mbeya is the **Mbozi meteorite** (adult/child Tsh10,000/5000),
one of the largest meteorites in the world. Weighing an estimated 25 metric tonnes, it's
around 3m long and 1m tall. Scientists are unsure when it hit the earth, but it is assumed
to have been many thousands of years ago, since there are no traces of the crater that it
must have made when it fell, nor any local legends regarding its origins.

Although the site was only discovered by outsiders in 1930, it had been known to
locals for centuries, but not reported because of various associated taboos. Like most
meteorites, the one at Mbozi is composed primarily of iron (90%), with about 8% nickel
and traces of phosphorous and other elements. It was declared a protected monument
by the government in 1967 and is now under the jurisdiction of the Department of Antiquities. The meteorite's dark colour is due to its high iron content, while its burnished
look comes from the melting and other heating that occurred as the meteorite hurtled
through the atmosphere towards earth.

To reach the site you'll need your own vehicle. From Mbeya, follow the main road towards Tunduma. About 50km from Mbeya there's a signposted turn-off to the left. From
here, it's 13km further down a dirt road (no public transport). During the wet season,
you'll need a 4WD. Otherwise, a 2WD can get through without difficulty, except perhaps
for a tiny stream about 2km before the meteorite.

From Mbeya, the trip to the lake can make an adventurous loop for those with their own 4WD transport. Head northeast along the edge of the Mbeya escarpment, passing World's End Viewpoint, with views over the Usangu catchment area (source of the Great Ruaha River). Once past Chunya (where there is a basic guesthouse), it's possible to continue via Saza and Ngomba to the shores of the lake. Return via Galula and Utengule Coffee Lodge (p306) towards Mbeya on a somewhat rougher road. Lake Rukwa is also accessible from Sumbawanga.

There are no facilities at the lake.

Tukuyu

📞 025 / POP 29,500

The small, peppy town of Tukuyu is set in the heart of a beautiful area of hills and orchards near Lake Nyasa. There are many hikes and natural attractions nearby, but only the most basic tourist infrastructure; for all excursions you'll need to rough it. There's compensation, though, in the lush surrounding hills, swathed in tea plantations and dotted with banana-palm groves, and the town itself has a lively daily market selling fruit, veg and clothes.

NBC (Main Rd; ⊙ 9am-4pm Mon-Fri) in the town centre has an ATM.

◎ Sights & Activities

Hiking opportunities abound, with Rungwe Tea & Tours and Bongo Camping the main options for organising something. Afriroots (p386) also does tours here. Expect to pay between Tsh20,000 and Tsh35,000 for most tours.

Daraja la Mungu (Bridge of God) BRIDGE

South of Ngozi Peak and west of the main road, this natural bridge 22km west of Tukuyu is estimated to have been formed around 1800 million years ago by water flowing through cooling lava that spewed out from the nearby Rungwe volcano. The bridge spans a small waterfall.

Ngozi Peak & Crater Lake HIKING

This lushly vegetated 2629m-high volcanic peak has a deep-blue lake – the subject of local legends – about 200m below the crater rim. It is about 7km west of the main road north of Tukuyu. To get here via public transport, take any dalla-dalla travelling between Mbeya and Tukuyu and ask to be dropped off; there's a small sign for Ngozi at the turn-off.

Once at the turn-off, if you haven't come with a guide, you'll be approached by locals offering their services; the going rate is about Tsh5000. If you're short on time, you can go about half the distance from the main road to Ngozi by vehicle and then walk the remainder of the way. Once at the base, it's about another steep hour or so on foot up to the crater rim.

Mt Rungwe HIKING

(entry per person US$10) This 2960m dormant volcano, much of which is protected as the Rungwe Forest Reserve, rises up to the east of the main road north of Tukuyu, adjoining Kitulo National Park. It marks the point where the eastern and western arms of the Rift Valley meet, and is an important centre of endemism.

With an early start, you can hike up and down in a day (allow about 10 hours), passing through pristine patches of tropical forest. There are several routes, although not all are always open. Paths are often overgrown and obscure, and it's easy to get lost, so a guide is essential. Before climbing, you need to go first to the **Ofisi za Muhifadi ya Milimani Rungwe**, in Tukuyu. It's in the Municipality Building (Majengo ya Halmashauri) opposite NMB bank (note: not NBC bank). There, you can pay the required fee and hire a guide (US$15 per group). It will also give you information about which route to use. Both Rungwe Tea & Tours and Bongo Camping can also help you organise a Rungwe climb.

⌁ Tours

Rungwe Tea & Tours HIKING

(📞 0754 767389, 025-255 2489; rungweteatours@gmail.com) This is an energetic one-man-show type of place, supported by Rungwe Fairtrade tea growers, where you can organise guides for hikes in the surrounding area. Prices start about Tsh15,000 per day including a guide and local community fee. It's in the Ujenzi area at the 'Umoja wa Wakulima Wadogo wa Chai Rungwe' building, behind the Landmark Hotel.

⊨ Sleeping & Eating

Bongo Camping CAMPGROUND $

(📞 0732 951763; www.bongocamping.com; camping with own/hired tent Tsh6000/8000; P) A backpacker-friendly place with a large, grassy area to pitch your tent, basic cooking facilities, hot-bucket showers, tents for hire and meals on order. It's at Kibisi village, 3.5km north of Tukuyu, and 800m off the main road (Tsh1000 in a taxi from Tukuyu bus stand).

English-speaking guides can be arranged for hikes of Mt Rungwe and for other excursions in the area.

DM Motel HOTEL $
(☑ 0764 061580, 025-255 2332; s/d/ste Tsh20,000/25,000/35,000, s without bathroom Tsh15,000; ℗) Clean rooms with a large bed (no same-gender sharing permitted) and meals on request. Thefts have been reported, so be careful with your belongings. It's just off the main road at the turn-off into Tukuyu town, and is signposted.

Landmark Hotel HOTEL $
(☑ 025-255 2400, 0782 164160; camping US$5, s/d US$40/45; ℗) Spacious, good-value rooms, all with TV and hot water, a small lawn where it's sometimes permitted to pitch a tent, and a slow but good restaurant. Doubles have two large beds. It's the large multistorey building at the main junction just up from NBC bank; the street is noisy, so ask for a room at the back.

Kivanga Lounge TANZANIAN $
(lunch Tsh5000; ⊙ 10am-9pm) Look out for this pinky-orange building with an open-air counter. It serves tasty and filling lunches: beef, chicken or fish with ugali or pilau rice and greens. Nothing fancy, but it's satisfying.

❶ Getting There & Away

Minibuses run several times daily between Tukuyu **bus station** (off Main St) and both Mbeya (Tsh2500, one to 1½ hours) and Kyela (Tsh2000, one hour).

Two roads connect Tukuyu with the northern end of Lake Nyasa. The main tarmac road heads southwest and splits at Ibanda, with the western fork going to Songwe River Bridge and into Malawi, and the newly paved eastern fork to Kyela and Itungi port. A secondary rough dirt road heads southeast from Tukuyu to Ipinda and then east towards Matema – only attempt this if you're in a 4WD.

Kasumulu

☑ 025 / POP 3000
Sitting just north of the Songwe River and Malawi, one-horse Kasumulu is the closest point to the border. If you get stuck overnighting here, try **Mala Green Campsite**

Park (☑ 0752 628635; malagcamp@yahoo.com; camping US$5, r US$10-20), about 3km before the border and 2km south of the main road, with basic bungalows and camping.

To reach Kasumulu from Mbeya, take a bus to Kyela, as these detour to the border en route. No buses make the border crossing, so you will need to decant yourself and your belongings to physically cross the border. Unless you have a lot of luggage, you won't need a motorbike (Tsh1000) for the short walk.

Lake Nyasa

Picturesque and unspoilt Lake Nyasa (also known as Lake Malawi) is Africa's third-largest lake after Lake Victoria and Lake Tanganyika. It's more than 550km long, up to 75km wide and as deep as 700m in parts. It also has a high level of biodiversity, containing close to one-third of the world's known cichlid species. The lake is bordered by Tanzania, Malawi and Mozambique. The Tanzanian side is rimmed to the east by the Livingstone Mountains, whose green, misty slopes form a stunning backdrop as they cascade down to the sandy shoreline. Few roads reach the towns strung out between the mountains and the shore along the lake's eastern side. To the north and east, the mountains lead on to the Kitulo Plateau.

Places of interest around the Tanzanian side of the lake include (from north to south) Kyela, Itungi, Matema, Liuli and Mbamba Bay.

Kyela

☑ 025 / POP 31,000
Kyela is the closest town to **Itungi** – the port 11km to the south where the Lake Malawi ferries used to begin and end their journey along the Tanzanian lakeshore. It's a scruffy, nondescript transit town, and there's no reason to linger. The surrounding region, much of which is wetlands dotted with rice paddies, is more appealing.

There are no ATMs; the best bet for changing money is with a local hotel proprietor or shop owner.

⌨ Sleeping & Eating

Kyela Beach Resort HOTEL $
(☑ 0784 232650, 025-254 0152; kyelaresort@ yahoo.com; camping US$4, s/d US$25/35; ℗ ✳) If you have your own transport, this is a good bet, with 18 simple but pleasant,

well-ventilated rooms (windows on both walls) set around a garden compound and a restaurant. It's about 1.5km north of town, signposted just off the Tukuyu road. Hot water can be a little unpredictable.

Sativa's Midland Hotel HOTEL $
(☑ 0768 660059; d Tsh25,000-30,000; ❋) An acceptable and clean town-centre option, Sativa's has reasonable facilities, and a decent restaurant and bar are around the corner.

⊙ Getting There & Away

Minibuses go several times daily from Kyela to Tukuyu (Tsh2500, 1½ hours) and Mbeya (Tsh5000, two to 2½ hours) from the minibus stand in the town centre immediately south of Sativa's Midland Hotel, many stopping also at the Malawi border. Pick-ups run daily between Kyela and Itungi port (Tsh500) in rough coordination with boat arrivals and departures.

For updated information on passenger ferry service from nearby Itungi port either call or ask at your hotel.

Matema
☑ 025 / POP 20,000

This quiet lakeside settlement is the only spot on northern Lake Nyasa that has any sort of tourist infrastructure, and with its stunning beachside setting backed by the Livingstone Mountains rising steeply up from the water, it makes an ideal and very family-friendly place to relax for a few days.

Here you can arrange walks and dugout canoe rides through your accommodation or simply lounge on the beach. On Saturdays, there's a **pottery market** at Lyulilo village, about 2km east of Matema village centre along the lakeshore, where Kisi pots from Ikombe are sold.

There's talk of an ATM, but at the time of writing there was nowhere in Matema to withdraw or change money, so bring enough cash with you.

⊨ Sleeping & Eating

Matema has the best accommodation in the area. Facing the water, turn right up the treelined road to find the resorts, which are typically simple and attractive places where the unspoilt lakeshore is the main focus.

★**Blue Canoe**
Safari Camp CAMPGROUND, COTTAGES $
(☑ 0783 575451; www.bluecanoelodge.com; camping US$9, s bungalows US$40-70, d bungalows US$60-90; ⓟ@⊞) ⍚ This lovely beachfront place has camping with spotless ablution blocks, and luxury bungalows with verandas overlooking the lake, polished wood floors and comfortable beds with spacious mosquito netting. There are also less-expensive standard bungalows. The bar is well stocked and the cuisine tasty. The operators arrange snorkelling, kayaking and birding excursions. It's 3.5km from Matema; pick-ups are possible with advance notice.

The owners have made many efforts to integrate their lodge with the local community, training local staff and using traditional building styles and materials from the area. The results are impressive.

Matema Lake Shore Resort COTTAGE $
(☑ 0782 179444, 0754 487267; www.mec-tanzania. ch; camping Tsh15,000, s/d/tr/f from Tsh30,000/ 40,000/75,000/80,000; ⓟ⚕) This recommended Swiss-built place has several spacious, breezy, comfortable two-storey beachfront family chalets, some smaller, equally nice double and triple cottages, and a four-bed option. All rooms front directly onto the lake – with lovely views – except the cheaper back ones. The restaurant serves decent, reasonably priced meals, and all self-contained rooms have minifridge and fan.

**Matema Beach
View Lutheran Centre** COTTAGE $
(☑ 0684 991030; camping Tsh4000, s/d/tr from Tsh40,000/40,000/50,000, tw/q without bathroom Tsh30,000/55,000; ⓟ) Rooms at this place – in brick *bandas* on or just back from the beach – are no frills, although the local ambience is agreeable. It serves a simple breakfast of tea or coffee and bread.

This is the closest accommodation action to town, just 700m west of Matema hospital and the village centre.

Landmark at Lake Nyasa COTTAGE $$
(☑ 0784 716749; s/d Tsh105,000/120,000; ❋☎) The new brick *bandas* constructed by this Tanzanian chain are comfortable enough, but little has been done to make them blend with the stunning natural surroundings, and the interiors are chain-hotel bland. A dramatic wide thatched bar is the most interesting feature, but food is below par for the price.

⊙ Getting There & Away

BOAT
There is currently no reliable passenger ferry service on the eastern side of Lake Nyasa. Once

it resumes, the boat stop for Matema is actually at Lyulilo village, about 25 minutes on foot from the main Matema junction. Just follow the main 'road' going southeast from the junction, paralleling the lakeshore, and ask for the *bandari* (harbour).

BUS

From Tukuyu, pick-ups to Ipinda via Ibanda and Kyela (Tsh2500, three hours) leave around 8am most mornings from the roundabout by the NBC bank. Although drivers sometimes say they are going all the way to Matema, generally they go only as far as Ipinda. Once in Ipinda, pick-ups run onwards to Matema (Tsh300, one hour, 35km). Returning from Matema, departures are in the morning. The only direct buses to Mbeya depart before dawn.

From Kyela, there are several vehicles daily from about 1pm onwards to Ipinda (Tsh1500), a few of which continue on to Matema (Tsh3000, two hours). Departures from Matema back to Kyela run in the morning. From Kyela, it's also fairly easy to hire a vehicle to drop you off at Matema (from about Tsh70,000).

There are also usually two direct buses daily between Mbeya's Nane Nane bus stand and Matema (Tsh10,000, six hours), departing Mbeya between 9am and 10am. All transport in Matema departs from the main junction near the hospital.

CAR & MOTORCYCLE

From Kyela, the signposted turn-off to Ipinda and Matema is about 3km north of the town centre. From here, it's about 14km to Ipinda, and another 25km to Matema along the newly paved road. Allow 30 minutes for the 40km stretch.

There's also a shorter, scenic, but very rough route directly from Tukuyu to Ipinda, which should only be attempted in a 4WD. About 20km out of Tukuyu en route to Ipinda off this road is Masoko Crater Lake, into which fleeing Germans allegedly dumped a small fortune of gold pieces and coins during WWI.

Mbamba Bay

📞 025 / POP 9500

The relaxing outpost of Mbamba Bay is the southernmost Tanzanian port on Lake Nyasa. With its low-key ambience and attractive beach fringed by palm, banana and mango trees, it makes a good spot to spend a few days waiting for a ferry across Lake Nyasa (once service resumes) or as a change of pace if you've been travelling inland around Songea or Tunduru.

On the steep and stunning road through *miombo* woodland between Mbamba Bay and Songea, in the heart of a major coffee-producing area, lies the small, prosperous town of **Mbinga**. Travelling to/from Mbamba Bay via public transport, you'll probably need to change vehicles there, and there's a scattering of guesthouses if you get stuck. It's a friendly place for an overnight, but there are no formal sights.

Most guesthouses can help organise dug-out canoe trips for exploring the nearby shoreline.

🛏 Sleeping

Mbamba Bay

Bio Camp Lodge   BANDA, CAMPGROUND **$**

(📞 0765 925255; www.mbambabay-biocamp. com; camping per tent Tsh20,000, s/d permanent tent Tsh30,000/75,000, s/d/q banda Tsh75,000/ 80,000/135,000) 🍽 Comfortable stone and thatched bungalows with bathrooms, plus some permanent tents on the beach under *makuti* (thatched palm leaf) roofing. You can also pitch your own tent. Local-style meals are available. It's on the beach about 5km north of Mbamba Bay. Walk, or hire a motorbike at the Mbamba Bay bus stand to bring you there.

Snorkelling around nearby islands can be arranged, as can boat trips, cultural dances and guided walks.

WHOSE LAKE IS IT?

Looking at Lake Nyasa, fringed by mountains and dotted with dugout canoes, it's hard to imagine it as a source of conflict. But claims to ownership of these otherwise tranquil waters have resulted in five decades of border dispute, which intensified in 2017 with Malawi's plan to take its northern neighbour to the International Court of Justice in the Hague.

The origins of the dispute lie in the colonial carve-up of territory by the British and Germans in the 1890s. Tanzania claims the true border cuts through the lake, while Malawians say that Lake Malawi, as they call it, is theirs except for the section that sits in Mozambique. While this is a matter of national pride, it's also a matter of money: as well as the fishy riches of the lake, both countries want to stake their claim to oil and gas resources found there in recent times.

Neema Lodge GUESTHOUSE $
(Mama Simba's; r without bathroom Tsh10,000) Basic rooms, basic meals and a pleasant setting overlooking the lake. Turn left just before the bridge as you enter town on the road from Mbinga.

St Benadetta Guest House HOSTEL $
(r Tsh25,000) This two-storey church-run place is set on a small rise overlooking the lake. It has simple rooms, a pleasant garden and meals on order.

ⓘ Getting There & Away

BOAT
There is currently no pasenger ferry service between Mbamba Bay and Matema. Previously, boats departed Mbamba Bay on Sunday (arriving Monday in Matema), and departed Matema on Thursday (arriving Friday in Mbamba Bay).

BUS
There's at least one direct vehicle daily from Songea (Tsh8000, five hours). Otherwise you will need to change vehicles at Mbinga.

CAR & MOTORCYCLE
From Mbamba Bay northbound, there are occasional 4WDs to Liuli mission station.

Between Liuli and Lituhi there is no public transport and little traffic, and from Lituhi northwards, there is no road along the lake, only a footpath.

There's also a rough track leading from Lituhi southeast towards Kitai and Songea, which opens the possibility of an interesting loop.

Liuli

Liuli is the site of an old and still active Anglican mission and the small St Anne's mission hospital, the major health facility on the eastern lakeshore. It's also notable for a (with some imagination) sphinx-like rock lying just offshore, which earned the settlement the name of Sphinxhafen during the German era.

For accommodation, head to **Joseph's** (☏ 0757 723559; d Tsh30,000) – simply and utterly idyllic, with a scattering of simple, thatched huts on the lakeshore, and meals of fish, rice and beans on order.

Until ferry service resumes on Lake Nyasa, the best way to get here is via motorbike taxi (about Tsh15,000, 30 minutes) or 4WD from Mbamba Bay.

THE MAJI MAJI REBELLION

The Maji Maji rebellion, which was the strongest local revolt against the colonial government in German East Africa, is considered to contain some of the earliest seeds of Tanzanian nationalism. It began around the turn of the 20th century when colonial administrators set about establishing enormous cotton plantations in the southeast and along the railway line running from Dar es Salaam towards Morogoro. These plantations required large numbers of workers, most of whom were recruited as forced labour and required to work under miserable salary and living conditions. Anger at this harsh treatment and long-simmering resentment of the colonial government combined to ignite a powerful rebellion.

The first outbreak was in 1905 in the area around Kilwa, on the coast. Soon all of southern Tanzania was involved, from Kilwa and Lindi in the southeast to Songea in the southwest. In addition to deaths on the battlefield, thousands died of hunger brought about by the Germans' scorched-earth policy, in which fields and grain silos in many villages were set on fire. Fatalities were undoubtedly exacerbated by a widespread belief among the Africans that enemy bullets would turn to water before reaching them, and so their warriors would not be harmed – hence the name Maji Maji (*maji* means 'water' in Swahili).

By 1907, when the rebellion was finally suppressed, close to 100,000 people had lost their lives. In addition, large areas of the south were left devastated and barren, and malnutrition was widespread. The Ngoni, a tribe of warriors much feared by their neighbours, put up the strongest resistance to the Germans. Following the end of the rebellion, they continued to wage guerrilla-style war until 1908, when the last shreds of their military-based society were destroyed. In order to quell Ngoni resistance once and for all, German troops hanged about 100 of their leaders and beheaded their most famous chief, Songea.

Among the effects of the Maji Maji uprising were temporary liberalisation of colonial rule and the replacement of the military administration with a civilian government. More significantly, the uprising promoted national identity among many ethnic groups and intensified anti-colonial sentiment, kindling the movement for independence.

Songea

📞 025 / POP 235,300

The sprawling town of Songea, situated at an altitude of just over 1000m, is capital of the surrounding Ruvuma region and will probably seem like a major metropolis if you've just come from Tunduru or Mbamba Bay. Away from the scruffy and crowded central market and bus stand area, it's a pleasant, attractive place, with shaded leafy streets, surrounded by rolling hill country dotted with yellow sunflowers and grazing cattle. The main ethnic group here is the Ngoni, who migrated into the area from South Africa during the 19th century, subduing many smaller tribes along the way. Songea takes its name from one of their greatest chiefs, who was killed following the Maji Maji rebellion.

About 30km west of town, in Peramiho, there's a large **Benedictine monastery** with an affiliated hospital, should you fall ill.

◎ Sights

Songea's colourful **market** (Soko Kuu) along the main road is worth a visit.

The impressive carved wooden doors on the **Catholic cathedral** diagonally opposite the bus stand are also worth a look, as are the bright painted wall paintings inside.

Maji Maji Museum　　　　　MUSEUM
(Tsh10,000; ⊙8am-4pm) About 1km from the town centre, off the Njombe road, is this small museum commemorating the Maji Maji uprising. Behind it is Chief Songea's tomb. Unmissable sights are the statues of 12 chiefs captured and killed by the Germans, which locals still hang with garlands. From town, take the first tarmac road to the right after passing CRDB bank and continue about 200m. The museum entrance is on the left with a pale-blue archway.

The Ngoni chief Songea, after whom the town is named, is buried nearby, alongside a mass grave for other victims of the uprising against the Germans.

🛏 Sleeping

Seed Farm Villa　　　　　B&B $
(📞0752 842086, 025-260 2500; www.seedfarm villa.com; s/d from Tsh75,000/85,000; 🅿️❄️📶) This place has modern, quiet rooms with TV set in tranquil garden surroundings away from the town centre in the Seed Farm area. It has a sitting room with TV, and a restaurant (advance order necessary). Head out of town along Tunduru Rd for 2.5km to the

signposted turn-off, from where it's 200m further.

Heritage Cottage　　　　　HOTEL $
(📞0754 355306; www.heritage-cottage.com; Njombe Rd; s/d Tsh75,000/90,000; 🅿️❄️🔌) This hotel has modern, clean rooms with TV (some with minifridge), a popular bar-restaurant, a large lawn area behind, and a playground for children. It's located 3km north of town along the Njombe Rd.

Anglican Church Hostel　　　　HOSTEL $
(📞025-260 0090; s/d Tsh8000/16,000) This long-standing hostel has no-frills rooms (some sharing a bathroom) set around a courtyard in a quiet area just off the main road. Food is usually available with advance order. To get to the hostel, head uphill from the bus stand, past the market to the Tanesco building. Go left and wind your way back about 400m to the Anglican church compound.

OK Hotels 92　　　　GUESTHOUSE $
(📞026-260 2640; Litunu St; d Tsh15,000-20,000) Small but decent rooms with variable hot water. From the bus stand, head uphill 400m past the market, take the second right (watch for the sign for the Lutheran church). After about 200m go right again, and look for the apricot-coloured house in a fenced compound to your left. Meals are available at Krista Park across the street.

🍴 Eating

Heritage Cottage　　　INTERNATIONAL, INDIAN $
(📞0754 355306; Njombe Rd; mains Tsh12,000-15,000; ⊙7am-10pm) This hotel restaurant has slow service, but provides tasty continental and Indian cuisine and a pleasant covered open-air dining area.

Krista Park Fast Food　　　　TANZANIAN $
(mains Tsh5000; ⊙6.30am-6.30pm Mon-Sat) Snacks and local-style meals, plus a small bakery. From the market, go uphill for about 400m, take the second right (there's a sign for the Lutheran church). After about 200m go right again; Krista Park is on your right.

Agape Cafe　　　　TANZANIAN $
(off Main Rd; snacks from Tsh2000; ⊙8am-5.30pm) Just uphill from the Catholic church, with pastries and inexpensive meals.

ℹ️ Information

IMMIGRATION

Immigration Office (Uhamiaji; Tunduru Rd; ⊙8am-4pm Mon-Fri) At the beginning of the

SELOUS NIASSA WILDLIFE CORRIDOR

The **Selous-Niassa Wildlife Corridor** (www.selous-niassa-corridor.org), or 'Ushoroba' in Swahili, joins the Selous Game Reserve with Mozambique's Niassa Reserve, forming a vast conservation area of about 120,000 sq km, and ensuring protection of one of the world's largest elephant ranges. In addition to the elephants, estimated to number about 85,000, the area is home to one of the continent's largest buffalo herds, more than half of its remaining wild dog population, a substantial number of lions and resting and nesting migratory birds.

The area also encompasses large areas of both the Rufiji and Ruvuma river basins, with the watershed running roughly parallel to the Songea–Tunduru road. Local communities in the area are the Undendeule, the Ngoni and the Yao, who have formed various village-based wildlife management areas to support the corridor. Several of these communities have started small ecotourism ventures, including Marumba, southwest of Tunduru. At the Chingoli Society office in the village centre, guides can be arranged for village tours and to visit **Jiwe La Bwana** (with views across the border into Mozambique) and **Chingoli Table Mountain** and caves, used by locals as a hiding place during the Maji Maji rebellion. Tourist infrastructure ranges from basic to non-existent, with a basic campsite just outside the village.

Tunduru Rd. Get your passport stamped here if you are travelling to/from Mozambique.

MONEY

CRDB (Njombe Rd; ⊘9am-5pm Mon-Fri) ATM.

NBC (⊘8.30am-4pm Mon-Fri, to 1pm Sat) Behind the market; ATM.

ⓘ Getting There & Away

Super Feo departs the **bus stand** daily from 5am to Iringa (Tsh19,000, eight hours) and Dar es Salaam (Tsh42,000, 13 hours), and at 6am to Mbeya (Tsh19,000 to Tsh24,000, eight hours) via Njombe (Tsh10,000, four hours). There are also departures to Njombe at 9.30am and 11am.

For Mbamba Bay, there's one direct vehicle departing daily by 7am (Tsh8000, five hours). Otherwise, get transport to Mbinga and from there on to Mbamba Bay.

To Tunduru (Tsh10,000, four hours), there's a daily bus departing by 7am. There's also one bus daily direct to Masasi (Tsh20,000 to Tsh21,000, six to seven hours), departing by 6am.

Transport to Mozambique departs from the Majengo C area, southwest of the bus stand and about 600m in from the main road; ask locals to point out the way through the back streets. If you're driving to Mozambique, head west 18km from Songea along the Mbinga road to the signposted turn-off, from where it's 120km further on an unpaved but decent road to the Mozambique border.

Tunduru

📞 025 / POP 38,000

Tunduru, halfway between Masasi and Songea, is in the centre of an important gemstone-mining region. The town is also a truck and transit stop, and you're likely to need to spend the night here if travelling between Masasi and Songea. The route between the two towns passes through the southern reaches of the forested Selous-Niassa Wildlife Corridor, which connects the Selous Game Reserve with the Niassa Reserve in Mozambique. This vital wildlife link has been the cause of a number of infamous man-eating lion incidents around Tunduru over the years.

Namwinyu Guest House GUESTHOUSE $
(📞0655 447225, 0786 447225; Songea Rd; r Tsh30,000; P❋) This is Tunduru's best accommodation, with clean, pleasant double-bedded rooms (no same-gender sharing) and tasty, inexpensive meals on order. It's along the north side of the main road at the western edge of town, and an easy 10-minute walk from the bus stand.

ⓘ Getting There & Away

There's at least one bus daily between Tunduru and Masasi, departing by 6am (Tsh8000 to Tsh9000, three to four hours) and also between Tunduru and Songea (Tsh10,000, four hours). The road from Tunduru in both directions is paved, although there are few villages, so bring some food and water. En route between Songea and Tunduru, you'll pass through the Selous-Niassa Wildlife Corridor, with wide views over the Ruvuma River Basin. About 65km east of Songea is the turn-off for Mbarang'andu Wildlife Management Area, an extension of the Selous ecosystem.

Southeastern Tanzania

Why Go?

Time seems to have stood still in Tanzania's sparsely popu-lated southeast. It lacks the development and bustle of the north and tourist numbers are a relative trickle. Yet, for sa-fari enthusiasts and divers, and for adventurous travellers seeking to learn about traditional local life, the southeast makes an ideal destination.

Among the southeast's highlights: Selous Game Reserve, with its top-notch wildlife watching; white-sand beaches and stunning corals around Mafia island; and the Kilwa Kisiwani ruins, harking back to days when the East African coast was the centre of trading networks stretching to the Far East.

Mafia and the Selous offer a good selection of comfortable accommodation and Western amenities. Elsewhere, tourist infrastructure is more limited, although there are some real gems to be found.

Best Places to Stay

➡ Old Boma at Mikindani (p339)

➡ Butiama Beach (p319)

➡ Chole Mjini (p320)

➡ Fanjove Private Island (p331)

➡ Rufiji River Camp (p324)

Best Places to Eat

➡ Pole Pole Bungalow Resort (p320)

➡ Siwandu (p324)

➡ Shamba Kilole Eco Lodge (p320)

➡ Kimbilio Lodge (p328)

When to Go
Mtwara

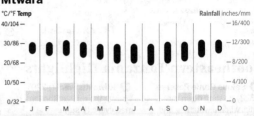

Mar–May Many Selous camps are closed; for those still open, birding is excellent.

Oct This is the prime time for diving and snor-kelling around the Mafia archipelago.

Nov–Feb See whale sharks swimming offshore from Kilindoni (Mafia).

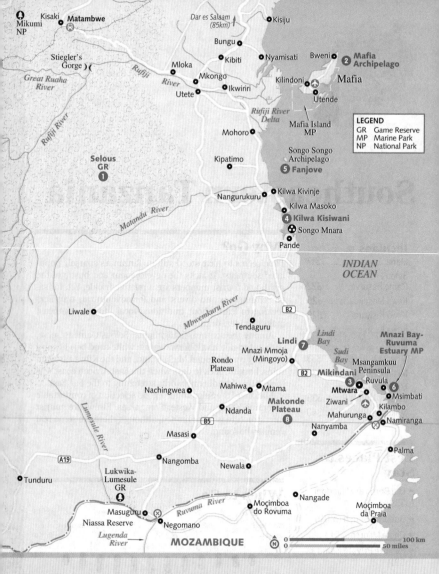

Southeastern Tanzania Highlights

1 Selous Game Reserve
(p322) Boating down the Rufiji, wildlife watching and birding.

2 Mafia (p317) Diving amid idyllic sandbanks and islets.

3 Mikindani (p338)
Exploring traces of bygone days at an old Swahili trading town.

4 Kilwa Kisiwani (p329)
Visiting the ruins of the famed medieval city-state.

5 Fanjove (p331) Relaxing on your own private island in the Songo Songo archipelago.

6 Mnazi Bay-Ruvuma Estuary Marine Park (p340)
Exploring colourful corals

and an amazing underwater world.

7 Lindi (p332) Immersing yourself in local life in this and other southeastern Tanzanian towns.

8 Makonde Plateau (p340)
Experiencing traditional life on this remote, isolated plateau.

Mafia

♪ 023 / POP 46,400

The green islands of the Mafia archipelago are strewn along the coast southeast of Dar es Salaam, surrounded by turquoise waters and glinting white sandbanks. Historically, the archipelago lay at a trade crossroads, with visitors from Kilwa and elsewhere on the mainland, as well as from the Zanzibar Archipelago, Comoros and Madagascar.

Now, this rich melting pot of historical influences, together with the archipelago's strong traditional culture, are among Mafia's highlights. Other draws include the archipelago's natural beauty, its outstanding marine environment, its tranquil pace and its fine collection of upmarket lodges.

History

In addition to Mafia island, the Mafia archipelago includes Juani (southeast of Mafia), Chole (between Mafia and Juani), Jibondo (south of Juani) and at least a dozen other islets and sandbars. The archipelago first rose to prominence between the 11th and 13th centuries in the days when the Shirazis controlled much of the East African shoreline. Thanks to its central buffer position between the Rufiji River delta and the high seas of the Indian Ocean, it made an amenable trading base, and the local economy soon began to thrive. One of the first settlements was built during this era at Ras Kisimani, on Mafia's southwestern corner, followed by another at Kua on Juani.

By the time the Portuguese arrived in the early 16th century, Mafia had lost much of its significance and had come under the sway of the Sultan of Kilwa. In the early 18th century, the island's fortunes revived, and by the mid-19th century it had come within the domain of the powerful Omani sultanate, under which it flourished as a trade centre linking Kilwa to the south and the Zanzibar Archipelago to the north. It was during this era that the coconut palm and cashew plantations that now cover much of the island were established.

Following an attack by the Sakalava people from Madagascar, Mafia's capital was moved from Kua to the nearby tiny island of Chole. Chole's star ascended to the point where it became known as Chole Mjini (Chole City), while the now-main island of Mafia was referred to as Chole Shamba (the Chole hinterlands). Mafia's administrative seat continued on Chole throughout the German colonial era. It was moved to Kilindoni on the main island by the British, who used Mafia as a naval and air base.

Today, farming and fishing are the primary sources of livelihood for Mafia's approximately 46,000 residents, most of whom live on the main island. While shopping in the markets, you'll find cassavas, cashews and coconuts in abundance.

◎ Sights

It doesn't take too much imagination to step back in time in the Mafia archipelago, with village life here much the same as during the island's Shirazi-era heyday. On Mafia island itself, there are small **beaches** interspersed with the mangroves around Chole Bay, and some idyllic nearby sandbanks; all the lodges arrange excursions. One of the closest is **Marimbani**, a popular picnic stop for snorkelling excursions. Further away is **Mange**, with beautiful white sand populated only by crabs and sea birds, and surrounded by crystal-clear aqua waters. At **Ras Mkumbi**, Mafia's windswept northernmost point, there's a lighthouse dating from 1892, as well as **Kanga beach**, and a forest that's home to monkeys, blue duikers and many birds.

There are **green and hawksbill turtle breeding sites** along Mafia island's eastern shores and on the nearby islands of Juani and Jibondo. To protect these and other local ecosystems, the southeastern part of the island, together with offshore islets and waters, has been gazetted as a national marine park (p319). **Whale sharks** (*potwe* in Swahili) visit Mafia between about November and February, and are best seen offshore near Kilindoni.

Away from Mafia island, intriguing destinations to explore include Chole, Juani and Jibondo islands.

Jibondo   ISLAND

Sparsely vegetated Jibondo is less aesthetically appealing than Mafia's other islands, and its inhabitants are traditionally unwelcoming towards visitors. However, it is intriguing in that it supports a population of about 3000 people despite having no natural water sources. Jibondo is renowned as a boat-building centre, with much of the wood coming from forests around mainland Kilwa. In Jibondo's village centre, look for the carved door frame on the mosque, said to come from the old settlement at Kua on Juani. Except during the peak rainy season

SOUTHEASTERN TANZANIA MAFIA

Mafia

INDIAN
OCEAN
Nyororo
Ras
Mkumbi
Nyamisati
(30km)
Bweni
Shungumbili
Mbarakuni
Kirongwe
Ras
Mbisi
Mafia
Baleni
Kilindoni
Chole Bay
Bwejuu
Mange
Ras
Chole
Kisimani
Utende
Kitoni
Kua
Juani
Mrima
Reef
Jibondo
Mange
Reef
Mafia Island
Kitutia
Reef
Boundary of
Marine Park
Mafia Island
Marine Park

(when rainwater is collected on the island from run-off), boats ply daily between Jibondo and Mafia island, transporting large yellow containers filled with water. The best time to watch all the activity is just after sunrise, at the Chole Bay beach near Kinasi Lodge (p320).

Juani
ISLAND, HISTORIC SITE

The large and heavily vegetated island of Juani, southeast of Mafia, has overgrown but evocative ruins at Kua. This includes the remains of several mosques dating from a Shirazi settlement during the 18th and 19th centuries, and crumbling palace walls. Also note the ablutions area just to the right of the main entrance to the settlement. Access to the ruins is only possible at high tide. South of here is a channel and a nearby lagoon for birding and swimming.

Chole
ISLAND, HISTORIC SITE

(day visit per person US$4) A good place to start exploring in the Mafia archipelago, especially around the crumbling but atmospheric ruins, dating from the 19th century. Also on Chole is what's probably East Africa's only **Fruit Bat Sanctuary** (Comoros lesser fruit bat), thanks to the efforts of a local women's group who bought the area where an important nesting tree is located.

🏃 Activities

Fishing

Long popular in deep-sea fishing circles, Mafia is known especially for its marlin, sailfish, tuna and other big-game fish. Conditions are best between September and March, with June and July the least-appealing months due to strong winds. Contact Big Blu or Kinasi Lodge (p320). Licences can be arranged through Mafia Island Marine Park Headquarters (p321) in Utende.

Diving & Snorkelling

Mafia offers divers fine corals, a variety of fish, including numerous pelagics, and relaxing, uncrowded diving, usually done from motorised dhows. You can dive year-round in Chole Bay at various sites for all levels, plus there is seasonal diving (October to February) outside the bay for experienced divers. The best month is generally October, and the least favourable months are April, May and early June, when everything shuts down due to the rains. Diver operators include Big Blu, Mafia Island Diving and the in-house dive instructors at Shamba Kilole Eco Lodge (p320).

Big Blu
DIVING

(☑ 0654 089659, 0787 474108; www.bigblumafia. com; Chole Bay) On the beach at Chole Bay, and under the direction of Moez, a veteran diver with long experience on Mafia. Offers diving, PADI dive-certification courses, snorkelling, excursions around Mafia and reasonably priced accommodation. Overall very good value.

Mafia Island Diving
DIVING

(☑ 0688 218569; www.mafiadiving.com; Mafia Island Lodge, Chole Bay) On the beach at Mafia Island Lodge (p320). Offers snorkelling, diving, PADI dive-certification courses and excursions around Mafia.

🛏 Sleeping & Eating

For all Chole Bay accommodation (including the Utende budget hotels located near the park gate and all accommodation on Chole island), you will need to pay daily marine-park fees, whether you go diving or not.

🛏 Kilindoni & Around

Whale Shark Lodge
GUESTHOUSE $

(Sunset Camp; ☑ 0659 696067, 0755 696067; carpho2003@yahoo.co.uk; Kilindoni; s/d US$25/50; @) This backpacker-friendly budget place, in a quiet, clifftop setting overlooking a prime whale-shark viewing area, is excellent value, with six simple, pleasant cottages with fan, mosquito net and bathroom. There's a large, lovely dining terrace with sunset views and local-style meals (US$7) on order. A short walk down the cliffside is a small beach with high-tide swimming.

It's 1.5km from Kilindoni town centre, behind the hospital and Tsh1500 in a *bajaji* (tuk-tuk).

New Lizu Hotel
GUESTHOUSE $

(📞 023-201 0180; www.newlizuhotel.blogspot.com; Kilindoni; s/d Tsh20,000/25,000; @) This long-standing local guesthouse has friendly staff, spartan, scruffy rooms with fan, cheap food on order and a noisy, central location at Kilindoni's main junction, less than a 10-minute walk from both the airfield and the harbour.

Bustani Bed & Breakfast
B&B $$

(📞 0682 982165, 0675 168893; www.bustanimafia.com; s/d incl airport transfers US$60/100; ❈ ▣) This good-value place on the outskirts of Kilindoni has attractive, tastefully decorated twin- and double-bedded rooms, a pool, a good restaurant and views to the water in the distance. It's under the same management as Butiama Beach and Big Blu, and is ideal for travellers looking to save some money while enjoying simple comforts and having easy access to excursions.

★ Butiama Beach
LODGE $$$

(📞 0787 474084; www.butiamabeach.com; s/d half board US$180/300; ☀ Jun-Mar; @) This lovely 15-room place is spread out in palm-tree-studded grounds on a fine stretch of beach near Kilindoni, about 2km south of the small harbour. Accommodation is in spacious, breezy, appealingly decorated cottages. It has delicious Italian-style dining, sea kayaks for exploring the birdlife in nearby creeks, sunset views and a warm, classy ambience. Very good value for money.

Mkaile Super Market
SUPERMARKET $

(Kilindoni; ☀ 8am-9pm) This small supermarket, diagonally opposite the market in the centre of Kilindoni, has a reasonable selection of basics.

Utende & Chole Bay

Big Blu
GUESTHOUSE $

(📞 0654 089659, 0787 474108; www.bigblumafia.com; Chole Bay; s/d tent US$30/50, s/d r from US$60/100; ☀ Jun-Mar; @) This friendly dive outfitter on the beach at Chole Bay has several tidy, simple beachside bungalows, plus a few tents set back from the beach. It's primarily for divers with Big Blu, although anyone is welcome. Special dive-accommodation packages are available. There's also a good beachside restaurant serving sandwiches, salads and other light meals.

Meremeta Guest House & Apartment
GUESTHOUSE $

(📞 0715 345460, 0787 345460; www.meremetalodge.com; Utende; s/d/tr US$40/50/75) This well-priced place has clean and pleasant budget rooms with fan, delicious meals (US$10 to US$15), and free coffee and tea. The helpful owner makes every effort to ensure his guests have a comfortable stay, and

SOUTHEASTERN TANZANIA MAFIA

MAFIA ISLAND MARINE PARK

At around 822 sq km, Mafia Island Marine Park (www.marineparks.go.tz; adult/child US$23.60/11.80) is the largest marine protected area in the Indian Ocean, sheltering a unique complex of estuarine, mangrove, coral reef and marine channel ecosystems. These include the only natural forest on the island and almost 400 fish species. There are also about 10 villages within the park's boundaries with an estimated 15,000 to 17,000 inhabitants, all of whom depend on its natural resources for their livelihoods.

The park has been classified as a multiuse area to assist local communities in developing sustainable practices so that conservation and resource use can coexist. Entry fees are payable by everyone, whether you dive or not. They are collected at a barrier gate across the main road about 1km before Utende, and must be paid by credit card (Visa or MasterCard), although if you show up with cash only, park staff will receive it and put your payment on a park credit card. Save your receipt, as it will be checked again when you leave. Mafia Island Marine Park Headquarters (p321) are in Utende.

The main way to explore the park is on a diving excursion with one of the Chole Bay dive operators.

also offers bicycle rental and good island excursions. Look for the pink building and local artwork.

Meremeta is on the main road in Utende, about 800m before the Mafia Island Marine Park entry gate, although still within the marine park area and hence subject to daily park fees.

Didimiza
COTTAGE $

(📞 0719 098598; hassanbakari@gmail.com; Utende; s/d/tr US$40/50/60) This very basic place is about 1km before the Mafia Island Marine Park entry gate, although still within the marine park area and subject to daily park fees. It has a few no-frills rooms; local-style meals (US$10 to US$15) and excursions can be arranged. The sea is about a 10-minute walk away through the mangroves. Transfers from Kilindoni cost US$15 per person.

★ Pole Pole Bungalow Resort
LODGE $$$

(www.polepole.com; Chole Bay; s/d full board plus daily excursion US$384/590; ☺ Jun-Mar; @ ✖) 🖋 This beautiful, low-key hideaway is set amid the palm trees and tropical vegetation on a long hillside overlooking Chole Bay. It strikes an excellent balance between luxury and lack of pretension with its quiet style, impeccable service, excellent cuisine and comfortable bungalows. Children under 10 years of age are not allowed.

Mafia Island Lodge
LODGE $$$

(📞 0763 527619, 0655 378886; www.mafialodge. com; Chole Bay; per person half board US$115-135; ☺ Jun-Apr; ❄ 🛜 ✖) This reliable, good-value place – the former government hotel – is set on a long lawn sloping down to the beach. There's a mix of pleasant 'standard' and nicer 'superior' rooms plus two spacious family suites. The restaurant, under a soaring thatched roof overlooking Chole Bay, serves delicious meals. There's also a beach bar and an attached dive centre.

Kinasi Lodge
LODGE $$$

(📞 0715 669145, 0777 424588; www.kinasilodge. com; Chole Bay; s/d full board from US$180/320; ☺ Jun-Mar; 🛜 ✖) A genteel choice, with 14 stone-and-thatched cottages set on a long, green, palm-shaded hillside sloping down to Chole Bay. The Moroccan-influenced decor is at its most attractive in the evening, when the grounds are lit by small lanterns. There's an open lounge area with satellite TV, a spa, a small beach, and a PADI and NAUI dive centre.

Shamba Kilole Eco Lodge
LODGE $$$

(📞 0753 903752, 0786 903752; www.shambakilole lodge.com; Utende; per person full board in chalet/ ste from US$170/220; 🛜 ✖) 🖋 Lovely Shamba Kilole is set in tranquil grounds on a small escarpment overlooking Kilole Bay, just southwest of Chole Bay. Its chalets are individually themed, all are tastefully decorated and the Italian owners – long-time Mafia residents – have put great effort into making the place a true ecolodge, with local sourcing and organic foods. There's also PADI dive instruction on-site.

🛏 Chole Island

Chole Foxes Guesthouse
GUESTHOUSE $

(📞 0715 877393, 0787 877393; per person US$35) Chole's only budget accommodation, this small, tranquil guesthouse has a lovely location on the southwestern edge of the island directly overlooking Chole Bay and Mafia island. The three rooms are simple but adequate – all opening onto the mangroves and water – and delicious local-style meals are available for about US$10.

It's in the Kilimani area of Chole, about 2.5km from the ruins. Wind your way through the palm trees and villages, and ask locals to point out the way, as there are many twists and turns in the road. If you book in advance (which you should do anyway), they will come and collect you with their boat at Utende, or they'll bring a bicycle and guide for you to the main dock in Chole.

★ Chole Mjini
TREEHOUSE $$$

(📞 0784 520799, 0787 712427; www.cholemjini. com; s/d full board US$265/420; ☺ Jun-Easter) 🖋 Chole Mjini is an upmarket bush adventure in synchrony with the local community and environment. Sleep in spacious, rustic and fantastic treehouses, eat fresh seafood, experience the real darkness of an African night without electricity, and take advantage of diving excursions, all while supporting Chole Mjini's work with the local community.

The concept of Chole Mjini grew out of the founders' commitment to the local community, and community development is still at the heart of the undertaking. A portion of earnings are channelled back into health and education projects, and over the almost two decades of the project's life, a health clinic, kindergarten and primary school have been established.

Work is also ongoing, together with the Tanzania Department of Antiquities, to rehabilitate the old German *boma* on Chole island as an extension of Chole Mjini.

ℹ Information

INTERNET ACCESS

Internet Café (Kilindoni; per hour Tsh3000; ⊙ 8am-6pm) At New Lizu Hotel.

MONEY

National Microfinance Bank (Kilindoni) Just off the airport road, and near the main junction in Kilindoni; has an ATM that takes Visa and MasterCard.

TOURIST INFORMATION

General tourist information concerning Mafia Island Marine Park is available at the entry gate along the main road into Utende. For more detailed technical information, **Mafia Island Marine Park Headquarters** (☑ 023-240 2690; ⊙ 8am-5pm Mon-Fri) are located about 1km further on next to Mafia Island Lodge.

ℹ Getting There & Away

AIR

Coastal Aviation (☑ 0713 325673, 0785 500229, 022-284 2700; www.coastal.co.tz; Mafia airport; ⊙ approx 8am-5pm, depending on flight schedules) flies daily between Mafia and Dar es Salaam (US$125), Songo Songo (US$150, minimum two passengers), Zanzibar Island (US$175) and Kilwa Masoko (US$190, minimum four passengers), with connections also to Selous Game Reserve and Arusha.
Tropical Air (☑ 024-223 2511, 0687 527511, 0715 364396; www.tropicalair.co.tz; Mafia airport; ⊙ approx 8am-5pm, depending on flight schedules) has a slightly cheaper daily flight between Mafia and Dar es Salaam with connections to Zanzibar.

All the Chole Bay hotels arrange airfield transfers for their guests (included in the room price at some, otherwise about US$15 to US$30 per person; enquire when booking).

BOAT

A small **ferry** sails daily in each direction between Mafia (Kilindoni port) and Nyamisati village on the mainland south of Dar es Salaam. Departures from Nyamisati are at 4am and from Kilindoni at 6am (Tsh16,000, about four hours). In Kilindoni, the ticketing office is at the top of the hill leading down to the port; buy tickets the afternoon before. In Nyamisati, buy tickets at the port on arrival. While a trickle of budget travellers reach Mafia this way, remember that there is no safety equipment on any of the boats. They are often crowded, and the ride can be windy and extremely choppy in the middle of the channel. Many boats have capsized on this route. If you want to try, it works better from Mafia to the mainland, as the entire journey is done in the daylight, and your hotel can help you get things sorted with the boat.

To reach Nyamisati, get a southbound dalla-dalla from Mbagala Rangi Tatu (Tsh5500), which is along the Kilwa road and reached via dalla-dalla from Dar es Salaam's Posta (Tsh400); allow up to four hours from central Dar to Nyamisati

To get to Kilndoni's town centre from the port, walk straight up the hill for about 300m. When arriving at Nyamisati, it's easy to find dalla-dallas north to Mbagala and central Dar es Salaam. Heading south from Nyamisati, you'll need to first get a vehicle to Bungu (Tsh3000) along the main Dar es Salaam–Mtwara road. Once in Bungu, you can get onward transport south to Nangurukuru (for Kilwa) and Mtwara. If you get stuck overnight in Nyamisati, ask for the 'mission', where you can sleep for Tsh10,000 per person.

ℹ Getting Around

Dalla-dallas connect Kilindoni with Utende (Tsh1000, 30 minutes) several times daily, and at least once daily with Bweni (Tsh4000, four to five hours). On the Kilindoni–Utende route, vehicles depart Kilindoni at about 1pm and Utende at about 7am; the last departure from Utende is about 4.30pm. Departures from Kilindoni to Bweni are at about 1pm, and from Bweni at about 7am. In Kilindoni, the transport stand is in the central 'plaza' near the market. In Utende, the start and end of the dalla-dalla route is at the tiny loading jetty between Mafia Island Lodge (p320) and Big Blu (p319).

It's also possible to hire taxis or *bajaji* (tuk-tuks) in Kilindoni to take you around the island. Bargain hard, and expect to pay from Tsh15,000

ℹ MAFIA INFORMATION

Kilindoni, where all boats and planes arrive, is Mafia's hub. Here you'll find a bank (with an ATM), port, market, small shops and several budget guesthouses. The only other settlement of any size is Utende, 15km southeast of Kilindoni on Chole Bay, where most upmarket lodges are located. The Utende–Chole Bay area is also the main divers' base. Mafia's western side is dotted with small villages, offshore islands and sandbanks, and stands of mangrove interspersed with patches of beach. Many lodges are closed in April and May. July and August can be very windy on the eastern side of the island.

between Kilindoni and Utende for a vehicle (Tsh10,000 for a *bajaji*).

The other option is bicycle, either your own (bring a mountain bike) or a rental (from about Tsh500 per hour for a heavy single-speed; ask around at the Kilindoni market).

To get between Utende and Chole island, most of the Chole Bay hotels provide boat transport for their guests, and transfers can be arranged with Mafia Island Diving (p318) and Big Blu (p319). Otherwise, local boats sail throughout the day from the beach in front of Mafia Island Lodge (p320; Tsh500). Boats also leave from here to Juani, and from Chole it's possible to walk to Juani at low tide. To Jibondo, you can usually catch a lift on one of the water transport boats leaving from the beach near Pole Pole Bungalow Resort (p320).

Selous Game Reserve

Selous Game Reserve (mtbutalii@gmail.com; adult/child US$59/35.40, plus daily conservation fee US$17.70-$29.50) is a vast, 48,000-sq-km wilderness area lying at the heart of southern Tanzania. It is Africa's largest wildlife reserve, and home to large herds of elephants, plus buffaloes, crocodiles, hippos, wild dogs, many bird species and some of Tanzania's last remaining black rhinos. Bisecting it is the **Rufiji River**, which winds its way more than 250km from its source in the highlands through the Selous to the sea, and boasts one of the largest water-catchment areas in East Africa. En route, it cuts a path past woodlands, grasslands and stands of borassus palm, and provides some unparalleled water-based wildlife watching. In the river's delta area, which lies outside the reserve opposite Mafia island, the reddish-brown freshwater of the river mixes with the blue salt water of the sea, forming striking patterns and providing habitats for dozens of bird species and passing dolphins.

Only the section of the reserve north from the Rufiji River is open for tourism; large areas of the south are zoned as hunting concessions. Yet, the wealth of Selous' wildlife and its stunning riverine scenery rarely fail to impress. Another draw is the Selous' relative lack of congestion in comparison with Tanzania's northern parks.

History

Parts of Selous Game Reserve were set aside as early as 1896. However, it was not until 1922 that it was expanded and given its present name (after Frederick Courteney Selous, the British explorer who was killed and buried in the reserve during WWI, and whose **grave** can still be visited). The area continued to be extended until 1975 when it assumed its current boundaries.

During the 1990s and thereafter, efforts were initiated to link Selous Game Reserve with the Niassa Reserve in Mozambique, with the first stages of the project – including establishment of a wildlife corridor – already functional.

Much of this progress is gradually being reversed by more recent developments within the reserve. These include poaching, uranium mining in the southern part of the Selous (leading to a redrawing of reserve boundaries) and government confirmation in mid-2017 that the Rufiji River – the heart and lifeblood of the Selous – will be dammed near **Stiegler's Gorge**, in the northwestern part of the reserve, in connection with a planned hydroelectric project.

In 2014, Unesco placed the Selous on its World Heritage in Danger list, and it reconfirmed this decision in 2017. If the dam project moves forward, complete delisting in the near future is a very real possibility. The Selous' only hope for survival now rests in the ability of concerned environmentalists in Tanzania and beyond to convince the government that it can achieve its goals of increasing Tanzania's electrical grid capacity and overall economic health through means other than exploiting one of its greatest natural treasures.

⊙ Sights & Activities

Boat safaris on the Rufiji or the reserve's lakes are offered by most camps and lodges. Most also organise walking safaris, usually three-hour hikes near the camps, with a night at a fly camp. **Vehicle safaris** are permitted in open safari vehicles – a welcome change from Tanzania's northern safari circuit.

Self-drive safaris are also possible. It's 75km through the Selous between Mtemere and Matambwe gates. Spending a few days on each side, linked by a full day's wildlife drive in between, is a rewarding option, although wildlife concentrations in the Matambwe area cannot compare with those deeper inside the reserve towards Mtemere. If you can only explore one area, eastern Selous is the best bet.

Selous Game Reserve (Northern Section)

N 0 ⸻ 10 km
   0 ⸻ 5 miles

Selous Game Reserve (Northern Section)

⊙ **Top Sights**
1 Selous Game Reserve B3

⊙ **Sights**
2 Selous Grave.. C2
3 Stiegler's Gorge.................................... B3

🛏 **Sleeping**
4 Beho Beho.. B2
5 Beho Beho Public Campsite................. B2

6 Lake Manze Tented Camp.................... C2
7 Lake Tagalala Public Campsite............ C2
8 Rufiji River Camp................................. D2
9 Sable Mountain Lodge.......................... A2
10 Sand Rivers Selous.............................. C3
11 Selous Impala Camp............................ C2
12 Selous Mbega Camp............................ D3
Selous River Camp........................ (see 12)
13 Siwandu C2
14 Special Campsite................................. C2

🛏 Sleeping & Eating

Just outside Mtemere gate are several reasonably priced camps, which make good options for budget travellers. There are also budget guesthouses in Mloka village, about 11km outside Mtemere gate, but these are only feasible for those with their own transport.

For self-catering, stock up in Dar es Salaam or Morogoro, although a small selection of basics is available in villages outside the Mtemere and Matambwe gates.

🛏 Inside the Reserve

All campsites must be booked and paid for on arrival at the gates. Bring all food and drink.

Lake Tagalala
Public Campsite   CAMPGROUND $
(mtbutalii@gmail.com; per adult/child US$35.40/ 23.60) Lake Tagalala campsite has basic but good facilities, including cold-water showers and covered cooking areas. There is usually water, but it is worth also filling up a container when entering the reserve. The campsite is located roughly midway between Mtemere and Matambwe gates on a low rise near Lake Tagalala.

Beho Beho Public Campsite   CAMPGROUND $
(mtbutalii@gmail.com; per adult/child US$35.40/ 23.60) Located at Beho Beho bridge, about 12km southeast of Matambwe and hence best accessed from Matambwe gate, with a lovely remote setting and basic ablutions.

Special Campsite
CAMPGROUND $

(mtbutalii@gmail.com; per adult/child US$59/35.40) Camping completely wild can be arranged in the area between Mtemere gate and Lake Manze (northeast of Lake Tagalala). You will need to be self-sufficient, including bringing all food and drink plus a large container to fill up for bathing and cleaning water at one of the entry gates.

★ Selous Impala Camp
TENTED CAMP $$$

(☑ 0753 115908, 0787 817591; www.selousimpala camp.com; per person with full board & excursions from US$670; ⊘ Jun-Mar; P 🛜 🛋) Impala Camp has eight well-spaced, nicely appointed tents in a prime setting on the river near Lake Mzizimia. Its restaurant overlooks the river and has an adjoining bar area on a deck jutting out towards the water, and the surrounding area is rich in wildlife.

★ Sand Rivers Selous
LODGE $$$

(☑ 0787 595908; www.nomad-tanzania.com; s/d with full board & wildlife excursions US$1365/2040; ⊘ Jun-Mar; P 🛋) Set splendidly on its own on the Rufiji south of Lake Tagalala, this is one of the Selous' most exclusive options, with some of Tanzania's most renowned wildlife guides. The eight luxurious stone cottages have full river views.

★ Rufiji River Camp
TENTED CAMP $$$

(☑ 0784 237422; www.rufijirivercamp.com; per person with full board & activities from US$410; ⊘ Jun-Mar; P 🛜 🛋) This long-standing, unpretentious camp is run by the Fox family who own camps throughout southern Tanzania. Set in a fine location on a wide bend in the Rufiji River about 1km inside Mtemere gate, it has tents with river views and a sunset terrace. Activities include boat safaris and overnight walking safaris.

The dining area and tents are also wheelchair accessible.

Beho Beho
LODGE $$$

(☑ in UK +44 1932 260618; www.behobeho.com; per person with full board & wildlife excursions US$1060; ⊘ Jun–mid-Mar; P 🛋) On a hillside northwest of Lake Tagalala, not overlooking any water, Beho Beho is nevertheless a fine option. It's especially recommended for repeat safari-goers who want to get to know the Selous in more depth. The spacious stone and thatched cottages have commanding views over the plains, guiding is excellent and there's the chance for a night in a private treehouse.

Siwandu
TENTED CAMP $$$

(Selous Safari Camp; ☑ 022-212 8485; www.selous. com; per person all-inclusive US$1014; ⊘ Jun-Mar;

ⓘ ESSENTIAL FEE INFORMATION: SELOUS GAME RESERVE

All fees are per 24-hour period and for single entry only. At the time of research, neither cash nor credit card were accepted at the reserve gates, although check before travelling as credit card payment at the reserve gates should be implemented in 2018. Meanwhile, payment of all reserve fees (including camping fees, if staying at reserve-run campsites) *must* be made in advance at any NBC bank branch into the following accounts:

➡ US dollar (US$) account: 012105021353

➡ Tanzanian shilling (Tsh) account: 012103011903

You will then need to present the bank receipt at Mtemere or Matambwe gate in order to be permitted to enter the Selous. Note that the above is mainly applicable to self-drive campers or to those arriving at the Selous without an advance booking. If you are staying in a lodge or tented camp, whether inside or outside the reserve, you can make payment arrangements in advance with them.

Admission US$59 per adult (US$35.40 per child aged five to 17 years)

Conservation fee US$29.50 per person for those staying at camps inside the Selous; US$17.70 per person for those staying at camps outside the Selous' boundaries

Vehicle fee Tsh23,600 for Tanzania-registered vehicles

Camping at ordinary campsite US$35.40 per adult (US$23.60 per child)

Camping at special campsite US$59 per adult (US$35.40 per child)

Wildlife guard (mandatory in camping areas) US$29.50

Guide US$47.20 (US$29.50 for walking- or boat-safari guides)

P @) This upmarket camp is set on a side arm of the Rufiji in a lush, beautiful setting overlooking Lake Nzelekela. It's divided into two separate camps, each with a half dozen spacious tents, giving a more intimate, exclusive feel. There's a raised dining and lounge area on one side, excellent cuisine and impeccable service throughout. No children under six years of age.

Lake Manze Tented Camp　　TENTED CAMP $$$
(☑ 022-260 1747; www.ed.co.tz; per person with full board & excursions from US$500; ◉ Jun-Mar; P) The rustic but comfortable Lake Manze is favourably situated, with 12 simple but pleasant tents in a good location along an arm of Lake Manze. The ambience is low-key with a bush feel, and the camp is recommended for those on tighter budgets, especially as part of the flight-accommodation deals with Coastal Travels (p68).

🛏 Outside the Reserve

Most lodges outside the gate can arrange boat safaris, walking tours outside the reserve and wildlife drives inside the Selous. Boat safaris are generally done along the stretch of river east of the reserve boundaries, although it's also possible inside the reserve. Reserve fees are payable only for the days you enter within the Selous' boundaries.

★ Selous River Camp　　TENTED CAMP $$
(☑ 0784 237525; www.selousrivercamp.com; camping US$10, s/d tent with full board US$100/155, s/d tr mud hut with full board US$230/300/348; ◉ Jun-Feb) This friendly place is the closest camp to Mtemere gate. It has cosy, river-facing 'mud huts' with bathrooms, plus small standing tents surrounded by forest with cots and shared facilities. The bar-restaurant area is lovely, directly overlooking the river at a particularly scenic spot. Overall, it's a great choice for budget travellers.

Selous Mbega Camp　　TENTED CAMP $$
(☑ 0784 748888, 0784 624664; www.selous-mbega-camp.com; s/d with full board from US$140/200, s/d backpackers' special with full board from US$95/140; ♿) This laid-back budget camp is located about 1km outside the eastern boundary of the Selous near Mtemere gate and just west of Mloka village. It has raised, no-frills tents set in the foliage overlooking the river, and reasonably priced boat and vehicle safaris. Pick-ups and drop-offs to and from Mloka are free.

ⓘ SELOUS GAME RESERVE

Why Go Rewarding wildlife watching against a backdrop of stunning riverine scenery; wonderful, small camps; excellent boat safaris and the chance for walking safaris.

When to Go The Selous is best visited from June through December. Many camps close from March through May, during the heavy rains.

Practicalities Fly or drive in from Dar es Salaam; drive in from Morogoro or Mikumi. Both Mtemere and Matambwe gates are open from 6.30am to 6pm.

Budget Tip Travel by bus from Dar es Salaam to Mloka village, and base yourself outside the Selous' boundaries, paying park fees only when you enter the reserve.

The 'backpackers' special' rate is for travellers arriving in Mloka or Kisaki by bus.

Sable Mountain Lodge　　LODGE $$$
(☑ 0713 323318, 0737 226398; www.selouslodge. com; s/d full board from US$250/390, all inclusive US$490/630; ◉ Jun-Mar; P @) Friendly and relaxed, Sable Mountain is about halfway between Matambwe gate and Kisaki village on the northwestern boundary of the reserve. There are cosy stone cottages, tented *bandas*, a snug for stargazing, walking safaris, wildlife drives and night drives outside the reserve.

ⓘ Getting There & Away

AIR

Coastal Aviation (www.coastal.co.tz) has daily flights linking Selous Game Reserve with Dar es Salaam (US$165 to US$195 one way), Zanzibar Island (US$210 to US$240 one way), Mafia (via Dar, US$275 to US$305 one way) and Arusha (via Dar, US$410 to US$440 one way), with connections to other northern-circuit airstrips. Coastal also flies between the Selous and Ruaha National Park (US$320 to US$350 one way).

Other airlines flying these routes for similar prices include **ZanAir** (www.zanair.com) and **Safari Airlink** (www.flysal.com). Flights into the Selous are generally suspended during the wet season from mid-March to May. All lodges provide airfield transfers.

BUS

Tokyo Bus Line runs a daily bus between Temeke's Sudan Market (Majaribiwa area) and Mloka village (Tsh12,000, seven to nine hours), which is about 10km east of Mtemere gate. Departures in both directions are between 5.30am and 6.30am. From Mloka, you'll need to arrange a pick-up in advance with one of the camps. Hitching within the Selous isn't permitted, and there are no vehicles to rent in Mloka.

If you are continuing from the Selous to Kilwa, Lindi or Mtwara, there's usually a daily dalla-dalla from Mloka to Kibiti junction, on the main road. It departs Mloka anywhere between 3am and 5am (four to six hours). Once at Kibiti, you'll need to flag down one of the passing buses coming from Dar es Salaam to take you to Nangurukuru junction (for Kilwa) or on to Lindi or Mtwara.

Coming from Morogoro: Tokyo Bus Line goes at least once daily between Morogoro's Msamvu transport stand and Kisaki village (Tsh9000, seven hours), departing in each direction between about 9am and 11am. From Kisaki, you'll need to arrange a pick-up in advance with the lodges to reach Matambwe gate, 21km further on. It's about 180km between Matambwe gate and Morogoro.

CAR

You'll need a 4WD with high clearance in the Selous. There's no vehicle rental at the reserve and motorcycles aren't permitted.

To get here via road, there are two options. The first: take the main tarmac road from Dar es Salaam to Kibiti, where you then branch south-westwards on a mostly decent dirt and sand track to Mkongo, Mloka and on to Mtemere gate (240km). The road's condition is reasonable to good, as far as Mkongo. Mkongo to Mtemere (75km) is sometimes impassable during heavy rains. Allow six hours from Dar es Salaam.

Alternatively, you can go from Dar es Salaam to Kisaki via Morogoro and then on to Matambwe gate (about 350km) via a scenic but rough route through the Uluguru Mountains. It's 141km from Morogoro to Kisaki and 21km from Kisaki on to Matambwe gate. This route has improved considerably in recent times, but is still adventurous. From Dar es Salaam, the road is good tarmac as far as Morogoro. Once in Morogoro, take the Old Dar es Salaam road towards Bigwa. About 3km or 4km from the centre of town, past the Teachers' College Morogoro and before reaching Bigwa, you will come to a fork in the road, where you bear right. From here, the road becomes steep and scenic as it winds its way through the dense forests of the Uluguru Mountains onto a flat plain. Allow five to six hours for the stretch from Morogoro to Matambwe, depending on the season. If you are coming from Dar es Salaam and want to bypass Morogoro, take the unsignposted left-hand turn-off via Mikese, about 25km east of Morogoro on the main Dar es Salaam road that meets up with the Kisaki road at Msumbisi.

Driving from Dar es Salaam, the last petrol station is at Kibiti (about 100km northeast of Mtemere gate), where you should top up. Otherwise try Ikwiriri, from where there is also an access road joining the Mloka track. There is no fuel thereafter. Coming from the other direction, the last reliable petrol station is at Morogoro (about 160km from the Matambwe ranger post). Occasionally you may find both petrol and diesel sold on the roadside at Matombo, 50km south of Morogoro, and at several other villages, although quality isn't reliable. If you plan to drive around the Selous, bring sufficient petrol supplies with you as there are none available at any of the lodges, nor anywhere close to the reserve.

Expect to pay from US$250 to US$300 per vehicle for a one-way transfer from Dar es Salaam via Mloka.

TRAIN

Train is an option for the adventurous, especially if you're staying on the northwestern side of the reserve. With luck, you may even get a preview of the wildlife from the train window. All **Tazara** (www.tazarasite.com) trains stop at Kisaki, which is about five to six hours from Dar es Salaam, the first stop for the express train, and the main station of interest. Ordinary trains also stop at Matambwe, near the Selous headquarters, as well as at Kinyanguru and Fuga stations.

It works best to take the train from Dar es Salaam to the Selous, though be sure you have a pick-up confirmed in advance, as the train generally arrives after nightfall. As it is not permitted to drive inside the Selous at night, this will only work for lodges based outside the reserve boundaries. Going the other way, delays are more common, and most lodges are therefore unwilling to collect travellers coming from the Mbeya side. There are several basic and unappealing local guesthouses in Kisaki, should you get stuck.

Kilwa Masoko

023 / POP 13,600

Kilwa Masoko (Kilwa of the Market) is a sleepy coastal town nestled amid dense coastal vegetation and several fine stretches of beach about halfway between Dar es Salaam and Mtwara. It's the springboard for visiting the ruins of the 15th-century Arab settlements at Kilwa Kisiwani and Songo Mnara, and, as such, is the gateway into one of the most significant eras in East African coastal history. The town itself is a relatively modern creation, with minimal historical appeal.

⊙ Sights & Activities

On the eastern edge of town is **Jimbizi Beach**, a short stretch of sand in a partially sheltered cove dotted with the occasional baobab tree. The best coastline is the long, idyllic palm-fringed open-ocean beach at **Masoko Pwani**, 5km northeast of town, and best reached by bicycle or *bajaji* (Tsh5000 one way). This is also where Kilwa Masoko gets its fish, and the colourful harbour area is worth a look, especially in the late afternoon.

Dhow excursions through the mangrove swamps on the outskirts of Kilwa – interesting for their birdlife and resident hippos – can be arranged with Kilwa hotels and with the Kilwa Islands Tour Guides Association (p328), as can a variety of other excursions. These include visits to the extensive limestone caves about 85km northwest of Kilwa at Kipatimo.

🛏 Sleeping & Eating

Kilwa Bandari Lodge　　GUESTHOUSE $
(☑0689 440557, 0717 397814; www.kilwabandari lodge.com; camping Tsh20,000, s Tsh39,000-49,000, d or tw Tsh49,000-59,000; ⓟ❄️🛜) Six tidy, modern rooms in the main building, plus several smaller but equally nice rooms in a back annex, make this a great budget bet. All rooms have fan, mosquito net and window screens, and tasty meals are available in the garden restaurant (meals from Tsh8000). It's about 1.5km south of the bus stand along the main road, shortly before the port gates.

Kilwa Seaview Resort　　LODGE $$
(☑0784 613335, 0784 624664; www.kilwa. net; Jimbizi Beach; camping US$10, s/d/tr/q US$90/110/130/150; ⓟ🛜🏊) This family-friendly place has spacious A-frame cottages perched above a rocky escarpment overlooking the eastern end of Jimbizi Beach. There's a restaurant built around a huge baobab tree serving tasty meals, and the swimming beach is just a short walk away.

If driving, the access turn-off is signposted from the main road. By foot from the bus stand, head south along the main road towards the port, then turn left near the police station, making your way past the police barracks to Jimbizi Beach. At the northeastern end of the beach is a small path leading up to the cottages. Transfers from Dar es Salaam or to the Selous cost from US$250 per vehicle one way.

Kilwa Masoko

Kilwa Masoko

⊙ Sights
1 Jimbizi Beach.............................. B2

🛏 Sleeping
2 Kilwa Bandari Lodge A3
3 Kilwa Pakaya Oceanic Resort B2
4 Kimbilio Lodge B2

🍴 Eating
5 Night Market B1

ℹ Information
6 Antiquities Office........................ A3
7 Kilwa Islands Tour Guides
　　Association B1
8 National Microfinance Bank B2

Kilwa Dreams　　BUNGALOW $$
(☑0784 585330; www.kilwadreams.com; Masoko Pwani; camping US$10, d/f bungalow US$90/110; ⓟ) This is a great spot for relaxing, with a handful of spartan but well-tended bungalows with cold water and no electricity in an idyllic setting directly on the long, wonderful beach at Masoko Pwani. There's also a beachside bar-restaurant (meals Tsh25,000 to 40,000). Take the airport turn-off and follow the signs along sandy tracks for about 4km to the beach. *Bajaji* charge Tsh5000 from town.

Kimbilio Lodge LODGE $$

(☎0713 975807, 0656 022166; www.kimbiliolodges.com; s/d US$80/120; P 🛜) This pleasant place has a good beachside setting on Jimbizi Beach. Accommodation is in six, spacious, tastefully decorated bungalows directly on the sand. It's warmly recommended. There's good Italian cuisine and, with advance notice, diving (no instruction). Snorkelling excursions and visits to the hippos and mangrove swamps can be arranged.

Kilwa Pakaya Oceanic Resort HOTEL $$

(☎0674 941112; www.kilwapakayahotel.co.tz; s/d US$75/95; P ❄ 🛜) Well-situated in the centre of Jimbizi Beach, Kilwa Pakaya has a beachside dining area, beach volleyball and small, reasonably comfortable rooms in a rather characterless multistorey block to the back. All have sea views plus fan and minifridge.

Mwangaza Hideaway LODGE $$$

(☎0765 289538, 0757 029244; www.kilwa-mwangaza.com; dm US$25, d/q with full board in bungalow/dhow house US$140/200; P ✕) Tranquil Mwangaza has good-value dorm accommodation (with breakfast included) in a refurbished six-bed house, plus a handful of open-style bungalows directly overlooking the mangroves, and a lovely four-person 'dhow house'. The restaurant serves excellent meals. It's on the western side of the peninsula and about 1km off the main road, reached via a signposted turn-off opposite the airfield.

Night Market MARKET $

(off Main Rd, behind bus stand; snacks Tsh500-2000; ⏲6-11pm) Kilwa's lively night market gets going each evening from around 6pm, with grilled *pweza* (octopus), *mishikaki* (grilled meat skewers) and other snacks.

ℹ Information

MONEY

National Microfinance Bank (Main Rd) ATM accepting Visa and MasterCard.

TOURIST INFORMATION

Kilwa Islands Tour Guides Association (Main Rd; ⏲8am-8pm) This small office at the bus stand is the hub of Kilwa's tourism scene. You'll need to stop here to arrange visits to Kilwa Kisiwani and Songo Mnara. It also provides assistance finding accommodation, and offers a range of excursions in the Kilwa area. Prices for most excursions start at about US$25 per person for a guide and transport (less with larger groups).

Antiquities Office (Idara ya Mambo ya Kale; Main Rd; ⏲7.30am-3.30pm Mon-Fri) This is where you get permits to visit Kilwa Kisiwani and Songo Mnara, though as you need to arrange everything through the Kilwa Islands Tour Guides Association anyway, it's easier to stop there first.

ℹ Getting There & Away

AIR

Coastal Aviation flies daily on demand between Kilwa and Dar es Salaam (US$275 one way), Zanzibar Island (US$330 one way) and Mafia (US$190 one way). All flights require a minimum of four passengers. Book through the Coastal Aviation office (p69) in Dar es Salaam. Kilwa Masoko's airstrip is about 2km north of town along the main road.

BOAT

Dhows to Songo Songo and other nearby islands are best arranged in Kilwa Kivinje. Boats to Kilwa Kisiwani and Songo Mnara depart from the small port (Main Rd) at the southern end of town. An intriguing option for those with time is the three-night sailing safari between Kilwa Masoko and Dar es Salaam, organised through Mwangaza Hideaway, or the **Slow Leopard** (theslowleopard@gmail.com) in Dar es Salaam (from US$485 per person).

BUS

To Nangurukuru (the junction with the Dar es Salaam–Mtwara road; Tsh2000, one hour) and Kilwa Kivinje (Tsh2000, 45 minutes), shared taxis and minibuses depart several times daily from the **transport stand** (Main Rd) just off the main road near the market. The transport stand is also the place to hire taxis or *bajaji* for local excursions.

To Dar es Salaam, there are several buses daily, usually stopping also in Kilwa Kivinje. Departures in each direction are between 5.30am and 10am (Tsh13,000, four to five hours). Book tickets the day before. All Kilwa departures are from the transport stand near the market. Departures in Dar es Salaam are from Mbagala Rangi Tatu, along the Kilwa road, which is also the end terminus for the bus on its run up from Kilwa. Coming from Dar es Salaam it's also possible to get a Mtwara-bound bus and get out at Nangurukuru junction, from where you can get local transport to Kilwa Kivinje (Tsh1000, 11km) or Kilwa Masoko (Tsh2000, 35km), although you'll usually be charged the full Dar es Salaam–Mtwara fare. This doesn't work as well leaving Kilwa, as buses are often full when they pass Nangurukuru (from about 11am). The best place to wait is at the large Starcom rest stop, along the main road about 200m north of Nangurukuru junction; most through buses stop here.

To Lindi, there's at least one direct bus daily (Tsh7000, four hours), departing Kilwa between 5am and 6am from the transport stand near the market; book a day in advance. There are no direct connections to Mtwara. Either get a shared taxi to Nangurukuru junction, and then try your luck catching a Mtwara-bound bus from there (wait at Starcom rest stop north of Nangurukuru junction) for the full Dar es Salaam–Mtwara fare. Otherwise, go first to Lindi, and take a minivan from there.

Kilwa Kisiwani

POP 1000

Kilwa Kisiwani ('Kilwa on the Island') is a quiet fishing village baking in the sun just offshore from Kilwa Masoko. In its heyday it was the seat of sultans and centre of a vast trading network linking the old Shona kingdoms and the goldfields of Zimbabwe with Persia, India and China. Ibn Battuta, the famed traveller and chronicler of the ancient world, visited Kilwa in the early 14th century and described the town as being exceptionally beautiful and well constructed. At its height, Kilwa's influence extended north past the Zanzibar Archipelago and south as far as Sofala on the central Mozambican coast.

While these glory days are now well in the past, the ruins of the settlement – together with the ruins on nearby Songo Mnara (p330) island – are among the most significant groups of Swahili buildings on the East African coast and a Unesco World Heritage Site.

History

The coast near Kilwa Kisiwani has been inhabited for several thousand years, and artefacts from the late and middle Stone Ages have been found on the island. Although the first settlements in the area date from around AD 800, Kilwa remained a relatively undistinguished place until the early 13th century. At this time, trade links developed with Sofala, 1500km to the south in present-day Mozambique. Kilwa came to control Sofala and to dominate its lucrative gold trade, and before long it had become the most powerful trade centre along the Swahili coast.

In the late 15th century, Kilwa's fortunes began to turn. Sofala freed itself from the island's dominance, and in the early 16th century Kilwa came under the control of the Portuguese. It wasn't until more than 200 years later that Kilwa regained its independence and once again became a significant trading centre, this time as an entrepôt for slaves being shipped from the mainland to the islands of Mauritius, Réunion and Comoros. In the 1780s, Kilwa came under the control of the Sultan of Oman. By the mid-19th century, the local ruler had succumbed to the Sultan of Zanzibar, the focus of regional trade shifted to Kilwa Kivinje on the mainland, and the island town entered a decline from which it never recovered.

◉ Sights

Thanks to funding from the French and Japanese governments, significant sections of the Kilwa Kisiwani ruins have been restored, and are now easily accessible, with informative signboards in English and Swahili.

The **ruins** (adult/student Tsh27,000/13,000) are in two groups. When approaching Kilwa Kisiwani, the first building you'll find is the **Arabic fort** (gereza). It was built in the early 19th century by the Omani Arabs, on the site of a Portuguese fort dating from the early 16th century. To the southwest of the fort are the ruins of the beautiful **Great Mosque**, with its columns and graceful vaulted roofing, much of which has been impressively restored. Some sections of the mosque date from the late 13th century, although most are from additions made to the building in the 15th century. In its day, this was the largest mosque on the East African coast. Further southwest and behind the Great Mosque is a smaller **mosque** dating from the early 15th century. This is considered to be the best preserved of the buildings at Kilwa and has also been impressively restored. To the west of the small mosque, with large, green lawns and placid views over the water, are the crumbling remains of the **Makutani**. Inside this large, walled enclosure is where some of the sultans of Kilwa lived. It is estimated to date from the mid-18th century.

Almost 1.5km from the fort along the coast is **Husuni Kubwa**, once a massive complex of buildings covering almost a hectare and, together with nearby **Husuni Ndogo**, the oldest of Kilwa's ruins. The complex, which is estimated to date from the 12th century or earlier, is set on a hill and must have once commanded great views over the bay. Watch in particular for the octagonal bathing pool. Husuni Ndogo is smaller than Husuni Kubwa and is thought to date from about the same time, although archaeologists are not yet sure of its original function. To reach these ruins, you can walk along the beach at low tide or follow the slightly longer inland route.

⚲ Tours

To visit the ruins, you'll need to be accompanied by a guide onto the island, arranged through the Kilwa Islands Tour Guides Association (p328), at the bus stand in Kilwa Masoko. The guide will also help you arrange and pay for the necessary permit at the Antiquities Office (p328), just uphill from the port in Kilwa Masoko. Ask for Idara ya Mambo ya Kale (Antiquities Office); the permit is issued without fuss while you wait. The Antiquities Officer is more likely to be there in the morning. On weekends, telephone numbers of duty officers are posted on the door, and officials are quite gracious about issuing permits outside working hours.

Prices for tours start at US$40 per person, and decrease with group size. There are sometimes also slight reductions if you use a non-motorised dhow to reach the island.

ⓘ Information

For detailed information in English about the ruins, look for a copy of HN Chittick's informative manuscript *A Guide to the Ruins of Kilwa with Some Notes on the Other Antiquities of the Region*. The Antiquities Office (p328) in Kilwa Masoko also sells some informative publications. The National Museum (p54) in Dar es Salaam has a small display on Kilwa Kisiwani.

ⓘ Getting There & Away

Local boats go from the port at Kilwa Masoko to Kilwa Kisiwani (Tsh200) whenever there are enough passengers – usually only in the early morning, at about 7am. However, they are not permitted to take tourists. As you are required to go with a guide to the islands, you'll need to pay their prices (US$40 per person including transport, guide fees and entry fee). With a good wind, in a sailing dhow the trip takes about 20 minutes.

Songo Mnara

The tiny island of **Songo Mnara** (adult/student Tsh27,000/13,000), about 8km south of Kilwa Kisiwani (p329), contains ruins at its northern end – including of a palace, several mosques and numerous houses – that are believed to date from the 14th and 15th centuries. They are considered in some respects to be more significant architecturally than those at Kilwa Kisiwani, with one of the most complete town layouts along the coast, although they're less visually impressive.

Together with Kilwa Kisiwani, they are a Unesco World Heritage Site.

Just off the island's western side is **Sanje Majoma**, with additional ruins dating from the same period. The small island of **Sanje ya Kati**, between Songo Mnara and Kilwa Masoko, has some lesser ruins of a third settlement in the area, also believed to date from the same era.

The only way for tourists to visit Songo Mnara is via boat from Kilwa Masoko, arranged through the Kilwa Islands Tour Guides Association (p328). Prices start at US$96 per person including transport, entry permit and guide, and decrease with a larger group size. Dhows between Kilwa Masoko and Songo Mnara take about two to three hours with a decent wind (1½ hours with motor). For combined full-day trips including both Songo Mnara and Kilwa Kisiwani, a guide plus motorised boat transport and entry permit fees costs US$148 for one person (US$247 for two).

After landing at Songo Mnara be prepared to wade through mangrove swamps before reaching the island proper.

Kilwa Kivinje

♪ 023

The slow-paced town of Kilwa Kivinje (Kilwa of the Casuarina Trees) owes its existence to Omani Arabs from Kilwa Kisiwani who set up a base here in the early 19th century following the fall of the Kilwa sultanate. By the mid-19th century the settlement had become the hub of the regional slave-trading network, and by the late 19th century, a German administrative centre. With the abolishment of the slave trade, and German wartime defeats, Kilwa Kivinje's brief period in the spotlight came to an end. Today, it's a crumbling, moss-covered and atmospheric relic of the past with a Swahili small-town feel and an intriguing mixture of German colonial and Omani Arab architecture.

In theory, Kivinje can only be visited after arranging a guide in Kilwa Masoko and paying for a permit (Tsh20,000). However, in practice it is usually easy enough to start directly in Kivinje and arrange a guide there.

◎ Sights & Activities

The most interesting section of town is around the old **German Boma** (administrative office). The street behind the *boma* is lined with small houses, many with carved Zanzibar-style doorways. Nearby is a **mosque**, which locals claim has been in continuous use since the 14th century, and a warren of back streets where you can absorb a slice of coastal life, with children playing on the streets and women sorting huge trays of *dagga* (tiny sardines) for drying in the sun. Just in from here on the water is the bustling **dhow port**, where brightly painted vessels set off regularly for Songo Songo, Mafia and other coastal ports.

Next to the hospital, about 1km west of town on the access road, is a small **monument** to the heroes of the Maji Maji rebellion (p312).

The best way to visit Kilwa Kivinje is as an easy half-day trip from Kilwa Masoko. The Kilwa Islands Tour Guides Association (p328) organises cycling trips from Kilwa Masoko for about US$25 per person.

Sleeping & Eating

King Peace Hotel   GUESTHOUSE $
(☑ 0753 372236, 0713 166626, 0784 615110; r Tsh40,000) This tidy guesthouse, about 800m west of town along the main access road, and diagonally opposite Kinyonga Hospital, has clean double-bed rooms, and tasty meals with advance notice (Tsh15,000). The rooms are all named after nearby islands, except 'Kinyonga' ('spot of executions'), which is named to remind visitors of those who lost their lives in the Maji Maji rebellion.

Getting There & Away

Kilwa Kivinje is reached by heading about 25km north of Kilwa Masoko (or 5km south of Nangurukuru junction on the main Dar es Salaam–Mtwara road) along a sealed road to the signposted access road. Follow this unpaved track for about 5km further, past Kinyonga Hospital, to Kilwa Kivinje.

Shared taxis travel several times daily to and from Kilwa Masoko (Tsh2000). Buses between Dar es Salaam and Kilwa Masoko also usually stop at Kilwa Kivinje. Chartering a private taxi from Kilwa Masoko will cost Tsh25,000 to Tsh30,000 return.

Kilwa Kivinje is an important regional dhow port. There are regular sailings from the colourful dhow port on the edge of town to Songo Songo (about Tsh2000, three to five hours; motorised boat Tsh7000 to Tsh10,000, two hours), from where it is easy to reach nearby Fanjove island. Departures for the motorised boats are usually from about 10am. For Mafia, take a bus up the coast towards Dar es Salaam and get a boat at Nyamisati.

Songo Songo

Coconut palms, low shrub vegetation, about 3500 locals, lots of birds, a beach and a major natural-gas field being exploited as part of the Songo Songo Gas to Electricity Project are the main attractions on this 4-sq-km island. Together with **Fanjove** and several other surrounding islets, it forms the Songo Songo archipelago, an ecologically important area for nesting sea turtles and marine birds. The surrounding waters also host an impressive collection of hard and soft corals. The archipelago, together with the nearby Rufiji River delta, the Mafia archipelago and the coastline around Kilwa Masoko have been declared a Wetland of International Importance under the Ramsar Convention. The best beach is in Songo Songo's southeastern corner, reached through a coconut plantation.

Sleeping & Eating

Kiliwani Guest House   GUESTHOUSE $
(r Tsh20,000) This small, local-style guesthouse a short walk east from where the dhows land has basic but adequate rooms. Meals can be arranged with advance notice.

★ **Fanjove Private Island**   LODGE $$$
(☑ 022-260 1747; www.ed.co.tz; s/d full board US$555/815; ◷ Jun-Mar) ◢ This small, private island has six rustic but comfortable eco-*bandas* directly on a lovely beach, showers open to the stars, and kayaking, snorkelling and other excursions. Everything is low-key, with the emphasis on minimising impact. It's unique, and highly recommended, especially in combination with Kilwa and Mafia, for anyone seeking an introduction to life on the Swahili coast.

Getting There & Away

AIR

Coastal Aviation (www.coastal.co.tz) flies between Songo Songo main island and Dar es Salaam (US$220 one way), Kilwa Masoko (US$160 one way) and Mafia (US$150 one way). If sleeping at Fanjove Private Island, the transfer from Songo Songo to Fanjove is done by boat (to be booked when you arrange your accommodation).

BOAT

Motorised dhows depart most days from about 10am from the Kilwa Kivinje dhow port for Songo Songo (Tsh7000 to Tsh10,000, two hours), from where you will need to continue over to Fanjove via boat transfer arranged with Fanjove Private Island (p331). It's also possible to arrange charter-boat transfer from Kilwa Masoko to Songo Songo through Kimbilio Lodge (p328), opening up the possibility for some appealing circuit itineraries.

Lindi

📞 023 / POP 78,800

In its early days, Lindi was part of the Sultan of Zanzibar's domain, a terminus of the slave caravan route from Lake Nyasa, regional colonial capital, and the main town in southeastern Tanzania. The abolishment of the slave trade and the rise of Mtwara as a local hub sent Lindi into a slow decline, from which it has yet to recover, although it again moved briefly into the limelight in the early 20th century when dinosaur bones were discovered nearby.

Today, Lindi is a lively, pleasant place and worth wandering around for a day or so to get a taste of life on the coast. Its small dhow port bustles with local coastal traffic, a smattering of carved doorways and crumbling ruins line the dusty streets, and a Hindu temple and Indian merchants serve as a reminder of once-prosperous trade routes to the east.

⊙ Sights & Activities

The old, historical part of town is the section along the waterfront, though you'll have to really hunt for the few still-standing remnants of the town's more glorious past. Look for the remains of the old **German boma**, ruins of an **Arab tower** and the occasional **carved doorway**. The small **Dhow Port** (Waterfront rd) on palm-fringed Lindi Bay is lively, colourful and worth a stroll. From some of the hills on the edge of town there are good views over large stands of palm trees and Lindi Bay, and across the Lukeludi River to **Kitunda peninsula** – ask locals to point you in the direction of Mtanda, Wailes ('Wire-less') or Mtuleni neighbourhoods. On Kitunda itself, which was formerly a sisal estate, there's nothing much now other than a sleepy village, but it's a pleasant destination for walking and offers a glimpse of local life. At the end of the peninsula behind the hill is a good beach (hire a local boat to get there).

About 6km north of town off the airfield road is **Mtema beach**, which is usually empty except for weekends and holidays. Take care with your valuables.

Salt production is the main local industry, announced by the salt flats lining the road

into town. There's also a sisal plantation in Kikwetu, near the airfield. The coral reef running from south of Lindi to Sudi Bay hosts abundant marine life, and the site has been proposed as a possible protected marine area.

🛌 Sleeping

Kadogoo Inn HOTEL $
(📞 0785 993999, 0716 152391, 023-220 2507; kadogooinn2007@gmail.com; Jamhuri St; r Tsh50,000-80,000, ste Tsh100,000-150,000) This smart, two-storey place stands out from Lindi's otherwise quite modest selection of local guesthouses. It's just a couple of blocks off the main roundabout with clean, modern rooms and meals.

Malaika Guest House GUESTHOUSE $
(📞 023-220 2880; Market St; r Tsh15,000) Malaika, in a convenient central location one block east of the market, is a long-standing place offering very basic and somewhat cramped but reasonably clean rooms with fan. There's also a good, inexpensive restaurant with pizza (sometimes) and local meals for about Tsh3000.

Vision Hotel GUESTHOUSE $
(📞 0687 111522; Makonde St; r Tsh25,000; ❄) This place, opposite the easy-to-find Brigita Dispensary, has clean rooms, all with fan, TV and one double bed. There's no food available.

Seaview Beach Resort HOTEL $$
(Oceanic Beach Resort; 📞 0657 737225, 023-220 2581; Waterfront Rd; r/ste Tsh120,000/250,000; 🅿❄🛜🏊) This hotel, in a prime waterfront location just down from the dhow port, has been completely renovated. It offers comfortable rooms with enormous beds, all facing towards the large swimming pool and the water. The suites have small balconies, and there's a restaurant. The main drawback: the often loud music from the waterside bar that sometimes goes late on weekends.

✖ Eating

Mbinga One AFRICAN $
(Market St; meals Tsh3000-6000; ⊙11am-10pm) This small, streetside place has inexpensive local-style meals.

Himo-One TANZANIAN $
(Jamhuri St; meals Tsh3000-6000; ⊙11am-9pm) This long-standing local favourite is on the scruffy side, but meals – chicken or fish and rice or chips – are quick and reliable. There's no alcohol. It's one block south of the market.

Lindi

Lindi Bay

Mtema Beach (6km); (20km)

Stadium

Brigita Dispensary

MIKUMBI

Market St

CRDB

Bus & Taxi Stand

Jamhuri St

Makonde St

Uhuru St

Shi'a Mosque

Amani St

Makongoro St

Ghana St

NBC

Boats to Kitunda

Kitunda (700km)

Lumumba St

Lukeludi River

Mingoyo Transport Junction (20km)

Lindi

◎ Sights
1 Dhow Port B1

🛏 Sleeping
2 Kadogoo Inn A2
3 Malaika Guest House A2
4 Seaview Beach Resort B2
5 Vision Hotel A1

🍴 Eating
6 Himo-One A2
7 Lindi Oceanic Hotel B2
8 Lindi Supermarket A2
   Mbinga One .... (see 8)

Kilwa Kivinje, north of Lindi, is a better spot to try to arrange dhow travel along the coast.

BUS
All transport departs from the bus and taxi stand on Uhuru St. Minibuses to Mtwara (Tsh4000, three hours) depart daily between about 5.30am and 11am. Otherwise, there are minibuses throughout the day to Mingoyo junction (Mnazi Mmoja; Tsh2000), where you can wait for a Masasi–Mtwara bus.

To Masasi (Tsh5500, three to four hours), there are two or three direct buses daily, departing between about 6am and 10am. Alternatively, go to Mingoyo junction and wait for onward transport there. The last Mtwara–Masasi bus passes Mingoyo about 2pm.

To Dar es Salaam, there are direct buses daily, departing Lindi at about 5am (Tsh21,000, eight hours), and terminating at Mbagala Rangi Tatu transport stand in Dar es Salaam, which is also where you need to go to catch transport heading south to Lindi. Some lines terminate at Temeke.

To Kilwa Masoko, there's at least one direct bus leaving Lindi daily by about 6am (Tsh7000, four hours).

ℹ Getting Around
Lindi is easily covered on foot. To arrange boats across the Lukeludi River to the Kitunda peninsula, go to the small jetty on the waterfront road near NBC bank.

Mtwara
📞 023 / POP 108,300
First an obscure fishing village, then an empty shell of a city after the failed East African Groundnut Scheme, sprawling Mtwara is now southeastern Tanzania's major town. The commercialisation of Mtwara's natural gas reserves that started in 2006 sparked a

Lindi Oceanic Hotel　　　　SEAFOOD $$
(📞023-220 2581, 0657 737225; Waterfront Rd; meals Tsh15,000-20,000; ◷11am-10pm Sun-Thu, to 11.30pm Fri & Sat) Lindi's most upmarket restaurant offers seafood grills plus some meat selections on a terrace overlooking the water.

Self-Catering
Lindi Supermarket　　　　SUPERMARKET $
(Market St; ◷8am-9pm) Lindi's main supermarket.

ℹ Information

MEDICAL SERVICES
Brigita Dispensary (📞023-220 2679; brigita_dispensary@yahoo.de; Makonde St; ◷9am-7pm) The Western-run clinic is the best place for medical emergencies. It's several blocks east of the market; anyone should be able to point you in the right direction.

MONEY
CRDB (Main roundabout) Has an ATM.
NBC (Lumumba St) On the waterfront; ATM.

ℹ Getting There & Away

BOAT
There is considerable local boat traffic to and from Lindi's bustling port, but for travellers,

BRACHIOSAURUS BRANCAI

Tendaguru, about 100km northwest of Lindi, is the site of one of the most significant palaeontological finds in history. From 1909 to 1912, a team of German palaeontologists unearthed the remains of more than a dozen different dinosaur species, including the skeleton of *Brachiosaurus brancai*, the largest known dinosaur in the world. The Brachiosaurus skeleton is now on display at the Museum of Natural History in Berlin. Scientists are unsure why so many dinosaur fossils were discovered in the region, although it is thought that flooding or some other natural catastrophe was the cause of the dinosaurs' demise.

Today, Tendaguru is of interest mainly to hardcore palaeontologists. For visitors there is little to see and access to the site is difficult.

flurry of building and investment. Now, however, with the construction of the gas pipeline to Dar es Salaam, many of the rapidly built high-rises are standing vacant, and the city's somnolent, sunbaked atmosphere is slowly returning. For travellers, Mtwara lacks the historical appeal of nearby Mikindani and other places along the coast. However, with its good infrastructure and easy access, it makes a useful stocking-up point between Tanzania and Mozambique. Mtwara has also become a popular resting point for those travelling between Dar es Salaam and Songea via the newly paved highway between Masasi and Tunduru.

Mtwara is loosely located between a business and banking area to the northwest, near Uhuru Rd and Aga Khan St, and the market and bus stand about 1.5km away to the southeast. The main north–south street is Tanu Rd. In the far northwest by the sea, and 30 to 40 minutes on foot from the bus stand, is the Shangani quarter, with a small beach. In the southeast, just past the market and bus stand, are the lively areas of Majengo and Chikon'gola.

History

Mtwara was first developed after WWII by the British as part of the failed East African Groundnut Scheme to alleviate a postwar shortage of plant oils. Grand plans were made to expand Mtwara, then an obscure

fishing village, into an urban centre of around 200,000 inhabitants. An international airport and Tanzania's first deep-water harbour were built and the regional colonial administration was relocated here from Lindi. Yet, no sooner had this been done than the groundnut scheme – plagued by conceptional difficulties and an uncooperative local climate – collapsed and everything came to an abrupt halt. While Mtwara's port continued to play a significant role in the region over the next few decades as an export channel for cashews, sisal and other products, development of the town came to a standstill, and for years it resembled little more than an oversized shell.

Natural gas reserves were discovered in the area in the 1980s. Commercialisation began in 2006, attracting high hopes for an economic boost for the city. Yet, a decade later, the controversial construction of a pipeline to Dar es Salaam removed much of the hoped-for gas business, and Mtwara today remains a relatively quiet town.

◎ Sights & Activities

In town, there's a lively **market** (Sokoine Rd; ◷ 6am-6pm) with wonderful textiles and a small traditional-medicine section next to the main building. **Aga Khan St** is lined with old Indian trading houses dating from the late 1950s and 1960s. Much of Mtwara's fish comes from Msangamkuu on the other side of Mtwara Bay, and the small dhow port and adjoining fish market are particularly colourful in the early morning and late afternoon.

The **beach** in Shangani is popular for swimming (high tide only); its gentle currents and general absence of sea urchins and other hazards make it ideal for children. For views over the bay and the white sands of Msangamkuu Peninsula, look for the tiny footpath leading to a viewpoint near the Southern Cross Hotel (p335).

Afri Mak Arts & Crafts Group   MUSEUM
(Sinani St; donation; ◷ 9am-6pm Mon-Sat, 1-5pm Sun) This tiny museum features masks, spears, tools and other cultural items from the Makonde, Makua and Yao tribes. All displays are labelled in English and Swahili. This is also the best place to get information on the annual **Makuya Festival**. From the small roundabout on Makonde Rd, go one block north, then turn right. It's the second building on the left.

Ayayoru Carvings & Tours TOURS
(☑0787 194196; www.mtwaratours.com; Sokoine Rd; ☺8.30am-5.30pm Mon-Sat) Moris Damian and his colleagues offer guided tours in and around Mtwara, including village visits with traditional dancing and drumming. Their small shop downhill from the market has a good selection of woodcarvings and other crafts.

🛌 Sleeping

Drive-In Garden & Cliff Bar GUESTHOUSE $
(☑0784 503007; Shangani Rd; camping per tent Tsh5000, r without breakfast Tsh20,000-25,000) This friendly place allows campers to pitch their tent in the leafy, bird- and butterfly-filled garden. There are also several simple, good-value rooms, plus a restaurant. It's just across the road from the beach, although for swimming you'll need to walk up to the main Shangani beach area near Shangani junction.

To get here go left at the main Shangani junction and continue, parallel to the beach, for 1.2km to the small signpost on your left.

Naf Blue View Hotel GUESTHOUSE $
(☑023-233 4465, 0656 107990; Sinani St; r Tsh50,000-80,000; ❇@☎) About 400m up (west) from the bus stand, this place is one of the better bets in the busy market area, with small, clean rooms with running hot water, satellite TV and meals on order. There are no mosquito nets.

Southern Cross Hotel HOTEL $
(☑0753 035809, 0712 035809; www.facebook.com/southerncrosshotelmtwara; Shangani waterfront; s/d Tsh60,000/75,000, s/d beach-facing bungalow Tsh120,000/135,000; P☎) This long-standing Mtwara establishment has a lovely setting, perched on a small, rocky outcrop overlooking the sea at the eastern end of Shangani beach. It has changed ownership and received a complete facelift. The pleasant rooms are either 'standard' (garden view) or sea facing, and there's a deservedly popular waterside restaurant. Breakfast costs Tsh10,000.

VETA HOSTEL $
(☑023-233 4094; Shangani; s/ste Tsh35,000/60,000; P❇🏊) This large compound has clean rooms, all with a large single bed, fan, TV and views towards the water. There's also a restaurant. It's in Shangani, about 200m back from the water (though there's no swimming beach here). From the T-junction in Shangani, go left and continue for about 2km. There's no public transport; *bajaji* charge around Tsh3000 from town.

Bambu Guest House GUESTHOUSE $
(cnr Sinani St & Makonde Rd; r Tsh15,000-20,000) This is one of the cheapest bets near the bus stand, with basic rooms – all with bathroom and fan – but no meals. Parking is available in the church compound across the street.

WORTH A TRIP

ST PAUL'S CHURCH

If you are in the Majengo area of Mtwara, it's well worth stopping in at **St Paul's Church** (800m southeast of the market) to view its remarkable artwork. The entire front and side walls are covered with richly coloured biblical scenes painted by a German Benedictine priest, Polycarp Uehlein, in the mid-1970s. In addition to their style and distinctive use of colour, the paintings are notable for their universalised portrayal of common biblical themes.

The themes were chosen to assist churchgoers in understanding the sermons and to relate the biblical lessons to their everyday lives.

The paintings, which took about two years to complete, are part of a series by the same artist that decorate churches throughout southern Tanzania and in a few other areas of the country, including churches in Nyangao, Lindi, Malolo, Ngapa and Dar es Salaam.

During the years he worked in Tanzania, Father Polycarp taught several African students. The best known of these is Henry Likonde from Mtwara, who has taken biblical scenes and 'Africanised' them. You can see examples of Likonde's work in the small church at the top of the hill in Mahurunga, south of Mtwara near the Mozambique border, and in the cathedral in Songea.

Mtwara

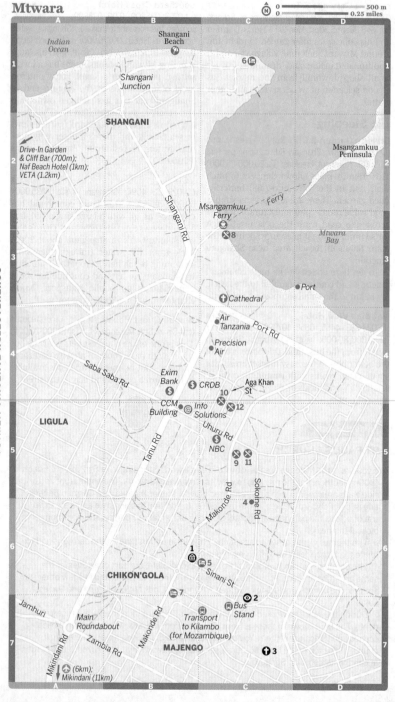

Mtwara

◎ Sights
1 Afri Mak Arts & Crafts Group B6
2 Market C7
3 St Paul's Church C7

⊕ Activities, Courses & Tours
4 Ayayoru Carvings & Tours C6

⊜ Sleeping
Bambu Guest House .... (see 1)
5 Naf Blue View Hotel C6
6 Southern Cross Hotel C1
7 Tiffany Diamond Hotel B6

⊗ Eating
8 Fish Market C3
9 Himo 2 Restaurant C5
10 Makonde Mini Market C4
11 Mtwara Super Market & Bakery C5
12 Senir Restaurant C5
Southern Cross Hotel .... (see 6)

Tiffany Diamond Hotel BUSINESS HOTEL $$
(☑0682 433379, 023-233 4801; www.tiffany
diamondhotels.com; Makonde Rd; r Tsh120,000; ✱
🔊❄) This soulless high-rise several blocks
from the bus stand is one of many in Mtwara
built to accommodate the hoped-for crowds
of business travellers connected with the
nearby gas fields. Rooms – all twin or double
bed – are reasonable value for money, and
there is a tiny pool.

Naf Beach Hotel HOTEL $$
(☑023-233 4706, 0655 703042; www.nafbeach
hotels.com; r US$50-90; 🄿✱🔊) Rooms in
this popular but unappealing high-rise have
one double bed, minifridge and satellite TV.
Some have sea views, and there's a restaurant, plus a charmless beachside bar across
the road featuring plastic tables and chairs
and an equally charmless bar-dining area
next to the main entrance.

Although it's just opposite the seafront, for
swimming you'll need to go about 1.5km east
to Shangani Beach. The hotel is about 1.8km
west of Shangani junction.

✗ Eating

Senir Restaurant INDIAN $
(☑0683 045678, 0682 985678; Aga Khan St, just
off Tanu Rd; mains Tsh5000-14,000; ◷10.30am-
10pm; 🖉) Tasty Indian cuisine (plus some
Chinese food) served inside or on a pleasant,
shaded streetside porch. Service is prompt
and meals – including a good selection of
vegetarian dishes – are well prepared.

Drive-In Garden & Cliff Bar TANZANIAN $
(☑0784 503007; Shangani Rd; meals Tsh12,000;
◷11am-2pm & 5.30-9pm) Simple, delicious and
generously portioned meals of grilled fish or
chicken and chips, plus cold drinks. It's in a
peaceful garden setting just back from the
water. Call in advance and place your order
to minimise waiting time.

Himo 2 Restaurant TANZANIAN $
(Makonde Rd; meals about Tsh5000; ◷6am-
9pm) This popular local-style eatery serves
good-value chicken, fish, beans, *mishikaki*
(marinated, grilled meat kebabs) and other
standard local fare, plus fruit juice. To get
here coming from town, take the first right
after NBC bank. Himo 2 is a few doors up
to the left.

Fish Market MARKET $
(off Shangani Rd; ◷6am-4pm) The fish market
at the Msangamkuu ferry dock is good for
street food, selling grilled *pweza* (octopus),
vitambua (rice cakes) and other delicacies.
Food is freshest in the early morning.

Southern Cross Hotel SEAFOOD, EUROPEAN $$
(☑0753 035809, 0712 035809; www.facebook.
com/southerncrosshotelmtwara; Shangani water-
front; meals Tsh25,000-35,000; ◷10am-11pm; 🔊)
Tasty seafood grills and other dishes, plus
good coffees, served on a lovely waterside
terrace with excellent views. It's also an ideal
spot for sundowners.

Self-Catering
Makonde Mini Market SUPERMARKET $
(Aga Khan St; ◷8.30am-1pm & 2-6.30pm Mon-
Sat, 9am-1pm Sun) Small but well-stocked
supermarket.

**Mtwara Super
Market & Bakery** SUPERMARKET $
(◷7.30am-9pm) Mtwara's largest super-
market.

❶ Information

INTERNET ACCESS
Info Solutions (Uhuru Rd; per hour Tsh2000;
◷8am-6pm Mon-Sat) On the side of the CCM
building.

MONEY
The following ATMs accept Visa and MasterCard.
CRDB (Tanu Rd)
Exim Bank (Tanu Rd) Also Mtwara's best place
to change cash.
NBC (Uhuru Rd; ◷8am-4pm Mon-Fri, 9am-1pm
Sat)

ⓘ Getting There & Away

AIR

There are five to six flights weekly between **Mtwara Airport** (MYW; off Mikindani Rd) and Dar es Salaam (from Tsh330,000 one way) on **Precision Air** (☏ 023-233 4116, 0782 818442; www.precisionairtz.com; Tanu Rd; ⊗8am-5pm Mon-Fri, 8am-2pm Sat) and three times weekly on **Air Tanzania** (☏ 0689 737212, 0782 737730; www.airtanzania.co.tz; Tanu Rd; ⊗8am-5pm Mon-Fri, 9am-2pm Sat).

BUS

All long-distance buses depart between about 5am and noon from the main **bus stand** (off Sokoine Rd) near the market.

Masasi (Tsh7000, three to four hours) There are roughly hourly departures between about 6am and 2pm.

Songea (Tsh25,000, 10 hours) There is at least one departure daily at 6am.

Lindi (Tsh7000, three hours) There are direct buses daily at 6am and again usually at 8am.

Kilwa Masoko There's no direct bus. You'll need to go first to Lindi and get onward transport from there, or take any Dar es Salaam–bound bus to Nangurukuru junction. For the latter option, you'll usually have to pay the full Dar price.

Newala (Tsh7500, six hours) Direct buses to Newala usually use the southern route via Nanyamba. Departures from Mtwara are between 6am and 8am daily. At the time of research rehabilitation work was starting on this route, so enquire before setting off. It's also possible to reach Newala via Masasi, and via Mtama (en route between Mnazi Mmoja junction and Masasi).

Dar es Salaam (Tsh23,000, eight hours) There are numerous departures daily in each direction between 6am and 10am, starting and terminating at Temeke's Sudan Market area, on Mbagala Rd, just east of Temeke Rd, where all the southbound bus lines also have booking offices. Book in advance. Some Dar es Salaam–Mtwara buses also start/terminate at Ubungo for approximately the same price.

Mozambique There are several pick-ups and at least one minivan daily to Mahurunga and the Tanzanian immigration post at Kilambo (Tsh5000), departing Mtwara between about 6am and 8am. This **transport to Kilambo** is from in front of Chilindima Guesthouse, one block southwest of the bus stand.

CAR & MOTORCYCLE

If you're driving to or from Dar es Salaam, there are petrol stations in Kibiti, Ikwiriri (unreliable), Nangurukuru, Kilwa Masoko, Lindi and Mtwara. The road is now all paved.

For self-drivers between Mtwara and the Mozambique border at Kilambo, the best places for updated information on the Ruvuma River crossing are Old Boma at Mikindani (p339) and Ten Degrees South Lodge (p339), both in Mikindani. At the time of research, Mozambique visas were being issued at the Kilambo border. However, this could change at any time, so get an update before setting your plans. There is no Mozambique consulate in Mtwara; the closest one is in Dar es Salaam (p372).

ⓘ Getting Around

Taxis can be difficult to find in Mtwara; you'll mostly need to rely on *bajaji* (tuk-tuks), which are everywhere. *Bajaji* 'stands' are at the bus stand, and near the CCM building at the intersection of Tanu and Uhuru roads. To and from the airport (6km southeast of the main roundabout) expect to pay about Tsh10,000 for a taxi and about half that for a *bajaji*. The cost for trips around town in a *bajaji* is Tsh1000 to Tsh2000 (Tsh3000 from the centre to Shangani).

There are a few dalla-dallas running along Tanu Rd to and from the bus stand.

To get to nearby Msangamkuu Peninsula, there is a ferry (off Shangani Rd) that runs daily between sunrise and sunset (Tsh300, about 15 minutes).

Mikindani

☑023

Mikindani – set on a picturesque bay surrounded by coconut groves – is a quiet, charming Swahili town with a long history. Although easily visited as a day trip from the nearby regional travel hub of Mtwara, many travellers prefer Mikindani to its larger neighbour as a base for exploring the surrounding area.

As well as seeing its various historical buildings, it's well worth just strolling through town to soak up the atmosphere and look at the numerous carved Zanzibar-style doors. With more time, make your way up Bismarck Hill, rising up behind the Old Boma, for some views.

History

Mikindani gained prominence early on as a major dhow port and terminus for trade caravans from Lake Nyasa. By the late 15th century, these networks extended across southern Tanzania as far as Zambia and present-day Democratic Republic of Congo (formerly Zaïre). Following a brief downturn in fortunes, trade – primarily in slaves, ivory and copper – again increased in the mid-16th century as Mikindani came under the domain of the Sultan of Zanzibar. In the 19th century, following the ban on the slave trade, Mikindani fell into decline until the late 1880s when the German colonial government made the town its regional headquarters and began large-scale sisal, coconut, rubber and oilseed production in the area. However, the boom was not to last. With the arrival of the British and the advent of larger ocean-going vessels, Mikindani was abandoned in favour of Mtwara's superior harbour, and now, almost a century later, seems not to have advanced much beyond this era. Much of the town has been designated as a conservation zone, and life today centres on the small dhow port, which is still a hub for local coastal traffic.

For David Livingstone fans, the famous explorer spent a few weeks in the area in 1866 before setting out on his last journey.

◉ Sights & Activities

Walking tours of town and local excursions can be organised at Old Boma at Mikindani and Ten Degrees South Lodge.

Boma HISTORIC BUILDING
The imposing German *boma,* built in 1895 as a fort and administrative centre, has been beautifully renovated as a hotel (p339). Even if you're not staying here, it's worth taking a look and climbing the tower for views over the town. It's just off the B2 (main road).

Slave Market HISTORIC BUILDING
Downhill from the *boma* is the old slave market building, which now houses several craft shops. Unfortunately, it was much less accurately restored than the *boma* and lost much of its architectural interest when its open arches were filled in. The original design is now preserved only on one of Tanzania's postage stamps.

Prison Ruins RUINS
These ruins are opposite the jetty, on the B2 (main road). Nearby is a large, hollow baobab tree that was once used to keep unruly prisoners in solitary confinement.

ECO2 DIVING
(☑ 0783 279446, 0784 855833; www.eco2tz.com; Main Rd) This good outfit offers PADI instruction (with advance reservation) and diving in both Mikindani Bay and at Mnazi Bay-Ruvuma Estuary Marine Park.

🛏 Sleeping & Eating

Mikindani has a tiny hotel scene consisting of just two (very good) hotels. Between them there is something for every budget. For self-catering, stock up in nearby Mtwara.

★**Old Boma at Mikindani** HISTORIC HOTEL $$
(☑ 023-233 3875, 0757 622000; www.mikindani.com; s US$60-110, d US$110-140; P@🛜🏊)
🍴 This beautifully restored building is on a breezy hilltop overlooking the town and Mikindani Bay. It offers spacious, atmospheric, high-ceilinged doubles and the closest to top-end standards that you'll find in these parts. There's a sunset terrace with magnificent views, a pool surrounded by bougainvillea bushes and lush gardens, a spa, attentive staff and an excellent restaurant.

Ten Degrees South Lodge LODGE $$
(ECO2; ☑ 0684 059381, 0766 059380; www.tendegreessouth.com; s/d US$60/70, with shared bathroom US$20/30; @🛜) This recommended budget travellers' base has four cheaper and simple but spacious and good-value rooms, all with large double beds and shared bathrooms, plus bay views and deckchairs up on the roof. Next door are a handful of newer, self-contained double-bed rooms with hot-water showers. There's also an outdoor restaurant-bar, with tasty wraps, pancakes, coffees and other delicacies from about Tsh15,000.

ⓘ Information

Both of Mikindani's hotel-restaurants offer free wi-fi access for their guests.

The closest banking facilities and ATMs are in Mtwara.

ⓘ Getting There & Away

Mikindani is 10km from Mtwara along a sealed road. Minibuses (Tsh500) run between the two towns throughout the day. *Bajajis* (tuk-tuks) from Mtwara charge about Tsh10,000 (it's about Tsh30,000 for a taxi).

Mnazi Bay-Ruvuma Estuary Marine Park

Mnazi Bay-Ruvuma Estuary Marine Park (www.marineparks.go.tz; adult/child US$23.60/11.80; ⊙7am-6pm) encompasses a narrow sliver of coastline extending from Msangamkuu Peninsula (just north and east of Mtwara) in the north to the Mozambique border in the south. In addition to about 5000 people, it provides home to more than 400 marine species. The plan is for the struggling park to become the core of a conservation area extending as far south as Pemba (Mozambique), although conservation and enforcement measures are sadly lacking.

The heart of the park is the **Msimbati Peninsula**, together with the bordering Mnazi Bay. Most visitors head straight to the tiny village of **Ruvula**, which is about 7km beyond Msimbati village along a sandy track (or along the beach at low tide), with a lovely stretch of sand and fine snorkelling. In addition to its beach (one of the few on the mainland offering sunset views) Ruvula is notable as the spot where British eccentric Latham Leslie-Moore built his house and lived until 1967, when he was deported after agitating for independence for the Msimbati Peninsula. His story is chronicled in John Heminway's *No Man's Land* and in *Africa Passion,* a documentary film. Today, Leslie-Moore's house stands in ruins; the property is privately owned.

Msangamkuu Peninsula, at the northern edge of the marine park and with a small beach, is best visited from Mtwara.

🛌 Sleeping & Eating

Ruvula Sea Safari   BANDA **$**
(📌0652 320183, 0788 808004; camping Tsh20,000, d banda Tsh50,000; 🅿) This is the only place to stay inside Mnazi Bay-Ruvuma Estuary Marine Park, with tatty beach-front *bandas* sharing equally tatty facilities, all redeemed, however, by a prime location directly on the sand. Tasty grilled-fish meals are available with advance notice (Tsh15,000). A few basic supplies are available in Msimbati village, but if you're camping, stock up in Mtwara and bring a torch.

Local boats can be arranged to Bird Island, directly opposite, and for exploring nearby mangrove channels. For the best snorkelling, walk left along the beach. The further you go, the better it gets.

Watch for the tiny sign marking the turn-off from the Msimbati–Ruvula road. Day visitors are charged Tsh5000 per person for beach use (the fee is waived if you eat a meal).

ℹ️ Information

At the time of research, marine-park entry fees were payable in cash only (Tanzania shillings or US dollars) and collected at the marine-park gate at the entrance to Msimbati village.

Most diving in the marine park is done in the waters near Msimbati. The best contact is ECO2 (p339) in Mikindani.

ℹ️ Getting There & Away

There is at least one pick-up daily in each direction between Mtwara and Msimbati (Tsh2500, one to two hours), departing Mtwara's main transport stand at about 8am. Departures from Msimbati are at around 9am from the police post near the park gate. Check on the latest times, as there was talk at the time of research that they would revert to 9am departures from Mtwara and 6am departures from Msimbati.

Driving from Mtwara, take the main road from the roundabout south for 4km to the village of Mangamba, branch left at the signpost onto the Mahurunga road and continue about 18km to Madimba. At Madimba, turn left again and continue for 20km to Msimbati; the road is unpaved, but in good condition. If you are cycling, the major village en route is Ziwani, which has a decent market.

Note that there is no public transport between Msimbati and Ruvula. On weekends, it's sometimes possible to hitch a lift. Otherwise, arrange a lift on a motorbike (about Tsh5000) with one of the locals or walk along the beach at low tide (one hour or more). Although sandy, the road is in reasonably good condition, and Ruvula Sea Safari can generally be reached in a regular 2WD taxi from Mtwara (from around Tsh60,000 round trip).

Small boats and a small ferry (p338) travel between the Shangani dhow port dock in Mtwara and Msangamkuu Peninsula throughout the day (Tsh300, about 15 minutes).

Makonde Plateau

This cool and scenic plateau, much of which lies between 700m and 900m above sea level, is home to the Makonde people, famed throughout East Africa for their exotic wood-carvings. With its comparative isolation, scattered settlements and seeming obliviousness to developments elsewhere in the country, it in many ways epitomises inland areas of southeastern Tanzania, and is worth a detour if you're in the area.

Roadworks are planned, but as at the time of research, all roads leading up the Makonde Plateau are rough. There is regular public transport connecting both Mtwara and Masasi with Newala (the main settlement on the plateau); allow plenty of time for journeys.

Masasi

📱 023 / POP 102,700

Masasi, a district centre and the birthplace of former Tanzanian president Benjamin Mkapa, stretches out along the main road off the edge of the Makonde Plateau against a backdrop of granite hills. It's a potentially useful stop for those travelling to or from Mozambique via the Unity Bridge. The history of the modern settlement dates from the late 19th century, when the Anglican Universities' Mission to Central Africa (UMCA) came from Zanzibar Island to establish a settlement of former slaves here. Today, it's notable primarily as a transport hub for onward travel west towards Tunduru, or north to Nachingwea and Liwale. About 40km northeast of Masasi, just off the main road, is the large Benedictine monastery of Ndanda, founded by German missionaries in 1906. Adjoining is a hospital, which serves as the major health clinic for the surrounding region.

About 70km east of Masasi off the main road is Mahiwa. This was the site of one of WWI's bloodiest battles in Africa, in which German and British Imperial forces (consisting of primarily Nigerian and South African troops) fought, and more than 2000 people lost their lives.

🛏 Sleeping & Eating

St Anne's Resthouse GUESTHOUSE $

(📱 023-251 0016; dactmasasi@yahoo.com; Mtandi; r Tsh45,000) This small, quiet guesthouse is run by the Anglican church. Rooms vary in size, but all are tidy and pleasant. Meals can be arranged with advance notice. It's about 1km from the town centre near the Anglican cathedral by Mtandi Hill, just north of the main road.

Rose Royal Hotel HOTEL $

(📱 0687 607733; just off Main Rd; r Tsh40,000; P ❄) This clean, straightforward place is conveniently located less than 10 minutes' walk east of the bus stand and about 200m off the main road. Rooms all have air-con, bathroom and double bed, and meals are available.

ℹ Information

MONEY
NBC (Main Rd) ATM at the eastern end of town.

THE MAKONDE

The Makonde, known throughout East Africa for their woodcarvings, are one of Tanzania's largest ethnic groups. They originated in northern Mozambique, where many still live, and began to make their way northwards during the 18th and 19th centuries. The Mozambican war sparked another large influx into Tanzania, with up to 15,000 Makonde crossing the border during the 1970s and 1980s in search of a safe haven and employment. Today, although the Makonde on both sides of the Ruvuma River are considered to be a single ethnic entity, there are numerous cultural and linguistic differences between the two groups.

Like many tribes in this part of Tanzania, the Makonde are matrilineal. Children and inheritances normally belong to the woman, and it's common for husbands to move to the village of their wives after marriage. Settlements are widely scattered – possibly a remnant of the days when the Makonde sought to evade slave raids – and there is no tradition of a unified political system. Each village is governed by a hereditary chief and a council of elders.

Due to their isolated location, the Makonde have remained insulated from colonial and post-colonial influences, and are considered to be one of Tanzania's most traditional groups. Even today, most Makonde still adhere to traditional religions, with the complex spirit world given its fullest expression in their carvings.

Traditionally, the Makonde practised body scarring and while it's seldom done today, you may see older people with markings on their faces and bodies. It's also fairly common to see elderly Makonde women wearing a wooden plug in their upper lip, or to see this depicted in Makonde artwork.

Most Makonde are subsistence farmers, and there is speculation as to why they chose to establish themselves on a waterless plateau. Possible factors include the relative safety that the area offered from outside intervention (especially during slave-trading days), and the absence of the tsetse fly.

TOURIST INFORMATION

Masasi Reserve Warden's Office (☑ 0713 311129, 0784 634972, 023-251 0364; Nachingwea Rd; ☺ 8am-4pm Mon-Fri) It's essential to stop here first to arrange permits if you're planning to visit Lukwika-Lumesule Game Reserve. The office is in Masasi's Migongo area, about 1km north of the main road en route to Nachingwea, on the left. Ask for Mali Asili (Natural Resources).

🛈 Getting There & Away

The bus stand is at the western edge of Masasi at the intersection of the Tunduru, Nachingwea and Newala roads.

The road between Masasi and Mtwara is in generally good condition. Buses travel between the two towns approximately hourly between 6am and 2pm daily (Tsh7000, three to four hours).

Transport leaves several times daily to Newala (Tsh5000, 1½ hours).

Newala

☑ 023

Bustling Newala is the major settlement on the Makonde Plateau. Thanks to its perch at 780m altitude, it offers a pleasantly brisk climate, and views over the Ruvuma River valley and into Mozambique. At the edge of the escarpment on the southwestern side of town is the old German *boma* (now the police station) and, nearby, the Shimo la Mungu (Hole of God) viewpoint. There are numerous paths from the edge of town leading down to the river. For any excursions, it's a good idea to carry a copy of your passport and visa (which you should carry around anyway in Newala, given its proximity to the border) and arrange a local guide. Bicycles can be rented near the market.

NMB (just off Main Rd) Has an ATM that takes Visa and MasterCard.

🛏 Sleeping & Eating

Kayanda Sun Hotel   HOTEL $
(☑ 0682 605704; Masasi Rd; r Tsh35,000-50,000; ❄) Clean, modern and comfortable rooms, a restaurant and a relatively convenient location about 1.8km from the bus stand make this a good choice.

**Country Lodge
Bed & Breakfast**   GUESTHOUSE $
(Sollo's; ☑ 0678 306003, 023-241 0355, 0784 950235; Masasi Rd; s/d/ste Tsh30,000/35,000/ 50,000; P ❄) This long-standing place features large-ish rooms – the doubles have two big beds – and a restaurant with the usual array of standard dishes. It's about a 1.5km walk from the bus stand.

🛈 Getting There & Away

Daily buses run from Newala to Mtwara (via Nanyamba; Tsh7500, six hours) and to Masasi (Tsh4000, two hours). There is usually also at least one vehicle daily between Newala and Mtama, east of Masasi on the road to Mtwara. The journeys to Masasi and Mtama offer beautiful views as you wind down the side of the plateau.

Lukwika-Lumesule Game Reserve

Tiny Lukwika-Lumesule Game Reserve is hidden away in the wild hinterlands southwest and west of Masasi. With luck you may see elephants, elands, crocodiles and hippos, though it's more likely you'll see none of these. The main challenge, apart from getting around the reserve, is spotting the animals through the often dense vegetation and dealing with the voracious tsetse flies.

Lukwika-Lumesule is separated from Mozambique's Niassa Reserve by the Ruvuma River, and animals frequently wade across the border. There are no real roads in the reserve, just overgrown bush paths. It's officially off-limits during the July–December hunting season, and unofficially off-limits during much of the rest of the year due to the rains. According to reserve officials, late June is the best time to visit. Before setting off, it's essential to stop by the Masasi Reserve Warden's Office in Masasi to get an entry permit.

🛏 Sleeping & Eating

Camping is allowed with your own tent; there's no charge. Water for bathing is normally available. Bring everything with you, including drinking water.

🛈 Getting There & Away

The entry point into Lukwika-Lumesule is about 2.5km southwest of Mpombe village on the northeastern edge of the reserve, and reached via Nangomba village, 40km west of Masasi.

There is no regular public transport, although you may occasionally be able to get a lift with a vehicle from the reserve warden's office in Masasi. Otherwise, you'll need your own 4WD transport. During the dry season, it's possible to drive around Lukwika-Lumesule, following a 'road' running along its periphery.

Understand
Tanzania

Tanzania Today

Tanzania today is moving fast and looking towards the future. Its urban areas are growing, it is one of Africa's top tourist destinations thanks to its national parks, and it possesses natural gas and mineral resources. Politically, the country's focus is on its new president, Dr John Magufuli, who is moving full steam ahead to eradicate corruption and yank Tanzania up by the bootstraps – to widespread acclaim in many quarters, accompanied by dismay in others at his hardline approach.

Best in Print

The Gunny Sack (MG Vassanji; 1989) Growing-up memoir told through the contents of a gunny sack.

Memoirs of an Arabian Princess from Zanzibar (Emily Ruete; 1888) Autobiography of a Zanzibari princess.

The Tree Where Man Was Born (Peter Matthiessen; 1972) Lyrical account of northern Tanzania's people and landscapes.

Nyerere and Africa – End of an Era (Godfrey Mwakikagile; 2002) Comprehensive study of Julius Nyerere.

Lions in the Balance: Man-Eaters, Manes, and Men with Guns (Craig Packer; 2015) A behind-the-scenes look into lion conservation politics in Tanzania.

Best on Film

Africa – The Serengeti (1994) Classic images of the Serengeti plains.

Tumaini (2005) AIDS devastation in a Tanzanian family.

People of the Forest – The Chimps of Gombe (1988) Gombe's chimpanzees up close.

As Old as My Tongue (2006) Story of legendary Zanzibari singer Bi Kidude.

Bongoland (2003) The USA life of a Tanzanian immigrant.

These Hands (1993) Life in a quarry near Dar es Salaam for Mozambican women refugees.

Nyerere's Legacy

Just past its half-century mark, Tanzania is still indebted to Julius Nyerere, who was at the country's helm for the first 25 years of its existence. Impelled by an egalitarian social vision, Nyerere introduced Swahili as a unifying national language, instilled ideals of *ujamaa* (familyhood) and initiated a tradition of regional political engagement. Thanks to this vision, Tanzania today is one of East Africa's most stable countries, and religious and ethnic conflicts are minimal.

Economic Challenges

On the economic front, the news is mostly good. Tanzania has been enjoying steady economic growth in recent years, and large natural gas reserves along the southeastern coast plus significant mineral resources in the north and west hold the potential for transforming its economy over the coming decades. However, major challenges remain. Tanzania is ranked near the bottom of the United Nations Development Programme's Human Development Index (151st out of 188 countries in the 2016 listing), and daily life for many remains a struggle. Unemployment averages about 10% and underemployment is widespread. Short-term austerity measures by the new government plus greatly stiffened revenue collection and regulatory measures mean that many Tanzanians are feeling an economic pinch. Yet if President Magufuli's plans are realised, the country may well experience an economic leap ahead within the next decade.

Shadow of Corruption

A major impediment to real progress has been corruption. In the most sweeping effort to date to combat it, President Magufuli has enacted tough anti-corruption measures, eliminating thousands of 'ghost workers' from government payrolls, firing anyone with even a suspicion of involvement in shady dealings, and in general succeeding in creating the seeds of a new mentality. Yet, while much progress has been made, there is still much to be done.

Family Squabbles

An ongoing challenge for the Tanzanian government is keeping ties happy between the mainland and the proudly independent Zanzibar Archipelago. While dialogue is generally amicable, the relationship requires ongoing attention. The most recent rough patch arose during the 2015 national elections, when the Zanzibar results – which were leaning towards the opposition Civic United Front (CUF) party – were suddenly annulled. The rerun elections held in March 2016 gave the ruling CCM a 91% majority on the islands, but were boycotted by most Zanzibaris.

A Lively Media

Tanzania's lively media has traditionally played an important role in political debate. While most of the main dailies are aligned to some degree with the governing CCM, the mainland local press has some independence, and Tanzania is ranked ahead of its neighbours in press freedom by Reporters Without Borders.

That said, enforcement of several restrictive laws has been significantly stepped up by President Magufuli's administration. Fear of running afoul of these laws has resulted in self-censorship and a sense of jitteriness, and Tanzania's press freedom rankings have dropped several points since 2016 as a result. Finding a way to allow for democratic pluralism while at the same time maintaining a hardline approach to economic reform is proving to be one of the new government's biggest challenges.

Due to distribution difficulties in rural areas and a countrywide illiteracy rate of approximately 30%, the influence of newspapers is primarily limited to urban centres.

Education for the Future

Perhaps the most significant determinant of Tanzania's future will be its educational system. Recent government administrations have elevated education to greater prominence on the national agenda, and Nyerere's goal of universal primary education is close to being realised. However, in many parts of the country, especially in rural areas, quality and standards are low and drop-out rates high.

Recent efforts by President Magufuli's government to improve teaching standards by removing teachers without proper credentials have resulted in some short-term shake-ups, but with the promise of long-term benefits. Nationwide, the primary student-to-teacher ratio is about 46 to one. At the secondary level, there is a shortage of schools, and an overall enrolment rate of less than 30% countrywide. Less than 2% of the eligible population is enrolled in university.

POPULATION: **52.5 MILLION**

LIFE EXPECTANCY: **63 YEARS**

MOBILE PHONES PER 100 PEOPLE: **74**

INTERNET USERS PER 100 PEOPLEINFLATION: **55.2%**

INFLATION: **5.2%**

belief systems
(% of population)

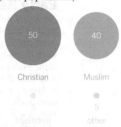

Christian 50

Muslim 40

traditional religions · 5

other · 5

if Tanzania were 100 people

64 would be under 25 years of age
33 would be between 25 and 64 years of age
3 would be 65 years of age or older

population per sq km

TANZANIA   KENYA   UK

🚶 ≈ 45 people

History

Tanzania's history begins with the dawn of humankind. It was here, in the 'cradle of humanity', that East Africa's earliest inhabitants lived. Over the millennia, what is now Tanzania became a backdrop for the great African population migrations, Arabic coastal settlement and European colonialism. The colonial era ultimately led to the growth of a strong independence movement before giving way to the modern-day United Republic of Tanzania.

Early Beginnings

About 3.6 million years ago, some of East Africa's earliest inhabitants trekked across the plains at Laetoli near Oldupai (Olduvai) Gorge in northern Tanzania, leaving their footprints in volcanic ash. The prints were discovered in 1978 by archaeologist Mary Leakey, who identified them as the steps of our earliest known ancestors, hominids known as *australopithecines*.

About two million years ago, the human family tree split, giving rise to *homo habilis*, a meat-eating creature with a larger brain who used crude stone tools. Its traces have also been found around Oldupai (Olduvai) Gorge. By 1.8 million years ago, *homo erectus* had evolved, leaving bones and axes for archaeologists to find at ancient lakeside sites throughout East Africa.

What is today Tanzania was peopled by waves of migration. Rock paintings possibly dating back 6000 years have been found around Kondoa. These are believed to have been made by clans of nomadic hunter-gatherers who spoke a language similar to that of southern Africa's Khoisan. Between 3000 and 5000 years ago, they were joined by small bands of Cushitic-speaking farmers and cattle-herders moving down from what is today Ethiopia. The Iraqw who live around Lake Manyara trace their ancestry to this group of arrivals. The majority of modern Tanzanians are descendants of Bantu-speaking settlers who began a gradual centuries-long shift from the Niger delta around 1000 BC, arriving in East Africa in the 1st century AD. The most recent influx of migrants occurred between the 15th and 18th centuries when Nilotic-speaking pastoralists

Swahili Ruins

Kilwa Kisiwani
Unesco World
Heritage site

Kaole Ruins,
Bagamoyo

Tongoni Ruins,
north of Pangani

Juani and Chole
Ruins, Mafia

TIMELINE	c 25 million BC	3.6 million BC	10,000–3000 BC
	Tectonic plates collide and the East African plains buckle. Formation of the Great Rift Valley begins, as do changes that result ultimately in the formation of Kilimanjaro and other volcanoes.	Some of our earliest ancestors amble across the plain at Laetoli in northern Tanzania, leaving their footprints for modern-day archaeologists to find.	Scattered clans of hunter-gatherers, followed by farmers and cattle herders, settle the East African plains, the well-watered highlands and the lakeshores of what is modern-day Tanzania.

from southern Sudan moved into northern Tanzania and the Rift Valley. Many of these people – ancestors of the Maasai – settled in the less fertile areas of north-central Tanzania where their large herds could have grazing space.

Monsoon Winds

As these migrations were taking place in the interior, coastal areas were being shaped by far different influences. Azania, as the East African coast was known to the ancient Greeks, was an important trading post as early as 400 BC. By the early part of the first millennium AD, thriving settlements had been established as traders, first from the Mediterranean and later from Arabia and Persia, came ashore on the winds of the monsoon and began to intermix with the indigenous Bantu speakers, giving rise to Swahili language and culture. The traders from Arabia also brought Islam, which by the 11th century had become entrenched. Over the next few centuries, the Arabic traders established outposts along the coast, including on the Zanzibar Archipelago and Kilwa Kisiwani. These settlements flourished, reaching their pinnacle between the 13th and 15th centuries, and trade in ivory, gold and other goods extended as far away as India and China.

The first travel guide to the Tanzanian coast was *Periplus of the Erythraean Sea*, written for sailors by a Greek merchant around AD 60. Third-century AD coins from Persia and North Africa have been found along the Tanzanian coast – proof of a long trading history with Arabia and the Mediterranean.

Arrival of the Europeans

One of the first Europeans to set foot in Tanzania was Portuguese sailor Vasco da Gama, who made his way along the coast in 1498 in search of the Orient. Portuguese traders kept to the coast until the early 18th century, when they were driven out by Omani Arabs. The Omanis took control of Kilwa and Zanzibar and set up governors in coastal towns on the mainland. Traders from the coast plied the caravan routes through the interior to the Great Lakes. They bought ivory and slaves in exchange for cheap cloth and firearms. The traders carried with them virulent strains of smallpox and cholera as well as guns. By the late 19th century, when Europe cast a covetous eye on Africa, East Africa was weakened by disease and violence.

SWAHILI

Although Swahili culture began to develop in the early part of the first millennium AD, it was not until the 18th century, with the ascendancy of the Omani Arabs on Zanzibar, that it came into its own. Swahili's role as a *lingua franca* was solidified as it spread throughout East and Central Africa along the great trade caravan routes. European missionaries and explorers soon adopted the language as their main means of communicating with locals. In the second half of the 19th century, missionaries, notably Johann Ludwig Krapf, also began applying the Roman alphabet. Prior to this, Swahili had been written exclusively in Arabic script.

1st century AD	1331	1498	c 1400–1700
Monsoon winds push Arab trading ships to the East African coast. They are followed later by Islamic settlers who mix with the local population to create Swahili language and culture.	Moroccan traveller Ibn Battuta visits Kilwa, finding a flourishing town of 10,000 to 20,000 residents, with a grand palace, a mosque, an inn and a slave market.	Searching for a route to the Orient, Portuguese sailors arrive on the East African coast and establish a coastal trade in slaves and ivory that lasts for 200 years.	In several waves, small bands of nomadic cattle herders migrate south from the Sudan into the Rift Valley – ancestors of today's Maasai.

European Control

The romantic reports of early-19th-century European travellers to East Africa, such as Richard Burton, John Speke, David Livingstone and Henry Morton Stanley, caught the attention of a young German adventurer in the late 19th century. In 1885, without obtaining his government's endorsement, Carl Peters set up a Company for German Colonization. From Zanzibar Island, he travelled into the mainland, collecting en route the signatures of African chiefs on a stack of blank treaty forms he had brought with him. In Berlin, Chancellor Bismarck approved the acquisition of African territory after the fact, much to the consternation of the British, who by now had established informal rule over Zanzibar.

In 1886 East Africa was sliced into 'spheres of influence' by the British and the Germans. The frontier ran west from the coast to Lake Victoria along the modern Kenya–Tanzania border. Needless to say, the Africans weren't consulted on the agreement, nor was the Sultan of Zanzibar. The Germans parked a gunboat in Zanzibar harbour until he signed over his claim to the mainland.

Portuguese influence is still seen in Tanzania's architecture, language and customs. The Swahili *gereza* (jail), from Portuguese *igreja* (church), dates from the days when Portuguese forts contained both edifices in the same compound.

The Colonial Era

Colonialism brought western education and health care to German East Africa, as well as road and rail networks. However, these developments benefited relatively few Africans, and the German administration was unpopular. Harsh labour policies, the imposition of a hut tax and numerous other measures contributed to the discontent. Local opposition began in earnest with the Abushiri Revolt in 1888, and culminated in the Maji Maji rebellion of 1905 to 1907, which decimated much of southern Tanzania and is considered to contain the first seeds of Tanzanian nationalism.

The German era lasted until the end of WWI, when German East Africa came under British administration as a League of Nations mandate and was renamed Tanganyika. This arrangement lasted until WWII, after which the area became a United Nations trust territory, again under British administration. To assist in its own postwar economic recovery effort, Britain maintained compulsory cultivation and enforced settlement policies. The development of a manufacturing sector was actively discouraged by Britain, which wanted to maintain the Tanzanian market for its own goods. Likewise, very few Africans were hired into the civil service.

The word 'Swahili' ('of the coast', from the Arabic word *sahil*) refers both to the Swahili language and to the Islamic culture of the peoples inhabiting the East African coast from Mogadishu (Somalia) down to Mozambique. Both language and culture are a mixture of Bantu, Arabic, Persian and Asian influences.

The Birth of TANU

In 1948 a group of young Africans formed the Tanganyika African Association to protest colonial policies. By 1953 the organisation was renamed the Tanganyika African National Union (TANU), led by a young teacher named Julius Nyerere. Its objective became national liberation. In the end, the British decamped from Tanganyika and Zanzibar rather abruptly

19th century	1840	1840s–60s	1856
Zanzibari slave trader Tippu Tip, tapping into the export slave trade that had thrived since the 9th century, controls a commercial empire stretching from the coast west to the Congo River.	The Sultan of Oman sets up court in a grand palace facing the lagoon on Zanzibar, from where he exerts his authority over coastal mainland Tanganyika.	The first Christian missionaries arrive from Europe. In 1868 the first mainland mission is established at Bagamoyo as a station for ransomed slaves seeking to buy their own freedom.	British explorers Richard Francis Burton and John Hanning Speke venture inland from Zanzibar Island, searching for the source of the Nile and finding Lake Tanganyika and Lake Victoria.

in 1961 and 1963, respectively. This was due at least as much to a growing European sentiment that empires were too expensive to maintain as to recognition of the fundamental right of all people to freedom from subjugation.

Independence

Tanganyikans embraced independence optimistically. However, Tanganyika embarked on the project of nation-building with few of the resources necessary for the task. The national treasury was depleted. The economy was weak and undeveloped, with virtually no industry. In 1961 there were a total of 120 African university graduates in the country.

Faced with this set of circumstances, the first autonomous government of Tanganyika, led by the 39-year-old Julius Nyerere, chose continuity over radical transformation of the economic or political structure. TANU accepted the Westminster-style parliament proposed by the British. It committed to investing in education and a gradual Africanisation of the civil service. In the meantime, expatriates (often former British colonial officers) would be used to staff the government bureaucracy.

Nyerere's political philosophy is set out in two collections of his major speeches and essays: *Freedom and Unity* (1967) and *Freedom and Socialism* (1968).

HISTORY INDEPENDENCE

JULIUS KAMBARAGE NYERERE

Julius Kambarage Nyerere, known as both Baba wa Taifa ('Father of the Nation') and simply as Mwalimu ('Teacher'), rose from humble beginnings to become one of Africa's most renowned statesmen. He was born in 1922 in Butiama, near Lake Victoria, son of a chief of the small Zanaki tribe. After finishing his education, including graduate studies in Scotland, he embarked on a teaching career. In 1953 he joined with a band of like-minded nationalists to form the Tanganyika African National Union (TANU), which he led to the successful liberation of Tanganyika from Britain and through its first two decades of government.

Nyerere gained widespread respect for his idealism, for his success in shaping a society which was politically stable and free of divisive tribal rivalries, and for his contributions towards raising Tanzania's literacy rate, which during his tenure became one of the highest in Africa. He also earned international acclaim for his commitment to pan-Africanism and for his regional engagement.

Despite criticisms of his authoritarian style and economic policies, Nyerere was indisputably one of Africa's most influential leaders, and the person almost single-handedly responsible for putting Tanzania on the world stage. He was widely acclaimed for his long-standing opposition to South Africa's apartheid system, and for his 1979 invasion of Uganda, which resulted in the deposition of the dictator Idi Amin Dada.

In his later years Nyerere assumed the role of elder statesman. He died in 1999 and was buried in his home village of Butiama, where many of his manuscripts and other memorabilia are on display at the Nyerere Museum.

1873	1885	5 October 1889	1890
Under pressure from the British Consul, the Sultan of Zanzibar agrees to abolish the Zanzibar slave market and the mainland trade in human beings.	German adventurer Carl Peters beats Henry Morton Stanley in a race to win the allegiance of the inland Kingdom of Buganda, claiming the territory of Tanganyika for Germany en route.	Mt Kilimanjaro is scaled by Yohani Kinyala Lauwo and Hans Meyer. Lauwo spent the remainder of his long life guiding trekkers up the mountain and training new guides.	Britain trades Heligoland in the North Sea to Germany for recognition of British control of Zanzibar. Between them, they divide up East Africa, with Tanganyika allocated to Germany.

As detailed by political scientist Cranford Pratt, the Nyerere government's early plans were drawn up on the assumption that substantial foreign assistance would be forthcoming, particularly from Britain. Yet this was not the case, and the new country was left scrambling for funds to stay afloat during the first rocky years of liberation. While grappling with fixing roads, running hospitals and educating the country's youth, the government managed to diffuse an army mutiny over wages in 1964. When Zanzibar erupted in violent revolution in January 1964, just weeks after achieving independence from Britain, Nyerere skilfully co-opted its potentially destabilising forces by giving island politicians a prominent role in a newly proclaimed United Republic of Tanzania, created from the union of Tanganyika with the Zanzibar Archipelago in April 1964.

Exhorting his compatriots to work hard, Nyerere quoted a Swahili proverb: 'Treat your guest as a guest for two days; on the third day, give him a hoe!'

Ujamaa – Tanzania's Grand Experiment

The events of the first few years following independence – the lack of assistance from abroad, rumblings of civil strife at home and the nascent development of a privileged class amid continuing mass poverty – led Nyerere to re-evaluate the course his government had charted for the nation.

Since his student days, Nyerere had pondered the meaning of democracy for Africa. In 1962 he published an essay entitled *Ujamaa [familyhood]: The Basis of African Socialism*. In it he set out his belief that the personal accumulation of wealth in the face of widespread poverty was antisocial. Africa should strive to create a society based on mutual assistance and economic as well as political equality, such as he claimed had existed for centuries before European colonisation.

The Arusha Declaration

In 1967 the TANU leadership met in the northern town of Arusha, where they approved a radical new plan for Tanzania, drafted by Nyerere. What became known as the *Arusha Declaration* outlined the Tanzanian government's commitment to a socialist approach to development, further articulated in a series of subsequent policy papers. The government vowed to reduce its dependence on foreign aid and instead foster an ethos of self-reliance in Tanzanian society. To prevent government becoming a trough where bureaucrats and party members could amass personal wealth, Nyerere passed a Leadership Code. Among other things, it prohibited government officials from holding shares in a private company, employing domestic staff or buying real estate to rent out for profit.

Throughout the country, in the wake of the *Arusha Declaration*, people turned out to help their neighbours build new schools, repair roads, and plant and harvest food to sell for medical supplies. Nyerere and his ministers made a regular practice of grabbing a shovel and pitching in.

The *Arusha Declaration* also announced the government takeover of industry and banking. It curtailed foreign direct investment and stated that the government would itself invest in manufacturing enterprises that could produce substitutes for imported goods. All land was henceforth

1905–07	1909–12	1919	1953
In the Matumbi Hills near Kilwa, a mystic called Kinjikitile stirs African labourers to rise up against their German overlords in what becomes known as the Maji Maji rebellion.	A team of German palaeontologists unearths the remains of various dinosaur species near Tendunguru, Lindi region. These include the skeleton of *Brachiosaurus brancai*, the world's largest known dinosaur.	At the end of WWI, Tanganyika is placed under the 'protection' of the British acting on behalf first of the League of Nations and then its successor, the UN.	A charismatic young school teacher named Julius Nyerere is elected President of the Tanganyika African National Union, an organisation dedicated to the liberation of Tanganyika from colonial rule.

to be common property, managed by the state. The government strove to provide free education for every child. School children were taught to identify themselves as Tanzanians with a shared language – Swahili – rather than just members of one of over 100 ethnic groups residing within the country's borders.

Socialist Leanings?

Nyerere himself was fascinated by Chinese economic development strategies, but dismissed Western fears that Tanzania was toying with doctrinaire Marxism, either Chinese- or Soviet-style. He argued in *Freedom and Unity – Essays on Socialism* (1967) that Tanzanians 'have no more need of being "converted" to socialism than we have of being "taught" democracy. Both are rooted in our own past – in the traditional society that produced us.' Nyerere's vision was enthusiastically embraced not only by the Tanzanian public, but by a body of Western academics and by aid donors from both East and West. Several of his policies nonetheless provoked the consternation of even his most ardent supporters abroad. In 1965 TANU voted to scrap the multiparty model of democracy bequeathed to it by Britain. As a consequence, Tanzania became a one-party state. Nyerere argued that democracy was not synonymous with multiparty politics and that the new country's challenges were so great that everyone had to work together. He advocated freedom of speech and the discussion of ideas, but banned opposition parties. Voters were given a choice of candidates, but they were all TANU party members. Furthermore, Nyerere authorised the detention of some individuals judged to be agitating against the best interests of the state. His defenders say he did his best to hold together a sometimes unruly cabinet and a country at a time when all over Africa newly independent states were succumbing to civil war and dictatorships. Critics say he turned a blind eye to violations of fundamental civil liberties.

The East African Community – originally formed in 1967 by Tanzania, Kenya and Uganda, and later revived after its 1977 collapse – now also includes Rwanda, Burundi and South Sudan. There has been some progress towards economic cooperation, but political federation is still far in the future.

'Villagisation'

Perhaps the most controversial of all government policies adopted post-Arusha was 'villagisation'. The vast majority of Tanzanians lived in the countryside, and the *Arusha Declaration* envisioned agriculture as the engine of economic growth. A massive increase in production was to be accomplished through communal farming, such as Nyerere argued was the practice in the old days. Beginning in 1967, Tanzanians were encouraged to reorganise themselves into communal villages where they would work the fields together for the good of the nation. Some did, but only a handful of cooperative communities were established voluntarily.

In 1974 the government commenced the forcible relocation of 80% of the population, creating massive disruptions in national agricultural

9 December 1961	1964	1967	1978–79
Tanganyika gains independence from British colonial rule, with Nyerere as president. The Zanzibar Archipelago follows suit in December 1963, establishing a constitutional monarchy under the Sultan.	Following a bloody coup on the islands of Zanzibar, in which several thousand Zanzibaris were killed, Tanganyika and the archipelago are united to form the United Republic of Tanzania.	At a gathering of TANU party faithful in Arusha, Julius Nyerere garners enthusiastic support for the *Arusha Declaration*, which sets out Tanzania's path to African socialism.	Ugandan dictator Idi Amin Dada invades Tanzania, burning villages along the Kagera River believed to harbour Ugandan rebels. Tanzania's army marches to topple Amin and restore Milton Obote to power.

production. The scheme itself, however, suffered from a multiplicity of problems. The new land was often infertile. Necessary equipment was unavailable. People didn't want to work communally; they wanted to provide for their own families first. Government prices for crops were set too low. To paraphrase analyst Goran Hyden, the peasantry responded by retreating into subsistence farming – just growing their own food. National agricultural production and revenue from cash crop exports plummeted.

Summing up the results of the *Arusha Declaration* policies, Nyerere candidly admitted that the government had made some mistakes. However, he also noted progress towards social equality: the ratio between the highest salaries and the lowest paid narrowed from 50:1 in 1961 to around 9:1 in 1976. Despite a meagre colonial inheritance, Tanzania made great strides in education and healthcare. Under Nyerere's leadership it forged a cohesive national identity. With the exception of occasional isolated eruptions of civil strife on the Zanzibar Archipelago, it has also enjoyed internal peace and stability throughout its existence.

Aid Darling to Delinquent

Post–*Arusha Declaration* Tanzania was the darling of the aid donor community. It was the largest recipient of foreign aid in sub-Saharan Africa throughout the 1970s and was the testing ground for every new-fangled development theory that came along.

TANZANIA ON THE WORLD STAGE

Throughout the 1960s to the 1980s, Nyerere, representing Tanzania, was a voice of moral authority in global forums such as the UN, the Organization of African Unity and the Commonwealth. He asserted the autonomy of 'Third World' states, and pressed for a fairer global economic structure.

Nyerere's government was also a vocal advocate for the liberation of southern Africa from white minority rule. From 1963 Tanzania provided a base for the South African, Zimbabwean and Mozambican liberation movements within its territory as well as military support, at great cost – both human and material – to itself.

While accepting Chinese assistance to build the Tazara Railway from Zambia to Dar es Salaam in the 1970s, throughout the Cold War Tanzania remained staunchly nonaligned, resisting the machinations and blandishments of both East and West.

Tanzania's lower profile on the world stage in recent decades can be attributed to the passing of the charismatic and revered Nyerere and to economic challenges. Nevertheless, Tanzania continues to open its doors to civilians fleeing violence in the countries that surround it. As of 2017, it was hosting over 300,000 refugees, mainly from Burundi and the Democratic Republic of the Congo (Zaïre), who are living in camps along Tanzania's western borders.

1985	1986	1992	7 August 1998
Julius Nyerere voluntarily steps down as president after five terms. This paves the way for a peaceful transition to his elected successor.	After resisting for several years, but with the economy in a downward spiral, Tanzania accepts stringent IMF terms for a structural adjustment program loan.	Opposition parties are legalised under pressure from the international donor community. The first multiparty elections are held in Tanzania in 1995 with 13 political parties on the ballot.	Within minutes of one another, Al Qaeda truck bombs explode at the American embassies in Nairobi and Dar es Salaam. Eleven Tanzanians die in the attack, with dozens more injured.

As the economy spiralled downward in the late 1970s and early '80s, the World Bank, International Monetary Fund (IMF) and a growing chorus of exasperated aid donors called for stringent economic reform – a dramatic structural adjustment of the economic system. Overlooking their own failing projects, they pointed to a bloated civil service and moribund productive sector, preaching that both needed to be exposed to the fresh, cleansing breezes of the open market. Nyerere resisted the IMF cure. As economic conditions continued to deteriorate, dissension grew within government ranks. In 1985 Nyerere resigned. In 1986 the Tanzanian government submitted to the IMF terms. The grand Tanzanian experiment with African socialism was over.

Structural Adjustment

As elsewhere on the continent, structural adjustment was a shock treatment that left the nation gasping for air. The civil service was slashed by over a third. Some of the deadwood was gone, but so were thousands of teachers, healthcare workers and the money for textbooks and chalk and teacher training. Economic growth rates slipped into the negative around 1974, where they languished for the next 25 years. In 1997 Tanzania was spending four times as much servicing its external debt than on healthcare, a situation that has improved only slightly during much of the past two decades.

Multiparty Democracy

In 1992, as part of a structural adjustment aid program, Western-style multiparty democracy was re-introduced, and the constitution was amended to legalise opposition parties. Since then, five national elections have been held, generally proceeding relatively smoothly on the mainland, less so in the Zanzibar Archipelago, where tensions between the CCM and the opposition Civic United Front (CUF) are strong.

In elections in 2015, Dr John Magufuli (CCM) was elected president with 58% of the vote. His main opposition was former CCM Prime Minister Edward Lowassa of the Party for Democracy and Progress (Chadema). Following the election, Dr Magufuli moved quickly to implement his program, and almost two years into his presidency was receiving considerable acclaim – especially among Tanzania's rural population – for his stiff anti-corruption measures and his determination to hold government officials accountable to their constituencies. At the same time, he was also being criticised in some quarters for his clamps on public debate and his stepped-up enforcement of restrictive laws governing freedom of the press. The next elections are scheduled for October 2020.

Historical Hotspots

Oldupai (Olduvai) Gorge Museum

Kondoa Rock-Art Sites

Natural History Museum, Arusha

National Museum, Dar es Salaam

Arusha Declaration Museum, Arusha

Nyerere Museum, Musoma

2000	2010	October 2015	2017
Contentious elections for the Zanzibari Legislature boil over into street violence and 22 people are shot by police during mass demonstrations protesting the results.	Jakaya Mrisho Kikwete is re-elected president with about 62% of the votes with a surprisingly strong showing by opposition candidates.	Dr John Pombe Magufuli (CCM) wins a hotly contested national presidential election with 58% of the vote.	At Jebel Irhoud (Morocco), fossil remains of early *homo sapiens* are found to date back 300,000 years, raising questions about East Africa's claim to be the 'cradle of humanity'.

People & Daily Life

A highlight of travelling in Tanzania is getting to know the people and becoming acquainted with the country's many cultures. Thanks to relatively widespread knowledge of English in urban and tourist areas, plus a strong tradition of hospitality, local customs and culture in Tanzania are generally quite accessible. If you're planning to travel in rural areas, it's well worth trying to learn some basic Swahili phrases in advance.

Tanzania's People

Tanzania is home to about 120 tribal groups, plus relatively small but economically significant numbers of Asians and Arabs, and a tiny European community. Most tribes are very small; almost 100 of them combined account for only one-third of the total population. As a result, none has succeeded in dominating politically or culturally, although groups such as the Chagga and the Haya, who have a long tradition of education, are disproportionately well represented in government and business circles.

About 95% of Tanzanians are of Bantu origin. These include the Sukuma (who live around Mwanza and southern Lake Victoria, and constitute about 16% of the overall population), the Nyamwezi (around Tabora), the Makonde (southeastern Tanzania), the Haya (around Bukoba) and the Chagga (around Mt Kilimanjaro). The Maasai and several smaller groups including the Arusha and the Samburu (all in northern Tanzania) are of Nilo-Hamitic or Nilotic origin. The Iraqw, around Karatu and northwest of Lake Manyara, are Cushitic, as are the northern-central tribes of Gorowa and Burungi. The Sandawe and, more distantly, the seminomadic Hadzabe (around Lake Eyasi), belong to the Khoisan ethnolinguistic family.

Tribal structures, however, range from weak to nonexistent – a legacy of Julius Nyerere's abolishment of local chieftaincies following independence.

About 3% of Tanzania's population lives on the Zanzibar Archipelago, with about one-third of these on Pemba. Most African Zanzibaris belong to one of three groups: the Hadimu, the Tumbatu and the Pemba. Members of the non-African Zanzibari population are primarily Shirazi and consider themselves descendants of immigrants from Shiraz in Persia (Iran).

The National Psyche

Partly as a result of the large number of smaller tribes in Tanzania, and partly as a result of the *ujamaa* (familyhood) ideals of Julius Nyerere, which still permeate society, tribal rivalries are almost nonexistent. Religious frictions are also minimal, with Christians and Muslims living side by side in a relatively easy coexistence. Although political differences flare, especially on the Zanzibar Archipelago, they rarely come to the forefront in interpersonal dealings.

Tanzanians place a premium on politeness and courtesy. Greetings are essential, and you'll probably be given a gentle reminder should you forget this and launch straight into a question without first inquiring as

Tanzania's literary scene is dominated by renowned poet and writer Shaaban Robert (1909–62). Robert, who is considered the country's national poet, was almost single-handedly responsible for the development of a modern Swahili prose style. An English-language introduction to his work is *The Poetry of Shaaban Robert*, translated by Clement Ndulute.

to the well-being of your listener and their family. Tanzanian children are trained to greet their elders with a respectful *shikamoo* (literally, 'I hold your feet'), often accompanied in rural areas by a slight curtsy, and strangers are frequently addressed as *dada* (sister) or *mama,* in the case of an older woman; *kaka* (brother); or *ndugu* (relative or comrade).

Daily Life

Family life is central, with weddings, funerals and other events holding centre stage. Celebrations are generally splashed-out affairs aimed at demonstrating status, and frequently go well beyond the means of the host family. It's expected that family members who have jobs will share what they have, and the extended family (which also encompasses the community) forms an essential support network in the absence of a government social security system.

Invisible social hierarchies lend life a sense of order. In the family, the man rules the roost, with the children at the bottom and women just above them. In the larger community, it's not much different. Child-raising is the expected occupation for women, and bread-winning for men, although a small but steadily growing cadre of professional women is becoming increasingly more visible. Village administrators (called *shehe* on Zanzibar Island) oversee things, and make important decisions in consultation with other senior community members.

The HIV/AIDS infection rate is about 4.7%. Public awareness has increased, with AIDS-related billboards throughout major cities. However, real public discussion remains limited, and in many circles AIDS deaths are still often explained away as 'tuberculosis'.

Tanzania is the only African country boasting indigenous inhabitants from all of the continent's main ethnolinguistic families (Bantu, Nilo-Hamitic, Cushitic, Khoisan). They live in closest proximity around Lakes Eyasi and Babati.

Religion

All but the smallest villages have a mosque, a church or both; religious festivals are generally celebrated with fervour, at least as far as singing, dancing and family gatherings are concerned; and almost every Tanzanian identifies with some religion.

Muslims, who account for close to 40% of the population, have traditionally been concentrated along the coast, as well as in the inland towns that lined the old caravan routes. There are several sects represented, notably the Sunni (Shafi school). The population of the Zanzibar Archipelago is almost exclusively Sunni Muslim.

Close to 50% of Tanzanians are Christians. Major denominations include Roman Catholic, Lutheran and Anglican, with a small percentage of Tanzanians adherents of other Christian denominations, including Baptist and Pentecostal. One of the areas of highest Christian concentration is in the northeast around Moshi, which has been a centre of missionary activity since the mid-19th century.

TANZANIAN STYLE

Tanzanians are conservative, and while they are likely to be too polite to tell you so directly, they'll be privately shaking their heads about travellers doing things such as not wearing enough clothing, sporting tatty clothes or indulging in public displays of affection. Especially along the Muslim coast, cover up the shoulders and legs, and avoid plunging necklines, skin-tight fits and the like.

Another thing to remember is the great importance placed on greetings and pleasantries. Even if just asking directions, Tanzanians always take time to greet the other person and enquire about their well-being and that of their families, and they expect visitors to do the same. Tanzanians often continue to hold hands for several minutes after meeting, or even throughout an entire conversation. Especially in the south, a handshake may be accompanied by touching the left hand to the right elbow as a sign of respect.

Maasai women

The remainder of the population follows traditional religions centred on ancestor worship, the land and various ritual objects. There are also small but active communities of Hindus, Sikhs and Ismailis.

Historically, the main area of friction has been between Tanzania's Muslim and Christian populations. Today, tensions, while still simmering, are at a relatively low level, and religion is not a major factor in contemporary Tanzanian politics. An exception to this is on the Zanzibar Archipelago, where increasing incidents of interreligious violence in recent years have cast a shadow.

The Role of Women

Women form the backbone of the economy, with most juggling child-rearing plus work on the family *shamba* (small plot), or in an office. However, they are frequently marginalised, especially in education. Fewer than 10% of girls complete secondary school, and of these only a handful go on to complete university. While secondary school enrolment levels are low across the board, girls in particular are frequently kept home due to a lack of finances, to help with chores or because of pregnancy.

Especially in rural areas, it's common for a woman to drop her own name, and become known as *Mama* followed by the name of her oldest son (or daughter, if she has no sons).

On the positive side, the situation is greatly improving. Since 1996 the government has guaranteed 20% of parliamentary seats for women, and just over one-third of members of the current National Assembly are women. The country's vice president is a woman, as are several cabinet ministers. In education, the 'gender gap' has been essentially eliminated at the primary level.

Arts
Music & Dance

Tanzania has an outstanding music and dance scene, mixing influences from its 100-plus tribal groups, from coastal and inland areas and from traditional and modern. Dar es Salaam is the hub, with the greatest variety of groups and styles, but search around anywhere in the country (asking locals is the best bet) to discover some real gems. Two good contacts are Tumaini University Makumira (www.makumiramusic.org) outside Arusha and Bagamoyo College of Arts (www.tasuba.ac.tz).

Traditional

Tanzanian traditional dance *(ngoma)* creates a living picture, encompassing the entire community in its message and serving as a channel for expressing sentiments such as thanks and praise, and for communicating with the ancestors.

The main place for masked dance is in the southeast, where it plays an important role in the initiation ceremonies of the Makonde (who are famous for their *mapiko* masks) and the Makua.

Modern

The greatest influence on Tanzania's modern music scene has been the Congolese bands that began playing in Dar es Salaam in the early 1960s, which brought the styles of rumba and soukous *(lingala* music) into the East African context. Among the best known is Orchestre Super Matimila, which was propelled to fame by the late Remmy Ongala (Dr Remmy), who was born in the Democratic Republic of the Congo (Zaïre), but gained his fame in Tanzania. Many of his songs (most are in Swahili) are commentaries on contemporary themes such as AIDS, poverty and hunger, and Ongala was a major force in popularising music from the region beyond Africa's borders.

Also popular are Swahili rap artists, a vibrant hip-hop scene and the hip-hop influenced and popular Bongo Flava. The easiest music to find is church choir music *(kwaya)*.

On the Zanzibar Archipelago, the music scene has long been dominated by *taarab*. Rivalling *taarab* for attention is the similar *kidumbak,* distinguished by its defined rhythms and drumming, and its hard-hitting lyrics.

Wedding Music

During the colonial days, German and British military brass bands spurred the development of *beni ngoma* (brass *ngoma*), dance and music societies combining Western-style brass instruments with African drums and other traditional instruments. Variants of these are still de rigueur at weddings. Stand at the junction of Moshi and Old Moshi Rds in Arusha

Swahili is famous for its proverbs. They're used for everything from instructing children to letting one's spouse know that you are annoyed with them. Many are printed around the edges of *kangas* (printed cotton wraparounds worn by many Tanzanian women). For a sampling, see www.glcom.com/hassan/kanga.html and www.mwambao.com/methali.htm.

NGOMA

The drum is the most essential element in Tanzania's traditional music. The same word *(ngoma)* is used for both dance and drumming, illustrating the intimate relationship between the two, and many dances can only be performed to the beat of a particular type of drum. Some dances, notably those of the Sukuma, also make use of other accessories, including live snakes and other animals. The Maasai are famous for their dancing, which is accompanied only by chants and often also by jumping.

Other traditional musical instruments include the *kayamba* (shakers made with grain kernels); rattles and bells made of wood or iron; xylophones (also sometimes referred to as *marimbas*); *siwa* (horns); and *tari* (tambourines).

BACK TO BASICS?

For a country that was founded by a teacher (Julius Nyerere is still referred to as Mwalimu, or 'Teacher'), Tanzania ranks near the bottom of the heap when it comes to education. It wasn't always like this. Nyerere was convinced that success for his philosophy of socialism and self-reliance depended on having an educated populace. He made primary education compulsory and offered government assistance to villagers to build their own schools. By the 1980s the country's literacy rate had become one of the highest in Africa.

Later, much of the initial momentum was lost. Although over 94% of children enrol at the primary level, about 20% of these drop out before finishing, and less than 15% complete secondary school. The reasons include not enough trained teachers, not enough schools and not enough money. At the secondary level, school fees are a problem, as is language. Primary school instruction is in Swahili, and many students lack sufficient knowledge of English to carry out their secondary-level studies.

any Saturday afternoon, and watch the wedding processions come by, all accompanied by a small band riding in the back of a pick-up truck.

Visual Arts

Painting

The most popular style of painting is Tingatinga, which takes its name from painter Edward Saidi Tingatinga, who began it in the 1960s in response to demands from the European market. Tingatinga paintings are traditionally composed in a square, with brightly coloured animal motifs set against a monochrome background, and use diluted and often unmixed enamel paints for a characteristic glossy appearance.

Sculpture & Woodcarving

In Tanzania, it's sometimes hard to know where the family ends and the community begins. Doors are always open, helping out others in the *jamaa* (clan, community) is expected and celebrations involve everyone.

Tanzania's Makonde, together with their Mozambican counterparts, are renowned throughout East Africa for their original and highly fanciful carvings. Although originally from the southeast around the Makonde Plateau, commercial realities lured many Makonde north. Today, the country's main carving centre is at Mwenge in Dar es Salaam, where blocks of hard African blackwood (*Dalbergia melanoxylon* or, in Swahili, *mpingo*) come to life under the hands of skilled artists.

Ujamaa (familyhood) carvings are designed as a totem pole or 'tree of life' containing interlaced human and animal figures around a common ancestor. Each generation is connected to those that preceded it, and gives support to those that follow. Tree of life carvings often reach several metres in height, and are almost always made from a single piece of wood. *Shetani* carvings, which embody images from the spirit world, are more abstract and even grotesque. The emphasis is on challenging viewers to new interpretations while giving the carver's imagination free reign.

Environment & National Parks

At over 943,000 sq km, or almost four times the size of the UK, Tanzania is East Africa's largest country. It encompasses a diversity of landscapes – forested mountains, open savannah lands, several major lakes and rivers, and a long coastline. It also hosts a wealth of animal and plant life, and has an exceptional collection of national parks.

Topography

Tanzania is bordered to the east by the Indian Ocean, with its wealth of corals, fish and sea turtles. To the west are the deep lakes of the Western Rift Valley, Lake Tanganyika and Lake Nyasa (Lake Malawi). Both have lush mountains rising up from their shores. Much of central Tanzania is an arid highland plateau averaging 900m to 1800m in altitude and nestled between the eastern and western branches of the Great Rift Valley. Savannah landscapes are best seen in the north, in Serengeti National Park.

Tanzania's mountain ranges are grouped into a sharply rising northeastern section, known as the Eastern Arc, and an open, rolling central and southern section known as the southern Highlands or Southern Arc. A range of volcanoes and extinct volcanoes known as the Crater Highlands rises from the side of the Great Rift Valley in northern Tanzania.

The country's largest river is the Rufiji, which drains the Southern Highlands en route to the coast, and which is scheduled to be dammed as part of the planned Steigler's Gorge hydroelectric power project. Other major rivers include the Ruvu, Wami, Pangani and Ruvuma.

About 6% (59,000 sq km) of mainland Tanzania is covered by inland lakes. The deepest is Lake Tanganyika, while the largest (and one of the shallowest) is Lake Victoria.

Wildlife

Zebras, elephants, wildebeest, buffaloes, hippos, giraffes, antelope, dikdiks, gazelles, elands and both greater and lesser kudus – these are just some of the 430 species and subspecies that make up Tanzania's

SAVING THE SEA TURTLES

Tanzania's sea turtle population is critically endangered, due to nest poaching, subsistence hunting and turtles getting caught in fishing nets. Sea Sense (www.seasense.org) has been working with coastal communities to protect turtles, as well as dugongs, whale sharks and other endangered marine species. It has made considerable progress, especially with its community nest protection program.

As part of this initiative, local community members are trained as 'turtle tour guides' to take visitors to nesting sites to watch hatchlings emerge and make their way to the sea. Places where this is possible include Dar es Salaam's South Beach, Ushongo beach (south of Pangani) and Mafia island. The modest fee is split between Sea Sense, to support its nest protection program, and local village environment funds. In this way, community members are able to benefit directly from their conservation efforts. If you'd like to watch a sea turtle nest hatching, contact Sea Sense (info@seasense.org).

THE EASTERN ARC MOUNTAINS

The ancient Eastern Arc mountains (which include the Usambara, Pare, Udzungwa and Uluguru ranges) stretch in a broken crescent from southern Kenya's Taita Hills down to Morogoro and the Southern Highlands. They are estimated to be at least 100 million years old, with the stones forming them as much as 600 million years old. Their climatic isolation and stability has offered plant species a chance to develop, and today these mountains are highly biodiverse and home to an exceptional assortment of plants and birds. Plant and bird numbers in the mountain ranges total about one-third of Tanzania's flora and fauna species, and include many unique species plus a wealth of medicinal plants.

In the late 19th century, population growth and expansion of the local logging industry began to cause depletion of the Eastern Arc's original forest cover, and erosion became a serious problem. It became so bad in parts of the western Usambaras that in the early 1990s entire villages had to be shifted to lower areas. The situation has now somewhat stabilised, with a reduction in logging and the initiation of several tree-planting projects. However, it remains a serious concern.

four-million-plus wild animal population. The country is famed in particular for its predators, with Serengeti National Park one of the best places for spotting lions, cheetahs and leopards. There are also hyenas and wild dogs (the latter in Ruaha National Park and Selous Game Reserve), and in Gombe and Mahale Mountains National Parks, chimpanzees.

Tanzania is notable for lying in a transition zone between the savannah lands of East Africa and the *miombo* (brachystegia) woodland habitats of southern Africa, and hosts species common to each area. This transition is best seen in Ruaha National Park, where East African highlights such as Grant's gazelle are found alongside more southerly ones such as Lichtenstein's hartebeest and greater kudu.

Complementing the country's wealth of large animals are over 1000 bird species, making Tanzania an ornithologist's dream. Commonly sighted birds include kingfishers, hornbills (around Amani in the eastern Usambaras), bee-eaters (along the Rufiji and Wami Rivers), fish eagles (Lake Victoria) and flamingos (Lakes Manyara and Natron). There are also many birds that are unique to Tanzania, including the Udzungwa forest partridge, the Pemba green pigeon, the Usambara weaver and the Usambara eagle owl.

In addition, Tanzania has over 60,000 insect species, about 25 types of reptiles or amphibians, 100 species of snakes and numerous fish species.

Endangered Species

Endangered species include the black rhino; Uluguru bush shrike; hawksbill, green, olive ridley and leatherback turtle; red colobus monkey; wild dog; and Pemba flying fox.

Plants

Top Spots for Botanists

Kitulo National Park

Amani National Reserve

Udzungwa Mountains National Park

Patches of tropical rainforest in Tanzania's Eastern Arc mountains provide home to a rich assortment of plants, many found nowhere else in the world. These include the Usambara or African violet *(Saintpaulia)* and impatiens, which are sold as house plants in grocery stores throughout the West. Similar forest patches – remnants of the much larger tropical forest that once extended across the continent – are also found in the Udzungwas, Ulugurus and several other areas. South and west of the Eastern Arc range are stands of baobab.

Away from the mountain ranges, much of the country is covered by *miombo* ('moist' woodland), where the main vegetation is various types of brachystegia tree. Much of the dry central plateau is covered with savannah, bushland and thickets, while grasslands cover the Serengeti Plains and other areas that lack good drainage.

National Parks & Reserves

Tanzania has 16 mainland national parks, 14 wildlife reserves, the Ngorongoro Conservation Area, three marine parks and several protected marine reserves. Until relatively recently, development and tourism were focused almost exclusively on the northern parks (Serengeti, Lake Manyara, Tarangire and Arusha National Parks), plus Kilimanjaro National Park for trekkers, and the Ngorongoro Conservation Area. All of these places are easily reached by road or air, and heavily visited, with a range of facilities. Apart from the evocative landscapes, the main attractions are the high concentrations, diversity and accessibility of the wildlife.

The southern protected areas (Ruaha National Park and Selous Game Reserve, plus Mikumi, Udzungwa Mountains and Kitulo parks) receive considerable attention, but still don't see the number of visitors that the north does. The wildlife, however, is just as impressive, although it's often spread out over larger areas. At Udzungwa Mountains and Kitulo, the main highlights are botanical.

In the west are Mahale Mountains and Gombe National Parks, where the main draws are the chimpanzees and (for Mahale) the remoteness. Katavi is also remote, and offers a wonderful opportunity to experience real wilderness. Rubondo Island National Park is set on its own in Lake Victoria, and is of particular interest for birding. Saadani, just north of Dar es Salaam, is the only terrestrial national park along the coast. Mkomazi, just off the Arusha–Tanga highway near Same, hosts a private sanctuary for black rhinos.

National Parks

Tanzania's national parks are managed by the Tanzania National Parks Authority (p165).

Best Places to Spot...

Black Rhino: Ngorongoro Crater

Uluguru Bush Shrike: Uluguru Mountains

Red Colobus Monkey: Jozani Forest, Zanzibar Island

Wild Dogs: Selous GR, Ruaha NP

Pemba Flying Fox: Pemba

ENVIRONMENT & NATIONAL PARKS NATIONAL PARKS & RESERVES

THE GREAT RIFT VALLEY

The Great Rift Valley is part of the East African rift system – a massive geological fault stretching 6500km across the African continent, from the Dead Sea in the north to Beira (Mozambique) in the south. The rift system was formed over 30 million years ago when the tectonic plates comprising the African and Eurasian landmasses collided and then diverged. As the plates separated, large chunks of the earth's crust dropped down between them, resulting over millennia in the escarpments, ravines, flatlands and lakes that characterise East Africa's topography today.

The rift system is notable for its calderas and volcanoes (including Mt Kilimanjaro, Mt Meru and the calderas of the Crater Highlands) and for its lakes, which are often very deep, with floors well below sea level although their surfaces may be several hundred metres above sea level.

The Tanzanian Rift Valley consists of two branches formed where the main rift system divides north of Kenya's Lake Turkana. The Western Rift Valley extends past Lake Albert (Uganda) through Rwanda and Burundi to Lakes Tanganyika and Nyasa, while the eastern branch (Eastern or Gregory Rift) runs south from Lake Turkana, past Lakes Natron and Manyara, before joining again with the Western Rift by Lake Nyasa. The lakes of the Eastern Rift are smaller than those in the western branch, with some only waterless salt beds. The largest are Lakes Natron and Manyara. Lake Eyasi is in a side branch off the main rift.

The escarpments of Tanzania's portion of the Rift Valley are most impressive in and around the Ngorongoro Conservation Area and Lake Manyara National Park.

Park entry fees range from US$30 to US$100 per adult per single entry per 24-hour period, depending on the park (US$10 to US$20 per child per single entry per 24 hours for children between five and 16 years of age), with Serengeti, Kilimanjaro, Mahale Mountains and Gombe parks the most expensive, and Mkomazi, Saadani, Mikumi, Udzungwa Mountains, Kitulo, Katavi and Rubondo Island parks the least expensive. The single-entry requirement means that it is not possible to exit a park and re-enter within 24 hours unless you pay entry fees again.

Park camping fees are US$30 per adult (US$5 per child) in public campsites and US$50 per adult (US$10 per child) in special campsites. Other costs include guide fees of US$20 to US$25 per group for walking safaris, plus vehicle fees (US$40 per foreign-registered vehicle and Tsh20,000 for Tanzania-registered vehicles). Note that a value-added tax (VAT) of 18% is applied to all park fees, including park entry, camping, guide and vehicle fees.

At all parks, all fees must be paid electronically with a Visa card or MasterCard. Especially at more remote parks, it is also advisable to bring cash, just in case the card machines are not working.

Wildlife Reserves

Wildlife reserves are administered by the **Tanzania Wildlife Management Authority** (TAWA; www.tawa.go.tz). Fees must be paid in advance, either through your lodge or tented camp or at any NBC bank branch. Selous Game Reserve (p322) is the only reserve with tourist infrastructure. Large areas of most others have been leased as hunting concessions, as has the southern Selous.

Marine Parks & Reserves

Mafia Island Marine Park (p319), Mnazi Bay-Ruvuma Estuary Marine Park (p339), Tanga Coelacanth Marine Park (p133), Maziwe Marine Reserve (p135) and the Dar es Salaam Marine Reserves (p73; Mbudya, Bongoyo, Pangavini and Fungu Islands) are under the jurisdiction of the Ministry of Natural Resources & Tourism's **Marine Parks & Reserves Unit** (Map p56; ☎022-215 0621; www.marineparks.go.tz; Olympio St, Upanga, Dar es Salaam; ☉8am-4.30pm Mon-Fri). Except for Mafia Island Marine Park, which accepts credit card only, entry fees for marine parks (US$20 per day per adult, US$10 per child) and marine reserves (US$10 per adult, US$5 per child) are payable in cash only.

Ngorongoro Conservation Area

The Ngorongoro Conservation Area (p181) was established as a multiple-use area to protect wildlife and the pastoralist lifestyle of the Maasai, who had lost other large areas of their traditional territory with the formation of Serengeti National Park. It is administered by the Ngorongoro Conservation Area Authority (p182). It is notable both for its superlative wildlife watching in the Ngorongoro Crater and for its rugged hiking in the surrounding highlands. Payment for entering the conservation area must be made with Visa or MasterCard, although it is advisable to bring cash as well.

Environmental Issues

Although Tanzania has one of the highest proportions of protected land of any African country (about 40% is protected in some form), limited resources and corruption hamper conservation efforts, and poaching, erosion, soil degradation, desertification and deforestation whittle away at the natural wealth. According to some estimates, Tanzania loses 3500 sq km of forest land annually as a result of agricultural and commercial clearing, and about 95% of the tropical high forest that once covered

---

Tanzania's Unesco World Heritage Sites: Mt Kilimanjaro National Park; Kondoa Rock-Art Sites; Ngorongoro Conservation Area; Ruins of Kilwa Kisiwani & Songo Mnara; Zanzibar Town's Stone Town; Serengeti National Park; Selous Game Reserve (currently listed as World Heritage in Danger)

Tanzania's montane forests contain 7% of Africa's endemic plant species on only 0.05% of the continent's total area. Check the Tanzania Conservation Group website (www.tfcg.org) for an introduction to the country's forests and the conservation of their exceptional biodiversity.

Zanzibar and Pemba Islands is now gone. Poaching has increased markedly in both the northern circuit parks and in Selous Game Reserve due to corruption, increased demand and insufficient enforcement. This, combined with inappropriate visitor use, especially in the northern circuit, is a serious threat to wildlife and ecosystems.

MAJOR NATIONAL PARKS & RESERVES

PARK	FEATURES	ACTIVITIES	BEST TIME TO VISIT
Arusha NP (p167)	Mt Meru, lakes & crater; zebras, giraffes, elephants	trekking, canoe & vehicle safaris, walking	year-round
Gombe NP (p271)	lakeshore, forest; chimpanzees	chimp tracking	Jun–Oct
Katavi NP (p277)	flood plains, lakes & woodland; buffaloes, hippos, antelope	vehicle & walking safaris	Jun–Oct
Kitulo NP (p302)	highland plateau; wildflowers & wilderness	hiking & horse riding	Dec–Apr (for wildflowers), Sep–Nov (for hiking)
Lake Manyara NP (p176)	Lake Manyara; hippos, water birds, elephants	vehicle safaris, walking, cycling & cultural activities, night drives	Jun–Feb (Dec–Apr for birding)
Mahale Mountains NP (p272)	remote lakeshore & mountains; chimpanzees	chimp tracking	Jun–Oct, Dec–Feb
Mikumi NP (p286)	Mkata flood plains; lions, buffaloes, giraffes, elephants	vehicle safaris, short walks	year-round
Mt Kilimanjaro NP (p233)	Mt Kilimanjaro	trekking, cultural activities on lower slopes	Jun–Oct, Dec–Feb
Mkomazi NP (p152)	semi-arid savannah; black rhinos & wild dogs (neither viewable by the general public), wonderful birding	vehicle safaris, short walks	Jun–Mar
Ngorongoro Conservation Area (p181)	Ngorongoro Crater; black rhinos, lions, elephants, zebras, flamingos	vehicle safaris, hiking	Jun–Feb
Ruaha NP (p297)	Ruaha River, sand rivers; elephants, hippos, kudus, antelope, birds	vehicle & walking safaris	Jun–Oct for wildlife, Dec–Apr for birding
Rubondo Island NP (p257)	Lake Victoria; birds, sitatungas, chimps	short walks, boating, fishing	Jun–Feb
Saadani NP (p130)	Wami River, beach; birds, hippos, crocodiles, elephants	vehicle safaris, short boat trips, short walks	Jun–Feb
Selous GR (p322)	Rufiji River, lakes, woodland; elephants, hippos, wild dogs, black rhinos, birds	boat, walking & vehicle safaris	Jun–Dec
Serengeti NP (p191)	plains & grasslands, Grumeti River; wildebeest, zebras, lions, cheetahs, giraffes	vehicle, walking & balloon safaris; walks & cultural activities in border areas	year-round
Tarangire NP (p172)	Tarangire River, woodland, baobabs; elephants, zebras, wildebeest, birds	vehicle safaris & night drives; walks, night drives & cultural activities in border areas	Jun–Oct
Udzungwa Mountains NP (p288)	Udzungwa Mountains, forest; primates, birds	hiking	Jun–Oct

RESPONSIBLE TRAVEL IN TANZANIA

Tourism is big business in Tanzania. Here are a few guidelines for minimising strain on the local environment:

➡ Support local enterprise.

➡ Buy souvenirs directly from those who make them.

➡ Choose safari or trek operators that treat local communities as equal partners and that are committed to protecting local ecosystems.

➡ For cultural attractions, try to pay fees directly to the locals involved, rather than to tour-company guides or other intermediaries.

➡ Ask permission before photographing people.

➡ Don't buy items made from ivory, skin, shells etc.

➡ Save natural resources.

➡ Respect local culture and customs.

In one of the most high-profile cases to date, Selous Game Reserve – a Unesco World Heritage site – is in danger of being de-listed due to government plans to go ahead with construction of a large dam and hydroelectric power project at Stiegler's Gorge on the Rufiji River. Part of the reserve's southern sector has already been de-gazetted due to uranium mining in the area.

The Mpingo Conservation & Development Initiative (www.mpingoconservation.org) and the African Blackwood Conservation Project (www.blackwoodconservation.org) are working to conserve *mpingo* (East African Blackwood) – Tanzania's national tree, and one of the main woods used in carvings.

Urban pollution is another serious concern, as the populations of major cities continue to expand without proper sewage treatment plants and air pollution controls. In Dar es Salaam it is estimated that the sewerage system – which drains in part into the sea – covers less than 15% of households. Air pollution, too, is a concern, with ever-increasing vehicle numbers, often poor-quality fuel and inadequate emissions controls.

In coastal areas, dynamite fishing remains a problem, although progress has been made. Mafia Isand Marine Park, for example, was created in 1995 in major part to curb dynamite fishing and other unsustainable fishing practices. Since its creation, dynamite fishing in the area has been largely eliminated, and the park has achieved considerable progress in promoting conservation measures alongside sustainable resource use by local communities.

On the positive side, there's growing involvement of communities directly in conservation, and local communities are now stakeholders in a number of lodges and other tourist developments. Zanzibar Island's Chumbe Island Coral Park is a good example, illustrating what long-term collaboration with local fishing communities can achieve in terms of conservation and environmental education. Manyara Ranch Conservancy (p174) is another example. Here, a collaborative relationship has been established in which the local Maasai communities are involved in and benefit from wildlife conservation.

Tanzanian Cuisine

It's easy to travel through Tanzania thinking that the country subsists on ugali (the main maize and cassava flour staple) and sauce. But there are some treats to be found. Tasty Indian cuisine is widely available. Along the coast, the Zanzibar Archipelago is one of East Africa's culinary highlights. Here, scents of coriander and coconut recall the days when the coast was a port of call on the spice route from the Orient. Elsewhere, lively local atmosphere and Tanzanian hospitality compensate for what can otherwise be a rather bland diet.

Tanzanian Specialities

Ugali is the Tanzanian national dish. This thick staple – which is made of cassava or maize flour, or both – is somewhat of an acquired taste for many foreigners. It varies in flavour and consistency depending on the flours used and the cooking. In general, good ugali should be neither too dry nor too sticky. It's usually served with a sauce containing meat, fish, beans or greens. Rice and *ndizi* (cooked plantains) are other staples, and chips are ubiquitous.

Mishikaki (marinated, grilled meat kebabs) and *nyama choma* (seasoned roasted meat) are widely available. Along the coast and near lakes, there's plenty of seafood, often grilled or (along the coast) cooked in coconut milk or curry-style.

Some Tanzanians start their day with *uji*, a thin, sweet porridge made from bean, millet or other flour. Watch for ladies stirring bubbling pots of it on street corners in the early morning. *Vitambua* – small rice cakes resembling tiny, thick pancakes – are another morning treat, especially in the southeast. On Zanzibar Island, try *mkate wa kumimina*, a bread made from a batter similar to that used for making *vitambua*. Another Zanzibari treat (you'll also find it in Dar es Salaam) is *urojo*, a filling, delicious soup with *kachori* (spicy potatoes), mango, limes, coconut, cassava chips, salad and sometimes *pili-pili* (hot pepper).

One of Zanzibar Island's great early-morning sights: coffee vendors carrying around a stack of coffee cups and a piping hot kettle on a long handle with coals fastened underneath, clacking together their metal coffee cups to attract custom.

DO'S & DON'TS

For Tanzanians, a shared meal and eating out of a communal dish are expressions of solidarity between hosts and guests.

➡ If you're invited to eat and aren't hungry, it's OK to say that you've just eaten, but try to share a few bites of the meal in recognition of the bond with your hosts.

➡ Leave a small amount on your plate to show your hosts that you've been satisfied.

➡ Don't take the last bit of food from the communal bowl, as your hosts may worry that they haven't provided enough.

➡ Never handle food with the left hand.

➡ If others are eating with their hands, do the same, even if cutlery is provided.

➡ Defer to your host for customs that you aren't sure about.

Ugali, fish and greens

Three meals a day is usual, although breakfast is frequently nothing more than *kahawa* (coffee) or chai (tea) and *mkate* (bread). The main meal is eaten at midday.

Drinks

Apart from the ubiquitous Fanta and Coca-Cola, the main soft drink is Tangawizi, a local version of ginger ale. Fresh juices are widely available, although check first to see whether they have been mixed with unsafe water or ice. Tap water is best avoided. Bottled water is widely available, except in remote areas, where it's worth carrying a filter or purification tablets.

With fruits and vegetables, it's best to follow the adage: 'Cook it, peel it, boil it or forget it.'

In the Tanga area and around Lake Victoria watch for *mtindi* and *mgando*, cultured milk products similar to yoghurt, and usually drunk with a straw out of plastic bags. Sweet or salty Indian-style lassi drinks are also available in many areas.

Tanzania's array of beers includes the local Safari and Kilimanjaro labels, plus Castle Lager and various Kenyan and German beers. Finding a beer is usually no problem, but finding a cold one can be a challenge.

Local brews fall under the catch-all term *konyagi*. Around Kilimanjaro, watch for *mbege* (banana beer). *Gongo* (also called *nipa*) is an illegal distilled cashew drink, but the brewed version, *uraka*, is legal. Local brews made from pawpaw (papaya) are also common.

Tanzania has a small wine industry based in Dodoma.

Dining Tanzanian-Style

Dining venues range from simple sidewalk stalls (*'Mama Lishe'*), where the local 'mama' prepares a plate of the day, to European-style restaurants. Throughout the country, there's usually no need to book tables in advance.

GOOD COFFEE

Tanzania has a long history of producing delicious coffee. Here are some places to try the local blends:

Zanzibar Coffee House (p91), in Zanzibar Town, with an award-winning Zanzibari barrista.

Utengule Coffee Lodge (p305), near Mbeya, with coffee tours also available.

Union Café (p229), in Moshi: an amenable spot to while away an afternoon.

Mr Kahawa (p112), Paje, Zanzibar Island: enjoy the local vibe.

Arusha Coffee Lodge (p161), on the outskirts of Arusha, in the middle of a scenic coffee plantation.

Fifi's (p162), in Arusha, with good company and good coffee.

Ridge Cafe (p305), in Mbeya: small and friendly, with good snacks.

Hotelis, Night Markets & Tearooms

For dining local style, sit down in a *hoteli* – a small, informal restaurant – and watch life pass by. Many *hoteli* have the day's menu written on a blackboard and a TV in the corner. Rivalling *hoteli* for local atmosphere are the bustling night markets found in many towns, where vendors set up grills along the roadside and sell *nyama choma* (barbecued meat), grilled *pweza* (octopus) and other street food. Especially in small towns and along the coast, you'll find 'tearooms' – great places to get snacks or light meals. Many feature Indian cuisine.

Restaurants

For Western-style meals, stick to cities or main towns, where there's a reasonable to good array of restaurants. Delicious Indian cuisine is also widely available. Most main towns have at least one supermarket selling various imported products such as canned meat, fish and cheese (but not speciality items such as trail food or energy bars). In coastal areas you can always find a fresh catch of fish and someone to prepare it for you; the best time to look is early morning.

Local Traditions

Tanzanian style is to eat with the hand from communal dishes in the centre of the table. There will always be somewhere to wash your hands – either a bowl and jug of water that are passed around, or a sink in the corner. Although food is shared, it is not customary to share drinks. Soft drinks are the usual accompaniment, and there will also usually be a pitcher of water, though this may be unpurified. Children generally eat separately. If there's a toast, the common salutation is *afya!* – (to your) health!

Street snacks and meals on the run are common. European-style restaurant dining, while readily available in major cities, is not part of local culture. More common are large gatherings at home, or at a rented hall, to celebrate special occasions, with the meal as the focal point.

In restaurants catering to tourists, it's usual to tip about 10% to 15%. Tipping isn't expected in small local establishments, though rounding up the bill is always appreciated.

Karibu Chakula

If you're invited to join in a meal – *karibu chakula* – the first step is hand washing. Your host will bring around a bowl and water jug; hold your

Food Glossary

chipsi mayai omelette with chips inside

kiti moto literally 'hot seat'; fried pork bits

mishikaki marinated, grilled meat kebabs

nyama choma barbecued meat

ugali staple made from maize and/or cassava flour

uji porridge

urojo Zanzibari soup

wali na maharagwe rice and beans

For more eating terms see p399

GOURMET TREATS

Staying at upmarket safari camps and hotels, you'll dine well. But for independent travellers or those on a limited budget, a diet of rice and sauce quickly gets tiresome. Following are some suggestions for treating yourself if you're craving something tasty and wholesome while travelling away from major centres:

Lushoto Homemade jam, wholegrain bread and cheese from Irente Farm Lodge (p146) and St Eugene's Lodge (p145).

Njombe Italian cheeses and fresh yoghurt at the Duka la Maziwa (p301).

Iringa to Makambako Gourmet cuisine and fresh farm produce at Kisolanza – The Old Farm House (p296).

Iringa Authentic Italian cuisine at Mama Iringa (p295); banana milkshakes and pancakes at Hasty Tasty Too (p294).

Tanga Fresh yoghurt and cheeses at Tanga Fresh (p139).

Tanzanian coast Fresh seafood everywhere, with Zanzibar Island's fusion of flavours a particular highlight.

Ololosokwan village (p200) Delicious honey harvested as part of a women's beekeeping project.

hands over the bowl while your host pours water over them. Sometimes soap is provided, and a towel for drying off.

The meal itself inevitably centres on ugali or rice and sauce. Take some with the right hand from the communal pot, roll it into a small ball with the fingers, making an indentation with your thumb, and dip it into the accompanying sauce. Eating with your hand is a bit of an art, but after a few tries it starts to feel natural. Don't soak the ugali too long (to avoid it breaking up in the sauce), and keep your hand lower than your elbow (except when actually eating) so the sauce doesn't drip down your forearm.

Except for fruit, desserts are rarely served; meals conclude with another round of hand washing. Thank your host by saying *chakula kizuri* or *chakula kitamu* – both local ways of saying that the food was tasty and delicious.

> The best 'fast food' is at night markets, where you can fill up on mishikaki, grilled pweza and other titbits, often for less than Tsh5000.

Vegetarian Cuisine

There isn't much in Tanzania that is specifically billed as 'vegetarian', but there are many vegetarian options and you can find *wali* (cooked rice) and *maharagwe* (beans) everywhere. The main challenges are keeping variety and balance in your diet, and getting enough protein, especially if you don't eat eggs or seafood. In larger towns, Indian restaurants are the best places to try for vegetarian meals. Elsewhere, ask Indian shop owners if they have any suggestions; many will also be able to help you find fresh yoghurt. Peanuts *(karanga)* and cashews *(korosho)* are widely available, as are fresh fruits and vegetables.

Survival Guide

Directory A-Z

Accommodation

Tanzania has a wide range of accommodation, from dingy rooms with communal bucket baths to luxurious safari and island lodges. It's generally not necessary to book in advance, except at holiday times and in popular beach and safari areas, where accommodation fills quickly.

Camping Campsites range from completely in the wild to reasonably well-outfitted places with running water and cooking facilities.

Hotels Vary from modest mid-range properties with en-suite rooms, often with air-con, right up to top-notch establishments.

Guesthouses Range from poorly ventilated cement-block rooms with shared bathroom to homey, simple but pleasant places with fan and private bathroom.

Camping

Carry a tent to save money and for flexibility off the beaten track. Note that camping in most national parks costs at least US$30 per person per night – as much as sleeping in park-run accommodation.

NATIONAL PARKS

All parks have campsites, designated as either 'public' ('ordinary') or 'special'. Most parks also have simple huts or cottages (sometimes called 'bandas'), several have basic resthouses and some northern circuit parks have hostels (for student groups, or for overflow, if the resthouses or cottages are full).

Public campsites These have toilets (usually pit latrines) and, sometimes, a water source, but plan on being self-sufficient. Most sites are in reasonable condition and some are quite pleasant. No booking required.

Special campsites These are smaller, more remote and more expensive than public sites, with no facilities. The idea is that the area remains as close to pristine as possible. Advance booking required; once you make a booking, the special campsite is reserved exclusively for your group.

ELSEWHERE

➡ There are campsites situated in or near most major towns, near many of the national parks and in some scenic locations along a few of the main highways

(eg Dar es Salaam–Mbeya and Tanga–Moshi).

➡ Prices average from US$10 per person per night to more than double this for campsites near national parks.

➡ Camping away from established sites is generally not advisable. In rural areas, seek permission from the village head or elders before pitching your tent.

➡ Camping is not permitted on Zanzibar Island.

Guesthouses

Almost every town has at least one basic guesthouse. At the bottom end of the scale, expect a cement-block room, often small and poorly ventilated, and not always very clean, with a foam mattress, shared bathroom facilities (often long-drop toilets and bucket showers), a mosquito net and sometimes a fan. Rates average Tsh10,000 to Tsh15,000 per room per night.

The next level up gets you a cleaner, decent room, often with a bathroom (although not always with running or hot water). Prices for a double room with bathroom average from about Tsh25,000 (from Tsh20,000 for a single).

Some tips:

➡ For peace and quiet, guesthouses without bars are the best choice.

➡ In many towns, water is a problem during the dry season, so don't be surprised

---

BOOK YOUR STAY ONLINE

For more accommodation reviews by Lonely Planet authors, check out http://lonelyplanet.com/tanzania/hotels. You'll find independent reviews, as well as recommendations on the best places to stay. Best of all, you can book online.

SLEEPING PRICE RANGES

The following price ranges refer to a standard double room with bathroom in high season. Unless otherwise stated, VAT of 18%, and continental breakfast, is included in the price. For midrange and top-end hotels, full breakfast is usually included.

$ less than US$50 (Tsh100,000)

$$ US50–US$150 (Tsh100,000–Tsh300,000)

$$$ more than US$150 (Tsh300,000)

if your only choice at budget places is a bucket bath. Many of the cheaper places don't have hot water. This is a consideration in cooler areas, especially during winter, although staff will almost always arrange a hot bucket if you ask.

➡ In Swahili, the word *hotel* or *hoteli* does not mean accommodation, but rather a place for food and drink. The more common term used for accommodation is *guesti* (guesthouse) or, more formally, *nyumba ya kulala wageni*.

➡ There are many mission hostels and guesthouses, primarily for missionaries and aid-organisation staff, though some are willing to accommodate travellers, space permitting.

➡ In coastal areas, you'll find bungalows or *bandas* (small thatched-roof cottages with wooden or stone walls) ranging from simple huts on the sand to luxurious en-suite affairs.

Hotels & Lodges

Larger towns offer from one to several midrange hotels with en-suite rooms (widely referred to in Tanzania as 'self-contained' or 'self-containers'), hot water, and a fan and/or an air-conditioner. Facilities range from not so great to quite reasonable value, with prices averaging from US$30 to US$100 per person.

At the top end of the spectrum, there's an array of fine hotels and lodges with all the amenities you would expect at this price level (from US$100 or more per person per night). Especially on the safari circuits there are some wonderful and very luxurious lodges costing from US$150 to US$500 or more per person per night, although at the high end of the spectrum prices are usually all-inclusive. Some park lodges offer discounted accommodation rates for those arriving with their own vehicles.

Tented Camps & Fly Camps

'Permanent tented camps' or 'luxury tented camps' stay in the same place from season to season. They offer comfortable beds in spacious canvas tents, with screened windows and most of the comforts of a hotel room, but with a wilderness feel. Most such tents also have private bathrooms with hot running water, as well as generator-provided electricity for at least part of the evening.

'Mobile' or 'fly' camps are temporary camps set up for one or several nights, or perhaps just for one season. In the Tanzanian context, fly camps are used for walking safaris away from the main tented camp or lodge, or to offer the chance for a closer, more intimate bush experience. Although fly camps are more rugged than permanent luxury tented camps (ie they may not have running water or similar features), they fully cater to their guests, including with bush-style showers (where an elevated bag or drum is filled with solar-heated water). They are also usually more expensive than regular tented camps or lodges, since provisions must be carried to the site.

Climate

Tanzania has a generally comfortable tropical climate year-round, although there are significant regional variations. Along the warmer and humid coast, the climate is determined in large part by the monsoon winds, which bring rains in two major periods. During the *masika* (long rains), from mid-March to May, it rains heavily almost every day, although seldom for the whole day, and the air can get unpleasantly sticky. The lighter *mvuli* (short rains) fall during November, December and sometimes into January. Inland, altitude is a major determinant of conditions; you'll need a jacket early morning and evening, especially in highland areas.

Customs Regulations

Exporting seashells, coral, ivory and turtle shells is

illegal. There's no limit on the importation or exportation of foreign currency, but amounts over US$10,000 must be declared.

Discount Cards

A student ID gets you a 50% discount on train fares and often on museum entry fees.

Electricity

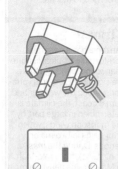

Type G
230V/50Hz

Embassies & Consulates

Most embassies and consulates in Dar es Salaam are open from 8.30am to 3pm Monday to Friday, often with a midday break. Visa applications for all countries neighbouring Tanzania should be made in the morning.

British High Commission (Map p56; ☑022-229 0000; www. gov.uk/government/world/ tanzania; Umoja House, cnr Mirambo St & Garden Ave)

Burundian Embassy (Map p62; ☑022-212 7008, 022-212 7007; burundiembassydar@yahoo. com; 1007 Lugalo St, Upanga) One-month single-entry visas cost US$90 plus a Tsh10,000 ap-

plication fee and two photos. The consulate in Kigoma also issues visas; allow one to two weeks.

Canadian High Commission (Map p56; ☑022-216 3300; www.canadainternational. gc.ca/tanzania-tanzanie; 38 Mirambo St)

Democratic Republic of the Congo Embassy (Formerly Zaïre) (Map p62; ☑022-215 2388; www.ambardc-tz.org; 20 Malik Rd, Upanga) Visas are only issued to Tanzania residents who have a Tanzania resident permit and who also have a letter of invitation from the DRC. Any Congolese visa issued in Tanzania will not be honoured on entry in the DRC unless you have a Tanzania resident's permit. Two-week single-entry limited gorilla trekking visas are available through www.visitvirunga.org.

French Embassy (Map p62; ☑022-219 8800; www.amba france-tz.org; 7 Ali Hassan Mwinyi Rd)

German Embassy (Map p56; ☑022-211 7409/15; www.dares salam.diplo.de; Umoja House, cnr Mirambo St & Garden Ave)

Indian High Commission (Map p56; ☑022-211 3094, 022-211 3079; www.hcindiatz.org; Shaaban Robert St)

Irish Embassy (Map p62; ☑022-260 2355, 022-260 0629; www. dfa.ie/irish-embassy/tanzania; 353 Toure Dr)

Italian Embassy (Map p62; ☑022-211 5935; www.ambdar essalaam.esteri.it; 316 Lugalo St, Upanga)

Kenyan High Commission (Map p62; ☑022-266 8286, 022-266 8285; www.kenyahighcomtz. org; cnr Ali Hassan Mwinyi Rd & Kaunda Dr, Oyster Bay) Kenyan visas should be applied for online in advance of travel at www.evisa.

go.ke. If this is not possible, they are readily issued at Kenya's borders with Tanzania for US$50 plus one photo. Transit visas (available online or at points of entry) cost US$20 and are valid for 72 hours. The Kenyan High Commission in Dar es Salaam does not issue visas.

Malawian High Commission (Map p62; ☑022-277 4220; www.malawihctz.org; Rose Garden Rd, Mikocheni A) Malawi visas issued in Dar es Salaam cost US$100 plus two photos. If application is made in the morning, they are sometimes issued on the same day.

Mozambique High Commission (Map p56; 25 Garden Ave; ⊙9am-3pm Mon-Thu, 9am-noon Fri) One-month single-entry visas cost US$60 plus two photos, and are issued within five days (US$100 for 24-hour service). In addition, you will require an application letter, a bank statement for the past six months, a return ticket, a hotel booking, a photocopy of your passport and a valid yellow fever certificate. As of mid-2017, Mozambique visas were being issued at the Kilambo, Negomano and Mtomoni borders with Tanzania. However, this situation could change at any time, so get an update before setting your plans.

Netherlands Embassy (Map p56; ☑022-219 4000; www.nether landsworldwide.nl/countries/ tanzania; Umoja House, cnr Mirambo St & Garden Ave)

Rwandan Embassy (Map p62; ☑022-260 0500, 0754 787835; www.tanzania.embassy.gov.rw; 452 Haile Selassie Rd) Three-month single-entry visas cost US$50 plus one photo, and are issued within four days.

Ugandan Embassy (Map p62; ☑022-266 7391; www.dares

PRACTICALITIES

Radio TBC Taifa, Radio One, Clouds

Newspapers *Guardian* and *Daily News* (dailies); *Business Times*, *Financial Times* and *East African* (weeklies).

Television ITV, EATV, TBC1

Weights and Measures Tanzania uses the metric system.

salaam.mofa.go.ug; 25 Msasani Rd) One-month single-entry visas cost US$50 plus two photos and are usually issued within 48 hours.

US Embassy (Map p62; 022-229 4000; https://tz.usembassy.gov; 686 Old Bagamoyo Rd)

Zambian High Commission (Map p56; 022-212 5529; ground fl, Zambia House, cnr Ohio St & Sokoine Dr; visa applications 9.30am-3.30pm Mon, Wed & Fri) One-month single-entry visas cost US$50 plus two photos, and are issued within two days or less. Visas can also be applied for electronically at http://evisa.zambiaimmigration.gov.zm, although the process takes longer. These e-visas are accepted for airport entry, as well as at the Nakonde border when arriving via train.

Gay & Lesbian Travellers

Homosexuality is illegal in Tanzania, including the Zanzibar Archipelago, and prosecutions have become more commonplace. In mid-September 2017, 20 people on Zanzibar Island were arrested while attending a HIV/AIDS education session. Public displays of affection, whether between people of the same or opposite sex, are frowned upon, and homosexuality is culturally taboo.

Insurance

Travel insurance covering theft, loss and medical problems is highly recommended. Some tips:

➡ Before choosing a policy, shop around; those designed for short package tours in Europe may not be suitable for the wilds of Tanzania.

➡ Read the fine print, as some policies specifically exclude 'dangerous activities', which can mean scuba diving, motorcycling and even trekking. A locally acquired

motorcycle licence isn't valid under some policies.

➡ Most policies for Tanzania require you to pay on the spot and claim later, so keep all documentation.

➡ Most importantly, check that the policy covers an emergency flight home.

Before heading to Tanzania, also consider taking out a membership with one of the following, both of which operate 24-hour air ambulance services and offer emergency medical evacuation within Tanzania:

➡ **African Medical & Research Foundation Flying Doctors** (www.flydoc.org) East Africa memberships available from US$16 per person per month.

➡ **First Air Responder** (www.knightsupport.com/first-air-responder) East Africa memberships from US$10 per week.

Worldwide travel insurance is available at www.lonelyplanet.com/travel-insurance. You can buy, extend and claim online anytime – even if you're already on the road.

Internet Access

There are internet cafes in all major towns, and wi-fi hotspots are widespread, except in rural areas. Prices at internet cafes average Tsh1000 to Tsh2000 per hour. Speed varies greatly; truly fast connections are rare. Almost all midrange and top-end hotels, including on the safari circuits, and some budget places have wireless access points; some are free, others charge a modest fee. The best

way to connect is either with your smartphone or by purchasing a wi-fi hotspot from one of the mobile providers (about Tsh70,000, including 10GB of initial credit). For topping up, various packages are available, averaging about Tsh35,000 for 10GB, valid for one month. Top-up credit vouchers are sold at roadside shops countrywide.

Language Courses

Tanzania is the best place in East Africa to learn Swahili, the country's official language, together with English. Swahili in coastal areas, especially the Zanzibar Archipelago, is generally considered more pure than the Swahili spoken inland. Some schools can arrange home stays.

ELCT Language & Orientation School (www.studyswahili.com; Lutheran Junior Seminary) This is a long-standing mission-run language school on the outskirts of Morogoro town.

KIU Ltd (Map p62; 0754 271263; www.swahilicourses.com) At various locations in Dar es Salaam, plus branches in Iringa and on Zanzibar Island.

Meeting Point Tanga (www.meetingpointtanga.net) Just south of Tanga.

MS Training Centre for Development Cooperation (027-254 1044, 0754 651715; www.mstcdc.or.tz) About 15km outside Arusha, near Usa River.

Legal Matters

Apart from traffic offences such as speeding and driving without a seatbelt (mandatory for driver and front-seat

---

EATING PRICE RANGES

The following price ranges refer to a standard single-course meal.

$ less than US$5 (Tsh10,000)

$$ US$5–US$10 (Tsh10,000–Tsh20,000)

$$$ more than US$10 (Tsh20,000)

passengers), the main area to watch out for is drug use and possession. Marijuana (*bangi* or *ganja*) is readily available in some areas and is frequently offered to tourists on the street in places like Zanzibar Island and Dar es Salaam, almost always as part of a set-up involving the police or fake police. If you're caught, expect to pay a large bribe to avoid arrest or imprisonment.

In Dar es Salaam, the typical scam is that you'll be approached by a couple of men who walk along with you, strike up a conversation and try to sell you drugs. Before you've had a chance to shake them loose, policemen (sometimes legitimate, sometimes not) suddenly appear and insist that you pay a huge fine for being involved in the purchase of illegal drugs. Protestations to the contrary are generally futile and there's little else you can do other than instantly hightailing it in the opposite direction if you smell this scam coming. If you are caught, insist on going to the nearest police station before paying anything and whittle the bribe down as far as you can. Initial demands may be as high as US$300, but savvy travellers should be able to get away with under US$50.

Maps

→ Good country maps include those published by Nelles and Harms-ic, both available in Tanzania and elsewhere, and both also including Rwanda and Burundi. Harms-ic also publishes maps for Lake Manyara National Park, the Ngorongoro Conservation Area and Zanzibar Island.

→ The **Surveys and Mapping Division's Map Sales Office** (Map p56; cnr Kivukoni Front & Luthuli St; ⊙8am-2pm Mon-Fri) in Dar es Salaam sells dated topographical maps (1:50,000) for mainland Tanzania. Topographical

maps for Zanzibar Island and Pemba are available in Stone Town.

→ Hand-drawn 'MaCo' maps (www.gtmaps.com) cover Zanzibar Island, Arusha and the northern parks. They're sold in bookshops in Dar es Salaam, Arusha and Zanzibar Town.

Money

→ Tanzania's currency is the Tanzanian shilling (Tsh). There are bills of Tsh500, Tsh1000, Tsh5000 and Tsh10,000, and coins of Tsh1, Tsh5, Tsh10 (although these three are rarely encountered), Tsh20, Tsh50, Tsh100 and Tsh200.

→ In 2011, bill design was changed for all amounts. Both the old and new styles are still accepted and in circulation.

→ A Visa or MasterCard is essential for accessing money from ATMs and for paying entry fees at most national parks.

→ Credit cards are not widely accepted for hotel payment, except at top-end establishments. Where they are accepted, it's often only with commissions. As a result, you will need to rely heavily on cash and ATMs.

→ US dollar bills dated prior to 2006 are not accepted anywhere. Post-2006 US dollars are generally accepted by larger establishments. For smaller local places you'll need to exchange them for Tanzanian shillings.

→ The easiest way to access money while travelling in Tanzania is at ATMs using a Visa card.

ATMs

ATMs are widespread in major towns, and all are open 24 hours. But they are occasionally out of service or out of cash, so you should have back-up funds. All internationally linked

machines allow you to withdraw shillings with a Visa or MasterCard. Withdrawals are usually to a maximum of Tsh300,000 or Tsh400,000 per transaction (ATMs in small towns often have a limit of Tsh200,000 per transaction) and with a daily limit of Tsh1.2 million (less in small towns). Some machines also accept other cards linked to the Cirrus/Maestro/Plus networks.

The main operators:

Barclays Dar es Salaam, Arusha, Moshi, Zanzibar Island, Tanga

CRDB Major towns

Exim Dar es Salaam, Arusha, Moshi, Mwanza, Tanga, Morogoro

National Bank of Commerce Major towns

Stanbic Dar es Salaam, Arusha, Moshi, Mbeya

Standard Chartered Dar es Salaam, Arusha, Moshi, Mwanza

In large cities, queues at ATM machines on Friday afternoons are notoriously long; take care of your banking before then.

If your ATM withdrawal request is rejected (no matter what reason the machine gives), it could be for something as simple as requesting above the allowed transaction amount for that particular machine; it's always worth trying again. Entering your PIN number erroneously three times results in a captured card.

Black Market

There's essentially no black market for foreign currency. You can assume that the frequent offers you'll receive on the street to change at high rates are a set-up.

Cash

US dollars, followed by euros, are the most convenient foreign currencies and get the best rates, although other major currencies are readily accepted in major centres. Bring a mix of large and small denominations, but note that US$50 and US$100 bills get better rates of exchange than smaller denominations. Old-style (small head) US bills and US bills dated prior to 2006 are not accepted anywhere.

Credit Cards

Bring a Visa card or Master-Card. These are essential for withdrawing money at ATMs; Visa is the most widely accepted. A Visa or MasterCard is also required for paying park fees at most national parks. Some upmarket hotels and tour operators accept credit cards for payment, often with a commission averaging from 5% to 10%. However, many don't; always confirm in advance.

Exchanging Money

➜ Change cash at banks or foreign exchange (forex) bureaus in major towns and cities; rates and commissions vary, so shop around.

➜ Forex bureaus are usually quicker, less bureaucratic and open longer hours than banks, although most smaller towns don't have them. They also tend to

accept a wider range of currencies than banks.

➜ The most useful bank for foreign exchange is NBC, with branches throughout the country. Countrywide, banks and forex bureaus are closed from noon on Saturday until Monday morning.

➜ To reconvert Tanzanian shillings to hard currency, save at least some of your exchange receipts, although they are seldom checked. The easiest places to reconvert currency are at the airports in Dar es Salaam and Kilimanjaro, or try at forex shops or banks in major towns.

➜ For after-hours exchange and exchanging in small towns, as well as for reconverting back to dollars or euros, many Indian-owned businesses will change money, although often at unfavourable rates.

➜ In theory, it's required that foreigners pay for accommodation, park fees, organised tours, upscale hotels and the Zanzibar ferries in US dollars, although

shillings are accepted almost everywhere at the going rate.

Taxes

Tanzania has an 18% value-added tax (VAT) that's usually included in quoted prices. While this has long applied to accommodation, as of July 2016 the tax also applies to ground transportation, guiding fees, park fees and camping fees. VAT refunds are not available.

Tipping

Restaurants Tipping is generally not practised in small local establishments, especially in rural areas. In major towns and in places frequented by tourists, tips are expected. Some top-end places include a service charge in the bill. Usually, however, either rounding up the bill or adding about 10% to 15% is standard practice.

Safaris and Treks On treks and safaris, it's common practice to tip drivers, guides, porters and other staff.

Taxis Tipping is not common practice, except for longer (full-day or multi-day) rentals.

WAYS TO SAVE MONEY WHILE TRAVELLING

➜ Travel in the low season, and always ask about discounted room and safari prices.

➜ Families: ask about children's discounts at parks and hotels.

➜ Travel in a small group for organised treks and safaris.

➜ Watch for last-minute deals.

➜ Stay outside park boundaries at those parks and reserves where you can do wildlife excursions in border areas.

➜ Enter parks around midday: as fees for wildlife parks are calculated on a 24-hour basis, you'll be able to enjoy prime evening and morning wildlife viewing hours for just one day's payment.

➜ Camp when possible.

➜ Focus on easily accessed parks and reserves to minimise transportation costs.

➜ Use public transport where possible.

➜ Do Cultural Tourism Programs rather than wildlife safaris.

➜ Eat local food.

➜ Stock up on food and drink in major towns to avoid expensive hotel fare and pricey tourist-area shops.

➜ Focus on off-the-beaten-track areas, where prices are usually considerably lower than in the northern safari circuit.

Travellers Cheques

Travellers cheques can no longer be changed anywhere in Tanzania.

Opening Hours

Opening hours are generally as follows:

Banks and government offices 8am to 3.30pm Monday to Friday

Restaurants 7am to 9.30am, noon to 3pm and 6.30pm to 9.30pm; reduced hours low season

Shops 8.30am to 5pm or 6pm Monday to Friday, 9am to 1pm Saturday; often closed Friday afternoon for mosque services

Supermarkets 8.30am to 6pm Monday to Friday, 9am to 4pm Saturday, 10am to 2pm Sunday

Photography

➡ Always ask permission first before photographing people and always respect their wishes. Sometimes, locals will ask for a fee (usually from Tsh1000 to Tsh10,000 and up) before allowing you to photograph them, which is fair enough.

➡ Don't take photos of anything connected with the government and the military, including army barracks, and landscapes and people anywhere close to army barracks. Government offices, post offices, banks, ports, train stations and airports are also officially off limits.

Post

Post is reasonably reliable for letters. Sending packages is at your own risk; for more assurance, use a courier service. General postal rates are available at www.posta.co.tz.

Public Holidays

The dates of Islamic holidays depend on the moon and are known for certain only a few days in advance. They fall about 11 days earlier each year and include Eid al-Kebir (Eid al-Haji), Eid al-Fitr and Eid al-Moulid (Maulidi).

New Year's Day 1 January

Zanzibar Revolution Day 12 January

Easter March/April – Good Friday and Easter Monday

Karume Day 7 April

Union Day 26 April

Labour Day 1 May

Saba Saba (Peasants' Day) 7 July

Nane Nane (Farmers' Day) 8 August

Nyerere Day 14 October

Independence Day 9 December

Christmas Day 25 December

Boxing Day 26 December

Safe Travel

Tanzania is in general a safe, hassle-free country. That said, you do need to take the usual precautions and keep up with government travel advisories (p378).

➡ Avoid isolated areas, especially isolated stretches of beach. In cities and tourist areas take a taxi at night.

➡ Only take taxis from established taxi ranks or hotels. Never enter a taxi that already has someone else in it other than the driver.

➡ Never pay any money for a safari or trek in advance until you've thoroughly checked out the company, and never pay any money at all outside the company's office.

➡ When using public transport, don't accept drinks or food from someone you don't know. Be sceptical of anyone who comes up to you on the street asking whether you remember them from the airport, your hotel or wherever. Take requests for donations from 'refugees', 'students' or others with a grain of salt. Contributions to humanitarian causes are best done through an established agency or project.

➡ Be wary of anyone who approaches you on the street, at the bus station or in your hotel offering safari deals or claiming to know you.

➡ In western Tanzania, especially along the Burundi border, there are sporadic outbursts of banditry and political unrest. Get an update locally before setting your plans.

➡ In tourist areas, especially Arusha, Moshi and Zanzibar Island, touts can be quite pushy, especially around bus stations and budget tourist hotels. Do what you can to minimise the impression that you're a newly arrived tourist: walk with purpose. Duck into a shop if you need to get your bearings or look at a map.

➡ Arriving for the first time at major bus stations, have your luggage as consolidated as possible, with your valuables well hidden under your clothes. Try to spot the taxi area before disembarking and make a beeline for it. It's well worth a few extra dollars for the fare. While looking for a room, leave your bag with a friend or reliable hotel rather

ISLAMIC HOLIDAYS

Following are approximate dates for celebration of Islamic holidays in Tanzania.

EVENT	2018	2019	2020
Ramadan begins	16 May	6 May	24 April
Eid al-Fitr (end of Ramadan, two-days)	14 June	4 June	23 May
Eid al-Kebir (Eid al-Haji)	22 Aug	12 Aug	31 July
Eid al-Moulid	20 Nov	10 Nov	29 Oct

than walking around town with it. Buy your bus tickets a day or two in advance (without your luggage).

➡ Carry your passport, money and other documents in a pouch against your skin, hidden under loose-fitting clothing. Or store valuables in a hotel safe, if there's a reliable one, ideally inside a pouch with a lockable zip to prevent tampering.

➡ Keep the side windows up in vehicles when stopped in traffic and keep your bags out of sight (eg on the floor behind your legs).

➡ When bargaining or discussing prices, don't do so with your money or wallet in your hand.

Telephone

The fast-fading Tanzania Telecom (TTCL) usually has its offices at the post office. TTCL ('landline') numbers are seven digits, preceded by a mandatory three-digit area code.

Tanzania's country code is 255. To make an international call, dial 000 followed by the country code, local area code (without the initial '0') and telephone number.

Mobile Phones

All mobile companies sell pre-paid starter packages for about US$2. Top-up cards are widely available from shops and roadside vendors throughout the country.

The mobile network covers major towns throughout the country, plus most rural areas, although signal availability can be erratic.

Mobile phone numbers are six digits, preceded by a four-digit provider code – either 07XX or 06XX; the major companies are currently Vodacom, Airtel, Tigo, Halotel and (on the Zanzibar Archipelago) Zantel. To reach a mobile telephone number from outside Tanzania, dial the country code, then the mobile phone code without the initial 0, and

TO BARGAIN OR NOT...

Bargaining is expected by vendors in tourist areas, particularly souvenir vendors, except in a limited number of fixed-price shops. However, at markets and non-tourist venues, the price quoted to you will often be the 'real' price, so in these situations don't immediately assume that the quote you've been given is too high. There are no set rules, other than that negotiations should always be conducted in a friendly, spirited and respectful manner. Before starting, shop around to get a feel for the 'value' of the item you want. Asking others what they have paid can be helpful.

then the six-digit number. From within Tanzania, keep the initial 0 and don't use any other area code. Dialling from your own mobile is generally the cheapest way to call internationally, especially if you purchase one of the international call bundles available from the major companies.

Time

Tanzania time is GMT/UTC plus three hours. There is no daylight saving.

Toilets

➡ Toilets vary from standard long-drops to full-flush luxury conveniences.

➡ Most non-budget hotels have flushable sit-down types.

➡ Budget guesthouses often have squat-style toilets, sometimes equipped with a flush mechanism, otherwise with a scoop and a bucket of water for flushing things down. Paper (you'll often need to supply your own) should be deposited in the can that's usually in the corner.

➡ Many upmarket bush camps have 'dry' toilets – a fancy version of the long drop with a Western-style seat perched on top.

Tourist Information

Tanzania Tourist Board (www.tanzaniatouristboard.com) The official tourism entity.

Travellers with Disabilities

While there are few facilities for travellers with disabilities, Tanzanians are generally quite accommodating and willing to offer whatever assistance they can. Some considerations:

➡ A small number of lodges have wheelchair accessible rooms. But, few hotels have lifts (elevators) and many have narrow stairwells, especially in Stone Town (Zanzibar Town) on Zanzibar Island, where they are often steep and narrow. Grips or railings in the bathrooms are rare.

➡ Many park lodges and camps are built on ground level. However, access paths – in an attempt to maintain a natural environment – are sometimes rough or rocky, and rooms or tents raised. Enquire about access before booking.

➡ As far as we know, there are no Braille signboards at any parks or museums, nor any facilities for deaf travellers.

➡ Minibuses are widely available on Zanzibar Island and on the mainland, and can be chartered for transport and for customised safaris. Large or wide-door vehicles can also be arranged through car-rental agencies in Dar es Salaam and with Arusha-based tour operators. Taxis countrywide are usually small sedans, and buses are not wheelchair equipped.

SWAHILI TIME

Tanzanians use the Swahili system of telling time, in which the first hour is *saa moja (asubuhi)*, corresponding with 7am. Counting begins again with *saa moja (jioni)*, the first hour, evening, corresponding with 7pm. Although most will switch to the international clock when speaking English with foreigners, confusion sometimes occurs, so ask people to confirm whether they are using *saa za kizungu* (international time) or *saa za kiswahili* (Swahili time). Signboards with opening hours are often posted in Swahili time.

Download Lonely Planet's free Accessible Travel guides from http://lptravel.to/Accessible Travel. Other contacts:

Access-Able Travel (www.access-able.com.au)

Accessible Journeys (www.disabilitytravel.com)

Disability Horizons (www.disabilityhorizons.com)

Go Africa Safaris & Travel (www.go-africa-safaris.com)

Mobility International (www.miusa.org)

National Information Communication Awareness Network (www.nican.com.au)

Safari Guide Africa (www.safariguideafrica.com/safaris-for-the-disabled)

Tourism for All (www.tourism forall.org.uk)

Visas

Almost everyone needs a visa, which costs US$50 for most nationalities (US$100 for US citizens) for a single-entry visa valid for a maximum of three months.

Officially, visas must be obtained in advance by all travellers who come from a country with Tanzania diplomatic representation. Single-entry visas (but not multiple-entry visas) are also currently issued on arrival (no matter what your provenance) at Dar es Salaam, Kilimanjaro and Zanzibar International Airports, at the Namanga border post between Tanzania and Kenya, and at Tunduma border (between Tanzania and Zambia). In practice, visas are currently also readily issued at most other major land borders and ports (US dollars cash only, single-entry only) with a minimum of hassle. Our advice: get your visa in advance if possible. If not possible, it's well worth giving it a try at the border.

When out and about in Tanzania, always carry at least a photocopy of your passport and visa or resident permit, and have the originals readily accessible.

Note that Tanzania is not currently a party to the East Africa Tourist Visa (EATV), and the EATV does not apply to travel in the country.

Visa Extensions

One month is the normal visa validity and three months (upon request) is the maximum. For extensions within the three-month limit, there are immigration offices in all major towns, including **Dar es Salaam** (Uhamiaji; Map p72; ☏022-285 0575/6; www.immigration.go.tz; Uhamiaji House, Loliondo St, Kurasini; ◷visa applications 8am-noon Mon-Fri, visa collections until 2pm), **Arusha** (Map p158; East Africa Rd; ◷7.30am-3.30pm Mon-Fri) and **Moshi** (Map p228; Boma Rd; ◷7.30am-3.30pm Mon-Fri); the process is free and generally straightforward. Extensions after three months are difficult; you usually need to leave the country and apply for a new visa.

Volunteering

Volunteering opportunities (generally teaching, or in environmental or health work) are usually best arranged prior to arriving in Tanzania. Note that the current cost of volunteer (Class C) resident permits is US$200 for three months. Also note that for any volunteering work involving children, you will require a criminal background check from your home country and/or previous countries of residence.

African Initiatives (www.african-initiatives.org.uk) Focuses on girls' education and women's rights, and offers several ways of getting involved, although most opportunities are outside Tanzania.

Frontier (www.frontier.ac.uk) Marine conservation work, primarily on Mafia island.

Indigenous Education Foundation of Tanzania (www.ieftz.org) Education work in Maasai areas of northern Tanzania.

Kigamboni Community Centre (Map p72; ☏0788 482684,

GOVERNMENT TRAVEL ADVICE

Government travel advisories can be good sources of updated security information:

Australian Department of Foreign Affairs (www.smartraveller.gov.au)

Canadian Department of Foreign Affairs (www.travel.gc.ca)

UK Foreign & Commonwealth Office (www.gov.uk/government/organisations/foreign-commonwealth-office)

US State Department (www.travel.state.gov)

0753 226662; www.kccdar.com; Kigamboni) Teaching and other volunteer opportunities in a rural community on the outskirts of Dar es Salaam.

Peace Corps (www.peacecorps. gov) USA voluntary organisation with placements in various countries, including Tanzania.

Responsible Travel.com (www. responsibletravel.com) Matches you up with ecologically and culturally responsible tour operators to plan a volunteer-focused itinerary.

Trade Aid (www.tradeaiduk.org/ volunteer.html) Skills training work in Mikindani village in southern Tanzania.

Voluntary Service Overseas (www.vso.org.uk) British voluntary organisation with placements in Tanzania.

Women Travellers

Women travellers are not likely to encounter many specifically gender-related problems. More often than not, you will meet only warmth, hospitality and sisterly regard, and find that you receive special treatment that you probably wouldn't be shown if you were a male traveller. That said, you'll inevitably attract some attention, especially if you're travelling alone, and there are some areas where caution is essential. A few tips:

➡ Dress modestly: trousers or a long skirt, and a conservative top with sleeves. Tucking your hair under a cap or scarf, or tying it back, also helps.

➡ Wearing sunglasses can help minimise hassles, as it's hard for hustlers to gauge your reactions and their level of success when they can't make eye contact. That said, keep in mind that wearing sunglasses when trying to chat or make friends with locals can be perceived as rude.

➡ Use common sense, trust your instincts and take the

SOLO TRAVEL IN TANZANIA

While solo travellers may be a minor curiosity in rural areas, especially solo women travellers, there are no particular issues with travelling solo in Tanzania, whether you're male or female. The times when it's advantageous to join a group are for safaris and treks (when going in a group can be a significant cost-saver) and when going out at night. If you go out alone at night, take taxis and use extra caution, especially in urban and tourist areas. Whatever the time of day, avoid isolating situations, including lonely stretches of beach.

usual precautions when out and about. Avoid walking alone at night. Avoid isolated areas at any time and be particularly cautious on beaches, many of which can become quickly deserted.

➡ If you find yourself with an unwanted suitor, creative approaches are usually effective. For example, explain that your husband (real or fictitious) or a large group of friends will be arriving imminently at that very place. Similar tactics are also usually effective in dealing with the inevitable curiosity that you'll meet as to why you might not have children and a husband or, if you do have them, why they aren't with you. The easiest response to the question of why you aren't married is to explain that you are still young (*bado kijana*), which whether you are or not will at least have some humour value. Just saying *bado* ('not yet') to questions about marriage or children should also do the trick. As for why your family isn't with you, you can always explain that you'll be meeting them later.

➡ Seek out local women, as this can enrich your trip tremendously. Places to try include tourist offices, government departments or even your hotel, where at least some of the staff are likely to be formally educated young to middle-aged women. In rural areas, starting points include women teachers at a local school, or staff at a health centre.

➡ On a practical level, while tampons and the like are available in major cities, women will likely come to appreciate the benefits of Western-style consumer testing when using local sanitary products.

Work

Unemployment and under-employment rates are high, and unless you have unique skills, the chances of lining up something are small.

➡ The most likely areas for employment are the safari industry, tourism, dive masters and teaching; in all areas, competition is stiff and the pay is low. Most teaching positions are voluntary and best arranged through volunteer agencies or mission organisations at home.

➡ The best way to land something is to get to know someone already working in the business. Also check safari operator and lodge websites, some of which advertise vacant positions.

➡ Work and residency permits should be arranged through the potential employer or sponsoring organisation; residency permits normally need to be applied for from outside Tanzania. Work permit regulations for foreigners have recently become more restricted, so be sure to inform yourself fully of the situation before setting your plans.

Transport

GETTING THERE & AWAY

Flights, cars and tours can be booked online at lonelyplanet.com/bookings.

Entering Tanzania

➡ Provided you have a visa, Tanzania is straightforward to enter.

➡ Yellow fever vaccination is required if you are arriving from an endemic area (which includes several of Tanzania's neighbours).

Air

Airports

Julius Nyerere International Airport (DAR; ☏022-284 2402; www.taa.go.tz) Dar es Salaam; Tanzania's air hub.

Kilimanjaro International Airport (JRO; ☏027-255 4252; www.kilimanjaroairport.co.tz)

(KIA) Between Arusha and Moshi, and the best option for itineraries in Arusha and the northern safari circuit. Not to be confused with the smaller Arusha Airport, 8km west of Arusha, for domestic flights.

Zanzibar International Airport (ZNZ, Abeid Amani Karume International Airport) Charter flights from Europe, as well as several international carriers.

Other airports handling regional flights include **Arusha Airport** (☏027-250 5920; www.taa.go.tz; Dodoma Rd), **Mtwara Airport** (MYW; off Mikindani Rd) and **Mwanza International Airport** (MWZ; ☏022-284 2402).

A useful website for researching and booking East African regional flights is www.tripindigo.com.

Airlines

Tanzania's flagship carrier is **Air Tanzania** (☏0782 737730, 0782 782732; www.airtanzania.co.tz), with domestic destinations, plus several regional destinations. Other useful

regional and international carriers include the following (all servicing Dar es Salaam, except as noted):

Air Kenya (☏in Kenya 020-391 6000; www.airkenya.com) Nairobi to KIA.

Egyptair (☏0789 516482; www.egyptair.com; Ali Hassan Mwinyi Rd, 1st fl, Viva Towers; ⏲9am-5pm Mon-Fri, 9am-1.30pm Sat)

Emirates (☏022-211 6100, 022-211 6101; Haidery Plaza, cnr Kisutu & India Sts; ⏲8am-4.30pm Mon-Fri, 8.30am-12.30pm Sat)

Ethiopian Airlines (☏022-211 7063, 0786 285899; www.ethiopianairlines.com; Ohio St, TDFL Bldg; ⏲8.30am-4.30pm Mon-Fri, 8.30am-1pm Sat) Also KIA.

Fastjet (☏0784 108900; www.fastjet.com) Johannesburg (South Africa), Harare (Zimbabwe) and Lusaka (Zambia) to Dar es Salaam.

Kenya Airways (☏0683 390008, 0786 390004, 0786 390005; www.kenya-airways.

CLIMATE CHANGE & TRAVEL

Every form of transport that relies on carbon-based fuel generates CO_2, the main cause of human-induced climate change. Modern travel is dependent on aeroplanes, which might use less fuel per kilometre per person than most cars but travel much greater distances. The altitude at which aircraft emit gases (including CO_2) and particles also contributes to their climate change impact. Many websites offer 'carbon calculators' that allow people to estimate the carbon emissions generated by their journey and, for those who wish to do so, to offset the impact of the greenhouse gases emitted with contributions to portfolios of climate-friendly initiatives throughout the world. Lonely Planet offsets the carbon footprint of all staff and author travel.

com; Ali Hassan Mwinyi Rd, 1st fl, Viva Towers; ⊙8.30am-5pm Mon-Fri) Also KIA.

KLM (☑0653 333446, 0789 777145, 022-213 9791; www. klm.com; Ali Hassan Mwinyi Rd, 1st fl, Viva Towers; ⊙8.30am-5pm Mon-Fri) Also KIA.

Linhas Aéreas de Moçambique (☑022-213 4600; www.lam. co.mz; Fast Track Tanzania, Bibi Titi Mohammed Rd; ⊙8.30am-5pm Mon-Fri, 8.30am-1pm Sat)

Malawi Airlines (☑022-213 6663; www.malawian-airlines. com; Fast Track Tanzania, Bibi Titi Mohammed Rd; ⊙8.30am-5pm Mon-Fri, 8.30am-1pm Sat)

Precision Air (☑022-219 1000, 0787 888417; www.precision airtz.com) Nairobi (Kenya) to Dar es Salaam and KIA.

Rwandair (☑022-210 3435; www.rwandair.com; Ali Hassan Mwinyi Rd, 2nd fl, Viva Towers; ⊙8am-5pm Mon-Fri, 9am-1pm Sat) Also KIA.

South African Airways (SAA; ☑0717 722772, 022-211 7045/7; www.flysaa.com; cnr Bibi Titi Mohammed Rd & Maktaba St; ⊙8.30am-4.30pm Mon-Fri, 8.30am-12.30pm Sat)

Swiss International Airlines (☑022-551 0020; www.swiss. com; 84 Kinondoni Rd; ⊙8am-4.30pm Mon-Fri, 8.30am-12.30pm Sat)

Land

Bus

➡ Buses cross Tanzania's borders with Kenya, Uganda and Rwanda. Visa fees aren't included in bus ticket prices for trans-border routes.

➡ For crossings with other countries, you'll need to take one vehicle to the border and board a different one on the other side.

Car & Motorcycle

To enter Tanzania with your own vehicle you'll need:

➡ vehicle registration papers

➡ driving licence

➡ temporary import permit (TIP; Tsh40,000 for one

month, purchased at the border) or a *carnet de passage en douane* (arranged in advance through your local automobile association). The *carnet* should also specify any expensive spare parts that you are carrying. The TIP is waived if your vehicle will be returning to its country of registration.

➡ road tax (US$25)

➡ third-party insurance (Tsh50,000 for three months, purchased at the border or at the local insurance headquarters in the nearest large town); the COMESA yellow card is accepted in Tanzania

➡ one-time fuel levy (Tsh10,000)

Burundi
BORDER CROSSINGS
The main crossings are at Kobero Bridge between Ngara (Tanzania) and Muyinga (Burundi), and at Manyovu (north of Kigoma).

BUS
For Kobero Bridge From Mwanza, there are buses daily at 5.30am to Ngara (Tsh20,000, seven to eight hours). Shared taxis also run all day from Nyakanazi to Ngara (Tsh10,000, two hours). Once in Ngara, there is onward transport to the Tanzanian border post at Kabanga.

For Manyovu Hamza Transport and several other lines (all ticket offices at Kigoma's Bero bus stand) have direct service between Kigoma and Bujumbura (Burundi; Tsh15,000 to Tsh20,000, seven hours) at 6.30am several times weekly. Otherwise, take a dalla-dalla (minibus) from Kigoma to Manyovu (Tsh6000, one to two hours), walk through immigration and find onward transport. There's always something going to Mabanda (Burundi), where you can find minibuses to Bujumbura, three to four hours away.

Kenya
BORDER CROSSINGS
The main route is the good sealed road connecting

Arusha (Tanzania) and Nairobi (Kenya) via the recently modernised Namanga border post (open 24 hours, with a bank and immigration inside the main building). There are also border crossings at Horohoro (Tanzania), north of Tanga; at Holili (Tanzania), east of Moshi; at Loitokitok (Kenya), northeast of Moshi; and at Sirari (Tanzania), northeast of Musoma. With the exception of the Serengeti–Masai Mara crossing (which is closed), there is public transport across all Tanzania–Kenya border posts.

TO & FROM MOMBASA
Modern Coast Express (www.modern.co.ke) goes daily between Dar es Salaam and Mombasa via Tanga, departing in the morning in each direction, and departing around 1pm from Tanga (Tsh15,000 to Tsh17,000, four hours Tanga to Mombasa; Tsh25,000, 10 to 11 hours Dar to Mombasa). There's nowhere official to change money at the border. Touts here charge extortionate rates, and it's difficult to get rid of Kenyan shillings once in Tanga, so plan accordingly.

TO & FROM NAIROBI
Bus The Dar Express (Libya St, Kisutu, Dar es Salaam; ⊙6am-6pm) goes daily between Dar es Salaam and Nairobi (Tsh60,000, 14 to 15 hours), departing about 6am in each direction. You can also board in Arusha (Tsh22,00 to 25,000, five hours), if seats are available. Dar Express also has Nairobi-bound buses that begin in Arusha, leaving at 2pm. Modern Coast goes daily between Mwanza and Nairobi, departing Mwanza at 2pm (Tsh33,000 to Tsh44,000, 14 hours).

Dalla-Dalla Comfortable nine-seater minivans (Tsh7000, two hours) and decrepit, over-crowded full-sized vans (which stop frequently along the way) go between Arusha's central bus station (they park at the north-ernmost end) and the Namanga border throughout the day from

6am. At Namanga, you'll have to walk a few hundred metres across the border and then catch one of the frequent matatus (Kenyan minibuses) or shared taxis to Nairobi (KSh500). From Nairobi, the matatu and shared-taxi depots are on Ronald Ngala St, near the River Rd junction.

Shuttle The best option between Moshi or Arusha and Nairobi is shuttle bus. These depart daily from Arusha and Nairobi at 8am and 2pm (six hours) and from Moshi (eight hours) at 6am and 11am. The non-resident rate is US$30 one way from Arusha (US$35 from Moshi), but with a little prodding it's usually possible to get the resident price (Tsh30,000/35,000). Pick-ups and drop-offs are at their offices and centrally located hotels. Depending on the timing, they may be willing to pick you up or drop you off at Kilimanjaro International Airport (US$15). Confirm locations when booking.

Impala Shuttle (☑0754 008448, 0754 678678, 027-254 3082) Leaves from the car park of Arusha's Impala Hotel and from in front of Chrisburger in Moshi.

Rainbow Shuttle (☑0754 204025, 027-254 8442; www.rainbowcarhire.com) Booking office and departure point in Arusha is at New Safari Hotel. Departures in Moshi are from the YMCA.

Riverside Shuttle (www.riverside-shuttle.com) Daily shuttle service between Moshi, Arusha and Nairobi. The Arusha departure point is just north of Hotel Impala. In Moshi, departures are from the YWCA building, just uphill from the Clocktower Roundabout.

TO & FROM VOI

Tahmeed Coach (www.tahmeedcoach.co.ke) goes daily from Moshi to Mombasa via Voi (Tsh20,000, seven to eight hours). Also, dalla-dallas go frequently between Moshi and the border town of Holili (Tsh2000, one hour). At the border (6am to 8pm) you'll need to hire a *piki-piki* (motorbike; Tsh1000) or bicycle to cross 3km of

no-man's land before arriving at the Kenyan immigration post at Taveta. From Taveta, sporadic minibuses go to Voi, where you can then find onward transport to Nairobi and Mombasa. If you're arriving/departing with a foreign-registered vehicle, the necessary paperwork is only done during working hours (8am to 1pm and 2pm to 5pm daily).

TO & FROM KISII

There are no direct buses over the border. Take one of the many daily buses between Mwanza and the Sirari–Isebania border post (Tsh15,000, five hours), and then get Kenyan transport on the other side to Kisii. Dalla-dallas also go daily from Musoma to the border (Tsh6000, two hours).

Malawi
BORDER CROSSINGS

The only crossing is at Kasumulu (Songwe River Bridge; 7am to 7pm Tanzanian time, 6am to 6pm Malawi time), southeast of Mbeya (Tanzania).

BUS

From Mbeya's Nane Nane bus stand, there are daily minibuses and 30-seater buses (known as 'coastals') to the border (Tsh5000, two hours). Once across, there's a 300m walk to the Malawian side, where there are minibuses to Karonga. There's also one Malawian bus daily from the Malawi side of the border to Mzuzu (Malawi), departing the border by mid-afternoon and arriving in Mzuzu by evening.

Some tips:

➡ Look for buses going to Kyela (these detour to the border) and verify that your vehicle is really going all the way to the border ('Kasumulu'), as some that say they are actually stop at Tukuyu (40km north) or at Ibanda (7km before the border). Asking several passengers (rather than the

minibus company touts) should get you the straight answer.

➡ Your chances of getting a direct vehicle are better in the larger 'coastals', which depart from Mbeya two or three times daily and usually go where they say they are going.

➡ The border buses stop at the Kasumulu (Songwe River) transport stand, about a seven-minute walk from the actual border; there's no real need for the bicycle taxis that will approach you.

➡ There are no cross-border vehicles from Mbeya into Malawi, although touts at Mbeya bus station may try to convince you otherwise. Going in both directions, plan on overnighting in Mbeya or Tukuyu; buses from Mbeya to Dar es Salaam depart between 6am and 7am.

Mozambique
BORDER CROSSINGS

The main vehicle crossing is via Unity Bridge over the Ruvuma at Negomano, reached via Masasi. There is also the Unity 2 bridge across the Ruvuma at Mtomoni village, 120km south of Songea. It's also possible to cross at Kilambo (south of Mtwara) via vehicle ferry. As of mid-2017, Mozambique tourist visas were being issued at all borders. However, this situation could change at any time; it's essential to get an update before setting your plans, as it's a long way from the border back to the closest consulate.

BUS

Vehicles depart daily from Mtwara beginning at about 6am to the Kilambo border post (Tsh6000, one hour) and on to the Ruvuma River, which in theory is crossed daily by the MV *Kilambo* ferry. The ferry, again in theory, takes half a dozen cars plus passengers (Tsh500 per person). However, its passage depends on tides, rains and mechanical condition. There is a faster passenger-only motorboat making crossings throughout the day between 7am and 6pm (Tsh1000). If neither of these are operating, you'll need to negotiate a ride in a dugout canoe (about Tsh5000, 10 minutes to over an hour depending on water levels, and dangerous during heavy rains). Although improved, the border remains a rough one, and it's common for touts to demand up to 10 times the 'real' price for the boat crossing in dugouts. Watch your belongings, especially when getting into and out of the boats, and keep up with the crowd.

Once in Mozambique, several pick-ups go daily to the Mozambique border crossing at Namiranga, 4km further on, and from there to Palma and Moçimboa da Praia (US$10, three hours).

Further west, one or two vehicles daily depart from Songea's Majengo C area by around 11am (Tsh12,000, three to four hours) to Mtomoni village and the Unity 2 bridge. Once across, you can get Mozambique transport on to Lichinga (Tsh30,000, five hours). It's best to pay in stages, rather than paying the entire Tsh40,000 Songea–Lichinga fare in Songea, as is sometimes requested. With an early departure, the entire Songea–Lichinga trip is easily doable in one day via public transport.

CAR
The main vehicle crossing is via the Unity Bridge at Negomano, southwest of Kilambo, near the confluence of the Lugenda River. From Masasi, go about 35km southwest along the Tunduru road to Nangomba village, from where a 68km good-condition track leads southwest down to Masuguru village. The bridge is 10km further at Mtambaswala. On the other side, there is a decent-in-the-dry-season 160km dirt road to Mueda

(slated to be paved by 2019). There are immigration facilities on both sides of the bridge. Entering Tanzania, take care of customs formalities for your vehicle in Mtwara.

The Unity 2 bridge south of Songea is another option. With a private vehicle the Songea to Lichinga stretch should not take more than about eight or nine hours.

At Kilambo, the **MV Kilambo** (per person/vehicle Tsh500/30,000) vehicle ferry operates most days around high tide. Enquire at **ECO2** (☎0783 279446, 0784 855833; www.eco2tz.com; Main Rd) or the **Old Boma** (☎023-233 3875, 0757 622000; www.mikindani.com) in Mikindani to confirm whether it is running.

Rwanda
BORDER CROSSINGS
The main crossing is at Rusumu Falls, southwest of Bukoba (Tanzania).

BUS
Trinity Express goes four times weekly between Dar es Salaam and Kigali via Dodoma, Singida and Kahama (Tsh80,000 to Tsh85,000, 30 to 35 hours). It's better to do the trip in stages. From Mwanza, there are daily buses via Kahama to Benaco (Nyakanazi), from where you can get transport to the border. After walking across the border, there is Rwandan transport on the other side to Kigali; reckon on about 12 to 14 hours and Tsh32,000 for the entire journey from Mwanza to Kigali.

For travellers entering Tanzania from Rwanda: in order to purchase a Tanzanian visa at the border, you must have US dollars or Tanzanian shillings. Rwandan francs will not be accepted, and they cannot be exchanged for Tanzania shillings at the border.

Uganda
BORDER CROSSINGS
The main post is at Mutukula (Tanzania), northwest of

Bukoba, with good tarmac on both sides. There's another crossing further west at Nkurungu (Tanzania), but the road is sparsely travelled. From Arusha or Moshi, travel to Uganda is via Kenya.

BUS
Kampala Coach has a daily bus from Arusha to Kampala via Nairobi (Tsh75,000, 20 hours). The cost to Jinja is the same as Kampala.

Several companies leave Bukoba at 6am and again at 12.30pm for Kampala (Tsh20,000, six to eight hours). Departures from Kampala are at 7am and again at 11am.

From Mwanza to Kampala, there is a daily direct connection via Bukoba (Tsh45,000, 16 hours).

Zambia
BORDER CROSSINGS
The main border crossing (7am to 8.30pm Tanzania time, 6am to 7.30pm Zambia time) is at Tunduma (Tanzania), southwest of Mbeya. There's also a crossing at Kasesya (Tanzania), between Sumbawanga (Tanzania) and Mbala (Zambia).

BUS
Minibuses go several times daily between Mbeya and Tunduma (Tsh4000, two to three hours), where you walk across the border for Zambian transport to Lusaka (about US$20, 18 hours).

The Kasesya crossing is mainly of interest for self-drivers as there's no direct transport; at least one vehicle daily goes to the border from each side (Tsh10,000, four to five hours from Sumbawanga to Kasesya). With luck you can make the full journey in a day, but since departures from both Sumbawanga and Mbala are in the afternoon, and departures from the borders are in the early morning, you'll likely need to sleep in one of the border villages.

CAR

If driving from Zambia into Tanzania: vehicle insurance is now available at the Kasesya border.

TRAIN

The **Tazara** (www.tazarasite. com) train line links Dar es Salaam with Kapiri Mposhi in Zambia twice weekly via Mbeya and Tunduma. The Mukuba express service departs Dar es Salaam at 3.50pm Friday (1st-class sleeping/2nd-class sleeping/super seater/economy class Tsh104,000/84,600/78,700/72,600, about 43 hours). The Kilimanjaro ordinary service departs Dar es Salaam at 11am on Tuesday (Tsh86,500/70,600/65,600/60,500, about 59 hours). Departures from Mbeya to Kapiri Mposhi (express 1st/2nd/super seater/economy class Tsh58,000/46,000/44,400/40,900, about 24 hours) are at 1.20pm Saturday (Mukuba express) and 2pm Wednesday (Kilimanjaro ordinary, about 32 hours). Students with ID get a 50% discount. From Kapiri Mposhi to Lusaka, you'll need to continue by bus. Departures from New Kapiri Mposhi are at 4pm Tuesday (express) and 11am Friday (ordinary). Visas are currently available at the border in both directions.

Sea & Lake

There's a US$5 port tax for travel on all boats and ferries from Tanzanian ports.

Burundi

Regular passenger ferry service between Kigoma and Bujumbura is suspended. Enquire at the passenger port in Kigoma for an update. However, once the situation settles in Burundi, it should be possible to travel on cargo ships between Kigoma's Ami port and Bujumbura (about Tsh10,000, 18 hours). Sailings are erratic, but average three times weekly. Lake taxis go once or twice weekly from Kibirizi (just north of Kigoma) to Bujumbura, but are not recommended as they take a full day and are occasionally robbed. However, you could use the afternoon lake taxis to Kagunga (the Tanzanian border post, where there's a simple guesthouse), cross the border in the morning, take a motorcycle-taxi to Nyanza-Lac (Burundi) and then a minibus to Bujumbura. Note that at the time of research, all Burundi travel was in flux due to the security situation there; check government travel advisories for an update.

Democratic Republic of the Congo (DRC, formerly Zaïre)

Cargo boats go roughly once weekly from Kigoma's Ami port to Kalemie (about US$10, deck class only, seven hours) or Uvira. Enquire at Ami port, or check with the Congolese embassy in Kigoma about sailing days and times. Bring food and drink with you, and something to spread on the deck for sleeping. Prior to travelling to the DRC, check government travel advisories for a security update, and keep in mind the difficulty of getting a visa.

Kenya

There is currently no passenger ferry service on Lake Victoria between Tanzania and Kenya. Dhows ply regularly between Mombasa and the Zanzibar Archipelago, but foreigners are prohibited.

Malawi

There are currently no passenger ferries operating between Tanzania's Mbamba Bay and Malawi's Nkhata Bay. Cargo boats (about Tsh10,000 to Tsh15,000, six hours) occasionally accept passengers, but safety standards are minimal and there have been several sinkings. There are no fixed schedules; ask at Immigration for information on the next sailing. Departures are often in the middle of the night to take advantage of calmer waters.

Mozambique

DHOW

Dhows between Mozambique and Tanzania (12 to 30 or more hours) are best arranged at Msimbati (Tanzania) and Moçimboa da Praia (Mozambique).

FERRY

There is currently no official ferry service between southwestern Tanzania and Mozambique. The main option is taking a cargo boat between Mbamba Bay and Nkhata Bay, and then the **MV Chambo** (www.malawitourism.com) on its weekly run from Nkhata Bay on to Likoma Island (Malawi), Cóbuè (Mozambique) and Metangula (Mozambique). There are also small boats that sail along the eastern shore of Lake Nyasa between Tanzania and Mozambique. However, Lake Nyasa is notorious for its severe and sudden squalls, and going this way is risky and not recommended.

There's an immigration officer at Mbamba Bay, Mozambique immigration posts in Cóbuè and in Metangula, and Malawi immigration officers on Likoma Island and in Nkhata Bay, although only the Cóbuè post is currently issuing visas.

In southeastern Tanzania, the **MV Kilambo** (per person/vehicle Tsh500/30,000) ferry crosses the Ruvuma River daily (in theory) between Namiranga (Mozambique) and Kilambo. A smaller passenger-only boat also does the trip daily. There are immigration posts at Kilambo and Namiranga.

Uganda

There is no passenger ferry service between Tanzania and Uganda on Lake Victoria.

Zambia

The venerable **MV Liemba** (028-280 2811) has been plying the waters of Lake Tanganyika for more than a century on one of Africa's classic adventure journeys. It connects Kigoma with Mpulungu in Zambia every other week (in theory), with prices for 1st/2nd/economy class costing US$105/95/75 (payment must be in US dollars cash). The trip takes at least 40 hours and stops en route at various lakeshore villages, including Lagosa (for Mahale Mountains National Park; US$40 for 1st class from Kigoma), Kipili (US$75) and Kasanga (southwest of Sumbawanga; US$100). In theory, departures from Kigoma are every second Wednesday at 4pm, reaching Mpulungu Friday morning. Departures from Mpulungu are (again, in theory) on every second Friday afternoon at about 2pm, arriving back in Kigoma on Sunday afternoon. Delays are common.

Food, soft drink, beer and bottled water are sold on board, but it's a good idea to bring supplements. First class is surprisingly comfortable, with two clean bunks, a window and a fan. Second-class cabins (four bunks) are poorly ventilated and uncomfortable. There are seats for third (economy) class passengers, but it's more comfortable to find deck space for sleeping. Keep watch over your luggage. Booking early is advisable, but not always necessary, as 1st-class cabins are usually available. There are also two VIP cabins, one with private bathroom.

There are docks at a handful of ports, including Kigoma, Kipili, Kasanga and Mpulungu, but at all other stops you'll need to disembark in the middle of the lake, exiting from a door in the side of the boat into small boats that take you to shore. While it may sound adventurous, it can be rather nerve-racking at night, or if the lake is rough.

For those coming from Zambia, there is usually a Tanzanian immigration officer on board to assist with processing visas.

At the time of writing the *Liemba* was scheduled to undergo major renovations, and schedules are likely to be curtailed or changed; enquire first before setting your plans, and stay flexible.

Tours

Australia & New Zealand

African Wildlife Safaris (www. africanwildlifesafaris.com.au) Customised trips to the northern circuit parks and Zanzibar Island.

Classic Safari Company (www. classicsafaricompany.com.au) Upmarket itineraries, including to Ruaha National Park and Selous Game Reserve.

Intrepid Travel (www.intrepid travel.com) ✐ Socially and environmentally responsible tours focusing on the northern circuit and Zanzibar Island.

Peregrine Travel (www.pere grineadventures.com) Northern circuit treks and safaris for all budgets; also Tanzania–Kenya combination itineraries.

South Africa

Africa Travel Co (www.africa travelco.co.za) Northern circuit and southern/East Africa combination itineraries.

Wild Frontiers (www.wild frontiers.com) A range of East Africa itineraries.

UK

Africa-in-Focus (www.africa -in-focus.com) Overland tours.

Baobab Travel (www.baobab travel.com) ✐ A culturally responsible operator with itineraries countrywide.

Camps International (www. campsinternational.com) Community-focused budget itineraries in the northern circuit and on Zanzibar Island.

Expert Africa (www.expert africa.com) A long-standing, experienced operator with a wide selection of itineraries.

Greentours (www.greentours. co.uk) Upmarket, botanically focused tours combining Kitulo and Udzungwa Mountains National Parks.

Responsible Travel.com (www. responsibletravel.com) ✐ Matches you up with ecologically and culturally responsible tour operators to plan an itinerary.

Tribes Travel (www.tribes.co.uk) ✐ Fair-traded safaris and treks, including in the south and west.

USA & Canada

Abercrombie & Kent (www. abercrombiekent.com) Customised northern circuit tours and safaris.

Africa Adventure Company (www.africa-adventure.com) Upmarket specialist safaris, including in southern and western Tanzania, and Kilimanjaro treks.

African Environments (www. africanenvironments.com) Top-end treks organised by one of the pioneering companies on Mt Kilimanjaro. Also northern circuit vehicle safaris, and cultural walking safaris, including in Ngorongoro Conservation Area and in Serengeti border areas.

African Horizons (www.african horizons.com) A small operator offering various packages focusing on northern Tanzania.

Deeper Africa (www.deeper africa.com) ✐ Socially responsible, upmarket northern circuit safaris and treks plus Tanzania with Kids itineraries.

Eco-Resorts (www.eco-resorts. com) ✐ Socially responsible itineraries in the north, south and west.

Explorateur Voyages (www. explorateur.qc.ca) Northern circuit treks and safaris.

Good Earth (📞0732 972655; www.goodearthtours.com; 1896 Moshono Baraa Rd, Arusha) Northern circuit safaris and treks.

International Expeditions (www.ietravel.com) Naturalist-oriented northern circuit safaris.

Mountain Madness (www. mountainmadness.com) ✐ Upmarket Kilimanjaro treks.

Thomson Family Adventures (www.familyadventures.com) Offers a handful of family-focused northern circuit itineraries.

GETTING AROUND

Air

Airlines in Tanzania

Sample one-way fares: Dar es Salaam to Mbeya from Tsh200,000; Dar to Mwanza from Tsh180,000; Dar to Kigoma about Tsh400,000; Dar to Arusha or Kilimanjaro International Airport (KIA) Tsh200,000 to Tsh600,000. Always reconfirm your flights.

Air Tanzania (☎0782 737730, 0782 782732; www.airtanzania. co.tz) KIA to Dar es Salaam and Zanzibar, and Dar to Mtwara, Tabora, Kigoma, Mbeya, Mwanza and Bukoba.

Air Excel (☎027-297 0248; www.airexcelonline.com) Arusha, Serengeti NP, Lake Manyara NP, Dar es Salaam, Zanzibar.

Auric Air (☎0783 233334; www.auricair.com) Bukoba, Mwanza, Zanzibar, Dar es Salaam, Iringa and other towns, plus Katavi and Rubondo Island national parks.

Coastal Aviation (☎022-284 2700, 0713 325673; www. coastal.co.tz; Julius Nyerere International Airport, Dar es Salaam, Terminal 1) Major towns and national parks, including Arusha, Dar es Salaam, Dodoma, Kilwa Masoko, Lake Manyara NP, Mafia, Mwanza, Pemba, Ruaha NP, Rubondo Island NP, Saadani NP, Selous GR, Serengeti NP, Tanga, Tarangire NP and Zanzibar.

Fastjet (☎0784 108900; www. fastjet.com) Dar es Salaam to Kilimanjaro, Zanzibar, Mbeya and Mwanza.

Flightlink (☎0782 354450, 0782 354448; www.flightlink. co.tz; Julius Nyerere International Airport, Dar es Salaam, Terminal 1) Dar es Salaam to Zanzibar, Selous GR, Dodoma,

Iringa, Serengeti NP and Lake Manyara NP.

Precision Air (☎022-219 1000, 0787 888417; www.precision airtz.com) Dar es Salaam to many major towns including Kilimanjaro, Mtwara, Mwanza and Zanzibar.

Regional Air Services (☎0754 285754, 0784 285753; www. regionaltanzania.com; Dodoma Rd, Arusha) Arusha, Dar es Salaam, Kilimanjaro, Lake Manyara NP, Ndutu, Serengeti NP and Zanzibar.

Safari Airlink (☎0783 397235, 0777 723274; www.flysal.com; Julius Nyerere International Airport, Dar es Salaam, Terminal 1) Dar es Salaam, Arusha, Katavi NP, Mahale Mountains NP, Pangani, Ruaha NP, Selous GR and Zanzibar.

Tropical Air (☎024-223 2511, 0777 431431; www.tropicalair. co.tz) Dar es Salaam to Zanzibar, Pemba, Mafia, Tanga and Arusha.

ZanAir (☎024-223 3670, 024-223 3768; www.zanair. com) Arusha, Dar es Salaam, Pemba, Saadani NP, Selous GR and Zanzibar.

Zantas Air (☎0688 434343; www.zantasair.com) Shared charters from Arusha to Katavi NP, Mahale Mountains NP and Kigoma.

Bicycle

Cycling is a seldom-used but fun way to explore Tanzania. When planning your trip, consider the following:

➡ Main sealed roads aren't good for cycling; there's usually no shoulder and traffic moves dangerously fast. Secondary roads are ideal.

➡ Distances are long, often with nothing in between. Consider picking a base, and doing exploratory trips from there.

➡ Carry all supplies, including water (at least 4L), food, a water filter, at least four spare inner tubes, a spare tyre and plenty of tube patches.

➡ Cycling is best in the drier, cooler winter season (June to August/September). Plan on taking a break from the midday heat, and don't count on covering as much territory as you might in a northern European climate.

➡ Other considerations include rampaging motorists (a small rear-view mirror is worthwhile), sleeping (bring a tent) and punctures (from thorn trees). Cycling isn't permitted in national parks or wildlife reserves.

➡ In theory, bicycles can be transported on minibuses and buses, though many drivers are unwilling. For express buses, make advance arrangements to stow your bike in the hold. Bicycles can be transported on ferries for no additional cost, although this might take some negotiation. Contacts include the following:

Afriroots (☎0787 459887, 0713 652642, 0732 926350; www. afriroots.co.tz; Dar es Salaam tours per person US$40-50) Budget cycling tours around Dar es Salaam, in southern Tanzania and in the Usambaras.

Arusha Bicycle Center (ABC; ☎0767 520790; http://arushabicyclecenter.strikingly.com/; ⏰9am-4.30pm Tue & Thu-Sat, noon-6pm Wed) ✂ Rental and purchase of good-quality bicycles.

Bluebikes Zanzibar (www. bluebikeszanzibar.com; bike per day/week US$15/75) Cycling tours in and around Stone Town on Zanzibar Island.

Cycling Association of Tanzania (http://cyclingtanzania.or.tz) Information on local cycling events.

Nungwi Cycling Adventures (☎0777 560352, 0778 677662; www.zanzibarcyclingadventures.com; per person US$25-40) Cycling tours in the villages around Nungwi on Zanzibar Island.

Summit Expeditions & Nomadic Experience (☎0787 740282; www.nomadicexperience.com)

Cycling excursions on Kilimanjaro's lower slopes and multiday rides through the Usambara Mountains.

Summits Africa (☎0784 522090; www.summits-africa.com) Multiday fully equipped bicycle safaris and combination bike-safari trips in northern Tanzania.

Wayo Africa (Green Footprint Adventures; ☎0784 203000, 0783 141119; www.wayoafrica.com) Upmarket cycling tours around Arusha and in the Lake Manyara area.

Boat

Dhow

Main routes connect Zanzibar Island and Pemba with Dar es Salaam, Tanga, Bagamoyo and Mombasa; Kilwa Kivinje, Lindi, Mikindani, Mtwara and Msimbati with other coastal towns; and Mafia with the mainland. However, foreigners are officially prohibited on non-motorised dhows, and on any dhow between the Zanzibar

Archipelago and the mainland; captains are subject to fines if they're caught, and safety is also a concern. A better option is to arrange a charter with a coastal hotel (many have their own dhows) or with **Safari Blue** (☎0777 423162; www.safariblue.net; Fumba; adult/child $65/35).

Ferry

Ferries operate on Lake Victoria, Lake Tanganyika and Lake Nyasa, although passenger ferry service on Lake Nyasa was temporarily suspended as of late 2017. Ferries also operate between Dar es Salaam, Zanzibar and Pemba, and between Pemba and Tanga. There is a US$5 port tax per trip.

For all ferry travel: don't get on a boat that appears overloaded, don't set off in bad weather, and poke around on deck to try and find a life jacket.

LAKE VICTORIA

There is a daily ferry service connecting Tanzanian ports on Lake Victoria between

Mwanza and Ukerewe Island. The MV *Victoria*, which formerly connected Mwanza with Bukoba, was not operating. Meanwhile, service on the Mwanza to Bukoba route began in January 2018 on the smaller MV *Bluebird*.

LAKE NYASA

At the time of research, there was no passenger ferry service on the Tanzanian side of Lake Nyasa. Two new cargo ferries – the MV *Njombe* and the MV *Ruvuma* – were launched in July 2017, and a passenger ferry was under construction. Until this new boat is completed, you will need to travel overland. Just as a guideline for timings and pricing, should the new boat actually be launched: the previous ferry, MV *Songea*, departed from Itungi port about noon on Thursday and continued down the coast via Matema, Lupingu, Manda, Lundu, Mango and Liuli to Mbamba Bay (18 to 24 hours between Itungi and Mbamba Bay) before returning again to Matema and Itungi port on

---

DHOW TRAVEL

With their billowing sails and graceful forms, dhows have become a symbol of East Africa for adventure travellers. Yet, despite their romantic reputation, the realities can be quite different. Before contemplating a longer journey, test things out with a short sunset or afternoon sail. Coastal hotels are good contacts for arranging reliable dhow travel. If you happen to find yourself in a local dhow:

➡ Be prepared for rough conditions. There are no facilities on board, except possibly a toilet hanging off the stern. Sailings are wind and tide dependent, and departures are often predawn.

➡ Journeys often take much longer than anticipated; bring extra water and sufficient food.

➡ Sun block, a hat and a covering are essential, as is waterproofing for your luggage and a rain jacket.

➡ Boats capsize and people are killed each year. Avoid overloaded boats and don't set sail in bad weather.

➡ Travel with the winds, which blow from south to north from approximately July to September and north to south from approximately November to late February.

Note that what Westerners refer to as dhows are called either *jahazi* or *mashua* by Tanzanians. *Jahazi* are large lateen-sailed boats. *Mashua* are smaller, and often with proportionately wider hulls and a motor. The *dau* has a sloped stem and stern. On lakes and inland waterways, the *mtumbwi* (dugout canoe) is in common use. Coastal areas, especially Zanzibar Island's east-coast beaches, are good places to see *ngalawa* (outrigger canoes).

Sunday (Tsh25,000/16,000 for 1st/economy class between Matema and Mbamba Bay). For an update on the ferry situation, ask in Kyela or at one of the Matema hotels.

Bus

Bus travel is an inevitable part of the Tanzania experience for many travellers. Prices are reasonable for distances covered, and there's often no other way to reach many destinations.

➡ On major routes, there's a choice of express and ordinary buses. Express buses make fewer stops, are less crowded and depart on schedule. Some have toilets and air-conditioning, and the nicest ones are called 'luxury' buses. On secondary routes, the only option is ordinary buses, which are often packed to overflowing, stop frequently and run to a less-rigorous schedule (and often not to any recognisable schedule at all).

➡ Book in advance, although you can sometimes get a place by arriving at the bus station an hour prior to departure. Each bus line has its own booking office, at or near the bus station.

➡ Express buses have a compartment below for luggage. However, it's best to keep your bag with you. Never put it up on the roof.

➡ Prices are basically fixed, although overcharging happens. Buy your tickets at the office and not from touts, and don't believe anyone who tries to tell you there's a luggage fee, unless you are carrying an excessively large pack.

➡ For short stretches along main routes, express buses will drop you on request, though you'll often need to pay the full fare to the next major destination.

➡ On long routes, expect to sleep either on the bus, pulled off to the side of the road, or at a basic guesthouse.

Minibus & Shared Taxi

For shorter trips away from the main routes, the choice is often between 30-seater buses ('coastals') and dalla-dallas or Hiace minivans. Both options come complete with chickens on the roof, bags of produce under the seats, no leg room and schedules only in the most general sense of the word. Dalla-dallas, especially, are invariably filled to overflowing. Shared taxis are rare. Like ordinary buses, dalla-dallas and shared taxis leave when full, and are the least safe transport option.

Truck

In remote areas, trucks sometimes operate as buses (for a roughly similar fare), with passengers sitting or standing in the back. Even on routes that have daily bus service, many people still use trucks.

Car & Motorcycle

Unless you have your own vehicle and/or are familiar with driving in East Africa, it's relatively unusual for fly-in travellers to tour mainland Tanzania by car. More common is to focus on a region and arrange local transport through a tour or safari operator. On Zanzibar Island, it's easy enough to hire a motorcycle for touring.

Driving Licence

On the mainland you'll need your home driving licence or (preferable) an International Driving Permit (IDP) together with your home licence. On Zanzibar, you'll need an IDP plus your home licence, or a permit from Zanzibar, Kenya, Uganda or South Africa.

Fuel & Spare Parts

Petrol and diesel cost about Tsh2100 per litre. Filling and repair stations are found in all major towns, but are scarce elsewhere, so tank up whenever you get the opportunity and carry a range of spares for your vehicle. In remote areas and for longer stays in national parks, it's essential to carry jerry cans with extra fuel. It can happen that petrol or diesel may be diluted with kerosene or water. Check with local residents or business owners before tanking up. It's also common for car parts to be switched in garages (substituting inferior versions

PERILS OF THE ROAD

Road accidents are perhaps your biggest safety risk while travelling in Tanzania, with speeding buses among the worst offenders. Overtaking blind is a problem, as are high speeds. Your bus driver may, in fact, be at the wheel of an ageing, rickety vehicle with marginal brakes on a winding, potholed road. However, he'll invariably be driving as if he were piloting a sleek racing machine coming down the straight – nerve-racking to say the least. Impassioned pleas from passengers to slow down usually have little effect. Many vehicles have painted slogans such as *Mungu Atubariki* (God Bless Us) or 'In God We Trust' in the hope that a bit of extra help from above will see them safely through the day's runs. To maximise safety, avoid night travel and ask locals for recommendations of reputable companies. If you have a choice, it's usually better to go with a full-sized bus than a minibus (the worst option) or a 30-seater bus.

for the originals). Staying with your car while it's being repaired helps minimise this problem. Also note your odometer and gas gauge readings before having your car serviced.

Hire

In Dar es Salaam, daily rates for a 2WD vehicle start at about US$80, excluding fuel, plus from US$30 for insurance and tax. Prices for 4WDs are US$100 to US$250 per day plus insurance (US$30 to US$45 per day), fuel and driver (US$20 to US$50 per day). There's also an 18% value-added tax.

Outside the city, most companies require you to hire a 4WD. Also, most will not permit self-drive outside of Dar es Salaam, and none currently offer unlimited kilometres. Charges per kilometre are around US$0.50 to US$1.20. Clarify what the company's policy is in the event of a breakdown.

Elsewhere in Tanzania, you can hire 4WD vehicles in Arusha, Karatu, Mwanza, Mbeya, Zanzibar Town and other centres through travel agencies, tour operators and hotels. Most come with driver. Rates average US$100 to US$250 per day plus fuel on the mainland. On Zanzibar Island, expect to pay from US$50 per day plus fuel for a 2WD.

For vehicle hire with driver, contact the Dar es Salaam-based **Jumanne Mastoka** (☑ 0659 339735, 0784 339735; mjumanne@ yahoo.com).

Road Conditions & Hazards

The Tanzanian government has been moving full-steam ahead on roadworks and all major routes plus many secondary roads are now sealed. The condition of unpaved secondary roads ranges from good to impassable, depending on the season. For most trips outside major towns you'll need a 4WD.

If you aren't used to driving in East Africa, watch out for pedestrians, children and animals on the road or running into the road. Especially in rural areas, many people have not driven themselves and aren't aware of necessary braking distances and similar concepts. Never drive at night, and be particularly alert for vehicles overtaking blind on curves. Tree branches on the road are the local version of flares or hazard lights and mean there's a stopped vehicle, crater-sized pothole or similar calamity ahead.

Road Rules

Driving is on the left (in theory), and traffic already on roundabouts has the right of way. Unless otherwise posted, the speed limit is 80km/h; on some routes, including Dar es Salaam to Arusha, police have radar. Tanzania has a seat-belt law for drivers and front-seat passengers. The standard traffic-fine penalty is Tsh30,000.

Motorcycles aren't permitted in national parks except for the section of the Dar es Salaam to Mbeya highway passing through Mikumi National Park, on the road between Sumbawanga and Mpanda via Katavi National Park and on the Bagamoyo to Pangani road through Saadani National Park.

Hitching

Hitching is generally slow going. It's prohibited inside national parks, and is usually fruitless around them. That said, in remote areas, hitching a lift with truck drivers may be your only option. Expect to pay about the same or a bit less than the bus fare for the same route, with a place in the cab costing about twice that for a place on top of the load. To flag down a vehicle, hold out your hand at about waist level, palm to the ground, and wave it up and down.

Expat workers or well-off locals may also offer you a ride. Payment is usually not expected, but still offer some token of thanks, such as a petrol contribution for longer journeys.

As elsewhere in the world, hitching is never entirely safe, and we don't recommend it. Travellers who hitch should understand that they are taking a small but potentially serious risk. If you do hitch, it's safer doing so in pairs and letting someone know your plans.

Local Transport

Dalla-Dalla

Local routes are serviced by dalla-dallas and, in rural areas, by pick-up trucks or old 4WDs. Prices are fixed and inexpensive (Tsh400 for town runs). The vehicles make many stops and are extremely crowded. Accidents are frequent, particularly in minibuses. Many accidents are caused when the drivers race each other to an upcoming station in order to collect new passengers. Destinations are either posted on a board in the front window, or called out by the driver's assistant, who also collects fares. If you have a large backpack, think twice about getting on a dalla-dalla, especially at rush hour, when it will make the already crowded conditions even more uncomfortable for the other passengers.

Taxi

Taxis, which have white plates on the mainland and a 'gari la abiria' (passenger vehicle) sign on Zanzibar, can be hired in all major towns. None have meters, so agree on the fare with the driver before getting in. Fares for short town trips start at Tsh2000 (Tsh5000 in Dar es Salaam). In major centres, many drivers have an 'official' price list, although rates shown on it are often significantly higher than what is normally paid. If you're unsure of the price, ask locals what it should be and then use this as a base for negotiations. For longer trips away from town, negotiate the fare based on distance, petrol costs and road conditions, plus a fair profit for the driver. Only use taxis from reliable hotels or established taxi stands. Avoid hailing taxis cruising the streets, and never get in a taxi that has a 'friend' of the driver or anyone else already in it.

Train

For those with plenty of time, train travel offers a fine view of the countryside and local life. There are two lines: **Tazara** (www.tazarasite.com), linking Dar es Salaam with New Kapiri Mposhi in Zambia via Mbeya and Tunduma, and **Tanzania Railways Limited Central Line** (☑022-211 6213, 0754 460907; www.trl.co.tz; cnr Railway St & Sokoine Dr, Dar es Salaam), linking Dar es Salaam with Kigoma and Mwanza via Tabora. A Central Line branch also links Tabora with Mpanda, and Tazara runs the Udzungwa shuttle twice weekly between the Kilombero/Udzungwa area and Makambako.

In general, Tazara is more comfortable and efficient than the Central Line. However, both lines are currently in the process of upgrading, and there have already been notable improvements. Central Line now has a comfortable weekly deluxe service. For longer stretches, bring extra food and drinks to

supplement the basic meals that are available on board.

Classes

Tazara has four classes: 1st class (four-bed compartments), 2nd class (six-bed compartments), 2nd-class sitting (also called 'super seater') and economy (3rd) class (benches, usually very crowded). Men and women can only travel together in the sleeping sections by booking the entire compartment. At night, secure your window with a stick, and don't leave your luggage unattended, even for a moment. Central Line has 1st class (four-bed compartments), 2nd class (six-bed compartments) and economy. There is also deluxe service on the Central Line (suspended temporarily as of mid-2017).

Reservations

Tickets for 1st and 2nd class should be reserved at least several days in advance, although occasionally you'll be able to get a seat on the day of travel. Economy-class tickets can be bought on the spot.

TAZARA

Departures from Mbeya to Dar are at 2.30pm Wednesday (express) and 8.20pm Saturday (ordinary). Travel time between Dar and Mbeya is approximately 21/26 hours for express/ordinary. Express-train fares between Dar es Salaam and Mbeya are Tsh47,200/39,200/36,300/33,300 for 1st-class sleeping/2nd-class sleeping/super seater/economy class (slightly less for ordinary trains). Linens are provided for sleeper cars.

Tazara's Udzungwa shuttle runs an economy-class (only) service twice weekly connecting Kilombero (Mkamba) and Mang'ula (site of Udzungwa National Park headquarters) with Makambako in the Southern Highlands. Departures from Mang'ula are at 5.30pm on Sunday and Thursday, and from Makambako at 7.30pm on Monday and Friday (Tsh11,800 Mang'ula to Makambako, 11 hours).

CENTRAL LINE

Central Line trains depart Dar es Salaam for Kigoma (1st-class sleeping/2nd-class sleeping/economy class Tsh75,700/55,400/27,700, approximately 40 hours) and Mwanza (Tsh74,800/54,700/27,200, approximately 40 hours) at 9pm Tuesday, Friday and Sunday. Departures from Kigoma and Mwanza are at 9pm on Tuesday, Thursday and Sunday. There is also a weekly express train between Dar and Kigoma, departing Dar at 8am on Thursday and departing Kigoma at 8am on Saturday (2nd-class sleeping/2nd-class sitting/economy Tsh79,400/47,600/35,700, about 34 hours), although service was temporarily suspended as of mid-2017. Sleeper cars are mattresses only (no linens).

Trains between Tabora and Mpanda (economy class only Tsh17,800, about 12 hours) depart from Tabora at 12.30am Monday, Wednesday and Saturday, and Mpanda at 8pm Tuesday, Thursday and Sunday.

There are frequent schedule adjustments, so get an update before travel.

Health

As long as you stay up-to-date with your vaccinations and take basic preventive measures, you're unlikely to succumb to most of the possible health hazards. While Tanzania has an impressive selection of tropical diseases on offer, it's more likely you'll get a bout of diarrhoea or a cold than a more exotic malady. The main exception to this is malaria, which is a real risk throughout much of the country. Road accidents are the other main threat to your health. Never travel at night, and choose buses or private transport over dalla-dallas (minibuses) to minimise the risk.

BEFORE YOU GO

➡ Get a check-up from your dentist and your doctor if you have any regular medication or chronic illnesses, such as high blood pressure or asthma.

➡ Organise spare contact lenses and glasses.

➡ Get a first-aid and medical kit together; arrange necessary vaccinations.

➡ Consider registering with the International Association for Medical Advice to Travellers (www.iamat.org), which provides directories of certified doctors.

➡ If you'll be spending time in remote areas, consider doing a first-aid course (contact the Red Cross or St John

Ambulance) or attending a medicine-in-remote-areas first-aid course, such as that offered by the Royal Geographical Society (www.wildernessmedicaltraining.co.uk).

➡ Carry medications in their original (labelled) containers.

➡ If carrying syringes or needles, have a physician's letter documenting their medical necessity.

Insurance

Check in advance if your insurance plan will make payments directly to providers or reimburse you later for overseas health expenditures. Most doctors in Tanzania expect payment in cash.

Ensure that your travel insurance will cover any emergency transport required to get you at least as far as Nairobi (Kenya), or (preferably) all the way home by air and with a medical attendant if necessary. It's worth taking out a temporary membership with the African Medical & Research Foundation's Flying Doctors program (www.flydoc.org) or First Air Responder (www.knightsupport.com/first-air-responder/).

RECOMMENDED VACCINATIONS

Regardless of destination, the World Health Organization (www.who.int/en) recommends that all travellers be covered for the following:

➡ diphtheria
➡ tetanus
➡ measles
➡ mumps

➡ rubella
➡ polio
➡ hepatitis B

The Center for Disease Control and Prevention (www.cdc.gov) also recommends the following vaccinations for Tanzania:

➡ hepatitis A
➡ hepatitis B
➡ rabies

➡ typhoid
➡ boosters for tetanus, diphtheria and measles

A yellow fever vaccination certificate is not officially required to enter Tanzania unless you're coming from an infected area, but carrying one is advised.

Medical Checklist

Carry a medical and first-aid kit with you, to help yourself in case of minor illness or injury. Following is a list of items to include:

➡ acetaminophen (paracetamol) or aspirin

➡ adhesive tape

➡ antibacterial ointment for cuts and abrasions

➡ antibiotics eg ciprofloxacin (Ciproxin) or norfloxacin (Utinor)

➡ antidiarrhoeal drugs (eg loperamide)

➡ antihistamines (for allergic reactions)

➡ anti-inflammatory drugs (eg ibuprofen)

➡ antimalaria pills

➡ bandages, gauze, gauze rolls and tape

➡ DEET-containing insect repellent

➡ digital thermometer

➡ oral rehydration salts

➡ Permethrin-containing insect spray for clothing, tents and bed nets

➡ pocket knife

➡ scissors, safety pins, tweezers

➡ self-diagnostic kit to identify from a finger prick if malaria is in the blood

➡ sterile needles, syringes and fluids if travelling to remote areas

➡ sun block (SPF 30+)

➡ water purification tablets

Websites

General information:

Fit for Travel (www.fitfortravel. nhs.uk)

International Travel and Health (www.who.int/ith) – a free online publication of the World Health Organization

Lonely Planet (www.lonely planet.com)

Government travel-health websites:

Australia (www.smartraveller. gov.au)

Canada (www.phac-aspc.gc.ca)

UK (www.nhs.uk/nhsengland/ healthcareabroad/pages/health-careabroad.aspx)

USA (www.cdc.gov/travel)

Further Reading

➡ *Wilderness and Travel Medicine* by Eric A Weiss (2012)

➡ *Essential Guide to Travel Health* by Jane Wilson-Howarth (2009)

➡ *Africa – Healthy Travel Guide* by Isabelle Young and Tony Gherardin (2008)

IN TANZANIA

Availability & Cost of Health Care

Good medical care is available in Dar es Salaam, and reasonable-to-good care is available in Arusha and in some mission stations. Otherwise, you'll need to go to Nairobi (Kenya), which is the main destination for medical evacuations from Tanzania, or return home. If you have a choice, try to find a private or mission-run clinic, as these are generally better equipped than government ones. If you fall ill in an unfamiliar area, ask staff at your hotel or resident expatriates where the best nearby medical facilities are; in an emergency contact your embassy. Larger towns have at least one clinic where you can get an inexpensive malaria test and, if necessary, treatment.

Pharmacies in major towns are generally well stocked for commonly used items, and rarely require prescriptions; always check expiry dates. Antimalarials are relatively easy to obtain in larger towns. However, it's recommended to bring anti-malarials, as well as drugs for chronic diseases, from home. Some drugs for sale in Tanzania might be ineffective; they might be counterfeit (especially antimalarial tablets and antibiotics) or might not have been stored under the right conditions. The availability and efficacy of condoms also cannot be relied upon; they might not be of the same quality as in your home country and might be incorrectly stored.

There is a high risk of contracting HIV from infected blood transfusions. The BloodCare Foundation (www.bloodcare.org.uk) is a good source of safe blood, which can be transported to any part of the world within 24 hours.

Infectious Diseases

The following are some of the diseases found in Tanzania. With basic preventative measures, it's unlikely that you'll succumb to any.

Cholera

Cholera is usually only a problem during natural or artificial disasters, such as war, floods or earthquakes, although outbreaks can also occur at other times. Travellers are rarely affected. It's caused by a bacteria and spread via contaminated drinking water. The main symptom is profuse watery diarrhoea, which causes debilitation if fluids are not replaced quickly. An oral cholera vaccine is available in the USA, but is not particularly effective. Most cases of cholera could be avoided by close attention to good drinking water and by avoiding potentially contaminated food. Treatment is by fluid replacement (orally or via a drip), but sometimes antibiotics are needed. Self-treatment is not advised.

Dengue Fever

Mini-epidemics of this mosquito-borne disease crop up with some regularity in Tanzania, notably in Dar es Salaam. Symptoms include high fever, severe headache and body ache (dengue used to be known as break-bone fever). Some people develop a rash and experience diarrhoea. There is no vaccine, only prevention. The dengue-carrying Aedes aegypti mosquito is active at day and night, so use DEET-mosquito repellent periodically throughout the day. See a doctor to be diagnosed and monitored (dengue testing is available in Dar es Salaam). There is no specific treatment, just rest and paracetamol – do not take aspirin as it increases the likelihood of haemorrhaging. Severe dengue is a potentially fatal complication.

Diptheria

Diphtheria is spread through close respiratory contact. It usually causes a temperature and a severe sore throat. Sometimes a membrane forms across the throat and a tracheotomy is needed to prevent suffocation. Vaccination is recommended for those likely to be in close contact with the local population in infected areas, but is more important for long stays than for short-term trips. The vaccine is given as an injection, alone or with tetanus, and lasts 10 years. Self-treatment: none.

Filariasis

Filariasis is caused by tiny worms migrating in the lymphatic system and is spread by a bite from an infected mosquito. Symptoms include localised itching and swelling of the legs and/or genitalia. Treatment is available. Self-treatment: none.

Hepatitis A

Hepatitis A is spread through contaminated food (particularly shellfish) and water. It causes jaundice and, although it is rarely fatal, it can cause prolonged lethargy and delayed recovery. If you've had hepatitis A, you shouldn't drink alcohol for up to six months afterwards, but once you've recovered there won't be any long-term problems. The first symptoms include dark urine and a yellow colour to the whites of the eyes. Sometimes a fever and abdominal pain are present. Hepatitis A vaccine (Avaxim, VAQTA, Havrix) is given as an injection: a single dose will give protection for up to a year, and a booster after a year gives 10-year protection. Hepatitis A and typhoid vaccines can also be given as a single-dose vaccine (Hepatyrix or Viatim). Self-treatment: none.

Hepatitis B

Hepatitis B is spread through sexual intercourse, infected blood and contaminated needles. It can also be spread from an infected mother to her baby during childbirth. It affects the liver, causing jaundice and sometimes liver failure. Most people recover completely, but some people might be chronic carriers of the virus, which could lead eventually to cirrhosis or liver cancer. Those visiting high-risk areas for long periods, or those with increased social or occupational risk, should be immunised. Many countries now routinely give hepatitis B as part of childhood vaccination. It is given singly or can be given at the same time as hepatitis A.

A course will give protection for at least five years. It can be given over four weeks or six months. Self-treatment: none.

HIV

Human immunodeficiency virus (HIV), the virus that causes acquired immune deficiency syndrome (AIDS), is a major problem in Tanzania, with infection rates averaging about 4.7%, and much higher in some areas. The virus is spread through infected blood and blood products, by sexual intercourse with an infected partner and from an infected mother to her baby during childbirth and breastfeeding. It can be spread through 'blood to blood' contact, such as with contaminated instruments during medical, dental, acupuncture and other body-piercing procedures, and through sharing used intravenous needles. At present there is no cure; medication that might keep the disease under control is available, but these drugs are too expensive, or unavailable, for many Tanzanians. If you think you might have been infected with HIV, a blood test is necessary; a three-month gap after exposure and before testing is required to allow antibodies to appear in the blood. Self-treatment: none.

Malaria

Malaria is endemic throughout most of Tanzania and is a major health scourge (except at altitudes higher than 2000m, where the risk of transmission is low, and on Zanzibar Island, where it has been eradicated). Infection rates are higher during the rainy season, but the risk exists year-round and it is important to take preventive measures, even if you will be in the country for just a short time.

Malaria is caused by a parasite in the bloodstream spread via the bite of the female anopheles mosquito. There are several types, falciparum malaria being the most dangerous and the predominant form in Tanzania. Unlike most other diseases regularly encountered by travellers, there is no vaccination against malaria (yet). However, several different drugs are used to prevent malaria. Up-to-date advice from a travel-health clinic is essential, as some medication is more suitable for some travellers than others. The pattern of drug-resistant malaria is changing rapidly, so what was advised several years ago might no longer be the case.

SYMPTOMS

The early stages of malaria include headaches, fevers, generalised aches and pains, and malaise, which could be mistaken for flu. Other symptoms can include abdominal pain, diarrhoea and a cough. Anyone who develops a fever in Tanzania or within two weeks after departure should assume malarial infection until blood tests prove negative, even if you have been taking antimalarial medication. If not treated, the next stage could develop within 24 hours, particularly if falciparum malaria is the parasite: jaundice, then reduced consciousness and coma (also known as cerebral malaria) followed by death. Treatment in hospital is essential, and the death rate might still be as high as 10% even in the best intensive-care facilities.

SIDE EFFECTS & RISKS

Many travellers are under the impression that malaria is a mild illness, that treatment is always easy and successful, and that taking antimalarial drugs causes more illness through side effects than actually getting malaria. Unfortunately, this is not true. Side effects of the medication depend on the drug being taken. Doxycycline can cause heartburn and indigestion; mefloquine (Lariam) can cause anxiety attacks, insomnia and nightmares and (rarely) severe psychiatric disorders; chloroquine can cause nausea and hair loss; and proguanil can cause mouth ulcers. These side effects are not universal and can be minimised by taking medication correctly, eg with food. Also, some people should not take a particular antimalarial drug, eg people with epilepsy should avoid mefloquine, and doxycycline should not be taken by

pregnant women or children younger than 12.

If you decide that you really don't want to take antimalarial drugs, you must understand the risks and be scrupulous about avoiding mosquito bites. Use nets and insect repellent, and report any fever or flu-like symptoms to a doctor as soon as possible. Malaria in pregnancy frequently results in miscarriage or premature labour and the risks to both mother and foetus during pregnancy are considerable. Travel in Tanzania when pregnant should be carefully considered.

STAND-BY TREATMENT

If you will be away from major towns, carrying emergency stand-by treatment is highly recommended, and essential for travel in remote areas. Be sure to seek your doctor's advice before setting off as to recommended medicines and dosages. However, this should be viewed as emergency treatment only and not as routine self-medication, and should only be used if you will be far from medical facilities and have been advised about the symptoms of malaria and how to use the medication. If you do resort to emergency self-treatment, seek medical advice as soon as possible to confirm whether the treatment has been successful. In particular, you want to avoid contracting cerebral malaria, which can be fatal within 24 hours. Self-diagnostic kits, which can identify malaria in the blood from a finger prick, are available in the West and are worth buying.

Meningococcal Meningitis

Meningococcal infection is spread through close respiratory contact and is more likely in crowded places, such as dormitories, buses and clubs. While the disease is present in Tanzania, infection is uncommon in travellers.

Vaccination is recommended for long stays and is especially important towards the end of the dry season. Symptoms include a fever, severe headache, neck stiffness and a red rash. Immediate medical treatment is necessary.

The ACWY vaccine is recommended for all travellers in sub-Saharan Africa. This vaccine is different from the meningococcal meningitis C vaccine given to children and adolescents in some countries; it is safe to be given both types of vaccine. Self-treatment: none.

Onchocerciasis (River Blindness)

This disease is caused by the larvae of a tiny worm, which is spread by the bite of a small fly. The earliest sign of infection is intensely itchy, red, sore eyes. It's rare for travellers to be severely affected. Treatment undertaken in a specialised clinic is curative. Self-treatment: none.

Poliomyelitis

This disease is generally spread through contaminated food and water. It is one of the vaccines given in childhood and should be boosted every 10 years, either orally (a drop on the tongue) or else as an injection. Polio can be carried asymptomatically (ie showing no symptoms) and could cause a transient fever. In rare cases it causes weakness or paralysis of one or more muscles, which might be permanent. Self-treatment: none.

Rabies

Rabies is spread via the bite or lick of an infected animal on broken skin. It is always fatal once the clinical symptoms start (which might be up to several months after an infected bite), so post-bite vaccination should be given as soon as possible. Post-bite vaccination (whether or not you've been vaccinated before the bite) prevents the virus from spreading to the central nervous system. Consider vaccination if you'll be travelling away from major centres (ie anywhere where a reliable source of post-bite vaccine is not available within 24 hours). Three preventive injections are needed over a month. If you have not been vaccinated you'll need a course of five injections starting 24 hours, or as soon as possible, after the injury. If you have been vaccinated, you'll need fewer post-bite injections, and have more time to seek medical help. Self-treatment: none.

Schistosomiasis (Bilharzia)

This disease is a risk throughout Tanzania. It's spread by flukes (parasitic flatworm) that are carried by a species of freshwater snail, which then sheds them into slow-moving or still water. The parasites penetrate human skin during swimming and then migrate to the bladder or bowel. They are excreted via stool or urine and could contaminate fresh water, where the cycle starts again. Swimming in suspect freshwater lakes (including Lake Victoria) or slow-running rivers should be avoided. Symptoms range from none to transient fever and rash, and advanced cases might have blood in the stool or in the urine. A blood test can detect antibodies if you might have been exposed, and treatment is readily available. If not treated, the infection can cause kidney failure or permanent bowel damage. It's not possible for you to infect others. Self-treatment: none.

Trypanosomiasis (Sleeping Sickness)

This disease is spread via the bite of the tsetse fly. It causes headache, fever and eventually coma. If you have these symptoms and have negative malaria tests, have yourself evaluated by a reputable clinic in Dar es Salaam, where you should also be able to obtain treatment for trypanosomiasis. There is an effective treatment. Self-treatment: none.

Tuberculosis (TB)

TB is spread through close respiratory contact and occasionally through infected milk or milk products. BCG vaccination is recommended if you'll be mixing closely with the local population, especially on long-term stays, although it gives only moderate protection. TB can be asymptomatic, only being picked up on a routine chest X-ray. Alternatively, it can cause a cough, weight loss or fever, sometimes months or even years after exposure. Self-treatment: none.

Typhoid

This is spread through food or water contaminated by infected human faeces. The first symptom is usually a fever or a pink rash on the abdomen. Septicaemia (blood poisoning) can sometimes occur. A typhoid vaccine (Typhim Vi, Typherix) will give protection for three years. In some countries, the oral vaccine Vivotif is also available. Antibiotics are usually given as treatment, and death is rare unless septicaemia occurs. Self-treatment: none.

Yellow Fever

Tanzania (including the Zanzibar Archipelago) requires you to carry a certificate of yellow-fever vaccination only if you are arriving from an infected area (which includes Kenya). However, it is a requirement in some neighbouring countries (eg Burundi, Uganda). Yellow fever is spread by infected mosquitoes. Symptoms range from a flu-like illness to severe hepatitis (liver inflammation), jaundice and death. The yellow-fever vaccination must be given at a designated clinic and is valid for life. It is a live vaccine and must not be given to immunocompromised or pregnant travellers. Self-treatment: none.

Travellers' Diarrhoea

It's not inevitable that you'll get diarrhoea while travelling in Tanzania, but it's likely. Diarrhoea is the most common travel-related illness, and sometimes can be triggered simply by dietary changes. To help prevent it, avoid tap water, only eat fresh fruits or vegetables if cooked or peeled, and be wary of dairy products that might contain unpasteurised milk. Although freshly cooked food can be a safe option, plates or serving utensils might be dirty, so be selective when eating from street vendors (make sure that cooked food is piping hot all the way through). If you develop diarrhoea, be sure to drink plenty of fluids, preferably an oral rehydration solution. A few loose stools don't require treatment, but if you start having more than four or five stools a day you should start taking an antibiotic (usually a quinolone drug, such as ciprofloxacin or norfloxacin) and an antidiarrhoeal agent (such as loperamide) if you are not within easy reach of a toilet. If diarrhoea is bloody, persists for more than 72 hours or is accompanied by fever, shaking chills or severe abdominal pain, seek medical attention.

Amoebic Dysentery

Contracted by eating contaminated food and water, amoebic dysentery causes blood and mucus in the faeces. It can be relatively mild and tends to come on gradually, but seek medical advice if you think you have the illness as it won't clear up without treatment with specific antibiotics.

Giardiasis

This is caused by ingesting contaminated food or water.

The illness usually appears a week or more after you have been exposed to the offending parasite. Giardiasis might cause only a short-lived bout of typical travellers' diarrhoea, but it can also cause persistent diarrhoea. Seek medical advice if you suspect you have giardiasis. If you are in a remote area you could start a course of antibiotics, with medical follow-up when feasible.

Environmental Hazards

Altitude Sickness

Reduced oxygen levels at altitudes above 2500m affect most people. The effect may be mild or severe and occurs because less oxygen reaches the muscles and the brain at high altitudes, requiring the heart and lungs to compensate by working harder. Symptoms of Acute Mountain Sickness (AMS) usually develop during the first 24 hours at altitude but may be delayed for up to three weeks. Mild symptoms include headache, lethargy, dizziness, sleeping difficulties and loss of appetite. AMS may become more severe without warning and can be fatal. It is a significant risk for anyone, no matter what their fitness level, who tries to ascend Mt Kilimanjaro or Mt Meru too rapidly. Severe symptoms include breathlessness; a dry, irritative cough (which may progress to the production of pink, frothy sputum); severe headache; lack of coordination and balance; confusion; irrational behaviour; vomiting; drowsiness; and unconsciousness. There is no hard-and-fast rule as to what is too high: AMS has been fatal at 3000m, although 3500m to 4500m is the usual range.

Treat mild symptoms of AMS by resting at the same altitude until recovery, which usually takes a day or two. Paracetamol or aspirin can be taken for headaches. If symptoms persist or become worse, however, immediate descent is necessary; even descending just 500m can help. Drug treatments should never be used to avoid descent or to enable further ascent.

The drugs acetazolamide and dexamethasone are recommended by some doctors for the prevention of AMS; however, their use is controversial. They can reduce the symptoms, but they may also mask warning signs and cause severe dehydration; severe and fatal AMS has occurred in people taking these drugs. In general we do not recommend them for travellers.

To prevent AMS, try the following:

➡ Ascend slowly. On Kilimanjaro, this means choosing one of the longer routes that allow for a more gradual ascent. Whatever route you choose, opt to take an additional rest day on the mountain, sleeping two nights at the same location, and using the day for short hikes. All operators can arrange this, and the extra money (a relative pittance in comparison with the overall costs of a Kili trek) will be money well spent.

➡ It's always wise to sleep at a lower altitude than the greatest height reached during the day ('climb high, sleep low').

➡ Drink lots of fluids. Mountain air is dry and cold,

TRADITIONAL MEDICINE

According to some estimates, at least 80% of Tanzanians rely in part or in whole on traditional medicine, and close to two-thirds of the population have traditional healers as their first point of contact in case of illness. The *mganga* (traditional healer) holds a revered position in many communities, and traditional-medicinal products are widely available in local markets. In part, the heavy reliance on traditional medicine is because of comparatively higher costs of conventional Western-style medicine, and because of prevailing cultural attitudes and beliefs, but also because it sometimes works. Often, though, it's because there is no other choice. In northeastern Tanzania, for example, it is estimated that while there is only one medical doctor to over 30,000 people, there is a traditional healer for approximately every 150 people. Countrywide, hospitals and health clinics are concentrated in urban areas, and most are limited in their effectiveness because of insufficient resources and chronic shortages of equipment and medicines.

While some traditional remedies seem to work on malaria, sickle-cell anaemia, high blood pressure and other ailments, most traditional healers learn their art by apprenticeship, so education (and consequently application of knowledge) is often inconsistent and unregulated. At the centre of efforts to correct these problems is the Institute of Traditional Medicine (http://itm.muhas.ac.tz). Among other things, the institute is studying the efficacy of various traditional cures, and promoting those that are found to be successful. There are also local efforts to create healers' associations, and to train traditional practitioners in sanitation and other topics.

and moisture is lost as you breathe. Evaporation of sweat may occur unnoticed and result in dehydration.

➡ Eat light high-carbohydrate meals for more energy.

➡ Avoid alcohol as it increases risk of dehydration.

➡ Avoid sedatives.

Heat Exhaustion

This condition occurs after heavy sweating and excessive fluid loss with inadequate replacement of fluids and salt, and is primarily a risk in hot climates when taking unaccustomed exercise before full acclimatisation. Symptoms include headache, dizziness and tiredness. Dehydration is already happening by the time you feel thirsty; aim to drink sufficient water to produce pale, diluted urine. Self-treatment: fluid replacement with water and/or fruit juice, and cooling the body with cold water and fans. The treatment of the salt-loss component consists of consuming salty fluids (as in soup) and adding a little more table salt to foods than usual.

Heatstroke

Heat exhaustion is a precursor to the much more serious condition of heatstroke. In this case there is damage to the sweating mechanism, with an excessive rise in body temperature; irrational and hyperactive behaviour; and, eventually, loss of consciousness and death. Rapid cooling by spraying the body with water and fanning is ideal. Emergency fluid and electrolyte replacement is usually also required by intravenous drip.

Hypothermia

Trekkers at high altitudes, such as on Mt Kilimanjaro or Mt Meru, will need to have appropriate clothing and be prepared for cold, wet conditions. Even in lower areas,

TAP WATER

Unless your intestines are well accustomed to Tanzania, don't drink tap water that hasn't been boiled, filtered or chemically disinfected (eg with iodine tablets), and be wary of ice and fruit juices diluted with unpurified water. Avoid drinking unpurified water from streams, rivers and lakes. The same goes for drinking from pumps and wells; some bring pure water to the surface, but the presence of animals can contaminate supplies. Bottled water is widely available, except in very remote areas, where you should carry a filter or purification tablets.

such as the Usambara Mountains, the rim of Ngorongoro Crater or the Ulugurus, conditions can be wet and chilly.

Symptoms of hypothermia are exhaustion, numb skin (particularly of the toes and fingers), shivering, slurred speech, irrational or violent behaviour, lethargy, stumbling, dizzy spells, muscle cramps and violent bursts of energy. Irrationality may take the form of sufferers claiming they are warm and trying to take off their clothes.

To treat mild hypothermia, first get the person out of the wind and/or rain, remove any wet clothing and replace it with dry, warm clothing. Give them hot liquids (not alcohol) and high-kilojoule, easily digestible food. Do not rub victims: allow them to slowly warm themselves instead. This should be enough to treat the early stages of hypothermia. Early recognition and treatment of mild hypothermia is the only way to prevent severe hypothermia, which is a critical condition.

Insect Bites & Stings

Bites from mosquitoes and other insects can cause irritation and infections. To avoid this, take the same precautions as you would for avoiding malaria. Bee and wasp stings cause real problems only to those who have a severe allergy to the stings (anaphylaxis), in which case, carry an adrenaline (epinephrine) injection.

Scorpions are found in arid areas. They can cause a painful bite that is sometimes life-threatening. If bitten by a scorpion, seek immediate medical assistance.

Bed bugs are often found in hostels and cheap hotels. They lead to very itchy, lumpy bites. Spraying the mattress with crawling insect killer after changing the bedding will get rid of them.

Scabies is also frequently found in cheap accommodation. These tiny mites live in the skin, particularly between the fingers. They cause an intensely itchy rash. The itch is easily treated with Malathion and permethrin lotion from a pharmacy; other members of the household also need to be treated to avoid spreading scabies, even if they do not show any symptoms.

Snake Bites

Avoid getting bitten! Don't walk barefoot or stick your hand into holes or cracks. However, 50% of those bitten by venomous snakes are not actually injected with poison (envenomed). If bitten by a snake, do not panic. Immobilise the bitten limb with a splint (such as a stick) and apply a bandage over the site with firm pressure, similar to bandaging a sprain. Do not apply a tourniquet, or cut or suck the bite. Get medical help as soon as possible so an antivenin can be given if needed. Try to note the snake's appearance to help in treatment.

Language

Swahili is the national language of Tanzania (as well as Kenya). It's also the key language of communication in the wider East African region. This makes it one of the most widely spoken African languages. Although the number of speakers of Swahili throughout East Africa is estimated to be well over 50 million, it's the mother tongue of only about 5 million people, and is predominantly used as a second language or a lingua franca by speakers of other African languages. Swahili belongs to the Bantu group of languages from the Niger-Congo family and can be traced back to the first millenium AD. It's hardly surprising that in an area as vast as East Africa many different dialects of Swahili can be found, but you shouldn't have problems being understood in Tanzania (or in the wider region) if you stick to the standard coastal form, as used in this book.

Most sounds in Swahili have equivalents in English. In our coloured pronunciation guides, ay should be read as in 'say', oh as the 'o' in 'role', dh as the 'th' in 'this' and th as in 'thing'. Note also that the sound ng can be found at the start of words in Swahili, and that Swahili speakers make only a slight distinction between r and l – instead of the hard 'r', try pronouncing a light 'd'. In Swahili, words are almost always stressed on the second-last syllable. In our pronunciation guides, the stressed syllables are in italics.

WANT MORE?

For in-depth language information and handy phrases, check out Lonely Planet's *Swahili Phrasebook*. You'll find it at **shop.lonelyplanet.com**, or you can buy Lonely Planet's iPhone phrasebooks at the Apple App Store.

BASICS

Jambo is a pidgin Swahili word, used to greet tourists who are presumed not to understand the language. If people assume you can speak a little Swahili, they might use the following greetings:

Hello. (general)	*Habari*	ha·ba·ree
Hello. (respectful)	*Shikamoo.*	shee·ka·moh
Goodbye.	*Tutaonana.*	too·ta·oh·na·na
Good ...	*Habari za ...*	ha·ba·ree za ...
morning	*asubuhi*	a·soo·boo·hee
afternoon	*mchana*	m·cha·na
evening	*jioni*	jee·oh·nee

Yes.	*Ndiyo.*	n·dee·yoh
No.	*Hapana.*	ha·pa·na
Please.	*Tafadhali.*	ta·fa·dha·lee
Thank you (very much).	*Asante (sana).*	a·san·tay (sa·na)
You're welcome.	*Karibu.*	ka·ree·boo
Excuse me.	*Samahani.*	sa·ma·ha·nee
Sorry.	*Pole.*	poh·lay

How are you?
Habari? ha·ba·ree

I'm fine.
Nzuri./Salama./Safi. n·zoo·ree/sa·la·ma/sa·fee

If things are just OK, add *tu* too (only) after any of the above replies. If things are really good, add *sana* sa·na (very) or *kabisa* ka·bee·sa (totally) instead of *tu*.

What's your name?
Jina lako nani? jee·na la·koh na·nee

My name is ...
Jina langu ni ... jee·na lan·goo nee ...

KEY PATTERNS

To get by in Swahili, mix and match these patterns with words of your choice:

When's (the next bus)?
(Basi ijayo) (ba·see ee·ja·yoh)
itaondoka lini? ee·ta·ohn·*doh*·ka lee·nee

Where's (the station)?
(Stesheni) iko (stay·*shay*·nee) ee·koh
wapi? wa·pee

How much is (a room)?
(Chumba) ni (choom·ba) nee
bei gani? bay ga·nee

I'm looking for (a hotel).
Natafuta (hoteli). na·ta·foo·ta (hoh·*tay*·lee)

Do you have (a map)?
Una (ramani)? oo·na (ra·ma·nee)

Please bring (the bill).
Lete (bili). lay·tay (bee·lee)

I'd like (the menu).
Nataka (menyu). na·ta·ka (may·nyoo)

I have (a reservation).
Nina (buking). nee·na (boo·keeng)

Do you speak English?
Unasema oo·na·*say*·ma
Kiingereza? kee·een·gay·*ray*·za

I don't understand.
Sielewi. see·ay·*lay*·wee

ACCOMMODATION

Where's a ...?	*... iko wapi?*	... ee·koh wa·pee
campsite	*Uwanja wa kambi*	oo·*wan*·ja wa kam·bee
guesthouse	*Gesti*	gay·stee
hotel	*Hoteli*	hoh·*tay*·lee
youth hostel	*Hosteli ya vijana*	hoh·*stay*·lee ya vee·*ja*·na

Do you have a ... room?	*Kuna chumba kwa ...?*	koo·na *choom*·ba kwa ...
double (one bed)	*watu wawili, kitanda kimoja*	wa·too wa·*wee*·lee kee·*tan*·da kee·*moh*·ja
single	*mtu mmoja*	m·too m·*moh*·ja
twin (two beds)	*watu wawili, vitanda viwili*	wa·too wa·*wee*·lee vee·*tan*·da vee·*wee*·lee

How much is it per ...?	*Ni bei gani kwa ...?*	nee bay *ga*·ne kwa ...
day	*siku*	see·koo
person	*mtu*	m·too

---

air-con	*a/c*	ay·see
bathroom	*bafuni*	ba·*foo*·nee
key	*ufunguo*	oo·foon·*goo*·oh
toilet	*choo*	choh
window	*dirisha*	dee·*ree*·sha

DIRECTIONS

Where's the ...?
... iko wapi? ... ee·koh wa·pee

What's the address?
Anwani ni nini? an·*wa*·nee nee *nee*·nee

How do I get there?
Nifikaje? nee·fee·*ka*·jay

How far is it?
Ni umbali gani? nee oom·*ba*·lee ga·nee

Can you show me (on the map)?
Unaweza oo·na·*way*·za
kunionyesha koo·nee·oh·*nyay*·sha
(katika ramani)? (ka·*tee*·ka ra·*ma*·nee)

It's ...	*Iko ...*	ee·koh ...
behind ...	*nyuma ya ...*	*nyoo*·ma ya ...
in front of ...	*mbele ya ...*	m·*bay*·lay ya ...
near ...	*karibu na ...*	ka·*ree*·boo na ...
next to ...	*jirani ya ...*	jee·*ra*·nee ya ...
on the corner	*pembeni*	paym·*bay*·nee
opposite ...	*ng'ambo ya ...*	ng·*am*·boh ya ...
straight ahead	*moja kwa moja*	*moh*·ja kwa *moh*·ja

Turn ...	*Geuza ...*	gay·*oo*·za ...
at the corner	*kwenye kona*	*kway*·nyay *koh*·na
at the traffic lights	*kwenye taa za barabarani*	*kway*·nyay ta za ba·ra·ba·*ra*·nee
left	*kushoto*	koo·*shoh*·toh
right	*kulia*	koo·*lee*·a

EATING & DRINKING

I'd like to reserve a table for ...	*Nataka kuhifadhi meza kwa ...*	na·ta·ka koo·hee·fa·dhee *may*·za kwa ...
(two) people	*watu (wawili)*	wa·too (wa·*wee*·lee)
(eight) o'clock	*saa (mbili)*	sa (m·*bee*·lee)

I'd like the menu.
Naomba menyu. na·*ohm*·ba may·nyoo

What would you recommend?
Chakula gani ni cha·*koo*·la ga·nee nee
kizuri? kee·*zoo*·ree

Do you have vegetarian food?
Mna chakula   m·na cha·koo·la
bila nyama?   bee·la nya·ma

I'll have that.
Nataka hicho.   na·ta·ka hee·choh

Cheers!
Heri!   hay·ree

That was delicious!
Chakula kitamu sana!   cha·koo·la kee·ta·moo sa·na

Please bring the bill.
Lete bili.   lay·tay bee·lee

I don't eat ...	Sili ...	see·lee ...
butter	siagi	see·a·gee
eggs	mayai	ma·ya·ee
red meat	nyama	nya·ma

Key Words

bottle	chupa	choo·pa
bowl	bakuli	ba·koo·lee
breakfast	chai ya asubuhi	cha·ee ya a·soo·boo·hee
cold	baridi	ba·ree·dee
dinner	chakula cha jioni	cha·koo·la cha jee·oh·nee
dish	chakula	cha·koo·la
fork	uma	oo·ma
glass	glesi	glay·see
halal	halali	ha·la·lee
hot	joto	joh·toh
knife	kisu	kee·soo
kosher	halali	ha·la·lee
lunch	chakula cha mchana	cha·koo·la cha m·cha·na
market	soko	soh·koh
plate	sahani	sa·ha·nee
restaurant	mgahawa	m·ga·ha·wa
snack	kumbwe	koom·bway
spicy	chenye viungo	chay·nyay vee·oon·goh
spoon	kijiko	kee·jee·koh
with	na	na
without	bila	bee·la

Meat & Fish

beef	nyama ng'ombe	nya·ma ng·ohm·bay
chicken	kuku	koo·koo
crab	kaa	ka
fish	samaki	sa·ma·kee
hering	heringi	hay·reen·gee
lamb	mwanakondoo	mwa·na·kohn·doh
meat	nyama	nya·ma
mutton	nyama mbuzi	nya·ma m·boo·zee
oyster	chaza	cha·za
pork	nyama nguruwe	nya·ma n·goo·roo·way
seafood	chakula kutoka bahari	cha·koo·la koo·toh·ka ba·ha·ree
squid	ngisi	n·gee·see
tuna	jodari	joh·da·ree
veal	nyama ya ndama	nya·ma ya n·da·ma

Fruit & Vegetables

apple	tofaa	toh·fa
banana	ndizi	n·dee·zee
cabbage	kabichi	ka·bee·chee
carrot	karoti	ka·roh·tee
eggplant	biringani	bee·reen·ga·nee
fruit	tunda	toon·da
grapefruit	balungi	ba·loon·gee
grapes	zabibu	za·bee·boo
guava	pera	pay·ra
lemon	limau	lee·ma·oo
lentils	dengu	dayn·goo
mango	embe	aym·bay
onion	kitunguu	kee·toon·goo
orange	chungwa	choon·gwa
peanut	karanga	ka·ran·ga
pineapple	nanasi	na·na·see
potato	kiazi	kee·a·zee
spinach	mchicha	m·chee·cha
tomato	nyanya	nya·nya
vegetable	mboga	m·boh·ga

SIGNS

Mahali Pa Kuingia	Entrance
Mahali Pa Kutoka	Exit
Imefunguliwa	Open
Imefungwa	Closed
Maelezo	Information
Ni Marufuku	Prohibited
Choo/Msalani	Toilets
Wanaume	Men
Wanawake	Women

Other

bread	mkate	m·ka·tay
butter	siagi	see·a·gee
cheese	jibini	jee·bee·nee
egg	yai	ya·ee
honey	asali	a·sa·lee
jam	jamu	ja·moo
pasta	tambi	tam·bee
pepper	pilipili	pee·lee·pee·lee
rice (cooked)	wali	wa·lee
salt	chumvi	choom·vee
sugar	sukari	soo·ka·ree

Drinks

beer	bia	bee·a
coffee	kahawa	ka·ha·wa
juice	jusi	joo·see
milk	maziwa	ma·zee·wa
mineral water	maji ya madini	ma·jee ya ma·dee·nee
orange juice	maji ya machungwa	ma·jee ya ma·choon·gwa
red wine	mvinyo mwekundu	m·vee·nyoh mway·koon·doo
soft drink	soda	soh·da
sparkling wine	mvinyo yenye mapovu	m·vee·nyoh yay·nyay ma·poh·voo
tea	chai	cha·ee
water	maji	ma·jee
white wine	mvinyo mweupe	m·vee·nyoh mway·oo·pay

EMERGENCIES

| Help! | Saidia! | sa·ee·dee·a |
| Go away! | Toka! | toh·ka |

I'm lost.
Nimejipotea. nee·may·jee·poh·tay·a

QUESTION WORDS

How?	Namna?	nam·na
What?	Nini?	nee·nee
When?	Wakati?	wa·ka·tee
Where?	Wapi?	wa·pee
Which?	Gani?	ga·nee
Who?	Nani?	na·nee
Why?	Kwa nini?	kwa nee·nee

Call the police.
Waite polisi. wa·ee·tay poh·lee·see

Call a doctor.
Mwite daktari. m·wee·tay dak·ta·ree

I'm sick.
Mimi ni mgonjwa. mee·mee nee m·gohn·jwa

It hurts here.
Inauma hapa. ee·na·oo·ma ha·pa

I'm allergic to (antibiotics).
Nina mzio wa (viuavijasumu). nee·na m·zee·oh wa (vee·oo·a·vee·ja·soo·moo)

Where's the toilet?
Choo kiko wapi? choh kee·koh wa·pee

SHOPPING & SERVICES

I'd like to buy ...
Nataka kununua ... na·ta·ka koo·noo·noo·a ...

I'm just looking.
Naangalia tu. na·an·ga·lee·a too

Can I look at it?
Naomba nione? na·ohm·ba nee·oh·nay

I don't like it.
Sipendi. see·payn·dee

How much is it?
Ni bei gani? ni bay ga·nee

That's too expensive.
Ni ghali mno. nee ga·lee m·noh

Please lower the price.
Punguza bei. poon·goo·za bay

There's a mistake in the bill.
Kuna kosa kwenye bili. koo·na koh·sa kwayn·yay bee·lee

ATM	mashine ya kutolea pesa	ma·shee·nay ya koo·toh·lay·a pay·sa
post office	posta	poh·sta
public phone	simu ya mtaani	see·moo ya m·ta·nee
tourist office	ofisi ya watalii	o·fee·see ya wa·ta·lee

TIME & DATES

Keep in mind that the Swahili time system starts six hours later than the international one – it begins at sunrise which occurs at about 6am year-round. Therefore, *saa mbili* sa m·bee·lee (lit: clocks two) means '2 o'clock Swahili time' and '8 o'clock international time'.

What time is it?
Ni saa ngapi? nee sa n·ga·pee

It's (10) o'clock.
Ni saa (nne). nee sa (n·nay)

Half past (10).
Ni saa (nne) na nusu. nee sa (n·nay) na noo·soo

morning	asubuhi	a·soo·boo·hee
afternoon	mchana	m·cha·na
evening	jioni	jee·oh·nee
yesterday	jana	ja·na
today	leo	lay·oh
tomorrow	kesho	kay·shoh
Monday	Jumatatu	joo·ma·ta·too
Tuesday	Jumanne	joo·ma·n·nay
Wednesday	Jumatano	joo·ma·ta·noh
Thursday	Alhamisi	al·ha·mee·see
Friday	Ijumaa	ee·joo·ma
Saturday	Jumamosi	joo·ma·moh·see
Sunday	Jumapili	joo·ma·pee·lee

TRANSPORT

Public Transport

Which ... goes to (Mbeya)?	... ipi huenda (Mbeya)?	... ee·pee hoo·ayn·da (m·bay·a)
bus	Basi	ba·see
ferry	Kivuko	kee·voo·koh
minibus	Daladala	da·la·da·la
train	Treni	tray·nee

When's the ... bus?	Basi ... itaondoka lini?	ba·see ... ee·ta·ohn·doh·ka lee·nee
first	ya kwanza	ya kwan·za
last	ya mwisho	ya mwee·shoh
next	ijayo	ee·ja·yoh

A ... ticket to (Iringa).	Tiketi moja ya ... kwenda (Iringa).	tee·kay·tee moh·ja ya ... kwayn·da (ee·reen·ga)
1st-class	daraja la kwanza	da·ra·ja la kwan·za
2nd-class	daraja la pili	da·ra·ja la pee·lee
one-way	kwenda tu	kwayn·da too
return	kwenda na kurudi	kwayn·da na koo·roo·dee

What time does it get to (Kisumu)?
Itafika (Kisumu) ee·ta·fee·ka (kee·soo·moo)
saa ngapi? sa n·ga·pee

Does it stop at (Tanga)?
Linasimama (Tanga)? lee·na·see·ma·ma (tan·ga)

I'd like to get off at (Bagamoyo).
Nataka kushusha na·ta·ka koo·shoo·sha
(Bagamoyo). (ba·ga·moh·yoh)

NUMBERS

1	moja	moh·ja
2	mbili	m·bee·lee
3	tatu	ta·too
4	nne	n·nay
5	tano	ta·noh
6	sita	see·ta
7	saba	sa·ba
8	nane	na·nay
9	tisa	tee·sa
10	kumi	koo·mee
20	ishirini	ee·shee·ree·nee
30	thelathini	thay·la·thee·nee
40	arobaini	a·roh·ba·ee·nee
50	hamsini	ham·see·nee
60	sitini	see·tee·nee
70	sabini	sa·bee·nee
80	themanini	thay·ma·nee·nee
90	tisini	tee·see·nee
100	mia moja	mee·a moh·ja
1000	elfu	ayl·foo

Driving & Cycling

I'd like to hire a ...	Nataka kukodi ...	na·ta·ka koo·koh·dee ...
4WD	forbaifor	fohr·ba·ee·fohr
bicycle	baisikeli	ba·ee·see·kay·lee
car	gari	ga·ree
motorbike	pikipiki	pee·kee·pee·kee

diesel	dizeli	dee·zay·lee
regular	kawaida	ka·wa·ee·da
unleaded	isiyo na risasi	ee·see·yoh na ree·sa·see

Is this the road to (Embu)?
Hii ni barabara hee nee ba·ra·ba·ra
kwenda (Embu)? kwayn·da (aym·boo)

Where's a petrol station?
Kituo cha mafuta kee·too·oh cha ma·foo·ta
kiko wapi? kee·ko wa·pee

(How long) Can I park here?
Naweza kuegesha na·way·za koo·ay·gay·sha
hapa (kwa muda gani)? ha·pa (kwa moo·da ga·ni)

I need a mechanic.
Nahitaji fundi. na·hee·ta·jee foon·dee

I have a flat tyre.
Nina pancha. nee·na pan·cha

I've run out of petrol.
Mafuta yamekwisha. ma·foo·ta ya·may·kwee·sha

GLOSSARY

(m) indicates masculine gender, (f) feminine gender and (pl) plural

ASP – Afro-Shirazi Party

bajaji – tuk-tuk

banda – thatched-roof hut with wooden or earthen walls; the term is also used to refer to any simple bungalow- or cottage-style accommodation

bangi – marijuana

bao – a board game widely played in East Africa, especially on Zanzibar

baraza – the stone seats seen along the outside walls of houses in Zanzibar's Stone Town, used for chatting and relaxing

boda-boda – motorcycle taxi (from 'border-border', as they are commonly used transport for bridging the no-man's land between country borders)

boma – a fortified living compound; colonial-era administrative offices

bui-bui – black cover-all worn by some Islamic women outside the home

Bunge – Tanzanian Parliament

chai – tea

chakula – food

Chama Cha Mapinduzi (CCM) – Party of the Revolution (governing party)

choo – toilet

Cites – UN Convention on International Trade in Endangered Species

Civic United Front (CUF) – main opposition party

Coastal ('thelathini') – 30-seater buses, commonly used on some routes instead of large, full-size buses; also known as coasters

dada – sister; often used as a form of address

dalla-dalla – minibus

Deutsch-Ostafrikanische Gesellschaft (DOAG) – German East Africa Company

dhow – ancient Arabic sailing vessel

duka – small shop or kiosk

fly camp – a camp away from the main tented camps or lodges, for the purpose of enjoying a more authentic bush experience

flycatcher – used mainly in Arusha and Moshi to mean a tout working to get you to go on safari with an operator from whom he knows he can get a commission. We assume the name comes from a comparison with the sticky-sweet paper used to lure flies to land (and then get irretrievably stuck) – similar to the plight of a hapless traveller who succumbs to a flycatcher's promises and then is 'stuck' (ie with their money and time lost in a fraudulent safari deal).

forex – foreign exchange (bureau)

ganja – see *bangi*

gongo – distilled cashew drink

hodi – called out prior to entering someone's house; roughly meaning 'may I enter?'

hotel/hoteli – basic local eatery

jamaa – clan, community

kahawa – coffee

kaka – brother; used as a form of address, and to call the waiter in restaurants

kanga – printed cotton wraparound worn by many Tanzanian women; Swahili proverbs are printed along the edge of the cloth

kanzu – white robe-like outer garment worn by men, often for prayer, on the Zanzibar Archipelago and in other Swahili areas

karanga – peanuts

karibu – Swahili for 'welcome'; heard throughout Tanzania

kidumbak – an offshoot of *taarab* music, distinguished by its defined rhythms and drumming, and hard-hitting lyrics

kikoi – cotton linen wraparound traditionally worn by men in coastal areas

kitenge – similar to a *kanga*, but larger, heavier and without a Swahili proverb

kofia – a cap, usually of embroidered white linen, worn by men on the Zanzibar Archipelago and in other Swahili areas

kopje – rocky outcrop or hill

kwaya – church choir music

maandazi – doughnut

makuti – thatch

marimba – musical instrument played with the thumb

mashua – motorised dhow

masika – long rains

matatu – Kenyan minivan

matoke – cooked plantains

mbege – banana beer

mgando – see *mtindi*

mihrab – the prayer niche in a mosque showing the direction to Mecca

mishikaki – meat kebabs

mnada – auction, usually held once or twice monthly on a regular basis

moran – Maasai warrior

mpingo – African blackwood

mtepe – a traditional Swahili sailing vessel made without nails, the planks held together with only coconut fibres and wooden pegs

mtindi – cultured milk product similar to yogurt

mvuli – short rains

Mwalimu – teacher; used to refer to Julius Nyerere

mzungu – white person, foreigner (pl *wazungu*)

nazi – fermented coconut wine

NCA – Ngorongoro Conservation Area

NCAA – Ngorongoro Conservation Area Authority

ndugu – brother, comrade

ngoma – dance and drumming

northern circuit – the northern safari route, including Serengeti, Tarangire and Lake Manyara National Parks and the Ngorongoro Conservation Area

nyika – bush or hinterland

orpul – Maasai camp where men go to eat meat

papasi – literally 'tick'; used on Zanzibar to refer to street touts

piki-piki – motorbike

potwe – whale shark

pweza – octopus, usually served grilled, at night markets and street stalls

public (ordinary) campsite – type of national park campsite, with basic facilities, generally including latrines and a water source

shamba – small farm plot

shehe – village chief

shetani – literally, demon or something supernatural; in art, a style of carving embodying images from the spirit world

shikamoo – Swahili greeting of respect, used for elders or anyone in a position of authority; the response is 'marahaba'

special campsite – type of national park campsite, more remote than *public campsites*, and without facilities

TAA – Tanganyika Africa Association, successor of the African Association and predecessor of TANU

taarab – Zanzibari music combining African, Arabic and Indian influences

Tanapa – Tanzania National Parks Authority

TANU – Tanganyika (later, Tanzania) African National Union

TATO – Tanzanian Association of Tour Operators

Tazara – Tanzania–Zambia Railway

tea room – a small shop, usually with a few tables, serving snacks and light meals

tilapia – a cichlid fish very common around Lake Victoria

Tingatinga – Tanzania's best-known style of painting, developed in the 1960s by Edward Saidi Tingatinga; traditionally in a square format with colourful animal motifs against a monochrome background

TTB – Tanzania Tourist Board

ugali – a staple made from maize and/or cassava flour

uhuru – freedom; also the name of Mt Kilimanjaro's highest peak

ujamaa – familyhood, togetherness

umoja – unity

Unguja – Swahili name for Zanzibar island

vitambua – rice cakes

wali – cooked rice

ZIFF – Zanzibar International Film Festival

ZNP – Zanzibar Nationalist Party

ZPPP – Zanzibar & Pemba People's Party

ZTC – Zanzibar Tourist Corporation

Behind the Scenes

SEND US YOUR FEEDBACK

We love to hear from travellers – your comments keep us on our toes and help make our books better. Our well-travelled team reads every word on what you loved or loathed about this book. Although we cannot reply individually to your submissions, we always guarantee that your feedback goes straight to the appropriate authors, in time for the next edition. Each person who sends us information is thanked in the next edition – the most useful submissions are rewarded with a selection of digital PDF chapters.

Visit **lonelyplanet.com/contact** to submit your updates and suggestions or to ask for help. Our award-winning website also features inspirational travel stories, news and discussions.

Note: We may edit, reproduce and incorporate your comments in Lonely Planet products such as guidebooks, websites and digital products, so let us know if you don't want your comments reproduced or your name acknowledged. For a copy of our privacy policy visit lonelyplanet.com/privacy.

OUR READERS

Many thanks to the travellers who used the last edition and wrote to us with helpful hints, useful advice and interesting anecdotes: Austin Oakley, Christian Arleth, Claerwen Snell, Edwin & Anne-Marie Schuurman, Hiroki Nishida, Isabel Fofana, Jolien Philipsen, Juergen Schweigler, Julie Syltern, Keisuke Mochida, Lynnae Ruttledge, Mark Peterson, Matthieu Kamerman, Mike Hawkins, Nathan Allinson, Nikitas van Maaren, Ondřej Černík, Robert Martyniecki, Rosy Danby, Rupert Wilkinson, Samantha Caselli, Valentina Schneck, Whitney Haruf, Zuberi Mabie

AUTHOR THANKS
Mary Fitzpatrick
Many people helped during the research and writing of this book. I'd especially like to thank Nassor in Newala, Sultan in Dar es Salaam, Abdullah in Somanga and Eustacia in Selous Game Reserve. My gratitude also to Destination Editor Matt Phillips and to my Tanzania co-authors. My biggest thanks goes to Rick, Christopher, Dominic and Gabriel for their entertaining company during research and their patience and good humour during write-up.

Ray Bartlett
My family. Matt P, editor extraordinaire. Sachi, Maha, Bintee, Dorocella, Zhen, Dawson, Ruge, Sauda, Paschal, Mr Gara, Happiness, Mr Bita, Mariam,

Hezron, Placilia, Will I Am, Jullyan, Novart, George, Rachel, Elizabeth, Megan and Evan, Eustocia, Ratna, Dharmesh, Loyce, Jacky, Clara, William, Peter, Paul, Gabriel, Enock, Chesco, Yusuph, Abdullah, Siwema, Khatib, Antonny, Jabiri, Charles, Juma, Francisco, Neema, Nixon, Novart, Nuru, Kalfan, Hussein, Chris and Louise, Miho-san, and the incredible people of Tanzania. Thank you for such a lovely time in your sweet, special country.

David Else
Many thanks go first to the travellers and Zanzibaris that I met along the way; their insights and stories were invaluable. Big thanks also to my old pal Peter Bennett for local knowledge. And the biggest thanks to Corinne, my wife, for keeping the home fires burning while I'm on the road.

Anthony Ham
Heartfelt thanks to Matt Phillips, my Africa friend and editor of long standing for continuing to entrust me with a corner of the earth I adore. Warmest thanks also to Peter Ndirangu Wamae, another companion of the African road over many years. Carole and Donald Boag were wonderful hosts in the Serengeti, and thanks to Mary Fitzpatrick for her enduring wisdom. Thanks also to Jörg Gabriel, Victor Swanepoel, Tara Walraven and so many others. To my family, Marina, Carlota and Valentina: thank you for sharing my love of Africa and for giving me so many special memories there.

Helena Smith

Asante Elidady for a warm welcome and Art for arranging it, Mwisho Msumai for the lowdown on Morogoro, and Joas Kahembe in Babati. In Iringa thanks to Bill Allen, Owen Flagel and Joan Mayer for a great night out, and Rajipa David for a great day out. Jessica Klink, Cori Van Dyke and especially Amy Glasser who shared knowledge of Mbeya and Matema. Thanks too to Amelia in Mbeya, Erica Zelfand for help with Tukuyu, and Moyo Jacob Mwagobele in Matema.

ACKNOWLEDGEMENTS

Climate map data adapted from Peel MC, Finlayson BL & McMahon TA (2007) 'Updated World Map of the Köppen-Geiger Climate Classification', Hydrology and Earth System Sciences, 11, 163–344.

Cover photograph: Elephants, Tarangire National Park, Licinia Machado/500px ©

THIS BOOK

This 7th edition of Lonely Planet's *Tanzania* guidebook was researched and written by Mary Fitzpatrick, Ray Bartlett, David Else, Anthony Ham and Helena Smith. The previous two editions were written by Mary Fitzpatrick, Tim Bewer, Stuart Butler, Anthony Ham and Paula Hardy. This guidebook was produced by the following:

Destination Editor Matt Phillips

Product Editor Grace Dobell

Senior Product Editor Anne Mason

Senior Cartographer Diana Von Holdt

Book Designer Wibowo Rusli

Assisting Editors Sarah Bailey, Judith Bamber, Michelle Bennett, Nigel Chin, Melanie Dankel, Andrea Dobbin, Alexander Knights, Kristin Odijk, Gabrielle Stefanos, Simon Williamson

Cartographer Mick Garrett

Cover Researcher Naomi Parker

Thanks to William Allen, Hannah Cartmel, Elizabeth Jones, Kirsten Rawlings, Tony Wheeler

Index

Map Legend

Sights

- Beach
- Bird Sanctuary
- Buddhist
- Castle/Palace
- Christian
- Confucian
- Hindu
- Islamic
- Jain
- Jewish
- Monument
- Museum/Gallery/Historic Building
- Ruin
- Shinto
- Sikh
- Taoist
- Winery/Vineyard
- Zoo/Wildlife Sanctuary
- Other Sight

Activities, Courses & Tours

- Bodysurfing
- Diving
- Canoeing/Kayaking
- Course/Tour
- Sento Hot Baths/Onsen
- Skiing
- Snorkelling
- Surfing
- Swimming/Pool
- Walking
- Windsurfing
- Other Activity

Sleeping

- Sleeping
- Camping
- Hut/Shelter

Eating

- Eating

Drinking & Nightlife

- Drinking & Nightlife
- Cafe

Entertainment

- Entertainment

Shopping

- Shopping

Information

- Bank
- Embassy/Consulate
- Hospital/Medical
- Internet
- Police
- Post Office
- Telephone
- Toilet
- Tourist Information
- Other Information

Geographic

- Beach
- Gate
- Hut/Shelter
- Lighthouse
- Lookout
- Mountain/Volcano
- Oasis
- Park
- Pass
- Picnic Area
- Waterfall

Population

- Capital (National)
- Capital (State/Province)
- City/Large Town
- Town/Village

Transport

- Airport
- Border crossing
- Bus
- Cable car/Funicular
- Cycling
- Ferry
- Metro station
- Monorail
- Parking
- Petrol station
- Subway station
- Taxi
- Train station/Railway
- Tram
- Underground station
- Other Transport

Routes

- Tollway
- Freeway
- Primary
- Secondary
- Tertiary
- Lane
- Unsealed road
- Road under construction
- Plaza/Mall
- Steps
- Tunnel
- Pedestrian overpass
- Walking Tour
- Walking Tour detour
- Path/Walking Trail

Boundaries

- International
- State/Province
- Disputed
- Regional/Suburb
- Marine Park
- Cliff
- Wall

Hydrography

- River, Creek
- Intermittent River
- Canal
- Water
- Dry/Salt/Intermittent Lake
- Reef

Areas

- Airport/Runway
- Beach/Desert
- Cemetery (Christian)
- Cemetery (Other)
- Glacier
- Mudflat
- Park/Forest
- Sight (Building)
- Sportsground
- Swamp/Mangrove

Note: Not all symbols displayed above appear on the maps in this book

Anthony Ham

Northern Tanzania Anthony is a freelance writer and photographer who specialises in Spain, East and Southern Africa, the Arctic and the Middle East. In 2001,
after years of wandering the world, Anthony finally found his spiritual home when
he fell irretrievably in love with Madrid on his first visit to the city. Less than a
year later, he arrived there on a one-way ticket, with not a word of Spanish and
not knowing a single person in the city. When he finally left Madrid 10 years later,
Anthony spoke Spanish with a Madrid accent, was married to a local and Madrid had become his
second home. Now back in Australia, Anthony continues to travel the world in search of stories.

Helena Smith

Central Tanzania, Southern Highlands Helena is an award-winning writer and
photographer covering travel, outdoors and food – she has written guidebooks
on destinations from Fiji to northern Norway. Helena is from Scotland but was
partly brought up in Malawi, so Africa always feels like home. She also enjoys
global travel in her multicultural home area of Hackney and wrote, photographed
and published *Inside Hackney,* the first guide to the borough. Her 1000-word
autobiography won *Vogue*'s annual writing contest and she's a winner of the *Independent on
Sunday*'s travel writing competition. As well as working as a guidebook author, Helena is a travel
and portrait photographer. She was senior photographer at the Edinburgh Film Festival, where she
worked for three consecutive years, and has exhibited her work at Rich Mix and Floradita.

OUR STORY

A beat-up old car, a few dollars in the pocket and a sense of adventure. In 1972 that's all Tony and Maureen Wheeler needed for the trip of a lifetime – across Europe and Asia overland to Australia. It took several months, and at the end – broke but inspired – they sat at their kitchen table writing and stapling together their first travel guide, *Across Asia on the Cheap*. Within a week they'd sold 1500 copies. Lonely Planet was born.

Today, Lonely Planet has offices in Franklin, London, Melbourne, Oakland, Dublin, Beijing and Delhi, with more than 600 staff and writers. We share Tony's belief that 'a great guidebook should do three things: inform, educate and amuse'.

OUR WRITERS

Mary Fitzpatrick

Curator, Dar es Salaam, Northeastern Tanzania, Southeastern Tanzania Originally from the USA, Mary spent her early years dreaming of how to get across an ocean or two to more exotic locales. Following graduate studies, she set off for Europe. Her fascination with languages and cultures soon led her further south to Africa, where she has spent the past two decades living and working as a professional travel writer all around the continent. She focuses particularly on East and Southern Africa, including Mozambique and Tanzania. Mary has authored and co-authored many guidebooks for Lonely Planet, including *Mozambique; Tanzania; South Africa, Lesotho & Swaziland; East Africa; West Africa;* and *Egypt.* Mary also wrote the Plan, Understand and Survival Guide chapters for this book.

Ray Bartlett

Western Tanzania, Lake Victoria Ray has been travel writing for nearly two decades, bringing Japan, Korea, Mexico, and many parts of the United States to life in rich detail for top-industry publishers, newspapers and magazines. His acclaimed debut novel, *Sunsets of Tulum,* set in Yucatán, was a Midwest Book Review 2016 Fiction pick. Among other pursuits, he surfs regularly and is an accomplished Argentine tango dancer. Follow him on Facebook, Twitter, Instagram, or contact him for questions via www.kaisora.com, his website. Ray currently divides his time between homes in the USA, Japan and Mexico.

David Else

Zanzibar Archipelago David is a professional freelance writer specialising in travel, trekking, cycling, walking and outdoor adventure activities. Since the 1980s he's been writing guidebooks for Lonely Planet and other publishers, plus a wide range of travel topics for magazines, newspapers and websites. In three decades of covering Africa, David wrote many Lonely Planet guidebooks including *West Africa* and *Southern Africa* and detailed guides such as *Malawi, Zambia, Gambia & Senegal* and *Trekking in East Africa.* He now lives in the UK, where he's worked on local LP titles including several editions of guides to Great Britain and England. Beyond guidebooks, David writes regular articles for lonelyplanet.com. His words and photos have also appeared in the travel section of *The Independent* newspaper, *Travel Africa* magazine, *Cycling Weekly* magazine and *Lonely Planet* magazine. David continues to travel widely – by train, plane, car, bike or on foot. Recent trips have taken him from France and Spain to Mexico and Morocco, via the ice-cold thrills of Greenland and the epic landscapes of India.

OVER MORE
PAGE WRITERS

Published by Lonely Planet Global Limited
CRN 554153
7th edition – Jun 2018
ISBN 978 1 78657 562 3
© Lonely Planet 2018   Photographs © as indicated 2018
10 9 8 7 6 5 4 3 2 1
Printed in Singapore